Special Edition
Using

Microsoft®
Excel 2000

Raised and lowered surfaces are also great for strategic positioning. The value index here shows coverage from easy to hard, and the titles show the coverage; the void in this market is shown as a sunken surface. The different surfaces and colors make the market opportunity clear.

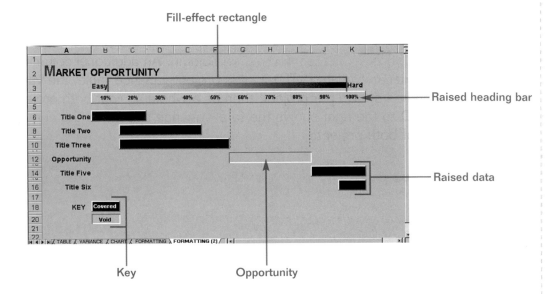

Fill-effect rectangle

Raised heading bar

Raised data

Key

Opportunity

Variance Tables

Variance tables show actual cost or sales against budgeted or forecast cost or sales. By creating a properly structured variance table, you can measure performance against projections at any level—day, week, month, quarter, year, and so on. Variance occurs over time, so you need time measurements (in this example, months in column C). Then show the budgeted or forecast numbers in one column, actual results one column to the right, and variance in the third column. An additional column can show variance to date (VTD). In this project variance table, the variance by month is shown per project, then as a whole against both projects. The total VTD to the right shows the total variance applied to the cumulative results of both projects.

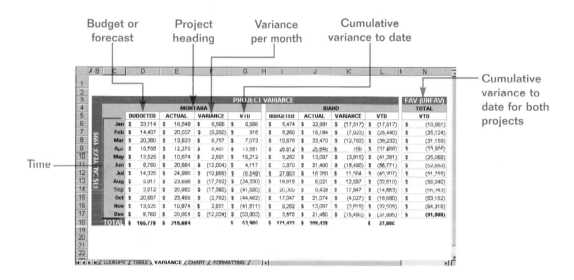

Budget or forecast Project heading Variance per month Cumulative variance to date

Time

Cumulative variance to date for both projects

Keys to proper variance table structure:

- Apply the categories or projects across from left to right.
- Apply the time measurement from top down along the left side of the table.
- Per category, dedicate the first column to budget or fore-cast, the second to actual, and the third to variance. The fourth category is variance to date, which is a cumulative of the variance per month.

Consistent Table Structure

The display of information in summary form is critical for making business decisions. Several types of tables can be used to view information once compiled. Two common tables are tiered timetables and variance tables.

Tiered Timetables

A *tiered timetable* organizes time breakouts from lowest level to highest level. This example is organized in months, then quarters, and finally the year. (Use the Merge and Center button to align the higher categories properly over the lower.) The projects are listed down the left side. You can also use fill shades to separate the categories.

Use borders to create distinction between categories and elbows.

Use shading to differentiate time categories.

Months, quarters, years, title

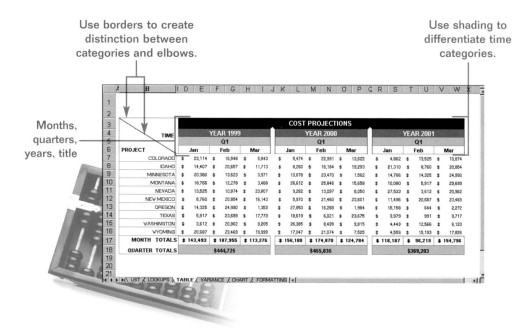

PROJECT	YEAR 1999 Q1 Jan	Feb	Mar	YEAR 2000 Q1 Jan	Feb	Mar	YEAR 2001 Q1 Jan	Feb	Mar
COLORADO	$ 23,114	$ 16,548	$ 5,843	$ 5,474	$ 22,991	$ 13,622	$ 4,962	$ 13,525	$ 10,874
IDAHO	$ 14,407	$ 20,657	$ 11,713	$ 8,260	$ 16,184	$ 19,293	$ 21,310	$ 8,760	$ 20,854
MINNESOTA	$ 20,380	$ 13,623	$ 3,971	$ 10,678	$ 23,470	$ 1,562	$ 14,766	$ 14,325	$ 24,990
MONTANA	$ 19,766	$ 12,279	$ 3,468	$ 26,612	$ 25,846	$ 15,658	$ 10,080	$ 5,917	$ 23,699
NEVADA	$ 13,525	$ 10,974	$ 23,807	$ 9,282	$ 13,097	$ 8,050	$ 27,533	$ 3,612	$ 20,962
NEW MEXICO	$ 8,760	$ 20,854	$ 16,143	$ 5,970	$ 21,460	$ 23,601	$ 11,496	$ 20,687	$ 23,469
OREGON	$ 14,325	$ 24,990	$ 1,353	$ 27,953	$ 16,289	$ 1,984	$ 15,158	$ 644	$ 2,272
TEXAS	$ 5,917	$ 23,699	$ 17,773	$ 18,619	$ 6,021	$ 23,675	$ 3,979	$ 991	$ 3,717
WASHINGTON	$ 3,612	$ 20,962	$ 3,205	$ 26,395	$ 8,439	$ 9,815	$ 4,443	$ 12,566	$ 6,133
WYOMING	$ 20,687	$ 23,469	$ 19,999	$ 17,047	$ 21,074	$ 7,525	$ 4,559	$ 15,193	$ 17,826
MONTH TOTALS	$ 143,493	$ 187,955	$ 113,276	$ 156,180	$ 174,870	$ 124,784	$ 118,187	$ 96,219	$ 154,796
QUARTER TOTALS	$444,725			$455,835			$369,203		

LIST / LOOKUPS \ TABLE / VARIANCE / CHART / FORMATTING

Keys to proper tier table structure:

- Merge and center headings to create the hierarchy or tiered time structure.
- Eliminate the table body lines if at all possible.
- Border the headings, and use light line colors to soften lines that don't need attention. By using border colors this way, you can also minimize clutter.
- Although spacing is good for separating categories, keep it to a minimum.
- Never use two font styles in the same table.
- Label categories. If the numbers in the body of the table represent widgets, note that they're widgets; if dollars, use the dollar symbol or note that they're dollars.

FOUR KEYS TO
SUCCESS WITH EXCEL

Few Excel books address the keys that make an everyday Excel user effective. Here are four quick keys that will help you become more effective at structuring, managing, and presenting information in Excel.

Proper List Structure

The most important aspect of managing information in Excel is the list structure, which is the foundation from which all information will eventually be extracted. The key is hierarchy. The foundation of a list should consist of categories broken down to the lowest level. The year is separated from the month, the capitalization is consistent, and each category is broken down to its lowest level. (For example, for a list where you need to see the cost per week for a project, the lowest level would be the week and project. The hierarchy would be structured as follows— week, month, quarter, year, and then project. All categories have their own columns and each row is filled in per line item.)

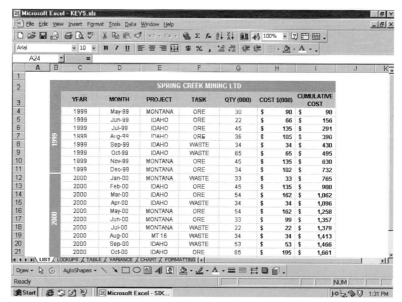

- If you use a legend, eliminate the legend border.
- The chart title should be bold, all caps, and two point sizes larger than the axis titles.
- The chart subtitle should be in initial caps and two point sizes smaller than the title.
- Use embedded charts if possible, rather than chart sheets. Embedded charts are far more flexible for formatting and comparison analysis.

Impressive Formatting

You can make a worksheet much more readable by creating a white "canvas" on which to apply numbers, text, colors, shapes, and grids. Select the appropriate region (or entire worksheet) and apply the white fill color. Adding "raised" and "lowered" surfaces to the worksheet can give it texture and dimension. You can apply these surfaces to create timelines, borders, headings, and so on.

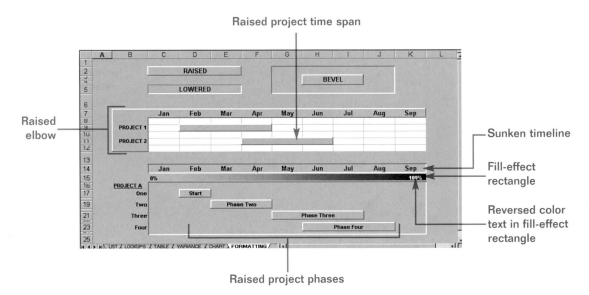

Raised project time span

Raised elbow

Sunken timeline

Fill-effect rectangle

Reversed color text in fill-effect rectangle

Raised project phases

Keys to proper list structure:

- Separate first and last names whenever possible.
- Use consistent case.
- Eliminate spacing. Don't insert blank rows and columns.
- Make sure that all line items have attachments. For example, don't place the year in a cell and then list items under that year. Each line item should have the year in a corresponding column and row cell.
- Don't separate column headings and the list body. If the column headings are in C3:I3, start the list body in cells C4:I4.

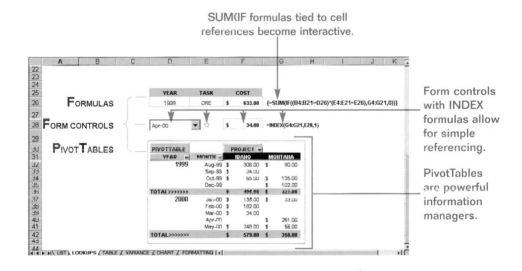

SUM(IF formulas tied to cell references become interactive.

Form controls with INDEX formulas allow for simple referencing.

PivotTables are powerful information managers.

With the proper list structure, formulas, form controls, and PivotTables become powerful list-management tools that can be used to look up and compile the information stored within the list.

Clean, Clear Charts

Standard techniques help create clean, effective presentations with charts. Although Excel offers a variety of tools, it's easy to get carried away and clutter the presentation. When a chart is viewed by an audience, you have only seconds to get the point across; eliminate any unnecessary information. This embedded chart shows everything in a clean, effective manner, with titles for the axes, dollar amounts emphasized, and shading applied from darkest to lightest on the categories for easy distinction.

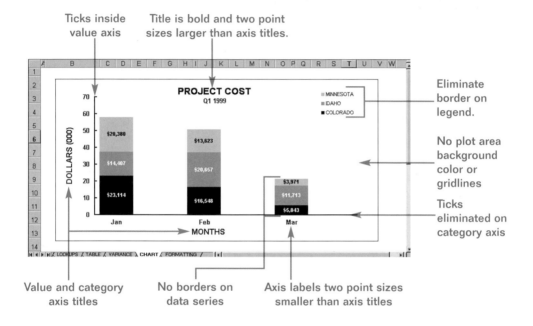

Keys to effective charts:

- Use Arial (or something comparable) for the font.
- The axis titles should be two point sizes larger than the axis labels.
- Eliminate the plot area background color.
- Eliminate the value axis gridlines, or change the color to light gray.
- When using colors or shades, use darkest to lightest.
- On column or bar charts, eliminate the series borders.

NEW AND IMPROVED EXCEL 2000 FEATURES

In addition to overall improvements in speed and user-friendliness over previous versions, you'll find the following new and improved features throughout Excel 2000.

NEW FEATURES	DESCRIPTION
Personalized Menus	By default, the Excel 2000 menus shuffle their commands so that the most recently used commands appear first on the menu. (If you continue to hold the menu open, or click the double arrow at the bottom of any menu, all the commands appear within a few seconds in their usual places.) This feature was added to help new users learn Excel quickly, without having to display features on the menu that they never use. If you're already familiar with Excel, you can turn off this setting, returning to static menus.
Office 2000 Clipboard	The new Office 2000 Clipboard supports up to 12 items, and will accept selections from all Office 2000 applications. You can paste everything from the Clipboard at once, or paste individual selections. A new Clipboard toolbar shows the number of selections on the Clipboard, with ScreenTips that show the text or numeric content of each selection, and a Clear Clipboard command to empty the Clipboard.
New Date Formats	Excel 2000 offers two new date formats for two- and four-character years, enabling you to create worksheets that are Y2K compliant.
New Toolbars	The 3D Settings and Shadow Settings toolbars offer greater ability to create graphics with visual depth, and a Clipboard toolbar provides access to the new 12-item Office 2000 Clipboard.
New Web/Email Features	Now you can email a worksheet right from the Standard toolbar. Click the E-mail button and choose to send the active worksheet as an attachment to an email message, or have the entire sheet appear as the body of the message.
	Improve your online meetings by sending worksheets for discussion with the File, Send To, Online Meeting Participant command.
	Adding to the Web focus of Office 2000, you can now choose to insert an HTML object with the Insert, Object command.
	Using the Microsoft Script Editor, you can build and edit Web scripts within worksheets, using a variety of script languages.
	On the Web tab in the Format Object or Format Picture dialog box, you can specify alternative text to display while a browser is loading the map, drawing, or other Excel object with a worksheet.
Automatic Office Repair	New and improved Help is here! The Detect and Repair command on the Help menu finds and fixes errors in the application—including replacing missing or deleted files.

Improved Features	Description
Toolbars	The Standard and Formatting toolbars now appear in one strip to give you more screen space for viewing your worksheet. Clicking the More Buttons button displays the additional tools that don't fit onscreen. You can turn off this default, returning to two distinct Standard and Formatting toolbars.
	To give you faster and easier access to the new Office 2000 clip art collection, the Drawing toolbar now includes the Insert Clip Art button.
Office Assistants	The default Clippit paper clip character has been improved, and several new characters are available, including F1 (a robot) and Links (a cat).
Saving Files in HTML	File, Save As Web Page replaces the previous Save As HTML command. You can choose to save the file in HTML format, or publish the worksheet data to a Web page.
PivotTables/PivotCharts	The PivotTable feature has been redesigned to make creating PivotTables much easier. Using the new PivotTable toolbar, you can drag and drop fields into (or out of) the PivotTable.
	The addition of PivotCharts to the PivotTables feature enables you to combine the power of Excel's extensive charting features with your PivotTables.
Clip Art	Adding clip art (as well as sounds and movies) is much easier in Excel 2000. No need to select and double-click the object in the dialog box—just drag the item onto your worksheet. The icons in the dialog box are also larger and easier to preview.

Special Edition Using Microsoft® Excel 2000

Patrick Blattner
Laurie Ulrich
Ken Cook
Timothy Dyck

201 W. 103rd Street
Indianapolis, Indiana 46290

Special Edition Using Microsoft® Excel 2000

International Standard Book Number: 0-7897-1729-8

Library of Congress Catalog Card Number: 98-85321

Printed in the United States of America

First Printing: May 1999

02   6

Interpretation of the printing code: The rightmost double-digit number is the year of the book's first printing; the rightmost single-digit number, the number of the book's printing. For example, a printing code of 99-1 shows that the first printing of the book occurred in 1999.

Trademarks

Executive Editor
Angie Wethington

Acquisitions Editor
Jamie Milazzo

Development Editors
Robin Drake
Jim Grey

Managing Editor
Thomas F. Hayes

Project Editor
Karen S. Shields

Copy Editor
Jill Bond

Indexer
Becky Hornyak

Proofreader
Maribeth Echard

Team Coordinator
Vicki Harding

Technical Editors
Kyle Bryant
Robert Rosenberg

Software Development Specialist
Andrea Duvall

Layout Technicians
Christy Lemasters
Eric S. Miller

Cover Designers
Dan Armstrong
Ruth Harvey

Book Designers
Louisa Klucznik
Ruth Harvey

Contents

ABOUT THE AUTHORS

Patrick Blattner has been using Excel for more than 12 years in corporate and private business. After graduating from Northeast Louisiana University, he started out in the contracting and gold-mining industry. He then branched off into product development where he received a United States Utility Patent (5,031,865) and set up manufacturing in China with international distribution. He has spent the last four years in interactive software development and is a member of The Academy of Interactive Arts and Sciences. Patrick currently works for Disney Interactive. He can be contacted at Patrick@BlattnerBooks.com or you can visit his site at www.Blattnerbooks.com.

Laurie Ulrich has been teaching computer classes for universities and corporate training centers for more than 10 years. She also runs her own firm, Limehat & Company, Inc., an organization that specializes in technical documentation, software education, Web page design, and Web site hosting. Her firm's primary focus is helping businesses to make the most of their computer investment—by shedding their fears of computerization, and remaining on the cutting edge of business software. In the last two years, Laurie has been a contributing author on several books, and authored four of her own for Que Publishing: *Using Microsoft Word 97, Using Microsoft PowerPoint 97, The Microsoft Office 97 Productivity Pack,* and *The Complete Idiot's Guide to Running a Small Office with Microsoft Office.* One of her upcoming titles includes *Sams Teach Yourself Microsoft Office 2000 in 21 Days.* She can be contacted at laurie@limehat.com or you can visit her site at www.limehat.com.

Ken Cook operates his own software training and consulting business, which he formed in 1989 in the central New Jersey area. He specializes in developing Microsoft Office custom solutions and training Microsoft Office as well as sales automation software for Fortune 500 companies. Ken's writing experience includes developing a custom training curriculum for his clients. Prior to consulting, Ken worked for five years at Prince Manufacturing, where he held marketing and operations positions that exposed him to all facets of the corporate environment. Ken holds a bachelor of science degree in marketing from Syracuse University.

Timothy Dyck has been using, supporting, and developing for Microsoft Office applications since 1984 (when he was blown away seeing Microsoft Word for DOS's onscreen italic for the first time). He is a Microsoft Certified Systems Engineer and has an honors degree in computer science from the University of Waterloo, Ontario, Canada. He is now a contributing editor for PC Week Labs, specializing in databases and Web-development tools.

DEDICATIONS

To my wonderful parents, Bill and Donna, and my older brothers, Scott and Chris, for your unwavering support.   p.b.

I dedicate my portions of this book with love to my great-aunt, Lillie Ulrich. She wouldn't understand too much of this book, but she'd think it was really cool that my name is on the cover. I love you and I miss you, Lil. See you later...   l.u.

ACKNOWLEDGMENTS

PATRICK BLATTNER

To write a book as complete and in depth as Que's *Special Edition Using Microsoft Excel 2000* takes a team of talented and dedicated individuals. I personally would like to take this opportunity to recognize each one of them for their valued contributions. Jamie Milazzo, your positive attitude, ability to recognize talent, and remarkable ability to pull things together and make it happen when it counts is a talent few possess and even fewer do well. Robin Drake, what a pleasure it's been working with you. You're a teacher and mentor in every sense of the word. Jill Bond, thank you for the countless corrections and professionalism throughout the process. In addition, I would like to thank Kyle Bryant and Robert Rosenberg for their technical contributions and expertise. Ken Cook, Tim Dyck, Jim Grey, Julia Kelly, Sherry Kinkoph, and Joyce Nielsen, thank you for the added value you brought to this book with your knowledge and experience. And finally, I would also like to thank the executives at Que: Angie Wethington, Jim Minatel, and John Pierce. Thank you for the opportunity and support.

LAURIE ULRICH

I'd like to thank our acquisitions editor, Jamie Milazzo, for giving me the opportunity to work on this book. It's been a great opportunity from a professional standpoint, and the scope and intricacies of the project have been very educational. A tremendous "thank you" must also go to Robin Drake, our development editor in this project. Her insightful edits whipped us all into shape, and I'm grateful for her years of experience and her straightforward personal style. On a personal note, I'd like to thank all of my Excel students, without whom writing my portions of this book would have been difficult. As a teacher, I learn every day from the needs and interests of my students, and I applied many of their teachings to my chapters.

TELL US WHAT YOU THINK!

As the reader of this book, *you* are our most important critic and commentator. We value your opinion and want to know what we're doing right, what we could do better, what areas you'd like to see us publish in, and any other words of wisdom you're willing to pass our way.

As the Executive Editor for the General Desktop Applications team at Que, I welcome your comments. You can fax, email, or write me directly to let me know what you did or didn't like about this book—as well as what we can do to make our books stronger.

Please note that I cannot help you with technical problems related to the topic of this book, and that due to the high volume of mail I receive, I might not be able to reply to every message.

When you write, please be sure to include this book's title and author as well as your name and phone or fax number. I will carefully review your comments and share them with the author and editors who worked on the book.

Fax: 317-581-4666

Email: feedback@quepublishing.com

Mail: Executive Editor
          General Desktop Applications
          Que
          201 West 103rd Street
          Indianapolis, IN 46290 USA

INTRODUCTION

Just as Microsoft Excel 2000 is the most comprehensive and powerful tool for creating spreadsheets, this book, *Special Edition Using Microsoft Excel 2000*, is the most comprehensive and powerful reference of its kind.

Written by a team of talented authors, this book represents decades of experience teaching, using, and developing spreadsheet solutions with Excel. We bring our expertise to you in this accessible yet extensive book and its accompanying CD-ROM.

Whether you'll use this book as a reference to solve problems and research new features or you plan to read it from cover to cover, this book is designed for people who've used Excel before. We don't want to exclude the new or self-taught user, however, so the first chapter has been designed to provide you with a great foundation in spreadsheet concepts and the basics of Excel.

We welcome you to our book!

NEW FEATURES AND ENHANCEMENTS IN EXCEL 2000

There are a variety of new and enhanced features in Excel 2000—some the result of Office-wide changes and additions, others found solely in Excel.

Enhancements and new features you'll find in Excel fall into the following categories:

- A true Web focus improves Excel's HTML document-creation and Web-publishing capabilities. Look for online collaboration tools as well.
- Improved data analysis tools to support decision-making include PivotTable enhancements such as AutoFormat and PivotCharts, and the capability to pivot data when saved as HTML. Access and use of data tables are improved through enhanced database queries
- Access to Enterprise Data enables you to create OLAP PivotTables, and use Excel's new OLE DB and ADO data access technologies in a SQL Server environment.

- Office Web Components allow Excel objects (worksheets, charts, PivotTables) to be manipulated through your Web browser.

- User interface improvements include new mouse pointers, better charting tools, improved AutoFill features, and year 2000 support.

- The Clipboard is enhanced to allow up to 12 selections, from any Office 2000 application, to be stored on the Clipboard at once. Paste them individually or as a group.

- Currency formatting now includes the new Euro, offering both the symbol and the ISO code.

- Another new feature in all of the Office 2000 applications is the combining of the Standard and Formatting toolbars into one toolbar. At the beginning of the book, you'll see the default single toolbar, and then as the authors move forward through their coverage of Excel, the default may be turned off and the two toolbars appear separately. You'll also notice a variety of Office Assistant characters throughout the book—this reflects the different authors' personal preferences.

HOW THIS BOOK IS ORGANIZED

Special Edition Using Microsoft Excel 2000 is divided into logically ordered and carefully divided sections. This makes it easier for you to find the topics you need, and ensures that the book flows from basic to advanced topics in a manner that enables you to read the book from start to finish, effectively building your Excel skills.

Part I: Workbook Basics

Chapters 1 and 2 introduce you to the Excel environment and discuss the process of building a worksheet. Although this book is designed for the intermediate user, basic users will also benefit from the content of these chapters as they build a solid Excel foundation. If you're a self-taught Excel user, you may find these chapters very useful in filling in the gaps that can occur without formal training.

Part II: Editing Worksheet Content

Chapters 3, 4, and 5 take you through the process of selecting, editing, and deleting worksheet entries, and using the Clipboard to move and copy worksheet content. Tools for moving, copying, and naming sections of your worksheet are discussed, improving your comfort level and the speed with which you navigate even your most complex worksheet.

Part III: Formatting and Printing Excel Worksheets

Chapters 6 through 9 help you add formatting, drawing shapes, and clip art to achieve a visually powerful worksheet environment for your data. Then learn to print your data—in sections, specific pages, or the entire workbook.

Part IV: Using Formulas and Functions

Chapters 10, 11, and 12 go to the real core of any worksheet—formulas and functions. Build your own formulas with your mouse and/or keyboard, or use named ranges and

Excel's built-in functions to simplify even the most complex or esoteric mathematical procedure. These chapters start from the ground up to make sure you're building your formulas correctly, and then pick up the pace to show you tools that will help you build any formula you need.

Part V: Creating and Modifying Charts

Chapters 13 through 16 take you on a comprehensive tour of Excel's considerable charting tools. From building a simple bar or pie chart to stacking multiple charts, you'll learn which chart type best depicts your data and how to manipulate its appearance and content to express your numeric data effectively. Learn professional techniques for making your charts stand out visually as well as in terms of their content, communicating complex data in a dynamic visual format.

Part VI: Analyzing and Managing Your Data

Chapters 17 through 22 focus on Excel's data analysis and data management features. Learn how to build a database or list, edit, sort, and filter the list, and create illuminating reports from the data you store. Take advantage of Excel's new and improved PivotTable and PivotChart tools for data analysis to support your business decisions. Improve your worksheets with form controls that make Excel work as a project-management program. Use the Goal Seek, Solver, and Analysis ToolPak tools to solve simple or complex business problems.

Part VII: Taking Excel to the Next Level

Chapters 23 and 24 show you new and creative ways to use Excel. Learn how to build dynamic Gantt charts in Excel for time and flow management. Employ Excel's drawing tools to build value chains for market analysis and strategic business planning. Create quadrants to compare product placement and market focus. By learning how to mix and combine Excel's tools, you'll start to see the true power and flexibility of Excel 2000.

Part VIII: Integrating Excel with Other Applications

Chapters 25 through 27 show you how to end your isolation and branch out—using Excel data in your Word documents, PowerPoint presentations, and Access tables. Work in the other direction, taking Word, PowerPoint, and Access content and using it to improve your Excel worksheets. Chapter 26 focuses extensively on Excel's database access capabilities and on retrieving data from the Web. Learn how to build database queries and retrieve information from Access and from other databases. Chapter 27 introduces you to OLAP PivotTables and data stores. Use Excel 2000's Cube Wizard to build and use cubes for quick data access and analysis offline.

Part IX: Customizing and Automating Excel

Chapters 28 through 31 focus on your ability to make Excel work the way you do—from resetting software defaults to writing and editing macros to collaborating with other Excel users on a network or the Web, these chapters show you how to tweak and automate Excel, unleashing your creativity and making you more productive.

Part X: Appendixes

Appendixes A and B are supplements that support and expand on topics covered in the rest of the book. Appendix A is a comprehensive guide to Excel's functions, providing information you'll find indispensable. Appendix B outlines the content of the CD-ROM that accompanies this book and tells you how to access and use the files and programs on the CD.

CONVENTIONS USED IN THIS BOOK

Que, as well as all of Macmillan Computer Publishing's various imprints, has more than 10 years' experience creating the most popular and effective computer reference books available. From trainers to programmers, Que's authors have invaluable experience using and—most importantly—*explaining* computer and software concepts. From basic to advanced topics, Que's publishing experience and their authors' expertise and communication skills combine to create a highly readable and easily navigated book.

Note	Notes contain extra information or alternate techniques for performing tasks that the author feels will enhance your use and/or understanding of the current topic.

Tip #1001 from *Laurie*	Found throughout the book's text, tips are just that—quick advice to help you make faster or more efficient use of Excel.

Caution	If there is a potential problem with a feature or something you should be aware of to avoid errors or unwanted results, you'll find both a description of the situation and how to resolve or avoid it in the Caution format.

ICONS

Whenever an icon is referred to in a discussion paragraph or step-by-step procedure, the icon will appear in the margin, next to the text that mentions it. This helps you find the icon on the toolbar and remember its location and function for future use.

UNDERLINED HOT KEYS

To assist you in using the keyboard to issue menu and dialog box commands, you'll find the underlined letters as they appear onscreen underlined in the text. For example, File, Print tells you that pressing Alt+F to open the File menu, followed by P will open the Print dialog box. After you're in the Print dialog box, Alt+E will tell Excel that you want to print the Current page.

KEYBOARD SHORTCUTS

Whenever a combination of keys can be pressed to execute a command, they'll appear paired by a plus sign, as in Ctrl+Home (to move to cell A1) or Ctrl+P (to open the Print dialog box). When using a keyboard shortcut, press the first key, and while that key is pressed, tap the second key.

TYPEFACES

Throughout this book, a variety of typefaces will be used, each one designed to draw your attention to specific text:

Typeface	Description
Monospace	Screen messages and VBA commands appear in this special typeface.
Italic	New terminology and emphasized text will appear in italic.
Boldface	References to text you should type will appear in boldface.

END-OF-CHAPTER EXAMPLES

At the end of many chapters, you'll find an example of how to use that chapter's features to improve the overall functioning, legibility, and/or effectiveness of your worksheets. Often appearing in the form of before-and-after figures with explanatory callouts, these samples offer advice and practical examples for your own implementation.

WORKBOOK BASICS

CHAPTER

1

GETTING STARTED WITH EXCEL

by Laurie Ann Ulrich
laurie@limehat.com

In this chapter

STARTING AND EXITING THE EXCEL PROGRAM

If you're new to Excel, it won't be long before you're accustomed to performing various spreadsheet tasks simply and quickly. You'll want to start the program with as much speed and simplicity as possible. Choose one of the following methods to start Excel:

- From the Start menu, choose Programs, and then select Microsoft Excel from the list. This method isn't the fastest, but you don't need to do anything special to use it—the menus are set up for you through your installation of Microsoft Office.

- Choose New Office Document from the Start menu, and choose the Blank Workbook icon from the General tab. Click OK to open Excel. Again, this isn't the fastest method, but the tools are already set up for you.

- Click the Excel icon on the Office Shortcut Bar. This opens Excel and a blank workbook for you. Many users may opt not to display this toolbar, but its presence on the desktop is part of the typical installation of Office. If left on the desktop, the Office Shortcut Bar provides a quick method for accessing all the applications in Office 2000.

- Open an existing Excel workbook from within Windows Explorer, My Computer, or by using a desktop shortcut to that particular file.

→ To learn how to open an existing workbook file, **see** "Opening a Saved File," **p. 51**

- Create and use a shortcut icon on the desktop that takes you right into Excel. This requires you to create the icon in the first place, but you would have to do that only once. From then on, you'd have the fastest method of starting Excel right on your desktop. To create a shortcut, follow these steps:

  1. Right-click any empty spot on your Windows desktop.

  2. Choose New, Shortcut from the shortcut menu.

  3. In the Command line text box, enter the path and filename for Excel, which may be in a Microsoft Office folder on your local drive. The default path is C:\Program Files\Microsoft Office\Office\Excel.exe.

Tip #1 from

Laurie

| If you're not sure of the exact location, click Browse. When you've found the program file (Excel.exe), double-click it or click Open to return to the Create Shortcut dialog box.

---

  4. Click Next.

  5. Type a name for your shortcut, or accept the default name as it appears in the Select a Name for the Shortcut text box.

  6. Click Finish. Your shortcut appears on the desktop. (You can tell a shortcut from a program icon that exists nowhere but the desktop by the small arrow in the lower-left corner of the icon image. Only shortcuts have this arrow.)

- Add Excel to your Startup folder so that the program begins as soon as you start your computer and Windows opens. This also must be set up, which takes time. Consider this method only if Excel is the first program you use each day, and the primary program you work with throughout the day. To add Excel to your Startup folder, follow these steps:

1. Choose Settings, Taskbar & Start Menu from the Start menu.
2. Click the Start Menu Programs tab.
3. Click the Add button to start the Create Shortcut dialog box.
4. Enter the path and filename for Excel (Excel.exe) in the Command Line text box.

   If you aren't sure of the exact path to your program file, click Browse, and then double-click the Excel program file, which probably is located in your C:\Program Files\Microsoft Office\Office folder.
5. Click Next.
6. Scroll down in the Select Folder to Place Shortcut In box, until you find Startup. Click it once.
7. Click Next.
8. Enter a name for the shortcut, as you want it to appear in the Start menu (or accept the default name).
9. Click Finish.

When you start Excel, you are immediately presented with a blank Excel workbook, ready for you to begin entering and editing your data.

Exiting Excel can be performed in any one of the following ways:

- Choose File, Exit. Any open and unsaved workbooks will result in a prompt, asking you whether you want to save your work. After you respond to these prompts, the program will close.
- Click the Close button in the upper-right corner of the Excel application window. Using this button also results in prompts asking you to save any unsaved work, after which the application will be shut down. If you see two Close buttons, be sure to click the one on the Excel title bar; otherwise, you'll just close the workbook window.
- Right-click the taskbar icon for each of your Excel workbooks (a separate button appears on the taskbar for each open workbook) and choose Close from the shortcut menu for each open workbook. When all workbooks are closed, right-click the remaining Excel application button on the taskbar, and choose Close. The application will now be closed.
- Press Alt+F4 to exit the program.

If you need to close only the workbook you're working on and want to keep Excel open to work on other workbook files, choose File, Close from the menu, or press Ctrl+F4. If you haven't saved your work, you'll be prompted to do so before the workbook is closed. Find out more about saving your workbooks in Chapter 2, "Entering and Saving Worksheet Data."

IDENTIFYING WORKBOOK ELEMENTS

Before you start entering any text or numbers into your blank Excel workbook, it's a good idea to become familiar with the entire Excel window. Your Excel window contains the following main elements:

- Title bar
- Menu bar
- Toolbars
- Formula bar
- Scrollbars
- Worksheet columns and rows
- Worksheet tabs
- Status bar

Figure 1.1 shows a typical blank Excel workbook.

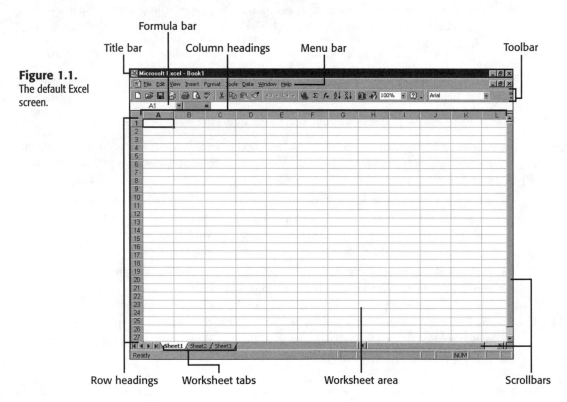

Figure 1.1.
The default Excel screen.

Formula bar

Title bar   Column headings   Menu bar   Toolbar

Row headings   Worksheet tabs   Worksheet area   Scrollbars

When a workbook is open, the Excel window contains two sets of Minimize, Maximize, and Close buttons. The uppermost set is associated with the Excel *application* (program), the lower set controls the workbook window.

Tip #2 from *Laurie*

> If you're using the Microsoft IntelliMouse or Microsoft IntelliMouse TrackBall, you can hold down the wheel button and drag up, down, left, or right within the window to scroll through your worksheet.

USING SCREENTIPS AND WHAT'S THIS? HELP

You can point to any element in your Excel window and, after a brief pause, a *ScreenTip* will appear to tell you the name of that particular element (see Figure 1.2).

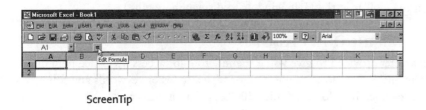

Microsoft Excel - Book1
A1
Edit Formula
ScreenTip

Figure 1.2. Use ScreenTips to help familiarize yourself with the names of your Excel window elements.

If you want to know more, press Shift+F1 or choose Help, What's This? on the menu, which turns on your *What's This? Help*. Your cursor then appears with a question mark attached to it. Point to any element and click. A pop-up description of the element (this is also called a ScreenTip) appears, as shown in Figure 1.3. Press Esc or click outside the ScreenTip to close the ScreenTip.

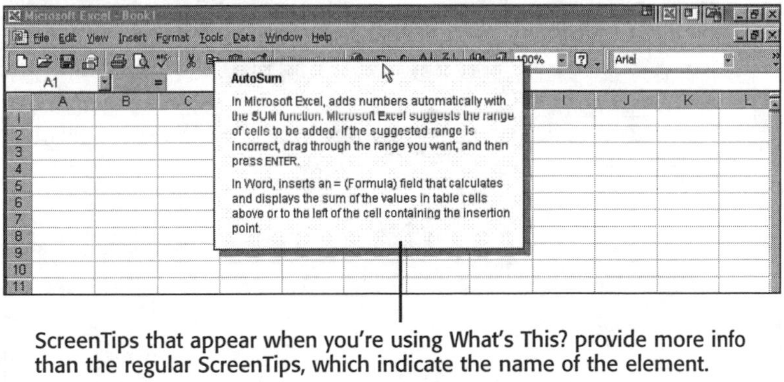
Microsoft Excel - Book1
File Edit View Insert Format Tools Data Window Help
AutoSum
In Microsoft Excel, adds numbers automatically with the SUM function. Microsoft Excel suggests the range of cells to be added. If the suggested range is incorrect, drag through the range you want, and then press ENTER.
In Word, inserts an = (Formula) field that calculates and displays the sum of the values in table cells above or to the left of the cell containing the insertion point.
ScreenTips that appear when you're using What's This? provide more info than the regular ScreenTips, which indicate the name of the element.

Figure 1.3. By pressing Shft+F1, you can turn your cursor into a point-and-click help tool.

Tip #3 from

Laurie

> What's This? Help is a great alternative to the standard Microsoft help because you don't need to know the name of a feature to find out more about it. Dialog boxes also include What's This? Help buttons that you can use to get information about the buttons, tabs, options, and so on, in the dialog box. The What's This? button displays a question mark, and is located next to the Close button in the upper-right corner of the dialog box.

To gain access to Excel's full set of help files, choose <u>H</u>elp, Microsoft Excel <u>H</u>elp or press F1. If the Office Assistant is enabled, this command displays the Assistant (see the next section for details). If the Office Assistant has been disabled or you're using the standalone version of Excel, this command displays the Help window.

In the Help window, you can search by topic using the <u>C</u>ontents tab, alphabetically using the <u>I</u>ndex tab, or by typing a question in the Answer Wizard tab. (If necessary, click the Show button on the toolbar in the Help window to display these tabs.)

GETTING ANSWERS WITH THE OFFICE ASSISTANT

An animated character provided to give you a friendly tool for accessing Office help files, the *Office Assistant* enables you to ask a question or type a series of keywords and follow a series of prompts to reach help for any Office 2000 application feature.

To access the Office Assistant, use one of the following methods:

- Click the Office Assistant button on the toolbar. The Assistant appears and prompts you to ask your question (see Figure 1.4). Right-click on the Office Assistant and select <u>C</u>hoose Assistant to obtain access to the Office Assistant <u>G</u>allery. Eight animated assistants are available.

Figure 1.4.
Type your request in question format, such as "How do I use formulas?" and a list of likely topics will be presented.

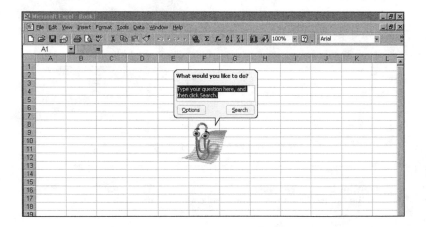

- Choose <u>H</u>elp, Show the <u>O</u>ffice Assistant. This method also opens the Office Assistant, and you can type your question or keywords.

- Press F1. Using this method does two things. It opens the Office Assistant and forces it to guess the topic for which you need help (see Figure 1.5). This context-sensitive help is based on the dialog box, menu, or feature that's in use at the time you press F1.

Tip #4 from

Laurie

If you prefer not to use the Office Assistant at all, choose the Options button in the Office Assistant's dialog box, or right-click the Assistant and choose Options. Deselect the option Use the Office Assistant.

If you want Excel to display the Help window when you press F1, rather than displaying the Office Assistant, deselect the Respond to F1 Key option in the Office Assistant dialog box.

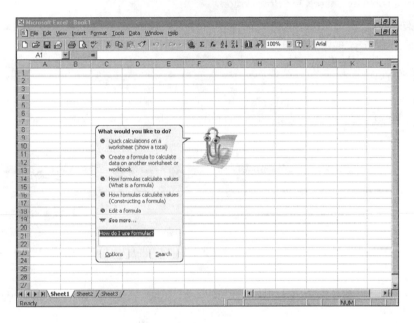

Figure 1.5.
Choose the topic that most closely matches your requested information. You can also type a new question and click Search.

When you're finished using the Office Assistant, you can right-click the Assistant character and choose Hide from the shortcut menu. If you don't hide the character, it will remain onscreen while you're working, and will become active if you press F1 or click the Office Assistant button on the toolbar. If you decide to leave the Assistant onscreen, it should change size or position automatically as necessary to move out of the way as you work. If the Assistant obscures a portion of the screen you need to see, however, just drag the Assistant out of the way.

VIEWING TOOLBARS

The Excel window opens with one toolbar displayed—a combination of the Standard and Formatting toolbars (see Figure 1.6). This toolbar contains buttons that represent the most frequently used Excel commands, as well as a great number of buttons that you'll recognize from other Microsoft Office programs, assuming that you installed Excel with Microsoft Office instead of installing Excel as a standalone program.

Figure 1.6.
The most commonly used buttons from the Standard and Formatting toolbars are displayed in one toolbar strip.

This toolbar configuration is new to Excel 2000, and although it's the default, you may prefer to see both toolbars at once. To reset your toolbars and turn off the default, choose Tools, Customize, and click the Options tab. Remove the check mark from the Standard and Formatting toolbars Share One Row option.

> **Note**
>
> In this book, most figures show the Standard toolbar appearing below the menu bar, followed by the Formatting toolbar on a separate strip.

This toolbar contains more buttons than can be displayed onscreen at one time. To view these obscured buttons, click the More Buttons button at the far-right end of the toolbar (see Figure 1.7).

Figure 1.7.
Tools for formatting appear in a tool palette when More Buttons is clicked.

Tables 1.1 and 1.2 list each of the toolbar buttons on the Standard and Formatting toolbars and briefly explain their functions.

TABLE 1.1. BUTTONS ON THE STANDARD TOOLBAR

Button	Name	Description
 New	New	Creates a blank workbook.
 Open	Open	Displays the Open dialog box, from which you can browse to find an existing file.
 Save	Save	For a first-time save, this tool opens the Save As dialog box, enabling you to give the file a name and choose a location to save it. After you save the file, this button updates the saved file to include your latest changes.
 Email	Email	Sends either the entire open workbook or the current worksheet as an email attachment.

Button	Name	Description
	Print	Sends the currently selected sheet(s) directly to the printer.
	Print Preview	Displays a thumbnail sketch of the worksheet.
	Spelling	Runs a spell check of the text in the workbook.
	Cut	Removes the selected content and places it on the Clipboard. Normally followed procedurally by pasting.
	Copy	Places a duplicate of the selected content on the Clipboard.
	Paste	Places the cut or copied content from the Clipboard to a new location.
	Format Painter	Copies formatting from one range of cells to another.
	Undo	Cancels the last action. You can undo multiple operations by clicking the down arrow and selecting from the list.
	Redo	Reverses previous Undo operation(s).
	Hyperlink	Opens a dialog box from which you can choose to create a link to a document on your local or network drive, or to a Web page on the Internet.
	AutoSum	Automatically sums a column or row of numbers. Click once to choose the numbers to be summed, click again or press Enter to perform the calculation and insert the result.
	Paste Function	Opens the Function Wizard, a series of dialog boxes that enable you to choose a mathematical function and then select the cells you want to use in the calculation.
	Sort Ascending	Performs an A–Z or 1–10 sort for a series of rows.
	Sort Descending	Performs a Z–A or 10–1 sort for a series of rows.
	Chart Wizard	Opens a wizard you can use to build a chart from selected cells in your worksheet.
	Map	Opens an application called Microsoft Map, which runs within Excel. Choose a region of the world, and a map is created. Mapping tools also appear, which you can use to format the map.
	Drawing	Displays the Drawing toolbar, a series of tools for creating and formatting hand-drawn shapes and lines.
100%	Zoom	Enlarges or reduces the display of your currently viewed worksheet area.
	Microsoft Excel Help	Activates the Office Assistant—an animated character you can use to get help on a variety of Excel topics. (Microsoft Office installations only.)

TABLE 1.2.   BUTTONS ON THE FORMATTING TOOLBAR

Button	Name	Description
Tahoma ▼	Font	Shows the font currently in use; click the down-arrow button to see a list of fonts that you can apply.
10 ▼	Font Size	Indicates the current point size; click the down-arrow button to see a list of available point sizes. Choose one from the list or type your own number.
B	Bold	Makes the selection bold.
I	Italic	Makes the selection italic.
U	Underline	Underlines the selection.
	Align Left	Text is left-aligned by default. Use this button to realign previously centered or right-aligned text or to left-align numeric content.
	Center	Moves text or numeric content to the center of the cell.
	Align Right	Aligns the content of selected cells along the right side of the cell.
	Merge and Center	Used primarily for titles, this button takes cell content in one cell and centers it across several contiguous (adjacent) cells, merging the cells into one long cell.
$	Currency Style	Turns standard numbers into currency by adding decimals, commas, and a dollar sign.
%	Percent Style	Turns standard numbers into a percent, with a percent sign.
,	Comma Style	Adds commas to numbers in excess of 999.99.
.00	Increase Decimal	Extends the display of numbers to the right of the decimal point. The number 5.6, for example, can become 5.58 or 5.579. Each click of the button extends the number one digit.
.00	Decrease Decimal	Reduces the number of digits to the right of the decimal point. Each click takes away one number.
	Decrease Indent	Moves the cell content in selected cells closer to the left side of the cell, if any indent had been applied in the cell.
	Increase Indent	Moves cell content to the right.
	Borders	Opens a palette of border options for placing borders on any side of a cell or block of cells, including thick and double bottom borders.

Button	Name	Description
	Fill Color	Applies or removes solid color fills in cell backgrounds.
	Font Color	Changes the color of text or numbers in selected cells.

Many of Excel's tools require that you select a cell or cells before using the tool, so that Excel knows where you want to apply the format or perform the action that the button represents. If you don't consciously select a cell or cells, the toolbar will act upon the active cell.

Tip #5 from

Laurie

Use What's This? Help to identify and get a brief description of the function of any toolbar button.

Although you may not feel the need to do so until you're more familiar with Excel, you can always add and delete toolbars from your Excel window. To see a list of the different toolbars available in Excel, right-click any of the displayed toolbars, or choose View, Toolbars. Click the name of the toolbar you want to add to the screen.

To remove a currently displayed toolbar, display the list of toolbars and select the name of the toolbar you want to remove. The toolbar list is a toggle list—select them once, they're on; select them again, they're off.

→ For more information on customizing Excel's toolbars, **see** "Modifying Toolbars," **p. 869**

WORKING WITH EXCEL MENUS

The Excel menus contain all of the same tools that are represented on the toolbars, and more. To access Excel menus, click the name of the menu, or press Alt plus the underlined letter in the menu name. To close a menu you opened accidentally, press Esc or click the menu name again.

Microsoft Office menus contain the following three main features:

- **Commands.** The words you click to make things happen. If the words are followed by an ellipsis (…), a dialog box will open. If the command is followed by a right-pointing triangle, a submenu will appear.
- **Toolbar reference icons.** To familiarize you with the toolbar buttons that match your menu commands, they're reiterated in the menus.
- **Keyboard shortcuts.** If a keyboard shortcut is assigned to a given command, that shortcut will appear to the right of the command text.

In case you prefer using the keyboard whenever possible, you can also issue menu commands by pressing the underlined letter in the command while the menu is displayed.

Tip #6 from

If Excel beeps repeatedly or refuses to insert entries as you type, you may have accidentally pressed the Alt key, which activates the menu bar without actually opening any particular menu. If one of the menu names looks different from the other menu names—boxed, or like a button—press Alt or Esc to deactivate the menu bar and return to the worksheet area.

A new feature in Office 2000 is the *personalized menus*, which are designed to be sensitive to the user. Each program begins by displaying a default set of commands when you open the menu; if you keep the menu open for a few seconds, additional (less used) commands also appear. As you use these less-common commands, they join the others in the default set; the menus thus adapt to match your use of the program. If you prefer to have your menu commands remain static rather than personalized, you can turn off this feature. Choose Tools, Customize, and turn off the Menus Show Recently Used Commands First option from the Options tab. Click Close to put this change into effect and close the dialog box.

Figure 1.8 shows a typical Excel menu.

Figure 1.8.
Although some commands are available only from the menus, most have toolbar and keyboard equivalents. Dimmed commands on menus are not available under the current circumstances.

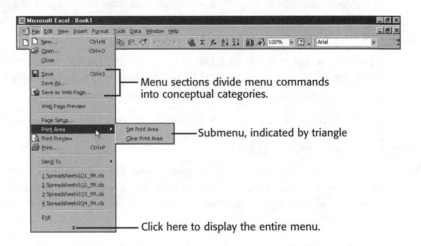

Menu sections divide menu commands into conceptual categories.

Submenu, indicated by triangle

Click here to display the entire menu.

Tip #7 from

When personalized menus are in use, you can display the entire menu immediately by double-clicking, rather than single-clicking, the top menu item (File, Edit, and so on). You also can click the last item on the open menu—a pair of downward-pointing arrows.

WORKING WITH SHORTCUT MENUS

Shortcut menus (also called *context menus*) are another type of menu that you'll find throughout Excel and all of the other Office 2000 applications. By right-clicking various items in your workbook window, you can open menus that offer context-sensitive commands. Figure 1.9 shows a typical shortcut menu that appears when you right-click any cell (or selected range of cells) in your worksheet.

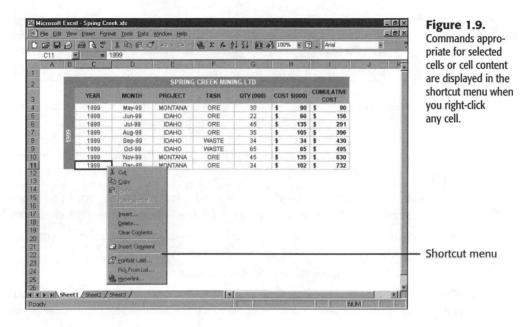

Figure 1.9.
Commands appropriate for selected cells or cell content are displayed in the shortcut menu when you right-click any cell.

Shortcut menu

WORKING WITH WORKBOOKS

It's important to understand one concept from the outset — Excel files are *workbooks*, each of which contains three *worksheets* by default. These worksheets can be accessed by clicking their *sheet tabs*, or by using the *tab scrolling buttons* to the left of the tabs, as shown in Figure 1.10.

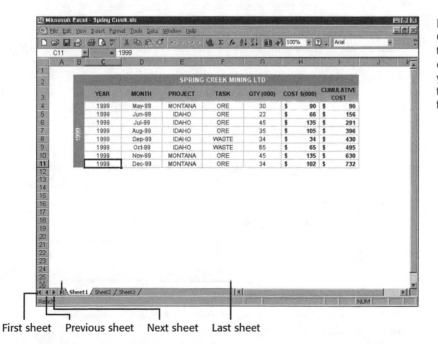

Figure 1.10.
Click a worksheet's tab to select it. If you can't see the sheet you want, click the tab scrolling buttons to bring it into view.

First sheet   Previous sheet   Next sheet   Last sheet

Tip #8 from

If you want to quickly select a sheet that's out of view, right-click the tab scrolling buttons to see a shortcut menu listing all the sheets in the workbook. Select the sheet you want by choosing its name from the list.

Why have separate sheets? That's a good and common question, as versions of Excel prior to 5.0 didn't have worksheets—each Excel file was one big spreadsheet, with just two dimensions—width and height. Since version 5.0, however, Excel files have had depth as well as vertical and horizontal dimensions. The following list describes standard workbook modifications:

- You can add sheets to the default three with which each workbook starts. The number of sheets per workbook is limited only by the amount of memory on your computer.

- You can change sheet names. Sheet1, Sheet2, and so on, are default sheet names. Worksheet names can be up to 31 characters long.

- You can rearrange worksheet order and delete sheets.

- If you need to create a new worksheet that resembles an existing worksheet, you can copy the existing worksheet, paste the copy into the workbook, and edit the copy to meet your needs.

- You can group your worksheets, and create several identical worksheets all at once. Or you can create one worksheet and make a copy of it.

After you've added sheets, you can go to any one of them quickly by right-clicking the sheet scrolling buttons and choosing the sheet by name.

Tip #9 from

You can change the default number of sheets that any new workbook opens with by choosing Tools, Options and clicking the General tab. Change the setting for Sheets in New Workbook, and click OK. For more information about customizing Excel to meet your needs, see Chapter 28, "Customizing Excel to Fit Your Working Style."

INSERTING AND DELETING SHEETS

If the three sheets that came with your blank workbook aren't enough for you, add new ones. To insert a new worksheet, choose Insert, Worksheet. A new sheet appears to the left of the currently active sheet. To delete a sheet, right-click the sheet tab and choose Delete; then confirm that you want to permanently delete the sheet.

New sheets are added chronologically. For example, if you add Sheet 4 and then delete it, the next new sheet will be called Sheet 5, even though Sheet 4 is no longer in the workbook.

NAMING WORKSHEETS

Numeric worksheet names (Sheet1, Sheet2) don't tell you about the content of your sheets. Unless you happen to remember what data you've entered on your individual sheets, you're likely to spend a lot of time clicking through the worksheets.

To name a worksheet, use the following methods:

- Choose Format, Sheet, Rename.
- Double-click the sheet tab or right-click it and choose Rename.
- Right-click the tab for the worksheet you want to rename and choose Rename from the shortcut menu.

All three techniques have the same result—the current sheet name is highlighted, and you can type the replacement text (see Figure 1.11). To confirm your entry, click in any cell on the current sheet, click another sheet tab, or press Enter. To keep the previous name, press Esc before confirming the new name.

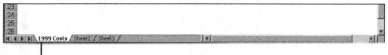

This sheet has been renamed from Sheet1 to 1999 Costs.

Figure 1.11.
Type a short and simple sheet name to identify the contents of that sheet for you and other users of the workbook.

REARRANGING WORKSHEETS

When you insert a new sheet, it's added to the left of the sheet that was active at the time. In many cases, this new sheet isn't in the position where you want it, relative to the existing sheets.

To move a sheet, click the sheet tab and drag it to a new position, watching the small down pointing triangle that appears and follows the tab as you move it left and right. Your mouse pointer also is accompanied by a small page icon. When the triangle is pointing to the spot where you want to place your tab, release the mouse. Figure 1.12 shows a sheet tab being moved.

GROUPING AND UNGROUPING SHEETS

Sheets can be *grouped* (connected) to facilitate creating or formatting two or more identical sheets. For example, you can create one sheet and copy it to two other sheets, or you can group three blank sheets and enter the sales report content once—no subsequent copying is required. Because the sheets are connected before any content is entered, all the content is automatically placed on all the grouped sheets.

To group sheets, click one of the tabs that you want in the group and press the Ctrl key. With the Ctrl key held down, click the remaining tabs in the intended group of sheets. All the grouped sheets' tabs will turn white, and the indicator [Group] will appear in the title bar after the workbook name, as shown in Figure 1.13.

Figure 1.12.
Rearrange your sheet tabs by dragging left and/or right until you find the correct location.

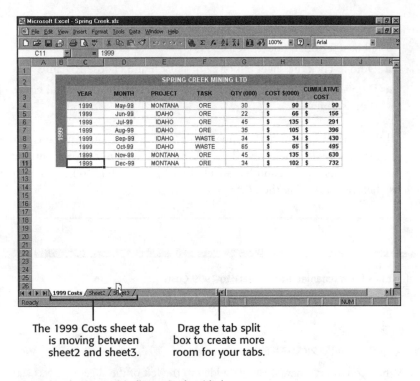

The 1999 Costs sheet tab is moving between sheet2 and sheet3.

Drag the tab split box to create more room for your tabs.

Notice the [Group] indicator in the title bar.

Figure 1.13.
Select as many sheets as you need for your group with the Ctrl key.

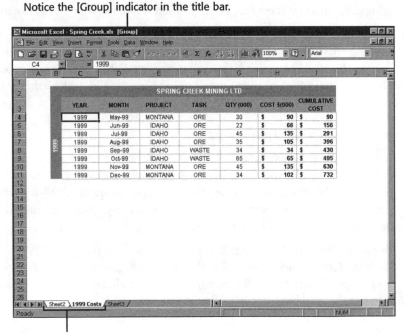

These two sheets are grouped.

Tip #10 from

You can group a series of sheets by pressing the Shift key as you click the first and then the last tabs in the series. All the sheets between the first and last tab will be included in the group.

You can group *all* the sheets in a workbook by right-clicking any sheet and choosing <u>S</u>elect All Sheets from the shortcut menu.

To *ungroup* your grouped sheets, click on a sheet tab outside of the group, or right-click any of the grouped tabs and choose <u>U</u>ngroup Sheets from the shortcut menu.

Caution

When entering group content, be sure to enter only the content that you want to be common to all of the sheets in the group. If the group of sheets are intended to be quarterly sales reports for two or more companies, for example, stop entering group content and ungroup the sheets before entering any content specific to any individual company.

NAVIGATING THE WORKBOOK

While you're entering data into a worksheet, you may be working in a confined area of the sheet and find that using the mouse and your arrow keys to make short-distance moves is completely adequate. When you start working with many columns and rows within a single worksheet or with multiple sheets, however, you'll want to make long-distance moves as quickly and easily as possible.

You can feel in control of a workbook and the worksheets within it only if you know how to move from one cell to another, one sheet to another, or to another open workbook and back again.

UNDERSTANDING CELL ADDRESSES

A cell's *address* is its location—an intersection of a *column* (vertical position) and a *row* (horizontal position). Cell C7, for example, is found at the intersection of column C and row 7, as shown in Figure 1.14. The Name box indicates the selected cell's address; the row and column headings for the selected cell appear bold and are "raised" to look like gray buttons.

Note

There are 256 columns in each worksheet—lettered A through Z, and then AA through IV. Use Alt+Page Down to page quickly across the width of your worksheet and familiarize yourself with the column letters.

When referring to a range of cells in a formula or to select them using the Go To dialog box, use a colon between the first and last cell in the range (see Figure 1.15).

For more information on selecting cells and ranges, see Chapter 3, "Selecting and Naming Cells and Ranges." To learn more about using and referring to cell addresses, see Chapter 10, "Constructing Excel Formulas."

The Name box indicates the selected cell's address (C4).

Cell pointer

Formula bar

Column letters

Figure 1.14.
Like coordinates on a map, a cell's address indicates its position within the worksheet.

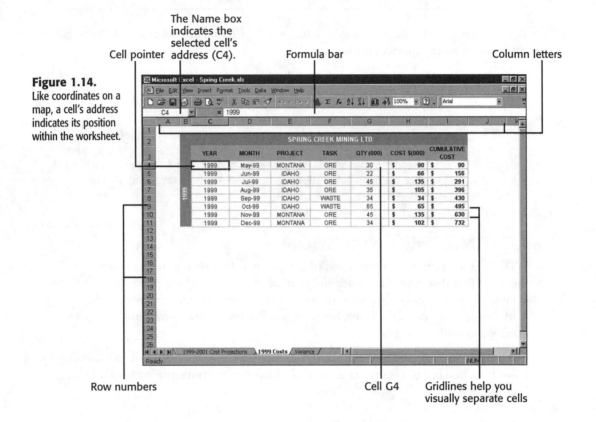

Row numbers

Cell G4

Gridlines help you visually separate cells

MOVING THROUGH A WORKSHEET

Worksheets are the major components of a workbook. There are over 16 million cells per worksheet. The columns range from A to IV and each worksheet includes 65,536 rows. Using your mouse and keyboard, you can move great distances—from cell A1 to IV65536 or right next door from A1 to A2. For most moves, you have more than one option.

Note

A standard three-sheet workbook includes over 50 million cells. You probably won't use even one percent of them in any of your worksheets, so don't worry about running out of space for your work!

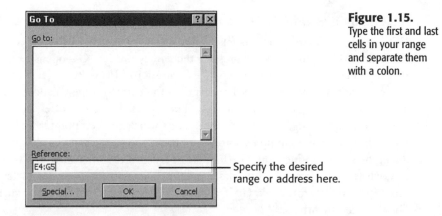

Figure 1.15.
Type the first and last cells in your range and separate them with a colon.

— Specify the desired range or address here.

USING WORKSHEET KEYBOARD SHORTCUTS

With more than 16 million cells in a single worksheet, it's important to get where you're going as quickly as possible. Table 1.3 lists the keyboard shortcuts you can use to move from cell to cell in a worksheet.

TABLE 1.3.   KEYBOARD WORKSHEET NAVIGATION

Keyboard Shortcut	Result
Tab	Moves one cell to the right.
Shift+Tab	Moves one cell to the left.
Enter	Moves one cell down.
Ctrl+Home	Moves back to cell A1 (called Home) from anywhere in the worksheet.
Ctrl+End	Moves to the last cell containing content in the worksheet.
Home	Moves to the beginning of the current row.
Page Down	Moves down one screen.
Page Up	Moves up one screen.
Alt+Page Down	Moves one screen to the right.
Alt+Page Up	Moves one screen to the left.
Ctrl+Page Down	Moves to the next worksheet in the workbook
Ctrl+Page Up	Moves to the previous sheet in the workbook.

ACCESSING CELLS WITH GO TO

While most keyboard shortcuts take you to a cell in relation to the cell you're in, the Go To shortcut—which you access by pressing the F5 key or Ctrl+G—opens a dialog box into which you can type any cell address (see Figure 1.16). Press Enter after typing the address, and you are automatically placed in that cell. You can also type an address in the Name box and press Enter to jump to that address. The Go To dialog box offers an advantage over the Name box; the dialog box displays the address where the cell pointer was located before you jumped, so it's easy to jump back to where you came from. You can also access the Go To dialog box by choosing Edit, Go To. The Special button opens the Go To Special dialog box, which lets you access formulas, conditional formatting, precedents, dependents, and more in an Excel workbook. Go To Special is also a good tool to use when auditing a workbook created by others.

Figure 1.16.
Use the Go To command to jump to cell references within a workbook.

Figure 1.17.
To access special formulas and features added to the workbook, use the Go To Special dialog box.

TROUBLESHOOTING

VIEWING MORE SHEET TABS

How can I see more of my sheet tabs?

After you've added and named sheets, you may find that not all of them are visible at the same time. You can do two things to avoid/rectify this situation. First, try to keep your sheet names short, using abbreviations such as `Qtr1 Sales/Exp` instead of `First Quarter Sales and Expenses`. Second, expand the sheet tab display area by clicking the *tab split box*—the little vertical bar at the left end of the horizontal scrollbar—and dragging it to the right. This reduces the width of the scrollbar, and allows more room for your tabs.

EXCEL IN PRACTICE

You can get rid of the gray lines a worksheet uses by default to show cell borders. Figure 1.18 shows these gray lines.

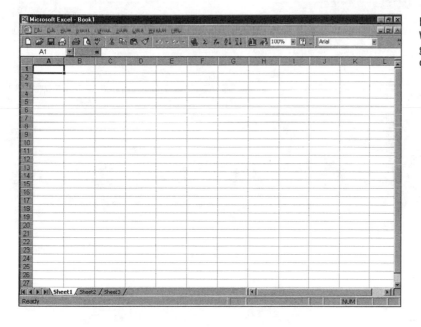

Figure 1.18.
Worksheets use gray grid lines to show cell boundaries.

To hide the gridlines, create a white background. Click the Select All button in the upper-left corner of the worksheet (it's to the left of the column A heading). Then click the arrow at the right of the Fill Color button in the Formatting toolbar, and choose white, as Figure 1.19 shows.

Figure 1.20 shows the resulting white background.

Figure 1.19.
After you select the entire sheet, click the Fill Color button and choose white.

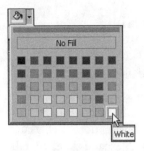

Figure 1.20.
The gridlines are no longer visible.

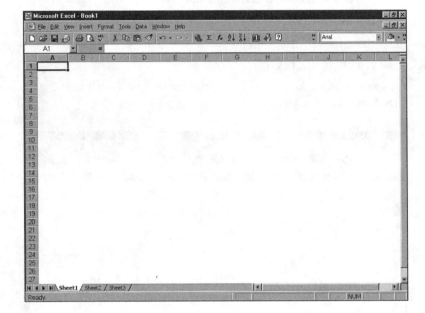

CHAPTER 2

ENTERING AND SAVING WORKSHEET DATA

In this chapter

by Laurie Ann Ulrich
laurie@limehat.com

PLANNING YOUR WORKSHEET

Whether your workbook will include one worksheet or hundreds, the process of building the workbook should begin with planning. You should have some mental picture of the workbook before you start entering data into the cells. For many spreadsheets, the structure you need is obvious; for others, you may go through a trial-and-error period where you find that the workbook you set up just doesn't meet your needs. Plenty of tools are available to help you reorganize and reuse your entries so that the restructuring process isn't too troublesome; they're discussed throughout this book.

Getting it right the first time is everyone's goal, but rarely happens. If you need to sketch your worksheet on paper before typing it in, do that. If you need to test some sample data before setting up hundreds of rows of data, do it. When you're confident that you know where and how to enter your worksheet content, roll up your sleeves and get started!

UNDERSTANDING CELL BASICS

Cells are the bricks that build your worksheets and workbooks, each playing an integral part in the storage and manipulation of your text and numeric data. You can think of each cell as an individual container capable of storing text, numbers, and so on. The following is a list of basic information about cells—things that you should know to improve your use and understanding of Excel:

- A cell can hold up to 65,000 characters, which can consist of text, numbers, formulas, graphics, or any combination of these. The amount of text you can view in a cell depends on the width of the column the cell is in and the formatting applied to the cell and its contents.

- Text, numbers, and formulas you type in a cell are immediately displayed in the Formula bar.

- Whenever a worksheet is active, at least one cell is also active (called the *active cell*). The active cell is designated by a heavy border around the cell, usually black. If the Excel window is the active application, and the workbook window is active within it, that one cell's content—or lack thereof in the case of an empty cell—will appear in the Formula bar. The address of the cell (or name, if you've named it) will appear in the Name box (see Figure 2.1).

- After you type data into a cell, press Enter to accept the entry and move down one cell, press the Tab key to accept the entry and move one cell to the right, or press an arrow key to accept the entry and move one cell in the direction of the arrow (pressing the up-arrow key, for instance, moves one cell up). During the time a cell's entry is unfinished (designated by a cursor blinking inside the cell or on the Formula bar), many of Excel's commands cannot be executed.

- If you change your mind about an entry prior to finishing it, press Esc or click the Cancel button (the red X on the formula bar) to nullify the entry and start over (see Figure 2.2).

Name box   Formula bar

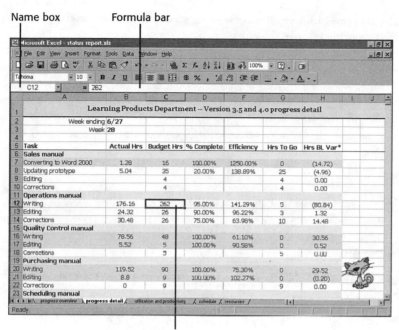

Figure 2.1.
Notice the address and content of the active cell. The active cell can be seen clearly here with its black border. The column letter and row number of the active cell are bold and appear as raised buttons to aid the eye in referencing the cell's location.

Active cell

Cancel button

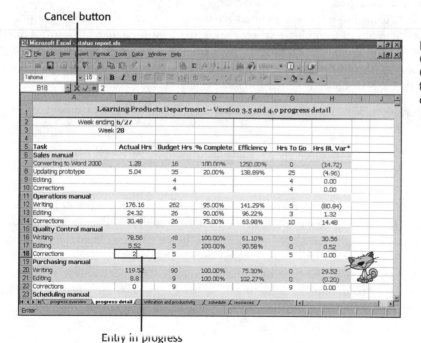

Figure 2.2.
Change your mind? Click the Cancel button or press Esc to delete the entry.

Entry in progress

- If you've already pressed Enter after completing an entry, you can reselect the cell and press Delete to quickly remove the entry.

Tip #11 from

Laurie

Almost everyone at one time or another forgets to finish entering data in a cell before attempting to access a command or some other object in the workbook. In many cases, Excel will finish entering the data for you. In some cases, though, Excel will beep.

If you can't access something that you think you should be able to access, check two things:

- Do you see the Cancel (red X) and Enter (green check mark) buttons on the Formula bar?
- Does the word Enter appear on the status bar at the bottom of the Excel window?

If the answer is yes, you forgot to finish entering data into a cell. Do so by pressing Enter, Tab, or using one of the arrow keys.

The remaining sections of this chapter discuss the intricacies of entering text and numbers into worksheet cells.

ENTERING TEXT

Text content in a spreadsheet seems like unnecessary fluff to some hard-core financial users. A necessary evil, text tells you which numbers are in which columns and rows, and which cells contain the results of formulas. For some users, that's more than enough text. For other users, however, Excel is a rich program capable of storing text in databases (names, addresses, comments), and can even be used for minor word processing. Figure 2.3 shows a worksheet that contains both minimal and more extensive use of text.

No matter how detailed or concise your text entries are, Excel applies the following defaults to text:

- Text is automatically left-aligned. This includes numbers that Excel perceives as text due to the inclusion of nonnumeric content, such as Social Security numbers that include hyphens.

- Text doesn't wrap unless you tell it to. If you type text that exceeds the width of the cell, text will appear to flow into the next cell. If there is already data in the adjacent cell, the overflow will be *truncated*, meaning that the excess won't display unless you widen the column (this technique is covered later in this chapter). Even if the column isn't widened, the truncated content is merely hidden—it isn't deleted, proof of which can be found by examining the cell's content in the Formula bar, which displays the active cell's entire content, including the hidden overflow (see Figure 2.4).

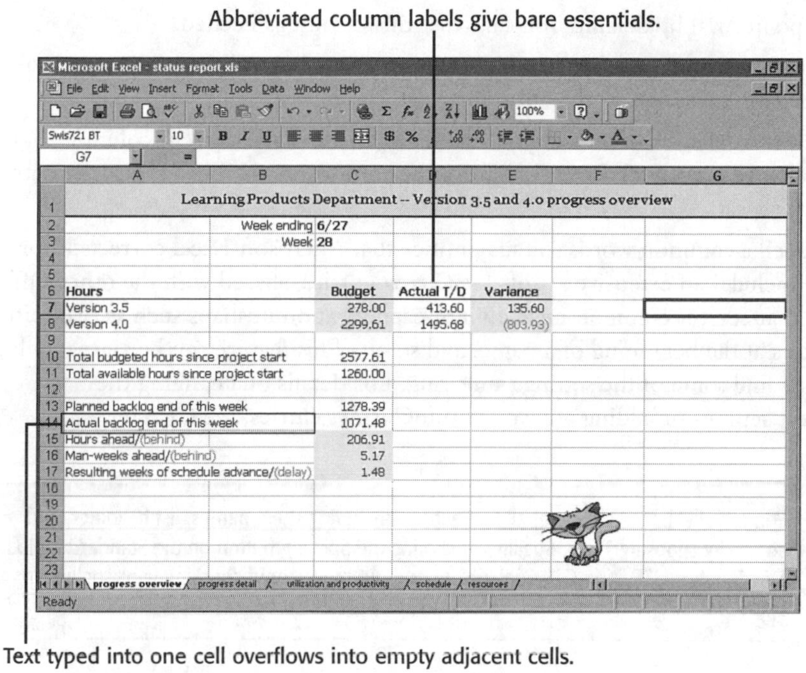

Abbreviated column labels give bare essentials.

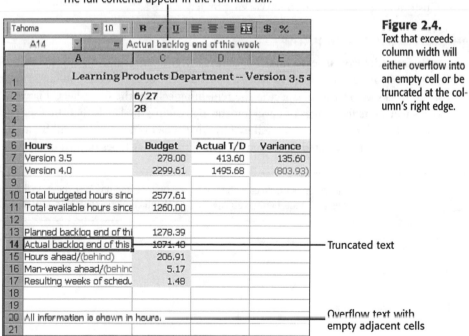

Figure 2.3.
Column and row labels can be as concise or detailed as you want. Text also can be used to explain and support the data on a worksheet.

Text typed into one cell overflows into empty adjacent cells.

The full contents appear in the Formula bar.

Figure 2.4.
Text that exceeds column width will either overflow into an empty cell or be truncated at the column's right edge.

Truncated text

Overflow text with empty adjacent cells

- Text is 10-point Arial by default. You can reset this default as needed.

- If you start to type an entry that resembles one you typed elsewhere in the same column, Excel may *AutoComplete* the entry for you.

- You can select from a list of entries you've already typed in the current column. Right-click the cell and select Pic<u>k</u> From List from the context menu. Then select the entry you want to repeat.

- If you misspell a common word, you may notice that Microsoft Excel corrects it for you. Excel includes an extensive set of *AutoCorrect* entries, shared with the other Office programs, that correct common misspellings, capitalization mishaps such as two initial capital letters at the beginning of a name, and so on. This feature can be a great help, but you may find some of the settings annoying. For details on changing the AutoCorrect settings or adding your own AutoCorrect entries, see Chapter 4.

Tip #12 from

Laurie

You can check the spelling of all text entries–including sheet names, list headings, and so on–by choosing <u>T</u>ools, <u>S</u>pelling or clicking the Spelling button on the Standard toolbar. See Chapter 4, "Editing Cell Content," to find out more about checking your spelling in Excel.

For more information on formatting the appearance and alignment of text, see Chapter 6, "Formatting Worksheets." To find out more about setting Excel defaults, see Chapter 28, "Customizing Excel to Fit Your Working Style."

LABELING COLUMNS AND ROWS

Aside from the worksheet's title (which normally goes into cell A1), the first cells you normally fill in are column and row labels. These are the cells that tell you (and any other users of the worksheet) what to expect in the remaining cells in the worksheet. Figure 2.5 shows a worksheet in its first stages of development. By reading the labels that the user has typed into strategic locations, you can tell exactly what type of information will be stored, and how it will be manipulated. You even have an idea of what types of formulas will be used.

Tip #13 from

Laurie

If the current worksheet's information will be repeated on other sheets in the workbook, group the sheets before you type the labels and common content to save time and effort.

→ To learn how to group and ungroup worksheets, **see** "Grouping and Ungrouping Sheets," **p. 23**

Column labels

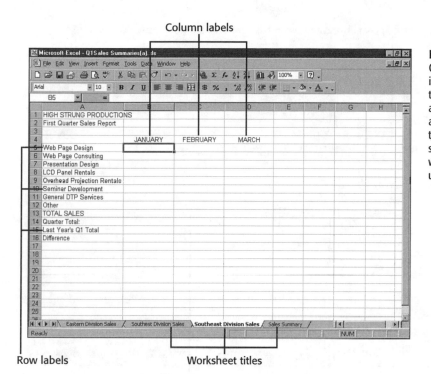

Figure 2.5.
Other than the use of in-house jargon, make the worksheet labels as clear and concise as possible, designing the sheet as though someone unfamiliar with the data will be using it.

Row labels   Worksheet titles

Tip #14 from

Laurie

First things first! Don't concern yourself with formatting the cells until the majority of the data is entered. Let the worksheet defaults for fonts, number formats, and alignment take over until you're ready to publish your efforts. When you're ready to make it look great, see Part III of this book, "Formatting and Printing Excel Worksheets."

ADJUSTING COLUMN WIDTH AND ROW HEIGHT

As you type the worksheet titles, column headings, and row labels (as well as the data in the worksheet), you may see the need to make columns wider or narrower, or to adjust the height of the rows. Figure 2.6 shows a worksheet with text and numeric content that requires some manual adjustment.

Excel will generally widen a column automatically to accommodate numeric entries (see the following Note), but text entries require manual adjustment. Row height will automatically increase if font size increases, but again, manual adjustments may become necessary from an aesthetic standpoint.

Text appears truncated when adjacent cells are not empty.

Overflow into empty adjacent cells requires no action.

Figure 2.6.
Truncated (chopped off) text, error messages, and a cramped appearance to the worksheet content are all reasons to adjust the column width and row height.

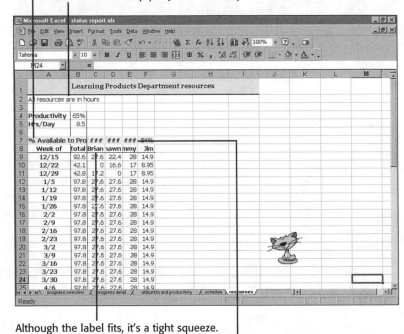

Although the label fits, it's a tight squeeze.

Numeric content that exceeds column width due to formatting will display as number signs.

Note

It's important to note when entering numbers that, regardless of what's displayed in the cell, Excel stores the entire number with a precision of 15 significant digits. Digits after 15 are also stored, but rounded to zero.

By default, cells in a new worksheet use General format, and Excel automatically adjusts column width to display numbers you type into cells. Except for date formats and certain custom formats, if you apply a particular number format to a cell, such as Currency with two decimal places, Excel widens the cell to accommodate the specified format, but may round the decimal places.

In General format, column width is automatically adjusted as follows when you enter numbers:

- Numbers containing decimals but with fewer than 11 total characters are rounded visually to fit the default column width. (Excel retains the entire number value, of course, as you can see in the Formula bar when the cell is selected.)

- Numbers containing more than 11 total characters appear in *scientific notation (page 41)*.

- Columns are widened to accommodate numbers entered with commas, dollar signs, or percent signs, regardless of the number of digits, although decimals may be rounded.

> - When numbers with fractions are entered, the column is adjusted to display the entire number, regardless of the number of digits (example: 111111111111111½). Digits beyond 15 are rounded to zero as usual.
> - Numbers consisting entirely of decimals are rounded to fit in the cell.

Excel provides several methods for adjusting the size of rows and columns, as shown in the following list:

- The *AutoFit* feature adjusts columns or rows to accommodate the longest or tallest entry, respectively. Using the row and column control buttons, double-click the bottom boundary on the selected row(s) or the right boundary on the selected column(s), as shown in Figure 2.7. The row/column will adjust to the size that fits the largest/widest entry. You also can invoke AutoFit by selecting the column(s) or row(s) and choosing Format, Column, AutoFit Selection or Format, Row, AutoFit.

Double-click here to adjust the entire set of selected columns.

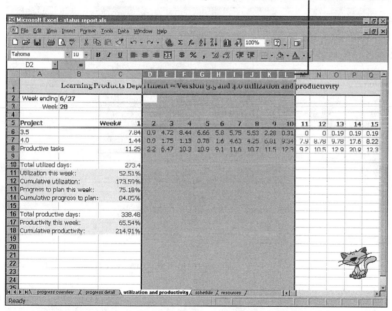

Figure 2.7.
Select a single column or row, or drag through a series of columns or rows, and adjust the width or height with one double-click.

- Choose Format, Column, Width or Format, Row, Height. In the resulting dialog box, enter an exact measurement for the selected column(s) or row(s). Figure 2.8 shows the Column Width dialog box.
- Drag the right boundary of a column or the bottom boundary of a row. When dragging, the direction you drag determines the column's or row's new dimensions—drag to the right to widen a column, drag down to make a row taller. If you select more than

one column or row, dragging the boundary of any column or row in the selection adjusts all of the columns or rows in the selection. Figure 2.9 shows a set of columns being widened by dragging.

Figure 2.8.
For column width, enter the number of characters you want to fit in the column.

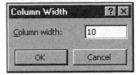

A ScreenTip shows the exact measurement as you drag the mouse.

A two-headed arrow appears when you point to the column's boundary.

Figure 2.9.
Drag the boundary of one of the selected columns or rows to adjust the whole selection. Drag left or right to change the width of the selected column(s) or drag up or down to change the height of selected row(s).

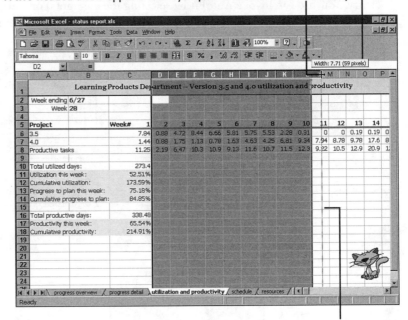

A vertical line shows the new column width.

Caution

If you adjust row height manually once and then make the content larger at a later time (requiring a taller row), the row will no longer adjust automatically. Once you have tinkered with row height, you can continue to adjust row height manually each time you increase/decrease the font size, or you can double-click the bottom boundary of the row(s) to return to using automatic adjustment.

- To AutoFit an entire worksheet with one double-click, select the entire worksheet by clicking the Select All button in the upper-left corner of the worksheet window (see Figure 2.10). Then double-click any boundary between column control buttons to AutoFit all the columns, or any boundary between row control buttons to AutoFit all the rows. Click any individual cell to deselect the worksheet after making the desired adjustments.

The Select All button   Double-click a boundary.

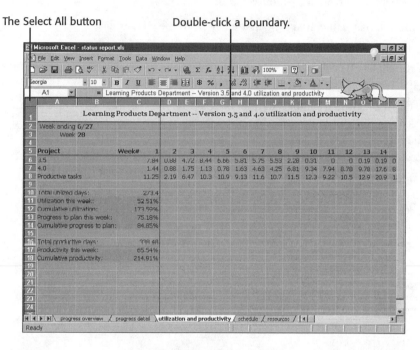

Figure 2.10.
You can make global adjustments by using AutoFit to adjust all rows and columns to fit their largest entries.

Caution

If cells display numbers in scientific notation, such as 78123E+12, AutoFit won't adjust the column to the width required to display the entire number. You may have to change the format of the cell for the number to display properly. See Chapter 7 for more information on formatting numeric entries.

USING CUSTOM LISTS TO SPEED DATA ENTRY

Excel provides a powerful and flexible tool for creating row and column labels, known as *custom lists*. Custom lists are lists of words installed with the Excel program that enable you to build a series of labels by typing just one of the words in the list. Excel's built-in custom lists include the following:

- Months of the year (spelled out or abbreviated)

- Days of the week (spelled out or abbreviated)

- Fiscal quarters (Q1, Qtr 1, Quarter 1, and so on)

If a worksheet tracks sales over a series of months, for example, the column headings for January through December need not be typed individually. You need only type January and follow the steps below to create a 12-month series:

1. Click in the cell that will contain the first entry from the custom list.

2. Type the first entry (in this case, January).

3. Point to the fill handle (the small black square located in the lower-right corner of the active cell). The mouse pointer will change into a black cross.

4. Holding down the primary mouse button, drag across the cells that will contain the labels, releasing the mouse when the number of cells through which you've dragged equals the number of labels you need (see Figure 2.11).

Figure 2.11.
The mouse pointer turns into a black cross when you point to the active cell's fill handle.

Fill handle

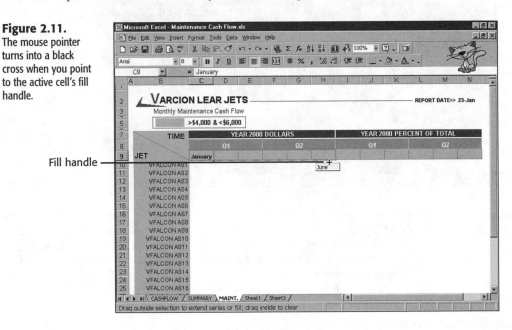

Excel is also able to recognize simple numeric patterns. Suppose that you're creating a pricing worksheet, and you want to show the price charged for quantity purchases of 10, 20, and 30 units, and so on. Rather than type the numbers 10, 20, 30, 40, and so forth, create a two-number pattern as an example, and use the fill handle to complete the list. This feature is called *AutoFill*. Figure 2.12 shows a worksheet with a numeric pattern created by dragging the fill handle. A series of decreasing numbers is created by selecting and dragging .25 and .20.

A series of decreasing numbers was created by selecting and dragging .25 and .20.

16						
17	Paper Grade	A	B	C	D	E
18	# of copies	0.25	0.20	0.15	0.10	0.05
19	1200	300	240	180	120	60
20	2500	625	500	375	250	125
21	5000	1250	1000	750	500	250
22						
23						

Figure 2.12.
Use a single-digit increment to create product or record numbers in the worksheet.

Follow these steps to create a pattern and fill in column or row labels of your own:

1. Click in the first cell that will contain a number in the series.

2. Type the first number, and then move to the cell that will contain the next number in the series.

3. Type the second number in the series. These two cells will be used to establish the pattern.

4. Highlight the two cells, and use the fill handle in the second cell to drag through the contiguous (adjacent) cells that will contain the series (see Figure 2.13).

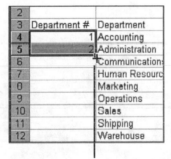

	Department #	Department
2		
3	Department #	Department
4	1	Accounting
5	2	Administration
6		Communications
7		Human Resourc
8		Marketing
9		Operations
10		Sales
11		Shipping
12		Warehouse

Fill handle in the second cell of the series, used to carry the pattern forward through the target cells

Figure 2.13.
When establishing a pattern, using the fill handle after both cells have been selected ensures that both cells are used in creating the series.

Based on the established pattern, the remaining cells are filled with numbers—increasing or decreasing in specific increments.

Tip #15 from

Laurie

AutoFill isn't just for numeric entries; you also can drag the AutoFill handle to repeat text entries. You can use the AutoFill handle to enter repeated content into contiguous cells. Select the cell containing the text (or numbers) that you want to repeat, and drag the AutoFill handle through any range of contiguous cells.

CREATING CUSTOM LISTS

What if Excel's custom lists aren't enough for you? For many users, they're not. Imagine that you have five divisions in your company, and you're repeatedly typing them in as row labels in various worksheets. They're always entered in the same order, and their names never change. The division names are a perfect choice for your own custom list. So are compass points, names of your staff or coworkers, or deliverables for a project.

To build your own custom list, follow these steps:

1. If you already have a group of entries listed in a range of cells, select the range.
2. Choose Tools, Options. The Options dialog box opens.
3. Click the Custom Lists tab (see Figure 2.14).

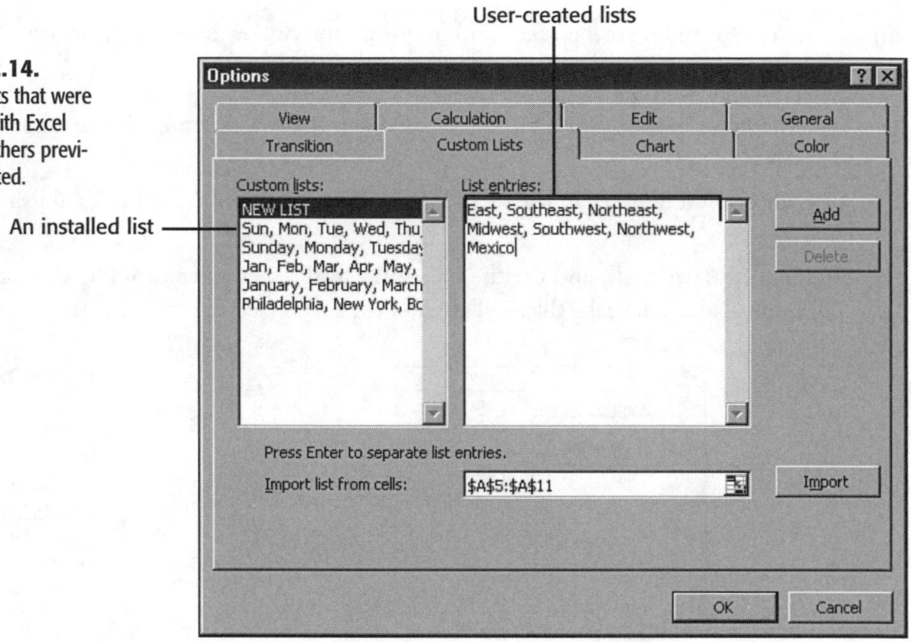

Figure 2.14.
See the lists that were installed with Excel and any others previously created.

4. With NEW LIST highlighted by default in the Custom Lists box, click in the List Entries box.
5. Type the list, each item separated by a comma and a space. (If you selected the list before opening the dialog box, you can click the Import button to immediately add the range to the list.)
6. Click Add.
7. Repeat steps 2 through 5 for any additional lists you want to create.
8. Click OK to close the dialog box.

Test your lists to make sure you spelled things right and that you have the items in the proper order. Remember that you can start the series anywhere—with the second or seventh item in the list, for example—and the filled series will continue from that item through to the end and start over. The number of cells through which you drag when filling the list determines whether the list begins again, as shown in Figure 2.15.

	A	B	C	D	E	F	G	H
1								
2	ERPmatic Quarterly Sales (millions)							
3								
4		1999		2000				
5		Q3	Q4	Q1	Q2	Q3	Q4	
6	Southeast	1.3	1.9	2.5	3.1	3.7	4.3	
7	Northeast	0.9	1.9	2.9	3.5	4.1	5.1	
8	Midwest	2.1	3.8	5.5	7.2	7.1	8.9	
9	Southwest	0.7	1.4	2.1	2.8	2.8	4.2	
10	Northwest	1.4	2.1	2.8	3.5	2.9	4.9	
11								
12								

Figure 2.15.
The fiscal quarters of the year end with 4 and start over with 1, through as many cells as you drag the series.

This series rolled over to its first value after reaching its last.

Tip #16 from

Laurie

For fiscal quarters, you can abbreviate Quarter as Q or Qtr (with or without a period). You also can spell the word out as Quarter. Other abbreviations, such as Qt, will be interpreted as quarts, or won't be recognized, and the fill series won't work properly.

To remove a custom list entry, select it in the Custom Lists box and click the Delete button.

ENTERING NUMERIC DATA

There's really no trick to entering numeric data—simply click in the cell that will contain the number, and type it, using either the number keys above the alpha-keyboard, or the numeric keypad (be sure NumLock is on). You'll notice that as soon as you press Enter or Tab (or the arrow keys) to move to another cell, the numeric content is automatically right-aligned. This is because columns of numbers are best viewed with their decimals (or lack thereof) lined up on the right, as shown in Figure 2.16.

Excel makes some formatting decisions of its own that you can either accept or reformat later, when all of the entries are made, or before you make any entries at all. It's a good idea to familiarize yourself with the following list of numeric tricks as performed by Excel:

- When entering dates, you'll find that Excel automatically formats them in M/D/YY format (if all three elements are provided) or in D-MMM format. Figure 2.17 shows a series of dates as entered, and as Excel formatted them.

- If you want to insert numeric content such as Social Security numbers or product numbers that contain dashes, slashes, or periods, the numbers will left justify because the nonnumeric content causes Excel to treat the entry as though it were text, which is automatically left-justified.

Figure 2.16.
If the numeric content doesn't automatically right align, check for nonnumeric content, improper comma use, or a previously applied number format.

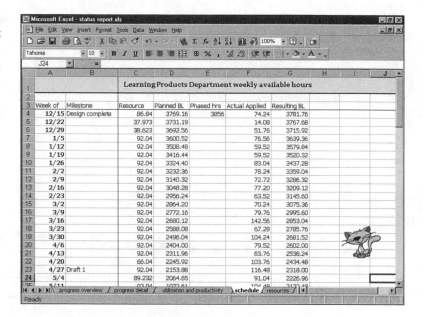

Figure 2.17.
The date format that Excel uses depends on how much of the date you enter, and what country you indicated you're in when Windows was installed.

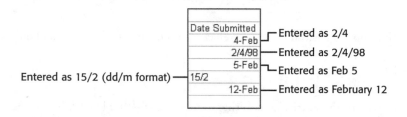

Tip #17 from
Laurie

> If you decide to type the commas into numbers greater than 999.99, be sure to place them correctly—if Excel sees improperly used commas, it will treat the numbers as text.

- Numeric content can contain as many decimal places as you want. If you type zeros at the end of the decimal place(s), however, Excel will chop off the zero(s) and display just the numbers prior to the zero(s).

Tip #18 from
Laurie

> You can format the cells containing zeros in the decimal places so that the decimals display in the cell. Click the Increase Decimal button on the Formatting toolbar.

- Unlike text, numbers must fit within the cell boundaries; they don't spill over into the next cell to the right. Earlier versions of Excel displayed number signs (#) instead of numbers if the number exceeded the cell width. In Excel 2000, Excel automatically resizes the column width to accommodate wider numbers (up to 11 digits) as you enter them. See the earlier section "Adjusting Column Width and Row Height" for details on how Excel automatically adjusts column width or cell entries to fit numbers.

> **Caution**
>
> If numbers exceed 11 digits, Excel displays the entry in *scientific notation*. If you enter 100000000000, for example, Excel displays 1E+11. The E+11 in the notation indicates that the decimal place actually goes 11 digits to the right. A notation of 1E-11 indicates that the decimal place goes 11 digits to the left.
>
> If the column width has been manually adjusted, number signs may be displayed when a number exceeding the column width is entered.

→ For more about formatting numeric worksheet content, **see** "Modifying Numbers and Dates," **p. 165**

PART

I

CH

2

SAVING EXCEL DATA

The first rule you should learn with regard to any computer application is to save your work early, and often. Excel is no exception to this rule, and is perhaps one of the applications where the rule is most important.

When is "early"? As soon as you've entered the worksheet title and column/row labels. Don't wait until you've entered all of the numbers and built the formulas. Why save so early? Because programs crash, power failures happen unexpectedly, and we all make mistakes, such as closing a file without saving.

How often is often? Whenever you've entered more data or performed more calculations or formatting than you'd want to repeat. Every five or ten minutes, depending on how fast you're working, isn't too often.

Excel, like all of the Microsoft Office applications, makes it easy to save your work, providing toolbar buttons, menu commands, and keyboard shortcuts to accommodate anyone's work style. In addition, you're prompted before exiting a file without saving, as shown in Figure 2.18. (If you have the Office Assistant turned on, it asks this question in a dialog balloon.)

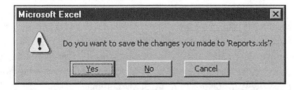

Figure 2.18.
If you never have saved the file or you have made changes since the last time you saved, this prompt appears when you choose to close a file.

PERFORMING A FIRST-TIME SAVE

The first time you save an Excel workbook (hopefully early in the worksheet development process), you'll need to name the file, choose a location for it, and in some cases choose a file format in which to save it.

A first-time save can be executed by any of the following methods:

- Choose File, Save.
- Choose File, Save As.
- Press Ctrl+S.
- Press Alt+F2, Alt+Shift+F2, or Shift+F12.
- Click the Save button on the Standard toolbar.

Whichever method you choose, the Save As dialog box opens the first time you save a file. Because Excel correctly assesses that the file hasn't been saved before, it opens this dialog box and gives you the opportunity to name the file and choose a folder in which to save it (see Figure 2.19).

Figure 2.19.
All Microsoft Office files will save to the My Documents folder by default. You can choose any folder you want.

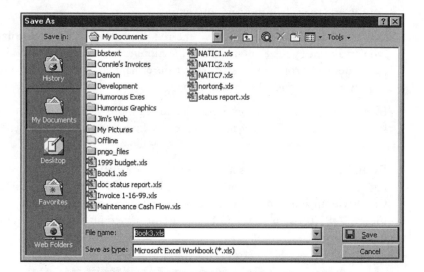

Tip #19 from

Laurie

It's a good idea to create subfolders (normally within a folder called My Documents) to categorize your files. By creating these folders, you make it easier to find the files, and simpler to copy or move them as a group to a backup disk or a network drive. You can create them within the Save As dialog box or through My Computer or Windows Explorer.

NAMING YOUR FILES

When the Save As dialog box opens, the default name (Book#) appears highlighted in the File Name box. With the default name highlighted, you can simply type over this name— no need to press Delete, just type the name you want to use—and then press Enter to accept the default My Documents folder as the location to save the file.

As in any other Microsoft Office application, an Excel filename can have up to 255 characters, including spaces. You can use dashes and exclamation points in filenames, but no slashes (/), question marks (?), or asterisks (*).

PART

I

CH

2

Tip #20 from *Laurie*	Keep filenames reasonably short, so that they're easy to read in the Explorer window and in Open dialog boxes. Also, if you'll be sharing files with users on a DOS-based network or in a Windows 3.1 environment, they won't see the whole filename—by keeping the filename short, you make the filename clearer to these users.

Note	You don't have to type the extension for the filename. Excel applies the default file extension, .xls, to whatever you type.

CHOOSING A DISK AND FOLDER FOR THE FILE

The default location for workbook files you create and save is My Documents. If you want to save the file to another folder, you can do so by following these steps:

1. After typing a name for the file, click the Save In list box, and choose the drive letter to which you want to save the file.

2. The folders on that drive are displayed. Double-click one of them to display the contents of that folder, including any subfolders.

3. Keep double-clicking subfolders until you reach the one into which you want to save the file. Then, click Save.

If you attempt to save any other workbooks during the current Excel session, the Save As dialog box will default to the last folder in which you saved a file. The My Documents default won't return until you close and then reopen Excel.

Tip #21 from *Laurie*	If you want to change the default folder in which workbook files are saved, choose Tools, Options, and click the General tab. In the Default file location text box, enter the path and folder name to which you want to save files, such as C:\My Documents\Workbooks, "Workbooks" being a subfolder you might have created to separate Excel files from other Office documents and presentations. See Chapter 28, "Customizing Excel to Fit Your Working Style," for more ideas on resetting Excel's options and defaults.

SAVING YOUR WORKBOOK WITH A PASSWORD

If the content of your workbook is confidential, you can apply a password that will keep others from opening and/or editing the workbook. This security measure would be in addition to any security afforded by your network or by the Excel Protection feature (as discussed in Chapter 18, "Using Excel's Data-Management Features").

A password can be set up on the first save, or by using File, Save As any time after that. Follow these steps to apply a password to the workbook:

1. In the Save As dialog box, open the Tools drop-down list and select General Options. The Save Options dialog box opens (see Figure 2.20).

2. To set a password that will be required each time the file is opened, type the password in the Password to Open box. The password will appear as asterisks to keep anyone from seeing what you've typed.

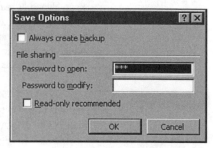

3. For further security, add a password for modification in the Password to Modify box. This option requires the user to enter an additional password in order to be able to edit the workbook.

Figure 2.20.

4. Click OK.

5. Reenter the password(s) in the Confirm Password dialog box, and click OK.

Caution

Don't forget your passwords! If you do, you won't be able to open and/or modify the file (depending on which functions you chose to secure with a password). There's no way to retrieve a forgotten password or reset it to a new password without the existing password.

Tip #22 from

Laurie

Choose a password you won't forget, but that others can't guess. Passwords of five to eight characters are long enough to be harder to decipher, but not so long you forget them. If you password-protect a lot of spreadsheets, you could keep a list of your passwords in a secure place, just in case you forget. Or you could always set your passwords to be the first five characters of the filename, but rotated forward some number of characters. For example, the password for Project Status.xls could be tvrni. T is four letters after p, y is four letters after r, and so on. With this method, all you must remember is your rule. Finally, you could simply use the same password for all your workbooks.

None of these methods provides unbreakable security—someone could find your password list, figure out your single password, or figure out your password system. But all of these methods deliver acceptable security for routine situations.

OPENING A SAVED FILE

After you've created, saved, and closed the file, you'll probably need to reopen it at some time in the future—to edit it, to print an extra copy, or to simply check it for important information. Excel (and Windows) provides a variety of ways to open existing workbook files:

- **Most recently used files.** The MRUs (as they're often called) appear at the end of the File menu (see Figure 2.21). By default, the four most recently used files are listed, numbered in order of use. You can click the name of the file you want, or just type the number to the left of the filename.

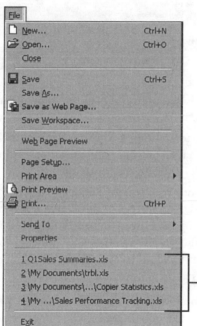

Figure 2.21.
The most recently used file will appear in the first position, followed by the last three files you used prior to that in the current session or previous Excel sessions.

The most recently used files appear at the bottom of the File menu.

Tip #23 from

Laurie

You can reset the default number of MRUs by choosing Tools, Options, and changing the Recently used file list setting on the General tab. The maximum number allowed is nine.

- **Use the Open dialog box.** Choose File, Open, and navigate to the folder that contains the workbook you want to open. From within the Open dialog box, you can choose to open the file as read-only or as a copy of the original by clicking the down-arrow button to the right of the Open button and selecting the option you want (see Figure 2.22). Opening a copy or in read-only mode allows you to protect the original version from any changes you might make. If you make changes to a read-only file, you must save the file with a new name in order to keep the changes.

Figure 2.22.
Open a file as read-only to prevent accidental changes or deletions as you review the worksheet.

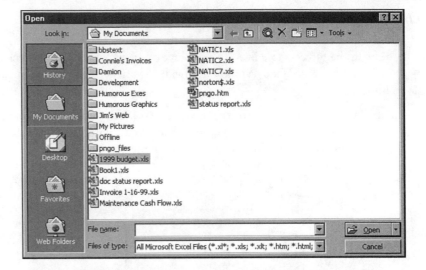

- **Use Windows Explorer or My Computer**. Open the folder containing the file, and double-click the file.

- **Click the Windows Start button and look in the Documents list**. If the desired file is one of the last 15 files you've used on your computer (not just in Excel), you'll find it in the Documents menu. Click the file in the list to open it.

If you have used previous versions of Excel, you may notice that the Open dialog box has changed quite a bit. One particularly nice feature of this dialog box is the vertical bar at the left side of the dialog box. By clicking the History button, you can display an extended list of Excel files you've opened recently, as well as shortcuts to folders you've used to open Office documents. If Excel files are stored on your company's intranet or Web server, the Favorites and Web Folders buttons also are handy for quick access.

At the top of the dialog box, the button with a left-pointing blue arrow (think of it as the Back button) goes back to the last folder you opened in the same session, the one before that, and so on. The ScreenTip for this button names the folder that will be displayed if you click the button.

UPDATING YOUR WORK

As you work on a previously saved workbook, you'll want to continue to save it periodically so that your additions and changes are reflected in the saved version of the file. To perform an update save, choose one of the following methods:

- **Press Ctrl+S**. This is a good choice if you're doing a lot of text and number entry. Your hands are already on the keyboard, so the time and extra thought required to click a button or menu with the mouse is avoided.

- Click the Save button on the Standard toolbar.

- Choose File, Save from the menu. Don't choose File, Save As unless you want to change the file name or location of the file.

None of these update save methods opens a dialog box to hinder your work. A progress bar and a floppy disk icon will flash briefly on the status bar in the Excel window. If the Office Assistant is visible, saving a file animates the Assistant briefly. You may not even notice these incidents, depending on the size of the file and the speed of the computer.

PART

1

CH

2

Caution

Don't assume that because you've saved recently you can answer No to the prompt that asks whether you want to save the file before closing it. Any entry or editing at all, no matter how slight (and even if you undo it), will result in the prompt appearing. Always answer Yes unless you specifically want to keep the current version of the file intact.

RENAMING AND RELOCATING FILES

At times, you may want to rename a saved file or save it to a new location. You might want to save the file with a new name to preserve the current version of the file, for example, or to create a duplicate file with a different name. You can always change a file's name and location by using Windows Explorer or My Computer, but you also can perform this task from within Excel.

To save a file with a new name or to a new disk/folder, follow these steps:

1. Choose File, Save As to open the Save As dialog box.

2. The file's current name appears in the File Name box (see Figure 2.23). If you want to save the file with a new name, type the new name.

3. As needed, click the Save In list box and choose a new disk or folder for the file.

4. Click Save or press Enter to save the file with a new name and/or to a new location.

Tip #24 from

Laurie

A popular method of creating a second version of a file is to append a 2 or an A to the original filename, so that the filenames resemble each other, but the second version is obvious.

When you save a file with a new name or new location, the previous version of the file is automatically closed, leaving the new version open. If you want to use the original version of the file, you must reopen it. The fastest method is to select it from the list of most recently used files in the File menu.

Figure 2.23.
No need to delete the current name—merely type the new name to replace the highlighted text.

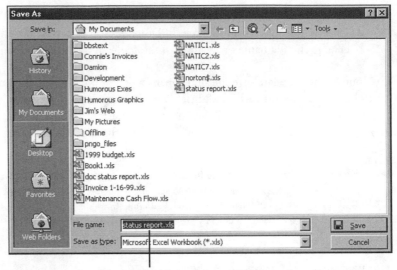

This filename will appear on the title bar when the file is open.

SAVING EXCEL FILES IN ALTERNATIVE FORMATS

Most of the time, you'll want to let Excel save your files in the default .xls format for the currently installed version of Excel. This ensures that you'll be able to open the file in the current version of the software, and that all the formatting will be preserved with the file.

Sometimes, however, you'll need to save files to another file format. Following are some reasons for this change:

- You're going to share the file with a user who has an older version of Excel. Each new release of Excel has features the previous release didn't. Saving to an older version strips out those features so that the recipient using an older version of Excel can open and use the file.

- You'll be sending the file via email, and you don't know what software the recipient has. Saving the file in tab-delimited text (.txt) format will enable the user to open the file in any word processing program, where the spreadsheet will appear as a block of tabbed text. When you save to this format, tabs are inserted between each cell so that the overall layout is preserved.

- You're sharing the file with someone who uses Lotus 1-2-3, Quattro Pro, Excel for the Macintosh, or dBASE. Choose the appropriate format for the software the recipient uses.

Tip #25 from

Laurie

> When saving a file in another spreadsheet software format (.WK1, .WKS, .WQ1, .DBF), if you're not sure of the version number, choose an older version (lower version number) so that you don't give the recipient a file that his or her version can't open or display properly.

- The current version of Excel is presenting problems and software errors, and it's been suggested that you save to a format that doesn't save the particular element that's causing problems. Normally, if this occurs, a Microsoft technical support person will tell you to save to the previous version of Excel or a tab-delimited text (.txt) format so you don't lose your work, reopen the file in the current version of Excel, and then try again.

- You're working on your company's intranet or Web server, or working internationally with other users and creating or saving files elsewhere via the Web. For these arrangements, you'll probably want to save the Excel files in HTML format (the language of the Web) rather than .xls format. To find out more about publishing Excel worksheets to the Web, read Chapter 31, "Using Excel on the Web."

PART

I

CH

2

To save a file to a new format, follow these steps:

1. Choose File, Save As.
2. If necessary, choose a location and type a name for the file.
3. Open the Save as Type list box and scroll through the formats, as shown in Figure 2.24.
4. Select a format by clicking it in the list. Excel appends the extension for the selected format to the filename in the File Name box.
5. Press Enter or click Save.

Tip #26 from

Laurie

> If you're creating a new version of the file in an alternative format (for sharing with another user or as backup), give the file a different name (perhaps including the format's extension in the filename). You could add a 2 or A to the existing filename so that even if you aren't displaying file extensions in the dialog boxes, you'll be able to tell the files apart.

PREVENTING AND RECOVERING FROM DISASTER—USING AUTOSAVE AND AUTOMATIC BACKUPS

When your computer and software are working well, it's easy to forget that at some point something will fail. A sudden power outage, a system crash, or even an incorrect response to a prompt can cause you to lose data that took time, thought, and effort to enter. The best preventive measure is to save your work early and often, as mentioned earlier. The next defense is to have backup files and be able to restore from them as needed.

Figure 2.24.
Excel offers dozens of different file formats. You may have fewer to choose from if you did a Minimum or Custom installation.

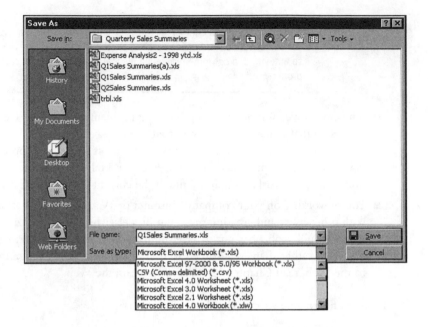

Setting Up the AutoSave Add-in

AutoSave is an add-in program that enables you to set up periodic saves of your open workbooks. This is an emergency program that often can recover most or all of a workbook file if the power goes off suddenly while you're working on the file in Excel. Because AutoSave is an add-in—not part of the typical installation of Excel or Office—you must install it separately.

First, check to see whether AutoSave is already running on your computer. If AutoSave isn't a menu command on the Excel Tools menu, then you need to install it using the following steps:

1. Choose Tools, Add-Ins to display the Add-Ins dialog box.
2. Select Autosave Add-in from the list of available add-ins (see Figure 2.25). Then click OK.
3. Excel asks you whether you want to install the add-in. Choose Yes. (If prompted, insert the Microsoft Office CD.)

   As Excel installs the add-in, you may see additional dialog boxes that indicate the progress of the installation. When the process is complete, the dialog boxes disappear and the AutoSave option is included on the Tools menu. The option is selected, as indicated by a check mark next to the option on the menu.

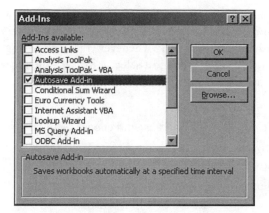

Figure 2.25.
In this dialog box, specify that you want to install the AutoSave add-in.

By default, AutoSave will save the active workbook in Excel every 10 minutes, and will prompt you to confirm the save process. To change the default settings for AutoSave, choose Tools, AutoSave to display the AutoSave dialog box (see Figure 2.26). Change the settings as desired and then click OK. To turn off the AutoSave feature completely, deselect the Automatic Save Every xx Minutes option. The AutoSave option will remain on the Tools menu, but won't be selected. To remove the option from the menu, choose Tools, Add-Ins to display the Add-Ins dialog box, and deselect Autosave Add-in. If the AutoSave add-in is installed but not currently enabled, you can activate it in the same dialog box.

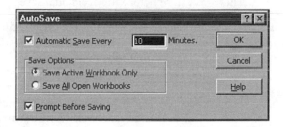

Figure 2.26.
You can change the AutoSave settings in this dialog box.

BACKING UP YOUR WORKBOOKS AUTOMATICALLY

By default, Excel does not make a backup copy when you save a file. If you tend to tinker with your worksheets—for example, creating different scenarios for use at a sales conference or experimenting with formatting of the worksheet—you may accidentally overwrite the original version of the file with the experimental version, and you can't undo a save operation.

With no backup copy, there's no easy way to recover from an accidental overwrite. To prevent this problem, you can tell Excel to automatically make a backup copy. This feature saves a second file (with the extension .xlk) whenever you save the original. (Unfortunately, this feature isn't universal; you must select it for each file for which you want backup copies.) Follow these steps:

1. Choose File, Save As.
2. In the Open dialog box, click open the Tools list and choose General Options.
3. In the Save Options dialog box, select the Always Create Backup option and choose OK to close the dialog box. Excel returns you to the Open dialog box.
4. Specify the filename and path, if necessary, and choose Save. If prompted, replace the existing version on disk.

After you have set up backups, Excel saves the previous version of the file to the .xlk format each time you save the file. Notice that the safety margin isn't huge. You can only recover from a single accidental save operation—if you save again, the original file now incorporates the new changes—but a workbook that needs this sort of protection usually is important enough that you'll realize it immediately when you've mistakenly saved.

If you need to restore a file from the backup version, open the backup file named Backup of *filename*, where *filename* is the name of the original file. Then choose File, Save As, and select *filename* (the original file). When prompted, choose Yes to replace the file with its backup copy. You're now back to where you were before the accidental save.

It's important to note that backup copies do take disk space, just like the original files. If you reach a point where disk space is at a premium, consider deleting backup files for workbooks that are complete, locked and protected, or no longer in active use.

Tip #27 from

Laurie

If you're careful not to save accidentally, you can experiment at will with your workbooks. Save the workbook to disk before you start fooling around with it. Then make any desired changes. When you're ready to get back to the original version, close the file without saving the changes, and reopen the original file. Alternatively, you can close the file after saving it and then open a copy for use in experimenting.

SAVING AN EXCEL WORKBOOK AS A REUSABLE TEMPLATE

If the workbook you've created is one that you can envision creating again in the future, it's a labor-saving idea to save it as a *template* in addition to saving it as a normal Excel file.

Why a template? Because templates are like cookie cutters for new workbooks. When a file is saved as a template, it becomes a potential foundation for future workbooks, containing all the text, numbers, formulas, and formats that the file has in it. By using the template to start a new file, you save yourself all the entry and formatting that went into the creation of the original file.

Note

Whether you realize it or not, you're already using a template. When you started Excel with a blank workbook, the blank workbook was based on a template called Blank Workbook.XLT, the *T* standing for *template*. This seemingly blank document contains all of the defaults you count on for consistency and to enable you to jump in and start typing the minute the workbook appears. Font sizes, alignment, custom lists, the number of blank worksheets you start with—these are all the products of this "blank" template!

CREATING TEMPLATE CONTENT

It's important that your template not contain data that isn't applicable to each use of the template. For example, if you're saving a sales report workbook as a template, make sure that when you save it, none of the specific sales numbers are in the cells. You want the column and row labels, a generic title, and the formulas to be part of the file, but not any esoteric information that will have to be changed or deleted when you use the template.

To save the current workbook as a template, follow these steps:

1. Choose File, Save As to open the Save As dialog box.

2. As needed, change the name of the file. Do not change the location, as Excel will dictate this as soon as you choose the Template format for the file.

3. Open the Save as Type list box and choose Template (.xlt) from the list. The Save In box automatically switches to the folder c:\Windows\Application Data\Microsoft\Templates, as shown in Figure 2.27.

4. Click Save.

Tip #28 from

Laurie

You can create subfolder(s) within the Templates folder to house new templates. Templates stored in the Templates folder appear on the General tab in the New dialog box; templates stored in a subfolder of Templates are listed on a separate tab named for the subfolder.

 If you've created or placed templates in a folder other than Templates and now can't see them, see "Why Save to the Templates Folder?" in the Troubleshooting section at the end of this chapter.

STARTING A NEW WORKBOOK FROM A TEMPLATE

Whether you're starting a new workbook from a template you created or one of the installed Excel templates, follow these steps:

1. Choose File, New. The New dialog box opens, as shown in Figure 2.28.

2. Click the tab that corresponds to the name of the subfolder in which the template file is stored.

The Save In list shows the location of the Templates folder.

Figure 2.27.
Don't redirect the Save In box to any other drive or folder other than Templates or one of its subfolders. If you do, you won't be able to access the template automatically in the future.

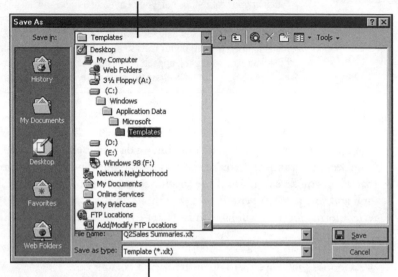

The .xlt format is selected.

Figure 2.28.
Excel looks for .xlt files in the Templates folder and all of its subfolders. It displays a tab for any folder found to contain an .xlt formatted file.

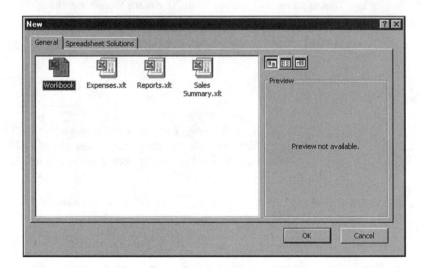

3. Double-click the template on which you want to base the new workbook, or click it once and press Enter.

   The new workbook opens, filled with whatever content and formatting was part of the template file.

Note

You aren't opening the template itself when you start a new workbook with a template. You're using the template as a foundation, creating a completely separate file that contains the information, content, and settings you established in the template. Notice that the file is named Book#, and the template filename doesn't appear on the title bar.

CONTROLLING THE WORKSHEET VIEW

Control means having things the way you want them. Controlling Excel means having the power to manipulate what you see on the worksheet. You can switch between open workbook windows to tile or cascade the open windows; you can freeze a row of column headings onscreen for simplified data entry, or even hide a column or row of confidential information (so that it's not visible onscreen). Figure 2.29 shows a project status report with frozen column headings and a hidden column. The following sections describe the techniques for freezing and hiding columns and rows, as well as how to split the window into multiple panes to focus in on multiple sections of the worksheet simultaneously.

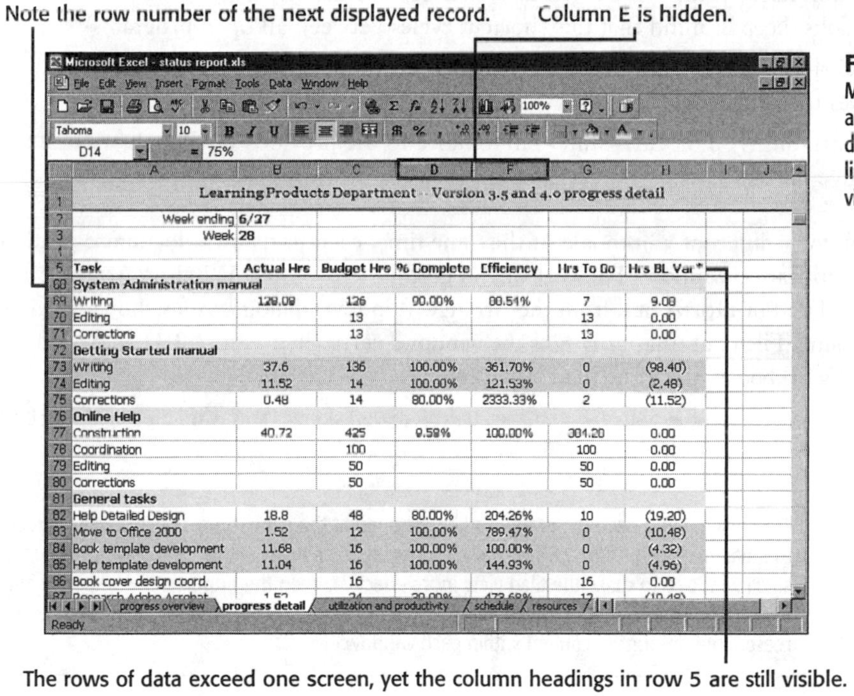

Note the row number of the next displayed record.   Column E is hidden.

Figure 2.29.
Make data entry easier and maintain confidentiality by controlling your worksheet view.

The rows of data exceed one screen, yet the column headings in row 5 are still visible.

SWITCHING BETWEEN OPEN WORKBOOKS

Windows gives you the power to have more than one program running at the same time, and within each program, more than one file open at a time. This capability would have little or no benefit if you couldn't also *switch* between those files and programs quickly and efficiently.

To switch between open Excel workbook windows, use one of the following methods:

■ Open the Window menu and choose the numbered workbook file from the list.

Caution

Watch out for slow responses, video pauses, or problems with screen colors when you have several workbooks open at the same time. The amount of memory in your computer will dictate how many workbooks you can have open without performance suffering. If you try to do too many things at once, Excel may crash or become unresponsive.

■ Click the Taskbar button for the workbook to which you'd like to switch. Office 2000 displays each open file with its own button on the Taskbar, not just a button for the application itself. With this new feature, you also can use Alt+Tab to switch between workbooks (keep in mind that this shortcut cycles between all open programs).

■ Press Ctrl+F6 or Ctrl+Tab to move to the next workbook. This workbook now becomes the active file.

■ Press Ctrl+Shift+F6 or Ctrl+Shift+Tab to move to the previous workbook, making it the active file.

You also can view different workbooks at the same time, each in its own document window within the application window. The best way to do this is to choose Window, Arrange, and then choose Tiled or Horizontal from the Arrange Windows dialog box, as shown in Figure 2.30. (Choosing Tiled automatically tiles the windows vertically.) Figure 2.31 shows the same pair of workbooks, this time tiled horizontally.

→ To learn how to copy content between workbooks, between worksheets, and within a single sheet, **see p. 116**

Tip #29 from

Laurie

Obviously, if you have too many workbooks open at the same time, tiling them will create too many small windows. It's virtually impossible to view an entire spreadsheet through a small window. To make the tiled view more effective, keep the number of workbooks open to three or less, so that each window gives you enough room to scroll around and see a reasonable amount of content within each window.

Each workbook has its own title bar.

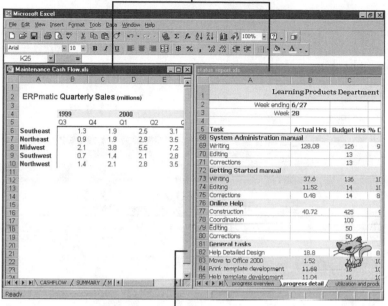

Figure 2.30.
Choose horizontal or vertical tiling based on the layout of the workbooks. In this example, the workbooks are tiled vertically.

The active workbook has a scrollbar, and the title bar may be a different color or shade.

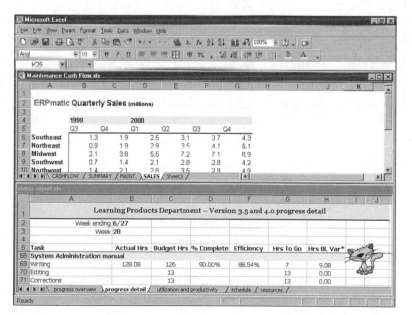

Figure 2.31.
Compare the contents of related workbooks or use the Clipboard to copy and paste between them.

FREEZING COLUMNS AND ROWS

Freezing part of a worksheet holds that part onscreen as you scroll the remainder of the worksheet. The most commonly frozen part of a worksheet is the row of column headings at the top of a long series of rows containing data, such as in a name and address list. By freezing this row of headings, you can still see what data goes in which cell as you scroll down the rows, as shown in Figure 2.32.

Figure 2.32.
Freezing keeps the column headings onscreen no matter how many rows of data you must enter or edit.

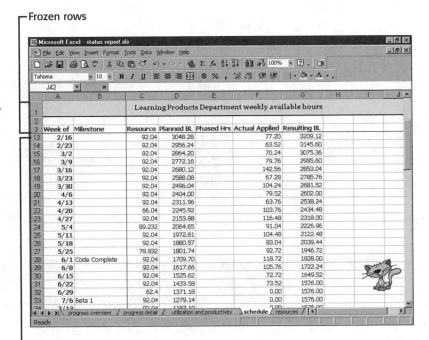

─Frozen rows

└ Note the row number of the next displayed record.

To freeze a row in the worksheet, follow these steps:

1. Click the row number *below* the row you want to freeze.

2. Choose <u>W</u>indow, <u>F</u>reeze Panes. Everything above the selected row is now frozen in place.

If you scroll through the rows, you'll see that the frozen rows remain onscreen, regardless of how far down you scroll.

Freezing a column (normally column A) keeps vertical headings onscreen so that you can enter data that exceeds screen width from left to right. To freeze a column, select the column to the right of the one you want to freeze, and choose <u>W</u>indow, <u>F</u>reeze Panes. When you scroll to the right, the frozen column remains onscreen.

Tip #30 from

Laurie

> You can freeze columns and rows at the same time by selecting a single cell and choosing Window, Freeze Panes. The rows above and columns to the left of the selected cell will be frozen. Use this technique to freeze row labels and column headings at the same time.

To unfreeze a frozen window, choose Window, Unfreeze Panes.

SPLITTING THE SCREEN

Splitting the Excel screen allows you to see two or four distinct parts of the same worksheet at the same time. You'll find this feature particularly useful when comparing content within a worksheet, or if you need to cut or copy content from one area to another. Imagine that you have a worksheet containing data for all four quarters of the year—by splitting the screen into four parts, each one displaying a different quarter, you can do a quick visual analysis of the entire year.

By splitting the screen, you create the effect of two or four "cameras" on the worksheet content, each aimed at a different section of the sheet. Each camera can scroll and pan around the section at which it's aimed, and of course, you can remove the split(s) when the need has passed. Figure 2.33 shows a worksheet window split into two parts.

PART

I

CH

2

The top two panes give context for the information in the bottom panes by showing the column headings.

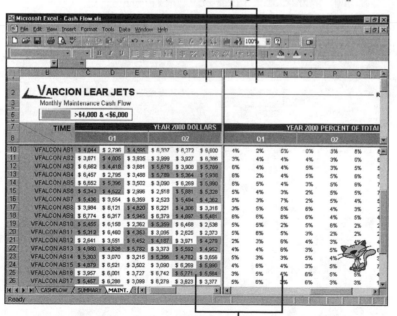

Figure 2.33.
If you need to compare or copy content from one area to another, split the worksheet window into two parts.

Scroll through the bottom two panes to compare maintenance cost to the percent each cost is of the total.

To split the worksheet window into two parts, follow these steps:

1. To split into two panes, select the row or column that will mark the split by clicking its number or letter, respectively. Or, to split into four panes, click in one cell.

2. Choose Window, Split.

The worksheet now has either two or four sets of scrollbars for each side of the split, enabling you to scroll up, down, left, or right, within each section of the screen. Conceivably, you can be looking at the same cells in both sides of the split.

After creating the split, you can scroll to any location in the worksheet from within any and all of the sections.

> **Note**
>
> With a four-pane window split, the panes scroll in pairs. When scrolling up and down, the two upper panes scroll together. When scrolling left and right, the two left panes scroll together, and the two right panes scroll together.

Moving the *split bars* enables you to increase or decrease the size of any of the sections. To move a split bar, point to the bar. The mouse pointer turns into a two-headed arrow, as shown in Figure 2.34. Horizontal bars can be moved up or down, vertical bars left or right.

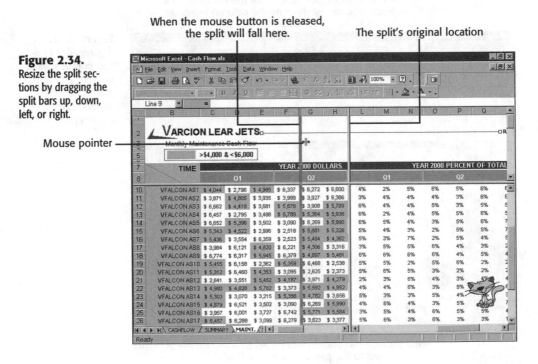

Figure 2.34.
Resize the split sections by dragging the split bars up, down, left, or right.

Tip #31 from

> To move all four sides of the split, point to the intersection of the vertical and horizontal bars. When the mouse pointer turns into a four-headed arrow, click and drag to move the intersection.

To remove the split, choose one of the following methods:

- Choose <u>W</u>indow, Remove <u>S</u>plit. All split bars will be removed.
- Double-click one split bar to remove it. To remove a four-way split, double-click the intersection of the two splits.
- Drag one of the split bars off the worksheet.

Tip #32 from

> Use the *split boxes*, small buttons at the top of the vertical scrollbar and to the right of the horizontal scrollbar, to insert and move split bars. If you can't see the split boxes, unfreeze the window—you can't split a frozen window.

HIDING AND UNHIDING ROWS AND COLUMNS

The word *hiding* can give the impression that something sneaky is happening, that something is being kept a secret. That may be your motive for hiding a column or row in your worksheet, but it's probably not the only one. Hiding rows and/or columns allows you to keep something from being printed if the content is of no interest to the person who'll be reading the printout (that may even be you), or to simplify the view of the worksheet, removing distracting or visually cluttering content while you work.

Tip #33 from

> Hiding content also can be used to make confidential content invisible, but there are better ways to do that, such as password-protecting a workbook or placing the file in a network drive to which only you have access.

To hide a column or row, you can choose from the following two methods:

- Resize the column or row until it is so narrow that it literally disappears.
- Select the row(s) or column(s) and choose F<u>o</u>rmat, <u>C</u>olumn (or <u>R</u>ow), <u>H</u>ide, or right-click the selection and choose <u>H</u>ide from the context menu.

When a column or row is hidden, a thick border appears between the headings of the visible rows or columns where the hidden number or letter would normally appear. Figure 2.35 shows the special split two-headed arrow that only appears on a boundary where one or more rows or columns are hidden.

PART

I

CH

2

Split two-headed arrow mouse pointer

Figure 2.35.
Make sure the mouse pointer is a split two-headed arrow before unhiding columns or rows.

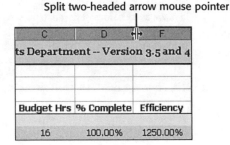

To reveal hidden columns or rows, choose one of the following methods:

- Point to the thick boundary between column letters or row numbers. When the mouse pointer turns into a split two-headed arrow, double-click (refer to Figure 2.34).

- Select the columns or rows that appear on either side of the hidden content, and choose Format, Column (or Row), Unhide.

Caution

Observe the two-headed arrow carefully—a solid two-headed arrow is used for resizing columns and rows, a split two-headed arrow is used for unhiding a column or row.

→ For more information on using protection to control changes to your workbooks, **see** "Protecting Your Data," **p. 520**

TROUBLESHOOTING

DISTINGUISHING ONE VERSION OF A FILE FROM ANOTHER

How do I determine which file is which?

Aside from doing a visual check for differences in content, you can distinguish two different versions of an Excel file by checking the date and time modified for each file. You can see this information in the Open dialog box, Windows Explorer, or My Computer (in Details view), or by choosing File, Properties when the workbook is active onscreen. The Statistics tab in the Properties dialog box shows the date and time the file was last modified.

CREATING A TEMPLATE FROM AN EXISTING WORKBOOK

What if I've already added data to the file that I want to use as a template?

Before you save the file as a template, save it one last time in its current format. Then delete any specific data, leaving only the labels, formulas, and any other text that you want to have on every worksheet created with the template. When you save the workbook as a template, the original file, prior to the deletions, will be left intact.

WHY SAVE TO THE TEMPLATES FOLDER?

I've placed my templates in a folder other than the Templates folder, and now I can't see them in the New dialog box. What do I do?

Only templates that are in the Templates folder or one of its direct subfolders (such as Spreadsheet Solutions) will appear in the New dialog box when you choose to create a new workbook based on a template. If you created or placed templates in some other folder, copy or move the templates—or the folder with its templates—to place them in c:\Windows\Application Data\Microsoft\Templates. If you prefer to keep the templates where they are, use the Open dialog box to open a template, and then immediately save it with its new workbook name before making any changes (to avoid changing the template).

PART

I

CH

2

EXCEL IN PRACTICE

You can use several of Excel's features to enhance any template you create. Beyond entering basic cell content to instruct or guide the template's users, adding settings such as frozen panes, prenamed sheet tabs, and hidden columns will help the user understand your goals for use of the template, not simply *how* to use it. Figures 2.36 and 2.37 show two different levels of template preparation.

Column headings indicate the type of data to be stored.

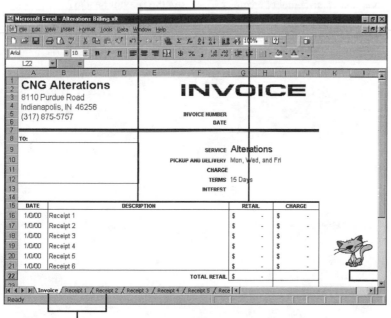

Figure 2.36.
This template is set up for a small alterations business to use for customer invoices.

Sheet tabs are named to guide the user through the template.

The Client Error? column is hidden to keep that information from printing.

Figure 2.37.
Saving the template with a frozen pane in place and the salary column hidden help the user make better use of the template.

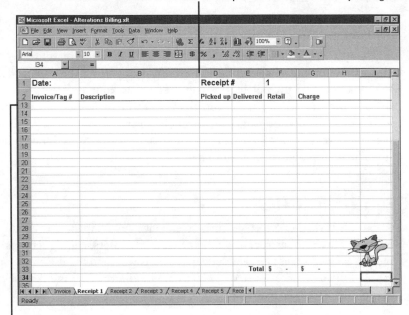

Note the row number under the frozen row—the user can enter more than a screenful of records and still see the column headings.

EDITING WORKSHEET CONTENT

SELECTING AND NAMING CELLS AND RANGES

In this chapter

by Laurie Ann Ulrich
laurie@limehat.com

SELECTING CELLS

After data entry, selecting worksheet content is probably the task most frequently performed in Excel. Selecting cells and ranges tells Excel where you are and what you're doing, and is an integral step in most formatting, calculation, and editing procedures. To select an individual cell, click on it or use any of the keyboard shortcuts shown in Table 3.1 for worksheet navigation to move to the desired cell.

TABLE 3.1. KEYBOARD SHORTCUTS FOR SELECTING INDIVIDUAL CELLS

Keyboard Shortcut	Selects
Enter	The cell below the current cell
Tab	The cell to the right of the current cell
Shift+Tab	The cell to the left of the current cell
Ctrl+Home	Cell A1
Home	The first cell in the current row

When a cell is *active* (the *current cell*), it appears with a thick border around it, as shown in Figure 3.1. This border, called the *cell pointer*, indicates the active cell. The Name box in the Formula bar displays the address of the active cell.

Figure 3.1.
Select a cell in preparation for entering or editing content, or to format the existing content of the cell.

The active cell is B7.

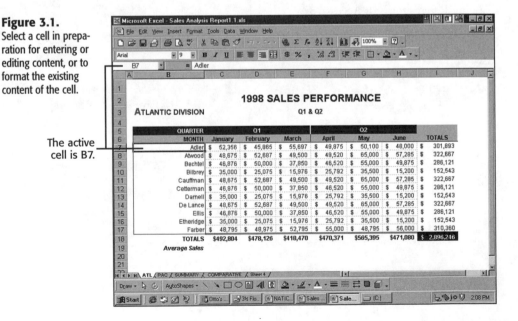

To select a range of cells, click and drag through them, dragging up, down, left, right, or a combination of these directions to select the desired range of cells. Release the mouse when the desired block of cells (two or more) is highlighted. Figure 3.2 shows a selected range of cells. The range in this example would have the address C7:H17—the colon representing the word *through*. The active cell is cell C7, which indicates that the range was selected from upper-left to lower-right; the cell pointer remains in the first cell selected. Notice that Excel highlights the row and column headings for the selected range, boldfacing the heading letter(s) or number(s) and displaying the headings as if they were buttons, with a "pushed-out" appearance.

As you select a *contiguous* range—a range in which all the cells are adjacent to one another—Excel displays information in the Name box to match the selection. In this case, the designation 11R x 6C indicates that the selection is eleven rows long and six columns wide. As soon as you complete the selection, the Name box goes back to displaying the address of the current cell.

The dimensions of the selected range appear in the Name box until you release the mouse button.

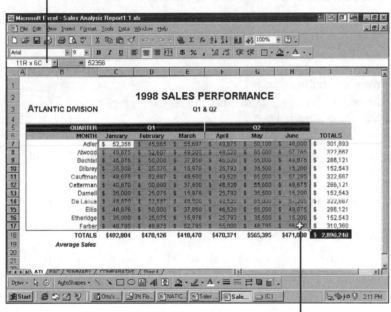

Figure 3.2.
The starting cell remains white. Other cells in the selected range show a transparent color (you can see the selected cells through the color).

Drag right and down to select this range.

Tip #34 from

Laurie

While this chapter's title lists them as two different things, both single cells and ranges of cells are considered ranges by Excel. You'll find this interchangeable terminology and concept in many areas, such as named ranges, covered later in this chapter.

Caution

Selected cells are vulnerable. If you accidentally press the spacebar or type a character while a cell or range of cells is selected, the content of the selection (in the one white cell of the range) will be deleted, replaced with a space or the character you typed. If this occurs, press Esc to cancel the entry if the cell is still selected. If you already accepted the entry, use the Undo feature to restore the original entry.

When a range of blank cells is selected, enter content by typing in the first cell and then pressing Enter. You automatically are moved to the next cell in the range. Continue typing content in each cell, and pressing Enter after each one. This procedure changes the normal effect of pressing the Enter key—normally the Enter key takes you to the cell below the current cell—and allows you to confine your edits to one area. If you select a block or range of cells for entry, using this method also will enable you to type entries without looking back at the worksheet to see where you are while typing. This is especially useful if you're referring to a printed document or written notes as a source for the entries.

Tip #35 from

Laurie

If you have selected a range that includes multiple rows, each press of the Enter key moves the cell pointer down until you reach the last row within the selection. Pressing Enter again moves the active cell to the top cell in the next column to the right. Use Shift+Enter to move backward in a selection.

Alternatively, you can move left to right in a selection by pressing the Tab key. Use Shift+Tab to move right to left.

You also can select a range of cells by using the keyboard. To select a block of cells, follow these steps:

1. Use the most appropriate keyboard shortcut or click in the first cell in the desired range.

2. Press and hold down the Shift key.

3. Use the arrow keys to select cells to the right of, left of, above, or below the starting cell. To select larger blocks of text, use PgUp/PgDn or Alt+PgUp/Alt+PgDn.

4. When the desired block of cells is selected, release the Shift key.

Tip #36 from

Laurie

It may be easier to use the Shift key and arrow keys to select a range when you're in the middle of a long data entry session—it saves you the time of using the mouse and dragging through cells when your hands are already on the keyboard.

SELECTING COLUMNS AND ROWS

Selecting a range requires highlighting a block of cells. You can drag to select all the entries in a column or row, but in many cases it's more efficient to select the entire row (all 256 cells) or column (all 65,536 cells), whether you're using the entire range of cells or not. To drag through an entire row or column could take several minutes, just to scroll to the ends of the worksheet. It's much easier to click the column letter or row number for the desired column or row, as shown in Figure 3.3.

Click here to select the entire column.

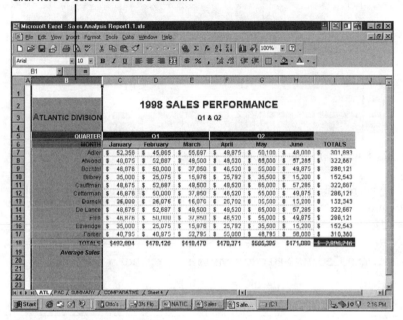

Figure 3.3.
Click the column letter to select all 65,536 cells in the column.

Notice that the color of the column or row heading is reversed when the entire column is selected. (This behavior may affect or be affected by background fills or patterns in the cells, however.)

 If your worksheet includes background fills or patterns, the selection color may look unusual. See "Color Selection Looks Odd" in the Troubleshooting section at the end of this chapter.

You can select multiple columns or rows by dragging through the column letters or row numbers, as shown in Figure 3.4.

Caution
Formatting an entire column or row tends to bloat the file size of the workbook because Excel must store the formatting information for every cell you selected, regardless of whether you ever enter any content in that cell. Apply global formatting only when necessary.

Figure 3.4.
Select a series of columns or rows to copy, move, format, or enter content for the entire selection.

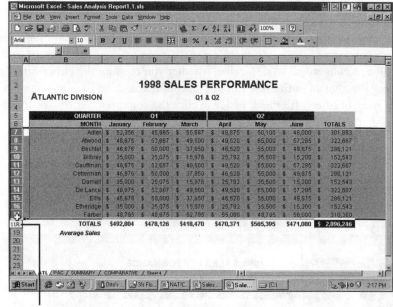

The ScreenTip indicates the number of rows selected.

Table 3.2 lists keyboard shortcuts you can use to select rows or columns in a worksheet. The Result column in the table assumes that the active cell is in the row or column you want to select *before* you use these shortcuts.

TABLE 3.2. ROW AND COLUMN SELECTION WITH THE KEYBOARD

Keyboard Shortcut	Result
Ctrl+Spacebar	Selects the entire column.
Shift+Spacebar	Selects the entire row.
Ctrl+Shift+Spacebar	Selects the entire worksheet.

Tip #37 from

You can select the entire worksheet by clicking the *Select All* button (the blank gray button at the intersection of the column letters and row numbers) just below the Name box.

SELECTING NONCONTIGUOUS RANGES

When edits, formatting changes, or deletions you want to make are in multiple separate areas of the worksheet, you can select these *noncontiguous ranges* by adding the Ctrl key to the selection procedure.

To select multiple ranges that don't share adjacent cells, follow these steps:

1. Select the first cell or range of cells.

2. Release the mouse, and press and hold down the Ctrl key.

3. Using the mouse again, select the next cell or range of cells.

4. Repeat steps 1 through 3 until you've selected all the ranges you need. Figure 3.5 shows a worksheet with three noncontiguous ranges selected: B6:B17, B6:H6, and C18:H18.

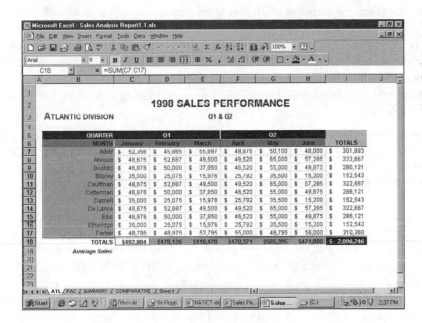

Figure 3.5.
Select the column and row labels, as well as the row of totals, so that you can apply formatting to all the selected cells at once.

After making these noncontiguous selections, you can delete or format all the selected areas at once.

Tip #38 from

Laurie

You can copy noncontiguous selections to the Clipboard only if all the selections are the same size and shape. For example, in Figure 3.5, you can select B7:E7, B11:E11, and B14:E14, and then copy that entire noncontiguous selection.

You'll notice that when you select the second range of cells, the active cell (starting cell) switches from the starting cell in the first range to the starting cell in the second range. The current cell will continue to move to each subsequent range you add to the group of selected ranges, ending up in the first cell of the last selected range.

SELECTING RANGES ON GROUPED WORKSHEETS

In addition to being able to select contiguous or noncontiguous ranges on a single worksheet, you might occasionally want to select the same ranges on multiple worksheets within a workbook. Why might you want to select cells/ranges from several sheets at once? The following list offers some suggestions:

- **To speed up and simplify formatting changes.** Want to make all titles on all sheets look the same? Select them all at once and then apply the formatting.

- **To expedite editing a series of cells.** You know that a selected range of cells can be edited, cell by cell, with the Enter key. What if you want to make changes to cell content on several sheets? Go through the workbook and select all the ranges, so that as you edit and press Enter, you're taken automatically to the next cell in the series to be edited. Keep in mind, though, that grouped worksheets have the same selections on every sheet; you can't select one set of ranges on one worksheet and a different set on another worksheet.

- **To make a quick deletion.** Assume that your worksheets include multiple references to a sales rep whom you no longer employ or a product you no longer sell. Select the cells and ranges that refer to this person or product, and then press Delete. All cell content in those cells—in all worksheets included in the group—will be removed.

The process of selecting worksheets is called *grouping*. It's important to note that you should group worksheets for formatting, data entry, or deletions only if all the worksheets are structured identically. For example, if you group Sheet1 and Sheet2, select the range B2:B7 on Sheet1, and then switch to Sheet2, you'll find that the same cell coordinates are selected on Sheet2. If you add a range to the selection while on Sheet2, the added selection will be echoed on Sheet1. For this reason, if the sheets *aren't* structured identically (everything in the same place on all sheets), restrict use of this feature to editing content—you can always press Enter to skip extra cells in the selection.

When working with grouped worksheets, you can select the ranges first and then group the worksheets, or group the worksheets and then make your selections. After all ranges are selected and the worksheets are grouped, you can make content changes, apply formatting, and so on.

To group worksheets, start by activating the first worksheet you want in the group. Then hold down the Ctrl key while clicking the sheet tab for each additional worksheet you want to include in the group. (If you want to include a set of contiguous sheets, you can display the first sheet, hold down the Shift key, and click the sheet tab for the last sheet.) The sheet tabs for grouped worksheets turn white, and a [Group] indicator appears in the title bar of the workbook window. Grouped worksheets remain grouped until you click the sheet tab for an ungrouped sheet or right-click the sheet tab for one of the grouped sheets and select Ungroup Sheets from the resulting context menu.

Group indicator

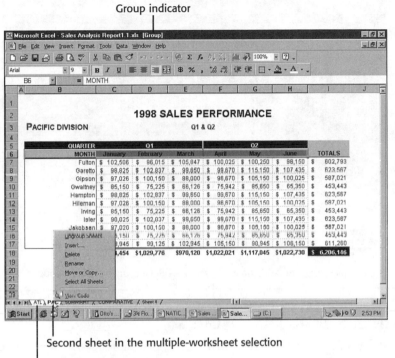

Figure 3.6.
Grouped sheets remain grouped until you ungroup them. Any changes are applied to all the grouped sheets.

Second sheet in the multiple-worksheet selection

First sheet containing selected cells

PART

II

CH

3

After sheets are grouped, you can switch freely between the grouped sheets by clicking the sheet tab for the sheet you want to see. Notice that if you select a new range on the active sheet, it's simultaneously selected on all other sheets in the group (see Figure 3.7).

Tip #39 from

Laurie

If you group a sheet you didn't want, simply Ctrl+click the sheet tab to remove it from the group.

These cells were selected on the PAC sheet.

Figure 3.7.
Selecting cells and ranges on grouped sheets makes it easy to edit and format cells within identical sheets.

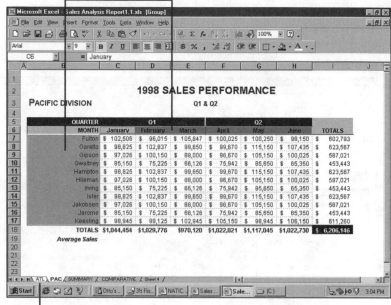

Cells selected on the PAC sheet will also be selected on the other grouped sheet.

NAMING RANGES FOR FAST ACCESS

After you enter some or all of a worksheet's content, you may find it easier to refer to cells and blocks of selected cells by name rather than cell address. Just as it's easier to find an employee by asking the receptionist for him or her by name than to comb the building on foot, looking in each cube or office, so finding cells and ranges by name is faster and easier than trying to find and remember cell addresses. Excel gives you the capacity to name individual cells or cell ranges so that you can find data by a logical name, and refer to the cells ranges in formulas, as described in Chapter 12, "Working with Named Ranges."

Tip #40 from
Laurie

It's a good idea to go through large or complex worksheets and name all the key cells or ranges to which you think you'll go often. Don't wait until you wish you had created a name for an often-accessed cell!

To name a cell or range of cells, follow these steps:

1. Select the cell(s), and choose Insert, Name, Define. This opens the Define Name dialog box, as shown in Figure 3.8.

2. In the Names in Workbook text box, type a name for the selected cell(s).

3. Click OK.

Tip #41 from

Laurie

You can type a range of cells or a single cell address into the <u>R</u>efers To box. This technique enables you to enter several ranges, clicking <u>A</u>dd after naming each one, without having to repeatedly close and then reopen the dialog box after selecting cells or ranges with the mouse.

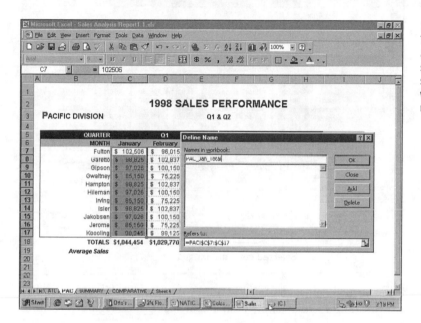

Figure 3.8.
Type the range name and click <u>A</u>dd to insert several ranges in one session, or OK if you want to add only one range name.

Tip #42 from

Laurie

A quick method for creating named ranges is to select the cell/range, and, using the Name box on the Formula bar, highlight the displayed cell address and replace it by typing a name for the cell/range. Press Enter to create the name.

Range names cannot begin with a number, resemble a cell address (such as FQ1999), or contain spaces or punctuation. You can use underscores in lieu of spaces, such as First_Quarter_1999. Although Excel allows range names to contain hundreds of characters, sticking to short names makes them easier to remember and use in formulas.

 Getting an error message when you type a range name? See "Range Naming Errors" in the Troubleshooting section at the end of this chapter.

When selecting cells to be named, they needn't be a contiguous range—use the Ctrl key to select several individual noncontiguous cells or ranges, and then give the group of selected cells a single name (see Figure 3.9). This could be used to find and sum various sales totals throughout the worksheet, for example, giving them one name, such as PAC Q's First Month.

The range name is typed into the Name box.

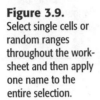

Figure 3.9.
Select single cells or random ranges throughout the work-sheet and then apply one name to the entire selection.

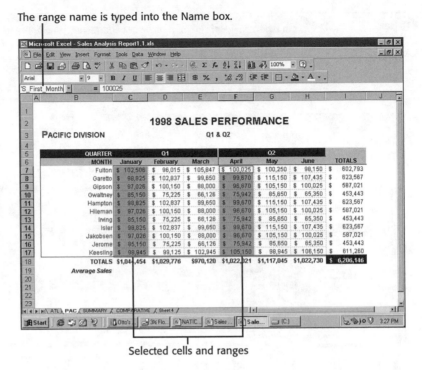

Selected cells and ranges

After you've added a named range, you can access it by opening the Name box on the Formula bar, or by pressing F3 to open the Paste Name dialog box. Figure 3.10 shows a series of named ranges.

Figure 3.10.
Select a range name from the list, and the cell or range it repre-sents is immediately selected.

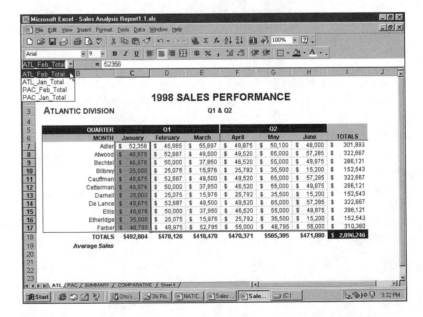

To remove a named range, choose Insert, Name, Define, and select the named range from the list. Click the Delete button, and then click OK.

TROUBLESHOOTING

COLOR SELECTION LOOKS ODD

When I select cells or ranges, the background color of my worksheet seems to go haywire.

If your worksheet includes colored background fills or patterns, a range selection may display in an odd color. The displayed color change is merely the temporary result of selecting the cells. Clicking away from the selected range to deselect it will display the cells with their normal formatting.

CAN'T COPY MULTIPLE SELECTIONS

After selecting several noncontiguous ranges, I try to copy them to the Clipboard but get the message That command cannot be used on multiple selections.

Excel can copy noncontiguous ranges only if they're the same size and shape. If you need to copy all the information in the various selections but nothing between, and you can't arrange the worksheet to make that data contiguous, try this trick: Apply a background fill or special format to the cells you don't want (a bright yellow or green fill works nicely). Then copy a contiguous block containing all the cells you do want as well as those you don't, and paste the copy into place in its target position. The cells that then need to be cleared are easily visible because of the fill or special format. Select those cells and choose Edit, Clear, All.

RANGE NAMING ERRORS

When I type the range name I want to create in the Name box, Excel displays the message You must enter a valid reference you want to go to, or type a valid name for the selection.

You're probably attempting to use a space in the range name or begin the range name with a number. Unfortunately, names such as 1999 Disbursements are not allowed. For this type of name, put the year at the end, and replace the space with an underscore: Disbursements_1999.

EXCEL IN PRACTICE

Excel's tools for selecting and naming ranges can be used to significantly reduce your setup time. Figure 3.11 shows a set of identical worksheets, created by grouping the sheets and selecting sections of their content. Simple formats were applied once, and that one action formatted all the sheets. This type of uniformity decreases the learning curve for users who have to work with the worksheets and makes it easier for you to build worksheets quickly and consistently.

Column headings, row labels, and totals are formatted on all the selected sheets.

Figure 3.11.
These sheets were grouped, and selections in all three sheets were simultaneously formatted to achieve a consistent look throughout the workbook.

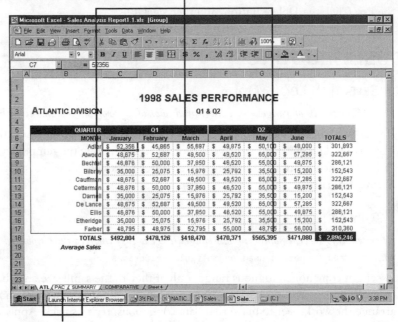

Grouped identical sheets

CHAPTER 4

EDITING CELL CONTENT

In this chapter

by Laurie Ann Ulrich
laurie@limehat.com

EDITING WITH THE KEYBOARD

When you click on a cell that already contains data, pressing virtually any key on your keyboard will replace your content with the character or code associated with the key pressed. In your use of Excel, you'll find that you can use this feature to your own benefit (for intentional replacements) or in error (by striking a key accidentally). To familiarize yourself with the keys that will edit your cell content, review the following:

- Alphanumeric keys (all the letters of the alphabet, the numbers 0 through 9, and all symbols and punctuation) will, when pressed, replace your selected cell content.

- The numeric keypad (active if Num Lock is on) will replace your content with numbers and mathematical symbols (/ * - +).

- The Spacebar will replace selected cell content with a space.

> **Caution**
>
> Pressing the spacebar in a cell doesn't delete the cell's contents—it replaces them with a space. To delete a cell's contents, select the cell and press the Delete key.

> **Tip #43 from**
>
>
>
> If a cell containing data is accidentally edited by your pressing a key on the keyboard, press the Esc key immediately to return to the cell's original content. If you have already pressed Enter, click the Undo button, choose Edit, Undo, or press Ctrl+Z to undo the changes.

EDITING A GROUP OF CELLS

You also can edit a group of selected cells, whether in a single block or a group of two or more noncontiguous selections. This enables you to edit several cells quickly, saving you the time of selecting and editing each cell individually.

To edit a group of selected cells, follow these steps:

1. Select the group of cells you want to edit. If the cells are noncontiguous, hold down the Ctrl key as you gather them into the selection.

2. Starting with the cell that remains white (the first cell in your most recent selection), type your corrected data and/or make your corrections using the Formula bar.

3. Press the Enter key to move to the next cell in the block (see Figure 4.1). If you'd prefer to move left to right through your selection, use the Tab key rather than Enter. Shift+Enter will move backward vertically, Shift+Tab will move backward horizontally.

4. Continue editing the cells in your selection, pressing Enter or Tab after each cell's edits are complete.

5. When you finish editing the cells, click any cell or use one of the arrow keys to deselect your block(s) of cells.

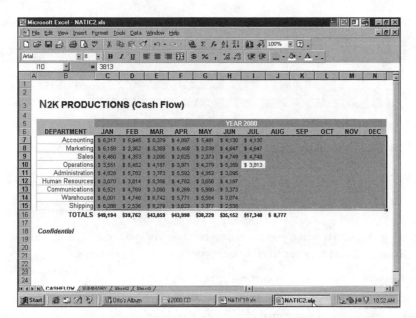

Figure 4.1.
Excel will move down the selected block's columns and then start at the top of the next column as you press the Enter key to complete each cell's edits.

Tip #44 from

Laurie

If you want to place the same entry in multiple cells, select the cells (contiguous or non-contiguous), type the entry in one of the cells or in the Formula bar, and press Ctrl+Enter to place the entry in all the selected cells.

Caution

If you don't click outside the selected cells or use an arrow key at the end of your editing session, you will cycle through the selected cells again. This risks reediting the first cells you edited in the current session.

To review the techniques for selecting cells in Excel, see Chapter 3, "Selecting and Naming Cells and Ranges."

→ For more information on keyboard shortcuts for navigating your Excel worksheet, **see** "Using Worksheet Keyboard Shortcuts," **p. 27**

EDITING USING THE FORMULA BAR

The Formula bar obviously displays more than formulas. If a selected cell contains text or a number that isn't the result of a formula, this content also appears in the Formula bar. Figure 4.2 shows the Formula bar content for a selected cell.

The I-beam pointer appears when you point to or click within the Formula bar content.

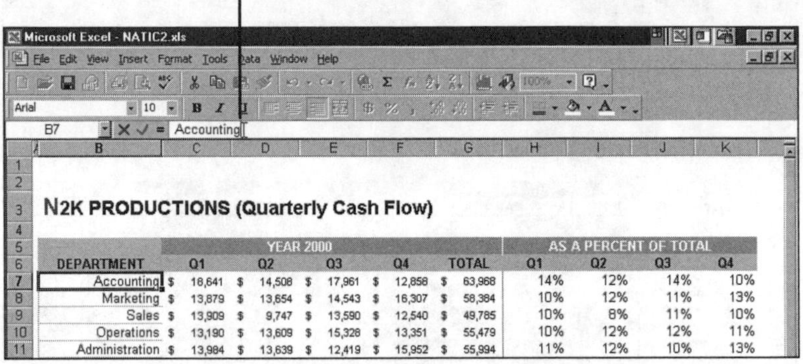

Figure 4.2.
The Formula bar gives you room to edit long titles, as well as complex numeric or formula content.

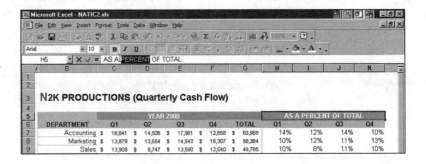

Excel's designers realized that when you're editing cell content, you might need a little elbow room. To use the Formula bar to edit cell content, follow these steps:

1. Click the cell you want to edit. Its content appears in the Formula bar.

2. In the Formula bar, use your mouse to select some or all of the cell's content (see Figure 4.3). You can select individual characters, words, or any portion of the cell content.

Figure 4.3.
In lieu of the mouse, you can use the Shift and arrow keys to select content on your Formula bar.

Tip #45 from
Laurie

> Use your Backspace or Delete keys to remove a cell's content, one character at a time, on the Formula bar.

3. Type the replacement content—this will simultaneously remove and replace the Formula bar's selected content.

4. Press Enter to place your edited content in the cell.

If your selected cell contains a formula, the result of the formula appears in the cell, but the formula itself appears in the Formula bar, as shown in Figure 4.4. To edit the formula, click in the Formula bar and delete/replace the numbers, operators, and cell addresses you need, and then press Enter. The formula will be recalculated, and the new result will appear in the cell.

The formula

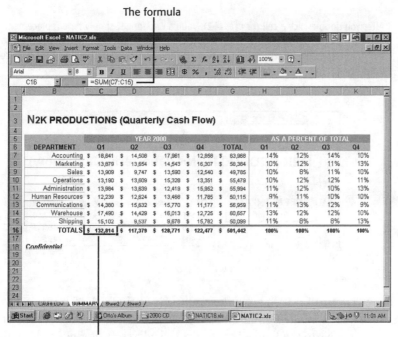

Result of the formula

Figure 4.4.
Always check the
Formula bar to see
whether the cell's con-
tent is a number that
was typed directly into
the cell or if the num-
ber is the result of a
formula.

For more information on building and using formulas in Excel, see Chapter 10, "Constructing Excel Formulas."

EDITING DIRECTLY IN THE CELL

While the Formula bar gives you more room, some users prefer a direct approach—editing the cell's content from within the cell itself. This can be done for text, numbers, or formula content. Use one of the following two methods to display the insertion point in the selected cell:

- Double-click the cell.
- After selecting the cell, press the F2 key.

Either method results in the insertion point blinking in the cell, at which point you can select specific cell content (characters, words, any portion of the content) for replacement or deletion, or use the Backspace and/or Delete keys to remove content (see Figure 4.5).

Note

When you double-click the cell, the insertion point appears at the position of the mouse pointer when you double-clicked. Because the white cross pointer is fairly large and it's common to use a relatively small font in Excel, the insertion point may not appear exactly where you expected. Be sure to check the insertion point's position before making changes. Use the arrow keys to move the insertion point as necessary.

PART

II

Cii

4

continues

continued

> After you double-click a cell (or press F2), you can no longer simply type replacement data and have it both delete the original cell contents and insert new content. If the cell's contents are active (the insertion point appears in the cell), you must highlight the cell's contents before typing your replacement characters.

Figure 4.5.
Press Enter or click into another cell after making your changes to the selected cell's content.

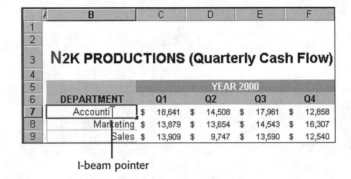

I-beam pointer

When editing directly in a cell that contains the results of a formula, the formula will appear in the cell (as well as on the Formula bar) as soon as you double-click the cell or press F2. In addition, thanks to the Range Finder, any cell addresses or ranges within the active worksheet that were used in the cell's formula will become highlighted with a colored border around the cells (see Figure 4.6). The formula being edited displays the cell addresses or ranges in the formula in matching colors. Each cell address in the formula will have a colored border, starting with blue for the first cell in the formula, green for the second, purple for the third, and so on. The Range Finder helps you edit the formula and is especially useful when you're working with a worksheet set up by someone else.

Figure 4.6.
Excel's Range Finder helps you edit a formula within the cell by placing an extra border around the cells referenced in your formula.

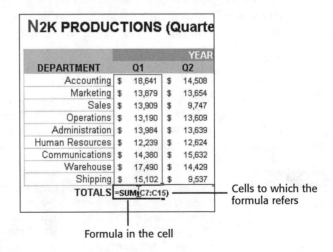

Formula in the cell

Tip #46 from

Laurie

To use the colored borders to edit your formula, you can drag the border from one cell to another, thus changing the cell address in the formula to the new cell. If your formula is currently =D6*E9 and you want to change E9 to E11, for example, drag the border from E9 to E11—the formula will update, becoming =D6*E11. Press Enter to recalculate the formula based on the new cell addresses.

Similarly, if you want to expand or narrow a range of numbers, drag the colored border's sizing handle. For example, to change the range A5:A10 to A5:A15, drag the sizing handle down to cell A15.

EDITING WITH THE MOUSE

Worksheets are complex documents, relying heavily on the exact and appropriate placement of text and numbers. Formula results and overall legibility can be adversely affected by numbers in the wrong cells or text that doesn't reflect the latest information. You may also need to repeat the content of one or more cells within the same worksheet and want to avoid retyping it.

While you can use the Clipboard to copy or move cell content, it often is easier to make minor changes in data location within a single worksheet by using the mouse. This feature, called *drag and drop*, is supported in all of the Microsoft Office applications—you may have used it in Microsoft Word, where it is especially useful in rearranging words in a sentence or sentences in a paragraph. These word processing examples should serve to remind you of a basic limitation of drag and drop—it works best within a small area, namely the portion of your worksheet that is currently visible onscreen.

→ Viewing separate sections of your worksheet is made easier by splitting your worksheet window into separate panes. **See** "Controlling the Worksheet View," **p. 61**

MOVING CELL CONTENT WITH DRAG AND DROP

Moving cell content, be it a single cell or a block of selected cells, is quite simple. You can drag any selection from one place to another by following these steps:

1. Select the cell or cells you want to move.
2. Point to the edge of the cell or block of cells, and look for your mouse to turn into a left-pointing arrow.

Note

You cannot move (or copy) noncontiguous selections with drag and drop.

3. Click and drag the cell(s) to the desired location on the worksheet (see Figure 4.7).
4. Release the mouse to drop the selection in its new location.

PART

II

CH

4

Figure 4.7.
If you let go of your
selection in the wrong
spot, choose Edit,
Undo, or press Ctrl+Z
to put it back in its
original location.

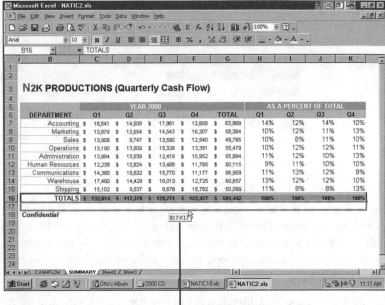

ScreenTips show cell addresses as you pass over cells with your mouse.

If you attempt to drop the moved cell(s) where data already exists, you'll be prompted to confirm your desire to replace the contents of the destination cells.

Tip #47 from
Laurie

If drag and drop doesn't seem to work, choose Tools, Options, click the Edit tab, and check Allow Cell Drag and Drop.

If you don't get the confirmation prompt after you drag and drop cells, the prompt is simply turned off. To turn it back on, choose Tools, Options, click the Edit tab, and check Alert Before Overwriting Cells.

Tip #48 from
Laurie

Although you can drag the selected cell(s) to a spot outside of the currently visible portion of the worksheet, you may find it difficult to control scrolling so that you arrive at your exact desired location. You may find that the sheet scrolls too fast.

There's an informal name for this unintended fast scrolling: the Roadrunner Effect. To counteract it, rein in how far off the grid you move your mouse. When dragging and dropping downward, for example, if your mouse pointer is in the sheet tab area, scrolling is relatively slow. But if you move the mouse pointer into the status bar, scrolling speeds up significantly. So don't just slam your mouse downward—keep it just off the edge of the grid.

If you need to move or copy cells between worksheets or workbooks, you can use <u>W</u>indow, <u>A</u>rrange, <u>T</u>ile or <u>C</u>ascade to position windows so that you can use drag and drop between them. If you prefer, you can use the Clipboard to move (cut) and copy, which is covered in Chapter 5, "Moving, Copying, Linking, and Embedding Information."

Tip #49 from

Laurie

You can drag and drop onto other worksheets in your workbook by holding down the Alt key and dragging the selected cells to the other worksheet's tab. That worksheet opens. Drag the selected cells to where you want them.

COPYING CELL CONTENT WITH DRAG AND DROP

Moving cell content implies that it isn't in the right place or that it's no longer needed in its current location. Copying, on the other hand, allows you to leave the original cell and its content right where it is, and place a duplicate elsewhere on the worksheet. Just like moving, you can use drag and drop to copy a cell or cells from one place to another on your worksheet—again, it's a task best performed within a small area.

To copy a cell or group of contiguous cells to another location on the active worksheet, follow these steps:

1. Select the cell or cells you want to copy.
2. Point to the edge of the selected cell(s). Your mouse pointer turns into a left-pointing arrow.
3. Press and hold the Ctrl key.
4. Drag your selected cells to another location, keeping the Ctrl key depressed as you drag. Figure 4.8 shows a block of cells being copied to another location.
5. When your desired location is reached, release the mouse.
6. Release the Ctrl key.

PART

II

CH

4

Caution

If you release the Ctrl key prior to releasing the mouse, your copy procedure turns into a move, and the selected cells will be taken from their original location and moved to the spot where you released the mouse. Be sure to release the Ctrl key after the cells' duplicates have been deposited in their new location.

When you attempt to move a cell's content to a cell that already contains data, you're prompted to confirm that this is your intention. Be aware that no such prompt appears when you drag and drop to copy a cell or cells, thus making it easy to accidentally overwrite data while copying.

Figure 4.8.
Because you're dragging a copy, a small plus sign (+) follows your mouse pointer to the target location.

Selected cells ———

Destination cells ———

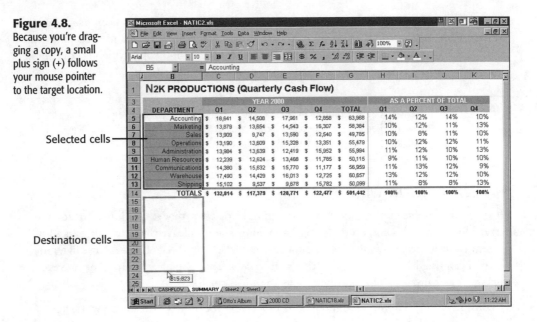

FINDING AND REPLACING DATA

Office 2000's Find and Replace feature enables you to search for a word or number and replace it with something else. This can be an invaluable tool for updating a worksheet to reflect current dates, or to make a sweeping change that eliminates outdated names or jargon within your workbook.

Find and Replace is performed on a per-worksheet basis, requiring that you repeat it for each worksheet in your workbook if the change you require is found throughout the entire book.

To search for and replace cell content, follow these steps:

1. Click in the first cell of the worksheet (A1) or press Ctrl+Home to select that cell.

2. Choose Edit, Replace.

3. In the Replace dialog box, type the content you want to replace in the Find what box (see Figure 4.9).

4. Type the replacement content in the Replace With box.

5. Choose your Search option: By Rows or By Columns.

6. As needed, choose the Match Case and/or Find Entire Cells Only options.

7. Click Find Next to go to the first occurrence of the Find What content.

8. If the first found occurrence needs to be replaced, click Replace, or click Find Next to skip this occurrence, leaving the original content intact in this cell.

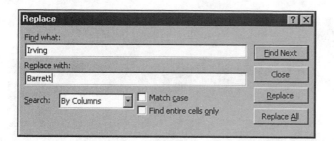

Figure 4.9.
Search for and replace text, numbers, or formulas. To avoid undesirable results, be sure to type your replacement content carefully.

Tip #50 from
Laurie

If you're sure you want to replace every occurrence of the content, click Replace All. Each occurrence will be replaced, and the Replace dialog box will close automatically.

Caution

When replacing numbers, avoid using the Replace All button. A global replacement of 1998 for 1997, for example, could result in the accidental replacement of $1997.58 with $1998.58, which would be an unwanted result.

9. Continue to click Find Next and then Replace (or Find Next) to move through your worksheet.

10. When all occurrences of the Find What content have been replaced, a prompt will appear, indicating that no more occurrences of the Find What content are found. Click OK.

Caution

If you don't replace every occurrence of the Find What content, Excel will continue to cycle through your worksheet each time you click Find Next. To avoid unnecessary repetitions and possible accidental replacements, click Close as soon as you see that you're going through cells that you've already skipped on a previous pass.

11. Click Close to close the Replace dialog box.

Tip #51 from
Laurie

If you want to make changes only within a specific area, select that area of the worksheet before opening the Replace dialog box. This technique avoids cycling back through found text that wasn't replaced. After Excel reaches the last cell in the selection, the search ends.

If you regret your replacements, you can use Edit, Undo (or Ctrl+Z) to reverse your actions, one by one. If this seems too laborious or will undo actions taken since the Replace procedure, you can reverse your Find What and Replace with entries and, using the Find Next and Replace buttons, put your original content back in specific cells. Replace All will replace all entries with their original content.

If you're just looking for cell content (perhaps you want to edit a formula or some text, and you can't find it), use Edit, Find. This opens the Find dialog box (see Figure 4.10).

Figure 4.10.
Use the Find dialog
box to locate text.

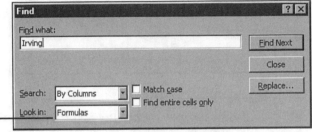

Click the Look In list box to
direct Excel to search your
Formulas, Values, or Comments.

After the content is found, you can click the Replace button to change the dialog box to a Replace dialog box, and enter the Replace with content you need.

DELETING THE CONTENTS OF A CELL

You'll want to delete cell content whenever you have entered content in error or need to take content from one place to another. Following are several methods available for deleting cell content—one or more of them will work depending on your particular situation:

- Select the cell or cells and press Delete. This removes the content of the cell(s), with no prompts from the software.

- Click in a particular cell and type replacement content. This deletes the original content and inserts new data.

- Delete the entire cell, which shifts cell content from other cells into the deleted area (covered in the next section).

- Select your cell or cells, and choose Edit, Clear. This menu command results in a sub-menu, offering options for you to indicate what you want to clear, as shown in Figure 4.11. (Alternatively, you can right-click the selection and choose Clear Contents.)

The method you choose depends on what you want to do. If you need to quickly remove content so that you can type something else in its place, just type the replacement text, achieving both goals. If you want the cell(s) left blank, press Delete. These two methods are fast and simple; they're best used when no formatting has yet been applied to those cells, and you have no doubts about how the deleted cell(s) will affect surrounding cells.

If you've already formatted those cells, applying fonts, colors, or numeric formatting (currency and decimal formatting for example), you may prefer to use Edit, Clear. This method gives you some control over what is deleted. You can, for example, leave the content, but remove a format that was applied in error, or leave your formatting intact while you delete your content.

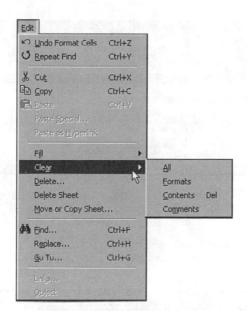

Figure 4.11.
Choose to clear just
the contents, just the
formatting, or every-
thing in the cell.

Tip #52 from

Laurie

Because deleting and/or replacing content is complicated by formatting, it's best to get most of your editing (deleting, moving, copying) out of the way before you attempt to format your worksheet.

PART

II

CH

4

You can find out more about cell formats in Chapter 6, "Formatting Worksheets," and Chapter 7, "Modifying Numbers and Dates."

DELETING CELLS, COLUMNS, AND ROWS

Unlike deleting a single cell's content to leave a cell blank or to replace it with new content, deleting groups of cells entirely is normally done to tighten up a worksheet or remove out-dated content. While you can't really delete a cell, column, or row (there are a fixed number in every worksheet), you can delete the content in a cell, row, or column, and have the surrounding cells move into the deleted cells' place. You can also remove sheets from workbooks and delete whole workbook files from disk. When you delete cell content, however, there can be unpleasant results. See the Troubleshooting section at the end of this chapter for information on potential pitfalls.

With cell(s) selected, choose Edit, Delete to remove the selected cells from the worksheet. This command will result in a question, appearing in the form of a dialog box as shown in Figure 4.12.

Figure 4.12.
Choose what you want done with the surrounding cells, or opt to remove the entire row or column that contains your selected cell(s).

Selected cells

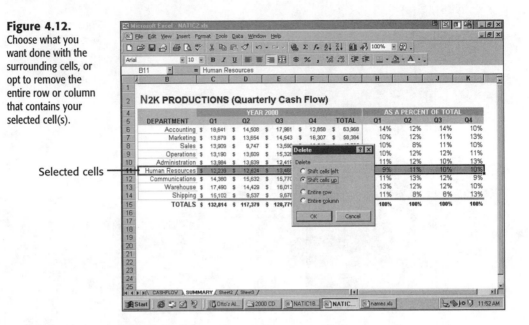

Why would you want to delete entire rows or columns? Imagine a list of monthly employee expenses, stored in Excel, as shown in Figure 4.13. Imagine further that one of the employees quit, so his expense information can be removed from the database. To quickly get rid of the information, you will want to delete the entire row.

Figure 4.13.
List databases are commonly edited by deleting columns and rows.

Click the row number to select the entire row.

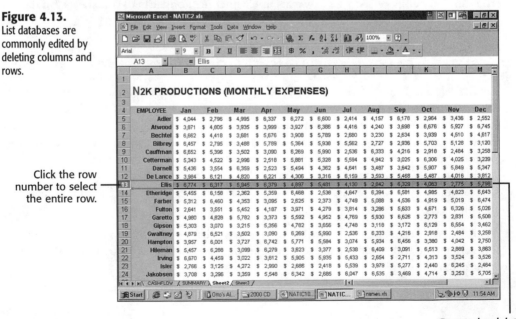

Row to be deleted

To delete a row or column, first select it.

- To select an entire row, click the row number.
- To select an entire column, click the column letter.

Column letters and row numbers are also referred to as *control buttons*, as in "row control button for row 3" or "column control button for column B."

After selecting the row or column, choose Edit, Delete. The selected row or column will disappear, and the surrounding cells will respond as follows:

- When a column is deleted, the column to its right moves left (and a new column IV is added at the far-right edge of the worksheet).
- When a row is deleted, the row below it moves up (and Excel adds a new row 65536 at the bottom of the worksheet).

You may find it faster to use the alternate method for deleting a row or column: Click a single cell in the row or column to delete. Right-click and choose Delete from the pop-up menu. The Delete dialog box appears. Click Entire Row or Entire Column, and then click OK.

Note

If you select a row or column and merely press the Delete key, the content in that row or column's cells will be deleted, but the row (now blank) will remain. You will be deleting content only, not the row or column itself.

You can also delete multiple rows and columns. To do this, you first must select them by dragging through their control buttons or holding down Shift or Ctrl and clicking the buttons. Figure 4.14 shows a series of contiguous rows selected, but you also can select non-contiguous rows or columns by holding down Ctrl and clicking on the control button for each row/column you want to select and subsequently delete.

Once selected, choose Edit, Delete to delete the selected rows/columns and move the surrounding cells into place.

You cannot delete rows or columns at the same time—separate sections that overlap cannot be deleted with the Edit, Delete command.

PART

II

CH

4

Figure 4.14.
Drag through row numbers or column letters to select a series of rows or columns.

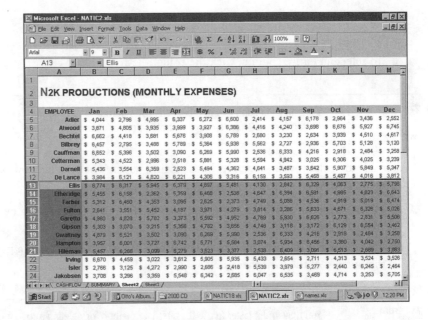

Caution

Before deleting an entire row or column, be sure it doesn't contain data you want to keep. To do a quick search on a seemingly empty row or column, select the row and choose Edit, Find, and search for * (asterisk). Excel will highlight any cell containing data.

List databases (where you'll find many uses for the deletion of rows and columns) are discussed in Chapter 17, "Setting Up a List or Database in Excel."

Tip #56 from

Laurie

If you want to repeat your last edit on another cell or range of cells, press Ctrl+Y or choose Edit, Repeat.

PROOFING YOUR SPELLING

Unlike Word, Excel does not automatically underline your spelling errors as you type them. For this reason, it's easy to forget to spell check, because you may not be aware that you've made any mistakes. It's a good idea to spell check any worksheet that you create (especially if it will be viewed by anyone else) as soon as you've completed the majority of your entries.

To perform a spell check in Excel, follow these steps:

1. To check your entire worksheet, press Ctrl+Home to move to the first cell in your worksheet. This saves you having to tell Excel to complete the spell check by starting over at the beginning should you begin the check with the active cell at any other point in your worksheet.

2. Choose <u>T</u>ools, <u>S</u>pelling, or click the Spelling button on the toolbar.

3. If Excel encounters a spelling error, the Spelling dialog box opens, as shown in Figure 4.15, displaying the first word that Excel doesn't find.

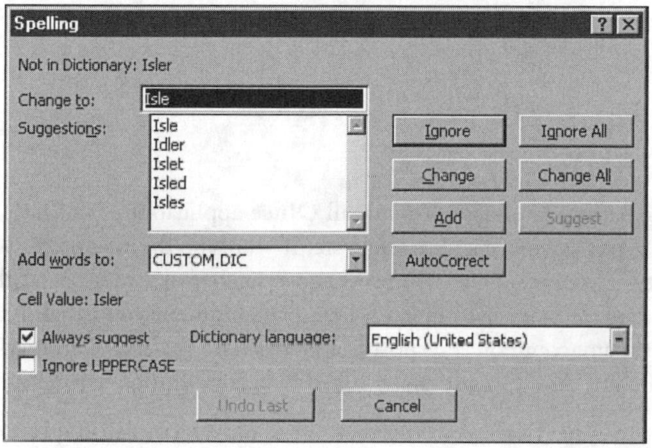

Figure 4.15.
Proper names, esoteric terms, and abbreviations may be correct as you've typed them, but if they're not in the dictionary, the Spelling tool will flag them as misspelled.

4. If Sugge<u>s</u>tions appear, choose one by double-clicking it, or by clicking it and then clicking the <u>C</u>hange button.

5. As each misspelled word is found, double-click a suggestion to change the misspelling to that suggestion. Or click <u>I</u>gnore to skip the word, or click <u>A</u>dd to add it to the custom dictionary.

6. After Excel spell checks the entire sheet, the Spelling dialog box disappears and a prompt appears. Click OK.

PART
II
CH
4

Tip #57 from
Laurie

If you think you've misspelled a word repeatedly in your worksheet, click Change A<u>l</u>l to change all occurrences of the error at one time. If you've decided to skip the word (because it's spelled correctly and is merely not in the dictionary), click I<u>g</u>nore All to ignore all occurrences in the worksheet. These steps will reduce your overall time spent spell checking your worksheet.

If you have content in your other worksheets, each sheet must be checked individually for spelling errors. Click the tab of the next sheet to check and repeat steps 1 through 6.

Tip #58 from
Laurie

It's a good idea to save your workbook after you check the spelling. If your computer or Excel were to crash, you risk losing your corrections. Upon reopening the file, you might forget that you didn't save your work since you ran the spell check.

Tip #59 from

Laurie

Turn on the Ignore UPPERCASE option in the Spelling dialog box so that acronyms (such as EPA or PETA) will be ignored. Also, if your worksheets contain a lot of product or serial numbers, make it a habit to use uppercase text—if you're using this option, it will cause these "errors" to be ignored as well.

USING AUTOCORRECT TO FIX MISTAKES AND ENTER CONTENT

AutoCorrect is an Office feature (available through all Office applications but Outlook) that fixes spelling errors and typos as you type. For example, if you type the word teh instead of the, AutoCorrect fixes it for you as soon as you press the Spacebar or Enter key at the end of the word (indicating that the word is complete). From the moment you install Excel, AutoCorrect can correct many common transposition errors (adn instead of and) and misspellings (alot instead of a lot). You can also teach AutoCorrect additional corrections.

Access AutoCorrect by choosing Tools, AutoCorrect. The AutoCorrect dialog box opens (see Figure 4.16) containing options for how AutoCorrect will be used, and enabling you to view, edit, delete, and add to the existing AutoCorrect entries.

Figure 4.16.
AutoCorrect will fix
your typing mistakes,
as well as adjust your
capitalization.

Turn these capitalization
AutoCorrect options on or
off to meet your needs.

Scroll through the entries
in the AutoCorrect list.

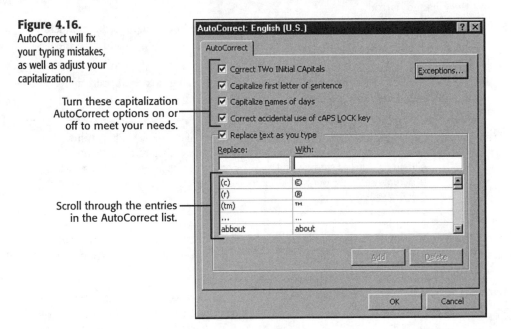

Note

The Exceptions button opens a dialog box that enables you to store words that you don't want fixed. For example, if you want to be able to enter an abbreviation such as "acctg." and follow it with another uncapitalized word, you can store "acctg." as an exception. Why would you need this sort of exception? Because the period at the end would indicate the end of a sentence, and by default, AutoCorrect would capitalize the next word, seeing it as the start of a new sentence.

You may want to add your own entries to the AutoCorrect list, enhancing Excel's capability to automatically fix your mistakes. Mistakes aren't the only thing that AutoCorrect can make easier for you to deal with, however. You can create AutoCorrect entries for abbreviations, initials, and phrases. The following is a list of some examples:

- **Your name.** Store your initials (such as "lau") to make entering your name much faster. When you type lau, AutoCorrect expands it to your full name.

- **Long department or company names.** If you work for the Department of State Funding for Animals, you might want to build an AutoCorrect entry such as DSFA, which when typed will expand to the full department name.

- **Phrases or terminology.** Instead of typing "caseworker assigned to this matter" over and over, create an AutoCorrect entry such as "cw" that will expand to the full phrase. This saves a lot of typing and reduces your margin for typos!

Tip #60 from

Laurie

Be careful not to create AutoCorrect entries that are real words (such as "as" for Ann Smith) or for abbreviations you want to use in their abbreviated form. If you work for the SPCA, you wouldn't want SPCA to be the AutoCorrect entry for Society for the Prevention of Cruelty to Animals, because you probably refer to your organization in the abbreviated form more often. Instead, try something like "SP" or "SPC" for when you want the full name.

PART

II

CH

4

To add an AutoCorrect entry, follow these steps:

1. Choose Tools, AutoCorrect.
2. In the AutoCorrect dialog box, click in the Replace box and type your error or abbreviation (see Figure 4.17).
3. Press the Tab key to move to the With box.
4. Type the content that you want filled in each time you type the error or abbreviation. The With entry can be text, numbers, or a combination thereof, and can be a single word, a phrase, or an entire sentence.
5. Click the Add button.
6. If you want to create more than one entry, repeat steps 2 through 5 for as many as you need to build.
7. Click OK to close the AutoCorrect dialog box.

Figure 4.17.
Type your error or
abbreviation and the
correction or expan-
sion you want.

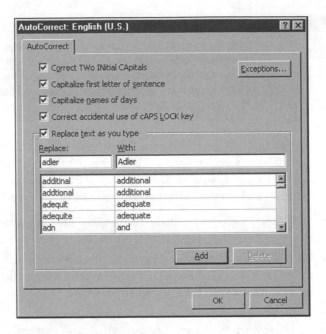

If your spell check session finds an error you feel you make often, click the appropriate
spelling from the suggested alternatives, and click the AutoCorrect button in the Spelling
dialog box. An AutoCorrect entry is made for you, consisting of the misspelled word and
your chosen replacement.

AutoCorrect entries can be deleted and edited as needed. To delete an entry, click on it in
the AutoCorrect dialog box list of entries, and click Delete.

To edit an entry, click to select it in the list, and edit the With content to meet your needs.
Click Replace (the button appears as soon as you've changed the With content for an existing entry, as shown in Figure 4.18) and then click Yes when prompted to confirm your
replacement.

After you delete an entry, the Replace and With text remains in the edit boxes. If you
immediately change your mind, just click Add to re-add the entry.

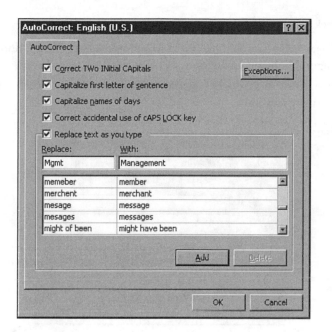

Figure 4.18.
If your entry was incorrect or needs to be updated, replace it by changing the <u>W</u>ith content.

If AutoCorrect makes unwanted changes to your worksheets, see "Handling Unwanted Results from AutoCorrect" in the Troubleshooting section at the end of this chapter.

TRACKING CHANGES MADE BY MULTIPLE USERS

If you work with a team to build, edit, and maintain a workbook or if your workbook passes through several hands on its way to completion, it can be useful to know who made which changes to the workbook content. By using Excel's Track Changes feature, you can see which person added which content, on which date, and at what time. You can also review changes others made, and keep only the changes you want.

Tip #63 from

Laurie

If you're a one-person editing team, you can track your own changes. Track Changes allows you to track not just who, but when a change was made, and that enables you to track your edits since your last save or after a certain date.

ENABLING AND DISABLING REVISION TRACKING

Track Changes must be turned on before you can begin tracking the evolution of your worksheet. If it isn't invoked, the changes someone else makes to your sheet will blend in with your content, and only your personal recollections will determine what's been added or changed.

To turn on and use Track Changes, follow these steps:

1. In the worksheet for which you would like to track multiple users' efforts, choose Tools, Track Changes, Highlight Changes.

2. The Highlight Changes dialog box opens (as shown in Figure 4.19). Click the Track Changes While Editing check box.

Figure 4.19.
Any edits or new entries made prior to turning on this feature will not be highlighted, nor will any data about their origin be saved or displayed.

3. Select the amount and type of tracking you want to perform by clicking in the check boxes next to When, Who, and/or Where. Figure 4.20 shows the choices for When.

Figure 4.20.
Click the When box to determine the starting point for tracking, such as Since I last saved or Since date to enter a particular date to begin tracking.

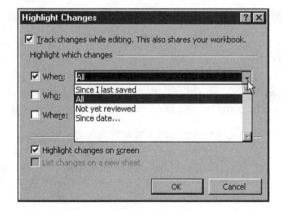

4. Leave on the Highlight Changes on Screen option (see Figure 4.21) so that cells containing new or edited content will be marked as such onscreen.

5. Click OK to close the dialog box and begin tracking changes.

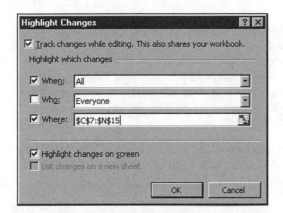

Figure 4.21.
To add visual indications of edits, choose to highlight them onscreen.

Use the Where option in the Highlight Changes dialog box to specify a range of cells in which to track changes. If a range is specified, Excel tracks changes only within that range.

Figure 4.22 shows a worksheet that has been edited by more than one user. The highlighted cells contain new/edited content, and the ScreenTip indicates who made the changes.

PART

II

CH

4

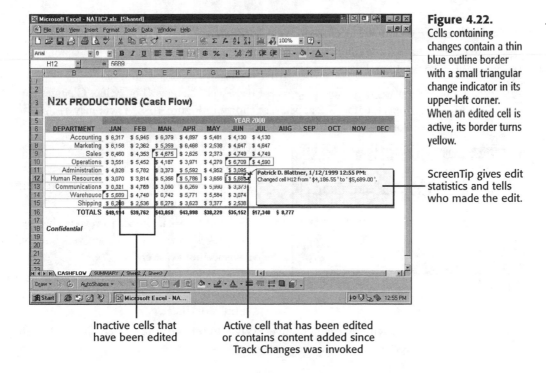

Figure 4.22.
Cells containing changes contain a thin blue outline border with a small triangular change indicator in its upper-left corner. When an edited cell is active, its border turns yellow.

ScreenTip gives edit statistics and tells who made the edit.

Inactive cells that have been edited

Active cell that has been edited or contains content added since Track Changes was invoked

Tip #65 from

The List Changes on a New Sheet option in the Highlight Changes dialog box enables you to store a record of what's been added or changed in your workbook on a separate sheet, so that all changes can be seen in one place. Otherwise, you must scroll through the entire book to find all the changes your team has made.

This list contains only changes made through the date and time you enabled this feature. To update the list of changes, save the workbook and reenable this feature.

You can turn off the Track Changes feature by opening the Highlight Changes dialog box and removing the check mark in the <u>T</u>rack Changes While Editing option box. A prompt appears to inform you that your workbook will no longer be in shared mode, which you must confirm by clicking <u>Y</u>es to turn off Track Changes.

Tip #66 from

You can change your tracking options midstream by using <u>T</u>ools, <u>T</u>rack Changes, Highlight Changes. For example, you can change from tracking changes throughout the worksheet to tracking changes only within a certain range of cells. When you change tracking options, however, previously changed cells are no longer marked as changed on the screen. Excel hasn't forgotten the changes—it merely doesn't mark them. To see those changes again, restore your previous tracking options.

ACCEPTING AND REJECTING CHANGES

After others have made their changes to your workbook, you can review the changes, keeping those you want and discarding those you don't.

1. Choose <u>T</u>ools, <u>T</u>rack Changes, <u>A</u>ccept or Reject Changes. The Select Changes to Accept or Reject dialog box appears, as shown in Figure 4.23. (Excel may ask you to save your workbook first. If so, click OK.)

Figure 4.23.

2. Decide what to review:

   - In the Whe<u>n</u> area, choose to review either changes you haven't reviewed yet, or changes made after a certain time.

   - In the Wh<u>o</u> area, choose to review changes made by all reviewers, all reviewers but you, or any specific reviewer.

   - In the Whe<u>r</u>e area, choose the range of cells to review. If you leave this blank, you'll review the entire worksheet.

3. Click OK to begin reviewing changes. When Excel finds the first change, it describes it in the Accept or Reject Changes dialog box (see Figure 4.24).

4. If more than one change was made to the cell, Excel lists them all. Click the one you want to keep.

5. Click <u>A</u>ccept to keep the change or <u>R</u>eject to keep the cell's original value.

6. Excel finds the next change. You can continue to accept

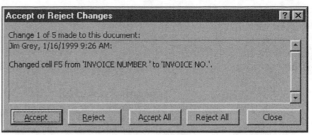

Figure 4.24.

or reject each change in turn. You can also click A<u>c</u>cept All to accept all the remaining changes in the workbook, or Re<u>j</u>ect All to keep each remaining changed cell's original value.

 If you accept a change, but later decide that you want to revert to the original value, see "Unaccepting Accepted Changes" in the Troubleshooting section at the end of this chapter.

USING COMMENTS TO EXPLAIN CELL CONTENT

Many times, the content we add to or edit in a cell requires more explanation or supporting information than we can easily add to the worksheet. Explaining, for example, that the price contained in a particular cell includes a 5% discount is easy enough to do by typing this text in an adjacent cell. If, however, the 5% discount is offered only to certain customers or will be going up to 8% within the next few days, this extra information might be too cumbersome to add as actual worksheet content. This explanation or parenthetical information can be added in the form of a comment, a box containing text that appears whenever the mouse is positioned over the cell that needs explanation (see Figure 4.25).

Tip #67 from

Laurie

Reviewers can also use comments to ask questions of the workbook's owner.

To add a comment to your worksheet, follow these steps:

1. Click in the cell for which a comment is needed.

2. Choose <u>I</u>nsert, Co<u>m</u>ment, or right-click the cell and choose Insert Com<u>m</u>ent from the shortcut menu.

3. A yellow comment box appears, containing your user name (as you provided it during the installation of Office). Click in the box to activate a cursor and begin typing your comment text.

4. Click in any other cell to close the comment box and store the entered comment text.

Tip #68 from

Laurie

You can format your comments so they look different from those others write. For example, if your comments have a light green background or use a different font, the person reviewing your comments will recognize yours just by the way they look. Use the Highlight tool on the Formatting toolbar to set a comment's background color. Use the font tools on the Formatting toolbar to change font attributes.

Figure 4.25.
Drag the comment box handles to increase the size of the box.

Comment box handles—

Default text—

Text added by user wraps— within the box.

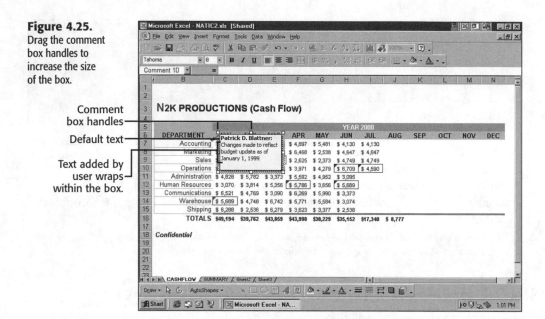

Cells that have an attached comment contain a small red triangle in the upper-right corner of the cell (see Figure 4.26). To view the comment, position your mouse pointer over the cell. The comment appears as long as your mouse remains over the cell.

Tip #69 from

You can set any comment so that it always displays. Right-click the cell and choose Show Comment. You can also set your worksheet so that all comments display. Choose Tools, Options, click the Options dialog box's View tab, and then click Comment & Indicator. (You can also click None to never show comments or comment indicators, or Comment Indicator to show indicators only.)

Tip #70 from

When you set any or all comments to always display, you can also print them with your workbook. Choose File, Page Setup, and then click the Sheet tab. Click the arrow at the end of the Comments box and choose either to print comments where they appear on the sheet, or to print comments at the end of the sheet. Click OK and then print the worksheet.

To delete a comment, right-click the cell and choose Delete Comment from the shortcut menu.

To edit a comment, right-click the cell and choose Edit Comment from the shortcut menu. The comment box becomes active, and you can click to position your cursor within it and begin editing.

Mouse pointer over
commented cell   Active cell

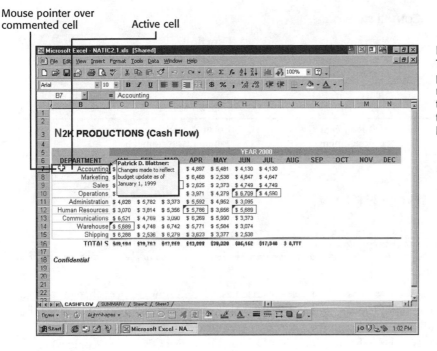

Figure 4.26.
The comment will display as long as your mouse hovers over the interior of the cell to which a comment has been attached.

The Reviewing toolbar helps you work with comments, especially when you're adding lots of them or when you're reviewing several comments others have made in your workbook. To turn it on, choose View, Comments. Table 4.1 shows the buttons on this toolbar.

TABLE 4.1. REVIEWING TOOLBAR BUTTONS

Icon	Name	Function
	Comment	Add a comment.
	Previous Comment	Find and show the previous comment.
	Next Comment	Find and show the next comment.
	Show Comment (or Hide Comment)	Cause the currently selected comment to always display, or hide the currently selected comment.
	Show All Comments (or Hide All Comments)	Display or hide all comments.
	Delete Comment	Remove the currently selected comment.

continues

PART

II

CH

4

TABLE 4.1. CONTINUED

Icon	Name	Function
	Create Microsoft Outlook Task	Make a task in Outlook out of the currently selected comment.
	Update File	Save new and changed comments in your workbook.
	Mail Recipient (as Attachment)	Email the workbook, with all its comments, to someone.

TROUBLESHOOTING

HANDLING UNWANTED RESULTS FROM AUTOCORRECT

I need to use the text (c) in my worksheet, but Excel keeps changing it to the copyright symbol. How do I work around this?

This is AutoCorrect at work. On a case-by-case basis, when AutoCorrect changes text you need left as you typed it, immediately choose Edit, Undo (or press Ctrl+Z) to restore the text. Alternatively, you can remove the item from AutoCorrect. Choose Tools, AutoCorrect. Highlight the item and click Delete. Then click OK. Do this only when you're sure you won't need the AutoCorrect entry elsewhere, however.

UNACCEPTING ACCEPTED CHANGES

What if I accept a change, but later decide I want the original value back?

Excel has no "undo change" function (as Word does). However, Excel still remembers all changes made to a cell, even after you accept a change in it. Hover your mouse over the cell to see a ScreenTip that lists all the changes. You can use this information to retype the value you want into the cell. It's unfortunate that this process isn't more automatic, but at least there is a way to restore original values.

WHERE DID THE CHANGE INDICATORS GO?

After you close a worksheet in which changes were tracked, the next time you open the worksheet, the change indicators don't appear.

This is because Excel assumes you only want to see changes since the last time you saved. To see all your changes, choose Tools, Track Changes, Highlight Changes. Then click the arrow at the end of the When box and choose All. Click OK. Change indicators appear for all changes made to the worksheet.

CHAPTER 5

MOVING, COPYING, LINKING, AND EMBEDDING INFORMATION

In this chapter

by Laurie Ann Ulrich
laurie@limehat.com

USING THE CLIPBOARD TO MOVE AND COPY DATA

You'll find a significant change in the use of the Clipboard in Office 2000. Rather than holding one cut or copied selection at a time, like the Windows Clipboard, the *Office Clipboard* can hold up to 12 selections, which can be pasted one at a time or as a group. In addition, you can display the new *Clipboard toolbar*, which contains an icon for each of the cut or copied selections. The toolbar displays a ScreenTip when you point to the icon, and you can drag the icon from the toolbar to the document to paste the selection in place. The Clipboard toolbar also contains buttons for copying, pasting, and clearing the Clipboard's contents (see Figure 5.1).

Note

Although the Office Clipboard keeps up to 12 items, the Windows Clipboard retains only the last selection cut or copied.

Figure 5.1.
Build a collection of up to 12 cut and copied selections on the Clipboard.

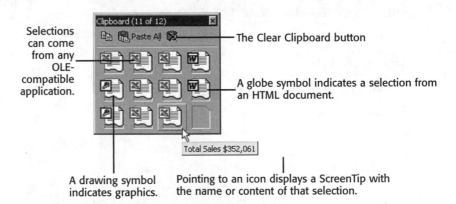

Selections can come from any OLE-compatible application.

The Clear Clipboard button

A globe symbol indicates a selection from an HTML document.

A drawing symbol indicates graphics.

Pointing to an icon displays a ScreenTip with the name or content of that selection.

Tip #71 from

Laurie

To display the Clipboard toolbar, right-click any existing toolbar and choose Clipboard from the shortcut menu.

When using the Clipboard in Excel, you can cut or copy selections and paste them within the same worksheet or into another worksheet within the same workbook. You also can paste them into another workbook entirely, or into another Office application, as discussed later in this chapter. Cut or copied selections can be pasted as many times as you'd like, remaining on the Clipboard until you clear it. Replace the items on the Clipboard with other items you've cut or copied, or exit all running Office 2000 applications.

The Office 2000 Clipboard can hold up to 12 selections, but you still can use it in the traditional way you use the Windows Clipboard. Perform the following steps for a single cut/copy and paste:

1. Select the cell or range of cells to be cut or copied.

2. Choose Cut or Copy from the Edit menu, or click the Cut or Copy button on the Standard toolbar.

3. Move to the cell into which you want to place the cut or copied content, and choose Edit, Paste.

Tip #72 from *Laurie*	Use the keyboard shortcuts Ctrl+X (Cut) or Ctrl+C (Copy) rather than the menu or toolbar. Ctrl+V is the keyboard shortcut to paste a single Clipboard selection.

Caution	When pasting a block of cells, you need only click in the first cell in the target block, and the pasted content will fill a block of cells that matches the dimensions of the cut or copied block. If cells in the target area are already filled with content, that content will be replaced by the pasted content.

If you cut or copy something to the Clipboard and then cut or copy a second selection, the Clipboard toolbar opens automatically, showing the second selection as a second icon on the toolbar. If you continue to cut and copy selections (in the current worksheet/workbook, other Office documents, or any other OLE-compatible program), the Clipboard toolbar remains onscreen, and new icons are added for each selection you make. (You can close the Clipboard toolbar at any time, or dock it on one of the sides of the window.)

To paste one of the Clipboard's selections, follow these steps:

1. Click in the cell in which you want to paste one of the Clipboard selections.
2. Click the icon on the Clipboard toolbar that represents the desired content.

Tip #73 from *Laurie*	If you're not sure which Clipboard toolbar icon represents which selection, point to (but don't click) the icons, one at a time. Each icon's ScreenTip displays, showing you the first several characters of the text or numeric content, the name of the graphic, and so on.

 You also can copy directly to the Clipboard toolbar. Make the desired selection in the worksheet and click the Copy button on the Clipboard toolbar.

If you want to paste all the selected items on the Clipboard toolbar, follow these steps:

1. Click in the first cell of the target block. This tells Excel where you want to begin inserting the pasted content.
2. Click the Paste All button on the Clipboard toolbar. A vertical series of cells will be filled with the Clipboard contents.

Paste All

Note	The Paste All option is not available when non-Office items are included on the Clipboard.

Tip #74 from

Laurie

Another way to place the most recently copied content in another location is to click in the desired target location and use the Insert, Copied Cells command. You can then choose to shift current content (in surrounding cells) down or to the right.

 If you've finished using the Clipboard's selections and don't want to use them again, you can empty the Clipboard by clicking the Clear Clipboard button on the Clipboard toolbar.

COPYING SHEETS

A typical Excel workbook is made of several worksheets, most of which you need only once in the workbook. At times, however, you may need to copy a sheet within a workbook or between workbooks, as in the following examples:

- To create an identical sheet in the same or a different workbook
- To preserve a copy of a sheet, enabling you to experiment with numbers in the duplicate version

→ If you just want to move a sheet to a different position, drag the sheet tab. For details, **see** "Rearranging Worksheets," **p. 23**

COPYING SHEETS IN THE SAME WORKBOOK

Moving worksheets in the same workbook is a lot like shuffling cards in a deck—you have the same group of cards, but you're changing their order. Although you can move sheets with a cut-and-paste operation and the Clipboard, it's much easier just to drag the sheet tabs, as described in Chapter 1, "Getting Started with Excel."

Copying sheets, on the other hand, duplicates the sheets and enables you to place the duplicates anywhere in the workbook, positioning the sheet or sheets in any order you require.

You can copy sheets by dragging the sheet tabs in much the same way as you move sheets, as explained in the following steps:

1. Click the sheet tab for the sheet you want to duplicate (copy).
2. Press and hold down the Ctrl key.
3. Drag the sheet tab to the left or right—a small triangle appears, as well as a page symbol with a plus sign (see Figure 5.2).

   If you drag just long enough to see the copy symbol and the triangle appear, the duplicate will appear next to the original. You also can drag to any other spot among the sheet tabs to copy and reorder the sheet at the same time.
4. When the triangle is pointing to the spot where you want to place the duplicate sheet, release the mouse button first, and then release the Ctrl key. Releasing the Ctrl key first will result in the sheet(s) being moved, not copied.

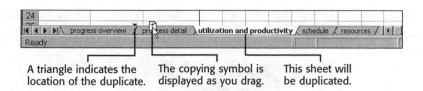

Figure 5.2.
Use the Ctrl key to make a copy of the selected sheet.

A triangle indicates the location of the duplicate.

The copying symbol is displayed as you drag.

This sheet will be duplicated.

Tip #75 from

Laurie

You can copy more than one sheet at a time by grouping the sheets before you copy them. Shift-click each sheet to include in the group and then press the Ctrl key as you drag the group. A duplicate set of sheets is created and positioned among the existing sheets.

MOVING AND COPYING SHEETS BETWEEN WORKBOOKS

For many users, the workbooks they create contain a lot of similar content—for example, a workbook for each of the company's divisions or a separate budget workbook for each fiscal quarter of the year. When workbooks contain similar data, it's often helpful to move data from one book to another if the data was placed in the wrong book or to copy a sheet from one book and use it in another.

Tip #76 from

Laurie

Moving and copying sheets saves time and effort, reducing the margin for error that retyping or moving/copying cell ranges presents. Rather than cutting or copying ranges of cells to a sheet in another workbook, work with the entire sheet. If small portions of the moved or copied sheet aren't required in the new location, they can be deleted easily.

MOVING SHEETS TO ANOTHER WORKBOOK

If one of your worksheets needs to move to a different workbook, you'll want to move it, all in one piece, as one sheet. To do so, follow these steps:

1. Open the workbook to which you want to move the worksheet.

2. In the workbook that currently contains the sheet, right-click the sheet tab for the sheet you want to move.

3. From the shortcut menu, choose Move or Copy (see Figure 5.3).

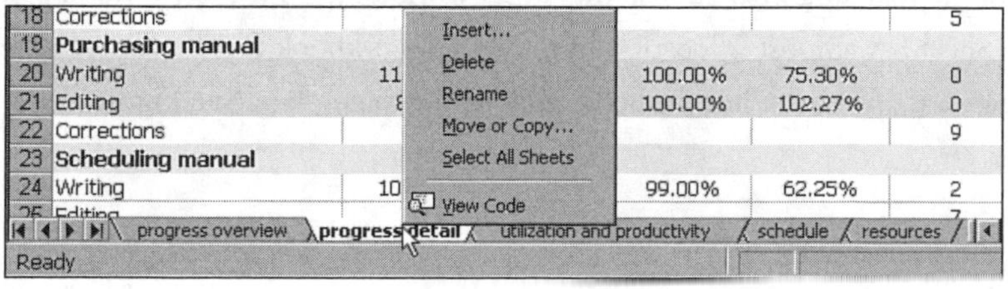

Figure 5.3.
The Move or Copy command gives you the choice between target workbooks and a position within that book's existing worksheets.

4. In the Move or Copy dialog box, choose from the To Book list the workbook to which you want to move the sheet (see Figure 5.4).

Figure 5.4.
Select another open workbook to receive the copied worksheet.

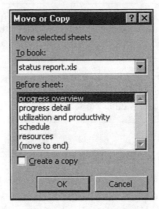

5. Choose a position for the sheet in the target workbook from the Before Sheet list.
6. Click OK.

Need to move several sheets at once? Select them as a group, and then right-click any one of the selected sheets in the group. You then can choose into which book to move them and where in the group of existing sheets to insert them.

COPYING WORKSHEETS BETWEEN WORKBOOKS

If your worksheet can be used in another workbook in addition to its current workbook, you'll need to copy it. Follow these steps to copy a worksheet in the current workbook to another workbook:

1. Be sure that both the workbook that currently contains the worksheet and the target workbook are open.
2. In the workbook that contains the sheet, right-click the worksheet tab for the sheet you want to copy.
3. Choose Move or Copy from the shortcut menu.
4. In the Move or Copy dialog box, choose the target workbook from the To Book list.
5. In the Before Sheet list, choose a location in the target workbook for the copied sheet.
6. Click the Create a Copy check box at the bottom of the dialog box (see Figure 5.5).
7. Click OK.

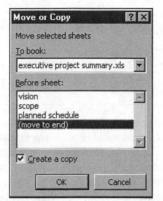

Figure 5.5.
Duplicate the sheet rather than your efforts by copying a worksheet between workbooks.

Clicking the Create a Copy option creates a duplicate of the active sheet and places it in the target workbook. You then can edit that duplicated sheet for any content that's inappropriate in the new workbook and save the target workbook to reflect the new sheet and any other changes.

If you want to copy several sheets from one book to another, group the sheets first. Right-click any of the sheets in the group, and then choose Move or Copy from the shortcut menu. Be sure to select the Create a Copy check box, and choose the workbook and location to which you want to copy the sheets.

> **Caution**
>
> Moving/copying sheets to other workbooks creates links in the target workbook if formulas in the moved/copied sheets refer to data in other sheets or workbooks. Check for such formula links before moving or copying worksheets, and be sure that you include any linked files if you're sending the new workbook to another user or placing it in a different folder or on a different drive.
>
> See the next section for details on linking sheets and files with Excel.

PART
II

CH
5

LINKING EXCEL DATA

So far, all the discussion of moving and copying has referred to content that exists in one or more locations, with no connection between the locations. Copying a section of a worksheet or an entire worksheet to another workbook saves you time and effort, but once the section or sheet is copied, the relationship between the source material and the target location may end (unless formulas are included that create links, as described shortly). If you go back to the source worksheet and change any of the data, the changes are not reflected in the place(s) to which the material was copied.

What if you want to establish a permanent relationship between the source material and the target? What if you need to copy a section of a worksheet to another workbook, and you want changes in the original (source) material to update the target (copied) material as well? To establish such a relationship, you must set up a *link* between the source and the target. Such a link uses *OLE* (*object linking and embedding*), a powerful Windows feature.

Caution

If the target workbook will be transferred to or used on another computer or network, be sure to send along the source workbook also, or the link between the files will be broken. Be sure to place the files in folders at the new location that match the folder names at the old location, so that the path between the files remains the same (unless both files are in the same folder, in which case you don't have a problem). You may find that copying both files to the new location and then re-creating the link simplifies this process. See the later section "Breaking Links Between Files" for details.

ESTABLISHING LINKS BETWEEN WORKSHEETS OR WORKBOOKS

The simple Edit, Paste command places copied content in a new location. Choosing Edit, Paste Special enables you to create a link between the source and target worksheets or workbooks.

Tip #77 from

You can establish one or more links within a single worksheet, enabling you to enter repeated information once and have it update to one or more additional cells automatically.

To copy and link content between worksheets or workbooks in Excel, follow these steps:

1. When copying between workbooks, be sure both workbooks are open and have been saved.

Caution

If you attempt to link source content from a workbook file that hasn't been saved, you'll be prompted to confirm your intention to do so. If you link to an unsaved file, the link may not be maintained if the source file is closed without saving, such as from a power outage or software crash.

2. Select and copy the source content in the source worksheet. This content will become the linked object.

3. Move to the target worksheet, select the cell where you want the linked data to begin, and choose Edit, Paste Special to open the Paste Special dialog box (see Figure 5.6).

4. Make any selections pertaining to the content and formatting you want to include in the pasted material. In most cases, the default All selection is exactly what you need.

5. Click the Paste Link button. Note that this button doesn't open another dialog box, as you might expect. Instead, it immediately executes the link.

Figure 5.6.
In most cases, use the
All option that's
selected by default
when creating a paste
link.

Note

The Operation section of the Paste Special dialog box offers tools for performing calculations when you paste numeric content onto target cells that already contain numeric data. Suppose that the source selection is a single cell containing the number 5, and the single target cell contains 10. If you choose Add in the Paste Special dialog box, the result is 15 in the target cell. If you choose Divide, the target cell will contain 2 (10 divided by 5).

After linking a source and target, test the link by switching to the source cells and making a change to their content. Check the target, and see that the change is reflected. When viewing the target, notice that the Formula bar shows the link, listing the source location, as shown in Figure 5.7. The workbook name appears in brackets ([ ]), followed by the worksheet name, and the entire workbook/worksheet name is enclosed in single quotation marks (') and followed by an exclamation point (!) and the range name or cell reference. In this example, the link is as follows:

```
='[status report.xls]progress overview'!E8
```

- The source workbook's name is "status report" (xls is the file's extension).
- The source worksheet is named "progress overview."
- The source cell is E8.

If the source workbook is closed, the link formula also includes the full path to the source file.

Source workbook filename

Worksheet name   **Cell address**

Figure 5.7.
When a target cell is selected, the Formula bar displays the source filename, sheet name, and cell address.

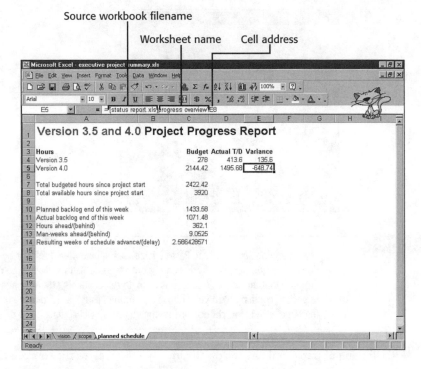

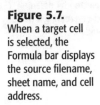

Tip #78 from

If you paste link blank cells, Excel displays 0 for the blank cell in the target location. To suppress the display of zeros, choose Tools, Options, click the View tab, and deselect the Zero Values option.

UPDATING LINKS TO A WORKBOOK

When you open a workbook that contains one or more links to other workbooks, you'll be prompted to update the links—that is, update the target to reflect any changes made in the source, as shown in Figure 5.8. If you prefer, you can choose to keep the file's existing content intact and update the links later, as needed.

Figure 5.8.
If you aren't the primary editor of the source document, it may be safer to choose No, and then check the source document before updating the linked data.

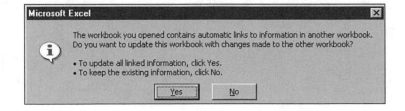

To update a link between two workbooks, follow these steps:

1. In the document containing the linked material (the target), choose Edit, Links to display the Links dialog box.

   Links can be edited only from within the target document. The Links command is disabled in the Edit menu if you attempt to access it from the source document or any unlinked workbook.

2. In the Links dialog box, click the link you want to update in the Source File list (see Figure 5.9).

3. Click the Update Now button.

4. Click OK.

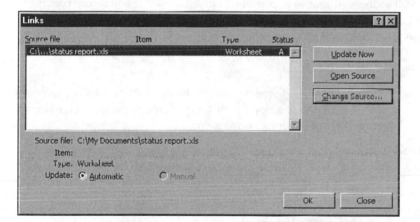

Figure 5.9.
It's a good idea to save the workbook before updating any links. If you regret having updated them, you can close the file without saving.

PART

II

CH

5

Tip #79 from

Laurie

To quickly update all links with one fast keystroke, press F9 in the workbook that contains linked data. Note, however, that this technique works only if the following conditions are met:

- The workbook containing the links has calculation set to Manual (choose Tools, Options, click the Calculation tab, and select Manual).
- The source workbook is open.

LOCKING LINKED EXTERNAL DATA

Worksheets may occasionally include links to OLE-compatible applications other than Excel. To prevent accidental updates of these links, you can lock the links. Choose Tools, Options to open the Options dialog box, and click the Calculations tab. Remove the check mark in the Update Remote References box. To resume updates in the future, turn the option back on.

Caution

> If you choose to lock links by turning off the Update Remote References option, you can't use the Automatic Update Option in the Links dialog box. This option enables you to choose whether the links will be updated automatically or manually each time you open the file and as changes are made to the source data.

REDIRECTING LINKS

If you rename a workbook to which other workbooks are linked, the links break. You can repair the broken links by redirecting them to the renamed file. To do so, move to the target document (the workbook that contains the links) and choose Edit, Links. Click the Change Source button, and choose the appropriate file from the Change Links dialog box. By default, the cell address(es) that were copied will be retained—if you linked content from cells C4:H9 to cells B5:G10, for example, the content in the new source file will come from C4:H9 and be placed in B5:G10. After selecting the new source file, click OK.

BREAKING LINKS BETWEEN FILES

Most broken links occur accidentally—the user changes the name of either the source or target file or moves one or both files to a new folder. Any change in name or location of either the source or target file will result in a broken link.

To purposely break a link, select the target cells (note that the link information appears in the Formula bar) and press Delete. You then can type new data into the cell(s) or leave them blank.

Note

> To establish a new link to another document, you must re-create a link from scratch, starting with copying the source data and using the Edit, Paste Special command to link the source data to the target cells.

Tip #80 from

Laurie

> You can replace linked cells with the values that the cells contain. Copy the linked cell(s), choose Edit, Paste Special, select Values in the Paste Special dialog box, and then choose OK.

COPYING EXCEL DATA TO OTHER APPLICATIONS

You can use Excel data to enhance Word and PowerPoint documents, saving you the time and effort required to reenter data you've already entered into your Excel workbooks. To share Excel information in other Office applications, use the Clipboard as described earlier in this chapter. Anything you copy to the Clipboard in Excel appears in the Clipboard in other Office applications.

Note

The following sections provide a brief review of the mechanics of sharing data among Excel and other Office applications. Chapter 25, "Using Excel with Word and PowerPoint," and Chapter 26, "Using Excel with Access and Other Databases," provide much more conceptual information and details on the issues involved.

Excel content can be used in many ways in Word and PowerPoint, including the following:

- **Reports**. Rather than retype the numbers from an Excel worksheet into a Word report, copy them from the worksheet right into the document. If it's a document you'll use repeatedly with ever-updating data, paste link the data so that it will always be current in the Word target.

- **Presentations**. Rather than typing existing Excel data into a PowerPoint datasheet to enter numeric data for a PowerPoint chart, paste numeric data from Excel right into the datasheet—the chart will build automatically, based on accurate and up-to-date content. You also can link or embed Excel data directly into PowerPoint slides.

- **Charts**. If you've already created a chart in Excel, don't re-create it in another application. Excel charts can be pasted into Word documents or PowerPoint presentations. If the chart is linked to the target file, any changes made to the Excel data that supports the chart will update the copies of the chart in Word and PowerPoint as well.

You can learn more about Excel charts in Chapter 13, "Building Charts with Excel."

Performing the Copy command when the target is a Word or PowerPoint document is no different than when an Excel worksheet is the target. Follow these simple steps:

1. Open the target application (Word or PowerPoint), and open or create the file that will eventually contain the Excel content.

2. In Excel, select the content you want and copy it to the Clipboard.

3. Position the insertion point in the document or slide where you want to paste the Excel material.

4. Choose Edit, Paste, or press Ctrl+V.

When you paste Excel data in table format into a Word document or a PowerPoint slide, the target application converts it to a native format—that is, Word table format or PowerPoint text format (but laid out like a table). This may not be the best or most effective approach for that data. If you prefer to keep the data in Excel format within Word or PowerPoint, use Edit, Paste Special in the target application to embed the data instead of pasting it in place. See the later section "Embedding Excel Data in Other Office Applications" for a brief discussion of the embedding technique; see Chapters 25 and 26 for complete details.

PART

II

CH

5

If the Clipboard toolbar is visible in Excel, it remains open when you switch to the target Office application, allowing quick access to the copied data.

LINKING DATA BETWEEN OFFICE APPLICATIONS

Beyond a simple copy-and-paste, you can create a link between an Excel worksheet and a Word or PowerPoint file. This will establish a connection that enables you to update your Excel data and have the updates reflected in the Word and/or PowerPoint target files.

Follow these steps to create a link between the Excel worksheet and a Word or PowerPoint file:

1. Copy the Excel content to the Clipboard.
2. Switch to the open Word or PowerPoint file that you want to contain the linked content.
3. Move to the location where you want to place the linked content.
4. Choose Edit, Paste Special.
5. In the Paste Special dialog box, click the Paste Link option (see Figure 5.10).

This part of the reference indicates the name of the source worksheet.

The range is indicated in R1C1 format—in this example, row 3 column 1 through row 20 column 5 (A3:E20).

Figure 5.10.
Click Paste Link to insert the linked content and close the dialog box.

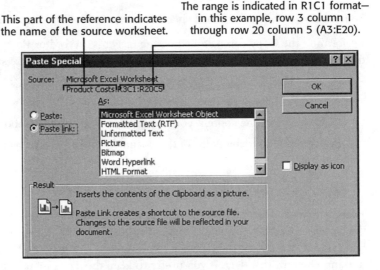

6. Select Microsoft Excel Worksheet Object from the As list.
7. Click OK to insert the pasted content and establish the link.

It's wise to test the link by changing the Excel content and verifying that it has changed in the target Word or PowerPoint file. Then undo the change in Excel.

If at any time you want to sever the link, you can delete the Excel content from within the Word or PowerPoint file, or choose Edit, Links from within the target application. Click the Break Link button, and then confirm your intention to do so when prompted (see Figure 5.11). If you choose this latter method, the linked content remains, but its link back to the source Excel worksheet is broken.

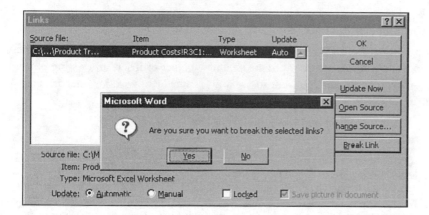

Figure 5.11.
Retain the linked content but break the link so that any updates to the Excel content aren't reflected in the Word or PowerPoint file.

EMBEDDING EXCEL DATA IN OTHER OFFICE APPLICATIONS

Embedding is the other half of OLE (object linking and embedding). As with linking, embedding places content from a source into a target document. Unlike linking, embedding also connects the source application itself to a target document. You could embed an Excel worksheet, for example, into a PowerPoint slide, giving you access to Excel's tools for creating a worksheet or using an existing worksheet to express important financial data. Because Excel's spreadsheet tools exceed those found in PowerPoint, this is a productivity-enhancing addition to the PowerPoint presentation.

PART
II

CH
5

KNOWING WHEN TO EMBED

Embed rather than link when you want the source data to become a permanent part of your target document, or when the source document will be unavailable (such as when the source document is on a file server and you're on the road, disconnected from the server).

An embedded object need not come from a file that has any actual content. You can use the embedded application to create content in the target application window, giving you the tools of the source application and the freedom to create something new. The choice to link or embed often is made purely on the basis of this concept. If the Excel content you need for a PowerPoint slide already exists in an Excel worksheet, you'd be better off linking the worksheet to the slide, and allowing the link to keep the slide updated. If you haven't created the worksheet, however, and you know you'll need Excel's tools to do it right, you can embed an Excel object in the PowerPoint slide, and avail yourself of Excel's tools to build the worksheet content you need.

PERFORMING THE EMBED OPERATION

To embed an Excel object in a Word document or PowerPoint presentation, follow these steps:

1. In the Word document or PowerPoint slide, choose Insert, Object.
2. The resulting dialog box differs between the two applications, but the concepts are the same. You indicate whether you want to create a new object or insert an existing object from a file. If you specify that you want to use a file, enter or browse for the path and filename.
3. Click OK to insert the object and close the dialog box.

Tip #83 from

Laurie

When inserting an object, you can choose to place the object as an icon. Using an icon enables you to save visual space in the target file and gives the file's users the choice as to whether to view the actual content. This is a good option to employ when you're inserting an object for the purpose of providing background or supporting data that the user may normally not need to see.

After you make this insertion, the Excel worksheet opens as an object within the Word document or PowerPoint slide. The object has selection handles, as though it were a graphic (see Figure 5.12).

Figure 5.12.
To resize the object, drag its handles. Drag them outward to make it larger, inward to make it smaller.

Handles

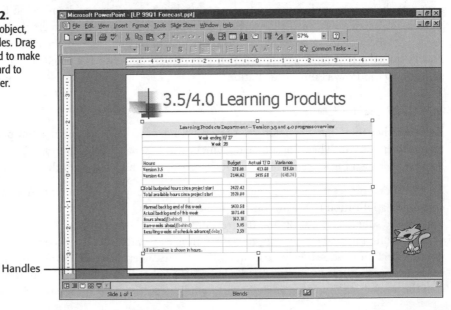

As soon as you double-click the object, the target application's menus and toolbars switch to Excel's. With the exception of the title bar, which still shows that you're in Word or PowerPoint, the application window appears to be an Excel window (see Figure 5.13).

PowerPoint's title bar   Excel's menu   Excel's toolbars

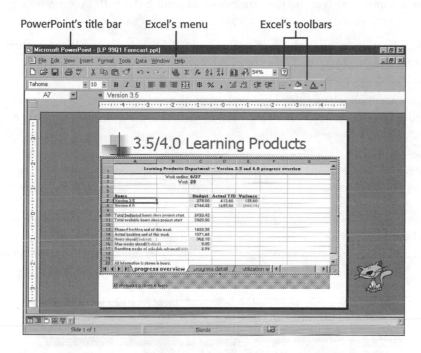

Figure 5.13.
Give yourself access to Excel's toolbars and menus by double-clicking the inserted object in the Word or PowerPoint window.

You can begin entering new Excel worksheet content or editing the existing content as soon as the object is inserted. Any Excel task can be accomplished—building formulas, formatting text and/or numeric content. When you've completed this development, merely click outside of the object to deselect it. The Word or PowerPoint tools return to the window.

To reactivate the object for further development, double-click the object. A single click selects the object for moving and resizing.

Caution

To remove an embedded object, click it once to select it, and press Delete. The object disappears. Perform this process with care—although you can undo it, if you decide you want the object back after the document has been saved and closed, it will be too late. Unlike links, which can be reestablished, an object created in a target document doesn't exist anywhere else.

PART
II

CH
5

EXCEL IN PRACTICE

The Clipboard can be a powerful ally in your pursuit of a truly great PowerPoint presentation or Word document. By combining existing content from Excel with PowerPoint or Word content, you achieve the following benefits:

- **Centralized access to multiple-application tools.** Adding Excel and Word content to a PowerPoint presentation, for example, gives you one window in which to access the tools from three powerful programs.

- **Speed and accuracy.** Rather than reenter a series of numbers and text in a Word table, use an existing section of an Excel worksheet. Don't risk typos and don't waste time typing.

- **More power.** No one program does it all, but by combining the products of each of these Office applications, you can create a presentation or document that makes an impact on your audience.

Figure 5.14 shows a PowerPoint slide that contains text from a Word document and a functioning Excel worksheet. The Word content is pasted rather than retyped because, in the case of contracts and other legal documents, even a minor typo can change the meaning of the text.

PowerPoint's template, titles, and text boxes bring it all together.

Excel content comes from an existing worksheet.

Figure 5.14.
Double-click the Excel worksheet to make quick changes to content and formatting.

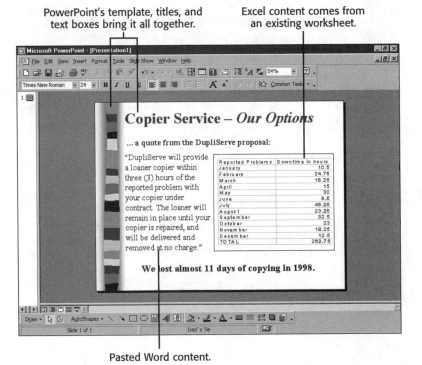

Pasted Word content.

FORMATTING AND PRINTING EXCEL WORKSHEETS

FORMATTING WORKSHEETS

by Laurie Ann Ulrich
laurie@limehat.com

WHY CHANGE THE FORMATTING?

You could build an entire workbook with no special formatting at all. Excel's default styles, fonts, alignments, and other settings for text and numbers are sufficient for the legible and accurate display and printing of worksheet data. As Figure 6.1 shows, a worksheet needs no special formatting to display text and numbers legibly.

Figure 6.1.
Excel's default font is 10-point Arial, a very generic font that works for most basic text requirements.

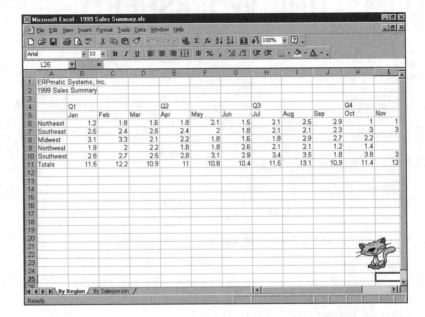

Many worksheets are never formatted, changed, or improved visually, because their users don't require any formatting to make the worksheets more interesting or informative. An equal number of worksheets, however, are formatted—different fonts applied, colors used, alignments changed, and titles dressed up—to make the data more interesting and easier to read. Figure 6.2 shows the same worksheet as shown in Figure 6.1, but some formatting has been applied. It's not hard or even time-consuming to apply this kind of formatting.

Note

It's important to understand that two different types of formatting are at work in any Excel worksheet: the visual formatting, which includes font choices, color, alignment, and so on; and the number formatting, which specifies how Excel stores, displays, and calculates the dates and numbers within a worksheet. Number formatting in Excel is not so much a matter of how the numbers look as how they work. Formatting numbers is discussed in the following chapter.

Even a small amount of formatting can make a worksheet easier to interpret—the formatting is used to draw the reader's eye to important information. Worksheets that will be published for customers, reports, or an Internet or intranet site will be much better received if they have a more polished, visually appealing look.

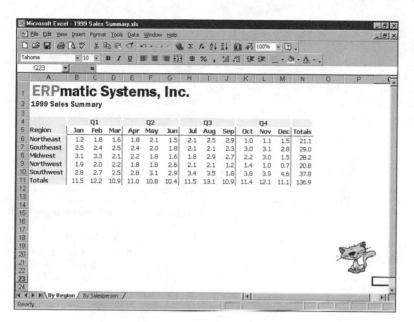

Figure 6.2.
The worksheet title is in an attractive display font, and the column and row headings are shaded and bolded. The worksheet also includes some number formatting.

Tip #84 from

Laurie

If you want readers to understand the overall content of the worksheet, see what information is being stored, and go right to the bottom line, make column headings and titles stand out through use of boldfacing or by applying a dynamic font, and draw attention to the bottom line—totals and the results of important formulas.

USING THE FORMATTING TOOLBAR

Excel's Formatting toolbar offers the most common tools used for changing the appearance of text. Table 6.1 shows the tools that change the appearance of text.

TABLE 6.1. TEXT FORMATTING TOOLS ON THE FORMATTING TOOLBAR

Button	Name	Method of Use/Formatting Effect
Tahoma ⏷	Font	Click the down arrow to see a list of fonts. Select a font from the list to apply to the selected cell(s), or text or numbers within a cell.
10 ⏷	Font Size	Click the down arrow to see a list of point sizes for the selected cell(s), or text or numbers within a cell. The larger the point size number in the Font Size box, the larger the text will be.

continues

TABLE 6.1   CONTINUED

Button	Name	Method of Use/Formatting Effect
B	Bold	Click the Bold button once to boldface the selected cell content, or selected text or numbers within a cell. If the selection is already bold, clicking this button removes the bold format.
I	Italic	Like the Bold button, the Italic button works by clicking it to apply the format. You also can click this button to remove italic formatting from a selection.
<u>U</u>	Underline	Click the Underline button to apply an underline to selected cell(s) or text or numbers within a cell. The underline spans spaces between words. Click the button again to remove the format. This is different from applying a bottom border to the entire cell, a technique discussed later in this chapter.
	Align Left	Text is left-aligned by default. You can apply this alignment to numeric content as well by selecting a cell or cells and clicking the Align Left button.
	Center	Useful for titles and column headings, centering cell content creates equal space to the left and right of the content in each selected cell.
	Align Right	Numbers are right-aligned by default. You also can apply right alignment to text. This format is especially effective for row headings.
	Merge and Center	Used primarily for worksheet titles, this button enables you to center text in a single cell that spans multiple columns.
A	Font Color	Change the color of the cell content. Click the button to see a palette of 40 different colors, and click one of the colors to apply it to the selected cell(s) or text or numbers within a cell.

The remaining tools on the Formatting toolbar are for number formatting, and their formats do more than change the appearance of the cell content. The Borders and Fill Color tools are discussed later in this chapter.

Tip #85 from

> When you're formatting a worksheet, it may be easier for you if you display the Formatting toolbar on its own. Choose Tools, Customize, click the Options tab, and turn off the Standard and Formatting Toolbars Share One Row option. Click Close to apply this change to the application window. This will give you full access to all of Excel's text formatting tools. Another method is to drag the Formatting toolbar by its move handle (the vertical bar at the left end of the toolbar) and position the toolbar floating or docked at any side of the window. Dragging the toolbar in this way also turns off the option in the Customize dialog box.

When applying formats from the toolbar, most tools toggle—one click to apply the format, a second click to remove it. For those that aren't toggles (alignment, color, Merge and Center), use the Undo button or press Ctrl+Z to remove the format.

Tip #86 from

> You can add buttons to the Formatting toolbar to make quick formatting easier. Two good button choices are the Increase Font Size and Decrease Font Size buttons—click them to change the selected text/numeric font size in small increments.

To find out more about number formats, see Chapter 7, "Modifying Numbers and Dates."

→ Find out more about customizing toolbars (adding, moving, and deleting buttons); **see** "Modifying Toolbars," **p. 869**

USING THE FORMAT CELLS DIALOG BOX

For more control and a preview of the formatting tools' effects before you apply them, you can use the Format Cells dialog box, opened by choosing Format, Cells or right-clicking a cell or selection and choosing Format Cells from the context menu. (Be sure to have the cells you want to format selected before opening the dialog box.)

The Format Cells dialog box contains six tabs, two of which apply to worksheet text:

- **Alignment.** Change not just the horizontal alignment (left, center, right) that you can adjust quickly from the toolbar, but the vertical alignment (top, center, bottom, and justified), and the orientation of the text (see Figure 6.3). You can rotate text up to 180°, an especially effective format for long column headings. You can also stack the text, useful for printing column headings vertically.

The Text Control settings on this tab also enable you to make selected cells' text wrap within the cell, shrink to fit the current cell dimensions, or merge the selected cells into one cell.

PART

II

CH

6

Figure 6.3.
Change the position of cell content with the Alignment tab's tools.

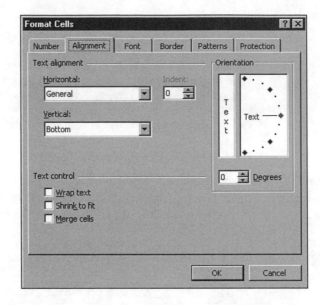

■ **Font**. Choose a font, size, style, and color for the selected cells' text. You can see a preview before applying the formats to the worksheet, as shown in Figure 6.4.

Note

The Underline options include double and single accounting-style underlines.

Figure 6.4.
Test drive font formats with the Font tab's Preview box.

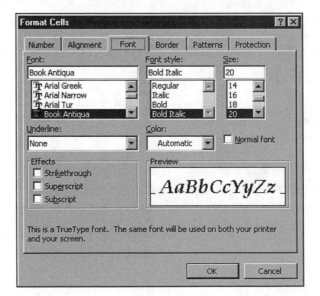

After making changes to the formats with one or both of these tabs, click OK to apply the changes to the selected cell(s) in the worksheet. You can undo any formatting by choosing Edit, Undo, or pressing Ctrl+Z.

Tip #87 from	If you can no longer Undo the formatting, select the cells that you want to "unformat" and choose Edit, Clear, Formats. The selected cell(s) revert to default formats.
Laurie	

CHANGING THE FONT, POINT SIZE, AND FONT STYLES

The default font in Excel—Arial, 10 points—is an effective generic font. It's available on virtually anyone's computer, and it's highly readable. Although you can format specific cells and cell ranges for visual impact, most users leave the majority of their cells, especially those containing numbers, in this default font. There's nothing wrong with that. But one of the simplest—and fastest—ways to dress up the worksheet and simultaneously draw attention to the more important text and numbers within the sheet is to make subtle changes to the font in certain areas of the worksheet. Fonts and font styles (bold, italic, and so on) can be applied with the Formatting toolbar or the Format Cells dialog box.

Tip #88 from	Avoid formatting entire columns or rows unless you plan to use all the cells. Excel must store the information for the thousands of cells involved in such formatting, which can enlarge the file size unnecessarily.
Laurie	

Caution	Make sure that you use only fonts that are installed on all of the other computers that will view your workbook. When Excel calls for a font that isn't installed, Windows replaces it with some other font, producing potentially unattractive results. For example, the title "ERPmatic Systems, Inc. 1999 Sales Summary" in Figure 6.2 is in Franklin Gothic Demi. On a computer that doesn't have this font installed, the text appears in Arial (but the Font drop-down box still says Franklin Gothic Demi). If you aren't certain what fonts are installed on your audience's computers, stick with Arial, Times New Roman, Garamond, and Courier New. These fonts are safe, if unexciting, bets because they come with Windows.

PART

II

CH

6

CHANGING THE FONT

The fastest way to change the font for a particular cell or range—including noncontiguous ranges—is to select the cell(s), click open the Font box on the Formatting toolbar, and click the font you want. Office 2000 shows each font's appearance (not just the name) in the drop-down list, as shown in Figure 6.5. TrueType fonts are indicated with a double T icon; printer fonts have a printer icon. (For more details on using fonts and printing with Windows, consult your Windows documentation.)

Figure 6.5.
The Font list shows the available fonts installed on your computer.

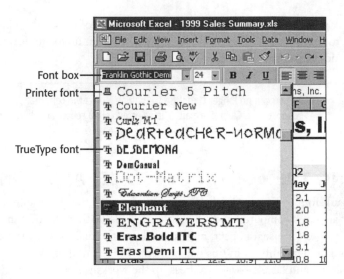

Font box

Printer font

TrueType font

If scrolling the list is too cumbersome, you can type the font's name in the Font box, although this technique works only when you know the font's exact name—if you want the Zurich XBlk BT font, you have to type it just like that. If you don't remember the exact name, you can click the arrow at the end of the Font box and type the first letter of the font you want, to jump to that part of the list. When you select a font in the list, it replaces whatever appears in the Font box.

Tip #89 from

Laurie

You can control whether to view font styles with their names. Choose Tools, Customize, click the Options tab, and select or deselect List Font Names in Their Font. If you have a slower PC, you might find that deselecting this setting will make the Font box work faster. Because this is an Office setting, changing it in one program changes it for all Office programs.

SETTING THE POINT SIZE

Measurements in typography are expressed in *picas* and *points*. There are six picas in an inch and 12 points in a pica, which means that there are 72 points in an inch.

Although many typographical measurements are absolute, font measurement is slippery. The size of type is measured in points—say, 11-point Times New Roman or 24-point Arial Black. This is a measurement from the top of an *ascender* to the bottom of a *descender* in the font. The letter d has an ascender—the *stem* that rises above the *bowl*, or round part, of the d. The letter g has a descender—that is, the stem that extends below the bowl of the g. If you superimpose a Times New Roman d over a Times New Roman g, the number of points between the top of the ascender and the bottom of the descender is the font's point size. Unfortunately, one 12-point font may not look to be the same size as another 12-point font.

Compare Arial to Times New Roman at the same point size. Arial appears to be much larger than Times New Roman. That's because your eye determines the "size" by looking at everything but the ascenders and descenders.

Note

Having a sense of this measurement will help you lay out a worksheet, and set up print areas that fit on a page without sacrificing legibility.

You can specify the desired point size for cells and ranges. The default point size is 10, which provides decent readability in the default Arial font. However, many users prefer titles to be larger, footnotes to be relatively tiny, and so on. The Size box, located next to the Font box on the Formatting toolbar, is a drop-down list that you can use to select the point size, or you can just type the desired point size (see Figure 6.6). Typing the point size offers the advantage of being able to specify a point size that isn't included in the list of default point sizes for that font—even in-between point sizes such as 10.5. However, keep in mind that this option isn't useful if your printer can't size the font to that specification.

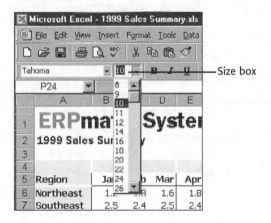

Figure 6.6.
Select or type the desired point size.

If you apply a larger point size, Excel automatically adjusts the height of the row to accommodate the new setting. The opposite isn't true, however; applying a smaller point size doesn't automatically reduce the row height unless you apply the point size to the entire row.

PART

II

CH

6

ADDING FONT STYLES

Now that you have the right font and point size in place, you may want to apply one or more *font styles* (also called *character styles*) to add emphasis to the text or numbers in the cell. The choices are reflected on the Formatting toolbar: bold (**B**), italic (*I*), or underline (<u>U</u>), as shown in Figure 6.7. Select the character(s) or cell(s) to which you want to apply the font style, and click the appropriate buttons. You can combine two or more font styles for additional emphasis.

Figure 6.7.
The Formatting tool-bar provides font style buttons for quick application.

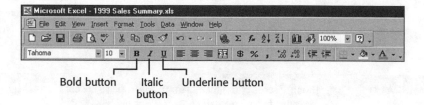

Bold button   Italic button   Underline button

Tip #90 from

Laurie

Some fonts offer special bold and italic styles that are "true" italics and bolds. Clicking the Bold or Italic buttons causes Windows to create a bold or italic version of the font. True italics and bolds generally look better than their created counterparts. For example, the Franklin Gothic Demi font (look back to Figure 6.2) also came with Franklin Gothic Heavy and Franklin Gothic Book variants. Book is essentially the normal typeface, whereas Demi is bold and Heavy is very bold.

You also can use shortcut keys to apply the font styles. Press Ctrl+B for bold, Ctrl+I for italic, or Ctrl+U for underline. The same shortcut keys toggle to remove the designated font style.

FORMATTING INDIVIDUAL CHARACTERS

Although you most likely will change the font, point size, or character style for entire cells, you can format individual characters, words, numbers, sentences, and so on within a cell. Simply select the character(s) and apply the formatting as desired.

You also can reverse the formatting for individual characters within a cell. If you have for-matted a particular cell as bold, for example, you can make one or more characters "not bold" by selecting those characters and clicking the Bold button to remove the boldfacing.

If you increase the point size for individual characters, Excel adjusts the row height to accommodate the new point size, just as if you had changed the entire cell.

RESETTING EXCEL'S DEFAULT FONT

If you don't like Arial as the default Excel font, or you prefer a larger font (you probably wouldn't want a smaller font for the default), you can change the default setting.

To reset Excel's default font and font size, follow these steps:

1. Choose Tools, Options. The Options dialog box opens.
2. Click the General tab.
3. Adjust the Standard Font setting and/or the Size setting as needed (see Figure 6.8).
4. Click OK to apply the changes.

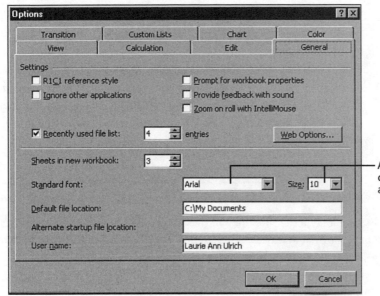

Figure 6.8.
Choose a legible font and an appropriate size as the new default for Excel worksheets.

Adjust these settings to change the default font and point size.

This change doesn't affect any open workbooks (it's not retroactive), and you must restart Excel before the changes can take effect.

 You can change the default font for just the active workbook. See "Changing the Default Font for the Active Workbook" in the Troubleshooting section at the end of this chapter.

Caution

Make sure you've selected a legible alternative for the default font—one that all users of your workbooks will have on their computers, and that can be read easily when printed, photocopied, and faxed. Also, choose a font that won't clash with any other fonts your organization uses in its letterhead or publications.

WORKING WITH STYLES

Styles are collections of formats, designed to make several formatting changes at once through the application of the style to a cell or range. For example, the Normal style—the default style that's applied to all new Excel content—consists of specific font, alignment, border, pattern, and other settings. To work with styles, choose Format, Style to open the Style dialog box shown in Figure 6.9.

Figure 6.9.
View the style defaults and edit them as needed.

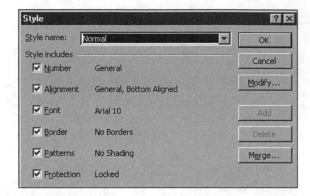

Normal is the only default style that includes all these settings. The other default styles specify only the number format and the alignment and placement of additional characters such as dollar signs, decimal points, and commas, as shown in the following list:

- **Comma and Comma (0).** These two styles add commas to numbers over 999.99. The Comma style displays two decimal places; Comma (0) displays none.

- **Currency and Currency (0).** These two styles add punctuation and currency symbols to match the regional settings for your computer. (Use the Regional Settings option in the Windows Control Panel to change the default monetary symbol, its position, and other currency properties as needed.) By default, Currency style for U.S. users displays two decimal places, commas for dollar amounts over $999.99, and the U.S. dollar sign ($). Currency (0) displays no decimal places.

- **Percent.** Displays the number with a percent sign (%). Percent amounts should be entered as decimals: .15, for example, is displayed as 15%.

The Comma, Currency, and Percent styles can be applied to selected cells by clicking the appropriate button on the Formatting toolbar: Comma Style, Currency Style, and Percent Style, respectively.

Tip #91 from

Laurie

Changing the number of decimal digits for cells formatted with Comma style or Currency style doesn't change the style to Comma (0) style or Currency (0) style. If you want to use either of the (0) styles, you must apply that style to the cell(s) with the Style dialog box. As a faster method, you can add the Style box to a toolbar and use it to apply styles. For details on customizing toolbars, see the section "Modifying Toolbars" in Chapter 28, "Customizing Excel to Fit Your Working Style."

EDITING THE DEFAULT STYLES

You can edit the default styles in the current workbook to apply the attributes you want. You might want cells formatted in Currency style to have a different background color, for example, so that they're more noticeable (or less). Changes to styles apply in the current workbook only.

 If you want to change the default styles permanently or create new styles that will apply to new workbooks, see "Creating Permanent Styles" in the Troubleshooting section at the end of this chapter.

To edit a style, follow these steps:

1. Choose Format, Style. The Style dialog box appears.

2. In the Style Name list, select the style you want to edit.

3. In the Style Includes section of the dialog box, turn any of the elements on or off by clicking the check boxes.

4. Click the Modify button to specify the settings for the selected options. This action opens the Format Cells dialog box, as shown in Figure 6.10.

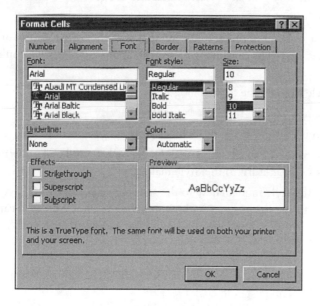

Figure 6.10.
You can change the font and alignment settings for the style, apply borders, add patterned or solid colored fills, or choose from a variety of number formats.

5. Using one or more of the six tabs in the Format Cells dialog box, select the new settings for the style.

6. Click OK to close the Format Cells dialog box and return to the Style dialog box.

7. Click OK. Excel immediately updates any cells with that style to reflect the formatting changes.

CREATING AND APPLYING CUSTOM STYLES

If you use Microsoft Word, you may already be comfortable with the process of creating custom styles to use for headings, bulleted lists, and so on. Excel's styles are comparable to those in Word, and offer just as many formatting possibilities. A common use for Excel styles is to create a certain "look" for worksheet titles used for a particular business. For worksheets disseminated outside your division or company, specific design standards may have been set up that require worksheets and charts to look alike. (In such circumstances, custom styles may already have been set up by someone else in your company. See the next section for details on how to combine those styles with yours.)

You create custom styles in either of the following ways:

- Design the style "from scratch" in the Style dialog box and Format Cells dialog box.
- Select a cell that already contains the formats you want to make into a named style, and use it as an example to establish the settings for the new style.

The methods are almost identical and are closely related to the technique for editing a default style. Follow these steps:

1. If you're creating a style by example, select a cell that uses the formats you want. If not, skip this step, or select any cells to which you want to apply the new style you're creating.
2. Choose Format, Style to open the Style dialog box.
3. Type a name for the new style in the Style Name box.
4. Select any settings you want in the Style Includes section of the dialog box.
5. Click the Modify button to open the Format Cells dialog box, and make any necessary changes. Then click OK to return to the Style dialog box.
6. If you want to apply the style immediately to the selected cells, click OK. If you just want to add the style to the list of styles without applying it, click Add. You can then close the dialog box with the Close button, or continue adding styles before you click the Close button.

To apply a style, select the cell(s) you want to format with the style, choose Format, Style, select the style in the Style Name list, and click OK.

MERGING STYLES FROM ONE WORKBOOK TO ANOTHER

The Merge button in the Style dialog box enables you to select another open workbook and merge any styles from that workbook with those in the active workbook. This feature saves time and effort by enabling you to create or edit styles in one workbook and then use them in other workbooks. For businesses with a standard set of styles, this feature also helps ensure consistency.

Merging the styles from one workbook to another overwrites existing styles with the same name (such as the default Normal style). Excel asks you to confirm this overwrite, but only once—you must either confirm or deny the overwrite for the entire set of styles.

To merge styles, follow these steps:

1. Open the source workbook containing the styles you want to merge.
2. Open or create the target workbook.
3. In the target workbook, choose Format, Style.
4. Click the Merge button to open the Merge Styles dialog box (see Figure 6.11).

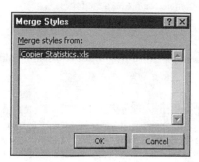

Figure 6.11.
Choose another open workbook's styles to merge with those in the current workbook. This helps create consistency throughout workbooks and their worksheets.

5. In the Merge Styles From list, select the source workbook whose styles you want to merge with the active workbook.
6. Click OK. Excel asks you to confirm that you want to merge styles that have the same name. This process will overwrite all existing styles with the same name.
7. Click Yes if you want to overwrite all existing styles with those in the source workbook. Click No if you don't.
8. Click OK or Close to exit the Style dialog box.

> **Caution**
>
> Merging styles can't be undone with Undo. Therefore, it's a good idea to review the styles in the workbook with which you want to merge like-named styles before performing the merge, and save the workbook before performing the merge. These extra steps can save you unexpected and potentially undesirable results (and enable you to go back to pre-merge status) should any of the formats be inappropriate for the current workbook. If you don't like the results, just close the workbook without saving, and reopen the saved version.

PART

II

CH

6

KEEPING WORKSHEETS LEGIBLE

Regardless of the method of applying fonts, font sizes, and formats, you'll want to make sure that these changes have the desired effect—to improve the overall appearance of the worksheets. Improving the overall appearance includes increasing (or at least not decreasing) legibility.

Caution

When you increase font sizes for numeric content for the first time, the column width adjusts automatically. Row height adjusts automatically to accommodate increases in both numeric and text content. If you adjust columns and rows manually, however, you'll have to continue to do so as changes are made to the font size, or use the AutoFit command to return to automatic adjustment.

→ Find out more about adjusting column width and row height, **see** "Adjusting Column Width and Row Height," **p. 37**

Tip #92 from

Laurie

Don't let the worksheet develop a cluttered look by allowing the gridlines to confine text and numbers, especially where you've applied elaborate fonts. Allowing some "breathing room" for worksheet content makes it easier to read and more pleasant to look at. Either turn off the gridlines if they're not needed (choose Tools, Options, click the View tab, and deselect the Gridlines option), or adjust the column width and row height to accommodate the size of cell contents.

If you have graphics software programs, games, and so on installed on your computer, you're likely to have a lot of fonts. Fonts also can be purchased on CD-ROM or downloaded from the Web and installed on your computer. A large selection of fonts certainly gives you a lot of choices when applying fonts to titles and column headings, or to important information to which you want to draw special attention. Don't let a variety of fonts lure you into one of the most common formatting mistakes, however. Don't create a circus-like atmosphere in your worksheets. Generally limit yourself to two or three fonts on one worksheet, and use fonts consistently throughout a workbook to maintain a visual theme among the worksheets.

Caution

Practical experience says it's best not to install more than 600 fonts on your computer. You might hear elsewhere that you should install no more than 1,000 fonts. Whatever the number, after you exceed it, you run the risk of experiencing system errors and of some programs not running properly.

CHOOSING COMPLEMENTARY FONTS

Following are some basic rules for the use of fonts in any business application, regardless of how creative the environment:

- Fancy or artistic fonts (also called *display fonts*) are best used sparingly. Avoid using more than one display font in any worksheet, and restrict usage to short titles for best readability. Figure 6.12 shows a worksheet with too many artistic fonts in use.

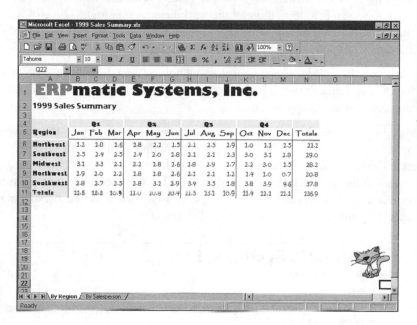

Figure 6.12.
A worksheet suffering from creeping fontitis. Compare this with Figure 6.2. Which looks more readable? Stick with two or three simple fonts for best results.

- Generally avoid using more than one serif or sans serif font in the same worksheet. Having one serif and one sans serif font in the same worksheet is effective, as these types of fonts complement each other. Having two or more of either type can create visual havoc. When you combine serif and sans serif fonts, use one type for headings and the other for data, as Figure 6.13 shows.

A serif font (Charter) creates a dignified look for labels.

A sans serif font (Arial) works well with numbers.

Region	Q1			Q2			Q3			Q4			Totals
	Jan	Feb	Mar	Apr	May	Jun	Jul	Aug	Sep	Oct	Nov	Dec	
Northeast	1.2	1.8	1.6	1.8	2.1	1.5	2.1	2.5	2.9	1.0	1.1	1.5	21.1
Southeast	2.5	2.4	2.5	2.4	2.0	1.8	2.1	2.1	2.3	3.0	3.1	2.8	29.0
Midwest	3.1	3.3	2.1	2.2	1.8	1.6	1.8	2.9	2.7	2.2	3.0	1.5	28.2
Northwest	1.9	2.0	2.2	1.8	1.8	2.6	2.1	2.1	1.2	1.4	1.0	0.7	20.8
Southwest	2.8	2.7	2.5	2.8	3.1	2.9	3.4	3.5	1.8	3.8	3.9	4.6	37.8
Totals	11.5	12.2	10.9	11.0	10.8	10.4	11.5	13.1	10.9	11.4	12.1	11.1	136.9

Figure 6.13.
The simplicity of a sans serif font is appealing when used with a more complex serif font.

Serif fonts have a flourish on the ends of the letters, as you see in the text of this paragraph. The term comes from *seraphim* (Latin for *angels*), and is applied to text with small "wings" on the ends of characters. *Sans serif* means "without serif," or no wings. Times New Roman (Word's default font) is a serif font, and Arial (Excel's default font) is sans serif.

PART

II

CH

6

SIZING FONTS

Choosing the appropriate size for fonts depends on two things—legibility and printing needs. Obviously, having fonts that are too small can make worksheets hard to read. On the other hand, small fonts can help to fit more of the worksheet on one page. The goal is to find a happy medium—the size of font that's easy to read but isn't so big that the worksheet requires an inordinate number of pages to print in its entirety.

For most worksheets, 10- or 8-point text is large enough to be read, but not so large that you waste paper. Column headings and row labels can be 12 or 14 points, and worksheet titles can be any size that seems appropriate.

Font size figures into the guideline of two or three fonts per worksheet. Arial 10 and Arial 12 are two fonts. Figure 6.14 uses five fonts: 24-point Franklin Gothic Demi, 12-point Franklin Gothic Demi, 10-point Tahoma Bold, 12-point Tahoma Bold, and 10-point Tahoma. You could consider "ERPmatic Systems" to be a logo, reducing the font count by one. This user made a judgment call that the grand sales total needed to be especially high-lighted, and used 12-point Tahoma Bold to accomplish the emphasis.

Figure 6.14.
Use font sizes as well as different fonts to format the work-sheet's overall appearance.

ERPmatic Systems, Inc.
1999 Sales Summary

Region	Q1 Jan	Feb	Mar	Q2 Apr	May	Jun	Q3 Jul	Aug	Sep	Q4 Oct	Nov	Dec	Totals
Northeast	1.2	1.8	1.6	1.8	2.1	1.5	2.1	2.5	2.9	1.0	1.1	1.5	21.1
Southeast	2.5	2.4	2.5	2.4	2.0	1.8	2.1	2.1	2.3	3.0	3.1	2.8	29.0
Midwest	3.1	3.3	2.1	2.2	1.8	1.6	1.8	2.9	2.7	2.2	3.0	1.5	28.2
Northwest	1.9	2.0	2.2	1.8	1.8	2.6	2.1	2.1	1.2	1.4	1.0	0.7	20.8
Southwest	2.8	2.7	2.5	2.8	3.1	2.9	3.4	3.5	1.8	3.8	3.9	4.6	37.8
Totals	11.5	12.2	10.9	11.0	10.8	10.4	11.5	13.1	10.9	11.4	12.1	11.1	136.9

Tip #93 from

Laurie

The user might have done equally well to use shading to put a colorful background behind the total instead, as Figure 6.15 shows. Bright yellow makes an excellent shade, by the way—not only does it display well, but it prints on a black-and-white printer as a shade of gray that doesn't interfere with text that appears on it. For more information about shading, see "Applying Borders and Shading," later in this chapter.

Figure 6.15.
Highlighting is a viable alternative to adjusting font size when you want to emphasize some-thing, such as this grand sales total.

ERPmatic Systems, Inc.
1999 Sales Summary

Region	Q1 Jan	Feb	Mar	Q2 Apr	May	Jun	Q3 Jul	Aug	Sep	Q4 Oct	Nov	Dec	Totals
Northeast	1.2	1.8	1.6	1.8	2.1	1.5	2.1	2.5	2.9	1.0	1.1	1.5	21.1
Southeast	2.5	2.4	2.5	2.4	2.0	1.8	2.1	2.1	2.3	3.0	3.1	2.8	29.0
Midwest	3.1	3.3	2.1	2.2	1.8	1.6	1.8	2.9	2.7	2.2	3.0	1.5	28.2
Northwest	1.9	2.0	2.2	1.8	1.8	2.6	2.1	2.1	1.2	1.4	1.0	0.7	20.8
Southwest	2.8	2.7	2.5	2.8	3.1	2.9	3.4	3.5	1.8	3.8	3.9	4.6	37.8
Totals	11.5	12.2	10.9	11.0	10.8	10.4	11.5	13.1	10.9	11.4	12.1	11.1	136.9

Highlighted cell

→ For information on setting print areas and printing worksheets in general, **see** "Adjusting Column Width and Row Height," **p. 37**

FORMATTING TITLES WITH MERGE AND CENTER

The worksheet title is usually the first thing someone notices when viewing a worksheet. The title normally tells the reader what sort of information will be found in the worksheet or what purpose the worksheet serves.

Making the title stand out is important for worksheets that will be published—on paper or on the Web. This chapter has discussed applying various formats to enhance worksheet text, and certainly those formats will be applied to the title. However, to place the title above and across the width of the worksheet is a popular effect, requiring use of Excel's Merge and Center tool. The Merge and Center effect is frequently enough to make titles stand out, even if no other special formatting is applied to the title text.

To center the title across the worksheet, follow these steps:

1. Assuming the title is in cell A1 or a cell to the left of and above the worksheet or a portion thereof, select the title and the blank cells to its right, as shown in Figure 6.16.

2. Click the Merge and Center button on the Formatting toolbar. The cells are merged into one cell, with the title centered across the cells (see Figure 6.17).

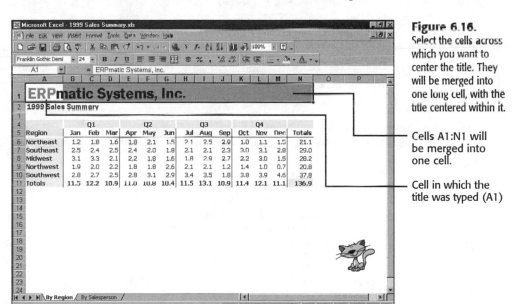

Figure 6.16.
Select the cells across which you want to center the title. They will be merged into one long cell, with the title centered within it.

Cells A1:N1 will be merged into one cell.

Cell in which the title was typed (A1)

Figure 6.17.
Keep the title visually separate from the rest of the worksheet content through the use of Merge and Center. (Merge and Center was applied to the subtitle, too.)

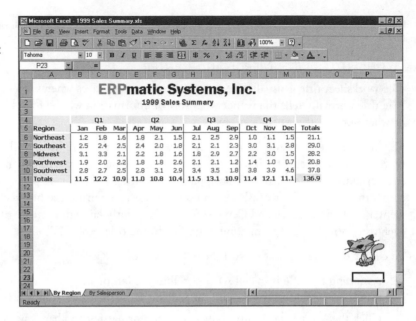

 If you select the whole row and then click Merge and Center, you'll get a surprise. See "Where Did the Worksheet Title Go?" in the Troubleshooting section at the end of this chapter.

ADJUSTING ALIGNMENT WITHIN CELLS, COLUMNS, AND ROWS

By default, Excel aligns text to the left, and numbers to the right. You can change the alignment of cell content by changing the number formats for numeric data, or by selecting a new alignment.

Why would you change cell alignment? The motivation is normally aesthetic, as changing alignment helps to change the worksheet's overall appearance and can help to set certain cells apart, such as column headings (see Figure 6.18).

Figure 6.18.
Centering the Q1, Q2, Q3, and Q4 headings helps make clear which months belong to which quarter. Right-aligning the month headings, however, makes clear their relationship with the numbers below.

Right-aligned   Centered

ERPmatic Systems, Inc.
1999 Sales Summary

Region	Q1			Q2			Q3			Q4			Totals
	Jan	Feb	Mar	Apr	May	Jun	Jul	Aug	Sep	Oct	Nov	Dec	
Northeast	1.2	1.8	1.6	1.8	2.1	1.5	2.1	2.5	2.9	1.0	1.1	1.5	21.1
Southeast	2.5	2.4	2.5	2.4	2.0	1.8	2.1	2.1	2.3	3.0	3.1	2.8	29.0
Midwest	3.1	3.3	2.1	2.2	1.8	1.6	1.8	2.9	2.7	2.2	3.0	1.5	28.2
Northwest	1.9	2.0	2.2	1.8	1.8	2.6	2.1	2.1	1.2	1.4	1.0	0.7	20.8
Southwest	2.8	2.7	2.5	2.8	3.1	2.9	3.4	3.5	1.8	3.8	3.9	4.6	37.8
Totals	11.5	12.2	10.9	11.0	10.8	10.4	11.5	13.1	10.9	11.4	12.1	11.1	136.9

For more information about applying number formats, see Chapter 7.

ALIGNING CELL CONTENT

To change the alignment of a single cell or any range of selected cells, you can use the Formatting toolbar or the Format Cells dialog box (choose Format, Cells or right-click the cell or range and choose Format Cells; then click the Alignment tab). The dialog box gives you more options for changing the cells' alignment, as described in the following list:

- **Horizontal.** This option in the Format Cells dialog box gives you choices ranging from General (meaning that alignment will be dictated by the type of content—text will be left-aligned, numbers right-aligned) to Center Across Selection.

Tip #94 from

Laurie

Center Across Selection is nearly the equivalent of the Merge and Center button on the Formatting toolbar, but not quite. If you use Merge and Center to place a title across A1:A5, clicking A1 selects the entire merged "cell" A1:A5. If you use Center Across Selection, clicking A1 just selects A1. Center Across Selection doesn't actually merge the cells; it just visually moves the title across the selection. The text remains in the first cell.

Center Across Selection is the way earlier versions of Excel handled centering titles. With Excel 97 came the Merge and Center feature, but it had a big drawback: You couldn't insert columns within a merged area, which was one of the reasons Microsoft kept the old Center Across Selection option. Excel 2000 has corrected this problem.

- **Vertical.** This setting enables you to align cell content to the top, middle, or bottom of a cell. By default, cells are bottom aligned.

 You can use the Decrease Indent and Increase Indent buttons to change the horizontal position of cell content within the cell. Before or after entering content into the active cell, click the Increase Indent button to move the content to the right, in small increments. To move the content to the left, click the Decrease Indent button.

ROTATING AND WRAPPING TEXT

The Alignment tab in the Format Cells dialog box also gives you access to tools for rotating text to any angle you need, and for choosing whether or not text will wrap in a cell.

Used primarily for column headings, the Orientation feature enables you to drag the wand to any position on the semicircle or enter a specific number of degrees of rotation for the text (see Figure 6.19). However, some fonts don't look very good when rotated, as Figure 6.20 shows. When you rotate text, be sure it's readable.

Wrapping text is frequently a better option than rotating it when you want it to fit a particular column width. Choosing Wrap Text enables you to type a phrase, sentence, paragraph, or more into a cell and have it wrap within the cell's current width. The cell grows taller to accommodate the wrapping text. You can also force Excel to wrap the text in the cell as you type—press Alt+Enter at the point where you'd like the text to wrap onto the next line. This is handy when you want line breaks to occur at specific points.

PART

II

CH

6

Figure 6.19.
Placing column headings on an angle reduces the need for wider columns.

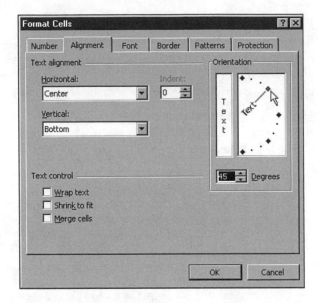

Figure 6.20.
Some fonts are hard to read when rotated. Notice how rotating the text also angles other cell formatting, such as shading.

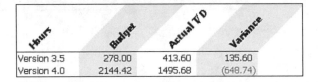

The Shrink to Fit and Merge Cells options are tools that give you more control over text placement. Shrink to Fit makes the text (or numbers) reduce in point size so that it fits in the cell's current dimensions. (Note that this can sometimes make cell entries unreadably tiny.)

Use Merge Cells to make one large cell out of two or more contiguous cells. You can do this before or after the selected cells have content.

Tip #95 from
Laurie

Merged cells in conjunction with a centered horizontal alignment is equivalent to the function of the Merge and Center button.

Tip #96 from
Laurie

Like fonts, alignment effects should be kept to a minimum. Using too many different alignments in a single sheet can be distracting for the reader.

APPLYING BORDERS AND SHADING

Using borders and/or shading in worksheets is an effective method for enhancing and improving a worksheet's appearance and highlighting important information.

Figure 6.21 shows a worksheet with borders and shading applied for both cosmetic and functional reasons.

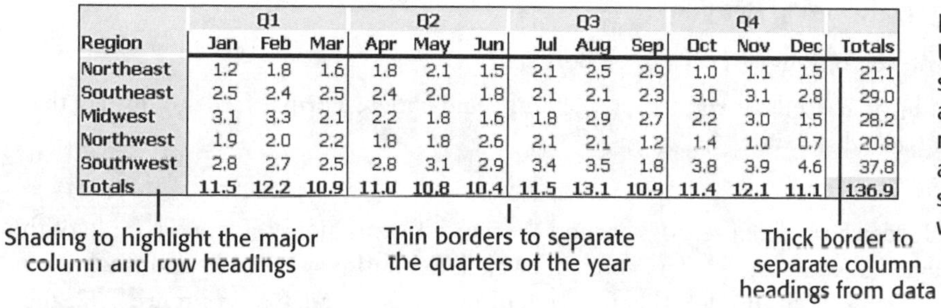

Region	Q1			Q2			Q3			Q4			Totals
	Jan	Feb	Mar	Apr	May	Jun	Jul	Aug	Sep	Oct	Nov	Dec	
Northeast	1.2	1.8	1.6	1.8	2.1	1.5	2.1	2.5	2.9	1.0	1.1	1.5	21.1
Southeast	2.5	2.4	2.5	2.4	2.0	1.8	2.1	2.1	2.3	3.0	3.1	2.8	29.0
Midwest	3.1	3.3	2.1	2.2	1.8	1.6	1.8	2.9	2.7	2.2	3.0	1.5	28.2
Northwest	1.9	2.0	2.2	1.8	1.8	2.6	2.1	2.1	1.2	1.4	1.0	0.7	20.8
Southwest	2.8	2.7	2.5	2.8	3.1	2.9	3.4	3.5	1.8	3.8	3.9	4.6	37.8
Totals	11.5	12.2	10.9	11.0	10.8	10.4	11.5	13.1	10.9	11.4	12.1	11.1	136.9

Shading to highlight the major column and row headings

Thin borders to separate the quarters of the year

Thick border to separate column headings from data

Figure 6.21.
Use borders and shading to draw attention to specific numbers or to create a barrier between sections in a worksheet.

Don't have a color printer? It's still worthwhile to add color to worksheets. Whether you're publishing the worksheet to the Web or simply sending it to another user to view onscreen, the use of color is never wasted. Even a black-and-white printout is enhanced by the use of color, as the colors are translated into subtly varying shades of gray.

USING BORDERS EFFECTIVELY

By default, worksheet gridlines don't print. This means that borders added to cells in a worksheet are the only lines that appear on the hard copy. You can turn gridlines on when you print, but with proper use of borders, your printouts will be much cleaner and more effective.

What purpose do borders serve? Borders draw attention, and borders create separations. Consider the following uses:

- Add a double border under the last number in a series of numbers to be totaled.
- Insert a border under the worksheet title.
- Use inside borders within a block of cells to create a visual table.
- Placing a full border around a single cell draws attention to a grand total or other important number.

To apply a quick border, you can use the Borders button on the Formatting toolbar. Follow these steps:

1. Select the cell or cells to which you want to apply a border.
2. Click the down-arrow button to the right of the Borders button to display a drop-down palette of border styles.
3. Choose one of the 12 border options from the Borders palette.

PART

II

CH

6

Notice that the button face changes to display the border style you selected. If you make another selection in the worksheet and click the button (instead of clicking the down arrow to display the list), Excel applies the border style shown on the button face to the new selection.

The Borders button applies thick, thin, or double lines to any cell or group of cells you select. If you want more variety, use the Borders tab in the Format Cells dialog box, as described in the following steps:

1. Select the cell or range of cells to be bordered.

2. Choose Format, Cells or right-click the range and choose Format Cells to display the Format Cells dialog box.

3. Click the Border tab.

4. In the Border box, click the sides around the word Text to indicate on which side of the selected cell(s) you want borders applied, or click the buttons that surround the box to choose which sides to border. If you have multiple cells selected, as in Figure 6.22, the word Text appears twice, and you can click the Inside button or click between the two words to insert borders between cells.

Figure 6.22.
The Border box serves as a tool for previewing borders as well as applying them.

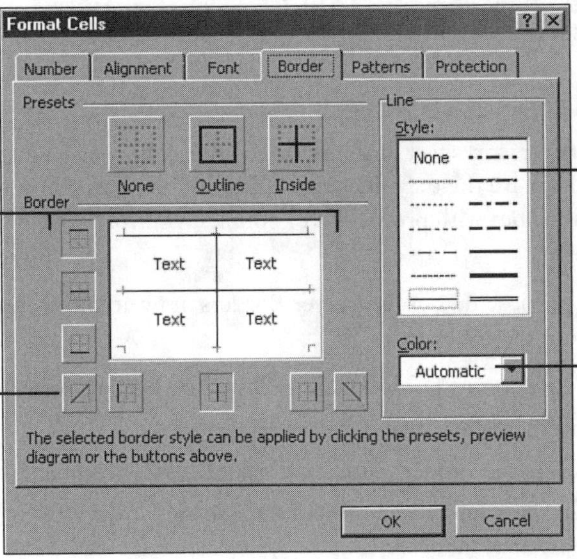

Click the border buttons or click within the box to add or remove borders.

Click these preset buttons for instant, simple borders.

Choose your line style.

Choose the border color.

5. Choose a line style, and if desired, a color for the border(s).

6. Click OK to apply the border(s) to the selected cell(s).

Tip #97 from

Laurie

To remove borders, select the cell(s), click open the Borders button, and select the No Border option in the upper-left corner of the palette.

USING COLORS, PATTERNS, AND TEXTURED FILLS

Shading cells can mean more than simply applying a shade of gray behind the cell content. Excel gives you 56 different solid colors and 18 different pattern fills to add visual interest and excitement to your worksheets.

To apply colors and patterns to selected cells, follow these steps:

1. Select the cell(s) and choose Format, Cells.
2. Click the Patterns tab (see Figure 6.23).

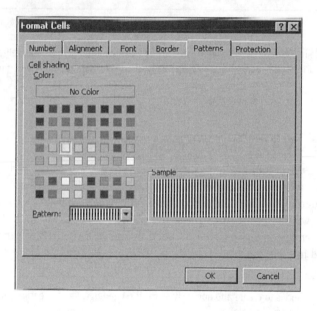

Figure 6.23.
Choose a color, a pattern, or both, and preview the selection in the Sample window.

3. To add color, click a solid color from the Color palette.
4. If desired, open the Pattern list box and choose a pattern. You can combine color and pattern by choosing a color and then a pattern, or vice versa.

Tip #98 from

Laurie

If you choose both a color and a pattern, the pattern will appear in black on top of the selected color. You can make a number of nice combinations by experimenting.

5. Click OK to apply the color and/or pattern to the selection.

PART

II

CH

6

To apply a fill color quickly, select the cell or cells to be colored, and click the Fill Color button on the Formatting toolbar. Choose one of the 40 colors on the palette.

To remove both fill color and pattern, select the cell(s), click open the Fill Color list, and choose No Fill on the palette. To remove one or the other, open the Format Cells dialog box, click the Patterns tab, and click No Color in the Color list or Solid in the Pattern list.

Caution

Be careful when choosing a fill color or pattern. Dark colors can make cell content difficult to read (requiring you to change the text color to white or yellow), and patterns can render the cell completely illegible. If you choose a light text color, be aware that text may be illegible when printed on a black-and-white printer. A good rule of thumb is to choose colors (for background and text) that will work in the majority of viewing and printing scenarios—don't create problems for yourself by applying formatting that requires very specific display or printing configurations.

Tip #99 from

If you're using Excel to create a fill-in form, using patterns in empty cells can tell the user not to use those cells, or simply create a visually interesting separation between parts of the form.

COPYING FORMATS WITH THE FORMAT PAINTER

Imagine you've formatted the column headings in one section of a worksheet with a different font, larger point size, a shaded background for the cells, and a thick border under the headings. That's four different formats you've applied. If you decide that you want the headings throughout the worksheet (or throughout the whole workbook) to look the same way, use the *Format Painter* to copy them from the section you've formatted to other sections you want formatted in the same way.

Tip #100 from

Another method is to create and apply styles for the headings. See the earlier section "Working with Styles" for details.

You can use the Format Painter to copy formats to one other location, or to several locations. To use the Format Painter, follow these steps:

1. Select the cell(s) containing the formatting you want to copy. These are the sample cells.

2. Click the Format Painter button. The mouse pointer changes to include a paintbrush symbol (see Figure 6.24).

3. Click on a single cell or drag through a range of cells that you want to format like the sample.

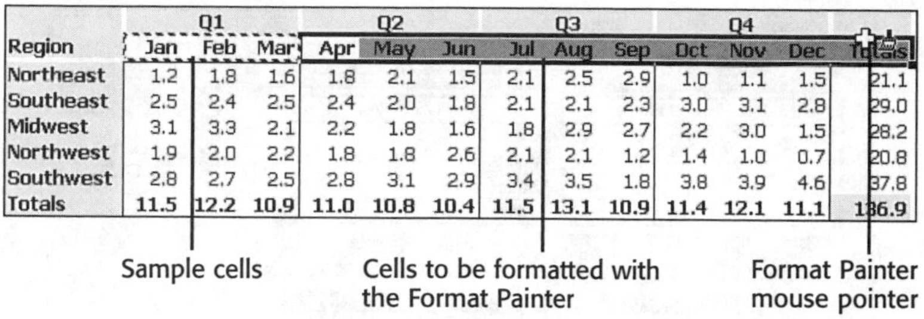

Region	Q1			Q2			Q3			Q4			Totals
	Jan	Feb	Mar	Apr	May	Jun	Jul	Aug	Sep	Oct	Nov	Dec	
Northeast	1.2	1.8	1.6	1.8	2.1	1.5	2.1	2.5	2.9	1.0	1.1	1.5	21.1
Southeast	2.5	2.4	2.5	2.4	2.0	1.8	2.1	2.1	2.3	3.0	3.1	2.8	29.0
Midwest	3.1	3.3	2.1	2.2	1.8	1.6	1.8	2.9	2.7	2.2	3.0	1.5	28.2
Northwest	1.9	2.0	2.2	1.8	1.8	2.6	2.1	2.1	1.2	1.4	1.0	0.7	20.8
Southwest	2.8	2.7	2.5	2.8	3.1	2.9	3.4	3.5	1.8	3.8	3.9	4.6	37.8
Totals	11.5	12.2	10.9	11.0	10.8	10.4	11.5	13.1	10.9	11.4	12.1	11.1	136.9

Sample cells   Cells to be formatted with the Format Painter   Format Painter mouse pointer

Figure 6.24.
Copy the formats (but not the content) from cell to cell with the Format Painter.

Tip #101 from

Laurie

To copy the sample format(s) to several noncontiguous locations throughout the worksheet or workbook, double-click the Format Painter button. Doing this leaves the tool "turned on" until you click the button again to turn it off.

USING AUTOFORMAT TO ENHANCE YOUR WORKSHEETS

If you'd rather not spend your time selecting fonts and choosing when and where to apply shading and borders, let Excel make these choices for you. Excel's *AutoFormat* feature offers a series of preformatted effects that you can apply to any range of cells within a worksheet.

To use AutoFormat, follow these steps:

1. Select the range of cells you want to format, keeping the following rules in mind:
   - You must have two or more contiguous cells selected in order to use AutoFormat.
   - AutoFormat can't be applied to multiple ranges.
2. Choose Format, AutoFormat.
3. Select a format from the list of samples (see Figure 6.25).

   Clicking the Options button displays a list of the formats that will be applied with the selected AutoFormat. You can deselect any of the options you don't want AutoFormat to apply.
4. Click OK.

PART
II
CH
6

Caution

If you've already sized columns and rows before using AutoFormat, deselect the Width/Height option. AutoFormat sizes the columns and rows to fit the widest/tallest entry, which may result in a cramped or crowded look for the worksheet.

In some cases, the size and content of the selected range and the AutoFormat you chose don't match—for example, a border might be applied indicating a total where you don't have one. If this occurs, simply remove the offending formatting effect or use Undo to remove the AutoFormat. At this point, you can reapply the AutoFormat, and choose not to apply the borders (or whatever format didn't work well with the selected cells).

Figure 6.25.
By default, the
AutoFormat's fonts,
sizing, shading, and
borders will be
applied as shown in
the sample.

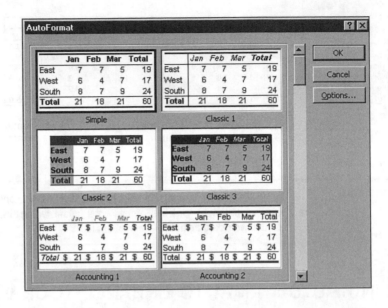

> **Note**
>
> If you find that you're turning off more than one or two of the formats to apply, this can be an indication that AutoFormat isn't appropriate for the currently selected range. Although AutoFormat is a time saver, it may not be the best formatting solution in every situation.

TROUBLESHOOTING

CHANGING THE DEFAULT FONT FOR THE ACTIVE WORKBOOK

How can you change the default font for the active workbook only?

Display the workbook whose default font you want to change. Choose Format, Style to open the Style dialog box, select the Normal style in the Style Name list, and click the Modify button to open the Format Cells dialog box. Click the Font tab, if necessary, and change the font as needed. Choose OK twice.

CREATING PERMANENT STYLES

I want to use styles I've created or modified in other workbooks. How do I do that?

Open the workbook whose styles you want to save permanently. Then open a new workbook and merge the styles to the new workbook. In the new workbook, choose File, Save As. In the Save As Type list, choose Template (*.xlt). In the File Name box, assign the file-name book. Store the file in the XLStart folder.

WHERE DID THE WORKSHEET TITLE GO?

I selected a row and clicked the Merge and Center button to merge the cells and center the title. Now I can't find the title, although it still appears in the Formula bar.

A common error when centering a title across the columns of a worksheet is selecting the entire row that contains the title. If you do this and then click the Merge and Center button, you'll merge all 256 cells of that selected row into one cell, and center the title across those 256 cells. Be sure to select only the cells that span the worksheet or a major portion of it.

EXCEL IN PRACTICE

The type of formatting you apply to a worksheet depends largely on its use and who will be seeing it. For worksheets that only you will see, formatting probably will be restricted to things that make the worksheet easier to read, such as increasing font size for onscreen viewing.

Worksheets that are shared with others often are formatted for clarity, visual impact, and a professional look. In some cases, you'll spend more time formatting than you did entering the data! To make the most of Excel's formatting tools without taking a lot of time, keep things simple (see Figure 6.26). Use shading to improve clarity and draw attention to important data, use borders and boldface to set column or row headings apart, and use fonts sparingly—you'll save time choosing them, and the worksheet won't look too "busy." It's a good idea to use the same formatting on many (if not all) of the worksheets—this strategy can help your work have a signature look that people will associate with you. Make it a good one!

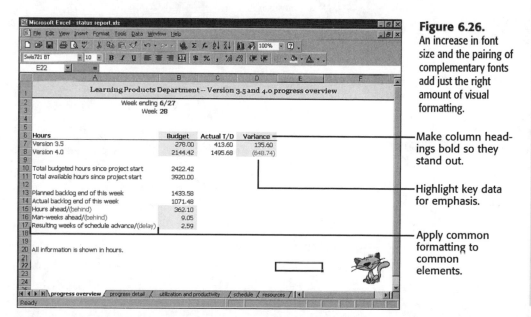

Figure 6.26.
An increase in font size and the pairing of complementary fonts add just the right amount of visual formatting.

Make column headings bold so they stand out.

Highlight key data for emphasis.

Apply common formatting to common elements.

PART

II

CH

6

MODIFYING NUMBERS AND DATES

by Laurie Ann Ulrich
laurie@limehat.com

In this chapter

APPLYING COMMON NUMERIC FORMATS FROM THE TOOLBAR

Numeric formatting changes the appearance of your numbers, converting them to currency, percentages, dates, and so forth. While this formatting may seem purely cosmetic, it also serves an important purpose in defining the nature of your numbers (do the sales figures represent dollar volume or number of units sold?). It also helps ensure that your numbers appear in a digestible format (reducing the number of decimals displayed in a percentage, for example) that doesn't crowd or complicate your worksheet unnecessarily.

The most commonly applied number formats are applied directly from the Formatting toolbar, and each is described in Table 7.1.

TABLE 7.1. NUMBER FORMATTING TOOLS

Button	Name	Formatting
$	Currency Style	Converts numbers to currency, adding dollar signs to the left of the number, and adding two decimal places to the right. Commas are used as a thousands delimiter.
%	Percent Style	Used for numbers that are the result of a formula that results in a percentage, this tool converts numbers from decimals to percentages, such as from .05 to 50 percent.
,	Comma Style	Use this tool to add commas to your numbers in excess of 999. A comma and two decimal places to the right are added to the number.
+.0 .00	Increase Decimal	Even if your decimals are currently zeros, this tool will add more of them. You can view a number to an unlimited number of decimal places with this tool, clicking once per desired decimal displayed.
.00 +.0	Decrease Decimal	If you've used the Increase Decimal tool and merely want to reverse your action or just want to see fewer numbers to the right of the decimal point, click this button. As you remove decimal places, numbers to the left of the removed numbers round up as required. For example, 5.682 becomes 5.68, then 5.7, and then 6 if the Decrease Decimal button is clicked three times.

→ Find out how to add the new Euro button to your Formatting toolbar; **see p. 169**

These buttons apply the default settings for each of these number formats. It is important to note that no matter what you do to the appearance of the format of your numeric content, the entire number you typed in is being stored and used by Excel. Remember that your formats merely adjust the way the number looks in the worksheet. You can customize the way each format is applied by using the Format Cells dialog box (see the following section).

Note

Scientific format allows you to display a shortened version of a number with many decimal places. This is useful for displaying scientific notation, as might a chemist entering the data on amounts of certain elements found in a sample compound. You can enter the number as it is (such as 2.3987900109299) or type the scientific format in (2.3E+12). You can also apply the Scientific format from the Format Cells dialog box—the category is found on the Number tab.

APPLYING BUILT-IN FORMATS

For many worksheets, Currency and Percentage formats will suffice. However, by using the Comma Style and Increase/Decrease Decimal buttons, a sufficient degree of customization is available through the toolbar should the defaults be inappropriate for a particular worksheet.

Should you need to use any additional number formats or want to adjust your defaults automatically, follow these steps:

1. Select the cells you want to format.
2. Choose Format, Cells or right-click the selection and choose Format Cells from the shortcut menu. The Format Cells dialog box opens.
3. Click the Number tab (see Figure 7.1).

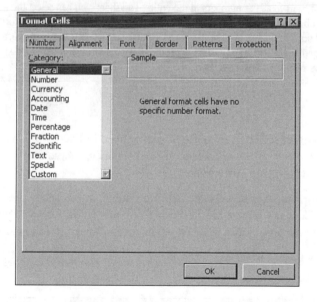

Figure 7.1.
There are 12 number-formatting categories available, most of which have their own set of options.

4. Select a Category by clicking the category name in the list.
5. For each category except General and Text, a different set of options appears. Figure 7.2 shows the settings for the Number category.

6. Select the appropriate settings for any options you want to customize, and click OK.

Figure 7.2.
Apply the Number format when your numeric data will require decimal places (or zeros after the decimal point) or commas.

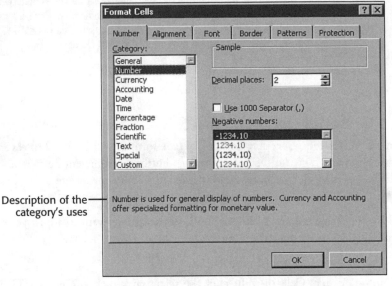

Description of the category's uses

Note

Your settings for the selected category apply only to the selected cells. To quickly apply numeric formats to all the numbers in the entire worksheet, you can select the entire worksheet before using the Format Cells dialog box. Be careful to apply only formats that will affect purely numeric content (no date formats), so that your text entries are not visually changed. If any unwanted results occur in a few cells throughout the worksheet, you can always reformat those cells later.

WORKING WITH CURRENCY

Currency is probably the most common numeric format applied in Excel worksheets. Many of the numbers you'll enter into your worksheets represent money, and you want that to be obvious to the people who view your worksheets.

Applying the Currency format is quick and easy, requiring only that you select the cells to be formatted, and click the Currency button on the Formatting toolbar. If, however, you want to customize the way your currency looks in the worksheet, you'll need to follow these steps:

1. Select the cells you want to format as currency.

2. Choose Format, Cells.

Tip #102 from

Laurie

If you've already applied the Currency format to your cells through the toolbar, you can follow these steps to customize the way the Currency category is applied to your previously formatted cells.

3. Click the Number tab.

4. Select Currency from the Category list.

5. Adjust the number of Decimal places as needed. You can type the number into the spin box, or use the triangles to increase or decrease the number.

6. Select a Symbol. If a U.S. dollar ($) symbol isn't appropriate (it's the default), scroll through the list and choose the monetary symbol to match the desired currency.

7. Choose how you want to see your Negative numbers displayed.

Tip #103 from

Laurie

> If you don't have a color printer, displaying your negative numbers in red (without parentheses) can make it hard to tell negative numbers on a printout. If you prefer red negative numbers and also want to be able to print on a black-and-white printer (without adjusting your print settings), choose the option to also add parentheses to red negative numbers.

---

8. View the Sample, which displays the content from your selected cell or the first cell in your selected range.

9. Click OK to apply your Currency settings and close the dialog box.

Figure 7.3 shows a worksheet with currency applied to the column totals from Jan through Jun. The format has been customized to show no decimals.

Caution

> When you choose to reduce the number of displayed decimal places, Excel rounds the displayed numbers up where needed. For example, 7.68 becomes 7.7 with one decimal place, and 8 with none. This can result in the appearance of numbers that don't equal your total where a SUM has been used. Don't worry! Your totals (and all other formulas that use the rounded cell content) are correct—Excel is using the number you entered; it's merely displaying it rounded.

 Converting to Euro Dollars

Excel 2000 supports the Euro dollar, the European Union's new currency. Unlike yen or pounds sterling, which are built into Excel, the Euro dollar requires enabling an add-in. Choose Tools, Add-Ins, and select Euro Currency Tools from the list of available add-ins. If you didn't install the add-ins when you installed Office 2000, selecting the add-in from the Add-Ins dialog box will spawn a series of dialog boxes that take you through the process of installing them. Once invoked, this add-in will place a Euro Dollar button on your Formatting toolbar.

FORMATTING FOR PERCENTAGES

The Percentage format normally is applied to the results of a formula that calculates a percentage. The format can be applied from the toolbar or the Format Cells dialog box, in which you can customize the way the format is applied.

Figure 7.3.
Currency formatting adds the currency symbol you use and lines up amounts in neat columns.

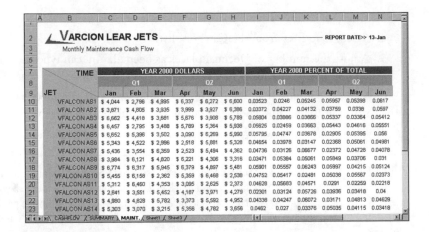

If you need to customize the Percentage format, choose Format, Cells, and in the Number tab, click the Percentage Category (see Figure 7.4).

Figure 7.4.
The Percentage format works best with numbers expressed as decimals or with numbers that are actually a calculated percentage.

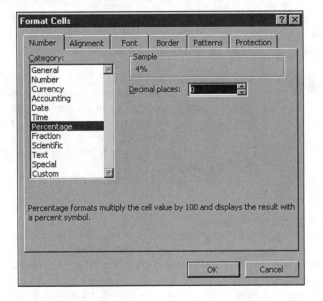

Your only Percentage format option is to adjust the number of decimal places added to the number. The default is two, and for most situations, this is appropriate. Figure 7.5 shows analysis to the right with calculated percentages, formatted in Percent Style.

Caution

If you apply the Percentage format to a number that isn't a calculated percentage, your results can be inappropriate. For example, in a cell containing the typed number 10, the 10 will change to 1000%.

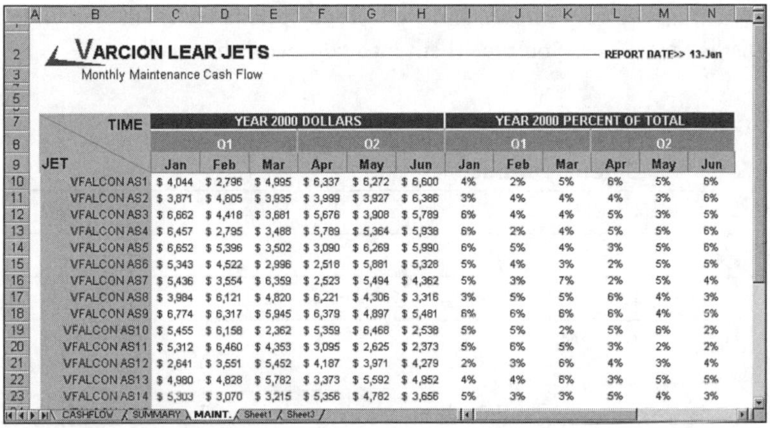

VARCION LEAR JETS — REPORT DATE>> 13-Jan

Monthly Maintenance Cash Flow

TIME / JET	YEAR 2000 DOLLARS						YEAR 2000 PERCENT OF TOTAL					
	Q1			Q2			Q1			Q2		
	Jan	Feb	Mar	Apr	May	Jun	Jan	Feb	Mar	Apr	May	Jun
VFALCON AS1	$ 4,044	$ 2,796	$ 4,995	$ 6,337	$ 6,272	$ 6,600	4%	2%	5%	6%	5%	6%
VFALCON AS2	$ 3,871	$ 4,805	$ 3,935	$ 3,999	$ 3,927	$ 6,386	3%	4%	4%	4%	3%	6%
VFALCON AS3	$ 6,662	$ 4,418	$ 3,681	$ 5,676	$ 3,908	$ 5,789	6%	4%	4%	5%	3%	5%
VFALCON AS4	$ 6,457	$ 2,795	$ 3,488	$ 5,789	$ 5,364	$ 5,938	6%	2%	4%	5%	5%	6%
VFALCON AS5	$ 6,652	$ 5,396	$ 3,502	$ 3,090	$ 6,269	$ 5,990	6%	5%	4%	3%	5%	6%
VFALCON AS6	$ 5,343	$ 4,522	$ 2,996	$ 2,518	$ 5,881	$ 5,328	5%	4%	3%	2%	5%	5%
VFALCON AS7	$ 5,436	$ 3,554	$ 6,359	$ 2,523	$ 5,494	$ 4,362	5%	3%	7%	2%	5%	4%
VFALCON AS8	$ 3,984	$ 6,121	$ 4,820	$ 6,221	$ 4,306	$ 3,316	3%	5%	5%	6%	4%	3%
VFALCON AS9	$ 6,774	$ 6,317	$ 5,945	$ 6,379	$ 4,897	$ 5,481	6%	6%	6%	6%	4%	5%
VFALCON AS10	$ 5,455	$ 6,158	$ 2,362	$ 5,359	$ 6,468	$ 2,538	5%	5%	2%	5%	6%	2%
VFALCON AS11	$ 5,312	$ 6,460	$ 4,353	$ 3,095	$ 2,625	$ 2,373	5%	6%	5%	3%	2%	2%
VFALCON AS12	$ 2,641	$ 3,551	$ 5,452	$ 4,187	$ 3,971	$ 4,279	2%	3%	6%	4%	3%	4%
VFALCON AS13	$ 4,980	$ 4,828	$ 5,782	$ 3,373	$ 5,592	$ 4,952	4%	4%	6%	3%	5%	5%
VFALCON AS14	$ 5,303	$ 3,070	$ 3,215	$ 5,356	$ 4,782	$ 3,656	5%	3%	3%	5%	4%	3%

CASHFLOW / SUMMARY / MAINT. / Sheet1 / Sheet3

Figure 7.5.
Percentage calculations that result in long numbers with many decimal places can be quickly converted to manageable numbers with the Percent Style format.

For more information on creating formulas (for calculating percentages and other operations), see Chapter 10, "Constructing Excel Formulas."

FORMATTING THE DATE AND TIME

Dates and times are normally included in worksheets for information, for calculation, or both. By default, Excel converts typed dates as shown in Table 7.2.

TABLE 7.2. DEFAULT DATE FORMATS

Typed Content	Default Result
4/7/66	4/7/66
4/7	7-Apr
April 7, 1966	7-Apr-66

If you want to have your typed dates formatted differently, follow these steps:

1. Select the cells that contain or will contain dates to be formatted.

> **Tip #104 from** *Laurie*
>
> If the cells that you want to format are scattered throughout your worksheet, use the Ctrl key to select them as a group before applying the format.

2. Choose Format, Cells.
3. Click the Number tab, and select the Date Category.
4. Select one of 15 date formats in the Type list.
5. After viewing the Sample, click OK.

The Time Category settings are very similar, and eight Type options are available. Table 7.3 shows the Excel defaults for times as you type them into your worksheet cells:

TABLE 7.3.   DEFAULT TIME FORMATS

Typed Content	Default Format
1:50:15	1:50:15
1:50 am	1:50 AM
1:50 a	1:50 AM
1:50 p	1:50 PM

The Type list contains formats in a 12- and 24-hour clock, with or without seconds, and with or without the date accompanying the time.

Note

If you'll be using your time entries in formulas, it will be easier to use the time in your formula if you apply a 24-hour format.

Tip #105 from

Laurie

The 24-hour clock starts at 0:00:01 and ends at 24:59:59. To figure out the 24-hour equivalent of a 12-hour-based time, add 12 if the time is PM. For example, 1:00PM is 13:00 in a 24-hour format. AM times are the same in both 12- and 24-clocks.

WORKING WITH DATES IN 2000 AND BEYOND

A source of concern among many users is how computers will deal with dates in and beyond the year 2000. Excel 97 and Excel 2000 were both designed to effectively deal with this issue, with some further enhancements added to the 2000 edition of Excel.

First, you don't need to worry about entering a date for 2000 or 2001 and having Excel interpret it as a date in the year 1900 or 1901. If you enter 5/28/19, Excel assumes you mean May 28, 2019. Second, you can choose from two date systems, each enabling you to successfully calculate dates after 1999:

- **The 1900 Date System.** The first date is 1/1/1900 (serial value 1) and the last is 12/31/9999 (serial value 2958525).
- **The 1904 Date System.** The first date is 1/2/1904 (serial value 1) and the last date is 12/31/9999 (serial value 2957063). (This choice is available for compatibility with output from Macintosh versions of Excel. The Mac uses the 1904 date system.)

To change your date system (it's 1900 by default), choose Tools, Options, and in the Calculation tab, click the 1904 Date System check box.

Excel 2000 offers an additional tool for making it clear which 00 year you're referring to—1900 or 2000—by giving you the option to display dates as four digits (regardless of their entry as two or four digits). To display your dates as four digits, choose one of the formats that show four-digit years, such as 3/14/1998, 14-Mar-1998, or March 14, 1998.

CREATING CUSTOM FORMATS

If Excel's built-in formats don't match what you're looking for, you can create a custom format. For example, say you want a date to show the weekday, month, date, and year, such as "Saturday, January 16, 1999." Or, say you want to make sure that if a number is less than 1, that Excel omits the zero to the left of the decimal point. In both cases, you create a custom format.

To create a custom format, you type a string of *formatting codes* (also simply called *codes*) that Excel interprets. Here are the details:

1. Select the cell(s) to format.

2. Choose Format, Cells, click the Number tab, and choose the Custom Category.

3. In the Type field, type your custom format. In the list box below the Type field, you can choose a custom format upon which to base yours. For example, you can type **dddd**, **mmmm dd**, **yy** to represent day-of-week, month, day, year, such as Tuesday, January 19, 1999. The rest of this section explains how to develop custom formats.

4. Click the OK button. Excel formats the cell(s) using your custom format, and adds your custom format to the list of available custom formats so you can use it again later.

The difficult part of this task is knowing what codes to type in step 3. The codes can be broken down into two groups: *date and time* codes and *number and text* codes.

WORKING WITH DATE AND TIME FORMATTING CODES

For custom date and time formats, type combinations of codes as Table 7.4 shows. For example, "dddd, mmm d, yyyy" changes 2/2/99 to Tuesday, February 2, 1999.

TABLE 7.4.   DATE AND TIME FORMATTING CODES

Code	Meaning
d	Day, from 1 to 31.
dd	Day, from 01 to 31.
ddd	Three-letter day of week, such as Tue.
dddd	Day of week, such as Tuesday.
m	Month, from 1 to 12; or minute, from 1 to 60.
mm	Month, from 01 to 12; or minute, from 01 to 60.

continues

PART
III

CH
7

TABLE 7.4. CONTINUED

Code	Meaning
mmm	Three-letter month, such as Aug.
mmmm	Month, such as August.
yy	Two-digit year, such as 99.
yyyy	Four-digit year, such as 2001.
h	Hour, from 0 to 23.
hh	Hour, from 00 to 23.
s	Second, from 0 to 59. Follow with .0 or .00 to add tenths or hundredths of a second, respectively.
ss	Second, from 00 to 59. Follow with .0 or .00 to add tenths or hundredths of a second, respectively.
AM/PM	AM or PM, as appropriate.
am/pm	am or pm, as appropriate.
A/P	A or P, as appropriate.
a/p	a or p, as appropriate.

Note

If you use one of the AM/PM, am/pm, A/P, or a/p codes, Excel formats time on a 12-hour clock. If you omit these codes, Excel formats time on a 24-hour clock.

Figure 7.6 shows a custom date format that shows a four-digit year followed by a two-digit month.

Figure 7.6.
Type your custom format in the Type box.

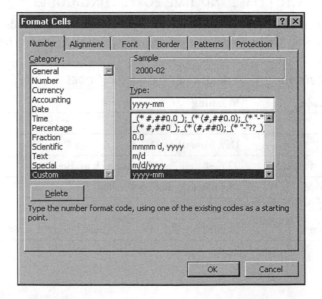

Tip #106 from

Laurie

You can add a left and right bracket around any time or date code to make Excel show elapsed time. For example, if cell A1 contains 8/12/2001 10:15 and cell A2 contains 8/13/2001 9:42, and cell A3 contains =A2-A1, formatting cell A3 with [h]:mm:ss shows you how many hours, minutes, and seconds elapsed between the two dates.

WORKING WITH NUMBER AND TEXT FORMATTING CODES

Creating custom number formats can be more challenging, because Excel gives you lots of flexibility. Table 7.5 shows the codes available for formatting numbers and text.

TABLE 7.5. NUMBER AND TEXT FORMATTING CODES

Code	Meaning
0	Digit placeholder. Use this code to ensure that the correct number of digits appears in a value. For example, if a cell contains .15 and you apply the format 0.000 to it, the cell will read 0.150. If the cell contained .15548, the 0.000 format would make it read 0.1555.
?	Digit placeholder. This is similar to the 0 placeholder, but places spaces instead of zeros on the right of the decimal point. 0.??? applied to a cell containing .21 would yield 0.21.
#	Digit placeholder. This is similar to the 0 placeholder, but does not pad a value with extra zeros. Use this placeholder mostly to show where to place commas. For example, #,### applied to a cell containing 123456789 yields 123,456,789.
.	Decimal point. Used in conjunction with other codes to signify decimal point placement. For example, 0.### applied to a cell that contains .1236 displays 0.124.
%	Percent symbol. This code multiplies the value by 100 and appends the percent symbol. Applying % to a cell containing 13 yields 1300%.
/	Fraction format. Use this code with the ? code to display numbers in fraction form. For example, applying ??/?? to a cell that contains 1.315 yields 96/73. Applying # ??/?? to the same cell yields 1 23/73. The more places you allow in the fraction, the more accurate it is. So ?/? applied to a cell containing .270 yields 2/7, while applying ??/?? yields 11/40.
,	Thousands separator, as well as rounding and scaling agent. When you surround a comma with #s, 0s, or ?s, the comma separates hundreds from thousands, thousands from millions, and so on. So #,### places a comma every third digit. When you place one comma at the end of a format, Excel rounds the number and displays it in thousands. When you place two commas at the end of a format, Excel rounds the number and displays it in millions. For example, #,###,###, displays 123456789 as 123,457 and #,###,###,, displays 123456789 as 123.

continues

PART

III

CH

7

TABLE 7.5.   CONTINUED

Code	Meaning
E+ E- e+ e-	Scientific notation. Use these formats in conjunction with ?, #, and 0 to cause numbers to display in scientific notation. For example, #.## e- ## applied to a cell that contains 545678132 displays 5.46 e 8. Also, E- and e- display - before negative exponents but no sign before positive exponents. E+ and e+ display - before negative exponents and + before positive exponents.
( ) $ - + / space	Literals. Excel places these characters directly into the value.
\	Literal interpreter. Precede any character with the backslash, and Excel places that character directly into the value. For example, \t inserts the character t (but not the backslash) into the format. (To insert several characters in a row, use "text", described below.)
_	Space inserter. This character leaves space equivalent to the width of the next character, to help you align elements. For example, _m leaves a space equal to the width of the m.
"text"	Literal string. For example, "Part No." inserts the text Part No. into the cell.
*	Repeater. Repeats the next character until the column is filled. Use only one asterisk per format.
@	Text placeholder. If a cell contains a text value, this character tells Excel where to show it. For example, if a cell contains the text "check," "Customer paid by "@"." displays Customer paid by check.
[color]	Color. Applies the specified color to the text. For example, [Red]#,###.## applied to a cell that contains 43567.4 displays 43,567.4 in red.

If a cell could contain a positive value, a negative value, zero, and/or text, you can apply a different format for each. Just write multiple formats, separating each with a semicolon. If you write two formats, the first applies to positive and zero values and the second applies to negative values. If you write three formats, the first applies to positive values, the second to negative values, and the third to zero. If you write four formats, they apply to positive, negative, zero, and text values, respectively. For example, you might write this format:

```
#,###; [red]#,###; "No balance"; "Note: "@
```

If the cell contains 2340, it displays 2,340. If the cell contains -4211, it displays 4,211 in red. If the cell contains zero, it displays No balance. If the cell contains the text "Non-negotiable," it displays Note: Non-negotiable. You might find it easier to use conditional formatting, described in the next section, to handle these kinds of situations.

CONDITIONAL FORMATTING

Most formatting is performed by you, selecting a cell or cells, and clicking the appropriate buttons or using a dialog box to execute your commands and customized options. You can, however, let Excel carry out your commands automatically by setting conditional formats.

Conditional formatting requires that you create a set of criteria, much like entering search criteria for a database. Using expressions such as "equal to" or "greater than" (expressed as = or >), you choose formats to apply to cells that contain text or numbers that match your criteria.

This can be a very useful tool, enabling you to apply visual formatting throughout a worksheet or an entire workbook, with one simple set of commands. To apply conditional formatting to your data, follow these steps:

1. Select the range of cells that you want to include in your conditional formatting.

Tip #107 from

Laurie

If you want the search for your conditional formatting criteria to encompass the entire worksheet, click the Select All button, located in the corner of the worksheet headings, between the column heading buttons and row heading buttons.

2. Choose Format, Conditional Formatting.

3. In the Conditional Formatting dialog box, choose between Cell Value Is and Formula Is (see Figure 7.7). Cell values can be text or numbers you typed into the cells, or the results of formulas.

Compress Dialog button reduces dialog box to give you access to the worksheet for selecting cells.

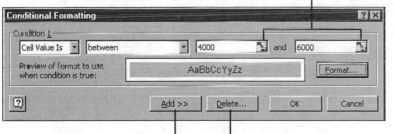

Figure 7.7.
Choose which conditions Excel should look for in your cells, and then which formats to apply.

Click Add to create a second set of conditions.   Click Delete to remove a condition.

4. Select an operator, or expression, such as equal to or greater than. You can choose from eight options.

5. Click the Compress Dialog button to access your worksheet, and click in a cell that contains the value you want Excel to search for and format. The cell address appears in the dialog box (see Figure 7.8).

Tip #108 from

Laurie

If you aren't sure where the conditional value is in your worksheet, you can type a value into the box.

PART

III

CH

7

Figure 7.8.
When you click in a cell, the cell address appears in the dialog box. The dollar signs indicate that all other cells should be compared to the contents of this one cell.

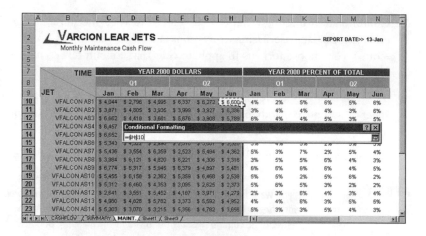

6. Click the Format button to establish the visual formatting for the cells that meet your criteria. The Format Cells dialog box opens, as shown in Figure 7.9, and you can assign a font style, color, or background shading to any cells that meet the defined conditions (click OK to return to the Conditional Formatting dialog box).

Figure 7.9.
When applying font formats, you cannot change fonts, but you can choose a style (such as bold or italic) or color. You also can apply borders or shading to the cells that meet your conditions.

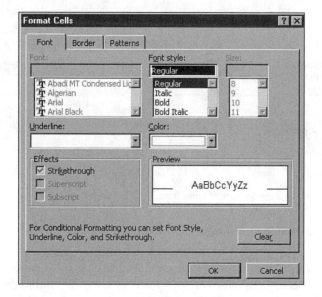

7. If you want to set up second or third sets of conditions, click the Add button.

8. After setting all your conditions and formats, click OK.

After you've set conditional formatting in a worksheet, any cells that you fill with content that matches the conditions you set will be formatted per your conditional formatting instructions. This will continue until you delete the instructions.

Figure 7.10 shows a worksheet formatted with cash flows that fall between $4,000 and $6,000 per month.

Cells containing values that meet the defined condition appear with the formatting you assigned.

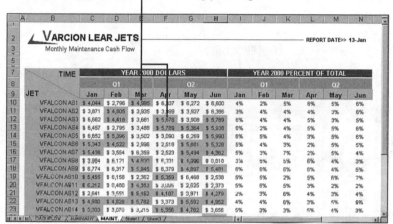

Figure 7.10.
Use conditional formats to call out numbers that meet certain criteria.

To delete the conditions from your worksheet (removing all formatting applied through conditional formatting and ending the continued application of your conditional formats), follow these steps:

1. Select the entire worksheet by clicking the Select All button.

2. Choose Format, Conditional Formatting.

3. Click the Delete button in the Conditional Formatting dialog box.

4. In the Delete Conditional Format dialog box that appears, place a check mark next to any conditions you want to delete (see Figure 7.11).

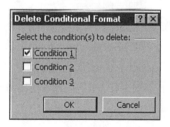

Figure 7.11.
Choose the conditions you no longer want to apply.

5. Click OK to return to the Conditional Formatting dialog box.

6. Click OK to remove the formatting applied through the deleted condition and close the dialog box.

PART

III

CH

7

Figure 7.12 shows a worksheet formatted with Conditional Formatting to show all the maintenance numbers that fall between $4,000 and $6,000, and those that don't. To help you or your intended audience understand the meaning of the conditional formatting, consider adding a legend to the worksheet. The formatting legend helps those who view the file onscreen or on paper understand how to interpret the formatting on this and any similarly formatted worksheets.

Formatting legend

Figure 7.12.
Be sure to include the formatting key in your print area when you print the worksheet, so others will know how to interpret the information.

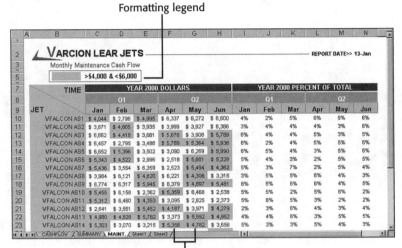

Conditional formatting applied a shaded background to these cells.

TROUBLESHOOTING

FORMATTING FORMULAS AS TEXT

I applied the text format to a cell that contains a formula. Why did other cells immediately display the #VALUE error?

If you apply the Text format to a cell that contains a formula, Excel recognizes the cell's contents as text—not as a formula. So, if cell A1 contains a formula formatted as text, and cell A2 contains a formula that references cell A1, then cell A2 will display the #VALUE error.

The only way around this is to never apply the text format to cells that contain formulas.

GETTING ELAPSED TIME

I'm trying to get elapsed time in minutes, but Excel says the custom format I've created is in error. I've typed [mm:ss]. What am I doing wrong?

In all elapsed-time formats, you place the square brackets around only the first code. Change this format to [mm]:ss and it will work fine.

CHAPTER 8

USING EXCEL'S DRAWING TOOLS

by Laurie Ann Ulrich
laurie@limehat.com

In this chapter

INTRODUCING THE DRAWING TOOLBAR

The *Drawing toolbar* is available through Excel, Word, and PowerPoint and offers the same set of tools in each application. The Drawing toolbar tools enable you to add shapes, lines, text boxes, artistic text, and clip art to your Office documents and manipulate them in terms of their size, placement, and colors.

Tip #109 from

Laurie

Be aware that while not all of the drawing tools and commands available are covered in this chapter (nor are they all typically used in an Excel worksheet context), they are worth exploring on your own, if only to improve your use of them with Word and PowerPoint. In addition, the PhotoDraw application, shipped with the Professional and Premium editions of Office 2000, gives you even more tools for manipulating graphics, as well as retouching photographs.

Note

This chapter covers the basic uses of drawing objects, AutoShapes, and so on. For more advanced uses of the drawing tools, see Chapter 15, "Formatting Charts," Chapter 16, "Professional Charting Techniques," and Chapter 24, "Professional Formatting Techniques."

The use of drawing objects, shapes, colors, and so on is governed by the capabilities of your equipment. If you plan to create elaborate designs on your worksheets, keep in mind that you'll need a monitor, printer, and/or projection system capable of handling graphics at that level.

You can also use the <u>I</u>nsert, <u>P</u>icture command to insert graphic images such as scanned photographs and logos. Several of the Drawing toolbar's tools can be used to affect placement and appearance of these items. This capability can enhance a product listing (with pictures of the products) or a financial report on a particular division (with a photo of the location).

Why add shapes, lines, and clip art to your Excel worksheets? In many worksheets, you can use shapes and lines to draw attention to or explain important cells or to add visual interest. Using clip art can add a message in the form of a picture, the image emphasizing the point made by your worksheet's data. Figure 8.1 shows a worksheet that contains drawn shapes, lines, and clip art.

Caution

It is very likely that if you're creating a worksheet, the thrust of the document is the numbers, not the look of the worksheet. Make sure that your graphic elements don't obscure the information that you're trying to convey.

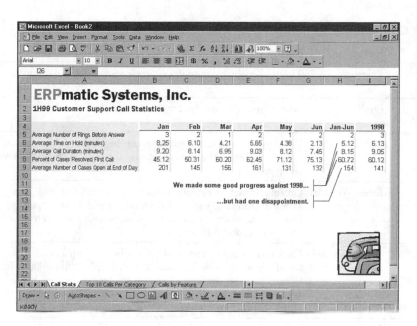

Figure 8.1.
Callouts, lines, and clip art, when used effectively, can make your worksheets more informative and interesting for your readers.

Table 8.1 describes each of the Drawing toolbar's tools.

TABLE 8.1. THE DRAWING TOOLBAR

Button	Name	Button Function
Draw ▾	Draw	Click this button to display a menu of commands that enable you to manipulate the placement of and relationship between your drawn objects.
	Select Objects	Use this arrow tool to click on drawn objects. Using this tool tells Excel that you're dealing with your drawn objects and not the worksheet's cell content.
	Free Rotate	Click this tool and then the object you want to rotate, and drag the object's handles in the direction you want to spin the object.
AutoShapes ▾	AutoShapes	Click this button to display a list of AutoShape categories, such as Basic Shapes and Flowchart. From these categories, choose shapes from a palette of drawing tools.
	Line	Use this tool to draw straight lines of any length. You can later format the lines to varying lengths and styles, as well as add arrowheads to make the line point to something.
	Arrow	If you know your line will be an arrow, draw one using this tool. You can later select arrowheads for one or both ends of the line.

continues

TABLE 8.1. CONTINUED

Button	Name	Button Function
	Rectangle	This tool enables you to draw simple rectangles and squares.
	Oval	Draw elliptical shapes and true circles with this tool.
	Text Box	When you need a text object that can be placed on top of your cells anywhere on the worksheet, use this tool to create the box and type the text.
	Insert WordArt	Create artistic text headlines and banners with this tool. The WordArt program, with its own toolbars and menus, opens to give you the ability to create text objects with a wide variety of color, shape, and fill options.
	Insert Clip Art	Click this button to view and insert objects from a categorized list of clip art images that were installed with Office 2000. The Office 2000 also contains extra clip art images that you can add from the CD as needed—navigate to your CD-ROM drive to access them.
	Fill Color	Choose from a palette of solid colors to fill your drawn shape.
	Line Color	Click the button to display a palette of colors that you can use to color your line, arrow, or the outline of a shape.
	Font Color	Apply a color to text box text or to text within your worksheet cells.
	Line Style	Choose from various line weights and styles for double and triple lines.
	Dash Style	If you want your line to be dashed, dotted, or a combination thereof, click this button and select a style from the palette.
	Arrow Style	Turn a simple line into an arrow or change the arrowheads on your existing arrow line. Choose from 10 styles.
	Shadow	Choose from 20 shadow settings, each with a different light source and angle. Applying a shadow gives your object depth, and it can be applied to shapes or lines.
	3D	Apply up to 20 3D effects to your shapes. Unlike a shadow, which merely repeats the object in a flat 2D state behind the original, 3D settings add sides and depth to your object, and shade the sides for a true 3D effect.

You can display the Drawing toolbar by right-clicking any existing toolbar and choosing Drawing from the list, or by choosing View, Toolbars, Drawing.

Tip #110 from

Laurie

You can turn your Drawing toolbar (or any toolbar, for that matter) into a floating toolbar by dragging it from the edge of the window onto your worksheet area. Click the left edge of the toolbar and drag the entire toolbar out onto the worksheet. After you release your mouse, the toolbar appears with its own title bar, which you can use to move the floating toolbar anywhere you want it onscreen.

When using the Drawing toolbar, keep the following concepts in mind:

- The Drawing toolbar's drawing tools (Line, Arrow, Rectangle, Oval, and all of the AutoShapes) work by clicking them and then drawing the associated shape or line.

- Each time you click and then use a drawing tool, the tool turns off as soon as the object is created. To draw another one, you must reclick the tool.

Tip #111 from

Laurie

To avoid having to reclick a drawing tool to draw another shape, double-click the drawing tool (Line, Arrow, Rectangle, Oval), and you can draw an infinite number of objects with that tool. To turn off the tool, click it again.

- Buttons with a down arrow (triangle) display a palette or menu when you click the down arrow (see Figure 8.2).

Figure 8.2.
Click the down arrow to the right of the color tools to see a palette of available colors. You also can access tools for more colors and fill effects.

- In the case of the Fill, Line, and Font Color tools, clicking the button itself will apply the color displayed on the button to the selected object. The button face changes to show any new color you select from the palette.

- The Line, Dash, and Arrow style tools display a palette although there is no triangle on/next to the button (see Figure 8.3).

- The Draw and AutoShapes buttons display a menu and submenus/palettes as opposed to performing a task or applying a format (see Figure 8.4).

Figure 8.3.
Choose a line style from the palette that appears when you click the button. The style will apply to the selected object.

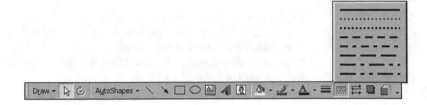

Figure 8.4.
Choose a Draw command to affect the placement of your drawn objects or their relationship to other shapes and lines.

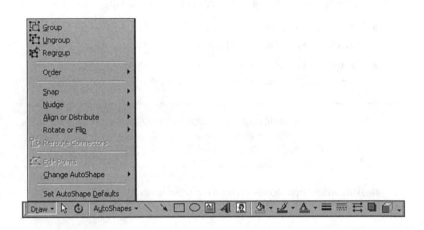

> **Caution**
>
> Drawn objects float over the worksheet content. Be careful to place them so that they don't obscure something important—they're intended to enhance your worksheet, not compete with it.

CREATING DRAWN SHAPES AND LINES

Drawing any shape or line is a simple process—click the tool and then move your mouse onto the worksheet. You'll notice, as shown in Figure 8.5, that your mouse pointer turns into a crosshair.

Crosshair mouse pointer

Figure 8.5.
The crosshair mouse pointer indicates that you're in drawing mode.

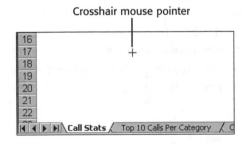

To draw the object, point, click, and drag your mouse diagonally away from your starting point. The farther you drag, the larger the object (or longer the line) becomes. The angle at which you drag will affect the dimensions of drawn shapes, determining their width and height (see Figure 8.6)

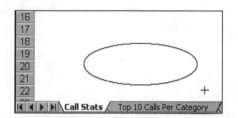

Figure 8.6.
You can see the shape's overall dimensions onscreen as you draw it.

Tip #112 from

Laurie

If you want your drawn shape to have equal width and height (to make perfect squares or circles, for example), press the Shift key as you draw the shape.

When using the Shift key as you draw a shape, be sure to release the mouse before you release the Shift key or you'll lose your shape's equal width and height.

As soon as you release the mouse, your shape appears onscreen, with handles on its sides and corners, as shown in Figure 8.7. You can use these handles to resize the shape. Handles will be discussed later in this chapter.

Default white fill

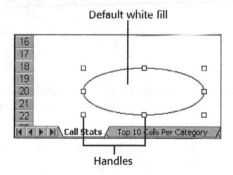

Handles

Figure 8.7.
A selected drawn object will have handles on its perimeter, enabling you to resize the object horizontally, vertically, or both.

As you draw your shapes and lines, Excel names and numbers them, and these names/ numbers appear in the Name Box at the left end of the formula bar (see Figure 8.8). You can rename these objects by selecting and replacing the automatic name with any text you desire.

Figure 8.8.
You can rename Line 13 to Average Time on Hold Reduced to make it clear what this line means and where it belongs.

Name box

Selected object

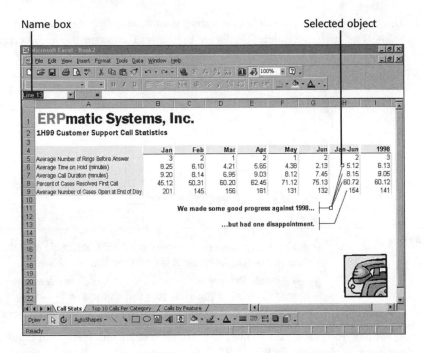

Tip #113 from

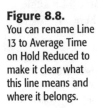

Renaming your shapes and lines makes it easier to differentiate between them. When you choose to rename them, make the name indicative of the purpose and/or placement of the object.

DRAWING RECTANGLES AND OVALS

Rectangles and ovals are the most commonly used shapes and, therefore, are represented by buttons on the main Drawing toolbar. Access other shapes, such as triangles and stars, through AutoShapes.

Because rectangles and ovals are so commonly used, you'll find many uses for them in even the simplest worksheet. Following are some of those uses:

- Place a rectangle between sections of your worksheet, acting as a visual separator. By using this technique (instead of adding color to the blank cells), you can more easily resize the rectangle to meet the needs of your changing worksheet and the size of its sections.

- Place a rectangle or oval behind your worksheet content to draw attention to the worksheet content on top. (Remember to use the Shift key while drawing a rectangle to make it a perfect square and while drawing an oval to make it a perfect circle.) Using an oval can be especially effective in this situation, as it doesn't look like you've merely colored in your cells. You'll find out more about how to do this later in this chapter.

Tip #114 from

Laurie

The Excel 2000 Drawing toolbar also gives you a quick way to create a circle or square without actually drawing the shape:

1. Click the Rectangle or Oval tool on the Drawing toolbar.

2. Click anywhere on your worksheet. A square or circle (depending on which tool you used) is inserted, with a white solid fill.

3. Continue to click and place shapes as you need them—place as many squares and/or circles as you need on the worksheet.

CREATING LINES AND ARROWS

Use the Drawing toolbar's Line and Arrow tools to add borders, underlines, directions (for flow charts or to visually link two sections of a worksheet, for example), or to connect a text box or clip art image to worksheet content to which it relates. Figure 8.9 shows an arrow pointing from one section of a worksheet to another.

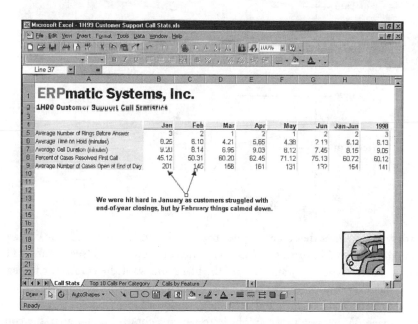

Figure 8.9.
Show direction, flow, or merely a relationship by pointing from one object to another.

You can draw lines at any angle, although pressing the Shift key as you drag and position the line will help you to place it at a 45- or 90-degree angle. After you draw a line, you can move it or resize it. You also can add arrowheads to the line at one or both ends.

Arrows have an arrowhead at the end by default. Also by default, your arrows point in the direction they were drawn. In Figure 8.9, both arrows were drawn from bottom to top, so the top end of the arrow has the arrowhead, pointing up. Although you can change the arrow's direction and arrowhead style later, it's easier to draw it in the proper direction first.

WORKING WITH AUTOSHAPES

Whether you're an artist with pen and paper or using Excel to create your art for your worksheets, you'll find that using the Drawing toolbar's AutoShapes tool will make it easier to draw polygons and other complex shapes than to create them with freehand line drawing tools or connected straight lines. There are seven AutoShapes categories, found by clicking the AutoShapes button on the Drawing toolbar:

- **Lines**. Choose one of six line types, from straight to squiggle, with or without arrowheads, as shown in Figure 8.10.

Figure 8.10.
Lines for every purpose—from straight directional lines to curved or freehand lines—are available.

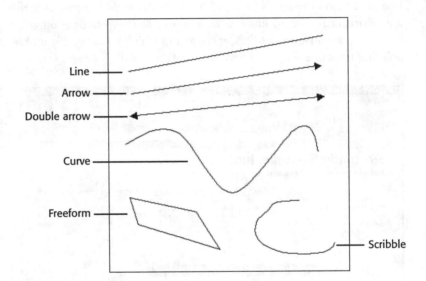

- **Connectors**. Create lines that connect one shape or line to another, with the connections highlighted by small boxes. Choose from nine connector types (see Figure 8.11). Select the connector type you want, click at the place you want the connector to begin, and drag to the place you want it to end. The connector snakes around as needed to connect the objects. You can click and drag the diamond-shaped handles to adjust a connector's shape. When you move an object to which a connector is drawn, the connector remains connected to the object, resizing itself as needed, as Figure 8.12 shows.

- **Basic Shapes**. Choose from 32 shapes, everything from triangles to hearts, from lightning bolts to crescent moons. The last seven of these shapes are a series of brackets and parentheses.

- **Block Arrows**. There are 28 arrows: straight, curved, bidirectional, and some that contain a box with an arrow melded into one shape. These are great for flow charts or any graphical depiction of a process or order of operations.

Selected connector

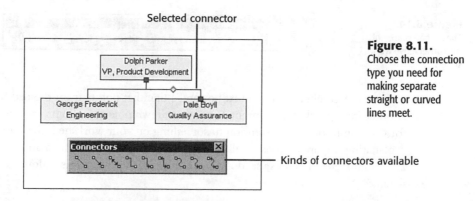

Figure 8.11.
Choose the connection type you need for making separate straight or curved lines meet.

Kinds of connectors available

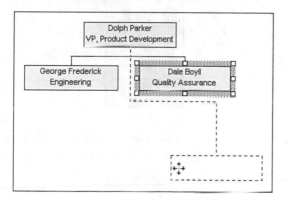

Figure 8.12.
When you move a connected object, the connector adjusts automatically.

■ **Flowchart**. If you're familiar with flowcharts and which shapes to use to indicate which point in a process, you'll find these symbols very useful (see Figure 8.13). You also can use them as simple geometric shapes.

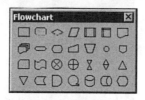

Figure 8.13.
Use these familiar flowchart shapes to describe a procedure.

Tip #115 from
Laurie

You can use connectors between shapes in your flowchart. That way, if you need to rearrange the flowchart, the connectors move with the flowchart shapes.

■ **Stars and Banners**. A total of 16 stars, sunbursts, explosions, and banner styles are available (see Figure 8.14).

Figure 8.14.
These shapes are not for conservative worksheets.

- **Callouts.** A combination of a text box and a line that points from the text box to another item (worksheet content or another drawn object), callouts are effective tools for drawing informative attention to something on your worksheet that needs further explanation. Figure 8.15 uses callouts to highlight important information. Choose from 20 callout styles. The next section, "Creating Callouts," explains callouts in more detail.

Figure 8.15.
Callouts emphasize and explain by combining text with a pointing line.

- **More AutoShapes.** Click this option to open a new window, displaying a list of 55 shapes—line drawings (see Figure 8.16). (This window is essentially the Clip Gallery window. It operates the same way.)

Figure 8.16.
Click a shape and then click the Insert Clip button that appears in the shortcut toolbar.

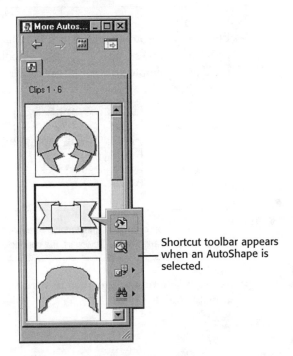

Shortcut toolbar appears when an AutoShape is selected.

After selecting the shape, follow these steps to create your AutoShape:

1. Move your mouse pointer onto the worksheet (note that the pointer has turned into a crosshair).

2. Click and hold the mouse button to establish your starting point for the shape.

Tip #116 from
Laurie

If you want your AutoShape's width to match its height, hold down the Shift key as you drag to draw the shape.

3. Drag diagonally away from your starting point, dragging until your shape is the desired height and width.

Tip #117 from
Laurie

If you're using the Shift key to achieve an object of equal height and width, be sure to release the mouse button and then the Shift key when you've completed your shape.

After drawing your shape, you can resize and move it as needed. If you need to delete the shape, click once on the shape to select it, and press the Delete key.

CREATING CALLOUTS

A *callout* is a combination of a drawn box and a line that points from the box to another object—part of the worksheet or even another drawn object. The box in the callout is a *text box*, a rectangle with an active cursor. You can type as much or as little text as you need into the text box, and you can move the callout as a unit, or move the box and line independently. Figure 8.17 shows a callout in a worksheet, used to explain data within the worksheet cells.

To create a callout, follow these steps:

1. Display the worksheet onto which you want to place the callout.

2. Click the AutoShapes button, and choose Callouts from the pop-up menu.

3. Choose a callout style by clicking a callout in the palette. When you move your mouse onto the worksheet, it changes to a crosshair.

4. Starting next to the item to which the callout points, drag diagonally until the callout is the appropriate size (see Figure 8.18).

5. As soon as a cursor appears in the text box portion of the callout, type your callout text (see Figure 8.19).

Figure 8.17.
Make your parenthetical statements or explanations with a callout.

Line component of callout that points to item

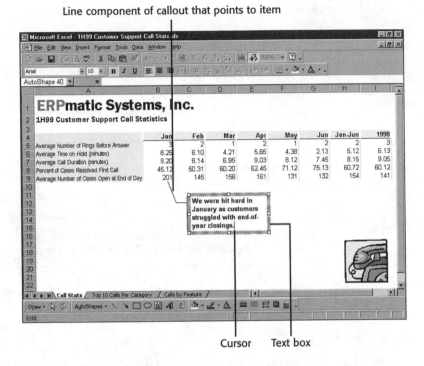

Cursor   Text box

Figure 8.18.
You can move and resize your callout after creating it, but try to get the approximate size and position from the start through careful dragging.

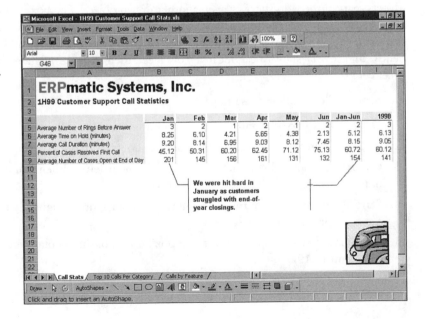

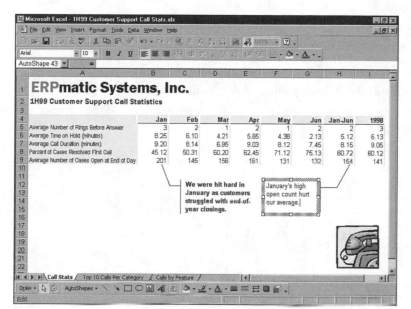

Figure 8.19.
The callout box text
you type will follow
your worksheet
defaults for font and
size. The installed
default is Arial, 10
points. However, you
can format callout text
as you like.

Note

When typing callout text, there is no need to watch the right margin within the text box. Type as you would in a table cell—the sides of the box will confine the text, causing it to wrap as you type. You need only press Enter if you want to create a new paragraph or type a list within the callout text box.

USING THE AUTOSHAPES LINE TOOLS

The AutoShapes Lines palette contains three straight-line tools and three curved-line tools. The first three, for drawing simple straight lines, single-headed arrows, and double-headed arrows, are drawn by clicking and dragging the mouse to create a line, as discussed earlier in this chapter. The last three enable you to draw with the mouse, creating s-curves, freeform shapes, and scribbled lines.

You'll use these tools to create lines that wrap around sections of your worksheet or to create shapes that can't be found through the other AutoShapes categories.

Tip #118 from

Laurie

Using the Freeform and Scribble tools requires some mouse control, so don't be surprised if your first attempts to use it don't result in the precision you're looking for.

DRAWING CURVES WITH THE AUTOSHAPE LINES TOOL

To create a line with the Curve tool, follow these steps:

1. Click the Curve tool, and move your mouse onto the worksheet.

2. Click to create your starting point, and drag to draw a line.

3. Click again to make the line curve, moving your mouse to adjust the curve of the line (see Figure 8.20).

Figure 8.20.
Your second click creates the curve, and the depth of the curve is determined by the distance you drag your mouse.

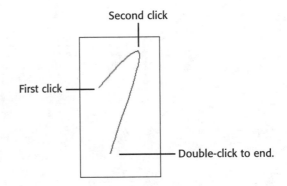

4. For a simple curve, double-click to end the line.

5. To continue creating waves or curves on a continued line, continue to click and move the mouse, creating curves, waves, or loops as required.

6. Double-click to stop the line and turn off the tool.

> **Note**
>
> Simple S-curves or arcs are the most common use of the Curve tool in an Excel environment. Typical worksheets don't require use of wavy or excessively curved lines. For an exception to this rule, see the section "Creating Visual Effects and Professional Pointing Devices" in Chapter 24, "Professional Formatting Techniques."

DRAWING FREEFORM SHAPES

While elaborate or wild shapes don't normally have a place in an Excel worksheet, you may need to create a shape that isn't found within the other AutoShape categories. You can use the Freeform tool in one of two ways:

- Click and drag the mouse, keeping the mouse button depressed as you draw a freeform shape with no straight sides. Come back to your starting point to create a closed shape (see Figure 8.21). By default, closed shapes are given a solid white fill.

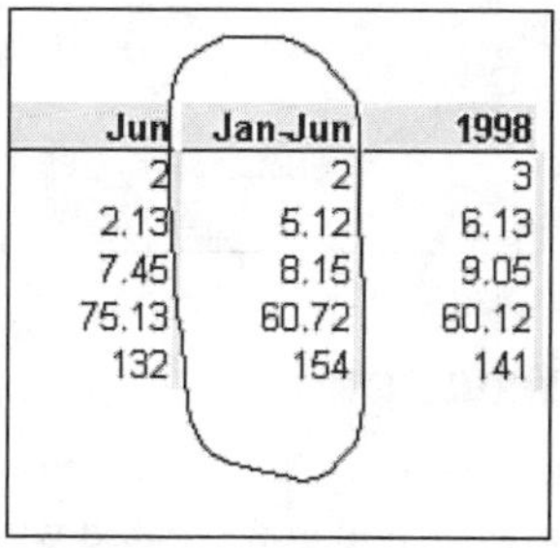

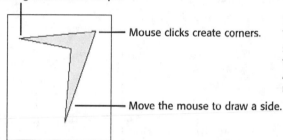

Figure 8.21.
Draw amoeba-like
shapes with the
Freeform tool.

- Create a polygon with straight sides by clicking and moving the mouse. Click again to create a corner, and move the mouse again to create a second side. Continue this process until you return to your starting point, creating a closed shape that can be filled with color (see Figure 8.22).

Finish at the beginning to close the shape.

Mouse clicks create corners.

Move the mouse to draw a side.

Figure 8.22.
You can draw closed
shapes when one of
the built-in closed
AutoShapes doesn't
meet your need.

Tip #119 from

By default, all closed shapes will be filled with white. Choose No Fill from the Fill Color button on the Drawing toolbar to keep your drawn shape from obscuring worksheet content.

 If the object you draw prints across two pages, see "Drawn Object Prints Across Two Pages" in the Troubleshooting section at the end of this chapter.

USING THE SCRIBBLE TOOL

The Scribble tool enables you to draw on your worksheet. Using this tool requires great mouse control in order to create legible or recognizable shapes. Unlike the Freeform tool, you need not close the shape—your scribbles can be curved or jagged lines (see Figure 8.23). To use the Scribble tool, click it, click and hold the mouse button on the worksheet, and drag to create your shape.

Figure 8.23.
Draw on your work-
sheet with the
Scribble tool.

EDITING THE POINTS OF A SCRIBBLE, CURVE, OR FREEFORM SHAPE

It's challenging to draw good freehand shapes with the mouse. Fortunately, Excel includes the Edit Points command. It changes a line or polygon created with the Scribble, Curve, or Freeform Shape to a series of points you can drag to reshape the object. To adjust the shape of a freehand line or freeform polygon:

1. Select the object.
2. Choose Draw, Edit Points. The object's points become visible.
3. Drag the points to adjust the shape.

Figure 8.24 shows a freeform shape with its points visible.

Figure 8.24.
This freeform shape
has four points.

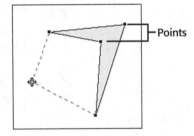

—Points

There are four kinds of points:

- **Auto Points** are the simplest kind of point. All you can do with an Auto Point is drag it to a new location. Points in curves are Auto Points by default. You can change any point to an Auto Point by right-clicking it and choosing AutoPoint from the pop-up menu.

- **Straight Points** are never created automatically; you must convert a point to a Straight Point by right-clicking it and choosing Straight Point from the pop-up menu. The line through which a straight point runs is smoothly and equally curved.

- **Smooth Points** are never created automatically; you must convert a point to a Smooth Point by right-clicking it and choosing Smooth Point from the pop-up menu. A smooth point creates gradual transitions along the line that flows through it.

- **Corner Points** create abrupt transitions in lines that flow through them. The Scribble tool always creates Corner Points. You can change any point to a Corner Point by right-clicking it and choosing CornerPoint from the pop-up menu.

All points but Auto Points display *vertex handles* when you select them. Click and drag a vertex handle to adjust the way the line flows through the point. Figure 8.25 shows the same shape as Figure 8.24, except the upper-right point has been converted to a Smooth Point and one of its vertex handles is being adjusted.

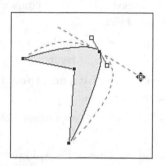

Figure 8.25.
Dragging a point's vertex handle lets you make fine adjustments to a shape.

ORDERING, GROUPING, MOVING, AND RESIZING DRAWN OBJECTS

After you draw lines and shapes on your worksheet, you'll probably want to move them around a bit so they line up just right, adjust their size, and even resolve unintended overlap of objects. Several techniques will help you.

CHANGING THE ORDER OF OVERLAPPING DRAWN OBJECTS

The objects you draw, if overlapping, will stack in the order in which they were drawn—first drawn on the bottom, last drawn on the top. Because you may not draw things in the order you need them to appear in overlapped groupings, you may want to change this order.

To restack your overlapping objects, follow these steps:

1. Click on the object that you want to move up or down in the stack of drawn objects. Figure 8.26 shows an object that is partially obscured by another object.

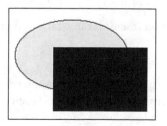

Figure 8.26.
If a buried object belongs on top, change its order in the stack.

2. Choose D_raw, O_rder, and select the command that matches your needs—moving the item to the very top or bottom, or moving it up or down one layer in the stack. Your choices are

- Bring to Fron_t. Takes the object from wherever it is in the stack and puts it on top of all other objects on the worksheet. This, of course, only affects items on top of which you later place the object.

- Send to Bac_k. Places the selected object on the bottom layer of all drawn objects, but it remains above the worksheet content layer.

- Bring _Forward. To move items one layer at a time (from fourth in the stack to second, for example), choose this command.

- Send _Backward. Move the selected object down toward the bottom, one layer at a time.

3. The object remains selected in its new stacking order, as Figure 8.27 shows. If moving one layer at a time (Bring _Forward or Send _Backward), you can repeat the command until the object is where it belongs.

Figure 8.27.
Selecting the oval and choosing D_raw, Order, Bring _Forward places it on top of the rectangle.

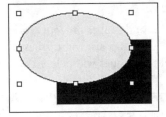

GROUPING DRAWN SHAPES AND LINES

After you've painstakingly aligned two or more objects in relation to one another, you don't want to accidentally move one of the objects out of place, changing its relative position. Or, perhaps you want to move the objects, but you want to move them as a group, so their relative positions remain unchanged. To accomplish this, the objects must be selected and grouped, so that Excel sees them as one unit.

To group two or more drawn shapes and/or lines on your worksheet, follow these steps:

1. Click on the first item in your group (the order in which you click the items is immaterial).

2. Press and hold the Shift key.

3. One at a time (with the Shift key still pressed), click on the other objects you want to include in the group. When the entire group of objects is selected (handles appear around each one of them, as shown in Figure 8.28), choose D_raw, _Group.

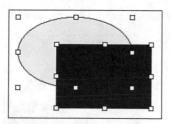

Figure 8.28.
As you build your group, handles appear on or around each selected item.

Once grouped, the entire group of items has one set of handles, as shown in Figure 8.29.

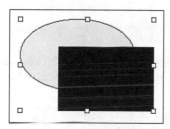

Figure 8.29.
One set of eight handles surrounds the entire group, even if the items in the group are scattered around a large area of the worksheet.

> **Note**
>
> Grouping is not the same as selecting multiple items for quick recoloring or resizing. Grouped objects remain a unit, even after you deselect them. If you click again on any item in the group, the entire group is selected.

You can ungroup your items at any time by selecting the group (click on any one item in the group) and choosing Draw, Ungroup. Use the Regroup command to put any one selected item back in a group with the items with which it was formerly grouped.

MOVING AND RESIZING DRAWN SHAPES AND LINES

Rarely are the shapes and lines you draw perfect from the start—you'll probably need to tweak them a bit, making them bigger, smaller, taller, wider, and/or moving them to a new spot on the worksheet.

Before you make any changes to the shapes and lines you've drawn, you must select them by clicking once on the object. You know an object is selected when you see handles appear on its perimeter, as shown in Figure 8.30.

Although a circle/oval doesn't technically have corners, it has corner handles.

Figure 8.30.
Handles appear on all four corners and in the middle of each side.

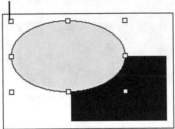

MOVING A SHAPE OR LINE

After you select a shape or line, follow these steps to move it:

1. Point anywhere on the shape or line (not on a handle). The pointer changes into a four-headed arrow (see Figure 8.31).

Figure 8.31.
Watch for the mouse pointer to turn into a four-headed arrow, indicating that you're in move mode.

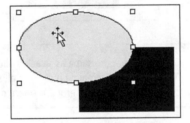

2. Click the mouse and drag the object to a new location. A dashed-bordered "ghost" of the object will follow your mouse movements, as shown in Figure 8.32.

Figure 8.32.
The object remains in its original location until you release the mouse at the desired new location.

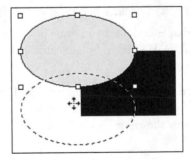

3. When the object is where you want it to be placed, release the mouse button.

RESIZING A SHAPE OR LINE

Making a shape larger or smaller or adjusting the length of a line requires dragging the object's handles. With regard to shapes, the handle you choose to drag from will determine the manner in which the shape is resized (see Figure 8.33).

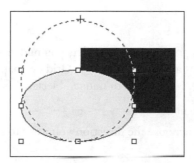

Figure 8.33.
For very specific sizing needs, you may need to drag from more than one handle, adjusting width first, and then height to achieve a shape that's "just right."

- Drag from a top or bottom side handle to make an object taller or shorter.
- Drag from a left or right side handle to make an object wider or narrower.
- Drag from a corner handle to adjust the width and height of your object at the same time.
- Dragging away from the center of an object makes it bigger. Dragging toward the center makes it smaller.

Note

If you want to maintain the object's current width-height proportions (also known as its *aspect ratio*), press and hold the Shift key as you resize. Release the mouse button first, and then release the Shift key when you have achieved the size you want.

Resizing lines and arrows requires dragging one of the two handles that appear when the line/arrow is selected. To make the line longer, drag away from the center of the line. To make the line shorter, drag toward the line's current center. Figure 8.34 shows a line being made longer, increasing its reach.

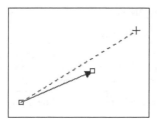

Figure 8.34.
Drag one of your line's handles to a point farther away from its current position, making the line longer.

Note

You can spin an arrow to make it point in another direction. Click and drag the handle on the end that has an arrowhead, and drag clockwise (or counterclockwise) until the arrow points in the desired direction. This is especially helpful when the object to which the arrow points has been moved.

NUDGING DRAWN OBJECTS INTO PLACE

If you're especially precise, you'll appreciate that Excel lets you nudge any object into place, one pixel at a time (or one grid point at a time, if Snap to Grid or Snap to Shape is turned on, as described in the next section). Here's how to nudge objects:

1. Select the object(s) you want to nudge.
2. Choose Draw, Nudge, and then choose the direction you want to nudge the object(s): Up, Down, Left, or Right.
3. Keep nudging until the objects are where you want them.

Tip #120 from
Laurie

If you are going to do a lot of nudging, tear off the Draw, Nudge submenu and let it float on your screen. That way, the nudge controls are always ready.

USING THE GRID AND OTHER OBJECTS TO LINE UP DRAWN OBJECTS

The intersections of the cell boundaries in your worksheet make a *grid* by which Excel can align drawn objects. You can turn on *Snap to Grid*, which lets you move and resize objects so that they always *snap* to the grid. You can also turn on *Snap to Shape*, which lets you move and resize an object so that, if another object is nearby, it snaps to the other object. To turn on Snap to Grid, choose Draw, Snap, To Grid. To turn on Snap to Shape, choose Draw, Snap, To Shape.

FLIPPING AND ROTATING DRAWN OBJECTS

You can flip and rotate drawn objects using the tear-off menu available when you choose Draw, Rotate or Flip. Table 8.2 explains the commands.

TABLE 8.2. THE ROTATE OR FLIP COMMANDS

Button	Name	Button Function
	Free Rotate	Click this tool and then the object you want to rotate, and drag the object's handles in the direction you want to spin the object. Figure 8.35 shows an object after this button was clicked.
	Rotate Left	Rotate the selected object 90 degrees counterclockwise.

Button	Name	Button Function
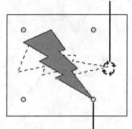	Rotate Right	Rotate the selected object 90 degrees clockwise.
	Flip Horizontal	Flip the selected object along its horizontal axis.
	Flip Vertical	Flip the selected object along its vertical axis.

Mouse pointer shows you're rotating.

Click and drag a rotate handle.

Figure 8.35.
When you choose to
free-rotate an object,
click and drag one
of the four rotation
handles.

FORMATTING DRAWN OBJECTS

After you've created a shape or line, you can change just about anything about it—its color, size, and relationship to the worksheet in which it resides. In addition, you can protect it from changes and specify how it will be represented on a Web page while the Web page loads.

To access these formatting tools in one dialog box, select the object (a shape or line), and choose Format, AutoShape. The Format AutoShape dialog box opens, as shown in Figure 8.36.

The dialog box is divided into the following five tabs:

- **Colors and Lines**. Choose the Fill and Line (outline) color for shapes, or just apply a Line format to lines and arrows. The same line and arrow styles you access through the Drawing toolbar are available here.

Note

To let anything that appears behind your shape—cell content or other shapes—show through the shape, click the Semitransparent option in the Format AutoShape dialog box. Found in the Colors and Lines tab, the option makes the object slightly see-through, as Figure 8.37 illustrates.

Figure 8.36.
The Format AutoShape dialog box offers one place to find many tools for manipulating your shapes and lines.

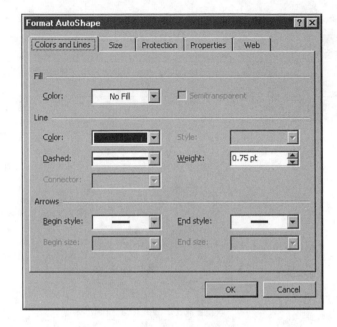

Figure 8.37.
The rectangle shows through the oval because the Semi-transparent option was set for the oval.

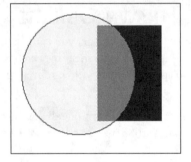

- **Size**. Adjust the Height, Width, and Rotation of your shape or line, as well as its scale (see Figure 8.38). You can increase your object's size by any percentage; numbers lower than 100% reduce it and greater than 100% make it larger.

Tip #121 from
Laurie

Click the Lock Aspect Ratio option to ensure that when you increase the Height, the Width adjusts to keep the object's current proportions.

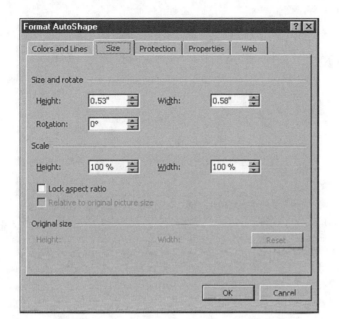

Figure 8.38.
More exact than the mouse, this dialog box can be used to enter precise measurements for your AutoShape.

Note

You also can use the Free Rotate tool to adjust the rotation of your AutoShape with the mouse. Click the shape/line and then the Free Rotate tool. Drag the green handles in a clockwise or counterclockwise direction.

- **Protection**. If your worksheet is protected, you can lock your selected shape, preventing it from being moved, resized, or in any way reformatted (see Figure 8.39). To protect your worksheet, choose Tools, Protect Sheet.

- **Properties**. This tab lets you control how Excel moves and sizes objects as you adjust cells (see Figure 8.40). Click the option that makes sense for your intended or potential worksheet modifications. Also, check or uncheck the Print object check box to control whether the object appears when you print the worksheet.

- **Web**. If you will publish your worksheet as a Web page, type the text that you want to appear in place of the AutoShape on your Web page (see Figure 8.41). This text will appear as the page loads through your browser, or in the event that the AutoShape is missing or the user has images turned off in the browser.

APPLYING SOLID COLORS AND FILL EFFECTS

When you need only apply a fill color to your shape, it may be easier to use the Fill Color tool on the Drawing toolbar. With your shape selected, click the triangle to the right of the Fill Color tool, and choose from a large palette of colors (see Figure 8.42).

Figure 8.39.
Click the Locked option to protect your selected AutoShape from inadvertent changes or deletion.

Figure 8.40.
Leaving the default option (Move and Size with Cells) turned on will save your moving and resizing your AutoShape when your worksheet is reformatted.

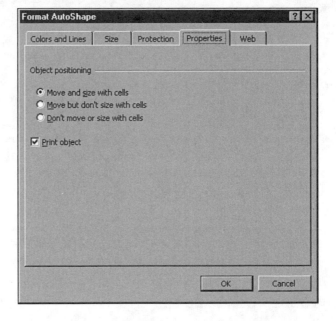

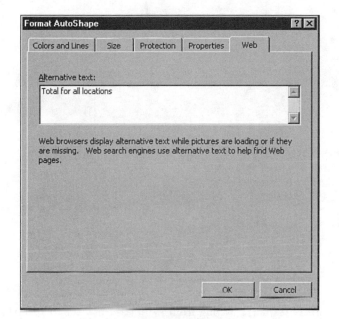

Figure 8.41.
If your worksheet will be part of a Web page, you'll want to add text to represent your AutoShape while the page loads onscreen.

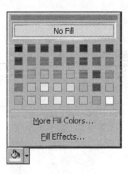

Figure 8.42.
Choose a solid color that will complement other colors you're using in the worksheet.

Not only does this tool give you quick access to a spectrum of solid colors with which to fill your AutoShape, it gives you access to a variety of fill effects, such as the following:

- **Gradient.** Choose One or Two Colors, or from a series of Preset gradient effects (see Figure 8.43). Apply a Shading Style and choose from four Variants to customize the way the gradient is applied to your shape.

Figure 8.43.
Apply a gradient when a subtle shading effect is desired.

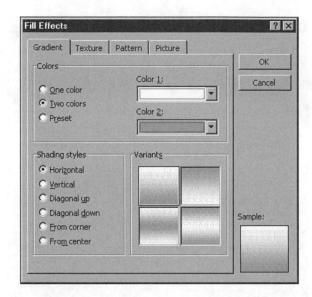

- **Texture**. Choose from 24 textures, ranging from White Marble to Paper Bag (see Figure 8.44). Select a texture that matches the tone of your worksheet, and that won't overwhelm your worksheet content or other drawn shapes.

Figure 8.44.
Textures are especially effective when your worksheet is viewed onscreen.

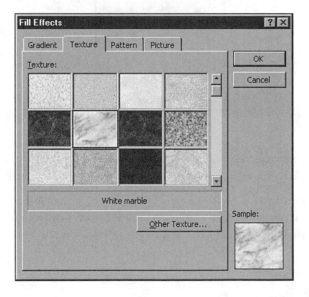

- **Pattern**. Select one of 42 two-color patterns, and choose a Foreground and Background color for it. View the Sample to be sure that you've chosen complementary colors (see Figure 8.45).

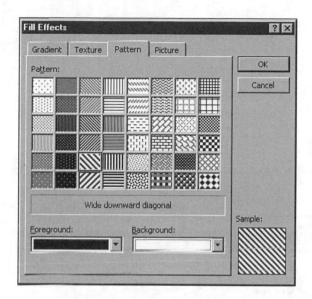

Figure 8.45.
Pattern fills are effective in black and white, especially if you don't have access to a color printer.

- **Picture.** Use any photographs or clip art images you have on your computer, by clicking the Select Picture button. Browse to the graphic file you want to work with, and see it used as the fill for your AutoShape.

> **Caution**
>
> Using Picture fills can increase your workbook file size significantly. Avoid using this type of fill effect whenever small file size is important to you in order to accommodate limited hard drive space, or when files will be transmitted via modem or on disk.

APPLYING COLOR TO LINES AND ARROWS

To quickly apply a color to your lines, arrows, or the outline of an AutoShape, click the Line Color button on the Drawing toolbar. The color displayed on the button at that time will be applied to your selected shape or line. If you want to choose from a palette of 40 colors, click the triangle to the right of the Line Color tool (see Figure 8.46).

> **Tip #122 from**
> *Laurie*
>
> To choose from an entire color wheel representing hundreds of colors, click the More Line Colors command on the Line Color tool menu.

If you want to apply a patterned line style, click the Patterned Lines command in the Line Color menu. Choose from 42 two-color patterns, and select the Foreground and Background colors for the patterns.

Figure 8.46.
Choose a color that won't clash with your other lines, colors used to fill worksheet cells, or the fill colors of your AutoShapes.

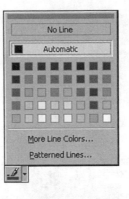

Tip #123 from
Laurie

A line pattern is a very subtle effect (if not wasted) when applied to a thin line.

APPLYING LINE AND ARROW STYLES

No matter how your line was created—with the Line, Arrow, Curve, or Scribble tools—you can change its appearance. You also can apply Excel's line-formatting tools to the outline of shapes, using dashes, dots, and/or varying line widths to change the appearance of your AutoShape.

To format your line, select it and use one or more of the following tools:

- **Line Style**. Choose from lines of varying widths, or make your line double or triple (see Figure 8.47).

Figure 8.47.
Applying a thick line style will make your drawn object stand out.

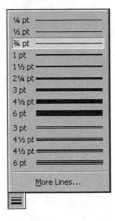

- **Dash Style**. Make a rectangle look like a coupon, or indicate a tentative relationship between sections of your worksheet with a dashed or dotted line (see Figure 8.48).

Figure 8.48.
Dashes, dots, or a combination thereof can create an interesting border or make a line less obtrusive in your worksheet.

- **Arrow Style**. Choose from arrowheads, circles, diamonds, or combinations thereof for one or both of your line's endpoints (see Figure 8.49).

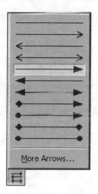

Figure 8.49.
Change a simple line into a pointer by adding an arrowhead.

WORKING WITH SHADOWS AND 3D EFFECTS

Applying a shadow or 3D effect to AutoShapes will make them appear to lift off the worksheet, whether viewed onscreen or on paper. Use them to create the look of depth and weight. Following are the options from which you can choose:

- **Shadow**. Click this tool and choose from 20 shadow styles for your selected object. The shadow style implies a light source, a direction from which light is shining on your drawn object, as Figure 8.50 shows.

Figure 8.50.
The most subtle visible shadow generally gives the best effect.

- **Shadow Settings**. Click this option to turn your shadow on or off, nudge the shadow up, down, left, or right, and choose a color for your AutoShape's shadow.

■ **3D**. This tool redraws your object as a 3D shape, with sides and a gradient fill on the top and sides (to imply a light source). Choose from 20 effects (see Figure 8.51).

Figure 8.51.
Use the 3D effect sparingly on your worksheets—its dynamic results can be overwhelming if applied too often within one sheet.

■ **3-D Settings**. Click this button to view a toolbar that enables you to adjust your 3D settings to meet your specific needs, as shown in Figure 8.52.

Figure 8.52.
Adjust the tilt, depth, angle, and light source for your 3D effect with the 3-D Settings toolbar.

CREATING TEXT BOXES

Text boxes are rectangles with text in them—the text and the box float on top of your worksheet, hopefully placed so as not to obscure worksheet content. Figure 8.53 shows a text box on a worksheet, used to display background information on a section of the worksheet's data.

To create a text box, click the Text Box tool and draw a rectangle the size you'll need for the text you'll be typing inside it. If you aren't sure how much room you need, draw the box and then resize it after you've started typing your text.

Tip #124 from

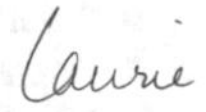

To create a quick text box on a chart, select the chart and just start typing. When you've finished typing the text, press Enter. Excel creates the text in a text box and displays it on the chart. You can resize and format the text box and text as desired.

ENTERING TEXT

As soon as you release the mouse after drawing your text box, a cursor appears in the box. You can begin typing immediately. Be sure to allow the text to wrap naturally, using the sides of the box to control the text flow. Don't press Enter unless you want to create a paragraph or type items in a list.

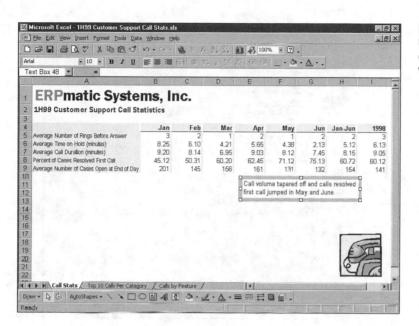

Figure 8.53.
Use your text box to
explain or support
worksheet data.

Tip #125 from

Laurie

While typing, you can use the Backspace and Delete keys to edit your text box content, as
well as use the mouse to select text for replacement/deletion.

Note

As you begin to type and your text wraps, you may notice that the text doesn't flow legibly.
If this happens, widen the box by dragging a left- or right-side handle away from the center of the box. Drag in small increments, checking your results between adjustments.

FORMATTING TEXT IN A TEXT BOX

You can format text box text with the Font and Size tools on the Formatting toolbar, or
through the Format AutoShape dialog box. To open this dialog box, select your text box,
and choose Format, Text Box. A series of eight tabs is offered, each one enabling you to
customize the way text looks and relates to the text box itself. Four of the tabs will look
familiar—you've seen them in the Format AutoShape dialog box. The three that pertain to
text box content are described here:

- **Font**. Choose a Font, Font style, Size, and Color for your text (see Figure 8.54). A
  Preview box enables you to see a sample of your formatting before you apply it to the
  text box text.

Figure 8.54.
Choose a font and size that will be legible in your text box, avoiding elaborate fonts or point sizes that are too small to read.

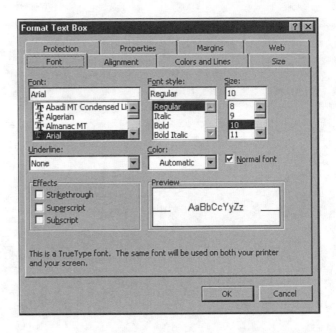

■ **Alignment.** Select a Horizontal and/or Vertical alignment for your text (see Figure 8.55). You also can choose an orientation for the text, changing the direction in which the text prints.

Figure 8.55.
If your text box contains a short phrase or single word, center it horizontally and vertically.

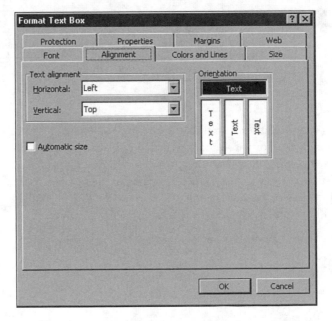

■ **Margins**. If you'd like to create some distance between the outline of your text box and its text content, increase the margins. Click the Margins tab and enter a small measurement in inches (don't type the inch marks), such as .01 for one-tenth of an inch (see Figure 8.56). Enter the measurement into the <u>L</u>eft, <u>R</u>ight, <u>T</u>op, and/or <u>B</u>ottom boxes, and click OK to apply them.

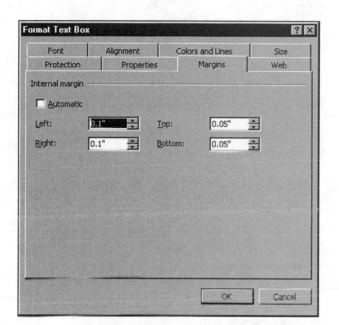

Figure 8.56.
Use very small increments to establish a margin between the text box borders and the text within the box.

Tip #126 from

Laurie

To return your text box to its original size (after resizing it), click the A<u>u</u>tomatic Size option on the Format AutoShape dialog box's Alignment tab.

USING WORDART TO CREATE ARTISTIC TEXT

Use WordArt for creating artistic text for a worksheet title, dynamic label, or simply a text-based graphic, used anywhere in your worksheet. Figure 8.57 shows a WordArt object used as a worksheet title.

Figure 8.57.
Choose a WordArt style that matches the tone of your worksheet.

WordArt ——

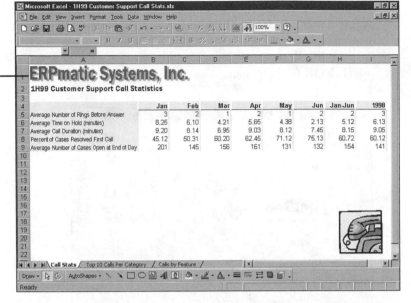

Caution

Although it's a lot of fun to experiment with WordArt's stranger options, remember that you want WordArt—any graphic, for that matter—to enhance your message, not detract from it. Use WordArt conservatively and sparingly in your worksheets.

To create WordArt, follow these steps:

1. Click the WordArt button to display the WordArt Gallery (see Figure 8.58).

Figure 8.58.
Choose a style for your WordArt object, selecting colors, shapes, and an overall look to match your worksheet.

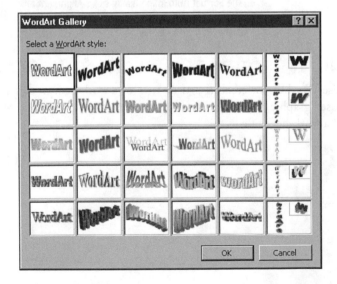

2. Choose a WordArt style by double-clicking one of the samples.

3. Type your text in the Edit WordArt Text dialog box (see Figure 8.59).

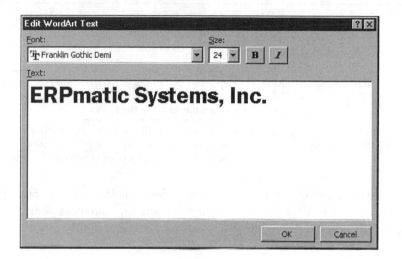

Figure 8.59.
Replace the sample text with your text—single words and short phrases work best as WordArt.

4. Choose a Font, Size, and apply Bold or Italic formatting if desired.

5. Click OK.

Your WordArt object is created and appears onscreen with handles on its perimeter. The WordArt toolbar appears, offering the tools described in Table 8.3:

TABLE 8.3.   THE WORDART TOOLBAR

Button	Name	Function
![Insert WordArt]	Insert WordArt	Creates a new WordArt object, starting the process of creating an object all over again. This button doesn't affect the selected WordArt object.
Edit Text...	Edit Text	Use this button to reopen the Edit WordArt Text dialog box. Edit the text within the dialog box and click OK to return to the object with the text edits reflected.
![Word Art Gallery]	Word Art Gallery	To choose a different WordArt style, click this button to redisplay the Gallery.
![Format WordArt]	Format WordArt	Open a four-tabbed dialog box, enabling you to adjust the fill and size of your WordArt.
![WordArt Shape]	WordArt Shape	Each WordArt style applies a shape to the text—arches, curves, and so forth. Click this button to choose a new shape for your text.
![Free Rotate]	Free Rotate	Use this button to spin your WordArt object clockwise or counterclockwise, changing its degree of rotation onscreen.

continues

TABLE 8.3. CONTINUED

Button	Name	Function
Aa	WordArt Same Letter Heights	If your text combines upper- and lowercase characters, make them all the same height with this button.
Ab bJ	WordArt Vertical Text	Change the orientation of your WordArt text to vertical, stacked text.
(icon)	WordArt Alignment	Align your WordArt text to the left, right, center, or by the Word or Letter. You also can Stretch Justify the text to spread out across the width of the object area.
AV	WordArt Character Spacing	Spread your characters out within each word in your WordArt object, or bring them close together. Choose from five spacing options, plus a custom percentage setting.

You can move and resize a WordArt image like any drawn object—point to it and drag it to a new location, or use one of its handles to make it larger or smaller. To remove your WordArt object, click it once, and press Delete. To change the angle of the WordArt text, drag the yellow adjustment handle.

INSERTING CLIP ART IMAGES

 The capacity to add clip art images from the Drawing menu is new to Office 2000. In previous versions of Office, you could insert clip art by selecting Insert, Picture, Clip Art (and you still can use this method in Office 2000), but having an Insert Clip Art button on the Drawing toolbar certainly makes this process faster and easier.

To insert clip art from the toolbar, follow these steps:

1. Click the Insert Clip Art button.
2. From the Insert Clip Art dialog box, select one of the 58 category buttons in the Pictures tab (see Figure 8.60).

Note

If you aren't sure which category to select, type keywords in the Search for Clips box and press Enter. Your keywords will be compared to stored keywords that accompany each clip art image. Images matching your keywords will be displayed.

3. An array of clip art images for the selected category appears. Click the image you want to use. (If you don't like any of the images, press Alt+Home to redisplay the categories.)
4. From the shortcut toolbar, click the Insert Clip button (see Figure 8.61).

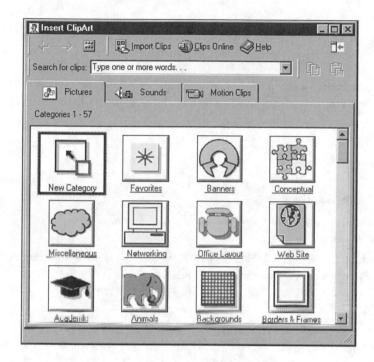

Figure 8.60.
Scroll through the
category buttons to
find one that seems
applicable to your
worksheet.

Insert Clip   Preview Clip

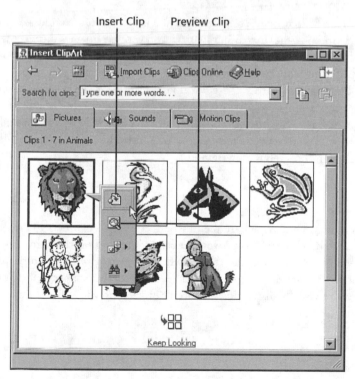

Figure 8.61.
You also can preview
your image in a full-
size preview window
by clicking the
Preview Clip button.

Note You also can right-click the image you want, and choose Insert from the shortcut menu.

After it is inserted, you can resize a clip art image by dragging its handles or move it by pointing to the image and dragging it to a new location on the worksheet. To delete a clip art image, click once on the image to select it, and then press Delete.

TROUBLESHOOTING

DRAWN OBJECT PRINTS ACROSS TWO PAGES

I drew a callout on my worksheet. But when I print the sheet, part of the callout is cut off and appears on a second page. Why?

You let the callout extend beyond a page break. It's easy to ignore the dashed lines that indicate the edge of a page's print area. Try moving and/or resizing the callout until it fits.

DRAWN OBJECTS AND EXCEL FILE SIZES

I added clip art to one of my workbooks, but it made the file so large it takes forever to email it to someone over my dialup Internet connection. Is there clip art available that doesn't take up so much disk space?

It is challenging to find "lean" clip art and photographs. The more elaborate an image, the more data it adds to the workbook file, increasing its size. You can use image-editing software to crop photographic images to reduce their size. You can also use image-editing software to convert bitmapped, nonphotographic images to use a smaller number of colors—for example, reducing a 16-bit color image to a 256-color image reaps a tremendous savings in file size. However, some images don't look right when you reduce the number of colors. Finally, the World Wide Web is rich with sites that offer clip art. You may be able to find something out there that will be attractive, effective, and economically sized. (Bear in mind that much clip art available on the Web is copyrighted.)

EXCEL IN PRACTICE

Graphic images that do more than decorate are the most effective choices when you're adding drawn shapes, lines, and clip art to your worksheets. Depending on the nature of your business, the audience for your work, and the content of your worksheet, pictures may be considered inappropriate. Figure 8.62 shows a worksheet with drawn shapes that detract from the worksheet—they're visually distracting and aren't in keeping with the serious nature of the data.

Smiley faces and starbursts are too lighthearted for many worksheets.

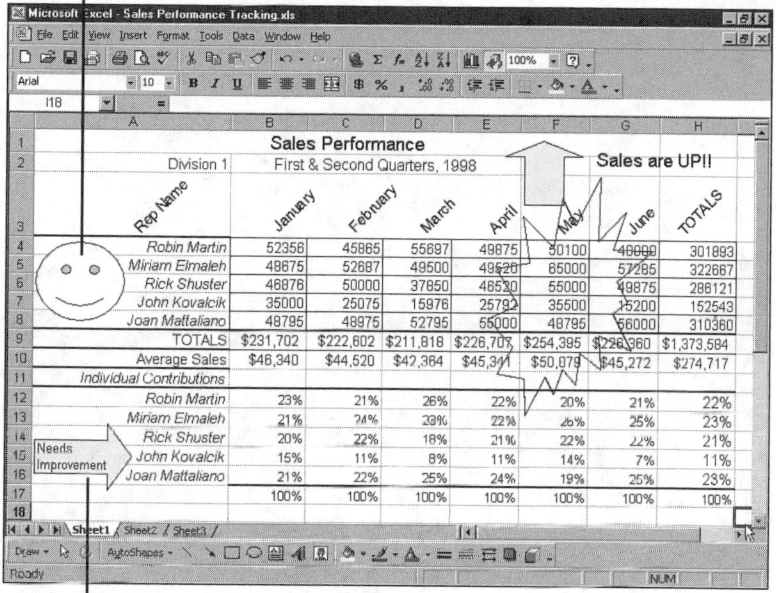

Figure 8.62.
Using fun shapes when the topic isn't fun can make your data seem less respectable, bringing your accuracy and understanding of the data into question.

Excessive ornamentation is distracting.

Take another look at Figure 8.1 at the beginning of this chapter for an example that uses drawn objects and clip art effectively. Those images enhance the worksheet and maintain the tone of the data.

CHAPTER 9

PRINTING EXCEL WORKSHEETS

In this chapter

by Laurie Ann Ulrich
laurie@limehat.com

PRINTING A WORKSHEET

While many worksheets will be viewed onscreen, the need to create tangible evidence of your spreadsheet content is undeniable. It's important to document your work as a backup, as well as for people with whom you share your work who might be without the use of or access to a computer. Some users find it easier to edit a worksheet on paper than onscreen, making notes and drawing on the worksheet to indicate changes in content, placement, and formatting. Printed worksheets also are handy for carrying to meetings, especially if you need to hand out copies to several people.

Printing your worksheet can be as simple as a click of a button, or it can be more complex, depending on what you want to print and how much control you want to have over the content and appearance of your printout. Excel gives you the tools for either approach, most of which can be accessed from within the Print dialog box.

> **Note**
>
> Charts can be printed with their worksheet content or on separate pages. For details, see the section "Printing Charts" in Chapter 13, "Building Charts with Excel."

 To print a single copy your active worksheet immediately, with standard Print options, click the Print button on the Standard toolbar.

To set Print options such as number of copies or which pages to print, choose File, Print. The Print dialog box opens, as shown in Figure 9.1.

Figure 9.1.
Use the Print dialog box to choose the printer, which pages, and the number of copies you want in your printout.

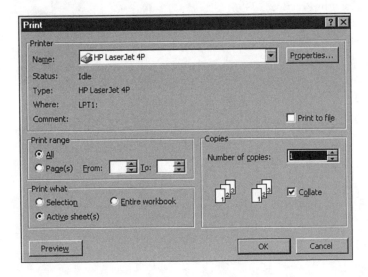

Tip #127 from

Laurie

You also can invoke the print dialog box by pressing Ctrl+P.

The Print dialog box both gives and asks for information. It is divided into the following four main sections:

- **Printer**. Set the default or currently selected printer that will generate your print job. You can choose an alternate printer as needed.

  The selected printer's properties—its settings, options, and capabilities—are available through the Properties button found in the Printer section of the Print dialog box.

- **Print Range**. Choose to print all pages of your worksheet or a select few.

- **Print What**. A powerful section of the Print dialog box, this enables you to print the Active Sheet or Sheets (if you've grouped two or more sheets) or print the Entire Workbook. You also can print just a Selection, a single cell or a range of cells from within the active sheet, or a selected chart.

- **Copies**. Choose the Number of Copies of the selected pages, sheets, or workbook you'll need. By default, Collate is turned on, and in the case of printouts consisting of two or more sets of the selected pages, you'll want to leave it on. (Collate prints a document in its entirety before it prints the next copy of a document; if you clear the Collate check box, Excel prints the selected Number of copies of each page, and you'll have to collate the separate pages into complete document sets by hand.)

Tip #128 from

Laurie

If you forgot to preview your worksheet before issuing the Print command, you can click the Preview button in the Print dialog box. To find out more about previewing before printing, see the section "Previewing the Print Job." [this chapter]

Detailed coverage of all the options found in the Print dialog box is provided throughout this chapter.

SELECTING A PRINTER

If you're on a network and have physical access through the network to more than one printer, you can choose an alternate printer before you begin your print job. If you're on a standalone computer but have more than one printer, you also can change printers before your printout is created.

To change printers, click the Name drop-down arrow in the Print dialog box to display a list of printers accessed by your computer and choose a different printer from the list, as shown in Figure 9.2.

You can click the Print to File check box in the Printer section of the Print dialog box to create a print job in the form of a computer file—the file then can be run through Windows Explorer, My Computer, or the Run command on the Start menu. By running the file, you will send the print job to the printer selected when the file was created. You needn't have Excel open to run the file.

Figure 9.2.
All your available printers are listed in the Name list.

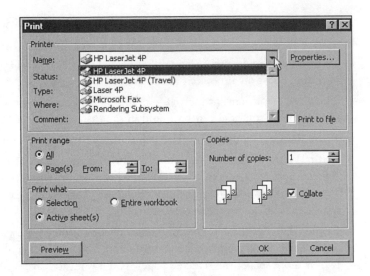

Tip #129 from

Laurie

Be sure you've previewed and set up your worksheet to print exactly the way you want it to before you print it to a file, because when you print the file later, you won't have the opportunity to preview it or change print settings.

CHOOSING THE PRINT RANGE

Don't confuse print range with print area, which will be covered later in this chapter. A *print range* refers to the pages within your worksheet that will be printed—the physical pages, determined by page breaks (both naturally occurring and forced by the user) within the worksheet content. The *print area* is a manually defined range of cells that you select and designate as a range to be divided into pages and printed. Setting a print area is done before you use the Print dialog box, and is discussed in greater detail later in this chapter.

Tip #130 from

Laurie

To quickly print a specific range of cells, select the range in the worksheet, and then click File, Print. In the Print dialog box, under Print What, click the Selection option, and then click OK.

Your print range choices are All or Page(s), the latter requiring a range (From and To) of page numbers be entered, as shown in Figure 9.3. To print a single page, enter that page number in both the From and To boxes. If you leave the default choice All selected, all the pages in defined print areas in the active worksheet will be printed; if you haven't defined print areas, everything in the active worksheet will be printed, including any empty rows and columns between ranges of data.

After you've set a Print range and any other options you want, send the file to the printer by clicking OK.

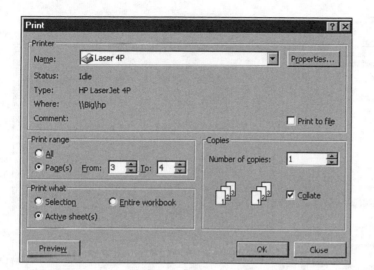

Figure 9.3.
If you don't want every page in your worksheet to print, select a range of pages by entering the From and To page numbers for your printout.

PREVIEWING THE PRINT JOB

What if you don't know how your worksheet has been broken into pages? While there are onscreen indications of page breaks, it can be hard to tell precisely where an integral section of information falls (see Figure 9.4). Excel's Print Preview feature lets you check your worksheet over before committing it to paper.

Other good reasons for previewing before printing are to check page headers and footers (make sure they're up-to-date and correct, and not overlapping the data area), and to make sure all the data is visible. Occasionally, numbers that are visible on your screen will be slightly too wide for the column on a printed page, and will print as ###### (before you waste time and paper, you can widen the column until all the numbers are displayed in Print Preview).

 To see what your printed page will look like, choose File, Print Preview, or click the Print Preview button on the Standard toolbar.

The Print Preview window shows you a small view of your first page, and a set of text buttons, as shown in Figure 9.5.

Use the Print Preview toolbar buttons to view subsequent and previous pages in your worksheet, and to alter the layout and appearance of your printout.

- **Next** and **Previous**. Use these buttons to move from page to page within your Preview.
- **Zoom**. If you need to be able to read your worksheet text, click the Zoom button to see a 100% view of your page. (Clicking the Zoom button is the same as clicking on the page with your mouse, which looks like a small magnifying glass when hovering over a page.)

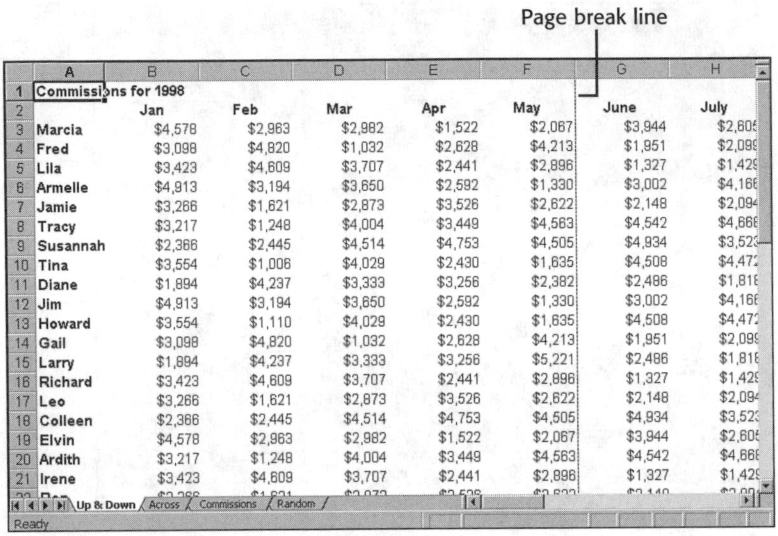

Page break line

Figure 9.4.
Look for dashed vertical and/or horizontal lines on your worksheet, indicating page breaks.

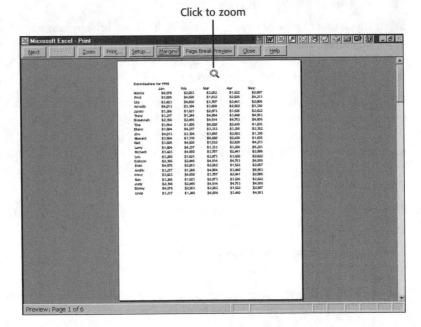

Click to zoom

Figure 9.5.
A bird's-eye view of your worksheet through Print Preview makes it easier to see what changes you need to make before printing.

- **Print**. This button opens the Print dialog box.
- **Setup**. This button opens the Page Setup dialog box (discussed later in this chapter).
- **Margins**. This button displays margin lines and column markers. You can use the mouse to quickly change margin and column widths by dragging the lines and markers.

Note

There are two sets of margins on your worksheet–the inner set are for the worksheet content, and the outer set (at the top and bottom) define the distance of your header and/or footer from the edge of the paper.

- **Page Break Preview**. To see and adjust how your page breaks were applied, click this button. This topic is covered in detail in the next section.

- **Close**. Click this button to return to your worksheet.

- **Help**. Click this button to access Print Preview-related help.

Tip #131 from

Laurie

Always look at a Preview of your worksheet before printing–you'll save paper by not printing things you don't want, and you'll save time by spotting and fixing problems before committing them to paper.

USING PAGE BREAK PREVIEW

As the data in your worksheet accumulates, it can exceed the size of a single page. The space allocated to a single page is determined by the size of your paper and the margins set within that page.

Page Break Preview gives you a big overview of how your worksheet breaks into pages. To enter Page Break Preview, choose View, Page Break Preview. Figure 9.6 shows the Page Break Preview of a four-page worksheet.

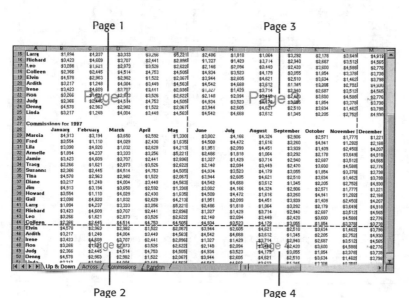

Page 1   Page 3

Page 2   Page 4

Figure 9.6.
Page Break Preview shows that this worksheet is not ready to be printed, because the pages break the lower table in half (the pages should break cleanly between the tables).

Tip #132 from

Laurie

> You also can see a Page Break Preview by clicking the Page Break Preview button in the standard Print Preview window of your worksheet.

To use Page Break Preview to adjust your page breaks, follow these steps:

1. Choose View, Page Break Preview. Page breaks appear onscreen as blue lines, running horizontally and vertically in the worksheet (see Figure 9.7).

2. Point to the page break that you want to adjust—you can adjust breaks side-to-side or up-and-down.

3. When your mouse pointer turns into a two-headed arrow, click and drag the page break borders to the desired location. Automatic page breaks (those that Excel sets using page margins) are broken blue lines; manual page breaks (those that you set) are solid blue lines.

Figure 9.7.
A nonprinting page number appears on each page of the worksheet. Broken blue lines are automatic page breaks; solid blue lines are manual page breaks.

Nonprinting page numbers

Page break border being adjusted

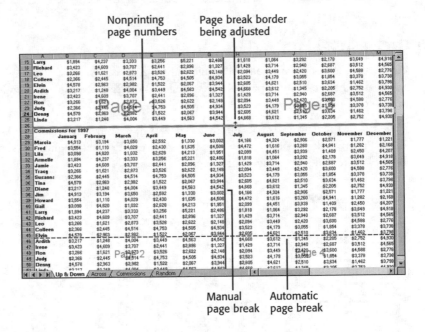

Manual page break

Automatic page break

4. Choose View, Normal to return to your worksheet.

Caution

> If you drag any of the page breaks beyond the page margins while using Page Break Preview, Excel accommodates you by shrinking the printed text so that everything you want to print on a single page will be printed on a single page. This is a quick and convenient way to adjust page *scaling*, which is covered later in this chapter.

WORKING WITH PAGE SETUP OPTIONS

After you've created and formatted your worksheet, you'll need to set up the printed pages so they'll resemble what you created onscreen. To set ground rules for the layout, content, and output of your printed pages, click File, Page Setup to open the Page Setup dialog box.

Tip #133 from

Laurie

> If you're looking at the pages in Print Preview and decide to change the page setup, click the Setup button on the Print Preview toolbar to open the Page Setup dialog box.

In the Page Setup dialog box, you'll find these four tabs:

- **Page.** Adjust the orientation, scaling, paper size, and print quality of your printed output (see Figure 9.8).

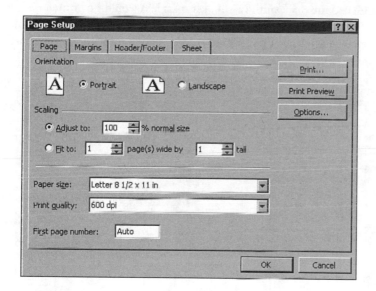

Figure 9.8.
Choose from four areas to control and adjust the appearance of your worksheet, both onscreen and on paper.

- **Margins.** While you can adjust them manually in Print Preview, this tab enables you to enter specific measurements for your margins (if you want margins identical side-to-side, it's easier to set them by measurement than by eye). You also can adjust your header and footer margins, and center the entire worksheet on the page both horizontally and vertically.

- **Header/Footer.** Click this tab to enter text or automatic entries into the header and/or footer of your worksheet printout.

- **Sheet.** This tab's settings enable you to choose a specific Print Area, set Print Titles for multiple-page worksheets, and choose the worksheet features (gridlines, column/row headings) that will be included in your printout.

Tip #134 from

Laurie

From within any of the Page Setup dialog box tabs, you can preview the changes you've made by clicking the Print Preview button.

WORKING WITH ORIENTATION

Your worksheet orientation determines how your worksheet content will be applied to the paper. By default, your worksheet orientation is 8.5"×11" and Portrait. If your worksheet, or the portion of it you want to print, is wider than it is long, you can switch to Landscape orientation by clicking the Landscape option under Orientation (shown in Figure 9.8).

A worksheet like the one in Figure 9.9, which contains commissions figures for several salespeople, will be printed most effectively in Landscape, because the worksheet's layout is wider than it is tall. If you were to print that same worksheet in Portrait orientation, any month columns that exceed the 8.5" width (within set margins) would be printed on a second page (see Figure 9.10). Worksheet content that flows unnecessarily to a subsequent page should be avoided whenever possible because readers find it annoying to shift back and forth between two pages.

Figure 9.9.
Keep an "aerial view" of your worksheet in mind when selecting an orientation.

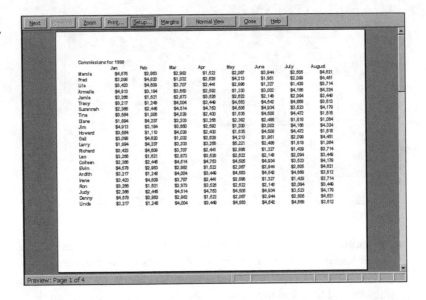

Tip #135 from

Laurie

Sometimes, a switch to Landscape orientation doesn't create enough width for your worksheet. Consider using legal-size paper for 14" of printed width, or scaling the worksheet down to fit on a single page.

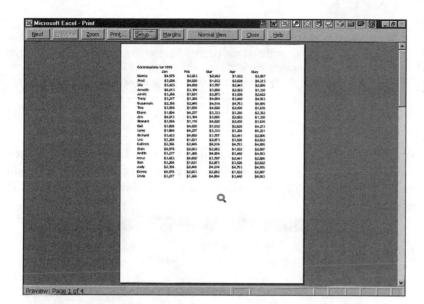

Figure 9.10.
For this data, portrait orientation is ineffective, as several of the columns don't fit on the page.

SCALING THE PRINTOUT

Another method of controlling the printed output of your worksheet is *scaling*. By scaling back, or shrinking, the size of your worksheet content—text, numbers, graphics—more of the worksheet fits on a page, thus reducing the number of pages in the entire printout. Reducing the number of pages, especially if it keeps as much of the worksheet as possible on one page, makes your printout easier to read.

To change the scale of your worksheet pages, follow these steps:

1. Choose File, Page Setup.

2. On the Page tab (shown in Figure 9.8), choose one of the following two scaling options:

   - **Adjust the percentage**. Use the spin box arrows to increase or decrease the percentage of original size or type a percentage. For example, reducing the number to 75% will give you 25% more worksheet on the page.

   - **Fit to a specific number of pages**. Your worksheet's pagination is based on the width and height of the worksheet. Choose how many pages wide and tall your printout will be. This is usually the most practical option—decide how many pages you want, and let Excel figure out the scale.

3. If you're finished setting up the page, click OK to close the Page Setup dialog box, or click Print to open the Print dialog box.

Tip #136 from

Laurie

Before adjusting your page scaling, it's a good idea to preview your worksheet with Print Preview so that you can see the current pagination, especially when using the Fit To option. Fit To causes Excel to squeeze the worksheet into the specified number of pages, potentially resulting in print so tiny that you'll want to change the settings immediately.

CHOOSING A PAPER SIZE

The default paper size for your worksheets is letter size, 8.5"×11" Excel gives you eight additional choices, including four envelope sizes, on the Page tab of the Page Setup dialog box. To display the sizes, open the Paper size drop-down list, as shown in Figure 9.11.

Figure 9.11.
Letter and legal size paper are the most common selections for users in the United States.

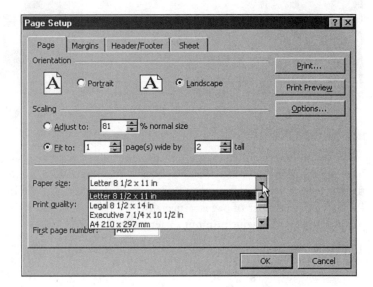

As you probably won't print your worksheets on envelopes, your main paper size options are as follows:

- Letter (8.5"×11")
- Legal (8.5"×14")
- A4 (210×297mm)
- Executive (7.25"×10.5")
- JIS B5 (182×257mm)

Note

A4 paper size is used primarily in Europe, and is slightly longer than Letter size. Be sure that the paper size you choose actually matches your paper so that none of your content is lost (prints off the page) or you fail to take advantage of the full paper size.

Bear in mind that you can adjust all the page setup options—changing orientation, scaling, and paper size—to meet the needs of your worksheet printout.

→ To find out more about changing orientation, **see** "Working with Orientation," **p. 234**

→ To find out more about scaling pages, **see** "Scaling the Printout," **p. 235**

ADJUSTING PRINT QUALITY

PART

III

CH

9

Print quality refers to the resolution of your printout and it's yet another option you can control on the Page tab. Click the Print Quality drop-down arrow to display a list of resolutions that reflect the capabilities of the printer or printers to which your computer can send output. If your printer is capable of 600 dpi (dots per inch) output, 600 and 300 (and perhaps 100 and 72, depending on your model printer) dpi output options will be offered in the list box. You cannot choose a dpi setting higher than your printer can handle.

> **Note**
>
> If you feel that your printer is capable of a higher dpi setting than is offered among your print quality settings, click the Options button in the Page Setup dialog box to view your selected printer's properties. (You can also use the Windows Control Panel to open the Printers window and check the Properties of your printer.) You may have the wrong driver set up for your printer or perhaps the settings for your printer have been changed from the default settings. Consult your printer's documentation before making any changes to the Properties settings.

> **Tip #137 from**
> *Laurie*
>
> Using a low dpi setting for draft prints can save printing time and toner or ink, with a result that's nearly as readable as a high dpi printout. When the worksheet is ready for a final print, switch the resolution to a higher resolution so it looks professional.

SETTING WORKSHEET MARGINS

The Margins tab in the Page Setup dialog box has options for setting specific numbers for your top, bottom, left, and right margins (see Figure 9.12). The default margins are 1 inch from the top and bottom, and .75 inch from the left and right.

To enter new margins for your worksheet, follow these steps:

1. Choose File, Page Setup.
2. Click the Margins tab.
3. In the Top margin box, type a new margin setting, or use the spin arrows to increase or decrease the number in .25" increments.
4. Set the Bottom, Left, and Right margins the same way.
5. Click OK to close the dialog box when you're finished, or Print to open the Print dialog box.

Figure 9.12.
While you can adjust your margins quickly from within Print Preview, this dialog box enables you to set more precise margins.

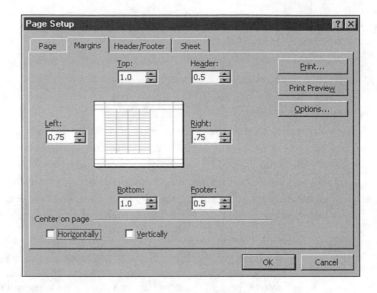

Tip #138 from

Laurie

In addition to using the spin box arrows to increase or decrease the margin settings, you can use the up and down arrows on your keyboard to adjust the number in .25″ increments.

SETTING HEADER AND FOOTER MARGINS

While in the Margins tab of the Page Setup dialog box, you'll notice that two additional spin boxes are offered. These settings let you control the placement of your header and footer content (if any) in relation to the edge of the paper. By default, these margins are set at .5 inch, just a half inch beyond the default top and bottom margins.

When setting new header and footer margins, keep your sheet margins in mind—if you've reduced your top and bottom margins to allow more worksheet content on the page, you'll have to reduce your header and footer margins, too. You need to reduce them enough so that they don't run into your sheet content, but not so much that they're off the page. Figure 9.13 shows reduced margins for the top, bottom, header, and footer on a worksheet. The header and footer margins are the topmost and bottommost margins on the page (if you point at a margin line and press the mouse button when you see the two-headed arrow, the status bar tells you at which margin you're pointing). The margins for the top and bottom of the data are the innermost margins.

To set header and footer margins, follow these steps:

1. Choose File, Page Setup, and click the Margins tab.

2. Type the Header setting you need, or use the spin box triangles to increment or decrement the measurement.

Header margin

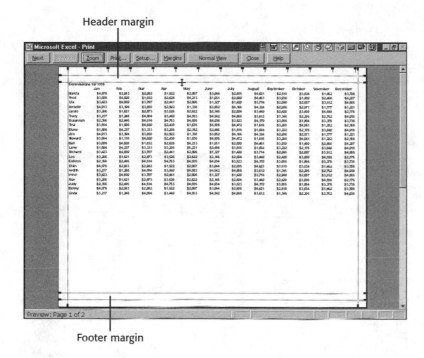

Figure 9.13.
Top and bottom margins of .5 inch require .25-inch header and footer margins.

PART

III

CH

9

Footer margin

3. Set the Footer margin the same way.

4. Click OK.

Note

Many worksheets don't require header or footer text–their content is either completely self-explanatory, or their use is informal. In any case, Excel inserts no header or footer content by default. Earlier versions inserted the worksheet name, but user requests resulted in Microsoft's deletion of that automatic insertion. The creation of header and footer content is covered later in this chapter.

→ To learn how to set header and footer text, **see** "Creating Headers and Footers," **p. 240**

CENTERING THE WORKSHEET ON THE PAGE

While technically unrelated to setting margins, the options for centering your worksheet on the page are found on the Margins tab. As shown in Figure 9.12, the Center on Page options are Horizontally or Vertically. You can select both options to place your worksheet in the actual center of the paper.

Caution

If your centering doesn't seem to work, check your margin settings. If your margins are not equal on opposite sides of the worksheet, your content will not appear centered on the page. You also may need to check your printer's settings; some printers have predefined margins on each side of the paper, and these settings may not be equal.

CREATING HEADERS AND FOOTERS

While not required for a worksheet printout, header and/or footer content can be very useful. Your worksheet already has space allocated for header and footer content, and you can use this space for information that will help your readers interpret your worksheet content. Figure 9.14 shows a worksheet with an informative header and footer.

Header

Figure 9.14.
Headers and footers are good places for company names and print dates.

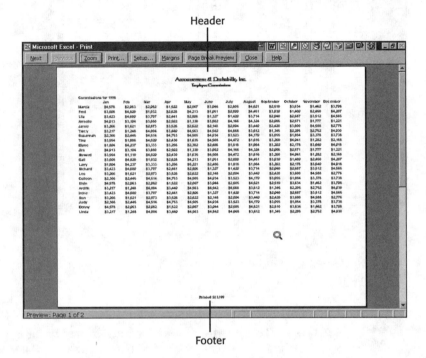

Footer

ENTERING HEADER AND FOOTER CONTENT

Headers are good places for information that identifies the document, such as a company name, department name, or report title. That kind of information can take up valuable screen space and interfere with data lists and tables if you place it on the worksheet; but, in a header, it appears where it's needed (on printed pages) and stays out of your way when you work with the data.

Footers are efficient places for automatic dates, times, and pages numbers. Automatic dates and times always print the date and time when the report was printed, so you know whether it's current, and page numbers tell you whether you've got the entire report. Like headers, footers place the information where it's needed (on the printed page) and out of your worksheet space.

Header and footer content can be totally automated. By clicking preset buttons, you can place the filename, worksheet name, current date, current time, page number, and total number of pages in the header or footer. Automated information is always correct and current, no matter what changes you make in the worksheet, and you can format it to be as elegant or mundane as you want.

To create header and/or footer content, follow these steps:

1. Choose File, Page Setup.
2. Click the Header/Footer tab, as shown in Figure 9.15.

Built-in headers   Header preview

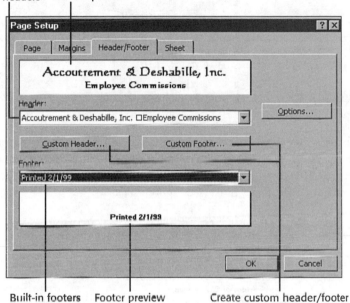

Built-in footers   Footer preview   Create custom header/footer

Figure 9.15.
You can choose built-in headers and footers, or create your own.

3. Choose from several built-in headers and footers in the Header and Footer drop-down lists, or follow steps 4–7 to create custom, formatted headers and footers.
4. Click the Custom Header button to open the Header dialog box, as shown in Figure 9.16.

Tip #139 from
Laurie

The ampersand is a field code character, and won't appear in your header/footer text. To include an ampersand (like the one in Figure 9.16), type two ampersands.

5. Each of the three boxes represents a section of the header. Type your text and use the field buttons to create custom header content.
6. Click OK.
7. Back in the Page Setup dialog box, click the Custom Footer button, and repeat steps 5 and 6 if you want to create a custom footer.
8. Click OK to close the Page Setup dialog box.

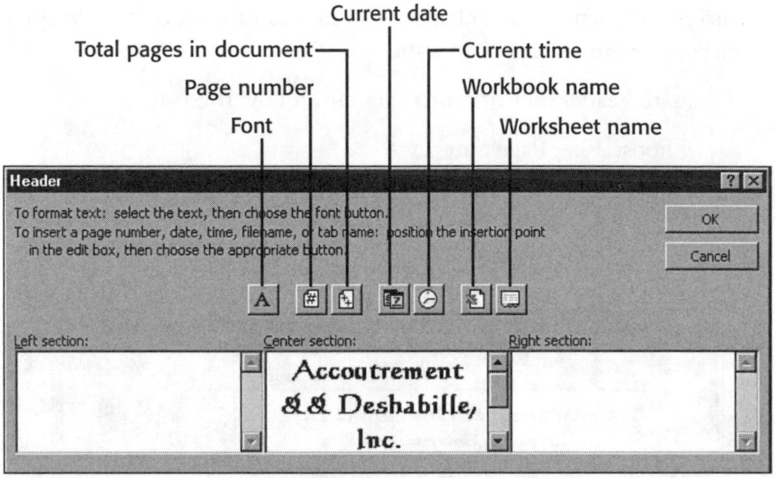

Figure 9.16.
Type your header text and/or click the field buttons to insert automatic content such as page numbers or the date.

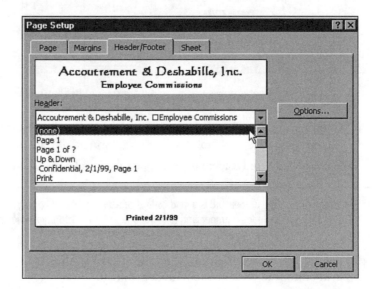

Your header and/or footer will appear whenever you print that worksheet, but only for that worksheet. If your header or footer is tall, you'll need to reset page margins so it doesn't overlap the worksheet area. If you want to delete the header or footer completely, click (none) in the He_a_der or _F_ooter drop-down list (see Figure 9.17).

Figure 9.17.
To delete your header and/or footer completely, choose (none) from the built-in He_a_der and _F_ooter lists.

INSERTING HEADER AND FOOTER FIELDS

Some of the automatic information that you may want to add to your header and footer is available through buttons in the Custom Header and Footer dialog boxes (shown in Figure 19.16). The following table describes each button.

TABLE 9.1.   HEADER AND FOOTER FIELD BUTTONS

Button	Name	Code	Function
A	Font		Opens a Font dialog box, from which you can format selected characters in the header or footer.
#	Page Number	&[Page]	Inserts the correct page number on each page of your printout.
	Total Pages	&[Pages]	Inserts the total number of pages in your printout.
	Date	&[Date]	Inserts the current date at the time of printing.
	Time	&[Time]	Inserts the current time at printing. This is especially useful in worksheets that are undergoing changes and updates on a daily basis—the time will help you be sure you have the most current copy.
	File Name	&[File]	Inserts the filename. If the file hasn't been saved, the default Book number will be inserted instead. If you subsequently save the file, the new filename will replace the default name.
	Sheet Name	&[Tab]	Inserts the sheet name. This is useful if you've named your worksheets.

Note

Use the Total Pages field button as an accompaniment to the Pages button. For example, type the word **Page**, and then click the Page Number button. Then type a space, type **of**, type another space, and then click the Total pages button. Your result looks like `Page 3 of 6`. This helps readers keep the pages in order and know immediately whether they're missing a page.

Caution

If it's important that a particular date be displayed in your header or footer, type the date rather than using the Date button. The Date button inserts the current date, which changes each time you open and print the file on a new date; but a date you type will remain the same, regardless of the date on which you print the file.

If you are inserting the current date or time, you are relying on your computer's system date and/or time (so keep in mind that your system clock needs to be correct).

Tip #140 from

Laurie

You can type the automatic field codes yourself, if you want to, but the buttons are faster and foolproof.

WORKING WITH SHEET SETTINGS

The Sheet tab, shown in Figure 9.18, in the Page Setup dialog box gives you more control over what appears on your printout. The dialog box is divided into the following main areas:

- **Print Area**. Click the Collapse Dialog button to reduce the dialog box, enabling you to drag through a range of cells in your worksheet, selecting them as your print area. This is not the fastest way to set print areas, but if the Page Setup dialog box is already open, you can set and change print areas here.

- **Print Titles**. If your data requires multiple printed pages, you can end up without labels to identify the columns and rows in your pages; setting print titles ensures that all the data in the printed pages is identified.

- **Print**. Choose which elements of your worksheet to print or not print (Gridlines, Row and Column Headings, and Comments), and how your printout will be processed in terms of color (Black and White, Draft Quality).

- **Page Order**. Choose the direction Excel will take in paginating your worksheet.

Figure 9.18.
You can set print areas in the Page Setup dialog box.

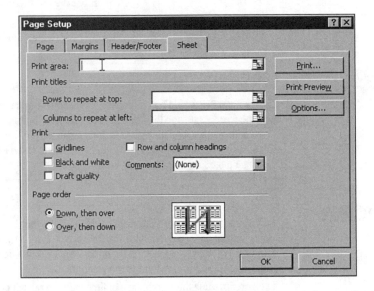

Tip #141 from
Laurie

You can move from tab to tab in any dialog box by pressing Ctrl+Tab or Ctrl+Shift+Tab.

SELECTING A PRINT AREA

If you don't want to print the entire worksheet, you need to set a print area. There are three ways to do this:

- Select a range of cells and choose File, Print Area, Set Print Area. The selected range becomes your print area. To set multiple print areas, select the first range, then press

Ctrl while you select the remaining ranges, and then choose File, Print Area, Set Print Area. Each of the print areas will be printed on a separate page, and they'll all print the worksheet's header and footer.

- To print a specific range quickly without setting a more permanent print area, select the range to print, then click File, Print, and then choose Selection from the Print What section of the Print dialog box.

- Click File, Page Setup. In the Sheet tab, click in the Print Area box, and drag to select a range of cells (use the Collapse Dialog button if the box is in the way). To select multiple print ranges, you can type a comma between each print range (see Figure 9.19), or press Ctrl while selecting additional print ranges.

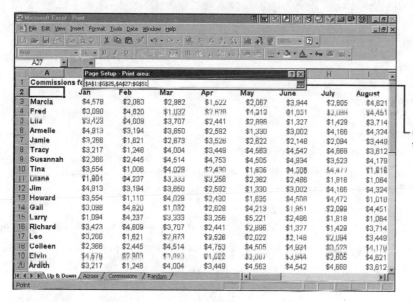

Figure 9.19.
Select multiple print areas by typing a comma between each range.

Click to expand the dialog box.

PRINTING TITLES AND ROW/COLUMN LABELS

If your worksheet is very large, some of your printed pages are not going to have the identifying row and column labels that a reader needs. For example, in the worksheet in Figure 9.20, page 1 shows both the month and employee name labels; for the rest of the pages, the data is meaningless. The solution is to set row and/or column labels as *print titles*, so that the data on every page is adequately identified.

> **Note**
>
> Print titles are not a replacement for headers and footers. A header or footer gets printed identically on every page of the document, but print titles print the row or column that corresponds to the displayed data on each page. You cannot use print titles to print identical information on each page.

Figure 9.20.
Only page 1 has all
the identifying labels
it needs; the rest
of the pages need
column and/or
row labels.

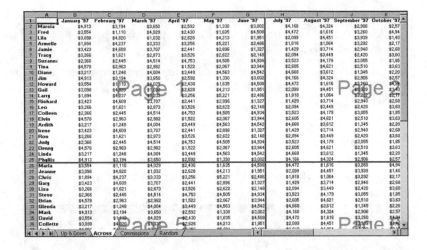

To set print titles, follow these steps:

1. Choose File, Page Setup.

2. Click the Sheet tab.

3. Under Print Titles, click in the Rows to Repeat at Top box.

4. In the worksheet, click or drag the row selectors for the rows that contain the column labels. These rows are printed at the top of each page's data.

5. Click in the Columns to Repeat at Left box.

6. In the worksheet, click or drag the column selectors for the columns that contain the row labels. These columns are printed at the left side of each page's data.

7. Click OK to close the dialog box, or Print Preview to see the results.

Tip #142 from

Laurie

Don't include the print title rows and columns in your print area, because, if you do, they'll be printed twice.

CHOOSING ELEMENTS TO PRINT

By default, your worksheet will print without gridlines. For many worksheets, this makes the data hard to read, especially if the worksheet is wide and the reader's eye must follow a row of data from left to right. If you don't want to format your data with borders (which look more professional but take more time), you can print the worksheet gridlines instead.

To print your worksheet gridlines (among other options), follow these steps:

1. Choose File, Page Setup.

2. Click the Sheet tab.

3. In the Print section of the dialog box, click to mark the check boxes next to <u>G</u>ridlines or Row and Co<u>l</u>umn Headings. If you want to print worksheet comments, choose how you want them printed.

Note

Comments are parenthetical references that you create and assign to a cell or range of cells. If you need to, you can choose to print them with your worksheet, choosing to have them appear at the end of the sheet or within the sheet, with the cells to which they refer.

PART
III
CH
9

4. Choose your color and print quality options (<u>B</u>lack and White or Draft <u>Q</u>uality).
5. Click OK.

Note

Use the Draft <u>Q</u>uality option if you want to create a quick printout that omits your graphic content. Use Draft quality for "rough" drafts or copies of your worksheet that will be edited. When you're ready to print a final copy that includes the graphic content, turn this option off.

➜ To find out how to create a worksheet comment, **see** "Using Comments to Explain Cell Content," **p. 111**

DETERMINING PRINT ORDER

Use the Page order option buttons at the bottom of the Sheet tab to determine print order. Excel's default print order is down, then over. This order numbers multiple worksheet pages down the left side first, and then up to the top and down again (as shown in Figure 9.21). If your data looks better printed over, then down (as shown in Figure 9.22), you can switch the print order.

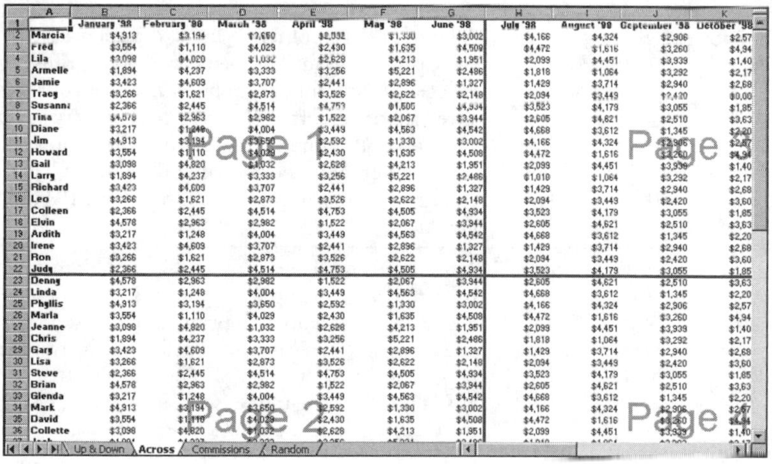

Figure 9.21.
This page order is down, then over.

Figure 9.22.
This page order is over, then down.

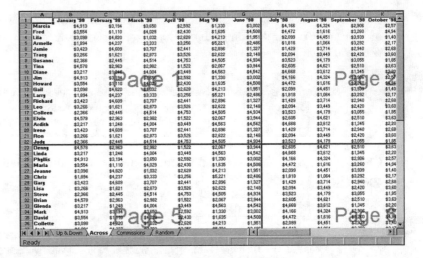

TROUBLESHOOTING

Printing problems are usually related to your printer rather than to the application through which you're printing (Excel, in this case). Some common printing problems and their potential solutions appear in Table 9.2:

TABLE 9.2. PRINTING PROBLEMS AND SOLUTIONS

Printing Problem	Possible Cause/Solution
One or two columns or rows flow onto a second or other unwanted subsequent page.	Too much data to fit on the page. Try reducing margins, or scaling the page to fit on a specific number of pages.
Printing takes too long.	A lot of graphic content—fonts, drawings, clip art. Increase the amount of memory in your printer or reduce the amount of graphic content in your worksheet, if possible. If you're on a network, try printing to a printer with more memory. If you have an ordinary laser printer, don't be surprised if it doesn't have enough memory to print even the smallest WordArt graphic.
Portions of your worksheet didn't print.	A print area has been defined that doesn't include the parts that are missing from your printout. Reselect the entire desired sections to print, and choose File, Print Area to reset. You can also redefine the print_area range name with an OFFSET formula so that the print area always fits the range (see Chapter 11, "Using Excel's Built-In Functions," to learn how).
Excel is ignoring the page breaks you set up.	Your Page Setup options may be in conflict with one another. Choose File, Page Setup, and on the Page tab, check the Fit To option, and specify the number of pages that your worksheet should print to.

If you're experiencing a lot of printing problems and none of the software-driven solutions seem to help, try reinstalling your printer driver. From the Start menu, choose Settings, Printers. Within the Printers window, double-click the Add Printer icon, and look for your printer's manufacturer and model. Follow the Add Printer procedure to install a new driver, which will appear as a copy of your original driver in the Printers window. You may need the original Windows 95/98 CD or disks in order to complete the process.

After the new driver is installed, delete the original icon for your printer so that your printer will utilize the newly installed driver, represented by the Copy icon. Restart your computer before printing again.

It's also a good idea to check your printer manufacturer's Web site periodically. Updated drivers are often available for free download.

EXCEL IN PRACTICE

Figure 9.23 shows a print preview of a worksheet that looked fine in the Excel window, but won't be easy to read when it's printed.

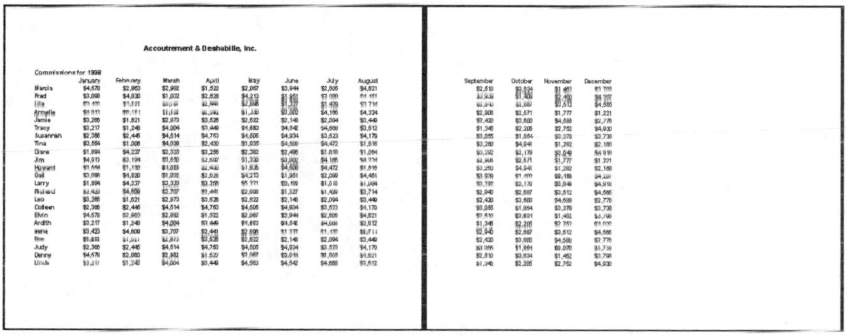

Figure 9.23.
The second printed page is missing important identifying information, and both pages are hard to read because there's too much unformatted data.

Because this table was the only table on the worksheet, I didn't need to set a Print Area. To make this report easy to read when it's printed, I've made the following changes (the finished report pages are shown in Figure 9.24):

- Moved the report title into the header, and formatted it differently from the worksheet text.

- Used the automatic worksheet name (Commissions) in the header.

- Added automatic page numbers to the header.

- Added an automatic date to the footer.

- Set row 1 (month names) and column A (employee names) as print titles.

- Formatted every other row a pale green to make them easier for the eye to follow across the page.

- Adjusted the top margin downward to make the page appear more visually balanced.

- Centered the data horizontally on the pages.
- Reset the page breaks equally, so six months appear on each page.

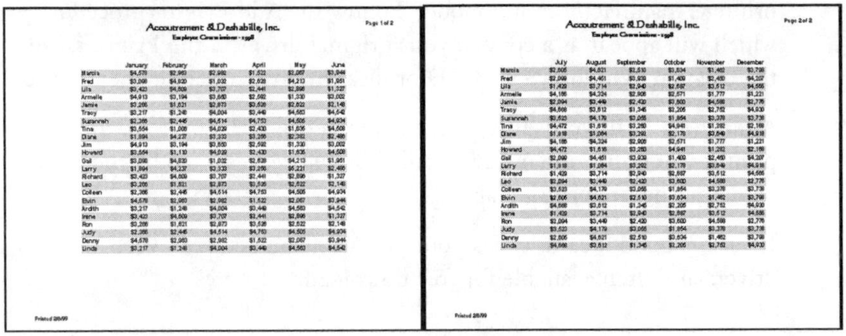

Figure 9.24.
This report is much
more readable and
professional.

Using Formulas and Functions

CHAPTER 10

CONSTRUCTING EXCEL FORMULAS

In this chapter

by Laurie Ann Ulrich
laurie@limehat.com

UNDERSTANDING BASIC FORMULA CONCEPTS

This chapter is about building your own mathematical formulas to calculate the data on a worksheet. Formulas, and the capability to build and edit them easily, are why you would want to use an electronic spreadsheet for storing and analyzing numeric data. Even if you're a mathematical genius, allowing Excel to do your calculations saves time, reduces the margin for error, and makes updating the results fast and easy. In addition, because numbers are stored in cells and you can refer to those cells in your formulas, the process of updating formulas with current data is automatic.

In Excel, you can write formulas from scratch or use a variety of automated features that write formulas for you. In this chapter, the focus will be on writing your own formulas to perform basic mathematical calculations in a worksheet; in Chapter 11, you'll use what you've learned about formula construction to write complex formulas that use *functions (page 265)* to perform more intricate calculations.

There are a few basic concepts that you need to understand and remember when you write Excel formulas.

Tip #143 from

> For users of other spreadsheet programs, such as Lotus 1-2-3, there are minor differences in how formulas are written. You'll want to learn how to write formulas the Excel way, but as an interim measure, you can tell Excel to accept formulas entered in Lotus 1-2-3 syntax: click Tools, Options, and on the Transition tab, check the Transition Formula Entry check box.

- All formulas begin with an equal sign (=).

- Formulas can use cell references and/or real numbers (called *constant values*) in their calculations.

- The mathematical operators Excel recognizes are + (addition), - (subtraction), * (multiplication), / (division), ^ (exponentiation), and % (percentage).

- You can add parentheses to control the order in which a formula carries out mathematical operations (when using parentheses, be sure you have complete sets of left and right parentheses).

- After a formula is entered, you'll see the formula in the Formula bar when the cell is active. The formula's result is displayed in the worksheet cell.

- When you edit a formula, you'll see the formula in both the Formula bar and the cell where you entered it, and you can edit the formula in either location.

- If you want to see all the formulas on your worksheet at once, instead of their results, you can switch the worksheet display. Press Ctrl+` (the grave accent in the upper left corner of your keyboard) to toggle between formulas and results, or click Tools, Options, and on the View tab, check the Formulas check box to show formulas (clear the check box to display results).

→ In addition to the mathematical operators, you can use Excel's built-in functions in formulas. **See** "Using Excel's Built-In Functions," **p. 279**

Note

If you use the Lotus 1-2-3 formula syntax (starting a formula with a plus [+] sign), Excel will change the syntax to begin with an equal sign after you enter the formula.

A formula can be as simple as =1+2. If you enter this formula into a worksheet, you'll get the result 3. But if you use cell references instead of values in your formulas, the formulas become much more flexible. For example, if you enter the value 1 in cell A1, and the value 2 in cell B1, you can write the formula =A1+B1 in any other cell, and the result will be 3. If you change the values in cells A1 and B1, the formula will continue to add the values in those cells and give you a correct result.

You can build on this principle by using cell references with other mathematical operators. For example, suppose you have a customer's invoice with a list of items and prices, and you want to add the sales tax to the subtotal. You can calculate the sales tax by multiplying the value in the subtotal cell by the sales tax. For example, in Figure 10.1, the tax rate is 5.5%, and the subtotal value is in cell E15. The formula =E15*5.5% in cell E16 calculates the correct tax whatever the subtotal.

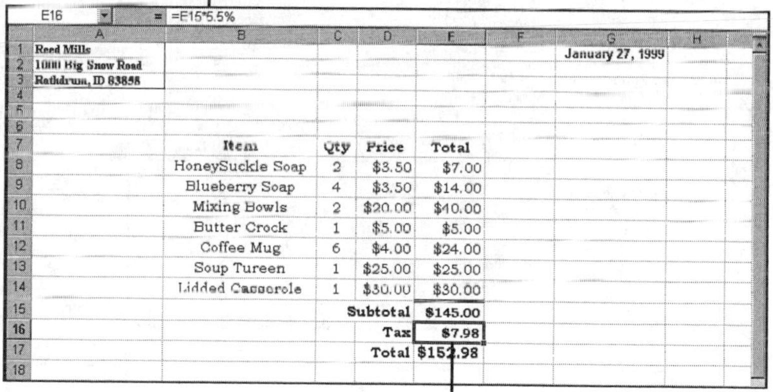

PART
IV
CH
10

The formula appears in the Formula bar.

Figure 10.1.
This formula multiplies a cell reference (E15) by a constant value (5.5%).

The result appears in the cell.

USING AUTOSUM TO TOTAL COLUMNS AND ROWS OF DATA

Because the most common worksheet calculation is the totaling of data in a list or table, Microsoft created the AutoSum toolbar button. AutoSum writes a formula that uses the SUM function to sum the values in all the cells referenced in the formula, and it writes the formula rapidly. (You'll learn more about functions in Chapter 11.)

AutoSum attempts to guess which cells you want to use in your SUM formula. But if it guesses wrong, you can change the referenced range quickly while you enter the formula.

You can use AutoSum to write quick SUM formulas using only your mouse, and you can write SUM formulas all the way across the bottom or down the side of a table in two clicks of a mouse.

To use AutoSum, follow these steps:

1. Click in the cell where you want to display the formula result.

2. Click the AutoSum button on the Standard toolbar.

   Excel guesses which cells you want to include, and surrounds them with an animated border (as shown in Figure 10.2).

3. If the formula doesn't have an obvious row or column to sum, or if it guesses wrong, drag to select the cells you want to sum. The animated border surrounds all the cells you drag.

4. When the range is correct, press Enter (or click the Enter button, the green check mark left of the Formula bar) to complete the formula.

The Enter button on the Formula bar   The AutoSum button   The SUM formula appears in the Formula bar.

Figure 10.2.
When you click AutoSum, an animated border surrounds the cells included in the formula.

Category	Qtr1	Qtr2	Qtr3	Qtr4	Total
Stony Keep Pottery Budget for 1998					
Office Supplies	$432.85	$476.14	$571.36	$485.66	=SUM(C5:F5)
Travel	$43.90	$48.29	$57.95	$49.26	
Telephone Charges	$528.36	$581.20	$697.44	$592.82	
Tax preparation	$69.96	$76.96	$92.35	$78.50	
Office Equipment	$555.12	$610.63	$732.76	$622.84	
Books/Publications	$574.57	$632.03	$758.43	$644.67	
On-Line charges	$150.15	$165.17	$198.20	$168.47	
Interest	$888.98	$757.88	$909.45	$773.04	
License	$110.00	$121.00	$145.20	$123.42	
Equipment Rental	$58.00	$63.80	$76.56	$65.08	
Total					

The SUM formula also appears in the cell.

If you want to write SUM formulas for several columns or rows in a table, follow these steps:

1. Drag to select all the cells that you want to display totals in, either across the bottom or down the right side of the table.

2. Click the AutoSum button.

   Each cell is automatically filled with a SUM formula that sums the contents of the column above it (as shown in Figure 10.3).

EDITING FORMULAS

When you need to change a formula, either the calculation or the referenced cells, there are several techniques from which to choose: You can edit the formula in the Formula bar or in the cell.

To edit in the Formula bar, click the cell that contains the formula, and then click in the Formula bar. Use regular text-editing techniques to edit the formula—drag to select characters you want to change; then delete or type over them. Press Enter to complete the formula.

To edit the formula in the cell, double-click the cell. The cell switches to edit mode and the entire formula is visible (as shown in Figure 10.4). You can select and edit the formula just as you would in the Formula bar.

Tip #144 from

Laurie

You can also press F2 to switch to edit mode for the selected cell you want to edit.

Note

If, when you double-click the formula cell (or press F2), the cell references are selected but the cell doesn't change to edit mode, click Tools, Options, and click the Edit tab. Click the Edit Directly in Cell check box to turn it on, and then click OK.

Whether you edit a formula in the Formula bar or in the cell, the references in the formula are highlighted in color, and the corresponding cell ranges on the worksheet are surrounded by borders that are color-matched to the range references in the formula, as shown in Figure 10.4. Although you can't see the actual colors in this figure, the callouts point them out, and you'll experience similar color highlights on your own screen.

Figure 10.4.
Follow the colors to
locate the referenced
ranges.

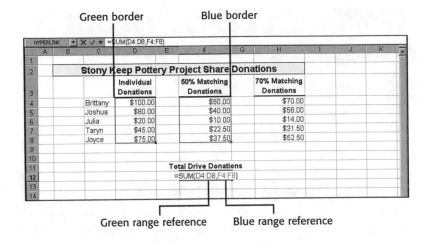

If you need to change the cell references so the formula calculates different cells, there are several techniques you can choose from. You can type new references, click and drag a new range on the worksheet, or use *range names (page 606)*.

> **Note**
>
> To get out of a cell without making any changes, or to undo any changes you've made before you enter them, press Esc or click the Cancel button (the red X left of the Formula bar).

DRAGGING CELLS TO REPLACE A REFERENCE

A quick and direct way to add or replace a range reference is to select the range you want on the worksheet. To add a new range to the formula, click in the formula to place the insertion point where you want to add the new range reference; then use your mouse to drag and select the range you want. If you're adding a new reference to one or more existing references, type a comma to separate the references.

> **Tip #145 from**
> *Laurie*
>
> To add several separate ranges all at the same time, drag to select the first range; then press and hold Ctrl while you drag to select the remaining ranges. This maneuver inserts the commas between the separate range references for you.

If you want to replace a cell or range reference, double-click the reference to highlight it in the formula (see Figure 10.5). Then click and drag the replacement cell or range on the worksheet.

When you finish editing the formula, press Enter to complete the formula and close the cell.

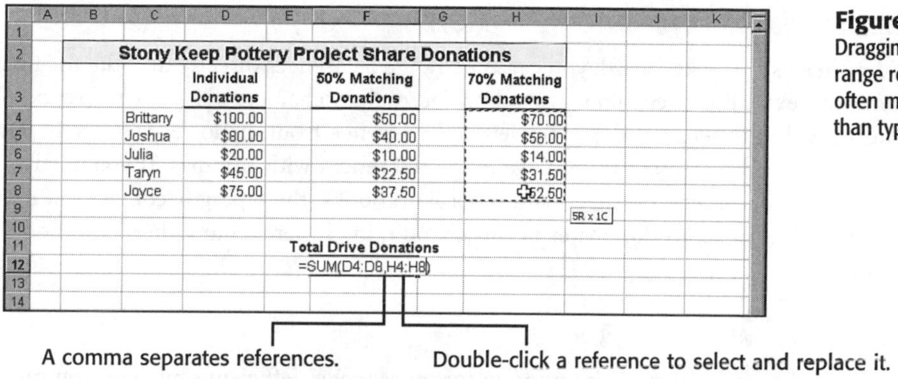

Figure 10.5.
Dragging to select range references is often more accurate than typing them.

A comma separates references.   Double-click a reference to select and replace it.

Tip #146 from

Laurie

When you drag to select cells, a ScreenTip appears to tell you how many rows and columns you've selected.

DRAGGING A RANGE BORDER TO CHANGE A REFERENCE

If you need to expand existing references (for example, if you added new columns or rows to a table and need to adjust the formula to include them), you can move or resize the colored range border to encompass the new cells. You can also move and resize the range border to reduce the range included in the formula.

To move a range border to surround different cells without changing its size, drag any side of the border. To expand or reduce the size of a range border, drag the *fill handle (page 261)* to change the size of the range (see Figure 10.6).

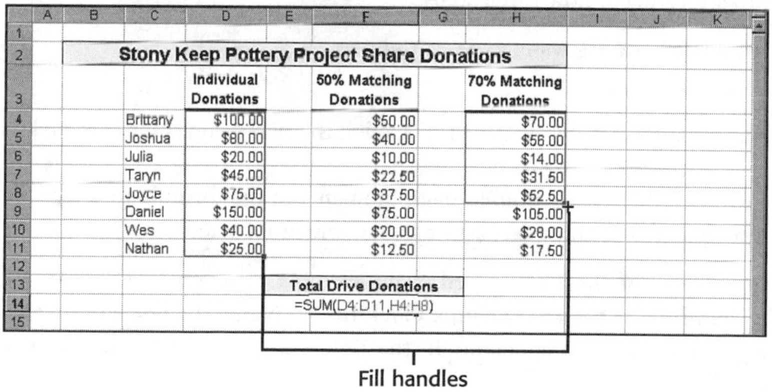

Figure 10.6.
You can edit a range reference by moving or resizing its colored borders.

Fill handles

TYPING REFERENCES DIRECTLY INTO A FORMULA

If you'd rather use your keyboard, you can type range references directly into the formula. Use common text-editing techniques to delete and replace characters in your references; be sure to use a colon to separate the upper-left cell reference from the lower-right cell reference in a range, and remember to separate range references with commas. If you need to reference ranges on other worksheets and other workbooks, the typing becomes a bit more complex; you'll learn about those later in this chapter, in "Referencing Other Workbooks and Worksheets."

TYPING A RANGE NAME INTO A FORMULA

If you named the ranges that you're using in formulas (a very efficient practice), you can type the range name in place of its reference.

→ To find out more about naming ranges, **see** "Naming Ranges for Fast Access," **p. 82**

It's useful to create range names that include some capital letters (such as Price or DecemberOrders), because the letter case will help you find misspelled range names. When you type a name into a formula, type it in all lowercase letters. If Excel recognizes the name, the characters will be converted to the case you created the name with; but if you mistype the name, the characters will remain lowercase and you'll get a #NAME? error. The lowercase name is your quickest clue to where the error is.

PASTING A RANGE NAME INTO A FORMULA

To be sure you don't misspell a range name when you add it to a formula (or if you don't remember exactly what the range name is), you can paste it from a list of all the range names in the workbook.

To paste a name into a formula, follow these steps:

1. Click in the formula where you want to paste the name.
2. Choose Insert, Name, Paste.
3. In the Paste Name dialog box (see Figure 10.7), click the name you want and click OK.

To replace a name with another name, double-click the name in the formula to select it, and then follow the preceding steps 2 and 3 to paste a new name in its place.

If you need to change the range that's calculated in the formula, don't change the formula; instead, change the definition of the range name. Click Insert, Name, Define, and in the Define Name dialog box, click the range name. In the Refers to box, change the range references, and then click OK.

Named range

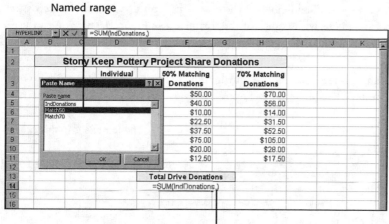

Figure 10.7.
Pasting a name prevents typing mistakes.

The pasted name will be inserted here.

→ To find out more about using named ranges in your formulas, **see** "Using Range Names in Formulas," **p. 326**

WRITING MULTIPLE COPIES OF A FORMULA

Suppose you have a table similar to the one shown in Figure 10.8, and you need to add identical formulas at the end of each row. Instead of entering each formula individually, there are a couple of ways to create copies of your formula quickly. One method uses AutoFill to copy a formula into several more cells. Another method creates multiple copies when you enter the formula.

COPYING FORMULAS WITH AUTOFILL

When you copy a formula using AutoFill, each formula adjusts its references automatically so that the calculation is correct. For example, when you write a formula that sums the values in the four cells to the left (like the formula in Figure 10.8), each copy of the formula will sum the values in the four cells to its left. This works because the formula uses *relative references (page 270)*.

→ To learn more about using relative references in your formulas, **see** "Using Relative, Absolute, and Mixed Cell References in Formulas," **p. 270**

To AutoFill a formula, follow these steps:

1. Enter your formula in the first cell (in this example, in the cell at the top of the column), as shown in Figure 10.8.

2. Select the formula cell. The active cell (or range) has a small black box in the lower-right corner called a *fill handle*.

3. Point the mouse at the fill handle; when the mouse pointer becomes a black cross, click and drag down to fill cells with copies of the formula (see Figure 10.8). You can use AutoFill to copy formulas in all four directions in your worksheet (up, down, left, and right).
4. At the end of range, release the mouse button. The cells you dragged are filled with copies of the formula, as illustrated in Figure 10.9.

The formula is in this cell.

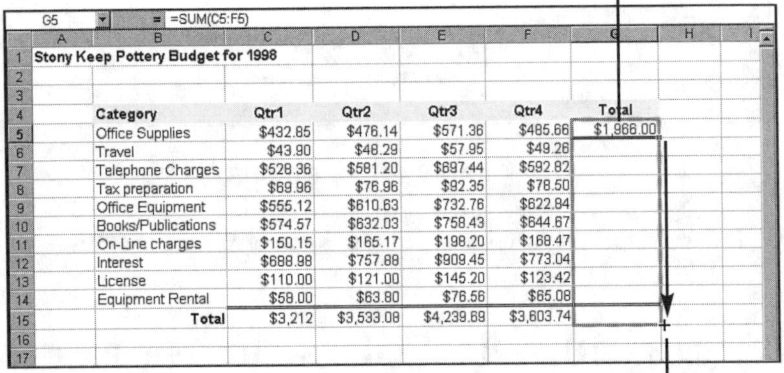
G5 =SUM(C5:F5)

	A	B	C	D	E	F	G	H
1	Stony Keep Pottery Budget for 1998							
2								
3								
4		Category	Qtr1	Qtr2	Qtr3	Qtr4	Total	
5		Office Supplies	$432.85	$476.14	$571.36	$485.66	$1,966.00	
6		Travel	$43.90	$48.29	$57.95	$49.26		
7		Telephone Charges	$528.36	$581.20	$697.44	$592.82		
8		Tax preparation	$69.96	$76.96	$92.35	$78.50		
9		Office Equipment	$555.12	$610.63	$732.76	$622.84		
10		Books/Publications	$574.57	$632.03	$758.43	$644.67		
11		On-Line charges	$150.15	$165.17	$198.20	$168.47		
12		Interest	$688.98	$757.88	$909.45	$773.04		
13		License	$110.00	$121.00	$145.20	$123.42		
14		Equipment Rental	$58.00	$63.80	$76.56	$65.08		
15		Total	$3,212	$3,533.08	$4,239.69	$3,603.74		
16								
17								

Drag the fill handle.

Figure 10.8. When your mouse pointer is a black cross, you can drag to AutoFill the formula to adjoining cells.

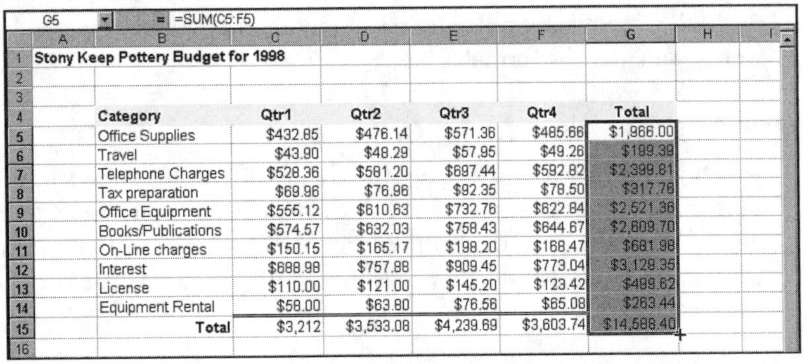
G5 =SUM(C5:F5)

	A	B	C	D	E	F	G	H
1	Stony Keep Pottery Budget for 1998							
2								
3								
4		Category	Qtr1	Qtr2	Qtr3	Qtr4	Total	
5		Office Supplies	$432.85	$476.14	$571.36	$485.66	$1,966.00	
6		Travel	$43.90	$48.29	$57.95	$49.26	$199.39	
7		Telephone Charges	$528.36	$581.20	$697.44	$592.82	$2,399.81	
8		Tax preparation	$69.96	$76.96	$92.35	$78.50	$317.76	
9		Office Equipment	$555.12	$610.63	$732.76	$622.84	$2,521.36	
10		Books/Publications	$574.57	$632.03	$758.43	$644.67	$2,609.70	
11		On-Line charges	$150.15	$165.17	$198.20	$168.47	$681.98	
12		Interest	$688.98	$757.88	$909.45	$773.04	$3,129.35	
13		License	$110.00	$121.00	$145.20	$123.42	$499.62	
14		Equipment Rental	$58.00	$63.80	$76.56	$65.08	$263.44	
15		Total	$3,212	$3,533.08	$4,239.69	$3,603.74	$14,588.40	
16								

Figure 10.9. When you release the mouse pointer, the cells are filled.

Tip #147 from *Laurie*

You can use AutoFill to fill out a table (for example, a loan payments table) by copying an entire row or column of entries and formulas. Select the range of cells you want to copy, and drag the fill handle on the lower-right corner of the range.

Also, if your table is extremely long, you can AutoFill an adjacent column by double-clicking the fill handle instead of dragging it.

→ To learn more about creating and using custom lists, **see** "Using Custom Lists to Speed Data Entry," **p. 41**

ENTERING MULTIPLE FORMULAS ALL AT ONCE

If you've already entered a formula and need to copy it across a row or down a column, AutoFill is quickest. But to enter multiple copies of a formula even faster, enter them all at the same time.

To enter the same formula in several cells at once, follow these steps:

1. Select all the cells you want to enter the formula in (see Figure 10.10). They can be in a single row or column, or in noncontiguous ranges (press Ctrl to select noncontiguous ranges).
2. Set up your formula by whatever means you normally use, but don't press Enter when you finish.
3. When the formula is complete, press Ctrl+Enter. The formula is entered in all the selected cells simultaneously (see Figure 10.11).

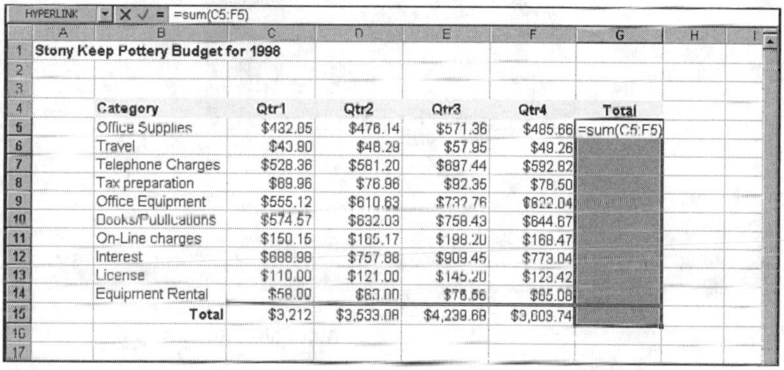

HYPERLINK =sum(C5:F5)

Stony Keep Pottery Budget for 1998

Category	Qtr1	Qtr2	Qtr3	Qtr4	Total
Office Supplies	$132.05	$476.14	$571.36	$485.66	=sum(C5:F5)
Travel	$40.90	$48.29	$57.95	$49.26	
Telephone Charges	$528.36	$581.20	$697.44	$592.82	
Tax preparation	$69.96	$76.96	$92.35	$78.50	
Office Equipment	$555.12	$610.63	$732.76	$622.04	
Books/Publications	$574.57	$632.03	$758.43	$644.67	
On-Line charges	$150.15	$165.17	$198.20	$168.47	
Interest	$688.98	$757.88	$909.45	$773.04	
License	$110.00	$121.00	$145.20	$123.42	
Equipment Rental	$58.00	$63.00	$76.56	$65.08	
Total	$3,212	$3,533.08	$4,239.68	$3,003.74	

Figure 10.10.
To enter multiple copies of a formula all at once, select all the cells first.

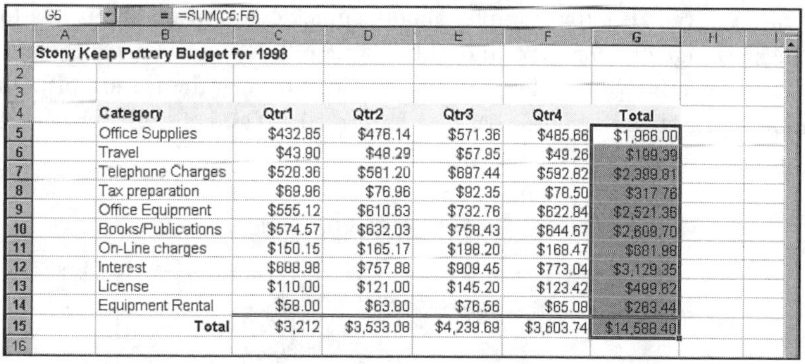

G5 =SUM(C5:F5)

Stony Keep Pottery Budget for 1998

Category	Qtr1	Qtr2	Qtr3	Qtr4	Total
Office Supplies	$432.85	$476.14	$571.36	$485.66	$1,966.00
Travel	$43.90	$48.29	$57.95	$49.26	$199.39
Telephone Charges	$528.36	$581.20	$697.44	$592.82	$2,399.81
Tax preparation	$69.96	$76.96	$92.35	$78.50	$317.76
Office Equipment	$555.12	$610.63	$732.76	$622.84	$2,521.36
Books/Publications	$574.57	$632.03	$758.43	$644.67	$2,609.70
On-Line charges	$150.15	$165.17	$198.20	$168.47	$681.98
Interest	$688.98	$757.88	$909.45	$773.04	$3,129.35
License	$110.00	$121.00	$145.20	$123.42	$499.62
Equipment Rental	$58.00	$63.80	$76.56	$65.08	$263.44
Total	$3,212	$3,533.08	$4,239.69	$3,603.74	$14,588.40

Figure 10.11.
Press Ctrl+Enter to enter the formula in all the selected cells.

If you use range references in the formula, they'll automatically adjust to the correct references in each copy of the formula (see the section "Understanding Cell References" later in this chapter to learn more). If you use range names or worksheet labels in the formulas, each copy of the formula will find its correct range (but be careful using worksheet labels—they can be a bit unpredictable and tricky).

USING AUTOCALCULATE FOR QUICK TOTALS

Sometimes you need a quick and impermanent calculation—you need to know right now what your expense account entries add up to, or how many items there are in a list. You can use *AutoCalculate* to get quick answers.

To use AutoCalculate, select the cells you want to calculate. The answer appears in the AutoCalculate box on the Status bar (see Figure 10.12).

Selected cells

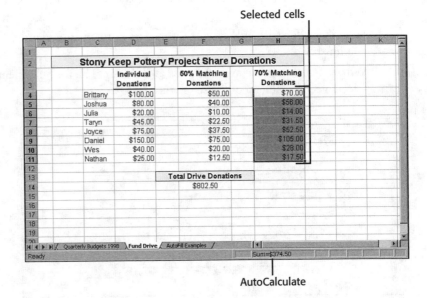

Figure 10.12.
Select two or more cells and see the automatic calculation of those entries displayed on the Status bar.

AutoCalculate

When you install Excel, AutoCalculate is set to calculate sums by default; but you're not limited to quick sums. You can also, for example, obtain a quick count of the items in a long product list or a quick average of your list of monthly phone bills. You can switch the calculation to Average, Count, CountNums, Max, or Min (or None to turn the feature off). To switch the calculation, right-click the Status bar (see Figure 10.13) and click the calculation you want on the shortcut menu.

Choose a calculation.

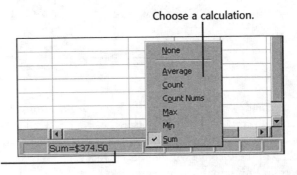

Figure 10.13.
Choose a different AutoCalculate function.

Right-click here.

Tip #148 from

Laurie

AutoCalculate retains whatever function you set until you change the function again.

AutoCalculate appears in the Status bar only when two or more calculable cells are selected. For example, if the AutoCalculate function is set to Sum and you select cells that contain only text entries, AutoCalculate won't appear (because there's nothing to sum).

AutoCalculate offers the following functions:

- **Average**—averages numeric values in the selected cells; ignores blank cells and nonnumeric values.

- **Count**—counts all entries, whether numeric, text, or logical; ignores blank cells.

- **CountNums**—counts only numeric values; ignores blank cells and nonnumeric values.

- **Max**—shows the single maximum numeric value in the selected cells.

- **Min**—shows the single minimum numeric value in the selected cells.

- **Sum**—sums numeric values in the selected cells; ignores blank cells and nonnumeric values.

PART

IV

CH

10

UNDERSTANDING FORMULA CONSTRUCTION

Earlier in this chapter, you began to learn about writing and editing formulas (writing simple formulas using both constant values and cell references, editing references, separating references with commas, and so forth).

In this section, you'll learn how to use arithmetic operators in your formulas, how to control the order in which Excel performs those operations, and how to fix error messages.

USING ARITHMETIC OPERATORS FOR SIMPLE MATH

To perform direct mathematical operations in a formula (as opposed to using *functions (page 280)*, which you'll learn about in Chapter 11), you use arithmetic operators. *Arithmetic operators* in a formula tell Excel which math operations you want to perform.

A simple formula might consist of adding, subtracting, multiplying, and dividing cells. Excel can also perform exponentiation, so you can enter a number and exponent (such as 5^4, or 5 to the fourth power) and Excel will use the ultimate value of the exponent in the formula calculation. You can use percentages in a formula the same way—instead of entering 25% as a fractional value (25/100) or a decimal value (0.25), you can enter 25% in a formula; Excel will calculate and use its decimal value in the math operation.

Excel's arithmetic operators are detailed in Table 10.1.

TABLE 10.1. ARITHMETIC OPERATORS	
Operator	**Description**
+ (plus sign)	Addition
- (minus sign)	Subtraction and Negation
* (asterisk)	Multiplication
/ (forward slash)	Division
^ (caret)	Exponentiation
% (percent)	Percentage

UNDERSTANDING THE ORDER IN WHICH EXCEL PERFORMS MATHEMATICAL OPERATIONS

If a formula performs more than one or two operations, you'll probably need to tell Excel in what order to perform those operations (or you may get a wrong answer).

For example, what's the answer to the equation 2+2*3? If you solve the equation left to right (perform the addition first, and then multiply), the answer is 12; but if you solve the equation using math rules (perform the multiplication first, and then the addition), the answer is 8. So how do you get Excel to solve the equation the way you want it solved, so you get the answer you want?

Excel follows standard math rules regarding which operations it performs first, next, and so forth; this is called the *order of operations*, and is shown as follows. To get the answer you want, you can use parentheses to divide the formula into segments and control the order of operations yourself.

- **Parentheses.** All calculations within parentheses are completed first.
- **Negation.** Making a number negative (such as −5) precedes any other operations, so that the negative value is used in the remaining calculations.
- **Percent.** Percentages (for example, 12%) are calculated next, so that the actual value (in this case, .12) is used in the remaining calculations.
- **Exponentiation.** Exponents (for example, 10^3 which means 10 cubed) are calculated next, so that the actual value is used in the remaining calculations.
- **Multiplication.** Performed after parenthetical operations and before all other calculations.
- **Division.** Follows any multiplication and is on the same level of precedence as multiplication.
- **Addition.** Performed after all divisions.
- **Subtraction.** Follows any additions and is on the same level of precedence as addition.

CONTROLLING THE ORDER OF OPERATIONS

Even though Excel follows a set order of operations when it calculates a formula, you can alter the order in a specific formula by using parentheses to break the formula into segments. Excel will perform all operations within sets of parentheses first, and you can use this to get exactly the order of operations you want.

If multiple operations are encased in multiple sets of parentheses, the operations are performed from inside to outside, then follow the order of operations, and then left to right. Table 10.2 shows results of rearranging parentheses within the same formula. Each parenthetical calculation is performed first; then the results of those first calculations are used for the second set of calculations, which follow the order of operations. All operations on the same level (in this case, all the additions) are then performed left to right.

TABLE 10.2. THE RESULTS OF REARRANGING PARENTHESES

Formula	Result
=(1+2)*3+4+5	18
=1+2*3+4+5	16
=1+2*(3+4)+5	20
=1+2*(3+4+5)	25
=(1+2)*(3+4)+5	26
=(1+2)*(3+4+5)	36

You must have balanced pairs of parentheses in any formula. If you forget a parenthesis, you'll see a message telling you there's an error. Sometimes Excel takes a guess at where you want the missing parenthesis (shown in Figure 10.14) and displays a prompt box. If the guess is right, click Yes; if it's wrong, click No and fix the formula yourself.

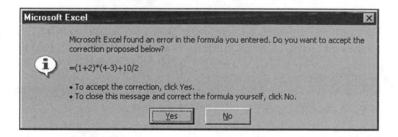

Figure 10.14.
Excel sometimes tries to guess what you want (but it may or may not guess correctly).

Tip #149 from

Laurie

If your formula is long and contains many sets of parentheses, it can be difficult to find the missing parenthesis by eye. Instead, open the formula for editing, and use the arrow keys to move the cursor (the insertion point) through the formula one character at a time. Whenever the cursor moves over a parenthesis, both parentheses in the pair are momentarily darkened. If the parenthesis is not temporarily darkened when the cursor passes over it, that's the one that's missing a matching parenthesis for the set.

NESTING CALCULATIONS WITHIN A FORMULA

Some calculations are more complex than can be handled with isolated sets of parentheses; they require parenthetical sets that are *nested*, or contained within larger parenthetical sets. This isn't so common in simple mathematical formulas, but is very common when you use functions (which you learn about in Chapter 11).

Nested calculations use parentheses to force Excel to follow the order of operations that you want, even as it follows the standard order of operations. Figure 10.15 shows a simple example of the changes you can make by nesting parentheses within other parentheses.

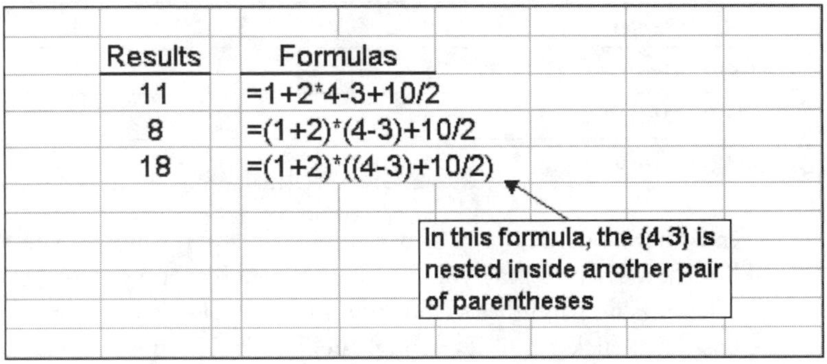

Figure 10.15.
Nesting parentheses within other parentheses alters the calculation even more.

Results	Formulas
11	=1+2*4-3+10/2
8	=(1+2)*(4-3)+10/2
18	=(1+2)*((4-3)+10/2)

In this formula, the (4-3) is nested inside another pair of parentheses

To simplify the principle: Excel calculates the innermost parentheses first, and then uses those quantities to calculate within the next outer level of parentheses, and so forth through all the nested levels. When all the parenthetical quantities have been calculated, Excel uses those quantities to calculate the formula by following the order of operations.

You'll see the real value of nested calculations in Chapter 11, where you learn about functions and how to nest them to make your worksheet work for you.

INTERPRETING FORMULA ERROR MESSAGES

When something prevents a formula from calculating, you'll see an error message instead of a result. The "something" might be a reference that was deleted from the worksheet, an invalid arithmetic operation such as dividing by zero, or a formula attempting to calculate a named range that doesn't exist.

Table 10.3 lists the error messages and their probable causes (some have several probable causes, and you must do some detective work to find the problem). But Excel has tools that can help you track down the source of an error.

TABLE 10.3. ERROR VALUES

This Error	Means This	To Fix It, Do This
#####	The column isn't wide enough to display the value.	Widen the column.
#VALUE!	Wrong type of argument or operand (for example, calculating a cell with the value #N/A).	Check operands and arguments; be sure references are valid.
#DIV/0!	Formula is attempting to divide by zero.	Change the value or cell reference so that the formula doesn't divide by zero.
#NAME?	Formula is referencing an invalid or nonexistent name.	Be sure the name still exists or correct the misspelling
#N/A	Most commonly means no value is available or inappropriate arguments were used.	In a lookup formula, be sure the lookup table is sorted correctly.
#REF!	Excel can't locate the referenced cells. (For example, referenced cells were deleted.)	Click Undo immediately to restore references and then change formula references or convert formulas to values.
#NUM!	Incorrect use of a number (such as SQRT(-1)), or formula result is a number too large or too small to be displayed.	Be sure that the arguments are correct, and that the result is between $-1*10^{307}$ and $1*10^{307}$.
#NULL!	Reference to intersection of two areas that do not intersect.	Check for typing and reference errors.
Circular	A formula refers to itself, either directly or indirectly.	Click OK and then look at the status bar to see which cell contains the circular reference. Use the Trace Precedents and Trace Dependents buttons on either the Circular Reference or Auditing toolbar to find the culprit references.

LOCATING ERRORS IN FORMULAS

To locate the source of an error in a formula, begin by checking the formula itself for typing and spelling mistakes. The error may be in the formula, or it may be in a source cell that's referenced by the formula.

To locate the source of an error, follow these steps:

1. Click Tools, Auditing, Show Auditing Toolbar.
2. Click the cell containing the error.
3. On the Auditing toolbar, click the Trace Error button.

If the error originated in a source cell rather than in the active cell, tracing arrows appear and guide you visually to possible sources of error (see Figure 10.16). Blue trace lines show referenced cells, and red trace lines lead to the cell that caused the error value.

If no error-tracing arrows appear, the source of the error is in the formula itself. Use the information in Table 10.3 to find the problem.

Even if there are no errors, you can trace the dependent and precedent cells in a formula by clicking the Trace Dependents and Trace Precedents buttons. Each time you click a Trace button, tracing arrows appear for the next level of precedents or dependents. The Remove Precedent Arrows and Remove Dependent Arrows remove the tracing arrows one level at a time.

Figure 10.16.
Tracing arrows show graphically where a cell's precedents and dependents are.

The precedents for D8

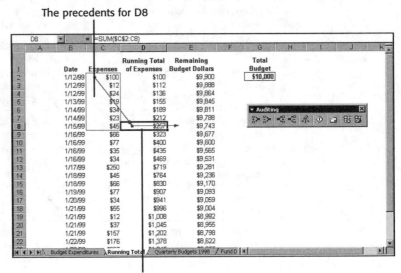

D8 points to its dependent.

USING RELATIVE, ABSOLUTE, AND MIXED CELL REFERENCES IN FORMULAS

Cells can have different types of references, depending on how you want to use them in a formula. Up until this point in the chapter, all the cell references written in the formula examples have been *relative* references. By default, Excel doesn't treat the cells you include in a formula as a set location. Instead, Excel considers the cells as a relative location. This type of referencing saves you from having to create the same formula over and over again. You can copy it and the cell references adjust accordingly. You saw this principle in action earlier in this chapter in the section on copying formulas ("Writing Multiple Copies of a Formula").

When writing AutoSum formulas, for example, formulas are written with relative references, and you can use AutoFill to quickly copy the formula to other cells. The copied formulas adjust themselves to the appropriate references. For example, if a relative reference in a formula refers to "the cell on my left," every copy of that formula refers to the cell on its left, no matter where you copy it.

Sometimes, however, you'll need to refer to the same specific cell on the worksheet in every copy of a formula. In a case like this, use an *absolute* reference. An absolute reference is fixed and never changes even if you move or copy the formula. Absolute references are denoted with dollar signs before the column and row address, such as $A$1.

For example, suppose you have a departmental budget and you like to keep a running total of what you've spent and what remains available. Figure 10.17 shows a column of running totals and a column of remaining budget dollars. The formulas use both absolute references and relative references. The formulas in the Running Total of Expenses column each sum the range from cell $C$4 to the cell left of the formula. The formulas in the Remaining Budget Dollars column each subtract the cell to the left from the Total Budget (cell $F$4). As the list of expenses in the Expenses column grows, the formulas in the Running Total and Remaining Budget columns can be quickly copied down with AutoFill.

Each Running Total formula starts in $C$4....

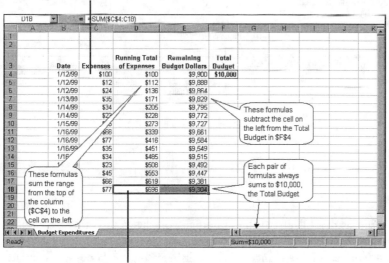

Figure 10.17.
Using absolute and relative references in the same formula enables you to create flexible lists.

...and sums down to its own row

PART
IV

CH
10

On occasion, you'll need a *mixed* reference. Mixed references can contain both absolute and relative cell addresses, such as $A4 or C$3. For example, if you want copies of a formula to refer to the value two columns left of the formula, but always in Row 3, you'd use a mixed reference with a relative column and an absolute row (such as A$3). Copies of the formula would always refer to a value in row 3, although which cell in row 3 would depend on where the formula was.

As mentioned previously, the default reference type is always relative, which means if you click and drag cells to add references to a formula, the references will be entered as relative. If you type them, you can type the dollar signs wherever you need to designate an absolute reference, but it's faster to type relative references and then change them to absolute or mixed.

You can quickly cycle through the reference types by pressing F4 on the keyboard. For example, if a formula uses the reference A1, pressing F4 will change the reference to $A$1, A$1, $A1, and A1 (in that order) with each press. Simply stop when the reference is the type you want to use.

To change the reference type, follow these steps:

1. Double-click the cell containing the formula (or select the cell and work in the Formula bar).

2. Within the formula, click in the cell reference you want to change (see Figure 10.18).

3. Press F4 until the reference changes to the type you want.

   Repeatedly pressing F4 cycles through all the possible reference types.

4. Press Enter to complete the change.

Click in the cell reference.

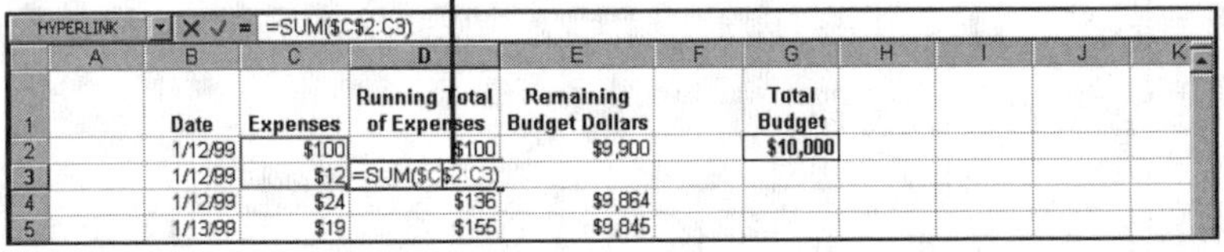

Figure 10.18.
To change the reference type, click in the cell reference; then, press F4.

REFERENCING VALUES IN OTHER WORKSHEETS AND WORKBOOKS

You can write formulas that calculate values in other worksheets and other workbooks, which is a common way to compile and summarize data from several different sources. When you write formulas that reference other worksheets and workbooks, you create links to those other worksheets and workbooks.

REFERENCING OTHER WORKSHEETS

Suppose you have a workbook that contains separate worksheets for each division in your company. You can combine data from each division's worksheet in a Summary sheet in that same workbook to compile and analyze data for the entire company. Formulas on the Summary sheet will need to reference data on the individual Division sheets (these are called *external references*). You can create external references by switching to the other worksheet and clicking and dragging the cells you want to reference, just as in a same-worksheet reference; the only difference is that the cells are located on a different worksheet.

To reference data from another worksheet in your formula, follow these steps:

1. Begin building the formula.

2. When you are ready to insert the reference from another worksheet, click the tab for that worksheet.

PART

IV

CH

10

Tip #150 from

Laurie

Sometimes it's easier to work in two windows, side by side on your screen. To open a second window, click Window, New Window. Click Window, Arrange, and in the Arrange Windows dialog box, click an arrangement (Tiled always works well), and click OK. Finally, select the second worksheet in one of the windows.

3. Locate the cell that you want to reference, and click it. If you're referencing a range, drag across the range to select it. The sheet name and cell reference appear in the Formula bar, as shown in Figure 10.19.

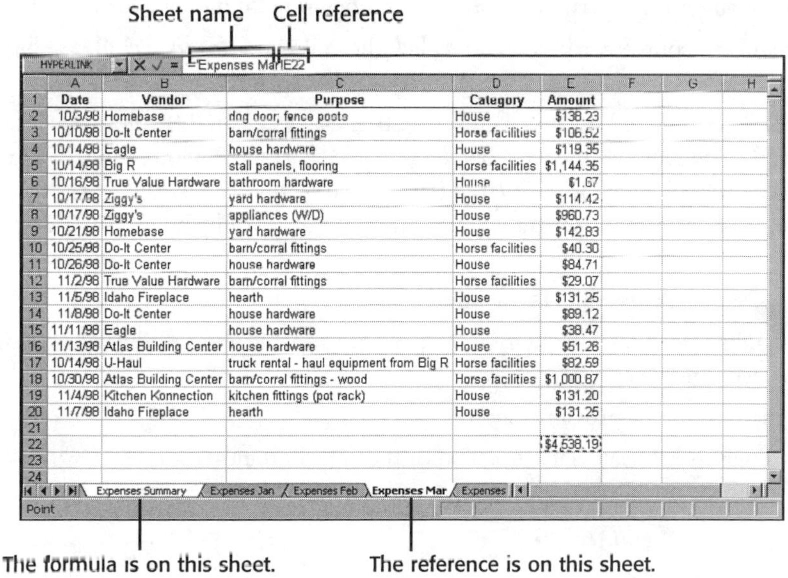

Sheet name   Cell reference

Figure 10.19.
An external worksheet reference is the sheet name, followed by an exclamation point, followed by the cell reference (which can be relative or absolute).

The formula is on this sheet.   The reference is on this sheet.

4. Continue building your formula by typing the remaining operators. If your formula requires cells from other worksheets (or from the original worksheet), repeat steps 2 and 3 to add them.

5. When the formula is complete, press Enter.

You can also enter external worksheet references by typing them. The syntax for an external worksheet reference is

`SheetName!CellReference`

If the sheet name contains spaces, enclose the sheet name in single quotes, like this:

`'Year End Summary'!CellReference`

If you change the sheet name after you've written formulas referencing it, no problem! Because they're in the same workbook, the formulas automatically update to show the current sheet name.

REFERENCING OTHER WORKBOOKS

If you need to reference data in another workbook (called a *source* workbook), you can write formulas with external workbook references. For example, employees in another city send you their Excel files with operational data for their division. The following steps show how to reference two additional workbooks. To write a formula using external workbook references, follow these steps:

1. Open the workbooks you want to use, including the source workbook(s) and the workbook in which you want to write the formula, and begin building your formula.

2. Click in one of the source workbooks, and click the cell you want to include in the formula.

   The cell reference is added to the formula, but because it's located in another workbook, the reference includes the workbook name and worksheet name, too (see Figure 10.20). The workbook name is in square brackets and is followed by the worksheet name; the worksheet name is separated from the cell reference by an exclamation point, like this:

   `[WorkbookName]WorksheetName!CellReference`

3. Continue building your formula by typing operators and clicking in other workbooks to enter the cell references.

4. Complete the formula by pressing Enter.

The formula in Figure 10.20 calculates the sum of the cells in the two source workbooks. All three workbooks are now linked by the formula.

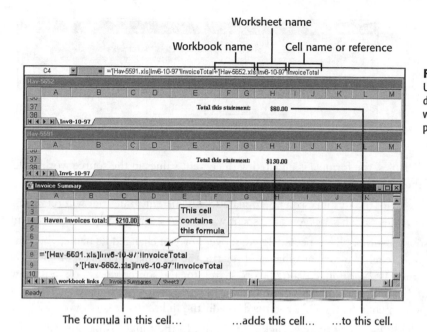

Figure 10.20.
Using multiple windows is the easiest way to work in multiple workbooks.

You can also enter external workbook references by typing them. The syntax for an external workbook reference is

```
[BookName.xls]SheetName!CellReference
```

If the book name or the sheet name contains spaces, enclose the entire book-and-sheet reference in single quotes, like this:

```
'[North Division.xls]Year End Summary'!CellReference
```

UPDATING VALUES IN REFERENCED WORKBOOKS

The workbook that contains the formula is called the *dependent* workbook, and the workbook that contains the data being referenced is called the *source* workbook. If the values in the source workbooks change, the formula that references them can update its results automatically.

If the source workbook is open when you open the dependent workbook, the formula is automatically updated with no questions. If the source workbook is closed when you open the dependent workbook, you'll be asked whether you want to update all linked information (as shown in Figure 10.21).

Figure 10.21.
If a workbook contains formulas that reference data in other closed workbooks, you'll be asked whether you want to update when you open the workbook.

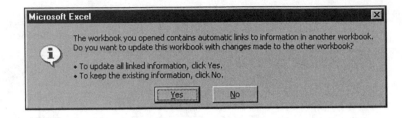

- If you click Yes, the formula is updated with current values in the source workbooks, even if those values have changed.

- If you click No, the formula won't be updated with current values but will retain its previous values, which saves you time spent waiting for a large workbook to recalculate.

- If the source workbook has been deleted, moved, or you changed its name, you can click No to retain the current values and rewrite the formula references, or click Yes and use the File Not Found dialog box to search for the source workbook in its new location. Searching for the file in the File Not Found dialog box is only a temporary fix; to permanently fix the link, you need to edit the links.

- To edit the links in a workbook, click Edit, Links. In the Links dialog box, click Change Source. In the Change Links dialog box, locate and click the name of the moved or renamed source workbook, and click OK. Click OK to close the Links dialog box, and the link is permanently fixed (until you move the source again).

Tip #151 from

Laurie

If you don't want the formula to recalculate, ever, or be bothered by the links that need updating every time you open the workbook, you can break the link and save the current formula result as a value. Select the formula cell and copy it; then (with the cell still selected) click Edit, Paste Special. Click the Values option, and click OK.

TROUBLESHOOTING

Formula errors are most often the result of a typo or the inclusion of a cell or range reference that doesn't contain appropriate values for the formula. Typos can include misspellings, missing or inappropriate operators, or missing parentheses. These rules may help you avoid formula errors:

- Type function names and range names in lowercase. You'll know immediately whether they're correct because Excel won't convert them to uppercase or proper case. Better yet, use the Paste Name and Paste Function dialog boxes to paste in the correct names.

- Watch out for range references that accidentally use a semicolon instead of a colon (better yet, click and drag to select cell and range references, because Excel won't enter a semicolon by mistake).

- Be sure that all nested functions, ranges, and arguments are held within a complete pair of parentheses, and that each left parenthesis has a matching right parenthesis.

- Don't type punctuation, such as dollar signs or commas, when you enter constant values into your formulas. For example, =B7*$5,000 will result in an error message (the correct formula would be =B7*5000).

- If you want to break the link between worksheets or workbooks, you can find the linking formulas by searching the worksheet for an exclamation point. Click Edit, Find, type ! in the Find what box, be sure Formulas is selected in the Look in box, and then click OK. To break a link, copy the cell that contains the link; then right-click the cell and click Paste Special, click Values, and click OK.

EXCEL IN PRACTICE

For presentation purposes, you can use Excel's auditing features to draw lines tracing references in your worksheet and then print the worksheet. The lines are printed along with the worksheet data, helping point out the connection between important data. Simply select the cell containing the formula to which you want to show the relationship of references; then display the Auditing toolbar (click Tools, Auditing, Show Auditing Toolbar). Use the Trace Precedents button to display tracing arrows. If any of the arrows obscure the view of data, enlarge the size of the row, as shown in Figure 10.22.

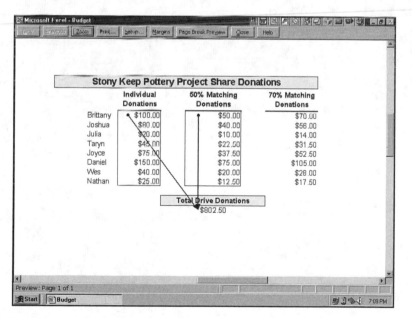

Figure 10.22.
If you leave the tracing lines on a worksheet, they'll print to show the formula's source values.

USING EXCEL'S BUILT-IN FUNCTIONS

by Laurie Ann Ulrich
laurie@limehat.com

UNDERSTANDING FUNCTIONS

Not all calculations are simple. Fortunately, with Excel's many functions, the program can handle just about anything you might throw its way.

Functions are built-in formulas that perform complex math for you. You enter the function name and any *arguments* (extra information) the function requires, and Excel performs the calculations. You saw the SUM function in action in Chapter 10, "Constructing Excel Formulas," and it's a simple, straightforward function that doesn't require any further elaboration. PMT (figures payments on a fixed-rate loan) and VLOOKUP (looks up a value in a table) are examples of common but more complex functions that I show you how to use in this chapter.

Tip #152 from	Many of the formulas you see in this chapter are written using cell or range names; if you need to learn more about naming cells and ranges, see Chapter 12, "Working with Named Ranges."
Laurie	

Excel comes with a slew of functions—some you use all the time, and some you'll be interested in only if you're an electrical engineer or nuclear physicist. Functions have specific names, such as SUM or AVERAGE or BETADIST, and function names must be spelled correctly or Excel won't recognize them; however, Excel provides dialog boxes that do the spelling for you and help you fill in the arguments each function requires.

Note	The more advanced (and less commonly used) functions are in the Analysis Toolpak. If you don't see the Analysis Toolpak add-in listed in the Add-Ins dialog box (open the Tools menu and select Add-Ins), you need to install the add-in from your Office 2000 or Excel 2000 CD-ROM.

BUILDING FUNCTIONS WITH THE PASTE FUNCTION DIALOG BOX

The easiest way to use a function in a formula is to use the Paste Function dialog box and the Formula Palette. These two integrated tools will walk you through the process of selecting and completing formulas using any of Excel's many functions.

To write a formula that uses a function, follow these steps:

1. Click the cell in which you want the results of the formula to appear.

2. On the toolbar, click the Paste Function button.

   The Paste Function dialog box appears (shown in Figure 11.1).

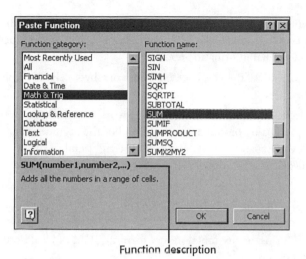

Figure 11.1.
The Paste Function dialog box briefly explains the selected function.

Function description

3. Click a category of functions, and then double-click the function you want to use from the list on the right. If you don't know which category to look in, click the All category and scroll through the alphabetical list of all functions.

The Formula Palette opens to help you complete the function (shown in Figure 11.2).

Tip #153 from
Laurie

Instead of scrolling through a very long list of functions, click any name in the Function Name list and then type the first letter of the function you want; the list will jump to that alphabetical section of the list.

Note

You can drag the *Formula Palette*—the dialog box in which you supply arguments for the formula—elsewhere on the worksheet to move it out of your way.

Arguments   Collapse Dialog button

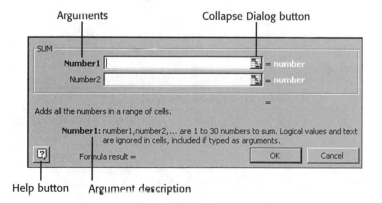

Figure 11.2.
The Formula Palette helps you fill in each argument.

Help button   Argument description

4. Click the top argument box and read the description of the argument to figure out what information is needed. (If this is the first time you've ever used the function, click the Help button for additional information about it.)

5. If the arguments call for cell references, click or drag worksheet cells to fill in arguments.

   To shrink the Formula Palette so that it doesn't cover worksheet cells you want to select, click the Collapse Dialog button at the right end of the argument and select the worksheet cells. Click the Expand Dialog button (at the right end of the collapsed argument box) to redisplay the Formula Palette and continue building your function.

6. When all the necessary arguments are added, click OK.

   The function is built and the formula is completed.

This is the basic procedure for using any function in a formula. Table 11.1 describes several of the most useful Excel functions.

Tip #154 from

Laurie

After you type an equal sign, the Name box to the left of the Formula bar becomes a drop-down list of recently used functions. If you click a function in the list, the Formula Palette appears for that function.

Note

After you get comfortable with formulas, you can often write them faster yourself, but you must spell the function name correctly. Try this tip: Type the function name in lowercase letters. If it's spelled correctly, Excel converts it to uppercase after you press Enter. (For example, sum is converted to SUM.) If it's spelled incorrectly, Excel won't convert it to uppercase; that's your clue that it's the function name that's causing a #NAME? error.

TABLE 11.1. USEFUL WORKSHEET FUNCTIONS

Function	Purpose
SUM	Add together the values in a selected range.
MIN	Find the minimum value in a selected range.
MAX	Find the maximum value in a selected range.
AVERAGE	Average the values in a selected range.
SUBTOTAL	Calculate the visible cells in a selected range; calculate filtered lists (11 calculations are available).
COUNT, COUNTA, and COUNTBLANK	COUNT counts the number of numeric entries in a range; COUNTA counts all the entries in a range; and COUNTBLANK counts the blank cells in a range.
COUNTIF	Count all values that meet specific criteria.
SUMIF	Add together all values that meet specific criteria.

Function	Purpose
VLOOKUP and HLOOKUP	Find a value in a table.
INDEX and MATCH	MATCH finds the position of a value in a single row or column; INDEX finds a value in a table when the position of the value is known. Used nested in one formula, they look up values in a table, similar to VLOOKUP and HLOOKUP.
IF	Display a value that depends on criteria you set.
ISBLANK, ISNUMBER, ISTEXT	Return logical (TRUE or FALSE) information about the value in a cell (usually nested in another function).
AND, OR, NOT	Return logical (TRUE or FALSE) values depending on whether arguments meet formula criteria (usually nested in another function).
PMT	Calculate the payment for a loan.
NOW	Return the current date and time.
TODAY	Return the current date.
CONCATENATE	Join multiple cell values together in a single cell.
LEFT and RIGHT	Return a specific number of characters from the left or right end of a cell's value.
UPPER, LOWER, and PROPER	Convert text strings to all uppercase, all lowercase, or each word to proper case (lowercase with the first letter capitalized).
OFFSET	Return a range specified by its arguments.
RAND	Generates random numbers between 0 and 1 (generates a new random number each time the worksheet recalculates).
DSUM, DGET, and DAVERAGE	Some of the several D-functions, they return values from a specific table column that are based on criteria you set. DSUM returns the sum of items that meet the criteria (similar to SUMIF), DGET returns a single item, and DAVERAGE returns the average of items that meet the criteria.

PART

IV

CH

11

WORKING WITH EXCEL'S MOST USEFUL FUNCTIONS

In this section, I show you examples of the functions in Table 11.1 (with the exception of the SUM function which you learned about in Chapter 10), with suggestions for using them in real-life worksheet situations. This short list of functions contains just a few of the hundreds of functions available in Excel. If you explore the list of functions in the Paste Function dialog box, you'll find functions that calculate sine, cosine, tangent, the actual value of pi, and functions for a lot of accounting and engineering equations, logarithms, and binomials.

If you want to use complex engineering and financial functions, you'll need to install the Analysis Toolpak. Click Tools, Add-Ins, mark the Analysis Toolpak check box, and click OK.

Tip #155 from

Laurie

When you first write a formula, you want to test it to be sure that it's calculating properly (that is, you want to be sure you entered all the arguments correctly and the results are accurate). To test your formulas, enter *mock data* (phony numbers) in the worksheet. Use mock data that's simple: short text that's quick to type, and round numbers so that you can do the math in your head and know quickly whether the results are accurate.

→ To learn more about cell references, **see** "Using Relative, Absolute, and Mixed Cell References in Formulas," **p. 270**

→ To learn how to use the AutoSum button to quickly sum ranges, **see** "Using AutoSum to Total Columns and Rows of Data," **p. 255**

MIN

The MIN function

```
MIN(number1,number2,...)
```

returns the minimum, or lowest, value in a range of numbers. Of course, if your range is a single column of numbers, you can also find the smallest value by sorting or filtering the list. If your range is a large table of numbers, such as the one in Figure 11.3, the MIN function comes in handy.

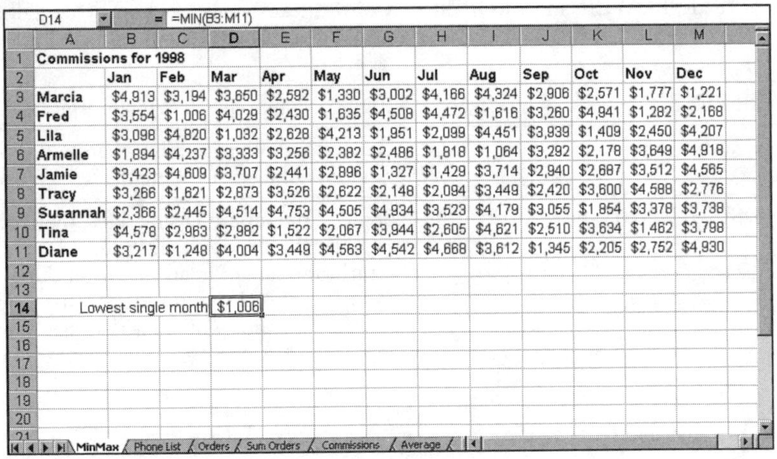

Figure 11.3.
The MIN function finds the minimum value in the selected table of data.

	A	B	C	D	E	F	G	H	I	J	K	L	M
1	Commissions for 1998												
2		Jan	Feb	Mar	Apr	May	Jun	Jul	Aug	Sep	Oct	Nov	Dec
3	Marcia	$4,913	$3,194	$3,650	$2,592	$1,330	$3,002	$4,166	$4,324	$2,906	$2,571	$1,777	$1,221
4	Fred	$3,554	$1,006	$4,029	$2,430	$1,635	$4,508	$4,472	$1,616	$3,260	$4,941	$1,282	$2,168
5	Lila	$3,098	$4,820	$1,032	$2,628	$4,213	$1,951	$2,099	$4,451	$3,939	$1,409	$2,450	$4,207
6	Armelle	$1,894	$4,237	$3,333	$3,256	$2,382	$2,486	$1,818	$1,064	$3,292	$2,178	$3,649	$4,918
7	Jamie	$3,423	$4,609	$3,707	$2,441	$2,896	$1,327	$1,429	$3,714	$2,940	$2,687	$3,512	$4,565
8	Tracy	$3,266	$1,621	$2,873	$3,526	$2,622	$2,148	$2,094	$3,449	$2,420	$3,600	$4,588	$2,776
9	Susannah	$2,366	$2,445	$4,514	$4,753	$4,505	$4,934	$3,523	$4,179	$3,055	$1,854	$3,378	$3,738
10	Tina	$4,578	$2,963	$2,982	$1,522	$2,067	$3,944	$2,605	$4,621	$2,510	$3,634	$1,462	$3,798
11	Diane	$3,217	$1,248	$4,004	$3,449	$4,563	$4,542	$4,668	$3,612	$1,345	$2,205	$2,752	$4,930
12													
13													
14		Lowest single month		$1,006									

D14 = =MIN(B3:M11)

You don't need the Formula Palette for a simple function such as MIN; to write the function yourself, follow these steps:

1. Click the cell in which you want to place the formula.

2. Type =.

3. Type min(.

4. On the worksheet, drag to select the cells you want to search for a minimum value (in this example, the range B3:M11, all the numbers in the table).

5. Type).

6. Press Enter.

The minimum value in the worksheet table shown in Figure 11.3 is $1,006, and it would have taken a bit more time to find it yourself.

Tip #156 from

Laurie

If your business requires monthly worksheets like the one in Figure 11.3, you could save yourself time by creating a template and including the MIN formula in it. When you open a copy of the template, the formula is already in place, and as you enter numbers, the formula finds the minimum value automatically.

Because the minimum value is the result of a formula, it continues to find the minimum value automatically, even if you change the numbers in the table.

→ To learn more about saving workbooks as templates, **see** "Saving an Excel Workbook As a Reusable Template," **p. 58**

MAX

The MAX function

`MAX(number1,number2,...)`

is the opposite of the MIN function and works exactly the same way. It finds the largest value in a selected range of cells. To write your own formula with the MAX function, you can follow the preceding procedure for the MIN function.

To write a MAX formula using the Formula Palette, follow these steps:

1. Click the cell in which you want to enter the formula.

2. Click the Paste Function button.

The Paste Function dialog box appears (shown in Figure 11.4).

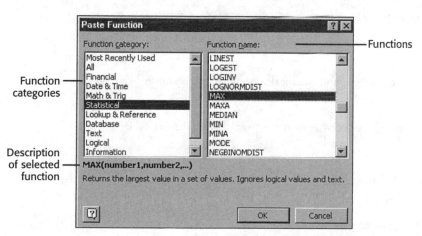

Figure 11.4.
The Paste Function dialog box helps you select and write a formula using any of Excel's many functions.

3. The MAX function falls under the Statistical category; click Statistical in the category list. (If you know the name of the function you want but don't know in which category to find it, click All.)

When you use the MAX or MIN function to determine the highest or lowest value in a large table, you still have to search to find where that value is located among all those numbers. You can make it jump out visually by combining the MAX or MIN function with conditional number formatting, which formats the number in the table with any formatting you choose. To learn more about conditional formatting, see Chapter 7.

4. Locate the MAX function in the function name list and double-click.

5. In the Formula Palette, highlight or delete any value in the Number1 argument text box and enter the entire table range by dragging to select the cells. In this example, the table range is A2:M11, but I previously named this range Commissions, so when I select the range, Excel inserts the range name, shown in Figure 11.5.

Figure 11.5.
Using a range name such as Commissions, instead of cell references, makes the formula more understandable.

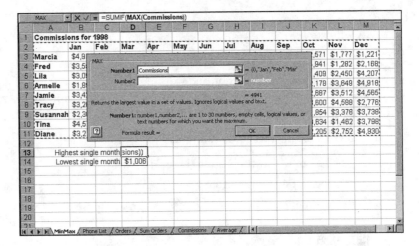

6. Click OK.

The formula is complete, and the maximum value in the range, 4941, is displayed (see Figure 11.6).

→ To learn more about conditional number formatting, **see** "Conditional Formatting," **p. 176**

AVERAGE

The AVERAGE function

```
AVERAGE(number1,number2,...)
```

is another common and easy-to-use function. It's as simple to write as the SUM, MIN, and MAX functions, so it's demonstrated here without using any dialog boxes.

The important thing to know about the AVERAGE function is that it gives a more correct result than you would get by adding cells and dividing by the number of cells. If you calculate averages by adding the cells together and then dividing by the number of cells, you'll occasionally get wrong answers because if a cell doesn't have a value in it, this method averages that cell as a zero. The AVERAGE function, however, adds the cells in the selected range and then divides the sum by the number of values; so any blank cells are left out of the calculation. (The comparison is shown in Figure 11.7. Cell comments show the formulas for each cell.)

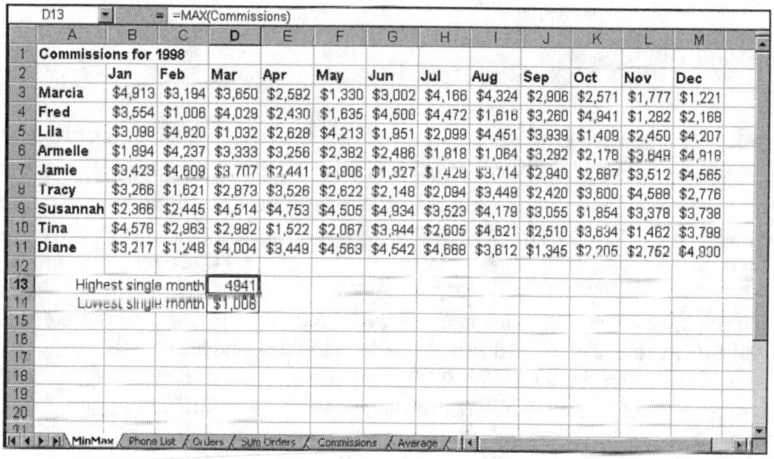

Figure 11.6.
Whether you use the Paste Function dialog box or write the formula yourself, the result is the same.

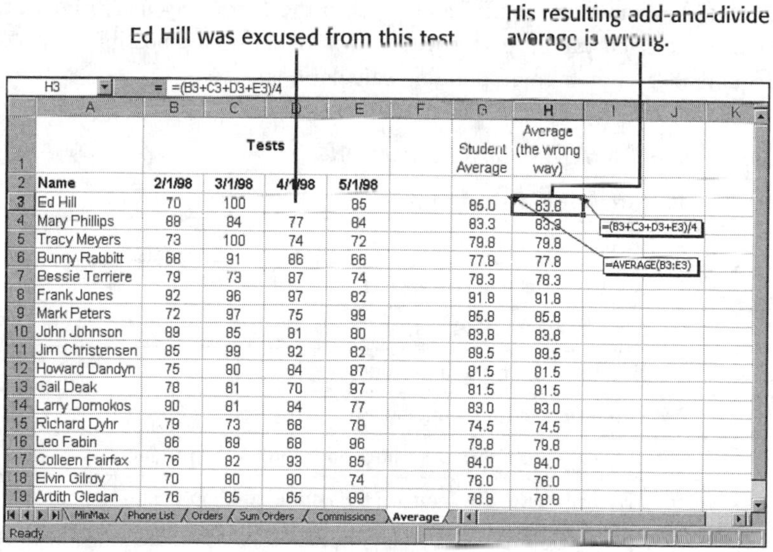

PART

IV

CH

11

Ed Hill was excused from this test

His resulting add-and-divide average is wrong.

Figure 11.7.
Adding and dividing don't always give the correct average, but the AVERAGE function does.

To write a formula using the AVERAGE function, follow these steps:

1. Click the cell in which you want to place the formula.
2. Type =AVERAGE(.
3. In the worksheet, drag the range of cells you want to average (or type the range name).
4. Type a closing parenthesis,).
5. Press Enter.

SUBTOTAL

The SUBTOTAL function

SUBTOTAL(function_num,ref1,...)

is particularly useful for calculating values in a filtered list, because it calculates only the visible cells in a range. If you use the SUM or AVERAGE functions, the entire table is calculated rather than the records you display with a filter. If, however, you use the SUBTOTAL function, the formula calculates the filtered, displayed records only, rather than the entire table.

Note

If you use the AutoSum button to create a SUM formula when the table is filtered, a SUBTOTAL formula is created instead of a SUM formula, and the new SUBTOTAL function calculates a sum. If you want the SUBTOTAL function to calculate an average instead of a sum, you need to change the calculation argument in the SUBTOTAL function.

The SUBTOTAL function can calculate several different functions, depending on the arguments you enter. The function requires a number in the function_num argument that determines what specific calculation it performs. Table 11.2 shows the possible SUBTOTAL function_num arguments and their corresponding calculations.

TABLE 11.2.   SUBTOTAL ARGUMENTS AND CALCULATIONS

This Argument	Performs This Calculation
1	AVERAGE (averages values)
2	COUNT (counts numeric values)
3	COUNTA (counts all values)
4	MAX (returns the maximum value)
5	MIN (returns the minimum value)
6	PRODUCT (multiplies the values and returns the product)
7	STDEV (calculates the standard deviation based on a sample)
8	STDEVP (calculates the standard deviation based on the whole population)
9	SUM (sums values)
10	VAR (calculates the variation based on a sample)
11	VARP (calculates the variation based on the whole population)

To illustrate how the SUBTOTAL function can be used, the next example sets up a SUBTOTAL formula that averages the filtered values in the Amount field of an expenses list. To write a SUBTOTAL formula, follow these steps:

1. Click a cell below the list in which you want to display the result of the formula, and click the Paste Function button.

Note

> If you click a cell next to the list, the cell is probably hidden when you filter the list; a cell below the list is still visible during a filter.

2. In the All or Math & Trig category, double-click SUBTOTAL.

   The SUBTOTAL dialog box appears (shown in Figure 11.8).

Calculation argument   Range to calculate

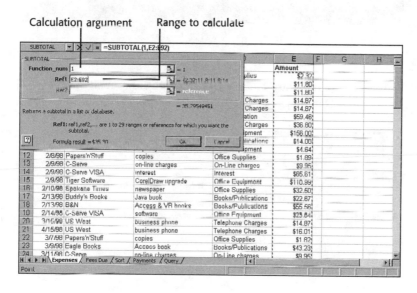

Figure 11.8.
This SUBTOTAL dialog box is set up to average whatever cells are displayed in the Amount column.

PART

IV

CH

11

3. In the Function_num box, type 1.

   The argument 1 tells SUBTOTAL to calculate an average. For a different calculation, look up the argument in Table 11.2.

4. In the Ref1 box, enter the range to calculate (in this case, the range E2:E92, in the Amount column).

5. Click OK.

   The SUBTOTAL formula calculates an average for the Amount cells that are displayed. Figure 11.9 shows the SUBTOTAL formula and the list filtered for Sprint charges.

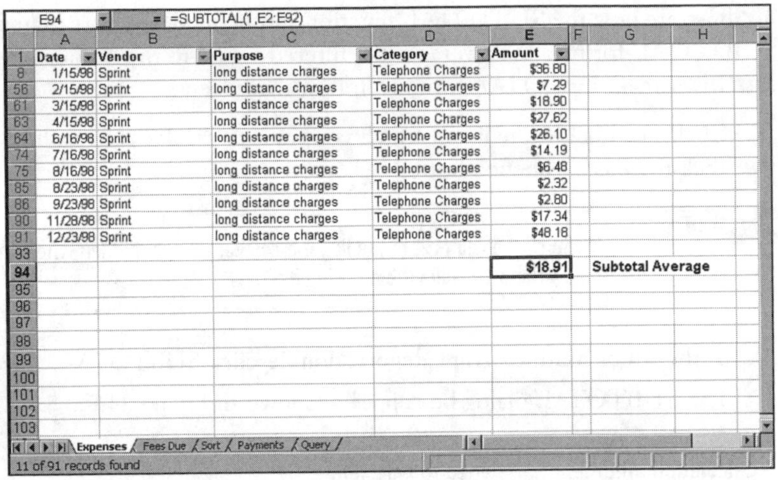

E94 | =SUBTOTAL(1,E2:E92)

	Date	Vendor	Purpose	Category	Amount
8	1/15/98	Sprint	long distance charges	Telephone Charges	$36.80
56	2/15/98	Sprint	long distance charges	Telephone Charges	$7.29
61	3/15/98	Sprint	long distance charges	Telephone Charges	$18.90
63	4/15/98	Sprint	long distance charges	Telephone Charges	$27.62
64	6/16/98	Sprint	long distance charges	Telephone Charges	$26.10
74	7/16/98	Sprint	long distance charges	Telephone Charges	$14.19
75	8/16/98	Sprint	long distance charges	Telephone Charges	$6.48
85	8/23/98	Sprint	long distance charges	Telephone Charges	$2.32
86	9/23/98	Sprint	long distance charges	Telephone Charges	$2.80
90	11/28/98	Sprint	long distance charges	Telephone Charges	$17.34
91	12/23/98	Sprint	long distance charges	Telephone Charges	$48.18
94					$18.91 Subtotal Average

Figure 11.9. Every time I change the filter, the SUBTOTAL formula recalculates an average for the displayed cells.

SUMIF

In the worksheet table shown in Figure 11.10, I want to know how much of the product named Celebes was sold in December.

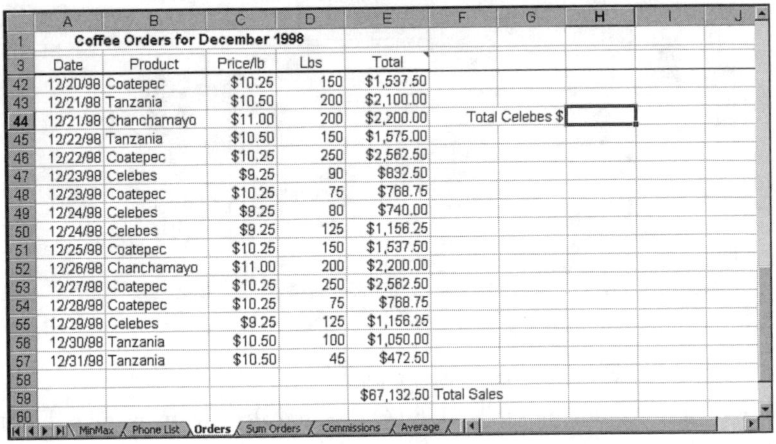

Coffee Orders for December 1998

	Date	Product	Price/lb	Lbs	Total
42	12/20/98	Coatepec	$10.25	150	$1,537.50
43	12/21/98	Tanzania	$10.50	200	$2,100.00
44	12/21/98	Chanchamayo	$11.00	200	$2,200.00
45	12/22/98	Tanzania	$10.50	150	$1,575.00
46	12/22/98	Coatepec	$10.25	250	$2,562.50
47	12/23/98	Celebes	$9.25	90	$832.50
48	12/23/98	Coatepec	$10.25	75	$768.75
49	12/24/98	Celebes	$9.25	80	$740.00
50	12/24/98	Celebes	$9.25	125	$1,156.25
51	12/25/98	Coatepec	$10.25	150	$1,537.50
52	12/26/98	Chanchamayo	$11.00	200	$2,200.00
53	12/27/98	Coatepec	$10.25	250	$2,562.50
54	12/28/98	Coatepec	$10.25	75	$768.75
55	12/29/98	Celebes	$9.25	125	$1,156.25
56	12/30/98	Tanzania	$10.50	100	$1,050.00
57	12/31/98	Tanzania	$10.50	45	$472.50
59					$67,132.50 Total Sales

Figure 11.10. For these December sales figures, I want to know the total revenues just for orders of Celebes coffee.

To find the answer, I use a SUMIF function

```
SUMIF(range,criteria,sum_range)
```

which sums values if they correspond to my criteria. (In this case, I write a formula that sums values in the Total column if they correspond to the value Celebes in the Product column.) A SUMIF formula can be written in one of two ways. You can use the Formula Palette, which is simpler and faster for single-criterion sums, or you can use the Conditional Sum Wizard, an add-in which is useful if you want to sum by two or more criteria. First, I'll show you how to write a simple SUMIF formula; then I'll show you how to use the wizard.

Note

> If you want to use more than one criterion in your conditional sum formula (for example, how much Celebes and Tanzania were sold in December), using the Conditional Sum Wizard is easier.

To use the Paste Function dialog box to write a SUMIF formula, follow these steps:

1. Click the cell in which you want to place the formula; then click the Paste Function button.

2. In the All or Math & Trig category, double-click SUMIF.

   The Formula Palette for SUMIF appears (see Figure 11.11).

Range containing criteria
(Product column)   Criteria (Celebes)

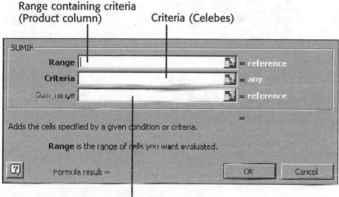

Figure 11.11.
The Formula Palette makes the SUMIF function reasonably easy to write.

Range containing values to sum (Total column)

3. In the Range box, enter the range of cells that contains the criteria (in this example, the Product column, because it contains the Celebes criteria).

Note

> My range entry, B:B, designates the entire column B as the range containing my criteria. It's important that there not be any other entries on the worksheet below this table, or the formula will calculate with those entries and get messed up. Also, the range reference B:B is a relative reference. If I wanted an absolute reference to column B, I'd type $B:$B.

You can drag the cells in column B (B3:B56), or you can enter the entire column (B:B), as I've done.

4. In the Criteria box, enter the criteria for which you want to sum values.

   ■ If it's a text string, as "Celebes" is, be sure to type quotation marks around it.

   ■ Alternatively, you can click a cell containing the entry Celebes, instead of typing the text string and quotation marks.

5. In the Sum_range box, enter the range of values you want to sum (in this example, column E, entered as the range E:E).

Your SUMIF dialog box should look similar to the one in Figure 11.12.

Figure 11.12.
The SUMIF dialog box, ready to sum only Celebes orders.

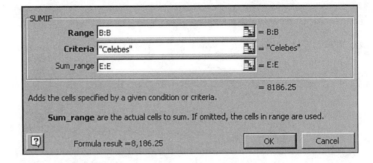

6. Click OK.

The SUMIF formula is complete (as shown in Figure 11.13). To find the total for Tanzania, open the cell and edit the formula. Change "Celebes" to "Tanzania" and press Enter.

Figure 11.13.
Celebes orders totaled $8,186.25 in December.

	A	B	C	D	E	F	G	H	I	J
	H44		= =SUMIF(B:B,"Celebes",E:E)							
1		Coffee Orders for December 1998								
3	Date	Product	Price/lb	Lbs	Total					
42	12/20/98	Coatepec	$10.25	150	$1,537.50					
43	12/21/98	Tanzania	$10.50	200	$2,100.00					
44	12/21/98	Chanchamayo	$11.00	200	$2,200.00		Total Celebes $	8,186.25		
45	12/22/98	Tanzania	$10.50	150	$1,575.00					
46	12/22/98	Coatepec	$10.25	250	$2,562.50					
47	12/23/98	Celebes	$9.25	90	$832.50					
48	12/23/98	Coatepec	$10.25	75	$768.75					
49	12/24/98	Celebes	$9.25	80	$740.00					
50	12/24/98	Celebes	$9.25	125	$1,156.25					
51	12/25/98	Coatepec	$10.25	150	$1,537.50					
52	12/26/98	Chanchamayo	$11.00	200	$2,200.00					
53	12/27/98	Coatepec	$10.25	250	$2,562.50					
54	12/28/98	Coatepec	$10.25	75	$768.75					
55	12/29/98	Celebes	$9.25	125	$1,156.25					
56	12/30/98	Tanzania	$10.50	100	$1,050.00					
57	12/31/98	Tanzania	$10.50	45	$472.50					
58										
59					$67,132.50	Total Sales				
60										

MinMax / Phone List / Orders / Sum Orders / Commissions / Average

The Conditional Sum Wizard is another way to get the same result, but you can switch the completed total to a different condition more easily. Instead of editing the formula, you type a different condition in the worksheet condition cell.

Note

If you don't see the Wizard command on your Tools menu, or if you don't see the Conditional Sum command on the Wizard submenu, you need to install the Conditional Sum Wizard add-in. Click Tools, Add-Ins, mark the Conditional Sum Wizard check box, and click OK.

To use the Conditional Sum Wizard, follow these steps:

1. Click anywhere in the table.

2. On the Tools menu, point to Wizard, and click Conditional Sum.

   The Conditional Sum Wizard starts (shown in Figure 11.14). If the selected range is wrong, change it by typing new references or dragging the range on the worksheet.

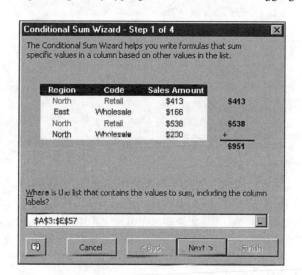

Figure 11.14.
The Conditional Sum Wizard assumes the table you clicked is the range you want.

3. Click Next.

4. In Step 2 of the wizard, choose the column you want to sum (in this case, Total) and the criteria.

   To set the criteria for this example, select Product, select =, and then select Celebes (shown in Figure 11.15).

5. Click Add Condition to add the condition to a list of conditions for the sum and then click Next.

6. In Step 3 of the wizard, you can choose to display just the sum or the sum and labels. Then click Next.

7. In the next few steps of the wizard, if you selected the "Formula and Conditional Values" option in Step 3 of the wizard, you can decide where the labels should be placed on the worksheet. In each step, click the wizard box and then click a cell on the worksheet for the criteria the wizard specifies; then click Next.

8. When you get to the last wizard step, click in the wizard box and then click the cell where you want the formula to be entered, and then click Finish.

Figure 11.15.
You can set multiple conditions by using the Conditional Sum Wizard; just keep adding conditions to the list in the dialog box.

Set criteria in these boxes.

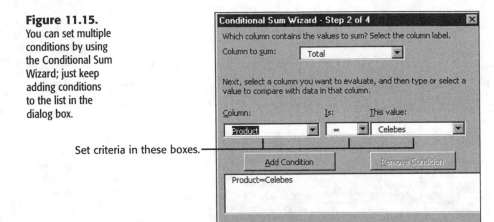

The wizard result is identical to the result of the SUMIF formula when you want to sum for a single condition (see Figure 11.16). The practical difference between a SUMIF formula you write and the SUMIF formula the wizard writes is that the wizard can use multiple conditions for selecting cells to sum, and the conditions can be changed by typing in the worksheet. For example, if you want to see the sum of Coatepec orders for December, replace **Celebes** in cell G46 with **Coatepec**.

Figure 11.16.
The SUMIF function or the Conditional Sum Wizard: Use the wizard to sum for more than one category.

H46		= {=SUM(IF($B$4:$B$57=G46,$E$4:$E$57,0))}								
	A	B	C	D	E	F	G	H	I	J
1	Coffee Orders for December 1998									
3	Date	Product	Price/lb	Lbs	Total					
41	12/20/98	Santo Domingo	$9.50	100	$950.00					
42	12/20/98	Coatepec	$10.25	150	$1,537.50					
43	12/21/98	Tanzania	$10.50	200	$2,100.00					
44	12/21/98	Chanchamayo	$11.00	200	$2,200.00		Total Celebes $	8,186.25		
45	12/22/98	Tanzania	$10.50	150	$1,575.00					
46	12/22/98	Coatepec	$10.25	250	$2,562.50		Celebes	$8,186.25		
47	12/23/98	Celebes	$9.25	90	$832.50					
48	12/23/98	Coatepec	$10.25	75	$768.75					
49	12/24/98	Celebes	$9.25	80	$740.00					
50	12/24/98	Celebes	$9.25	125	$1,156.25					
51	12/25/98	Coatepec	$10.25	150	$1,537.50					
52	12/26/98	Chanchamayo	$11.00	200	$2,200.00					
53	12/27/98	Coatepec	$10.25	250	$2,562.50					
54	12/28/98	Coatepec	$10.25	75	$768.75					
55	12/29/98	Celebes	$9.25	125	$1,156.25					
56	12/30/98	Tanzania	$10.50	100	$1,050.00					
57	12/31/98	Tanzania	$10.50	45	$472.50					
58										
59					$67,132.50	Total Sales				

MinMax / Phone List \ **Orders** \ Sum Orders / Commissions / Average /

Conditional Sum Wizard result   SUMIF result

COUNT, COUNTA, AND COUNTBLANK

These functions count the number of values in a range that meet each function's built-in criteria.

The COUNT function

```
=COUNT(range)
```

counts the number of numeric values in a range, and ignores all nonnumeric values and blank cells.

The COUNTA function

```
=COUNTA(range)
```

counts all values in a range that are not empty (if you need to count text values, use COUNTA).

The COUNTBLANK function

```
=COUNTBLANK(range)
```

counts all the cells in a range that are empty.

These functions are most often used nested in other functions. The value returned by the nested function becomes the value used as another function's argument.

To write a formula using any of the COUNT functions, use the same procedures as for MIN, MAX, SUM, or AVERAGE. To use these functions nested in another function, insert the function (without its equal sign) in place of the argument whose value it supplies (you'll see an example of this in the OFFSET function, later in this chapter).

PART

IV

CH

11

COUNTIF

The COUNTIF function

```
COUNTIF(range,criteria)
```

counts the number of values in a range that meet a specific criterion, such as "How many orders were there for Celebes coffee in December?"

Tip #159 from

Laurie

> Another way to get a quick answer to this question is to filter the table to show only Celebes and then take a count of the orders by using AutoCalculate's COUNT function.

→ To learn about AutoCalculate, **see** "Using AutoCalculate for Quick Totals," **p. 264**

→ To learn about filters, **see** "Filtering a List," **p. 513**

The COUNTIF function works like the SUMIF function but without a wizard alternative (nor is there any need for one).

To write a COUNTIF formula, follow these steps:

1. Click the cell in which you want to place the result; then click the Paste Function button.
2. In the All or Statistical categories, double-click the COUNTIF function.

   The Formula Palette opens with the COUNTIF function arguments (shown in Figure 11.17).

Figure 11.17.
COUNTIF requires only a range to search and what to count in that range.

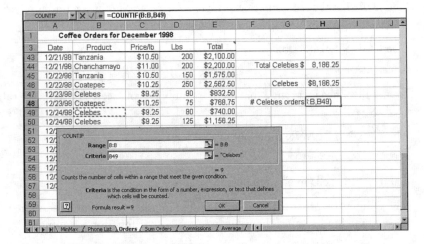

3. In the Range box, enter the range of cells to search (in this case, I've entered column B).
4. In the Criteria box, enter the criteria for counting cells (in this case, I've clicked cell B49, a Celebes entry, so the function counts all identical entries).
5. Click OK.

   The formula is complete (shown in Figure 11.18). I can find the average Celebes order by dividing the sum by the count.

Figure 11.18.
COUNTIF counts the number of Celebes orders in the list.

	A	B	C	D	E	F	G	H	I	J
		H48		= =COUNTIF(B:B,B49)						
1		Coffee Orders for December 1998								
3	Date	Product	Price/lb	Lbs	Total					
43	12/21/98	Tanzania	$10.50	200	$2,100.00					
44	12/21/98	Chanchamayo	$11.00	200	$2,200.00		Total Celebes $	8,186.25		
45	12/22/98	Tanzania	$10.50	150	$1,575.00					
46	12/22/98	Coatepec	$10.25	250	$2,562.50		Celebes	$8,186.25		
47	12/23/98	Celebes	$9.25	90	$832.50					
48	12/23/98	Coatepec	$10.25	75	$768.75		# Celebes orders	9		
49	12/24/98	Celebes	$9.25	80	$740.00					
50	12/24/98	Celebes	$9.25	125	$1,156.25					
51	12/25/98	Coatepec	$10.25	150	$1,537.50					
52	12/26/98	Chanchamayo	$11.00	200	$2,200.00					
53	12/27/98	Coatepec	$10.25	250	$2,562.50					
54	12/28/98	Coatepec	$10.25	75	$768.75					
55	12/29/98	Celebes	$9.25	125	$1,156.25					
56	12/30/98	Tanzania	$10.50	100	$1,050.00					
57	12/31/98	Tanzania	$10.50	45	$472.50					
58										
59					$67,132.50	Total Sales				
60										
61										

MinMax / Phone List / Orders / Sum Orders / Commissions / Average /

Number of Celebes orders in list

→ To learn more about AutoFilter, **see** "Managing the List with AutoFilters," **p. 513**

VLOOKUP AND HLOOKUP

Sometimes you need to look up a value in another table. For example, in an invoice, you might want Excel to look up the state tax rate for the shipping address, or if you're a teacher keeping grade sheets, you might want Excel to look up the letter grades corresponding to your students' test score averages.

A good function for looking up values in another table is VLOOKUP

```
VLOOKUP(lookup_value,table_array,col_index_num,range_lookup)
```

(or its transposed equivalent, HLOOKUP)

```
HLOOKUP(lookup_value,table_array,row_index_num,range_lookup)
```

These two functions are quite similar, the only difference being that one works vertically (VLOOKUP) and the other works horizontally (HLOOKUP) in the table. I'll demonstrate VLOOKUP, and when you understand VLOOKUP, you'll be able to figure out HLOOKUP if you ever need it.

Write a VLOOKUP formula.

1. Create a lookup table that contains the values you want to look up (such as a state tax rate table or the letter grades table I use in this example).

   The table needs to be set up so that the values you are looking up (in this example, the test averages) are in the leftmost column (as shown in Figure 11.19) and sorted in ascending order. The table can have several columns in it, as long as the values you look up are on the left.

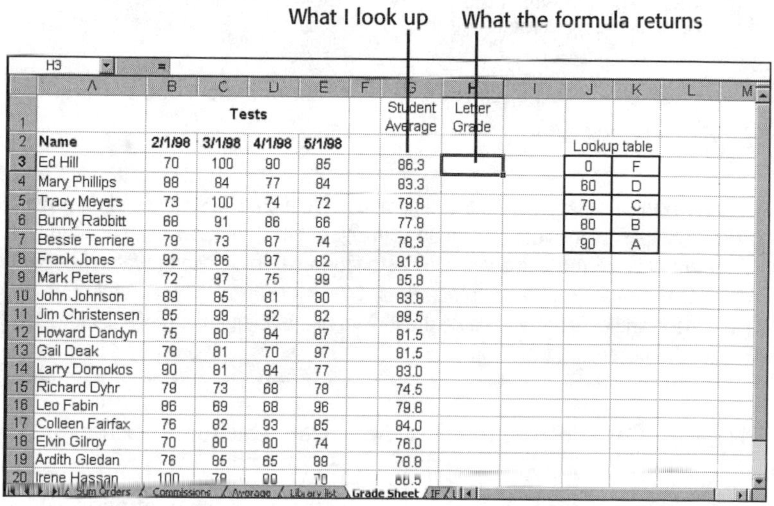

PART

IV

CH

11

What I look up   What the formula returns

Figure 11.19.
In my lookup table, the values I want to look up (test scores) are in the leftmost column (column J), and the table is sorted in ascending order.

Tip #160 from

Laurie

A lookup table can be on the same worksheet, another worksheet, or in another work-book. For example, if you need several identical worksheets that all look up values in the same table, you can create one table on its own worksheet and use that table in the VLOOKUP formulas on all the other worksheets.

For greater convenience, you can name the table and refer to it by name in the for-mula.

2. Click the cell in which you want the result to appear; then click the Paste Function button.

3. In the All or Lookup & Reference categories, double-click the VLOOKUP function. The VLOOKUP dialog box appears (shown in Figure 11.20).

Figure 11.20.
The VLOOKUP dialog box is the easiest way to write the function until you become familiar with it.

What to look up   Where to look it up

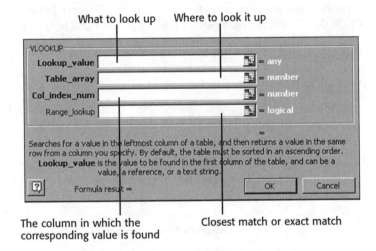

The column in which the   Closest match or exact match
corresponding value is found

4. Click the Lookup_value box and click the cell that contains the value you want to look up (in this case, the test average).

Note

If you're using a range reference instead of a range name, be sure you change the range reference types to absolute (as I've done in Figure 11.21); otherwise, the lookup table range adjusts incorrectly in every copy of the formula. To change the reference type, open the formula, click the reference, press F4 to cycle through types, and press Enter to finish the formula. Better yet, name the lookup range—then if the range is moved for any reason, the formulas can still find it.

5. Click the Table_array box and drag to select the lookup table (or enter the range name if you named the table).

6. In the Col_index_num box, type the number of the lookup table column in which Excel is to find a corresponding value. Think of the table columns as numbered left to right,

starting with 1. In this example, the corresponding values (the letter grades) are in Column 2 of the lookup table.

7. In the Range_lookup box, decide whether you want to find the closest match or an exact match. For the closest match (which is appropriate in this case), leave the box empty. For an exact match (for example, in an unsorted list), type **false**.

In this case, each score you look up has a closest match, but probably not an exact match. The lookup table is sorted in ascending order, and VLOOKUP looks down the column for the closest match that's less than the test score value that it looks up.

For this example, the VLOOKUP dialog box should look like the one in Figure 11.21.

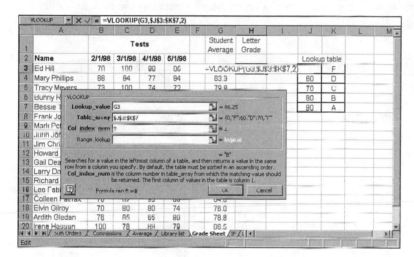

Figure 11.21.
The VLOOKUP dialog box is ready to look up a letter grade for the test score average.

PART

IV

CH

11

8. Click OK.

The VLOOKUP function looks up the score in the lookup table, finds the closest match, and returns the letter grade in the second column.

9. To copy the formula quickly down the side of the table, position the mouse pointer over the AutoFill handle and double-click.

Double-clicking the AutoFill handle works if the column is adjacent to the table, as shown in Figure 11.22. The formula is copied down the length of the table.

MATCH AND INDEX

The MATCH function

```
MATCH(lookup_value,lookup_array,match_type)
```

looks for a specific value in a single column or row, and returns a number that indicates the value's position in the list. The MATCH function is most often used in conjunction with other functions, such as INDEX (examples of the MATCH function alone and nested in an INDEX function are shown in Figure 11.23). The lookup_value argument is the value you are looking for; the lookup_array argument is the row or column being searched; and the match_type argument tells the function whether the row or column is sorted. The three match_type arguments are

- **0**—searches for an exact match; used in unsorted lists; returns #NA if an exact match isn't found.
- **1**—searches for the largest value less than or equal to the lookup_value; list must be sorted in ascending order. If omitted, the argument is assumed to be **1**.
- **–1**—searches for the smallest value greater than or equal to the lookup_value; list must be sorted in descending order.

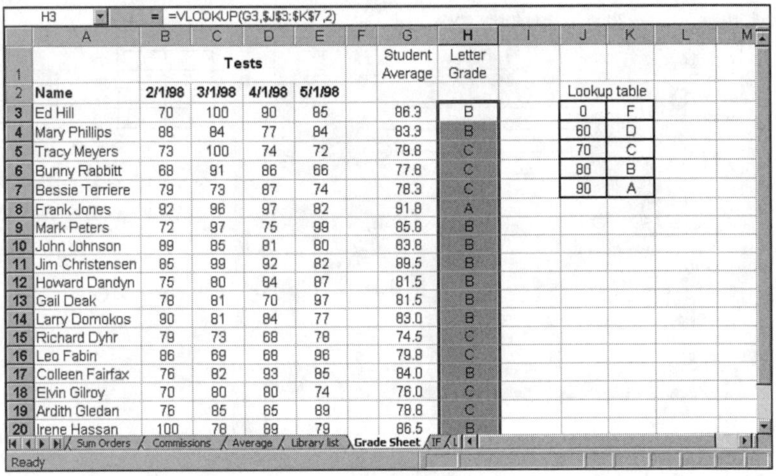

H3 = =VLOOKUP(G3,$J$3:$K$7,2)

	A	B	C	D	E	F	G	H	I	J	K
1		Tests					Student Average	Letter Grade			
2	**Name**	**2/1/98**	**3/1/98**	**4/1/98**	**5/1/98**					Lookup table	
3	Ed Hill	70	100	90	85		86.3	B		0	F
4	Mary Phillips	88	84	77	84		83.3	B		60	D
5	Tracy Meyers	73	100	74	72		79.8	C		70	C
6	Bunny Rabbitt	68	91	86	66		77.8	C		80	B
7	Bessie Terriere	79	73	87	74		78.3	C		90	A
8	Frank Jones	92	96	97	82		91.8	A			
9	Mark Peters	72	97	75	99		85.8	B			
10	John Johnson	89	85	81	80		83.8	B			
11	Jim Christensen	85	99	92	82		89.5	B			
12	Howard Dandyn	75	80	84	87		81.5	B			
13	Gail Deak	78	81	70	97		81.5	B			
14	Larry Domokos	90	81	84	77		83.0	B			
15	Richard Dyhr	79	73	68	78		74.5	C			
16	Leo Fabin	86	69	68	96		79.8	C			
17	Colleen Fairfax	76	82	93	85		84.0	B			
18	Elvin Gilroy	70	80	80	74		76.0	C			
19	Ardith Gledan	76	85	65	89		78.8	C			
20	Irene Hassan	100	78	89	79		86.5	B			

Sum Orders / Commissions / Average / Library list / Grade Sheet / IF

Ready

Figure 11.22.
AutoFill is the fastest way to copy the formula down the length of the table.

The INDEX function has two syntaxes:

```
INDEX(array,row_num,column_num)
```

is the appropriate function for looking up a value in a single range, and

```
INDEX(reference,row_num,column_num,area_num)
```

is the appropriate function for looking up a value in multiple noncontiguous ranges. The INDEX function searches a range for a specific row and/or column position, and returns the value at that position. The only difference between the two forms of the INDEX function is that in the second form, INDEX can search multiple ranges, and you supply a number (1, 2, 3, and so forth) that tells the function which range to search. Examples of the INDEX function alone and with nested MATCH functions are shown in Figure 11.23.

MATCH and INDEX used together are similar to VLOOKUP, and useful for automating lookups on a worksheet. To write a nested INDEX/MATCH formula using the Formula Palette, follow these steps:

1. Set up input cells where you can type values for the MATCH functions (as shown in Figure 11.23).

2. Click in the cell where you want the result, and then click the Paste Function button.

3. In the Lookup & Reference category, double-click INDEX.

4. In the Select Arguments dialog box, select the upper row of arguments and click OK (the lower row is used for indexing multiple noncontiguous ranges). The Formula Palette opens.

5. In the Array argument, enter the name or range reference for the table where you want to look up a value.

6. Click in the Row_num argument, and then select MATCH from the drop-down function list at the left end of the Formula bar (if you don't see MATCH listed, select More Functions and then double-click MATCH in the Paste Function dialog box). The Formula Palette changes to MATCH, and the MATCH function is nested in place of the Row_num argument in the Formula bar.

7. Click in the Lookup_value argument; then click to select the row input cell in the worksheet.

8. Click in the Lookup_array argument; then type or drag to select the row where the MATCH function looks up the Lookup_value.

9. In the Match_type argument, type **0**.

10. In the Formula bar, type a comma between the two closing parentheses. The comma tells Excel you're not finished with the formula, and the Formula Palette returns to the INDEX function. The Row_num argument will be filled in with a nested MATCH function.

11. Repeat steps 6 through 9 to write a MATCH function for the column input.

12. Before you click OK, inspect the formula in the Formula bar. Excel may have entered an unnecessary comma between the two closing parentheses. Delete the comma in the Formula bar, and the Formula Palette returns to the INDEX function, fully filled in.

13. Click OK. The formula is entered, and returns the value found at the intersection of your two input cells. If you change the entries in the input cells, the INDEX/MATCH formula looks up the new values.

After you understand how the INDEX and MATCH functions work, you may find it easier to write them yourself without the Formula Palette.

PART

IV

CH

11

Tip #161 from

Laurie

If a formula is long and complex, write the nested functions separately, and then copy and paste the nested functions (without their equal signs) into the larger formula.

Figure 11.23.
Nested together,
MATCH and INDEX
are useful for
automating lookups
in a worksheet.

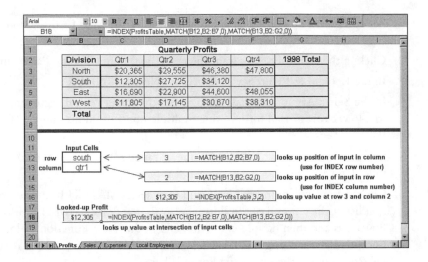

IF

The IF function

IF(logical_test,value_if_true,value_if_false)

is another way to determine a cell value based on criteria you set. The IF function works like this: IF a statement is true, THEN return this first value; OTHERWISE, return this second value. (Figure 11.24 shows several examples of the IF function in action.)

Figure 11.24.
You can use the IF
function in a lot of
creative ways. Each
formula in column C
is spelled out begin-
ning in column D.

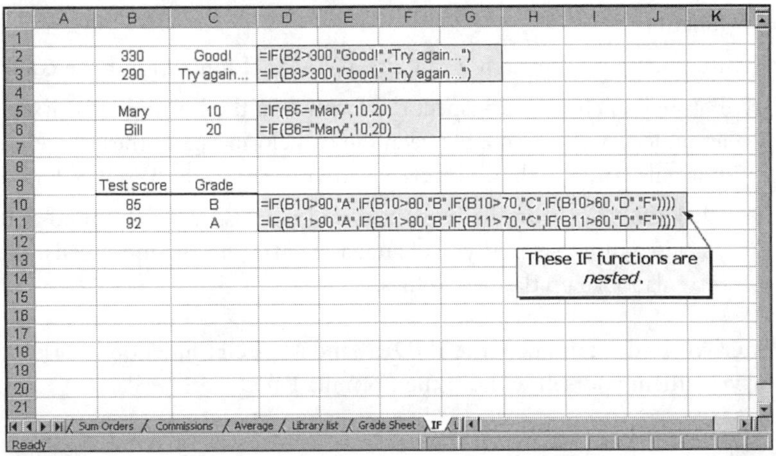

As you can see in Figure 11.24, IF functions can be *nested* or combined within other IF functions to make them even more useful. In fact, any function can be nested in another function, up to seven levels deep, which enables you to be creative with worksheet calculations. After you get comfortable writing formulas, you'll probably find it easiest to write IF formulas manually, but you can also use the Formula Palette.

To write an IF formula using the Formula Palette, follow these steps:

1. Click the cell in which you want to place the result, and then click the Paste Function button.

2. In the Logical category, double-click the IF function. The Formula Palette appears.

3. In the Logical_test box, type the condition the function is testing for. For example, in Figure 11.23, the formula in cell C2 uses a logical operator (>) to test whether the value in B2 is greater than 300.

4. In the Value_if_true box, enter the value to return if the logical test result is true. For example, in Figure 11.23, the formula in cell C2 returns the text Good! if the value in B2 *is* greater than 300.

5. In the Value_if_false box, enter the value to return if the logical test result is false. For example, in Figure 11.23, the formula in cell C2 returns the text Try again... if the value in B2 *is not* greater than 300.

6. Click OK to complete the formula.

When you nest functions, each nested function takes the place of an argument. For example, in Figure 11.24, rows 10 and 11, each nested IF function takes the place of the value_if_false argument in the higher-level IF function, until the last and most internal IF function, which has a value_if_false argument of "F."

You'll find worksheet examples of the IF function with nested logical and information functions in the section "IF, Information, and Logical Functions."

ISBLANK, ISNUMBER, AND ISTEXT

ISBLANK, ISNUMBER, and ISTEXT are called *information* functions, and are used nested in other formulas. Each of them returns either TRUE or FALSE, and the formula in which the function is nested uses that value to continue its calculation. You'll find the Information functions in the Information category in the Paste Function dialog box.

The ISBLANK function

```
ISBLANK(value)
```

tests whether a cell is empty, and if so, returns TRUE (if there is a value in the cell, it returns FALSE).

The ISNUMBER function

```
ISNUMBER(value)
```

tests whether a cell's value is numeric, and if so, returns TRUE (if the value is anything other than numeric, it returns FALSE). The value can be an entry or the result of a formula in the cell.

The ISTEXT function

```
ISTEXT(value)
```

tests whether a cell's value is text, and if so, returns TRUE (if the value is anything other than text, it returns FALSE). The value can be an entry or the result of a formula in the cell.

Used alone, information functions add little to a worksheet, but they're useful when nested in other functions and invaluable in programming procedures. You'll find worksheet examples of the IF function with nested information functions in the section " IF, Information, and Logical Functions."

AND, OR, and NOT

AND, OR, and NOT are called *logical* functions, and are used nested in other formulas. Each of them returns either TRUE or FALSE, and the formula in which the function is nested uses that value to continue its calculation. You'll find the Logical functions in the Logical category in the Paste Function dialog box.

The AND function

```
AND(logical1,logical2,...)
```

tests whether *all* of its arguments are TRUE; if so, it returns the value TRUE (if any of its arguments are FALSE, it returns FALSE). In plain language, AND asks whether argument1 *and* argument2 *and* argument3 are TRUE—if so, it returns TRUE; if not, it returns FALSE.

The OR function

```
OR(logical1,logical2,...)
```

tests whether *any* of its arguments are TRUE; if so, it returns the value TRUE (if all of its arguments are FALSE, it returns FALSE). In plain language, OR asks whether argument1 *or* argument2 *or* argument3 is TRUE—if so, it returns TRUE; if not, it returns FALSE.

The NOT function

```
NOT(logical)
```

tests whether a criterion is *not* true. If the criterion is *not* true, the function returns TRUE; if the criterion *is* true, the function returns FALSE. For example, an IF formula that calculates a discounted subtotal in an invoice might read, "*If* the value in cell SubTotal is *not* greater than $500, then return the value in SubTotal; otherwise, return 90% of the value in SubTotal." This formula would look like this:

```
=IF(NOT(SubTotal>500),SubTotal,SubTotal*.9)
```

Of course, there are always other ways to write any formula, and another way might make more intuitive sense to you, but this example demonstrates how the NOT function works.

Used alone, logical functions add little to a worksheet, but they're useful when nested in other functions and invaluable in programming procedures. You'll find worksheet examples of the IF function with nested logical functions in the section "IF, Information, and Logical Functions."

IF, INFORMATION, AND LOGICAL FUNCTIONS

The Information and Logical functions become useful when they're nested in other functions, by providing the values TRUE and FALSE as arguments for those functions.

Figure 11.25 shows the ISBLANK, ISNUMBER, AND, and OR functions at work in a worksheet. Their TRUE and FALSE results are used as arguments in the formulas in Figure 11.26.

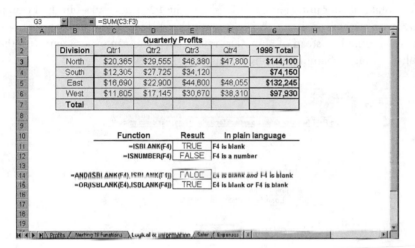

Figure 11.25.
Logical and Information functions test cell values and return TRUE or FALSE.

In Figure 11.26, the Logical function ISNUMBER checks whether the cell values are numbers, and the AND function checks whether the cell values are *all* numbers. The If formula says, IF cell C3 *and* D3 *and* E3 *and* F3 are numbers, then sum their values, otherwise display the text "Data incomplete". The opposite formula, using OR and ISBLANK functions, gives the same results in this situation.

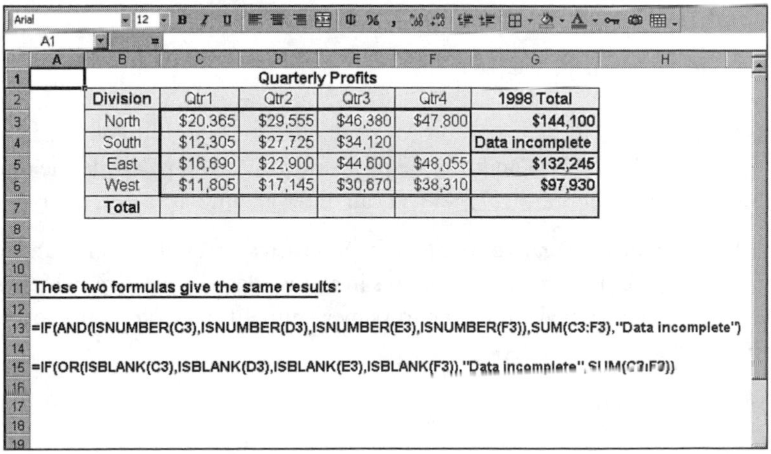

	A	B	C	D	E	F	G	H
1				Quarterly Profits				
2		Division	Qtr1	Qtr2	Qtr3	Qtr4	1998 Total	
3		North	$20,365	$29,555	$46,380	$47,800	$144,100	
4		South	$12,305	$27,725	$34,120		Data incomplete	
5		East	$16,690	$22,900	$44,600	$48,055	$132,245	
6		West	$11,805	$17,145	$30,670	$38,310	$97,930	
7		Total						

These two formulas give the same results:

=IF(AND(ISNUMBER(C3),ISNUMBER(D3),ISNUMBER(E3),ISNUMBER(F3)),SUM(C3:F3),"Data incomplete")

=IF(OR(ISBLANK(C3),ISBLANK(D3),ISBLANK(E3),ISBLANK(F3)),"Data incomplete",SUM(C3:F3))

Figure 11.26.
The TRUE and FALSE results from Logical and Information functions tell the IF formula what to do.

PMT

If you're shopping for a house, car, boat, or anything else that's expensive enough to require a loan, a key bit of information you want to know is the monthly payment. The PMT function

```
PMT(rate,nper,pv,fv,type)
```

figures it out for you quickly if you provide the annual interest rate, number of monthly payments, and total loan amount. (Figure 11.27 shows the PMT formula—in the Formula bar—filled out with the appropriate cells in the worksheet.) If you use cell references or named cells in the formula instead of numerical values, then you can experiment with the formula results by simply changing the input values on the worksheet.

Figure 11.27.
Use the PMT function to calculate how much of a loan you can afford.

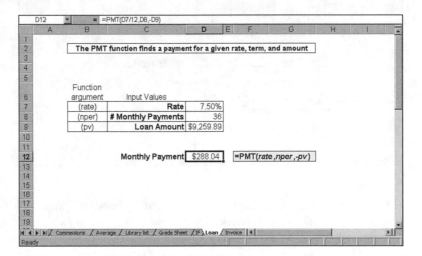

Two things to be aware of when you use the PMT function are

- Match the rate to the terms.
- The function calculates a negative payment.

If the interest rate is annual (as most are), and your payments are monthly, you need to divide the rate by 12 to make the rate and terms equivalent. It's easiest to divide the function argument by 12 (as shown in Figure 11.27), so you can enter an annual rate in the rate cell.

The PMT function calculates a negative payment for a positive amount, or a negative amount for a positive payment. To make the figures in the worksheet positive (which is what folks are accustomed to seeing), make the function's pv argument negative in the formula (as shown in Figure 11.27).

NOW AND TODAY

The NOW function returns the current date and time. The TODAY function returns the current date. They're useful to have in the corner of a worksheet so that you can always tell how current (or old) the information in a printed page is.

> **Note**
>
> If you want to see the serial number for a date, enter the date, and then format the cell as General. The serial numbers for dates begin with the number 1 on January 1, 1900; the serial number 100,000 corresponds to the date October 14, 2173. Time is determined by numbers on the right side of the decimal point in the serial number. For example, the decimal .5 corresponds to 12:00:00 noon.

> **Note**
>
> All the Office 2000 programs can format dates with four-digit years. If a two-digit year is from 00 through 29, the year is interpreted (and calculated) as 2000 through 2029. If the two-digit year is from 30 through 99, the year is interpreted (and calculated) as 1930 through 1999. If your data has dates that fall within the range 1900 through 1929, use four-digit years to keep your calculations correct.

NOW and TODAY have no arguments; to write them, you type =now() or =today(), and press Enter. (Be sure you include the parentheses and don't type anything between the parentheses.) The resulting value is actually a serial number for the number of days since January 1, 1900. It's displayed as a date or time because the cell has a date or time format.

PART
IV
CH
11

> **Tip #162 from**
>
> *Laurie*
>
> A quick trick to keep track of how long you've been working in a workbook uses a couple of NOW formulas. Pick two unused cells in the corner of the workbook, and enter the NOW formula in both of them. Copy one of the NOW formulas and paste it in place as a value. In a third cell, write a formula that subtracts the value cell from the active formula cell. Every time the workbook recalculates (or you press F9), the third cell shows the elapsed time since you wrote the formulas.

To learn more about converting formula results to values, see the later section "Converting Formula Results to Values." To learn more about formatting numbers, see Chapter 7, "Modifying Numbers and Dates."

LEFT AND RIGHT

Text functions such as LEFT and RIGHT

LEFT(text,num_chars)

RIGHT(text,num_chars)

seem rather pointless unless you have a real-life use for them; then, they're quite useful. The LEFT and RIGHT functions work similarly, except that LEFT forms a text string and RIGHT extracts the rightmost characters.

The list in Figure 11.28 is a stock list for a bookstore. The bookstore's owner wants to add a column of author codes that begin with the first three letters of the author's last name.

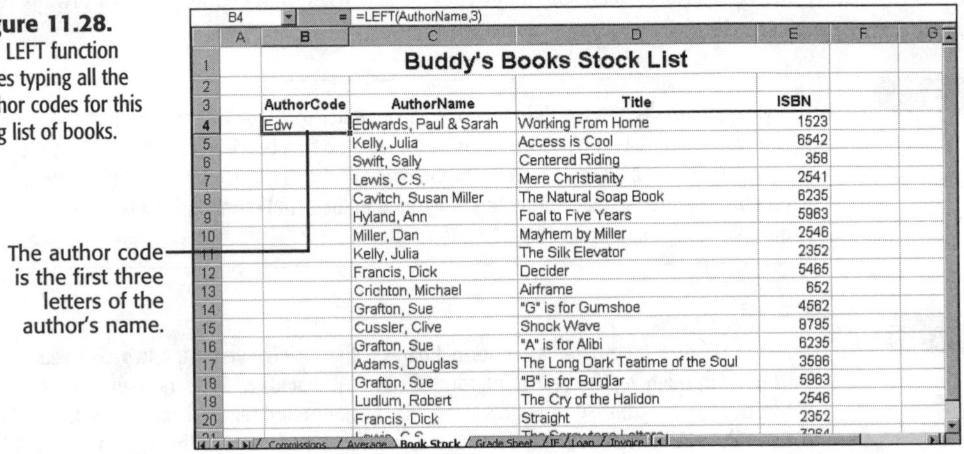

Figure 11.28.
The LEFT function saves typing all the author codes for this long list of books.

The author code is the first three letters of the author's name.

	B4	▼	=	=LEFT(AuthorName,3)		
	A	B	C	D	E	F	G
1			Buddy's Books Stock List				
2							
3		AuthorCode	AuthorName	Title	ISBN		
4		Edw	Edwards, Paul & Sarah	Working From Home	1523		
5			Kelly, Julia	Access is Cool	6542		
6			Swift, Sally	Centered Riding	358		
7			Lewis, C.S.	Mere Christianity	2541		
8			Cavitch, Susan Miller	The Natural Soap Book	6235		
9			Hyland, Ann	Foal to Five Years	5963		
10			Miller, Dan	Mayhem by Miller	2546		
11			Kelly, Julia	The Silk Elevator	2352		
12			Francis, Dick	Decider	5465		
13			Crichton, Michael	Airframe	652		
14			Grafton, Sue	"G" is for Gumshoe	4562		
15			Cussler, Clive	Shock Wave	8795		
16			Grafton, Sue	"A" is for Alibi	6235		
17			Adams, Douglas	The Long Dark Teatime of the Soul	3586		
18			Grafton, Sue	"B" is for Burglar	5963		
19			Ludlum, Robert	The Cry of the Halidon	2546		
20			Francis, Dick	Straight	2352		
21			Lewis, C.S.	The Screwtape Letters	7284		

At this point, the LEFT function saves a lot of redundant typing.

To write a formula by using the LEFT function, follow these steps:

1. Click the cell where you want the result of the function (in this case, the book's author code) to appear.

Note

> Remember, typing a function name in lowercase letters is a good way to catch spelling errors. If the function name is spelled correctly, Excel converts it to uppercase when you complete the formula.

2. Type =left(.

3. Click the cell containing the value from which you want to extract characters (in this case, the AuthorName cell next to the formula).

4. Type a comma (,), and then type the number of characters you want to extract (in this case, 3, for the leftmost three characters).

5. Type) and press Enter.

   The formula is complete, and it extracts the three leftmost characters in the AuthorName cell next to it.

6. Use AutoFill to copy the formula down the length of the list.

   As you can see in Figure 11.29, this saves a lot of typing.

Tip #163 from

Laurie

To combine the extracted letters in the Author Code column with the numbers in the ISBN column (an industry code which specifically identifies each book), combine the text function with a concatenate function. In Figure 11.30, enter this formula in cell B4 and AutoFill it down the column: =LEFT(C4,3)&E4. (See the "Concatenate" section later in this chapter to learn more.)

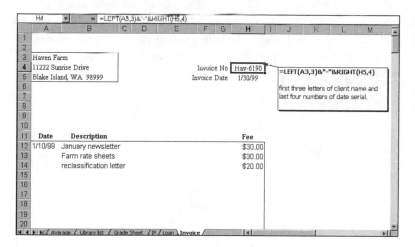

	A	B	C	D	E	F	G
				Buddy's Books Stock List			
1							
2							
3		**AuthorCode**	**AuthorName**	**Title**	**ISBN**		
4		Edw	Edwards, Paul & Sarah	Working From Home	1523		
5		Kel	Kelly, Julia	Access is Cool	6542		
6		Swi	Swift, Sally	Centered Riding	358		
7		Lew	Lewis, C.S.	Mere Christianity	2541		
8		Cav	Cavitch, Susan Miller	The Natural Soap Book	6235		
9		Hyl	Hyland, Ann	Foal to Five Years	5963		
10		Mil	Miller, Dan	Mayhem by Miller	2546		
11		Kel	Kelly, Julia	The Silk Elevator	2352		
12		Fra	Francis, Dick	Decider	5465		
13		Cri	Crichton, Michael	Airframe	652		
14		Gra	Grafton, Sue	"G" is for Gumshoe	4562		
15		Cus	Cussler, Clive	Shock Wave	8795		
16		Gra	Grafton, Sue	"A" is for Alibi	6235		
17		Ada	Adams, Douglas	The Long Dark Teatime of the Soul	3586		
18		Gra	Grafton, Sue	"B" is for Burglar	5963		
19		Lud	Ludlum, Robert	The Cry of the Halidon	2546		
20		Fra	Francis, Dick	Straight	2352		

B20 = =LEFT(AuthorName,3)

Figure 11.29.
After the formula is written using relative references, AutoFill copies the formula down the length of the table.

The LEFT and RIGHT functions are also useful for creating an invoice numbering system, like the one in my invoice in Figure 11.30.

H4 = =LEFT(A3,3)&"-"&RIGHT(H5,4)

	A	B	C	D	E	F	G	H	I	J	K	L	M
1													
2													
3	Haven Farm												
4	11222 Sunrise Drive					Invoice No		Hav-6190					
5	Blake Island, WA 98999					Invoice Date		1/30/99					
6													
7													
8													
9													
10													
11	**Date**	**Description**						**Fee**					
12	1/10/99	January newsletter						$30.00					
13		Farm rate sheets						$30.00					
14		reclassification letter						$20.00					

=LEFT(A3,3)&"-"&RIGHT(H5,4)

first three letters of client name and last four numbers of date serial.

Figure 11.30.
The text functions work with the date serial number to help me create unique invoice numbers for good recordkeeping.

To create this unique numbering system for my invoices, I combined the date serial number in the Date cell with the LEFT and RIGHT functions, as described in the following steps:

1. Create a Date cell (in this case, cell H5) and a Client Name cell (in this case, cell A3).

2. Click the cell in which you want to display the formula result (in this case, the labeled Invoice No cell).

3. Enter the following formula:

   ```
   =LEFT(A3,3)&"-"&RIGHT(H5,4)
   ```

This formula extracts the leftmost three characters from the Client Name cell (A3), joins or *concatenates* a dash character, and then extracts the rightmost four characters from the serial number in the Date cell (H5). In the next section, you learn more about concatenation. This makes the invoice number for each invoice unique. Because I save invoices by using the invoice number as a filename, I get a clue about how ancient or recent an invoice file is when I scan a list of filenames in a My Computer window.

CONCATENATE (&)

The CONCATENATE function joins together the displayed values in two or more cells. It can also join a text string to the displayed value in a cell.

> **Note**
>
> Unlike most other functions, the CONCATENATE function name can be either spelled out (CONCATENATE) or abbreviated to an ampersand (&), which is much easier.

A situation in which the CONCATENATE function comes in handy is shown in Figure 11.31. I want to join the first and last name columns into a single column of full names. I can do this slowly and inefficiently by laboriously copying and pasting every name, or I can write a single CONCATENATE formula that AutoFill copies down the length of the FullName column.

Figure 11.31.
To join each pair of names into a single cell, use the CONCATENATE function.

	A	B	C	D	E	F	G	H	I	
1		FirstName	LastName	FullName	Phone					
2		Julia	Abovian		555-9201					
3		George	Andersen		555-0482					
4		Robin	Bahir		555-8393					
5		Johnny	Baker		555-0784					
6		William	Balogh		555-3213					
7		Dick	Bedrosian		555-9720					
8		Jim	Christensen		555-1234					
9		Howard	Dandyn		555-1122					
10		Gail	Deak		555-0120					
11		Larry	Domokos		555-3123					
12		Richard	Dyhr		555-2721					
13		Leo	Fabin		555-1403					
14		Colleen	Fairfax		555-1330					
15		Elvin	Gilroy		555-0967					
16		Ardith	Gledan		555-9062					
17		Irene	Hassan		555-2425					
18		Ron	Kajetan		555-1970					
19		Judy	Karayan		555-1230					
20		Denny	Keleos		555-3019					
21		Mick	Kirkegar		555-2991					

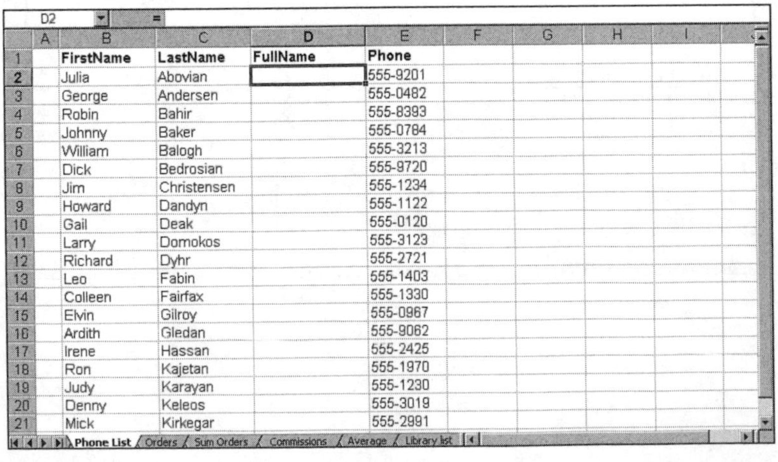

To do this in your own worksheet, follow these steps:

1. Create a column in which the joined value will be displayed (in this case, the FullName column).

2. Type = and click the first cell to be joined (in this case, the FirstName cell in the same row).

3. Type &.

> **Note**
>
> If you later want to delete the original cells (in this case, the FirstName and LastName columns), convert the CONCATENATE formulas to values first, or you get a column full of #REF! errors because the cells to which the formulas refer are gone. To learn how to convert formula results to values, see the section "Converting Formula Results to Values" later in this chapter.

4. Insert a space between the two names by typing " " (two quote marks with a space between them).

5. Type & again.

> **Tip #164 from**
>
> *Laurie*
>
> You can also join a text string such as Mr. to each cell value. To join, or concatenate, Mr. to the LastName values in Figure 11.31, click cell F2 and enter the formula ="Mr. "&" "&C2 (this formula joins Mr. and a space and the last name), and then use AutoFill to copy the formula down the list. (Of course, you'd have to edit the women's titles in this example, but it still saves time.)

6. Click the second cell to be joined (in this case, the LastName cell in the same row).

7. Press Enter to complete the formula.

The final formula is shown in Figure 11.32 in the Formula bar. The formula has been copied down the column.

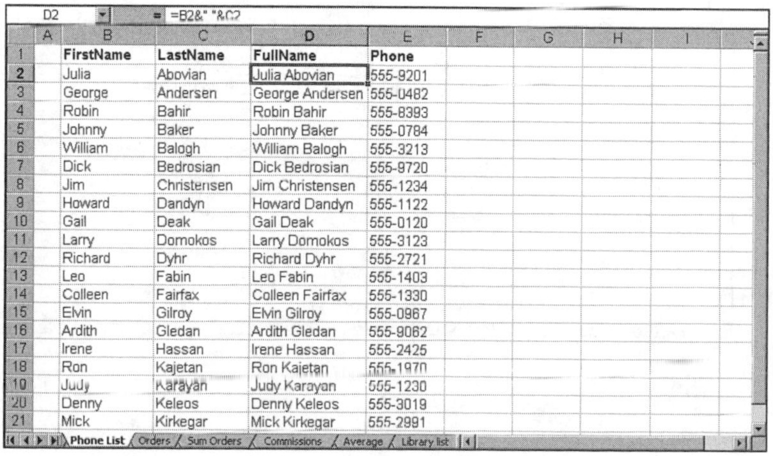

Figure 11.32.
CONCATENATE makes it easy to join cell values.

To learn how to convert formula results to values, see the later section "Converting Formula Results to Values."

Note

To separate a column of full names into separate first and last name columns, insert a new column to the right of the column you want to split. Then select the column and click Data, Text to Columns. Follow the steps in the Convert Text to Columns Wizard to split (or parse) the column into separate columns.

UPPER, LOWER, AND PROPER

The text functions UPPER, LOWER, and PROPER are useful for converting text strings in data that's been queried from external databases.

The UPPER function

```
UPPER(text)
```

converts all letter characters in a text string to uppercase (capital letters). The *text* argument can be a cell reference or a typed string of characters. Figure 11.33 shows an example of a column of names converted to uppercase by using the UPPER function.

The LOWER function

```
LOWER(text)
```

converts all letter characters in a text string to lowercase. The *text* argument can be a cell reference or a typed string of characters. Figure 11.33 shows an example of a column of names converted to lowercase by using the LOWER function.

Figure 11.33.
The UPPER, LOWER, and PROPER functions change the letter case of text strings in the referenced cell.

D9 = =LOWER(C9)

	A	B	C	D	E	F
1		FullName	UPPER CASE	lower case	Proper Case	
2		Julia Abovian	JULIA ABOVIAN	julia abovian	Julia Abovian	
3		George Andersen	GEORGE ANDERSEN	george andersen	George Andersen	
4		Robin Bahir	ROBIN BAHIR	robin bahir	Robin Bahir	
5		Johnny Baker	JOHNNY BAKER	johnny baker	Johnny Baker	
6		William Balogh	WILLIAM BALOGH	william balogh	William Balogh	
7		Dick Bedrosian	DICK BEDROSIAN	dick bedrosian	Dick Bedrosian	
8		Jim Christensen	JIM CHRISTENSEN	jim christensen	Jim Christensen	
9		Howard Dandyn	HOWARD DANDYN	howard dandyn	Howard Dandyn	
10		Gail Deak	GAIL DEAK	gail deak	Gail Deak	
11		Larry Domokos	LARRY DOMOKOS	larry domokos	Larry Domokos	
12		Richard Dyhr	RICHARD DYHR	richard dyhr	Richard Dyhr	
13		Leo Fabin	LEO FABIN	leo fabin	Leo Fabin	
14		Colleen Fairfax	COLLEEN FAIRFAX	colleen fairfax	Colleen Fairfax	
15		Elvin Gilroy	ELVIN GILROY	elvin gilroy	Elvin Gilroy	
16		Ardith Gledan	ARDITH GLEDAN	ardith gledan	Ardith Gledan	
17		Irene Hassan	IRENE HASSAN	irene hassan	Irene Hassan	
18		Ron Kajetan	RON KAJETAN	ron kajetan	Ron Kajetan	
19		Judy Karayan	JUDY KARAYAN	judy karayan	Judy Karayan	
20		Denny Keleos	DENNY KELEOS	denny keleos	Denny Keleos	
21		Mick Kirkegar	MICK KIRKEGAR	mick kirkegar	Mick Kirkegar	

Logical & Information / Sales / Expenses / Local Employees

The PROPER function

```
PROPER(text)
```

converts all letter characters in a text string to proper case (lowercase letters with initial capitals). The *text* argument can be a cell reference or a typed string of characters. Figure 11.33 shows an example of a column of names converted to proper case by using the PROPER function.

RAND

Some situations call for a table of random numbers to use as mock data, or a random assortment of items in a list. The RAND function generates random numbers between 0 and 1 each time the worksheet recalculates. An easy way to create a random sort order for a list is to add a column of RAND formulas to a list, and sort it repeatedly.

By nesting the RAND function in an INT formula (which returns whole numbers, or integers) and then multiplying by 10 or 100, you can create a table full of usable random numbers for mock data.

The RAND function takes no arguments. To fill a table with RAND formulas, select all the cells and type

```
=RAND()
```

Then press Ctrl+Enter to enter the formula in all the selected cells. A formula that generates random numbers between 0 and 1 to 15-digit precision is entered in the new column. Every time the worksheet recalculates, new random numbers are generated.

To freeze the random numbers, copy them and then paste them in place as values (see the section "Converting Formula Results to Values" at the end of this chapter).

To generate random numbers that are integers between 100 and 999, use this formula:

```
=int(rand()*100)
```

OFFSET

The OFFSET function

```
OFFSET(reference,rows,cols,height,width)
```

defines a range on a worksheet. The arguments in the function define the upper-left corner of the range, the number of columns in the range, and the number of rows in the range. You can use this function to write a formula that defines a *dynamic* worksheet range, a range that automatically changes its defined size to include all adjacent rows and columns. It uses nested COUNTA functions to tell the OFFSET function how many rows and columns to include in the range. Because it's a somewhat long and complex formula, you can save yourself time by *naming* the formula and then using the formula name in your worksheet (or as a source range for a print area, PivotTable, or chart).

To name a formula, click Insert, Name, Define, type a name in the Names in Workbook box, and type the formula in the Refers To box (as shown in Figure 11.34).

A simple OFFSET formula looks like the one I've laid out in Figure 11.34. To select the range, click in the Name box, type the name of the formula, and press Enter; or open the Edit menu, select Go To, type the name of the formula in the Reference box, and click OK.

Figure 11.34.
A simple OFFSET formula defines this worksheet range.

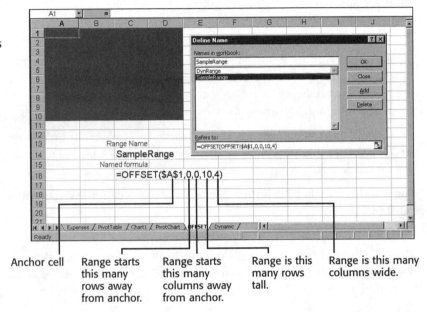

In Figure 11.34, I created a named formula, SampleRange, that defines the range I've colored in. If I filled the range with numbers, the formula =SUM(SampleRange) would sum all the numbers in the range. This named formula is a simple example of the OFFSET function. The range it defines is not *dynamic*; it's always the same size and location, just like a named range.

To make the range *dynamic*, I'll change the fourth and fifth arguments in the formula so that instead of the range being 10 rows tall and 4 columns wide, the range is as many rows tall as there are entries in column A and as many columns wide as there are entries in row 1. To do this, the formula nests a couple of COUNTA functions in the OFFSET function. (Figure 11.35 shows the dynamic range formula named DynRange.)

Note

For a dynamic range to work correctly, make sure that you have no entries in column A or row 1 other than those in the table because the dynamic range counts all the entries in the entire column and row.

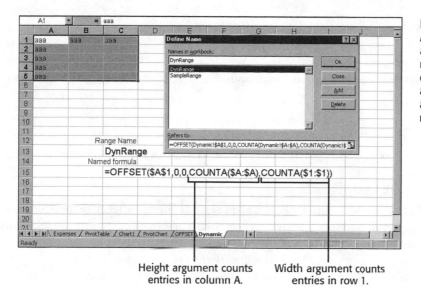

Figure 11.35.
A dynamic range always has as many rows as there are entries in column A and as many columns as there are entries in row 1.

Height argument counts entries in column A.

Width argument counts entries in row 1.

To create a dynamic range with a named formula, follow these steps:

1. On the worksheet where you want to create the named dynamic-range formula, choose Insert, Name, Define.

2. In the Define Name dialog box (shown in Figure 11.35), type a name for your dynamic-range formula under Names in Workbook.

PART
IV

CH
11

Tip #165 from

Laurie

> When I write a long, complex formula like this, I find it easier to write it in a cell without an = because I can easily see and edit the entire formula and then copy the formula and paste it into the Define Name dialog box.

3. Type the OFFSET/COUNTA formula in the Refers To box.

4. Click OK.

Note

> The formula name won't appear in either the Name box list or the Go To dialog box; however, both recognize the name, so if you type it in either the Name box or the Go To dialog box, the dynamic range is selected.

5. To test your dynamic-range formula, click the Name box (left of the Formula bar), type the formula name, and press Enter. If the formula is written correctly, the dynamic range is selected. (Be sure there are entries in column A and row 1 for the formula to count.)

If you're wondering where this is useful, you can use it to define a print area or a PivotTable source range in which the source range changes (you'll never have to redefine the source range).

→ To learn more about PivotTables, **see** "Using PivotTables and PivotCharts," **p. 555**

To use your dynamic range in a PivotTable, type the range name in the <u>R</u>ange box in Step 2 of the PivotTable and PivotChart Wizard. When you click the Refresh Data button, a dynamic-range PivotTable is updated with both changed data and newly added rows and columns.

To use your dynamic range in a print area, write the formula and name it Print_Area. Excel recognizes the name Print_Area (in fact, if you set a print area in a worksheet, and then choose <u>I</u>nsert, <u>N</u>ame, <u>D</u>efine, you'll find the name Print_Area has been defined).

DSUM, DAVERAGE, AND DGET

The DSUM, DAVERAGE, and DGET functions are D-functions (they're located in the Database category in the Paste Function dialog box). They extract data from a table or list (called a database in the function arguments) based on criteria you set, similar to the SUMIF function but more flexible. They all work the same way and use the same arguments, but differ in what they return. In the D-functions, the argument *database* is the table or list you are extracting values from. The *field* argument is a column in the *database* table, and the *criteria* argument comes from a criteria range you set up on the worksheet.

The DSUM function

```
DSUM(database,field,criteria)
```

sums the numbers in the column (field) you specify that meet the conditions (criteria) you specify.

The DAVERAGE function

```
DAVERAGE(database,field,criteria)
```

averages the numbers in the column (field) you specify that meet the conditions (criteria) you specify.

You specify criteria by placing a criteria range on the worksheet (as shown in Figure 11.36). The criteria range can include any or all of the fields (columns) in the table, and must have labels identical to those in the table. The criteria range must have at least one row below the column labels.

The D-functions are like filters that calculate, and you can set up AND and OR criteria in your criteria range. To set up OR criteria (as shown in Figure 11.36), put the criteria on separate rows in the criteria range. To set up AND criteria (for example, to calculate records that show Tanzania in the Product field AND more than 100 in the Lbs field), put the criteria on the same row in the criteria range. When you change criteria in the criteria range, the D-functions recalculate automatically.

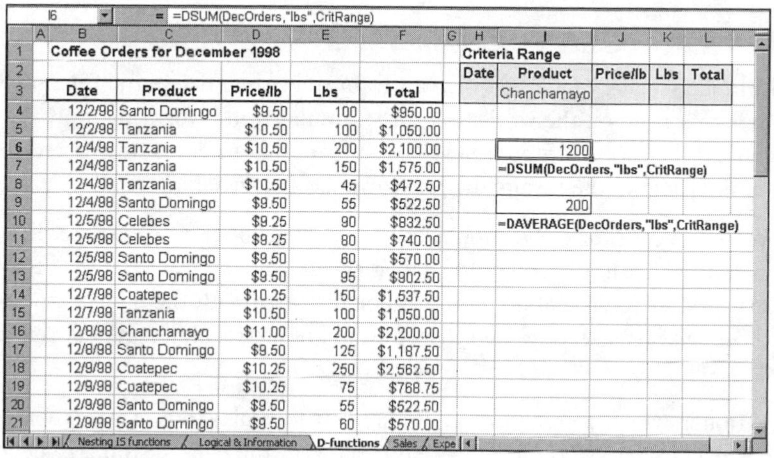

I6 =DSUM(DecOrders,"lbs",CritRange)

Coffee Orders for December 1998

Date	Product	Price/lb	Lbs	Total
12/2/98	Santo Domingo	$9.50	100	$950.00
12/2/98	Tanzania	$10.50	100	$1,050.00
12/4/98	Tanzania	$10.50	200	$2,100.00
12/4/98	Tanzania	$10.50	150	$1,575.00
12/4/98	Tanzania	$10.50	45	$472.50
12/4/98	Santo Domingo	$9.50	55	$522.50
12/5/98	Celebes	$9.25	90	$832.50
12/5/98	Celebes	$9.25	80	$740.00
12/5/98	Santo Domingo	$9.50	60	$570.00
12/5/98	Santo Domingo	$9.50	95	$902.50
12/7/98	Coatepec	$10.25	150	$1,537.50
12/7/98	Tanzania	$10.50	100	$1,050.00
12/8/98	Chanchamayo	$11.00	200	$2,200.00
12/8/98	Santo Domingo	$9.50	125	$1,187.50
12/9/98	Coatepec	$10.25	250	$2,562.50
12/9/98	Coatepec	$10.25	75	$768.75
12/9/98	Santo Domingo	$9.50	55	$522.50
12/9/98	Santo Domingo	$9.50	60	$570.00

Criteria Range

Date	Product	Price/lb	Lbs	Total
	Chanchamayo			

1200
=DSUM(DecOrders,"lbs",CritRange)

200
=DAVERAGE(DecOrders,"lbs",CritRange)

Figure 11.36. These D-formulas calculate the sum and average of all records that have Chanchamayo OR Tanzania in the Product field.

The DGET function

`DGET(database,field,criteria)`

is just a bit different from the other D-functions. It extracts a single record that meets the conditions (criteria) you specify. If several records meet your criteria, you'll get a #NUM! error.

Figure 11.37 shows a DGET formula extracting a phone number from a list. The list, including heading labels, is named Contacts, and the criteria range is named PhoneCriteria. The DGET formula looks in the Contacts list, in the Phone field, for the record matching the criteria in the PhoneCriteria range.

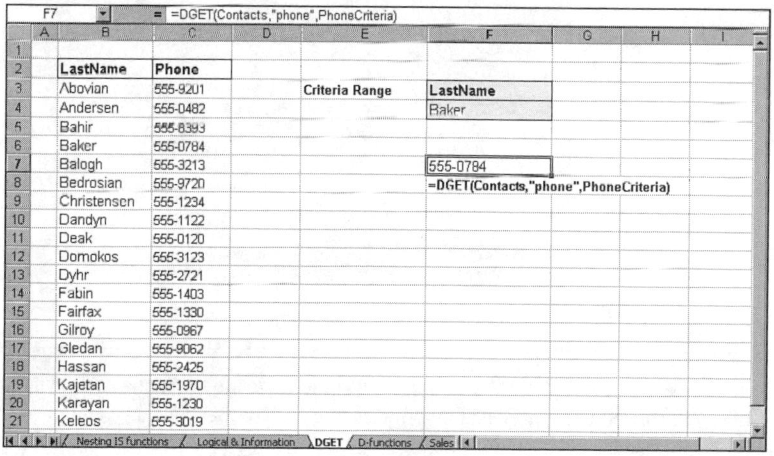

F7 =DGET(Contacts,"phone",PhoneCriteria)

LastName	Phone
Abovian	555-9201
Andersen	555-0482
Bahir	555-8393
Baker	555-0784
Balogh	555-3213
Bedrosian	555-9720
Christensen	555-1234
Dandyn	555-1122
Deak	555-0120
Domokos	555-3123
Dyhr	555-2721
Fabin	555-1403
Fairfax	555-1330
Gilroy	555-0967
Gledan	555-9062
Hassan	555-2425
Kajetan	555-1970
Karayan	555-1230
Keleos	555-3019

Criteria Range

LastName
Baker

555-0784
=DGET(Contacts,"phone",PhoneCriteria)

Figure 11.37. The DGET function extracts a single record. If more than one record matches the criteria, the DGET function returns a #NUM! error.

CONVERTING FORMULA RESULTS TO VALUES

If you write a formula, such as a CONCATENATE formula, then delete the referenced cells that you no longer need on the worksheet, the formulas won't work any more. You can, however, convert the formula results to values so that you can delete the unnecessary source cells without changing the results that the formulas produced.

Another situation which calls for conversion is breaking a workbook or worksheet link. If you've written formulas that link workbooks or worksheets and you want to break the links because you don't need the links and don't want to be bothered with the update messages, you can break those links by selecting the cells with the linking formulas and converting them to values.

Yet another situation in which you might want to convert formulas to values is when you fill a table with mock data using RAND formulas, and you want the data to stop recalculating new random numbers.

Convert formula results to values.

1. Select the formulas.

2. Click the Copy button (or use your favorite copy method).

3. From the Edit menu, click Paste Special.

4. In the Paste Special dialog box (shown in Figure 11.38), click the Values option.

Figure 11.38.
Use the Paste Special dialog box to convert formulas to values; then you can delete the source cells without affecting the formula results.

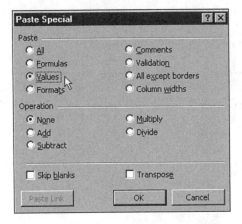

> **Note**
>
> In a worksheet like Figure 11.32, you might want to leave the last name column in place after you convert the concatenation formulas to values so that you can continue to sort the list by last name.

5. Click OK.

The formulas are replaced by their resulting values, and you can delete the source cells. If the moving border bothers you, you can remove it by pressing Esc.

TROUBLESHOOTING

If you build formulas by using the Paste Function dialog box and the Formula Palette, you'll have far fewer problems with your formulas. But when you get more comfortable with functions and start writing formulas by typing them yourself, here are some tips to help you avoid or fix problems.

- Be sure your parentheses are paired and balanced.
- Use the appropriate type of data in each function argument.
- Be sure all required arguments in the function have been filled in, and if you still don't get the results you expect, you may need to fill in optional arguments.
- Don't nest more than seven levels deep in any function.
- Make sure that any external references (to other worksheets or workbooks) are spelled correctly and in the correct syntax.
- Don't type punctuation such as dollar signs or commas in argument values—use plain numbers. (If you type a percent symbol or a caret symbol, Excel recognizes it as an arithmetic operator and uses it in the calculation.)
- See Table 10.3 in Chapter 10 for help with specific formula errors.

EXCEL IN PRACTICE

You can combine formulas with other Excel features to make your worksheets do more work for you. For example, if you have a large table of numbers like the one in Figure 11.39, and you want to highlight the minimum and maximum values, you can write MIN and MAX formulas. Then combine them with conditional formatting, so that you can instantly see where the minimum and maximum values lie in the table. When the numbers in the table change, both the formulas and the conditional formatting continue to calculate and display the values you want to see.

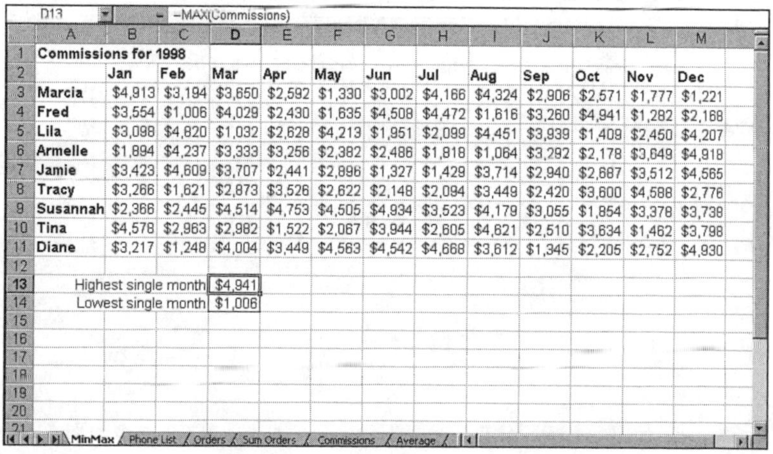

	A	B	C	D	E	F	G	H	I	J	K	L	M
1	Commissions for 1998												
2		Jan	Feb	Mar	Apr	May	Jun	Jul	Aug	Sep	Oct	Nov	Dec
3	Marcia	$4,913	$3,194	$3,650	$2,592	$1,330	$3,002	$4,166	$4,324	$2,906	$2,571	$1,777	$1,221
4	Fred	$3,554	$1,006	$4,029	$2,430	$1,635	$4,508	$4,472	$1,616	$3,260	$4,941	$1,282	$2,168
5	Lila	$3,098	$4,820	$1,032	$2,628	$4,213	$1,951	$2,099	$4,451	$3,939	$1,409	$2,450	$4,207
6	Armelle	$1,894	$4,237	$3,333	$3,256	$2,382	$2,486	$1,818	$1,064	$3,292	$2,178	$3,649	$4,918
7	Jamie	$3,423	$4,609	$3,707	$2,441	$2,896	$1,327	$1,429	$3,714	$2,940	$2,687	$3,512	$4,565
8	Tracy	$3,266	$1,621	$2,873	$3,526	$2,622	$2,148	$2,094	$3,449	$2,420	$3,600	$4,588	$2,776
9	Susannah	$2,366	$2,445	$4,514	$4,753	$4,505	$4,934	$3,523	$4,179	$3,055	$1,854	$3,378	$3,738
10	Tina	$4,578	$2,963	$2,982	$1,522	$2,067	$3,944	$2,605	$4,621	$2,510	$3,634	$1,462	$3,798
11	Diane	$3,217	$1,248	$4,004	$3,449	$4,563	$4,542	$4,668	$3,612	$1,345	$2,205	$2,752	$4,930
12													
13		Highest single month		$4,941									
14		Lowest single month		$1,006									

Figure 11.39.
Who has the maximum, and who has the minimum?

In Figure 11.39, I've written a MAX formula and a MIN formula, and I've selected the entire table to apply conditional formatting.

→ To learn more about conditional formatting, **see** "Conditional Formatting," **p. 176**

I'll apply bold, italic, and green formatting to cells in the range that are equal to the value in the cell with the MAX formula; I'll apply bold, italic, and red formatting to cells in the range that are equal to the value in the cell with the MIN formula (see Figure 11.40). Separately, I'll format the cells that contain the MAX and MIN formulas so they match the conditionally formatted cells in the range (see Figure 11.41).

Tip #166 from	To match the formatting quickly, click a conditionally formatted cell, then click the Format Painter button, and then click the matching formula cell.
Laurie	

Figure 11.40.
Apply conditional formatting to the table, using the formula results as a condition.

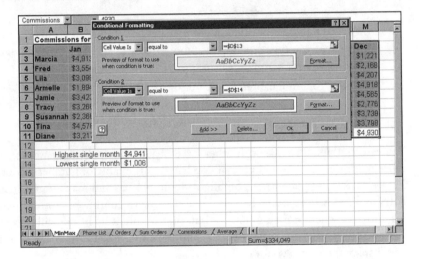

Figure 11.41.
It's easy to see the results at a glance when the formula results and matching values in the table have the same formatting.

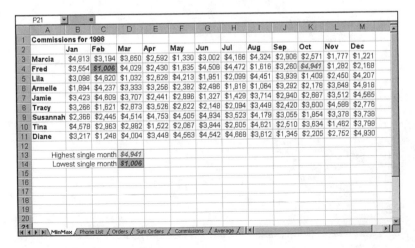

CHAPTER 12

WORKING WITH NAMED RANGES

In this chapter

by Laurie Ann Ulrich
laurie@limehat.com

MANAGING NAMED RANGES

Named ranges, which represent a single cell or a range of cells, are a significant tool in your mastery of Excel. As you learned in Chapter 3, moving from one location to another in a worksheet is made easier by range names, and finding a specific cell in a large or complex worksheet virtually requires them. But what else can they do for you? Assigning descriptive names to cells and ranges will save you a great deal of time when building formulas and functions, making it easier for you to remember what cell or range a formula refers to. As you build a worksheet, you should name significant ranges—important cells that contain information you'll want to find quickly or that you know you'll be using in formulas and functions.

If your Excel data is set up in a list or database format, for example, you could assign the name Database to the entire list, including the field names. This enables you to use the specified range name in Database functions that refer to the database. In addition, the Database range name is automatically updated to accommodate records that you add while using the data form.

As you modify or update your worksheets, you will occasionally find the need to rename, delete, or edit existing range names. Before you use range names in a formula or print a list of range names used in a worksheet, you'll want to ensure that they're up to date and relevant to your worksheet. Some simple worksheet maintenance will help you achieve that goal. Excel provides several commands and tools for helping you work with and manage the named ranges in your worksheets.

→ To learn how to create named ranges, **see** "Naming Ranges for Fast Access," **p. 82**

→ To learn more about Excel database design and using the data form, **see** "Using Excel As a Database Program," **p. 486**

RENAMING RANGES

Your list of named ranges will be only as static as your worksheet—as your worksheet grows and changes, be sure the named ranges remain relevant and complete. As you use your worksheet, you may find that the names you originally assigned are too short or vague (you aren't sure what they refer to) or too long (making them difficult to type into formulas).

To change the name of an existing range, follow these steps:

1. Choose Insert, Name, Define. The Define Name dialog box appears.

2. In the Names in Workbook list box, click the name you want to change. The name you select appears in the text box (see Figure 12.1).

3. Select the entire name in the Names in Workbook text box, then type the new name for the reference, and click the Add button.

4. Click the original name in the Names in Workbook list box, and then click the Delete button.

5. Click OK to close the Define Name dialog box.

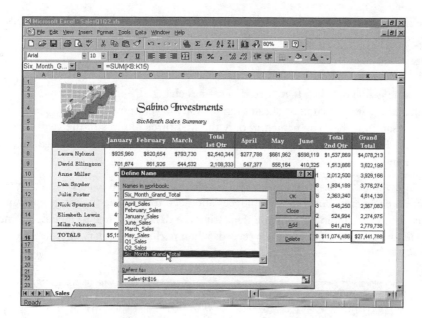

Figure 12.1.
Range names cannot contain spaces. You can use an underscore to show separations between words.

Tip #167 from

Laurie

Keep your range names descriptive, yet short enough to remember them when you type them into formulas. Remember, you cannot use range names that are the same as cell references, such as Q4 or BL1999.

Caution

Excel enables you to give the same cell or range a new name without deleting the old one if you use the Insert, Name, Define method. When creating new ranges, ensure that the range doesn't already have another name—Excel will display only the first name assigned in the Name box. Check the Define Name dialog box to see whether you have any duplicates.

PART

IV

CH

12

DELETING RANGE NAMES

When you copy or cut a named cell or range to the Clipboard, the range name moves with it when you paste the data. Cells that are dragged and dropped in another location take their names with them as well. If you delete named cells from one location and reenter them elsewhere, however, the names aren't transferred—they remain in their original location. In these instances, you may want to remove the old range name to avoid possible confusion.

To remove a range name that is no longer valid, follow these steps:

1. Choose Insert, Name, Define.
2. In the Names in Workbook list, click the range name you want to remove.
3. Click the Delete button; the name disappears from the list.
4. Click OK to close the Define Name dialog box.

If you delete the wrong range name, you can restore it if you click the Undo button immediately after you close the Define Name dialog box.

REDEFINING AN EXISTING RANGE NAME

What if the name is fine but the range it represents has changed? This is a common situation—imagine that your column of sales figures for the year now includes the first six months of the year, but when you named it, only the first three months of the year were entered. You need to extend the range to include an additional three months' worth of cells, but keep the name.

Figure 12.2 shows another instance of when you would want to redefine an existing range name. You've recently hired some new employees and need to redefine the range containing all of the records in the employee database. Updating the database range to include the new employees will enable you to include their records when performing salary subtotals by location, sorts, and other data analysis tasks.

Figure 12.2.
By entering the first and last cell addresses in the range, you can rebuild a named range from within the Define Name dialog box.

Name of the selected range

Current dimensions of the range

Rows that need to be added to the range

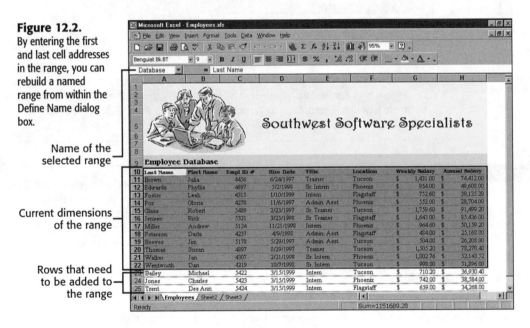

To redefine the boundaries of your named range, follow these steps:

1. Choose Insert, Name, Define.
2. Click once on the name you want to redefine.
3. In the Refers To box, edit the cell addresses (or use the Collapse Dialog button) to reflect your new range, as shown in Figure 12.3).
4. Click OK to close the dialog box and apply your changes.

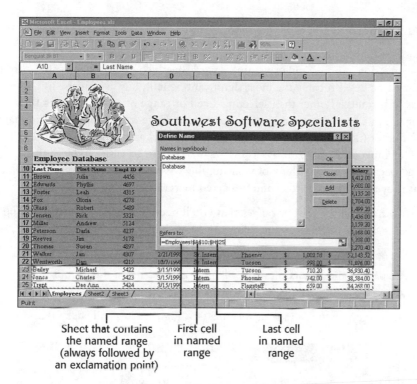

Figure 12.3.
Part of the range as it appears in the Refers To box is the name of the sheet on which the range is found.

Sheet that contains the named range (always followed by an exclamation point)

First cell in named range

Last cell in named range

Caution

Be careful when editing the range in the Refers To box—if you accidentally delete or move one of the symbols (parentheses, exclamation points, colon, dollar signs), your redefinition won't work. Excel will not warn you that you've made a mistake—your changes simply won't be applied.

If you've forgotten what a specific name in your worksheet refers to, you can click the name whose reference you want to check in the Names in Workbook list; then view the referenced cells in the Refers To box. You also could select the name from the Name box to see the range name highlighted in the worksheet.

All ranges you name in one worksheet of your workbook will be available in all sheets of that same workbook. As a result, you cannot use the same name twice in the same workbook, which is somewhat limiting—especially if you have similar information throughout your sheets.

Tip #168 from

Laurie

Don't forget to add a sheet name followed by an exclamation point when creating single-sheet range names—it's key to Excel's interpretation of your range name as a single-sheet name.

USING RANGE NAMES IN FORMULAS

The benefits of naming ranges have been extolled throughout this chapter and in Chapter 3—navigation, editing, and explaining a worksheet's content is made easier through the use of named ranges. Probably the most significant benefit, however, is the use of named ranges in formulas. Rather than selecting a cell or range of cells (or typing their cell addresses) for use in a formula, you can select the named range from a list. This eliminates the margin for error (unless you named the range incorrectly) and makes it easier to edit a formula. The formula =(Sales_Total*Proj_Increase)*.85 can be easier to build than =(C8*M25)*.85 because you don't think of your numbers as C8 and M25—you think of them as what they are: your sales total and projected increase.

If you effectively name all the cells or ranges that you'll need to use in formulas, creating a formula can be as simple as shown in the following steps:

1. Click in the cell that will contain the formula.
2. Type an equal sign (and a function name, if applicable) to begin the formula.
3. Choose Insert, Name, Paste. The Paste Name dialog box displays.
4. Click the named range to use in your formula (see Figure 12.4) and click OK.

Figure 12.4.
The benefits of creative and relevant range names are reaped now—when you're selecting them for use in formulas.

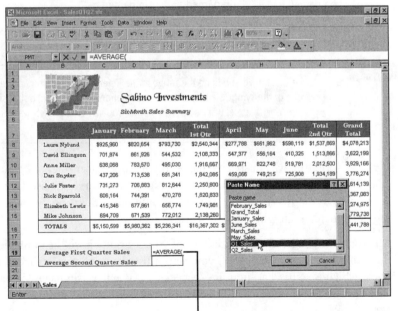

This cell will contain the formula.

5. If necessary, type the arithmetic operator.
6. Retrieve any other named ranges by repeating steps 3 and 4, as needed.
7. Complete your formula by adding any needed parentheses, and then press Enter (see Figure 12.5).

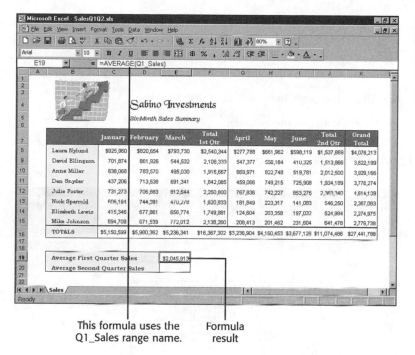

Figure 12.5.
A formula's construction is the same, whether or not named ranges are used. The names merely mask the cell addresses.

This formula uses the
Q1_Sales range name.

Formula
result

If you create your formulas by clicking in cells to add them to your formula, and if the cells have names, the names will be inserted into the formula automatically. On the other hand, if you type the cell addresses into the formula (rather than clicking the cells), names applied to those cells will not appear in the formula.

Tip #169 from

Laurie

When using the Paste Function dialog box to create a formula, you can type range names directly into the argument boxes rather than selecting them (with the Collapse Dialog button) or typing cell addresses.

You can find out more about proper formula construction, with or without the use of named ranges, in Chapter 10, "Constructing Excel Formulas."

→ To learn more about using range names with complex formulas, **see** "Using Named Ranges in Long or Complex Formulas," **p. 606**

PASTING NAMES INTO EXISTING FORMULAS

Using named ranges in your formulas does more than make your formula creation and editing process easier. It also makes it easier for another user (or you!) to see what your formulas actually do, as opposed to just seeing which cells they use in the calculation. When you first create a worksheet, you'll probably remember what everything in the formula represents. However, a week or a year from now, those formulas may seem a little obscure without named ranges.

If your formulas are currently based on cell addresses that you named after the formula was created, you can use the Insert, Name, Paste command to replace the cell addresses with range names. This command is also useful when correcting names that were mistyped in a formula.

Follow these steps to paste a range name in a formula:

1. Click in the cell that contains the formula.

2. In the Formula bar, select the cell address that will be replaced by a named range (see Figure 12.6).

Figure 12.6.
Edit your formula cell by cell, replacing cell addresses with named ranges.

Range to be replaced by new range name

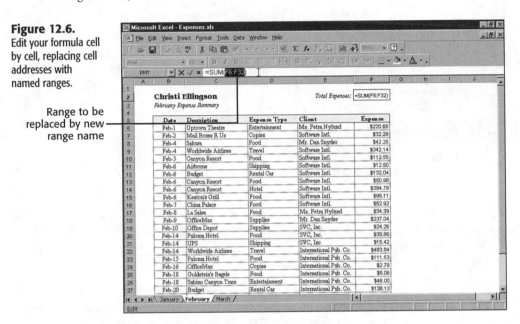

3. Choose Insert, Name, Paste. You also can type the range name if you're sure of its spelling.

4. Click the name you want to use, and click OK.

5. Press Enter to complete the formula (see Figure 12.7).

Tip #170 from

Laurie

It's a good idea to save your worksheet before replacing cell addresses with named ranges—any errors you make while selecting names will adversely affect your formulas' results.

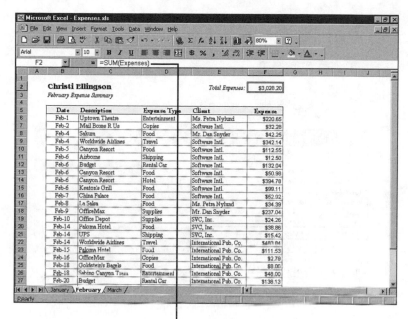

Figure 12.7.
The formula has been updated to include the new range name.

The formula now includes the "Expenses" range name.

REPLACING CELL REFERENCES WITH RANGE NAMES

If you build a formula after you've named all of your ranges throughout the worksheet, any named ranges used in the formula will appear by name in the formula. But what if you created the formula before creating or defining named ranges? Another method for updating your formulas to include range names is to use the Insert, Name, Apply command. This command provides additional options for inserting names in formulas other than the Insert, Name, Paste command that you read about in the preceding section.

To replace your cell addresses with names in an existing formula using the Apply command, follow these steps:

1. Select the formula that contains cell addresses you want to replace with named ranges.

2. Choose Insert, Name, Apply.

3. In the Apply Names dialog box, click the names you want to update in your formula (see Figure 12.8).

   You can click on as many names you want in the Apply Names list. Click the name a second time to deselect it if you make an error.

4. Click OK to apply the name(s) to your formula.

PART

IV

CH

12

Figure 12.8.
Make use of your named ranges by updating formulas built before the names were created.

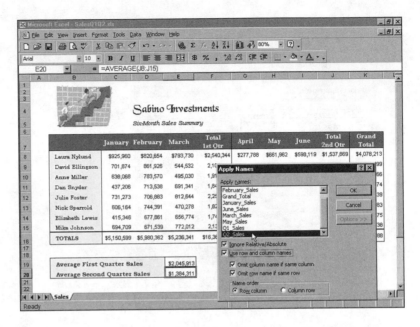

If you click the Options button in the Apply Names dialog box, the dialog box shows several ways Excel can apply your names to the selected formula. Table 12.1 lists the options for replacing cell references and explains their uses.

TABLE 12.1.   CELL REFERENCE REPLACEMENT OPTIONS

Apply Names Option	Description/Suggested Use
Ignore Relative/Absolute	If checked, this option ignores the absolute or relative reference status of the cells when inserting names. If you remove the check mark, absolute references will be replaced with an absolute reference name (including dollar signs), as will mixed reference cells.
Use Row and Column Names	If names for cells in the formula can't be found, column and row names will be used instead. The two Omit check boxes (for columns and rows) enable you to choose whether to use the column name, row name, or both.
Name Order	When applying names from column and row names, choose the order in which they're applied—Row Column or Column Row.

USING WORKSHEET LABELS IN PLACE OF RANGE NAMES IN FORMULAS

Excel provides a built-in shortcut that enables you to use existing column and row labels in worksheet formulas. This feature saves you the step of defining range names for use in formulas, as long as your worksheet is set up with labels at the top of columnar data and to the left of each row. Excel doesn't recognize these labels used in formulas by default.

You must first enable this feature by performing the following steps:

1. Choose Tools, Options; then click the Calculation tab.
2. In the Workbook options area, click the Accept Labels in Formulas check box to select it (see Figure 12.9).

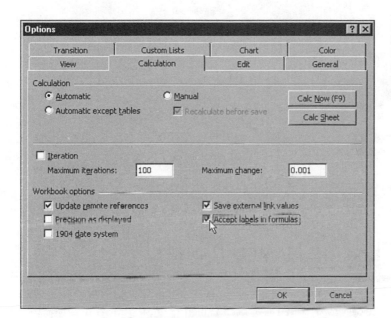

Figure 12.9.
Select this option to allow Excel to automatically accept worksheet labels in your formulas.

3. Click OK to close the Options dialog box, and accept your changes.

After you've enabled this feature by performing the preceding steps, you can use the row and column labels in formulas that refer to corresponding data. In Figure 12.10, for example, the formula =AVERAGE(January) was entered in cell C16. Although no range names have been set up in the worksheet, this formula produces the correct result because Excel is using the "January" label to determine which data to reference in the formula. After you enter the first formula, you can copy the formula across the row of cells; Excel adjusts the argument in the function to reflect data in the current column. If you copy the formula in cell C16 to cell C17, for instance, the formula in cell C17 appears as =AVERAGE(February).

Note

If you try using worksheet labels in formulas without first selecting the Accept Labels in Formulas option, your formula will result in the #NAME? error value.

 For more information on the #NAME? error value, see "Avoiding the #NAME? Error Value" in the Troubleshooting section at the end of this chapter.

PART

IV

CH

12

Figure 12.10.
If you use a worksheet setup similar to this, you can save time by using row and column labels in formulas instead of range names.

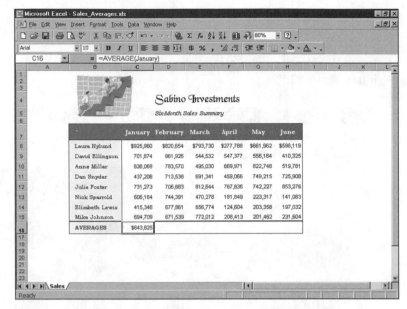

PASTING A LIST OF NAMED RANGES

You've named your ranges and used them in formulas, and they're a big part of your daily use of your worksheets. You use them to find cells, to quickly go to remote cells in your more complex worksheets. What more can named ranges do for you? If you'll be submitting the worksheet to other people in the form of a printout rather than an electronic file, the printout can be enhanced by including a list of your named ranges that shows the names and the cell addresses they represent.

In addition to helping others interpret your worksheet, appending your worksheet with a list of the named ranges used in that sheet can help you set up subsequent sheets that will be based on your current worksheet. That list of named ranges can save you from reinventing the wheel.

Tip #171 from

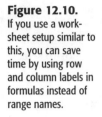

Display your formulas instead of their results in your worksheet cells, providing a map of your worksheet for use in developing a similar sheet or training someone in its use. Be sure to save this map with a different name to protect your working version of the worksheet.

To paste a list of named ranges in a worksheet, follow these steps:

1. Click in a cell at the end or bottom of the active area of your worksheet. You'll be pasting the list here, so it should be out of the way of your other data.

2. Choose <u>I</u>nsert, <u>N</u>ame, <u>P</u>aste. The Paste Name dialog box appears (see Figure 12.11).

3. Choose the Paste <u>L</u>ist button.

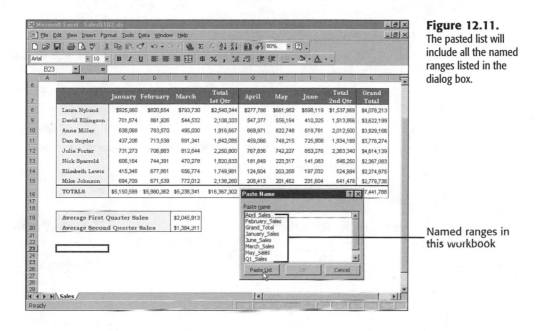

Figure 12.11.
The pasted list will include all the named ranges listed in the dialog box.

Named ranges in this workbook

The entire list of range names—for the entire workbook and any that you set up for one particular sheet—appear in a block of cells adjacent to the active cell (see Figure 12.12).

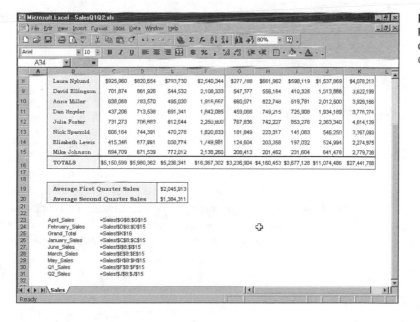

Figure 12.12.
Place the list outside of the worksheet's content.

When the worksheet is printed, you can print the list along with it, giving the recipient of the printout some idea of how you've structured the foundation of your worksheet. You also have a reference to use in building other worksheets based on this worksheet.

Using Range Names to Speed Formatting

Imagine that your workbook or worksheet contains many named ranges, and that several of those named ranges contain similar information. Perhaps you've named each of your individual months' sales totals or you've named each cell that contains summary information from your company's divisions.

These cells that contain similar information are likely to be formatted similarly as well, and Excel makes it easy to select these like ranges and apply formats to them all at once. To make a multiple-range selection, follow these steps:

1. Click the Name box drop-down list to display the list of named ranges in your worksheet.

2. Select one of the ranges you want to reformat; the named range is highlighted in the worksheet.

3. Press the Ctrl key and click the Name box drop-down list again to redisplay the list of names.

4. With the Ctrl key pressed, click another named range. This named range becomes highlighted as well.

5. Repeat steps 3 and 4 until all of the desired named ranges are highlighted onscreen.

6. Release the Ctrl key, and apply the desired formatting to the selected cells.

Tip #172 from

Laurie

You can also use this multiple-range selection technique to select cells for editing or deletion.

Troubleshooting

Avoiding the #NAME? Error Value

I just typed a formula that included a range name from my worksheet, but when I pressed Enter, the label #NAME? appeared in the cell. What did I do wrong?

Ensure that you spelled the range name correctly. Although named ranges aren't case sensitive, you may have typed (or omitted) a punctuation mark that is part of the defined range name. Check the Name box to see whether the name you typed in the formula appears there. If it doesn't, it's possible that you deleted the range name or the cells that it once referenced. Create the named range again, and the #NAME? error message should disappear.

EXCEL IN PRACTICE

Named ranges make it easy for you to find information that may not be visible, without scrolling down or across (or both) within your worksheet's rows and columns. Click the drop-down arrow in the Name box (left of the Formula bar) to see a list of named ranges in a workbook, and then click a name to see the dimensions of a particular range highlighted in the worksheet. You can use existing range names to quickly create formulas and also enable others viewing your worksheet to more easily identify the source data used in a formula.

Range names also make it easier for other people to navigate your worksheets. For example, you can immediately jump to a named range in the worksheet by pressing F5 to display the Go To dialog box and then double-clicking the named range. While you can go overboard in naming ranges, it's better to risk that than to spend too much time referring to cells and ranges by their cell addresses. Figure 12.13 shows a worksheet that contains several named ranges created for use in formulas, to explain cell content, and for the purpose of quick formatting of similar sections of data.

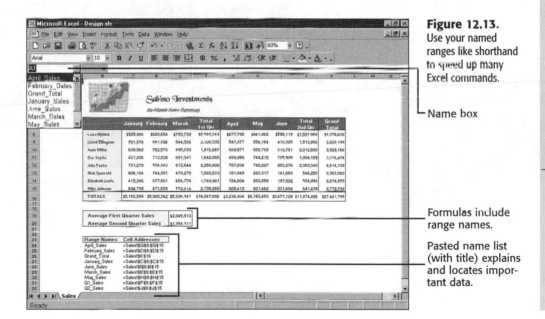

Figure 12.13.
Use your named ranges like shorthand to speed up many Excel commands.

— Name box

Formulas include range names.

Pasted name list (with title) explains and locates important data.

PART

V

CREATING AND MODIFYING CHARTS

BUILDING CHARTS WITH EXCEL

by Patrick D. Blattner
Patrick@BlattnerBooks.com

AN OVERVIEW OF EXCEL CHARTS

Creating charts in Excel gives you the power to transform numbers into pictures that ultimately tell a story. All too often, charts are created "just because." But charts can be the basis of decision making in business; effective charts can ultimately express a business's current situation and future needs. In addition, charts presented and formatted properly can create impact. If done correctly, many charts can tell a story without any additional explanation.

Before creating a chart, ask yourself the question, "What story do I need to tell?" The answer(s) usually can help you to decide what type of chart you need, as well as how to present it effectively. Consider the following examples:

- **You want to show the sales force the results of the previous year's performance against projected performance for this year.** Use a combination clustered column to show the actual sales and a line chart to show the projected sales.

- **You need to project the number of employees needed for the next three years.** Use a stacked column chart to show the base number of employees, with the projected future numbers stacked on top of the base.

- **You need a presentation that shows current market share.** Use a pie chart and show the percentages as data labels.

Tip #173 from	The CD in the back of this book includes all workbooks for all figures shown in this book. You may find it helpful to open and explore the chart examples shown here to learn exactly how they work.

CHART BASICS

Excel offers several ways to create charts. You can create a chart from the Insert menu with the Chart Wizard, from the toolbar with the Chart Wizard button, or by selecting the data and pressing F11 on your keyboard. You even can create a Microsoft Graph 2000 chart with the Insert, Object command.

You can embed your chart in the same worksheet with its source data or create the chart on a separate *chart sheet*. (By default, pressing F11 creates the new chart on a new sheet automatically.) See the later section "Choosing a Chart Location" for details on positioning charts.

Structuring Your Data for Automatic Charting

Excel makes it easy to create charts from information laid out in the proper manner. For example, structure your data in a simple grid, with titles along the left in the first column of the grid, and category information along the top in the first row. (Although category info certainly isn't a requirement, it's usually helpful in charts.)

Make sure that there are no blank rows or columns between the title and category headings and the body of the data, or Excel will plot the blank spaces. The cell where the headings cross—in the upper-left corner of the grid—should be blank.

If the data is formatted properly, as shown in later examples in this chapter, you can create an automatic chart instantly just by pressing F11. After you get the hang of the default Excel chart settings, you may find this feature to be a real time-saver.

By knowing all the chart elements and how to format your chart, you can create charts with visual impact rivaling that of drawing programs.

CHART TERMS

It's important for you to become familiar with the charting terminology. Then you can respond appropriately to the Chart Wizard prompts, and you'll know what to change when you want to edit a chart.

A basic chart offers a pictorial view of data, with the *Y-axis* (usually vertical) indicating the amount or quantity of the information in the chart, and the *X-axis* (usually horizontal) showing the categories. For example, the quarters in a year might be the category for a company or a division of a corporation.

> **Note**
>
> In a three-dimensional chart, Excel refers to the Y-axis as the *Z-axis*.

With multiple categories, a *legend* usually accompanies the chart. The legend provides a reference for the audience viewing the charted information, illustrating with text and a small sample of pattern or color exactly what category each pattern or color represents in the chart.

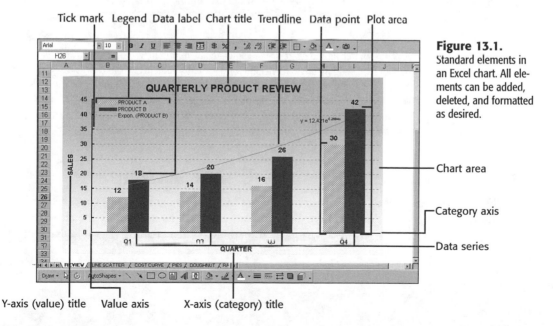

Figure 13.1.
Standard elements in an Excel chart. All elements can be added, deleted, and formatted as desired.

PART
V

CH
13

Table 13.1 describes each basic chart element. In addition to these basic elements, certain chart types have other special features that we'll discuss later in the chapter.

TABLE 13.1. CHART ELEMENTS

Element	Description
Data point	The plotted value associated with the category.
Data labels	Text or values displayed at data points to indicate the specific value or category.
Data series	The plotted value range.
Chart title	The title associated with the chart.
Value axis	The (usually vertical) axis that shows the values by which the data series are measured.
Category axis	The (usually horizontal) axis that plots the categories of the data series.
Legend	A text-and-graphics description of the data series in a chart.
Tick marks	Separators on both the category and value axes. Tick marks act as guide markers for visual comparison.
Plot area	The area in which data series are plotted and graphed.
Chart area	The total area of the chart. All elements are included in the chart area.
X-axis (category) title	Describes the category of the plotted data.
Y-axis (value) title	Describes the value against which the data is plotted.
Z-axis (value) title	In 3D charts, displays the value of the plotted data.
Trendline	Marks the trend of the selected data series.
Series labels	Labels the category name of the data on the plotted chart.

Tip #174 from

Minimize clutter on the chart. Try to eliminate any information that just takes up space without really adding anything helpful for the chart's audience. If the chart's categories are obvious without the legend, for example, perhaps you can live without it. You probably don't need both data points and data labels. This chapter and the next three show alternative ways to construct charts, with creative uses of color, pattern, text, and drawing tools.

CREATING CHARTS WITH THE CHART WIZARD

The Chart Wizard enables you to create a chart, step by step, and provides options along the way to help you tailor the chart. You can always go back in and modify the chart after it's created, so don't worry if you've missed something. When creating the table that will be the source information for the chart, make sure that you've structured the data in a manner that Excel understands (see the earlier sidebar "Structuring Your Data for Automatic Charting"). For example, create the table with the title information in the left column and the category information across the top, or vice versa. Include the title and category information in the selection when creating the chart.

Setting Up the Source Table for a Chart

Don't include cells containing totals in the selection when creating the chart. Unless you're showing a graph with categories as a percent of the total, this will create a distorted view of the data.

It's also a good idea not to place data in the upper-left cell of the selection you want to plot. Excel may interpret the data below or to the left of the upper-left cell as a series and plot it.

Excel may plot row and column headings that are entered as numbers. For example, if you track sales over a period of years and enter year numbers for either the row or column headings, Excel will plot the years as numbers. One way to avoid this problem is to place an apostrophe (') in front of each heading that Excel may interpret as a number.

After creating the source table—including the title and category information—open the Chart Wizard. The wizard defaults to certain chart types if you don't make a specific chart type selection, so you essentially can click Finish in step 1 and the default chart will appear.

To create a chart with the Chart Wizard, simply follow these steps:

1. Create the table you want to chart.

2. Select the table (see Figure 13.2).

3. Choose Chart from the Insert menu, or click the Chart Wizard button on the Standard toolbar.

4. Follow the steps in the Chart Wizard dialog boxes, filling in any details as needed. Click Finish when you're ready to create the chart.

The Chart Wizard button

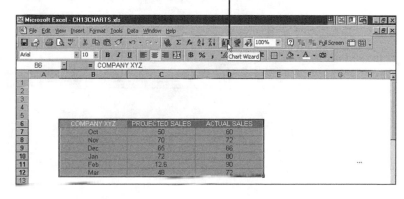

Figure 13.2.
The structure in which you create your table is important. For simplicity, it's best to create a table without empty cells.

Tip #175 from

Sometimes it's easier to dump a chart and start over than to fix it up. You may see immediately after clicking Finish that you should have selected more or different options in the Chart Wizard. Unfortunately, you can't undo a chart insertion. However, if the chart is embedded and still selected, you can just press the Delete key. If the chart is placed on a chart sheet, delete the new chart sheet. Select the table, click the Chart Wizard button, and then begin again.

Another option is to select the chart (if it isn't still selected), click the Chart Wizard button to open the Chart Wizard, change the settings, and then click Finish.

SELECTING THE CHART TYPE

The first step in creating a chart with the Chart Wizard is to select a chart type and sub-type. (See the later section "Excel Chart Types" for details.) To use one of the default chart types, click the Standard Types tab, scroll the Chart Type list as needed, and click the desired chart type. As shown in Figure 13.3, the sub-type list changes to provide variations of the chart type selected in the Chart Type list.

Figure 13.3.
The first step in the Chart Wizard gives you the opportunity to select the chart type and sub-type. You also can select a custom type.

You can see a sample of the chart using the selected data by clicking and holding down the Press and Hold To View Sample button in the Chart Wizard dialog box under the Chart Sub-type list. Although this is a pretty tiny sample, it can help keep you from wasting time with a chart type that clearly won't give the audience the information you want to convey.

Clicking the Custom Types tab gives you an additional set of variations on the standard Excel charts (see Figure 13.4). For details on using custom charts, see the later section "Excel Chart Types."

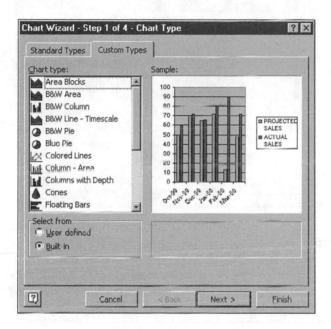

Figure 13.4.
The Custom Types tab enables you to select from predesigned custom charts or define your own by selecting User Defined in the Select From section of the dialog box.

After you make your selection, you can either go to step 2 of the Chart Wizard, or you can click Finish and Excel will select the default options for you.

SPECIFYING THE CHART SOURCE DATA

Although you'll typically select the data that you want to *plot* (display in the chart) before starting the Chart Wizard, you may decide after starting the wizard that you need to change the *data range* you selected. Or you may have forgotten to select the range before launching into chart creation. Step 2 of the Chart Wizard dialog box enables you to change the data range to be used in the chart (see Figure 13.5). The preview on the Data Range tab shows how the selected range will look in the chart. To adjust the range, change the settings shown in the fields on the Data Range tab.

Figure 13.5.
Use the Data Range settings to change category orientation from rows to columns.

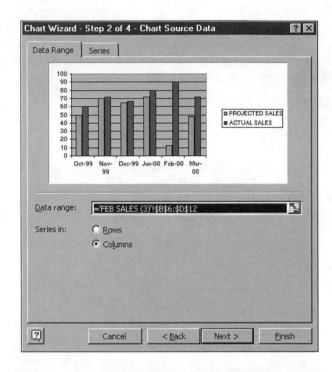

Tip #176 from

If you neglected to select a range before starting the Chart Wizard but left the cell pointer somewhere in the range you want, you may be surprised to see a preview of your chart in the Step 2 dialog box, with the appropriate data selected for you. If you formatted the data correctly (see the earlier section, "Chart Basics"), Excel can be pretty good at guessing exactly what you had in mind.

By default, a *data series* is one category of your table. By selecting one of the columns in the chart, you've selected a data series. You can change the *orientation* of the data from rows (the default) to columns. Figures 13.6 and 13.7, for example, show two different versions of the same chart in the preview window. In Figure 13.6, the data is plotted in rows; in Figure 13.7, the data is plotted in columns. If you change a series to plot from rows to columns, Excel changes the data from a clustered series with no spaces between the columns to individual columns. Excel usually plots the orientation of your data correctly, but if it's incorrect or not what you were expecting, you can change it in this dialog box.

⚡ *If you are having problems selecting specific chart elements, see "Selecting Chart Element" in the Troubleshooting section at the end of this chapter.*

On the Series tab, you can manipulate the series in a chart by either adding or removing a series of a chart (see Figure 13.8). For example, if you've selected the entire range of a table and decide you want to view one data series only (to focus the audience), you can remove the data series by selecting it and clicking the Remove button. Conversely, you can add a series to the chart by clicking the Add button, and then specify the details for the new series by using the other options on the Series tab.

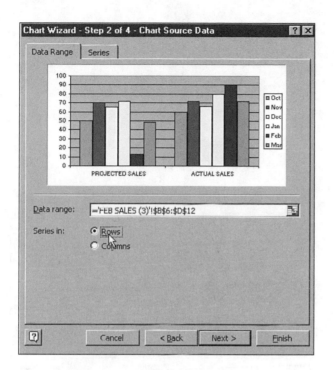

Figure 13.6.
When the Series In option is set to Rows, Excel plots each row as a data series, with each row heading appearing in the legend. The column headings appear as category labels along the X-axis of the chart.

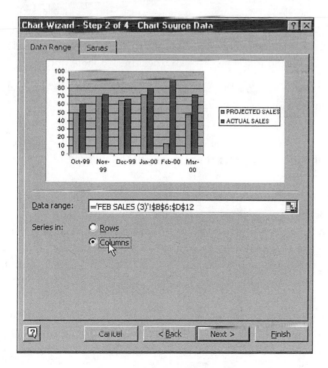

Figure 13.7.
Setting the Series In option to Columns plots each column as a data series, with each column heading appearing in the legend. Row headings now represent the categories that appear along the X-axis of the chart.

PART

V

CH

13

Figure 13.8.
The Series tab gives you the options of adding and removing data series. In addition, you can redefine the address from which Excel is retrieving names, values, and category labels.

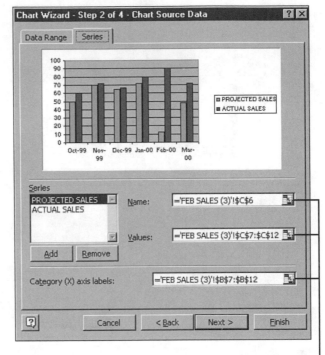

Collapse Dialog buttons

The options in this dialog box change depending on the type of chart and the series selected in the Series list box. The following list describes the available options:

- **Series, Add or Remove.** You can add a series to the chart by clicking the Add button and specifying the details. Remove a series by clicking Remove.

- **Name.** When you select a series in the Series list at the left side of the dialog box, this entry changes to show the address of the cell(s) containing the title for that series—for example, the name of a month or other time period, or the division or other category name used as a heading for that column or row.

  In Figure 13.8, for example, the series name (PROJECTED SALES) comes from the heading in cell C6 on the Feb Sales (3) sheet, as indicated in the Name box. Don't be thrown by the ='Feb Sales (3)'! designation; for dialog box options that list cell addresses, Excel lists the entire address, including the worksheet name. For example, if the worksheet name was Sales and the category title was in cell A2, the location formula would look like this: =Sales!$A$2. If the sheet name contains more than one word, Excel encloses it in single quotes (').

- **Values.** The Values box provides the address containing the values for the selected series. The values are the data used to build the columns. For some chart types, the Chart Wizard displays an X Values box and a Y Values box.

- **Category (X) Axis Labels.** This box shows the cell reference for the X-axis categories. In Figure 13.8, for example, the X-axis labels refer to the months listed in column B. As with the other options on this tab, you can select or type a different address or range for use as labels.

- **Second Category (X) Axis Labels.** Specifies the location of cell(s) containing the labels to be used for the second X-axis—for example, in stock charts or column-area custom charts.

 If after completing your chart you want to add data labels to a series, see "Adding Data Labels" in the Troubleshooting section at the end of this chapter.

Tip #177 from

If X-axis labels aren't located on a worksheet, you can type the labels in the Category (X) Axis Labels or Second Category (X) Axis Labels box, separating the labels with commas. Excel converts the labels to a formula, placing each label in quotes (") and surrounding all the labels with a set of braces ({ }).

- **Sizes.** In bubble charts, this option indicates the cell containing a value to indicate the size of bubble markers.

For options in which Excel lists a range, you can change the range if Excel hasn't guessed the address correctly. Select the option by clicking in the text box. Then use one of the following methods to change the range:

- Type the new range or name in the text box.

- Click outside the dialog box. Excel collapses the dialog box and enables you to select a new range.

- Click the *Collapse Dialog* button. This button squeezes the dialog box down to display just the option, as shown in Figure 13.9. Type or select the new range and then click the Collapse Dialog button again to return to the full-size dialog box.

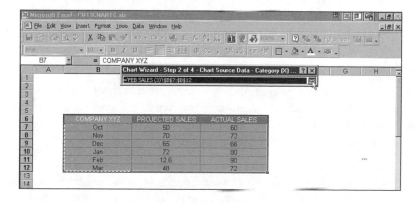

Figure 13.9.
The collapsed dialog box activates the range represented and enables you to drag over a new location on the worksheet.

PART

V

CH

13

After you make your selections, you can either go back to step 1 of the Chart Wizard, go on to step 3, or click Finish and Excel will select the default options for you.

Tip #178 from

If your column or row headings tend to be long, use an abbreviated version for titles, legends, and so on in the chart. You can change these items when you finish the chart, or create the abbreviations in a separate area of the worksheet and change the settings in the Series tab of the Chart Wizard to refer to these special cells. On the other hand, if you tend to abbreviate column and row headings to squeeze as much information as possible into a worksheet, you can expand the titles and legends for use in charts.

 If you want to add a trendline to a data series, see "Adding a Trendline" in the Troubleshooting section at the end of this chapter.

CHOOSING THE CHART OPTIONS

Step 3 of the Chart Wizard dialog box enables you to tailor your chart in several ways. You can add and delete features at will; however, note that you must finish the chart before you can format the features added. (To learn about formatting parts of the chart, see Chapter 15, "Formatting Charts.") This dialog box also enables you to view the chart as you're adding the features to understand how the final chart will look with the changes you've made.

Caution

Keep the chart clean and drive home a point. Too much information on a chart detracts from the focus of the chart. All too often, people try to put everything on the chart; before long, the story they're trying to tell gets lost. Excel offers more features with each new edition of the program, but just because it's there doesn't mean you should use it. As a test, show someone the information and see whether they can grasp the point within five seconds—ultimately, that's all the attention time you'll get for your chart. For example, if you have five or six callouts on a chart with multiple colors, the reader will need several minutes just to read through the data.

CHART TITLES

The Titles tab of the Chart Wizard - Step 3 of 4 dialog box enables you to insert a chart title, name the category axis, and name the value axis, as shown in Figure 13.10. If you have a dual-axis chart, the dialog box also displays options for naming the second category (X) axis and (Y) axis. The preview in the dialog box adds the new title a few seconds after you stop typing or click another option.

For most charts, I recommend adding each of the elements listed in the Titles tab. The chart title represents the total picture of the information in the chart. In Figure 13.11, for example, an appropriate title that describes the information might be "Corporate Sales." This title clearly describes what the information represents. Keep the title short and to the point.

Tip #179 from

If you complete the Chart Wizard, add a subtitle to the chart if needed; for this example, "Projected Six Month" would clarify further the information contained in the chart.

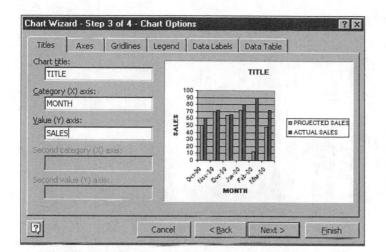

Figure 13.10.
The Titles tab enables you to add a chart title and provide titles for the chart's axes for easier reading.

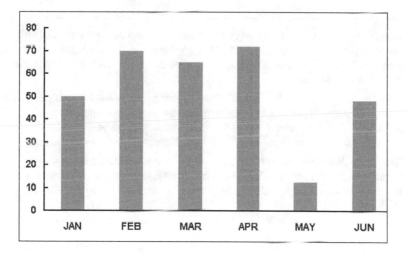

Figure 13.11.
A chart without a chart title and X- and Y-axis titles can draw blank stares.

I can't stress enough the importance of naming the value (Y) axis. All too often, I see graphs with no Y-axis title, and information that looks to be in the thousands of dollars can easily be misinterpreted as hundreds of thousands of dollars. In Figure 13.11, are you measuring sales in units or dollars? This should be part of the value (Y) title. In many cases, the category (X) axis title is self-explanatory; however, for consistency, it's good practice to name that axis as well. Without the titles, what's the story?

Figure 13.12 shows another version of the same chart, with titles added to clarify the information.

Figure 13.12.
With the proper titles in place, the chart now tells a clear story without any additional explanation.

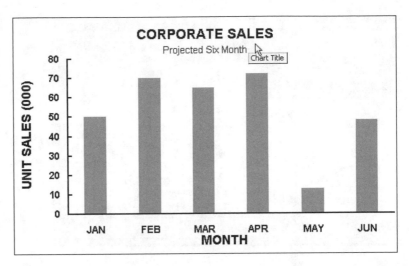

Tip #180 from

You can use the Display Units option in the Format Axis dialog box to specify what unit denomination you want to use, without adding a Y/Z-axis title. The advantage to using this feature is that Excel automatically changes the values on the Y/Z-axis to reflect whatever denomination you specify.

For example, if the source data contains values in millions, by default the scale values also appear in millions. However, if you specify millions for your display units, the word Millions will appear in the Y/Z-axis title and all scale values will be divided by one million. Thus 250,000,000 is displayed as 25 on the Y/Z-axis.

To specify a display unit, finish creating your chart. Then select the Y/Z-axis and choose Format, Selected Axis, or right-click the axis and select Format Axis from the context menu. In the Format Axis dialog box, click the Scale tab, and select the desired unit from the Display Units list box.

You may have noticed that the examples to this point use all uppercase letters for titles. Why? It's clean. The subtitle, on the other hand, should have initial caps, and you should drop the font size by two points to draw attention to the title first and subtitle second. The X- and Y-axis titles should be bold and two point sizes larger than the descriptions along the axis. (There's no absolute rule that says what's right and wrong, but experience has shown these practices to work well.)

Tip #181 from

Check the spelling! Misspelled titles will get far more attention than you'd like. Excel can spell-check these items for you after the chart is complete. With the chart selected, choose Tools, Spelling. For details on the Spelling feature, see Chapter 4, "Editing Cell Content."

AXES

The Axes tab, as shown in Figure 13.13, automatically displays data with a time-scale format if the data is date formatted. By deselecting the Category (X) Axis option, you can remove the axis labels, as shown in Figure 13.14. If the Category (X) Axis option is selected, the selected radio button below the option indicates what the axis will display.

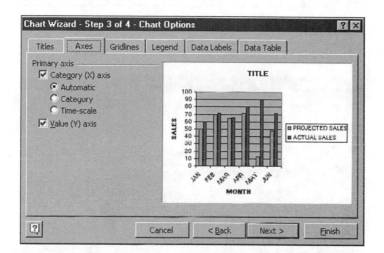

Figure 13.13.
The Axes tab enables you to show or hide values and text associated with the corresponding axis. You can also change the category axis to time-scale display.

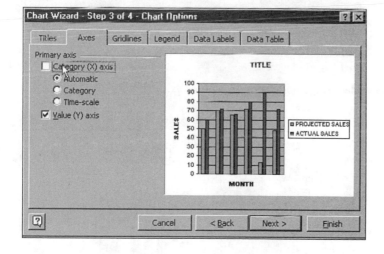

Figure 13.14.
By deselecting the Category (X) Axis option, you can hide the X-axis labels.

PART

V

Cн

13

Figure 13.15 shows an example of time scale. When the Time-Scale option is selected on the Axes tab, Excel converts the category from a text format to a date format. (If your date text crosses over year thresholds, convert the date format to time scale.)

> **Caution**
>
> If the date text isn't in a specific date format, Excel may not initially display the dates in the desired format. For example, if dates consist of month and year only (such as 5/98), Excel may initially display the dates as years only.
>
> You can change the date format after finishing the Chart Wizard. (To learn about formatting parts of the chart, see Chapter 15, "Formatting Charts.")

You also can add or delete the value (Y) axis. For example, if you're going to attach value labels to a data series, there's no need for the Y-axis.

Figure 13.15.
When the Time-Scale option is selected, Excel converts the text format to a date. If the date is formatted to show the month name in text, however, or you have data that crosses over years, you may want to convert the category to time-scale format to show the years.

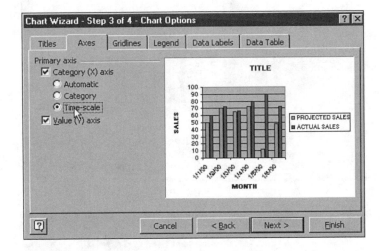

GRIDLINES

The Gridlines tab enables you to add major and minor axis gridlines (see Figure 13.16).

Figure 13.16.
The Gridlines tab enables you to apply vertical and horizontal gridlines to the plot area.

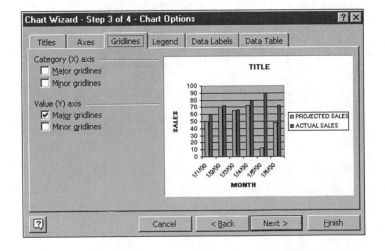

It's best to avoid gridlines to keep the chart clean. Normally, you would want to keep the major gridlines for the value (Y or Z) axis, but not apply additional gridlines. If formatted properly, however, gridlines can actually enhance and not detract from or clutter the chart.

Figure 13.17 shows major gridlines added to carry across and intersect the projected line when combining two chart types (this is a combination line chart and column chart).

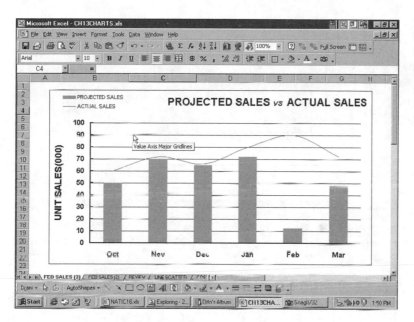

Figure 13.17.
By adding only major gridlines to a chart, and creating a lighter tone for the format of the gridlines, you can add organization without creating clutter.

In Figure 13.18, minor value gridlines and major category gridlines have been added to create a grid effect when showing incremental shifts. You also can lighten the grid effect by selecting the gridline and choosing Selected Gridlines from the Format menu. This example uses drawing tools to further illustrate the shift or decline over time on the chart.

→ To add drawing shapes to a chart, **see** "Enhancing Charts with Drawing Objects," **p. 427**

The last example, in Figure 13.19, uses white gridlines to carry across and highlight a specific month of data. Drawing tools were also added to the chart to call out the month increase.

LEGEND

The legend in a chart acts like a "map," with callouts to the different data series in a chart. If the chart consists of several categories, a legend is needed to pinpoint the pattern or color of each category. The Legend tab in the Chart Wizard dialog box enables you to apply or delete a legend (see Figure 13.20). You also can place the legend in different locations on the chart. Placement options just specify where the legend appears initially; you can move and/or resize the legend after the chart is created. For example, if you want the audience to focus on the chart itself, you may want to reduce the font size of the legend and place it in an inconspicuous place on the chart.

PART

V

CH

13

Figure 13.18.
Minor value gridlines and major category gridlines can be used when highlighting incremental shifts where callouts are needed.

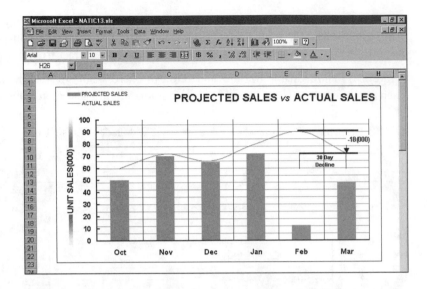

Figure 13.19.
The gridlines in this example are actually white, and a drawing tool rectangle sent to back was used to enhance the February sales increase. The chart area fill and the plot area fill are set to none.

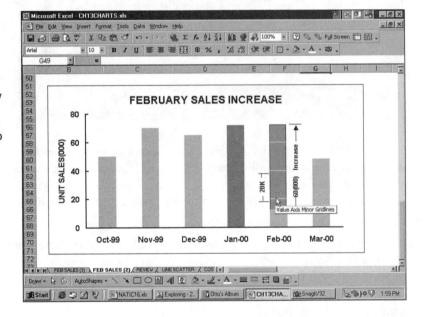

You can erase the borders of the legend to allow the legend to blend in with the rest of the chart. To erase the legend borders, select the legend after it's created on the chart (the sizing handles should be showing), choose Format, Selected Legend, and then set Border to None on the Patterns tab.

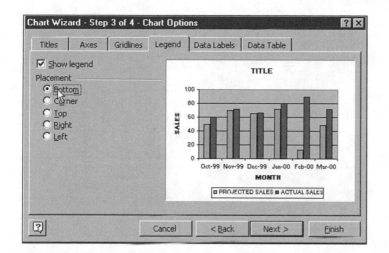

Figure 13.20.
The Legend tab enables you to delete the legend or place it in a different location on the chart.

Legends don't always have to be on the perimeter of the chart. Formatted properly, a legend can be placed within the plot area. Notice that in Figure 13.21 the legend actually sits better in the plot area than it would in any other region on the chart. This strategy also allows you to use the total landscape of the chart area.

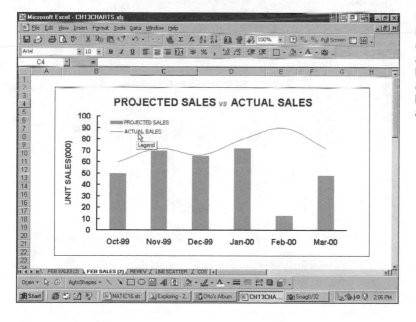

Figure 13.21.
By dragging the legend to the plot area and erasing the legend borders, you can take advantage of the total landscape of the chart area.

DATA LABELS

The Data Labels tab in the Chart Wizard dialog box gives you the option of showing labels or values next to each data series in the chart (see Figure 13.22).

Figure 13.22.
The Data Labels tab enables you to attach labels or values to the data series.

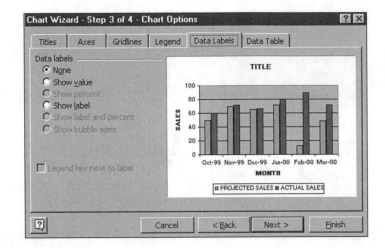

Figures 13.23 and 13.24 show examples of ways to use data labels. In Figure 13.23, notice how the data labels parallel the actual sales line. In Figure 13.24, by making the line white and adding the data labels, the months now represent the actual sales line.

Figure 13.23.
Data labels added to the actual sales line can distinguish the line or add more information.

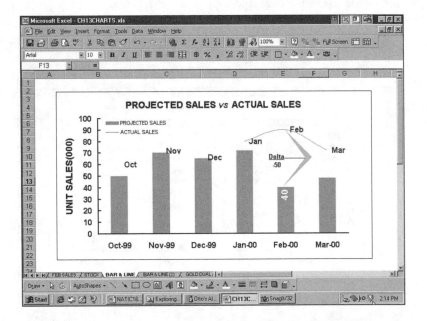

Tip #182 from

Patrick

Data labels can even be used to create an entire chart. For example, you can completely eliminate the category axis and replace it with data labels, thus providing more landscape for callouts and text.

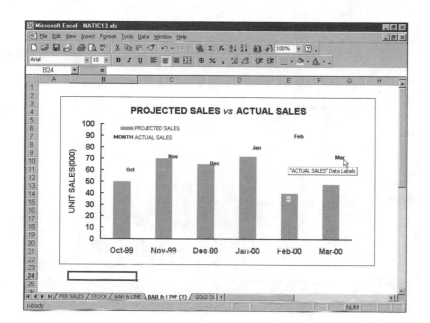

Figure 13.24.
Here the data labels
take the place of the
actual sales line in the
chart.

DATA TABLE

The Data Table tab in the Chart Wizard dialog box enables you to place a table below the X-axis (see Figure 13.25). This feature aligns the numeric data under the corresponding data series. This is one way to display data labels without cluttering the plot area (see Figure 13.26). It's also a handy way to combine a chart and its data into a single compact form—for example, for embedding on a PowerPoint slide.

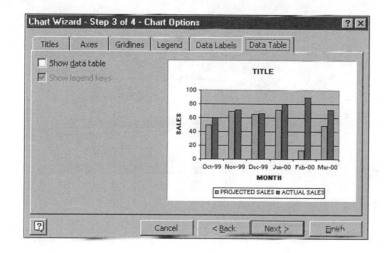

Figure 13.25.
The Data Table tab
places data series val-
ues under the X-axis.

Figure 13.26.
Notice that the data table aligns directly below the categories.

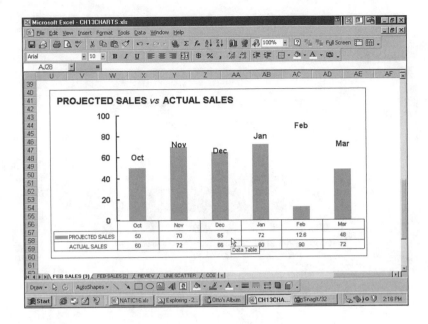

CHOOSING A CHART LOCATION

In step 4 of the Chart Wizard dialog box (the final step), you can use the following options to specify where you want to place the new chart (see Figure 13.27):

- As Object In. By default, this option embeds the chart in the worksheet containing the chart's source data (see Figure 13.28). You also can specify another sheet in the workbook by opening the drop-down list and selecting the sheet onto which you want to embed the chart.

Figure 13.27.
Specify whether you want to create the new chart as a chart sheet or embedded on a worksheet you select.

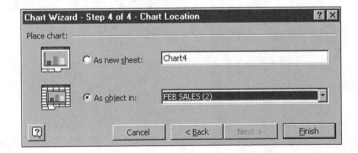

- As New Sheet. This option creates an independent *chart sheet* in the workbook (see Figure 13.29). With this option, the Chart Wizard automatically inserts a new sheet named Chart1. As with any other sheet tab, you can change this name to something more informative.

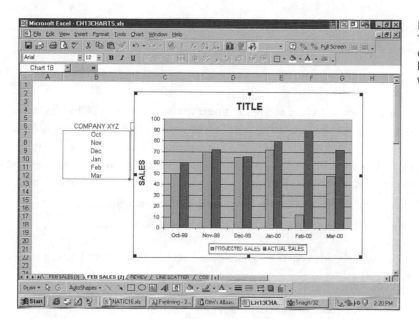

Figure 13.28.
This chart is embedded at your specified location within the worksheet.

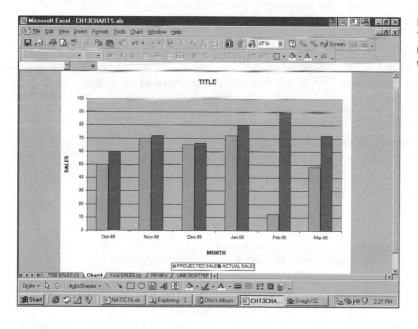

Figure 13.29.
The chart on a separate worksheet created within the workbook.

Although it may seem minor, the placement of the chart on the worksheet is critical. When combining a chart with additional data or tables on worksheets, it's important to place the chart in a manner that makes sense to the reader. The following sections describe the considerations for each placement.

EMBEDDED CHARTS

There are many advantages to creating embedded charts:

- You can move and manipulate the size of the chart, as well as change locations by just cutting and pasting the chart.

- You can drag and size the chart and place it next to the source data. Changes in the data are immediately reflected in the chart, so you can experiment by watching the chart as you make changes.

- At times, you'll need to view multiple sets of chart information at once; with embedded charts, you can size and place all the info on the same sheet within a single window.

- An embedded chart enables you to easily print data and chart together.

- You can connect chart and data with drawing items and comments.

On the downside, an embedded chart is easy to delete accidentally when deleting rows or columns.

CREATING THE CHART ON A SEPARATE CHART SHEET

Creating a chart on a separate worksheet doesn't offer as many advantages as creating embedded charts:

- When displaying a chart on a chart sheet, movement of the chart is limited.

- A chart sheet isn't as convenient as an embedded chart for viewing the chart with the data. It requires extra steps to see data changes reflected in the chart.

And on the other hand:

- All the options for changing the chart's appearance are still available, except for being able to grab the chart itself and move it around the worksheet.

- A chart sheet gives the chart more room in the window so that you can view and edit it more easily.

- It makes for easy printing of the chart on its own page.

 If you want to move a chart from a sheet to an embedded chart, see "Changing a Chart Sheet to an Embedded Chart" in the Troubleshooting section at the end of this chapter.

EXCEL CHART TYPES

Excel offers a wide variety of chart types because certain data works better with some chart types than others. For example, if you're plotting sales figures over a period of months, it's better to use a clustered column chart or line chart than a radar chart. The different chart types and the data that works best with the charts can be confusing, so it's important to understand which is the best chart for the information. The Chart Wizard suggests a certain type based on the data, but that doesn't mean that the suggested type is the best type to represent the data.

At some point, you'll probably want to experiment with each chart type to see how it plots data. This section shows the types that probably will be most beneficial in real-world use. After you become familiar with the different charts and what they're best suited for, you can even combine chart types for complex charting.

The following sections explore the various chart types. Rather than showing the standard version of each chart type (you can see these in the Chart Wizard dialog boxes), I'll provide plenty of examples of how you can make your charts more interesting, readable, or effective with the special charting features available in Excel. These features are covered in detail in the next three chapters on charting (Chapters 14, "Modifying Excel Charts," 15, "Formatting Charts," and 16, "Professional Charting Techniques"), and some more specialized techniques are described in Chapters 23, "Innovative Ways to Use Excel," and 24, "Professional Formatting Techniques."

Tip #183 from

Excel charts can be created in two-dimensional (2D) or three-dimensional (3D) format. (Many supposedly 3D charts actually are just 2D charts with perspective added to give a 3D effect. A true 3D chart has three axes.)

If you're not sure whether you want your data portrayed in 2D or 3D, or you have already created a chart and want to experiment with a different look, then use the Chart Wizard to change the chart type or sub-type and watch the results in the preview window.

Caution

Adding a third dimension to a 2D chart makes it more visually interesting, but also can make it more difficult to understand or leave it open to interpretation. Frequent use of 3D charts also can dilute their effectiveness with your audience. Use 3D sparingly.

COLUMN CHARTS

A *column chart* has vertical bars and plots as separate points over time (noncontiguous). Column charts are good for showing value amounts and quantities over time (see Figure 13.30). I would suggest becoming familiar with this chart type—knowing it well can dramatically improve your communication of data to others.

In this example, I've separated the categories by displaying the value (Y) axis between categories on the X-axis. The method is simple: Right-click the X-axis, choose Format Axis, click the Scale tab in the Format Axis dialog box, and select the Value (Y) Axis Crosses Between Categories option. This actually is a good way to visually represent two distinct categories—by separating them with the value axis.

Another type of column chart is the *stacked column chart*. A stacked column chart would work well in the following situation: Your division must report personnel needs for the next two years to corporate headquarters, and a maximum headcount is in place that you can't exceed (see Figure 13.31). Notice that the additional personnel needed per department is called out in the dark stacked region, and a line chart is applied to show the maximum headcount per department.

Figure 13.30.
A column chart with the value axis repositioned.

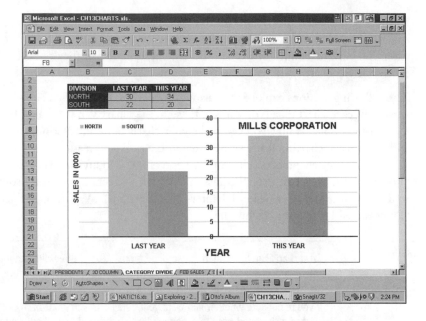

Figure 13.31.
A stacked column chart is a good way to show growth over current base. The use of drawing tools also can greatly enhance the story of the chart.

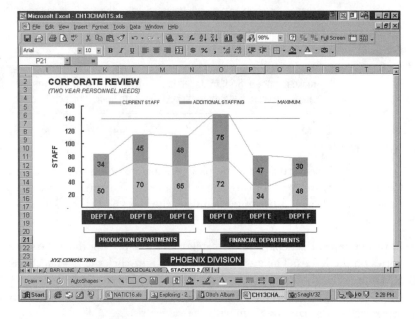

→ If you create 3D rather than 2D column charts, you have more formatting options to consider. For details, **see** "Formatting 3D Charts," **p. 436**

BAR CHARTS

A *bar chart* is similar to a column chart in that it plots bars as separate points; however, it plots the bars in a horizontal format. The bars can be placed side-by-side, as a cluster, stacked, or 3D. The bar chart was the original chart used for data display in the 1700s; the column chart came shortly after. When Excel plots a bar chart from your data, you'll notice that information normally viewed right-to-left translates to bottom-to-top.

→ To reverse a bar chart for top-to-bottom viewing, **see** "Changing the Series Order," **p. 399**

Bar charts are great tools for showing measurement, such as the percentage of a project completed (see Figure 13.32). In this example, an overlay effect helps pinpoint actual results against projected results.

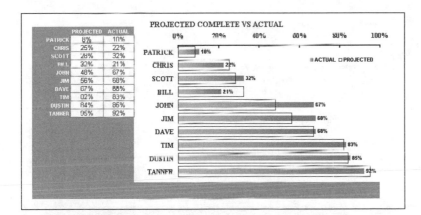

Figure 13.32.
A bar chart plots bars horizontally as separate points.

Bar charts originally were used to display events over time, and they're still great for that purpose, as shown in Figure 13.33. By adding a data label to the data series and applying no formats to the bars, the events become the chart. You can add drawing objects to further illustrate the point.

LINE CHARTS

Line charts serve well for measuring or plotting continuously over time. They make a good combination with column charts, or in multiple-line fashion. Line charts also are great for showing information that involves trends or change over time with one or two sets of data.

PART

V

CH

13

Tip #184 from

If you have more than two sets of data in a line chart, you'll need to be creative with line styles; otherwise, they start to blend together.

Figure 13.34 shows a typical line chart. Notice that the example shows the cost of a project to date against the projected cost.

Figure 13.33.
Use bar charts to illustrate events over time. By creating white borders and background on the bars and adding the data labels, the labels act as the chart.

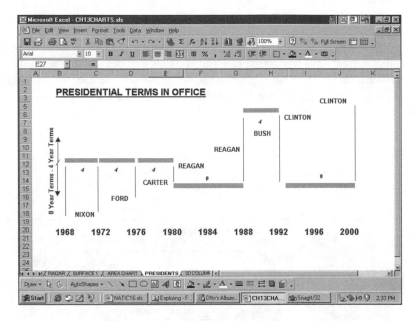

Tip #185 from

Think in terms of cumulative cost or production over time. If weekly values aren't combined, it may be difficult to see the visual impact of the total variance.

Figure 13.34.
Lines charts work well when showing variance analysis. Notice how drawing tools can be used as guide markers to the value (Y) axis.

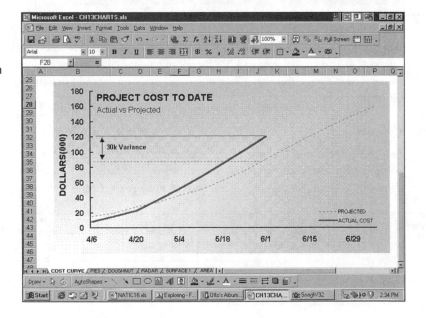

PIE CHARTS

Pie charts are used for showing a percentage of the whole. The pie chart types available are the standard 2D pie chart; exploded 2D pie; 3D pie; exploded 3D pie; *pie of a pie*, which extracts a subset of a pie slice; and *bar of a pie*, which extracts a subset of a pie and plots it as a stacked column chart.

One of the great features Excel offers with pie charts is that you can select the data point and drag it away from the whole pie, thereby *exploding* the slice—also called a *piece* or *wedge*—to highlight a certain data point.

Suppose that your company has been in business for 20 years and your market share was 20% twenty years ago. Now your market share has grown a single percentage point, to 21%, but in those twenty years, the value of that market share went from $20 million to $200 million. The 1% change would look very minor in some chart types. Shown in a pie chart, however, it's actually quite dramatic. Figure 13.35 shows this situation, using a combination of two pie charts of different sizes and a line chart. The line chart in the background displays the market over time. From this example, you can see how flexible combination charts can be.

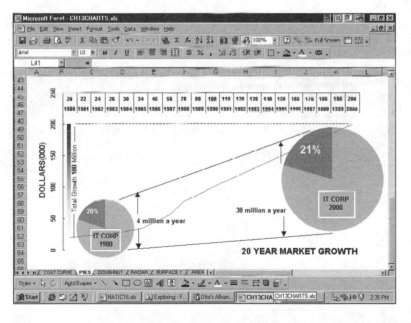

Figure 13.35.
The market grew from $4 million to $38 million; in this case, a single-digit percentage increase is substantial, considering the growth of the total market. By distorting the pie sizes, you create a visual image that represents the change in value.

PART

V

CH

13

If you need to plot several data series and insist on using a pie shape, I suggest using a doughnut chart (see the next section for details). Pie charts are designed specifically for one set of data, and doughnut charts are for two sets of data compared in pie form.

Caution

If you have more than 10 points of data in your data series, don't use a pie chart. With too much information, it's easy for the reader to become lost.

DOUGHNUT CHARTS

Doughnut charts are variations of pie charts. The difference is that doughnut charts are for multiple sets of data—sort of like plotting several pie charts against one another. One way to use a doughnut chart is to compare a fiscal year cycle of projected sales versus actual sales. The doughnut chart is a natural choice for this type of data because a year cycle is often thought of as a circle.

In Figure 13.36, the doughnut slice of actual sales takes up 60 percent of the doughnut's total area. If projected sales and actual sales were the same value, the slices of the doughnut would be equal in size.

The unit value associated with the 20 percent increase in actual versus projected sales is 25,000 units. I've called out this increase on the doughnut chart by using drawing tools.

Figure 13.36.
You can use doughnut charts to compare sets of stacked data or data sets over time.

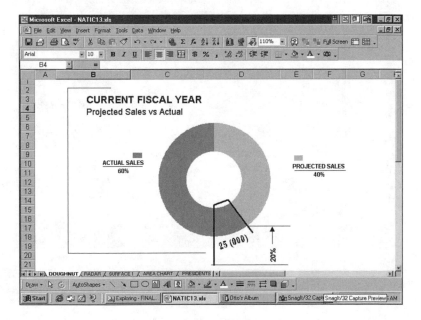

Scatter Charts

Scatter charts are used for plotting data over uneven time intervals. This chart style is mostly seen in the scientific and engineering arenas. However, the use of scatter charts can definitely cross over into other areas, as shown in Figure 13.37. This chart shows scatter charts plotted against industry averages. The industry average is in the form of a line chart (unchanging), and the names of the students are plotted in scatter form against time and against the industry average.

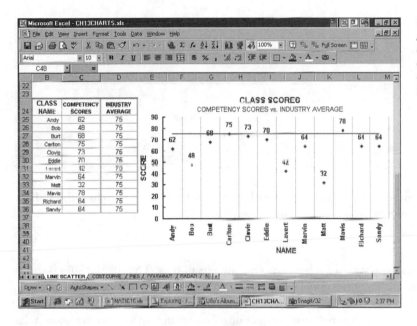

Figure 13.37.
A scatter chart for competency scores is combined with a line chart displaying the industry average.

Using the same approach, notice that Figure 13.38 has the same chart types, but the data is sorted from lowest scores to highest scores. When creating charts with random plotted points, a better approach may be to sort the information from smallest to largest so that the audience can grasp the information in a shorter period of time.

Area Charts

Area charts are used much like line charts, in that area charts plot data over time in a continuous manner. The only difference is that the area is filled, hence the name area chart (see Figure 13.39).

Tip #188 from

When plotting multiple areas against one another on the same graph, consider using extreme differences in shading colors so the areas don't blend together. An example of this would be to use the lightest shade of gray first and then darker and darker as the layers get deeper.

Part V
Ch 13

Figure 13.38.
Sort the scores in the worksheet from smallest to largest before creating the chart. This way, it's easier to compare the class scores against the industry average.

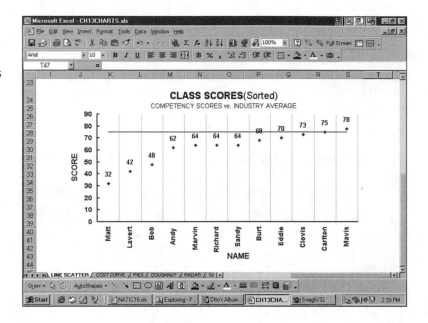

Avoid using more than five sets of data with this chart type. It's easy to lose the audience's focus if too much information is presented at once.

RADAR CHARTS

Radar charts show relationships between separate sets of data. The relationship is shown against the whole of a series, similar to the way a doughnut chart plots a data series against the whole of a series. Suppose that you want to compare the consumer spending in four categories of your market against your product distribution and focus. You can use a radar chart for market analysis in the form of a quadrant to analyze your current product focus against the consumer dollar spending, as shown in Figure 13.40. Radar charts help you to establish market comparatives for quick decision making, as well as refocus your audience's efforts and business strategy.

→ To learn more about quadrants, **see** "Using Drawing Tools to Create Quadrants," **p. 683**

SURFACE CHARTS

Surface charts measure two changing variables in the form of a topographical map, providing a great 3D representation of the highs and lows. There are two types of surface charts, with two variations of each type. The *3D surface* provides variations in color, and the *3D wire frame* gives the topographical contour without color variations.

Assume that you have several variables that you want to display, such as time, profit, season, loss, breakeven, and so on. It can almost become confusing. However, with a 3D surface chart, you can measure certain sets of data and use drawing tools to analyze the rest. (Always think in terms of combining Excel's tools to enhance your graph. You'll run into situations that will practically require chart embellishment.)

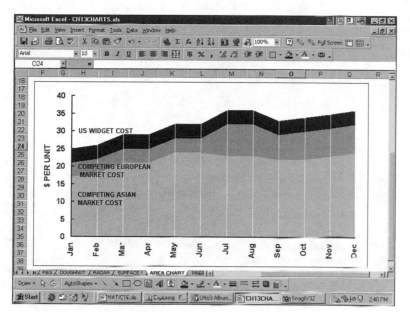

Figure 13.39.
When comparing global markets over time, area charts can effectively represent the differences between the markets.

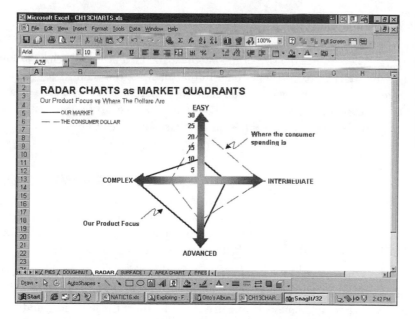

Figure 13.40.
Radar charts can be valuable tools in comparative analysis. This example helps the audience refocus its efforts and move its product focus closer to the consumer spending.

PART

V

CH

13

Figure 13.41 shows a surface chart and uses Excel's flexibility with drawing tools to tell the rest of the story. From this 3D view, you can see the average span of the season, the breakeven in mined ounces, and a profit scale above breakeven. There's a lot of information crammed into this small chart.

Figure 13.41.
You can use surface charts to show several levels of information that a two-dimensional chart would convey only with difficulty.

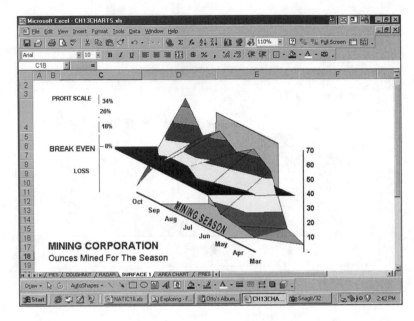

BUBBLE CHARTS

Bubble charts compare values in sets of three. The first two sets are actually used in the chart; the third value determines the size of the bubble markers. The bubble chart in Figure 13.42 represents the average ore mined per pod. In this example, you want to visually display the ounce concentration level per pod and show its respective location on the area map. If you have a picture of the map, you could paste it into the chart (in this case, however, it was drawn in). The highest concentration levels are formatted to be darker.

STOCK CHARTS

Stock charts are designed by default for the stock market and come in four varieties: high low close, open high low close, volume high low close, and volume open high low close. It might sound a little confusing; however, Excel indicates the order of the information in the chart sub-type in the Chart Wizard dialog box. For example, this type of chart can indicate the date and the high mark for the day, or the low mark and close for the day.

Often, you'll see *stock diaries* in publications that track information relative to the stock market's overall performance over the year or a specific period of time. The stock diary enables you to see the stock market's volume performance aligned against the high, low, and close for the specified period(s). You can create stock diaries in Excel as well. Notice the example in Figure 13.43, which consists of two charts: one for volume, and the other for the high, low, and close.

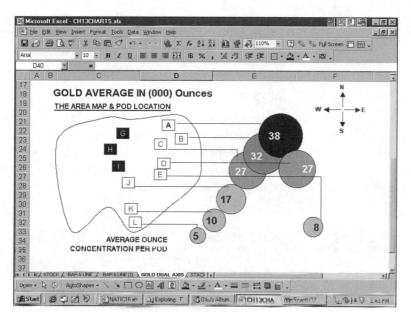

Figure 13.42.
The bubble chart example shows the ounce concentration per pod and its respective location on the mining grid or area map.

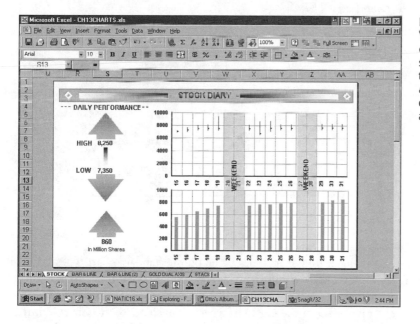

Figure 13.43.
You can create stock charts in Excel to measure performance over time. You also can align two charts, one over the other, to create a stock diary.

Rather than using two charts, you could plot this data on one chart with dual axes, but for simplicity it's easier to view it as two charts. Notice that I've aligned the two charts, used drawing tools to call out the key points for each day's performance, and blocked out the weekends.

Tip #189 from

Stock charts are also very handy for charting temperature variances for scientific or medical studies, crop yield projections, product analyses, and so on.

CYLINDER, CONE, AND PYRAMID CHARTS

Cylinder charts, *cone charts*, and *pyramid charts* are 3D charts with unique shapes. Where a standard column chart provides a rectangle effect in cluster column form, the cylinders, cones, and pyramids are shaped in the form of their names (see Figure 13.44). Sub-types include cluster column, stacked column, clustered bar, and stacked bar. If you like, you can create two forms of columns on the same chart—the example shows a column with a cylinder effect.

Figure 13.44.
A formatted cylinder chart can be great when a presentation is as much about the graphics as the supporting data.

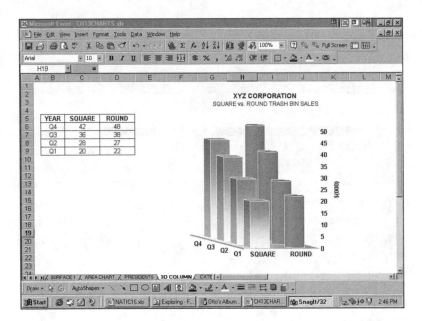

CUSTOM CHARTS

Excel offers many built-in custom chart types based on the standard chart types. Most of the custom chart types are formatted to add some pizzazz to a presentation or to put a little variety into a basic dull chart. To view what your data would look like as one of Excel's built-in custom chart types, select the Custom Types tab in step 1 of the Chart Wizard, or choose Chart Type from the Chart menu.

Chances are you probably won't use any of the custom types; however, they can provide ideas on how you can format your chart. Remember that charts are pictures that tell stories; it's easy to get carried away with all of the tools and formatting options in Excel. Be cautious; you can easily lose focus with too much on the chart at once.

CREATING A PERSONALIZED CUSTOM CHART

After formatting a chart, you can save the format as a custom type. You'll probably save several types of charts as custom types, so be sure that your title description fits the chart. To save charts as a custom type, follow these steps:

1. Select the chart you want to save as a custom chart.
2. Choose Chart Type from the Chart menu to open the Chart Type dialog box.
3. Click the Custom Types tab.
4. Select the User Defined option in the Select From section (see Figure 13.45).
5. Click the Add button to open the Add Custom Chart Type dialog box (see Figure 13.46).
6. Type a name for the new chart type and supply a description, if desired.
7. Click OK. The custom type now appears on the Chart Type list on the Custom Types tab. If you want this custom chart type set as the default chart type for use in Excel, click the Set as Default Chart button and respond Yes in the message box that appears.

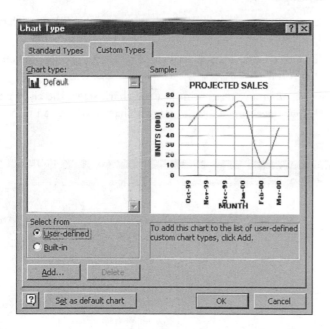

Figure 13.45.
The Custom Types tab in the Chart Type dialog box enables you to save a chart as a custom type.

To delete a custom chart type, select it in the Chart Type list on the Custom Types tab, click the Delete button, and click OK when asked for confirmation.

Figure 13.46.
Naming the custom
chart type.

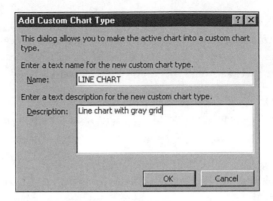

PRINTING CHARTS

Before printing a chart, it's good practice to preview the chart (see Figure 13.47). You can preview a chart in the following ways:

- If you created the chart on a chart sheet, activate or select the chart sheet. Select Print Preview from the File menu; a preview of the printed chart appears onscreen.

- If the chart is embedded on a worksheet, select Print Preview to preview the entire worksheet with the chart on it.

- If the chart is embedded and you want to print just the chart, select the chart and choose File, Print Preview. Excel previews the selected chart and you can print it as you would a chart sheet.

Figure 13.47.
The Print Preview
feature enables you
to review the chart
on the embedded
worksheet before
you print it.

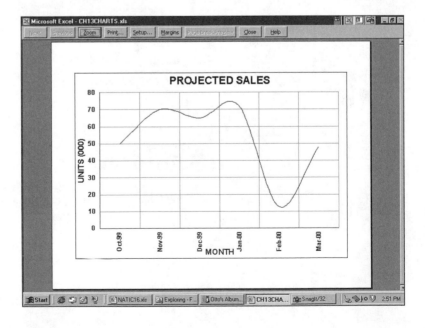

Whether you're printing on a color or a black-and-white printer (using *grayscale*), be sure to print a test copy and review it before distributing the chart. Remember that every printer is different, and that Print Preview shows you only Excel's projection of how the printout will look. If you create the chart in color but are printing in grayscale, the different colors on the chart may appear similar in shade when printed. Data series should stand apart from one another; be sure to use contrasting shades or switch from using color to using black-and-white patterns. Even when printing in color, be aware that color monitors and color printers don't "think" in the same colors. The colors may turn out to be more red, blue, and so on than you expected. Also note that the print quality of the printer, the paper, and the toner/cartridge/ribbon all affect the results you get.

When printing a chart on a chart sheet or printing a selected chart embedded on a worksheet, you can click the Print button on the Standard toolbar to send the chart directly to the printer, using the default print settings. Note that Excel resizes the chart as necessary to occupy the whole sheet of paper; this may not be exactly what you had in mind. Using the File, Print command, on the other hand, displays the Print dialog box as usual, but the Print What section of the dialog box gives you only one option: Selected Chart. While an embedded chart is selected, you can't opt to print the worksheet with the chart. If you want both, cancel the dialog box, deselect the embedded chart, and then issue the Print command from the menu or the toolbar button.

TROUBLESHOOTING

SELECTING A CHART ELEMENT

Excel won't let me select a specific chart element.

Excel gives you two ways to select chart elements:

- Click the element so the selection handles are showing.
- Click open the Chart Objects button on the Chart toolbar and select the desired element from the drop-down list.

CHANGING A CHART SHEET TO AN EMBEDDED CHART

I can't move a chart sheet next to my data table.

Excel defaults to creating a chart as a worksheet, but you can change the chart worksheet to an embedded chart. Select Chart, Location to open the Chart Location dialog box. Select As Object In and use the drop-down list to specify the worksheet you would like the chart to be embedded in.

ADDING A TRENDLINE

How do I add a trendline to a data series?

Trendlines can only be added to two-dimensional charts. To add a trendline, select the data series you want the trendline to represent. Choose Chart, Add Trendline to open the Add Trendline dialog box. On the Type tab, select the type of trendline you want and then choose OK.

ADDING DATA LABELS

The chart is complete, but I want to add data labels to a series.

Select the series of data for which you want to add labels. Then choose Format, Selected Data Series to display the Format Data Series dialog box. On the Data Labels tab, select the Show Label option. To add data labels to all the series at once, click anywhere in the chart and choose Chart, Chart Options to open the Chart Options dialog box. Click the Data Labels tab and select the Show Label option. Click OK.

EXCEL IN PRACTICE

Choosing the correct chart type to display information is critical to comprehension. Figure 13.48 shows a typical clustered column chart that displays additions to each department's headcount as a separate column. Although the information being conveyed is clear, the ramifications aren't obvious; the audience must do a bit of quick calculating to figure out the results. In Figure 13.49, the stacked chart type displays additions to each department as stacks on top of the current headcount stack. When displaying information that's in addition to another column but within the same data set, stacked charts work much better for getting the point across.

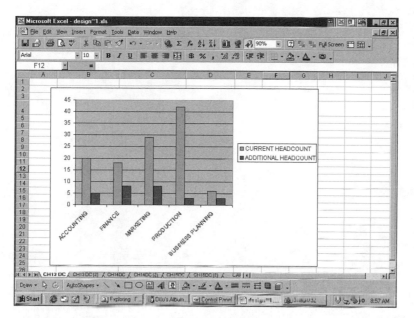

Figure 13.48.
Displaying the current and projected amounts in separate columns requires the audience to do a little math in their heads.

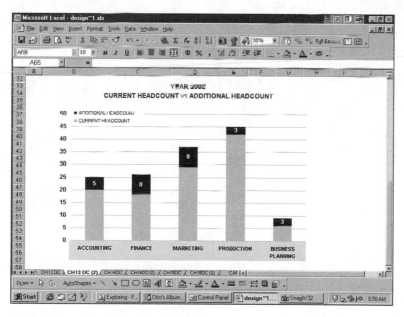

Figure 13.49.
The stacked chart shows at a glance the contrast between current and projected counts, and makes it instantly obvious which department is hoping to gain how much additional staff.

CHAPTER **14**

MODIFYING EXCEL CHARTS

In this chapter

by Patrick D. Blattner
Patrick@BlattnerBooks.com

OPTIONS FOR IMPROVING YOUR CHARTS

After you create a chart, you probably will want to add information or change elements of the chart. Excel enables you to manipulate any part of the chart, as well as add elements to the chart. If you saved the chart as an embedded chart and now want to change it to a chart on a separate chart sheet, you can do that, too. Many times, however, you must go into an existing chart, delete a series of data, and replace it with data from a new location, or even change the chart type to give the chart a different look and feel.

Information in a newly created chart almost always will have to be modified to get your point across. The better you become at presenting information to achieve your goals, the better off you'll be.

Excel provides numerous tools and techniques to manipulate a chart to make it serve the specific needs of the audience. Some of these techniques are discussed in Chapter 15, "Formatting Charts," and Chapter 16, "Professional Charting Techniques." For now, it's important to learn the fundamentals of building and modifying charts. This section begins by discussing the fundamentals of adding information and changing existing information on a chart.

MOVING AND RESIZING EMBEDDED CHARTS

When an embedded chart is complete, you probably will want to move or resize the chart so that it fits better with the data on the worksheet.

To resize a chart, select the chart by placing the mouse pointer over the embedded chart and clicking. Small black boxes called *sizing handles* appear around the perimeter of the chart. Point to one of the handles. When the pointer changes to display a two-headed black arrow, drag away from the center of the chart to enlarge, or toward the center of the chart to reduce. While resizing, Excel displays a dotted box to give you an indication of the final size of the chart.

Tip #190 from

Patrick

Dragging a corner handle resizes height and width simultaneously.

You may decide at some point that an embedded chart should have been placed in a different location: somewhere else in the current worksheet, on a different worksheet entirely, or on a separate chart sheet. Perhaps you chose the wrong option in the Chart Wizard, or you just changed your mind and want to move the chart from one place to another. As usual, multiple methods are available; the following methods are the easiest:

- Move the chart from one worksheet location to another with a quick cut-and-paste. Select the chart, cut it to the *Office Clipboard (page 116)*, position the cell pointer in the new worksheet location, and paste the chart into place.

- To drag the chart elsewhere on the current sheet, select the chart so that the handles are visible. Then click somewhere in the chart area (a ScreenTip says Chart Area), but not on any of the individual elements of the chart—in other words, don't click the title, axes, and so on—and watch for the mouse pointer to display the typical selection arrow. Drag the chart to its new position, and drop it there.

■ To move the chart from one worksheet to another or to a separate chart sheet, select the chart and choose Chart, Location to open the Chart Location dialog box. Specify whether you want to place the chart on a separate chart sheet or as an object in another worksheet in the current workbook (select from the drop-down list).

SELECTING PARTS OF A CHART FOR EDITING

It's very likely that you'll need to change particular aspects of a new or existing chart—removing a particular data marker, adding text boxes, adjusting line size and color, and so on. The first step to changing features within the chart is to select the chart so that the sizing handles are showing. After the chart is selected, place the mouse pointer over almost any item in the chart to display a *ScreenTip (page 844)* that indicates which object on the chart you're pointing to. To select the specified object, click it.

Chart objects such as data series and data points are grouped; clicking any one selects the entire set. If you need to change a particular one of the set, click it a second time to display handles around that item alone. Don't double-click; just click once to select the set, wait briefly, and then click the individual item.

Tip #191 from

Patrick

> If the chart is small or somewhat crowded, you may find yourself squinting at the screen or increasingly frustrated as you attempt to click tiny elements in the chart. Instead, use the Zoom feature to enlarge the view so that you can see what you're clicking. If the chart is embedded, click outside the chart—anywhere in the worksheet—to enable the Zoom feature. Make your selections and changes, and then restore the original Zoom setting, if desired.

The Chart toolbar can be very helpful when you want to edit a chart—particularly if you're having difficulty selecting individual parts of a chart because you can't remember what they're called. Table 14.1 describes the buttons on the Chart toolbar. If the toolbar isn't displayed, right-click the menu or any toolbar and choose Chart from the context menu that appears.

TABLE 14.1. BUTTONS ON THE CHART TOOLBAR

Button	Name	Description
Category Axis ▼	Chart Objects	Displays a drop-down list of the objects and data points within the chart. Click the drop-down arrow and select the one you want from the list.
(icon)	Format *<object>*	Displays the Format dialog box for the selected object on the chart. (The ScreenTip name for this button changes to show the name of the selected object.)

continues

TABLE 14.1.   CONTINUED

Button	Name	Description
	Chart Type	Displays a drop-down palette of chart types; click the type you want to apply to the current chart. The face of the button changes to show the last chart type selected.
	Legend	Toggles adding and removing a legend on the chart.
	Data Table	Toggles adding and removing a data table below the category (X) axis.
	By Row	Plots each row of data as a series in the chart.
	By Column	Plots each column of data as a series in the chart.
	Angle Text Downward	Changes the angle of selected text to 45 degrees downward. Use for data markers, axis labels, and so on.
	Angle Text Upward	Changes the angle of selected text to 45 degrees upward. Use for data markers, axis labels, and so on.

Tip #192 from

You can often save time by right-clicking the item in the chart and using the context menu rather than the main menu. You also can double-click the desired element of the chart to display the Format dialog box for that element.

CHANGING THE CHART TYPE

No matter how much time you spend deliberating before creating a chart about what type of chart to use, occasionally the result just isn't what you need. You can change the chart type very easily to some other type that works better for the data. Excel even lets you combine chart types by changing individual data series to a different type from the rest of the chart. For example, when comparing trends or different sets of data, it can be quite helpful to separate the data series with different chart types on the same chart to show distinct differences between two sets of information. Figure 14.1 shows projected sales in a line and actual sales in columns. In this example, displaying the projected sales as a line clearly emphasizes by how much sales fell short of projection.

The methods are basically the same for changing the chart type for the entire chart or for selected data series. The only difference is that if you want to change just a data series, you select the data series first. You can use any of the following methods to change the chart type:

- Choose Chart, Chart Type to open the Chart Type dialog box, and then select the desired chart type and sub-type (see Figure 14.2).
- Right-click any data point in the series (or anywhere else in the chart if you want to change the entire chart), and select Chart Type from the context menu to open the Chart Type dialog box. Change the settings as desired.

- Click the Chart Type button on the Chart toolbar, and select a new chart type from the displayed palette.

- Click the Chart Wizard button on the Standard toolbar to open the Chart Wizard - Step 1 of 4 - Chart Type dialog box. Select a new chart type and sub-type, and click Finish. This method changes the entire chart; it doesn't work for individual data series.

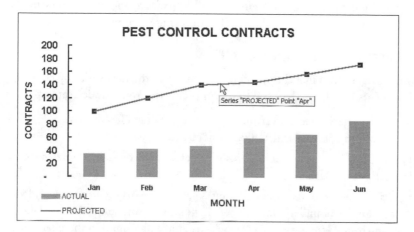

Figure 14.1.
The result of the changed series is in the form of a line chart.

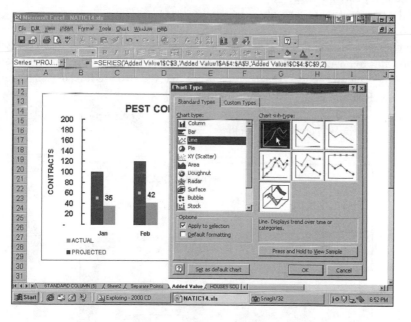

Figure 14.2.
Use the Chart Type dialog box to select a different chart type and sub-type.

Tip #193 from

The advantage of using the Chart Wizard to change the chart type for an entire chart is that you can use the Press and Hold to View Sample button to preview the data in the new chart format. This can save some steps if you need to try several chart types before you find the best type.

CHANGING A DATA SERIES

A *data series (page 342)* is represented by the bars in a bar chart, the columns in a column chart, and so on. For example, if you have a column chart and a set of the individual columns is one color, all the columns of that color together represent a data series.

In addition to formatting data series by changing the color, pattern, and so on, you can add or remove data series in the chart, as described in the following sections.

SELECTING A DATA SERIES OR DATA POINT IN A CHART

To modify or format a data series in a chart, you first must select the data series by clicking any one of the data points (a column, bar, and so on) in the series. You'll notice three things:

- When the mouse pointer is placed over the data series, a ScreenTip displays a description of the series and the particular data point under the mouse pointer.

- When a data point is clicked, the whole series is selected, and the sizing handles show up on the data series as square dots.

- When a data series is selected, its corresponding data in the worksheet is surrounded by colored Range Finder boundary lines. A purple boundary surrounds the axis labels, a green boundary surrounds the series labels (the ones normally found in the chart's legend), and a blue boundary surrounds the data series entries.

You also can change an individual data point in a data series. With the series selected, click the point you want to change (see Figure 14.3). To change the value of the data point and its corresponding value in the worksheet—remember that the two are linked—select the data point in the chart and drag it to the desired value.

 If you want to change the chart type for a series, see "Changing the Chart Type of a Data Series" in the Troubleshooting section at the end of this chapter.

Figure 14.3.
By selecting a single data point in a data series, you can format or change the value of the data point.

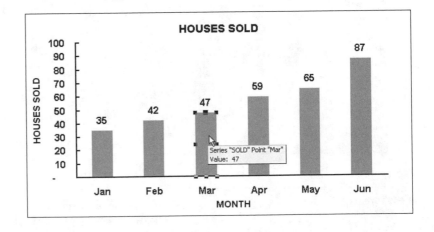

One reason you may want to change values this way is for visual emphasis. If you're trying to drive home a point and the actual value isn't static or exact, you may want to drag the value or data point to look a certain way (for example, very low or very high) as opposed to registering an exact value.

REMOVING A SERIES FROM A CHART

When displaying information with charts, you often want to analyze the information with and without different sets of data. For example, in a chart that shows actual versus projected sales for the year, you may want to display just the actual sales and then just the projections. To remove a data series from a chart, select the data series so that the handles are showing, and then press the Delete key, or choose Edit, Clear, Series. It's that simple.

ADDING OR ADJUSTING SOURCE DATA

Because business needs change, you may sometimes have to add data series to a chart—for example, to include a new division or product—or adjust existing data series or data points to include new information. You can build a new chart or just add data to the existing chart, as described in the following sections.

ADDING DATA POINTS OR DATA SERIES

Excel gives you the flexibility of adding data to a chart in several ways:

- Adjust the source data, as described in the following section.

- Select the chart and choose Chart, Add Data to display the Add Data dialog box (see Figure 14.4). Specify the range of the data you want to add. You can use the *Collapse Dialog button (page 529)* to reduce the size of the dialog box, or just drag the dialog box out of the way to see the worksheet. When the range is correct, click OK. You also can use this method to add data from a different worksheet.

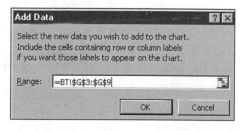

Figure 14.4.
Use the Add Data dialog box to add new series to an existing chart.

- Copy the data in the worksheet, select the chart, and paste the data into the chart. You can use the Paste command on the context menu; choose Edit, Paste; click the Paste button on the Standard toolbar; or press Ctrl+V With the paste command, Excel selects the format for the new series automatically.

- If you want more control of how Excel pastes the new data, choose Edit, Paste Special to display the Paste Special dialog box, in which you can indicate how you want the new data to appear (see Figure 14.5).

PART
V

CH
14

Figure 14.5.
The Paste Special dialog box gives you options for plotting information as new points or in a new series, as well as by rows or columns.

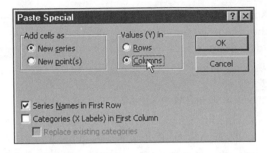

In the example in Figure 14.6, the new data is added as a series and plotted in the form of columns along the Y-axis—the same result as you would get with a simple paste. In Figure 14.7, on the other hand, the data is added as new points, thereby plotting the data separately, as a second category on the X-axis.

Figure 14.6.
The new information is pasted as a new series in columns.

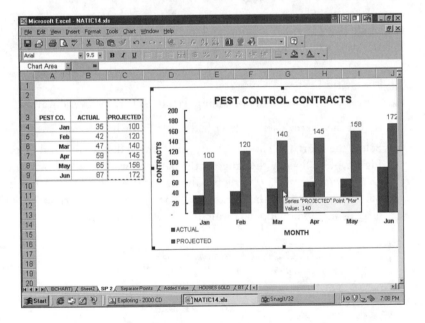

You can choose from the following options in the Paste Special dialog box:

- **New Series**. Adds the copied data to the chart as a new data series.
- **New Point(s)**. Adds the copied data to the chart as an additional data series along the same axis.
- **Rows** or **Columns**. Creates an additional data series from the contents of each row or column in the copied selection.
- **Series Names in First Row**. Uses the first row or column of the copied data as the label for the selected data series.

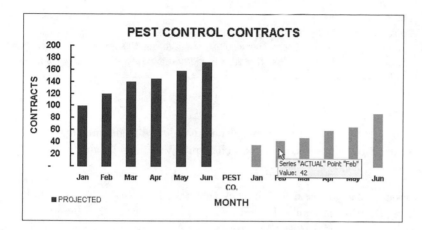

Figure 14.7.
The result of pasting information in as new points along the same category axis.

- **Categories (X Labels) in First Column**. Uses the first row or column of the copied data as category labels on the X-axis.

- **Replace Existing Categories**. Replaces the existing category labels with the category labels you want to paste in. For example, you could use this option to change existing labels January through December to 1 through 12.

Note

Choose Undo if the results aren't what you had in mind.

- Use the drag-and-drop method to add data to a chart. Select the data you want to add. Move the mouse pointer over the edge of the selection until the pointer changes to an arrow. Click and drag the data anywhere inside the chart; then release the mouse button.

  If the data is on a different worksheet from the chart, hold down the Alt key and drag the data down to the tab for the worksheet containing the chart. When the destination worksheet appears, release the Alt key and drag the data into the chart.

  If the data is in a different workbook, open the workbook and use the Window, Arrange command to display both workbooks onscreen. Display the worksheet containing the data and the worksheet containing the chart. Then select and drag the desired data from the source worksheet window into the chart. Data added from another workbook creates links to that workbook in the destination chart.

→ For details on working with worksheet links, **see** "Linking Excel Data," **p. 121**

Note

You may be prompted with the Paste Special dialog box if Excel can't define the new data automatically.

Tip #194 from

Avoid adding too many data series to one chart. You can easily lose the point if too much information is presented at once. Another alternative is to create two charts and embed them on the same sheet, and then use drawing tools and/or text to help the reader compare them.

CHANGING THE DATA SOURCE

Sometimes you don't need to add a data series—just adjust some that are already included in the chart. You can change the source data for a chart in any of the following ways:

- Add data points or data series as described in the preceding section.

- With the worksheet data visible behind it, click an embedded chart (you may need to move the chart nearer to the source data for this method to work). Then drag the selection handles for the colored lines that surround the source data, headings, and labels. If the mouse pointer is an arrow, dragging moves the selection rectangle. If the pointer is a black cross, dragging expands or contracts the selection. As you adjust the colored lines, the chart changes to reflect the new selection.

- Select the chart, start the Chart Wizard, and click Next in the Step 1 of 4 dialog box. In the Step 2 of 4 dialog box, change the data source as needed; then click Finish.

- Select the chart and choose Chart, Source Data, or right-click the chart and choose Source Data from the context menu. The Source Data dialog box opens (see Figure 14.8). Select the Data Range tab. From here, you can change the absolute address from which the data is derived.

Figure 14.8.
The Source Data dialog box enables you to change the address of your chart data.

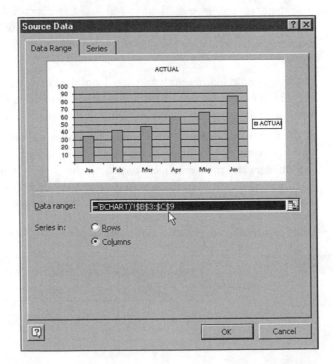

ADDING A SECONDARY AXIS TO THE CHART

More often than not, you'll run into a situation where you need to use a chart to compare two sets of data that are extremely different in value, such as unit output and dollars sold. One way to display this type of information is with a *secondary axis*. In most cases, the values would be extremely different, so you would want the units on one Y-axis, and the dollars represented on another Y-axis (see Figure 14.9).

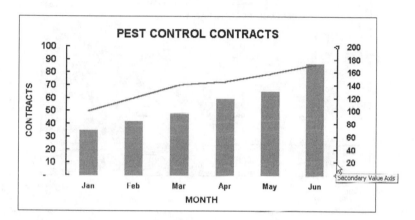

Figure 14.9.
Plotting series on two different Y-axes.

To create a dual-axis chart, follow these steps:

1. Select the data series that you want to plot on the secondary axis. In Figure 14.10, the dollar line is selected.

2. Choose Format, Selected Data Series to open the Format Data Series dialog box, as shown in Figure 14.11.

3. Select the Axis tab.

4. Under Plot Series On, choose Secondary Axis.

5. Click OK.

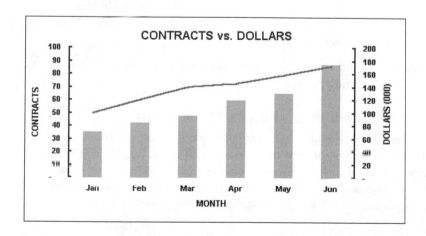

Figure 14.10.
In this example, the line chart will be plotted against the new secondary axis.

Figure 14.11.
Use the Format Data
Series dialog box to
set up the secondary
axis.

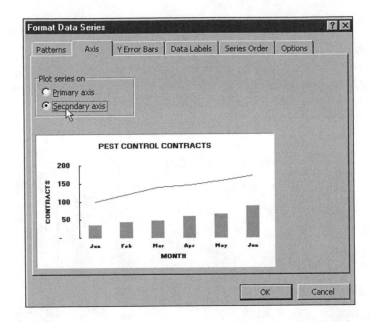

Tip #195 from

Use a secondary axis when you have two types of information with extremely different low
and high values. If plotted on the same axis, the category with the lower values may not be
visible.

VALUE AXIS SCALING

The *scaling* of the axes in a chart can control the chart's visual characteristics, and thereby
the assumptions that the audience makes based on viewing the chart. The X- and Y-axes in
a chart have different scaling options because they represent different things; usually, the
X-axis represents categories of data, and the Y-axis represents the values corresponding to
those categories. You can adjust the scale of the axes by constraining visual highs and lows:
the place where the two axes intersect (called the *origin*), the maximum value displayed, and
the unit iteration between values.

The following sections describe scaling the value axis; see the later section "Category Axis
Scaling" for details on adjusting the X-axis.

CHANGING THE MAXIMUM, MINIMUM, AND TICK MARK VALUES

In Figure 14.12, the sales represented look quite substantial. If you want to make the bars
appear smaller, you can change the scale of the axis to reduce the visual size of the columns.
Increasing the maximum value of the Y-axis makes the columns look shorter; decreasing the
maximum value makes them look taller. If the column value is 100, for example, and you set
the maximum Y-axis value at 100, the column extends to the maximum height of the Y-axis,

making it appear as if that data point is at peak value. Conversely, if you set the maximum value at 1000, the column value of 100 is only one-tenth the height of the Y-axis, minimizing the visual value of the column. In the example in Figure 14.13, the maximum value of the Y-axis is constrained to 100, and the column sizes appear less substantial in size, giving the change from this year to last year less impact than in Figure 14.12, in which the maximum value is 40.

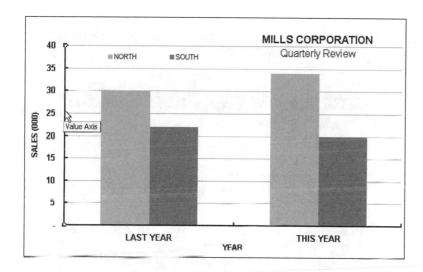

Figure 14.12.
By default, Excel places the origin at zero.

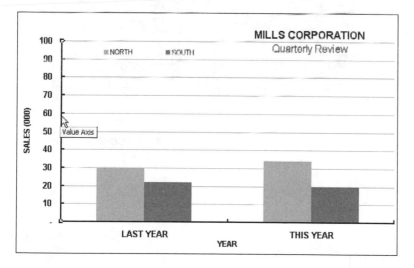

Figure 14.13.
By scaling the axis, you can control the visual size of the columns within the chart.

Caution

Obviously, skewing the visual elements in a chart also can skew the audience's perception of the chart's message. Be sure you understand exactly what information the chart is conveying.

If the maximum value is 10 and for some reason the value changes to 20, Excel automatically adjusts the value axis to accommodate for the increase in value. By changing the Maximum value setting on the Scale tab in the Format Axis dialog box, you can force Excel to use a particular maximum value you prefer (see Figure 14.14). For example, changing the maximum from the default of 40 to 100 for the chart in Figure 14.14 really diminishes the results visually.

Caution

When you set the maximum value, the Y-axis becomes static, showing plotted data series only to the maximum value that you specified.

Figure 14.14.
The Scale tab in the Format Axis dialog box enables you to adjust the Y-axis scaling.

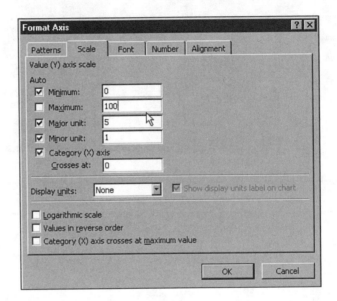

Figure 14.15.
The result of applying a maximum value to the chart is a reduced column visual.

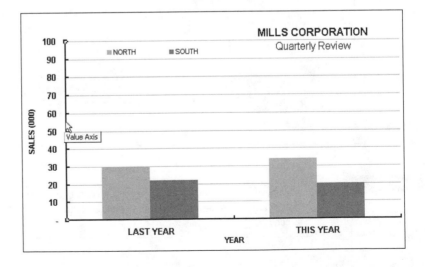

You also can use the settings on the Scale tab in the Format Axis dialog box to adjust the minimum unit to plot, as well as major and minor units that allow for interval adjustments. Suppose the Y-axis plots every 20 units, but you want it to plot every 10 units. Just change the Major Unit setting from 20 to 10. The Minor Unit setting controls the unit interval of the *tick marks (page 342)* on the minor gridlines. To space minor gridlines over three ticks, for example, set the Minor Unit setting to 3. The gridlines will appear at every third tick mark on the value axis.

If you're using the Logarithmic Scale option, the default origin is at 1, and the Minimum, Maximum, Major Unit, and Minor Unit settings are calculated as powers of 10 for the value axis, based on the data range plotted in the chart.

RESIZING THE PLOT AREA

In addition to axis scaling, you can resize the *plot (page 345)* area—changing the height or width—to change the visual message of a chart. Suppose a line chart shows a certain amount of growth over a period of time, and you want the increase to look much steeper or flatter. Narrowing or reducing the height of the plot area may give you exactly the look you want.

In Figure 14.16, for example, the chart on the left shows three different versions of a line chart—all of which represent the same value, plotted against the same Y-axis. The plot size in each case has been changed to give each line a different look. Figure 14.17 reverses this process; by adjusting the height of the plot downward, you can visually lessen the growth line.

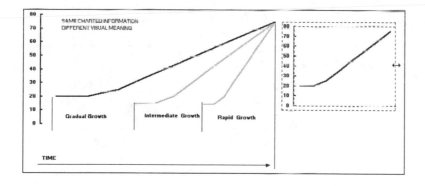

Figure 14.16.
By adjusting the plot area, you can change the visual steepness of a line chart. This can give a false sense of growth, but also help in providing the right look for the audience in a given situation.

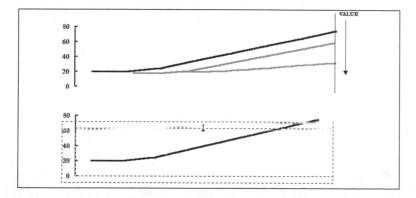

Figure 14.17.
You also can adjust the height to a level that reduces the steepness of the line (which "planes" or levels it out) by adjusting the plot area height.

CHANGING THE ORIGIN

You can change where the category and value axis cross. By default, the value axis intersects the category axis at zero (the origin); however, you can adjust the origin by specifying the value at which you want the category axis to meet the value axis.

Suppose that you're showing scores in a competition for qualifying entrants for the current year and last year. The chart in Figure 14.18 shows a typical column chart setup (sometimes called a *waterfall chart*) that you might use. However, by moving the origin from 0 to 70, as shown in Figure 14.19, you can use the axis to display the breakeven point. In this case, 70 is the minimum qualifying score.

Figure 14.18.
A typical column chart, also called a *waterfall* chart. Notice that the origin is positioned at 0 in this example.

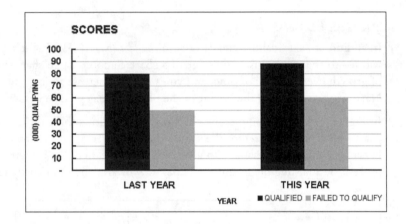

Figure 14.19.
The category axis now takes on two roles: the year and the minimum qualifying score.

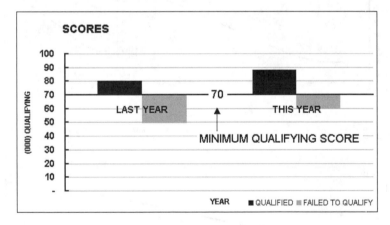

This technique is useful for any kind of pass/fail data. Charts like this are often used to represent value indexes with healthcare coverage plans, or other industries comparing corporate plans and their measured coverage. Even though the index reads positive, by placing the category axis at a certain point along the value axis, any value that reads below the line is viewed as less coverage, poor in rating, and so on.

To change where the category axis meets the value axis, select the Y-axis and change the Crosses At setting on the Scale tab in the Format Axis dialog box.

Note	If you're using the Logarithmic Scale option, the default origin is at 1.

Tip #196 from	For an unusual look, you can set the X-axis to cross the Y-axis at the maximum value rather than the minimum value. Select the option Category (X) Axis Crosses at Maximum Value on the Scale tab in the Format Axis dialog box. Because this chart arrangement is more difficult for the audience to interpret, however, you may need to add more explanatory text.

CATEGORY AXIS SCALING

The category axis scaling options act much like the value axis scaling options described in previous sections. You can adjust the settings to help define the story you're using the chart to tell.

To access the category (X) axis settings, select the axis and choose Format, Selected Axis, or right-click the axis and choose Format Axis from the context menu. Either action opens the Format Axis dialog box. Click the Scale tab to display the scaling options for the X-axis. The following sections describe the options.

REPOSITIONING THE AXES

The Y-axis doesn't have to cross the X-axis at the corner of the plot area; you can reposition the Y-axis along the X-axis between categories. The example in Figure 14.20 shows a standard column chart. You could create more of a division between this year's numbers and last year's by positioning the Y-axis between the two sets of columns, as shown in Figure 14.21. In this example, you set the Y-axis to intersect at the second category of the X-axis.

PART

V

CH

14

Figure 14.20.
Standard positioning
for the axes.

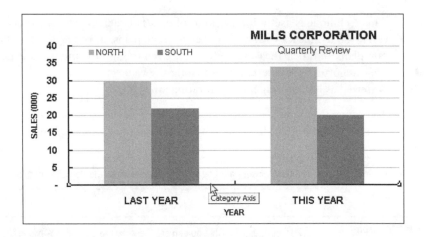

Figure 14.21.
Change the position
where the category
axis and value axis
cross to separate the
years.

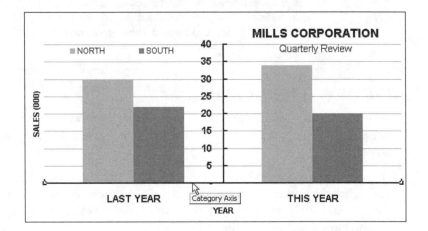

To change the position where the axes cross, change the setting for the option Value (Y) Axis Crosses at Category Number (see Figure 14.22). Two other options also affect the positioning of the Y-axes on the X-axis:

- **Value Y Axis Crosses Between Categories**. This option places the Y-axis at the edge of the category indicated in the box for the option Value (Y) Axis Crosses at Category Number. If this option is selected, data points are plotted between tick marks; if not, points are plotted at the tick-mark positions.

- **Value Y Axis Crosses at Maximum Category**. This option places the Y-axis after the last category on the X-axis.

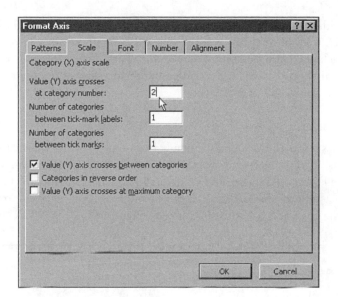

Figure 14.22.
Set the category number to move the value axis along the category axis.

CHANGING TICK MARKS AND LABELS

The option Number of Categories Between Tick-Mark Labels on the Scale tab specifies the frequency with which you want category labels to appear on the X-axis. For example, if a chart showing 40 years of sales figures displays a label for every year, you might decrease the number of labels so that they appear every fourth or fifth year, or just mark the decades.

The option Number of Categories Between Tick Marks specifies the number of categories you want to appear between each pair of tick marks. To place a minor tick mark between every category on the X-axis, set Number of Categories Between Tick Marks to 1.

Tip #197 from

Patrick

If category labels are long, or the chart includes quite a few labels, they can become too crowded on the axis to be easily readable. You can adjust the angle of the category labels by setting the *orientation (page 346)* on the Alignment tab in the Format Axis dialog box.

CHANGING THE SERIES ORDER

By changing the series order, you can manipulate the set of data the viewers' eyes will see first. Why do this? It's really a form of advertising—if you want to get a point across without getting lost in a conversation about all of the other elements, you place the data in the

PART

V

CH

14

most viewable place within a chart, which is the first series. Because people generally look at information from left to right or top to bottom, this will naturally allow you to flow into a discussion about which data set is most important in the chart. There are ways to draw focus using formatting that far outweigh series order, but series order is an important tool to gain control over the chart and the audience.

REVERSING THE CATEGORIES

Reversing the data series is a trick that comes in handy from time to time, particularly with bar charts. For example, if you create a bar chart with quarters, Excel plots the last series of quarters at the top (see Figure 14.23). Because we naturally view information in a top-down manner, you'll probably want to reverse the order in which the series are viewed, so that Q1 appears at the top of the chart and Q4 at the bottom (see Figure 14.24).

Figure 14.23.
The default category axis order clearly needs to be reversed because we view information from the top down.

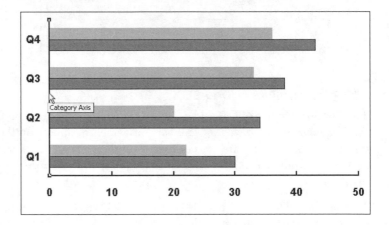

Figure 14.24.
Reversing the categories.

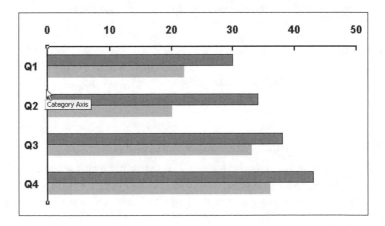

To display categories on the X-axis in the opposite direction, select the axis, open the Format Axis dialog box, click the Scale tab, and select the Categories in Reverse Order option (see Figure 14.25).

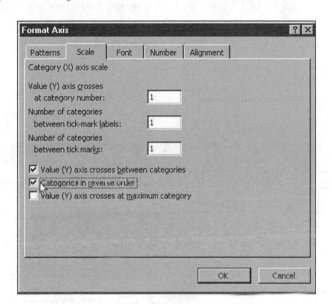

Figure 14.25.
The Format Axis dialog box enables you to reverse the order of the plotted data series.

REVERSING THE VALUES

Sometimes less is better. Using golf scores as an example, you might want a player with a lower score to have a more prominent column on a column chart. In this case, you would want to have zero or negative values at the top of the value axis and the largest number crossing at the category axis. In this reversed approach, the player with the lowest score would also be perceived as having the most prominent column on the chart. Selecting the Values in Reverse Order option on the Scale tab in the Format Axis dialog box for the value axis reverses the direction of values on scatter, column, and bar charts.

ADDING A TRENDLINE TO A DATA SERIES

Adding *trendlines* in Excel helps you understand where you've been and where you're potentially headed. Using *regression analysis*, you can plot trends against a data series and plot out periods of time going forward. You can even specify the number of periods for which you would like to project.

Note

Trendlines can only be added to certain types of charts: area, column, line, bar, and scatter.

To add a trendline to your chart, follow these steps:

1. Select the chart or select the data series to which you want to add the trendline.

2. From the Chart menu, choose Add Trendline to display the Add Trendline dialog box (see Figure 14.26).

3. From the Type tab, select the type of trendline you want to add.

4. Click OK.

Figure 14.27 shows a power trendline added to product B, showing the trend over fiscal quarters.

Figure 14.26.
The Add Trendline dialog box enables you to choose from six types of trends using regression analysis.

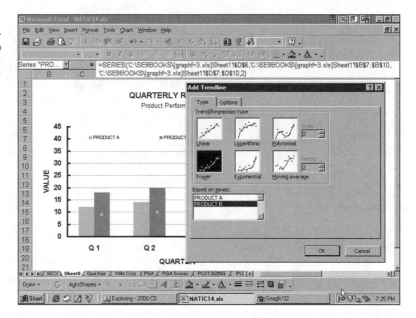

Figure 14.27.
By adding a trendline, you can graphically display the trend of a series of information.

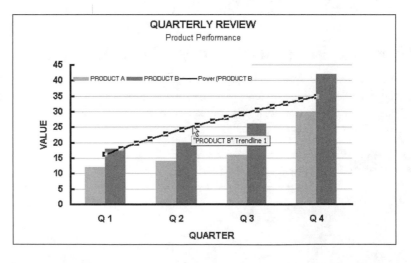

Table 14.2 describes the regression analysis trendline options available in the Add Trendline dialog box. The specific regression analysis equations and their explanations can be found by searching Excel's help for *Equations for calculating trendlines*.

TABLE 14.2.   TRENDLINE SETTINGS

Option	Function
Linear	Inserts a linear trendline.
Logarithmic	Inserts a logarithmic trendline.
Polynomial	Inserts a polynomial or curvilinear trendline.
Power	Inserts a power trendline.
Exponential	Inserts an exponential trendline.
Moving Average	Inserts a moving average trendline. The number of points in a moving average trendline equals the total number of points in the series, minus the number you specify for the period.
Order	By entering a number in the Order box, you specify the highest polynomial order. The value is expressed as an integer between 2 and 6.
Period	By entering a number in the Period box, you specify the number of periods you want to use to calculate the moving average.
Based on Series	Selects the series in which the trendline will be displayed.

Caution

When you start to add elements to a chart, there's a point where you must begin subtracting elements to eliminate the clutter. Be cautious when adding trendlines; avoid making your chart more difficult to interpret.

FORMATTING THE TRENDLINE

As with many other chart elements, quite often you'll want to format the trendline to fit within the visual aspects of the chart you're creating. Excel offers many options to create the look and feel you need for the trendline to fit into the picture. By selecting or activating the trendline, you can format the trendline as you would any other element of the chart (see Figure 14.28).

To format a trendline, follow these steps:

1. Select or activate the trendline.

2. From the Format menu, choose Selected Trendline to open the Format Trendline dialog box.

Tip #198 from

You can also double-click the trendline to access the Format Trendline dialog box.

Figure 14.28.
This trendline has a custom format.

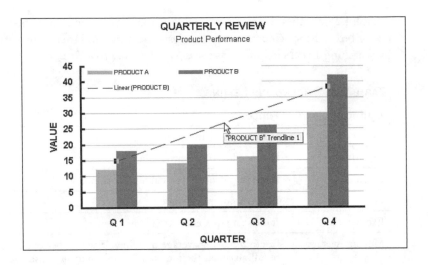

3. From the Patterns tab in the Format Trendline dialog box, select formatting options to create the desired visual effect (see Figure 14.29).

4. Click OK.

Figure 14.29.
On the Patterns tab, select the format style to apply to the trendline.

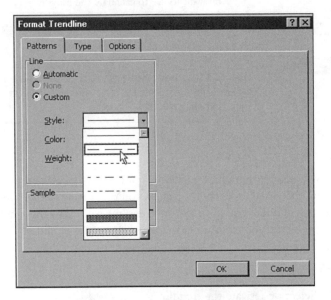

Tip #199 from

Patrick

Trendlines should be formatted differently from other plotted data series to make the trendline stand out. It's also good practice to format trendlines as dotted. The dotted lines suggest that the data is forecasted or trend data; solid lines are viewed as real or actual data.

The following list describes some of the formatting options available for trendlines:

→ For details on using line formats in Excel charts, **see** "Formatting Lines: Axes, Tick Marks, High/Low Lines, and Error Bars," **p. 410**

- **Automatic.** Applies the default Excel settings to the selected line or object.
- **Custom.** Enables you to customize the style, color, and weight of the selected trendline.
- **Style**. Specifies a style for the selected line or border.
- **Color**. Designates a color for the selected line or border.
- **Weight.** Indicates the weight (thickness) of the selected line or border.

As you make selections, watch the Sample box to see how the line or border will look with the options selected.

TRENDLINE OPTIONS

The settings on the Options tab in the Format Trendline dialog box enable you to further customize a trendline (see Figure 14.30).

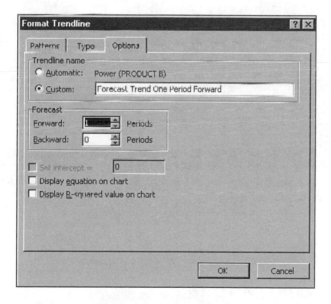

Figure 14.30.
The Options tab in the Format Trendline dialog box enables you to further customize the trendline with names and forecasting modes, as well as display the equations used.

The options are described in the following list:

- **Trendline Name.** Specify whether you want Excel to provide a name for the trendline, based on the trend chosen (<u>A</u>utomatic), or select the <u>C</u>ustom option and type your own name.

- **Forecast**. Use the options in this section to specify the number of periods to chart, going forward or backward. For example, based on the current or historical information from the charted series, Excel can plot out the trend of future periods (see Figure 14.31).

- **Set Intercept = ___**. By setting the *intercept*, you specify where you want the trendline to meet the Y-axis.

- **Display Equation on Chart** and **Display R-Squared Value on Chart**. Use these options to post regression equations or R-squared values on the chart. If you have several scenarios of trendlines, for example, you may want to show the values for each trendline.

Figure 14.31.
The trendline forecast out one period.

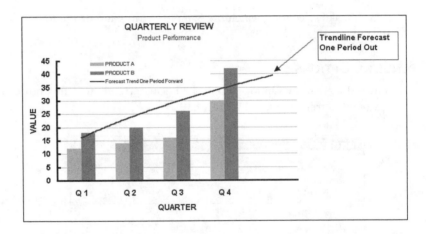

By default, trendlines are not the same color as the data series they're plotted against. Whenever possible, try to format the trendline to the color or shade of the series that the trendline represents. Doing this helps the audience to understand instantly which series the trendline is tied to, without additional explanation.

Tip #200 from

TROUBLESHOOTING

CHANGING THE MAXIMUM VALUE FOR THE VALUE AXIS

How can I make data appear smaller on the chart?

Select the value axis, choose F̲ormat, S̲elected Axis, select the Scale tab, and replace the Ma̲ximum value with a higher number.

CHANGING THE CHART TYPE OF A DATA SERIES

How do I change the chart type of just one of the data series in a chart?

Select the data series you want to change, choose Chart T̲ype from the C̲hart menu, select the desired chart type, and click OK. Note that some chart types can't be combined, but Excel will warn you if you choose a chart type that won't work with the existing chart.

CHARTING DRAMATICALLY DIFFERENT VALUES ON THE SAME CHART

I have two data series on my chart with extremely different values. How do I compensate for this?

Use a secondary axis to plot one of the series. Select the data series to plot on the secondary axis. Then choose F̲ormat, S̲elected Data Series, click the Axis tab, and choose S̲econdary Axis.

EXCEL IN PRACTICE

When data series on a chart have extremely different values, as shown in Figure 14.32, but they still must be viewed on the same chart, use the secondary axis feature as shown in Figure 14.33. Select the data series to plot on the secondary axis and choose Se̲lected Data Series from the Fo̲rmat menu. Click the Axis tab and choose S̲econdary Axis.

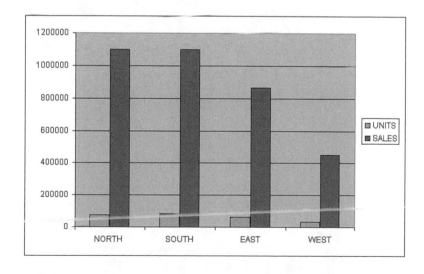

Figure 14.32.
The numbers for units and sales are widely divergent, making the chart look awkward and difficult to read.

PART

V

CH

14

Figure 14.33.
Plotting series on two different axes enables you to compare related series with different value sets.

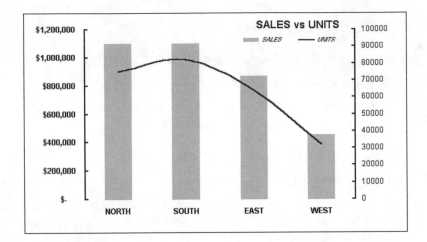

CHAPTER 15

FORMATTING CHARTS

In this chapter

by Patrick D. Blattner
Patrick@BlattnerBooks.com

AN OVERVIEW OF FORMATTING CHARTS

Formatting charts is as important as the data behind the chart. What you display says a lot about your skills and your ability to translate information to others. All too often, people clutter charts and the message gets lost in all the data. Because Excel offers such a wide variety of options, people want to use them all in graphic presentations. Actually, the less you try to cram onto the chart, the more easily understood your chart will be.

It's important to understand the characteristics and functions of the chart elements, as well as how to minimize or maximize their visual presence on a chart. You can format each chart element; understanding this, you can fade in and fade out elements. *Fading in* means darkening and *fading out* means lightening the element. An *element* is anything that can be selected on the chart with your mouse. Fading just adds or reduces emphasis on a chart element, and because all chart elements can be selected individually, you can create or take away emphasis on any element.

> **Note**
>
> Formatting options differ for different types of charts. For example, you can't format the axes of a pie chart, because it doesn't have any.

> **Tip #201 from**
>
> *Patrick*
>
> Use a standard format across all your charts. This will keep the focus on the information and away from trying to understand the new format with every chart presented. If the presentation is onscreen, the use of colors can be effective, but for most people, black and white is the standard form in which charts are presented.

FORMATTING LINES: AXES, TICK MARKS, HIGH/LOW LINES, AND ERROR BARS

Excel allows you to format just about any line element of a chart. The axes, for example, can be boldfaced and/or displayed with dots or dashes, colors, patterns, or different line weights. The same formatting options apply to high/low lines, tick marks, and error bars. Tick marks on the value or category axis can be removed from the axes altogether, placed inside the axes, crossed over the axes, or moved to the outside.

For radar charts, doughnuts, pies, and other nonrectangular charts, formatting options are available that don't apply to rectangular charts, such as *column charts (page 363)* or *bar charts (page 365)*. See the later section "Formatting Data Series" for details.

FORMATTING THE Y-AXIS, SECONDARY Y-AXIS, AND Z-AXIS

Formatting value axes in different ways can either draw attention to or away from the axes. Why would you want to change the format of the value axis? The default formats Excel chooses are fine; however, when presenting information, you might want to adjust the default formats for a more effective and clean presentation.

Tip #202 from

Format primary and secondary Y-axes to look at least somewhat alike, although the value, major units, and minor units may be extremely different.

Figure 15.1 shows the most common ways to format the value axis.

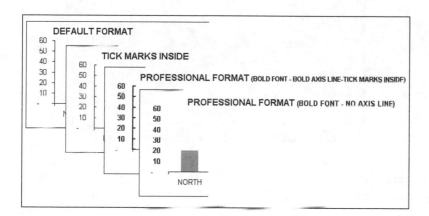

Figure 15.1.
These options are among the most common ways to format the value axis.

→ In most cases, you'll create a standard axis format that you'll use time and time again. Rather than reformatting repeatedly, you can save the chart as a custom type. For details, **see** "Creating a Personalized Custom Chart," **p. 375**

Tip #203 from

The default setting automatically places *tick marks* outside the axis. The tick marks generally reference the numeric or text value on the axis, so the general direction of the tick mark points to the number or text. However, considering the information you're referencing is usually on the inside of the plot area, you'll probably want to change the direction of the tick marks in most cases.

To format the Y-axis in the "professional" format shown in Figure 15.1, follow these steps:

1. Select the Y-axis so that the selection handles are showing.
2. From the Format menu, choose Selected Axis to display the Format Axis dialog box.
3. Select the Patterns tab.
4. Select the heavy weighted line, as shown in Figure 15.2.
5. Under Major Tick Mark Type, choose Inside.
6. Select the Font tab in the Format Axis dialog box.

Figure 15.2.
The Patterns tab in the Format Axis dialog box enables you to format the Y-axis line type and style, as well as customize the tick marks.

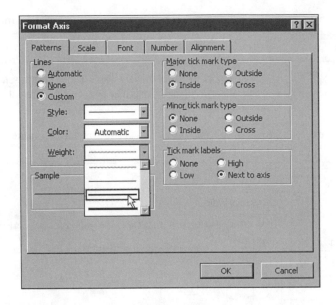

7. Under Font, choose Arial, as shown in Figure 15.3. (If Arial is your default font for Excel, this step can be skipped.)

Figure 15.3.
The Font tab in the Format Axis dialog box enables you to change the font type, style, and size.

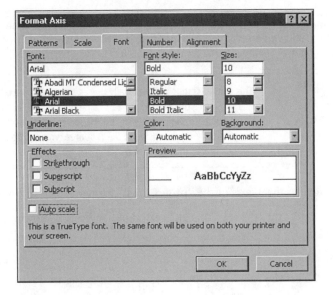

8. Under Font Style, select Bold.

9. Under Size, choose 10. (The size should be dependent on the size of the chart.)

10. Deselect Auto Scale.

11. Click OK.

PART

V

CH

15

Tip #204 from

Patrick

> The reason for deselecting the Auto Scale option is that you'll be changing the chart size on many occasions. If Auto Scale is selected, all the fonts on that axis will change proportionally when you size the chart. This generally is a time-saving issue only.

FORMATTING THE X-AXIS

Similar to formatting the value axis, formatting the category (X) axis can draw attention to or away from the axis. The number of categories ultimately dictates how you format the axis. For example, if you have several dates along the category axis, consider formatting the alignment vertically, so that Excel will wrap the text or change the number of labels displayed (see Figure 15.4). To make this type of change, use the *Orientation (page 346)* settings on the Alignment tab in the Format Axis dialog box (see Figure 15.5). By aligning the information correctly and formatting the text size, you can usually keep all labels visible on the chart.

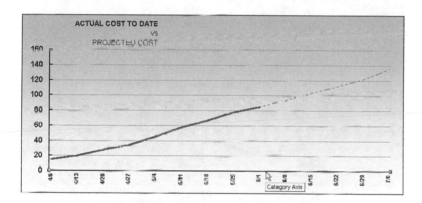

Figure 15.4.
This label orientation was changed to allow for a vertical view of the dates along the category axis.

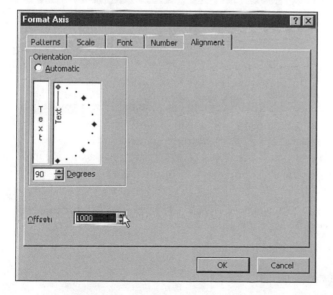

Figure 15.5.
You can change the orientation to vertical and offset the dates from the line or axis with the Offset option.

The <u>O</u>ffset option on the Alignment tab enables you to change the *offset*, which means how far the category labels are positioned from the line or axis. Usually Excel places labels next to the axis. By changing the offset, you can move the labels away from the axis, thus providing more room between the axis line and the labels. Figure 15.6 shows newly aligned axis labels; Figure 15.7 shows one way you can use the additional space between offset labels and the axis.

Figure 15.6.
The offset here has been set to its maximum value of 1000, moving the dates far away from the axis.

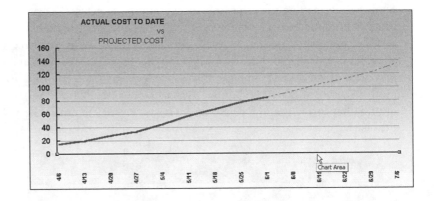

Figure 15.7.
The <u>O</u>ffset setting can give you additional room to apply elements to the chart between the axis and the labels.

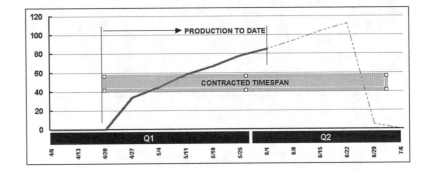

In addition to the alignment and offset, you can format the labels and axis in multiple ways. Figure 15.8 shows some of the most popular ways to format the axis.

The default setting automatically places tick marks outside the axis. If you only have a few categories on the X-axis, it's good practice to get rid of the tick marks altogether. Figure 15.8 shows only four categories, so you don't need guidelines to tell you where the categories separate—it's quite obvious. To remove the X-axis, tick marks, or tick mark labels from view, choose None for the appropriate option in the Format Axis dialog box (see Figure 15.9).

 If you want to remove the axis, but keep the axis labels, see "Eliminating the Axis While Keeping Axis Labels" in the Troubleshooting section at the end of this chapter.

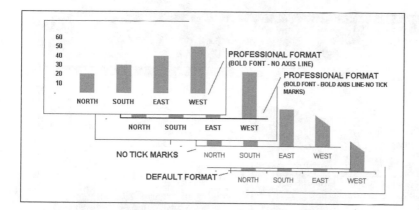

Figure 15.8.
Some common formatting options for the X-axis.

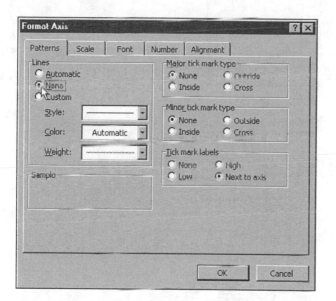

Figure 15.9.
The Patterns tab in the Format Axis dialog box enables you to choose multiple formatting combinations.

Looking at the final result of the X-axis in Figure 15.10, you can see how formatting the axis can provide a clean visual. The difference between the default chart format and the formatted axis is a much cleaner and more professional-looking chart.

FORMATTING AXIS LABELS

Besides changing the font style of the labels on an axis, you also can change the labels' number style and alignment. In addition, Excel enables you to display the units on the axis with different measurement units (see Figure 15.11).

Figure 15.10.
A comparison of the default chart and a chart with a formatted axis.

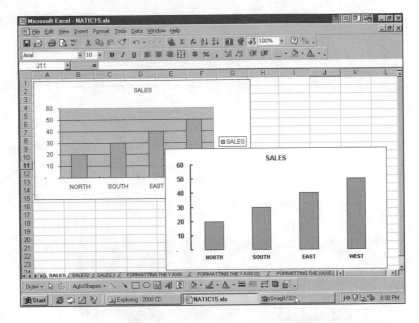

Figure 15.11.
Excel enables you to display units in the measurement amounts shown in the drop-down list.

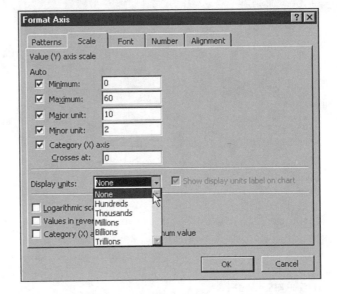

Figure 15.12 shows a comparison of some formatting options of the Y-axis labels. Because there are so many variations, these are just a few of the option combinations available. To create the combination of settings that you want, select the axis and then use the options in the Format Axis dialog box, on the Format menu, and on the Chart and Formatting toolbars.

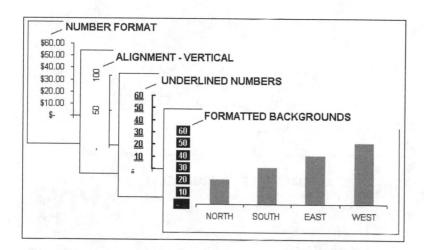

Figure 15.12.
A comparison of value formats on the Y-axis. Excel allows for multiple combinations.

Figure 15.13 shows some additional comparisons in formatting of the X-axis labels. Try to keep the labels as clean as possible, because the labels act as the reference point for the viewer. You'll notice that some of these label formats are combined with the X-axis line formats shown earlier (refer to Figure 15.8). When you start combining the formatting techniques shown, you become more effective in presenting the information.

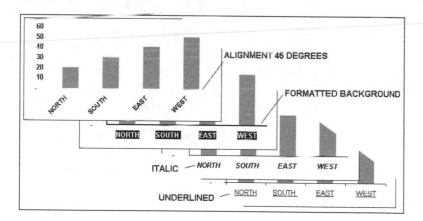

Figure 15.13.
A comparison of category formats on the X-axis. These are just a few of the formatting options available in Excel.

ADDING HIGH/LOW LINES

High/low lines generally are used for 2D stock charts that extend from the highest value to the lowest value in each category. High/low lines can help the chart reader distinguish the highs and lows of a data series. Figure 15.14 shows high/low lines as a guide from the lowest score to the highest score extending to the category axis. You can use high/low lines even if you're not creating a stock chart. (All options can cross over into other categories.)

Try to think out of the box when being creative with charts.) To add high/low lines, follow these steps:

1. Select the data series.
2. From the Format menu, choose Selected Data Series.
3. Select the Options tab in the Format Data Series dialog box.
4. Check the High-Low Lines check box.

Figure 15.14.
You can use high/low lines in other ways besides stock charts. Here, they serve as a guide to the category axis.

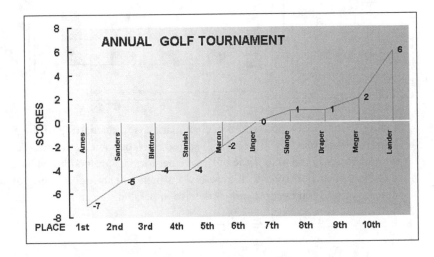

 Want to format a single data point? See "Formatting a Single Data Point" in the Troubleshooting section at the end of this chapter.

ADDING ERROR BARS

The Y Error Bars tab in the Format Data Series dialog box enables you to show error amounts that you set, or you can use the standard error of the plotted values as the error amount for each data point. You most often see error bars associated with sample polls, where there's a possibility of error plus or minus. For example, a poll might indicate the number of people who drink milk on a daily basis, with a possibility of error plus or minus 3% from the results shown.

This option is not available for 3D charts (except for bubble charts), or for any pie, doughnut, or surface charts.

X-axis error bars also are available with scatter charts and bubble charts, where you have values that are horizontal as well as vertical.

To access the Format Data Series dialog box, select the data series and choose Format, Selected Data Series (see Figure 15.15). Figure 15.16 shows error bars added to a typical sales chart. As Figure 15.17 shows, you can format the error bars, just like any other line in a chart. In this example, the error bars are simply boldfaced with the Bold button.

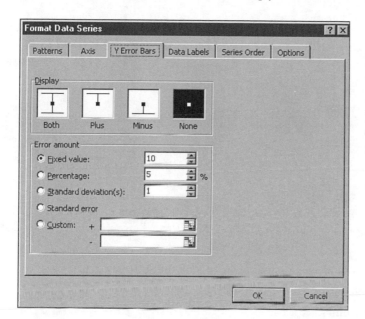

Figure 15.15.
Y error bars enable you to show plus or minus errors or deviations from the plotted data point.

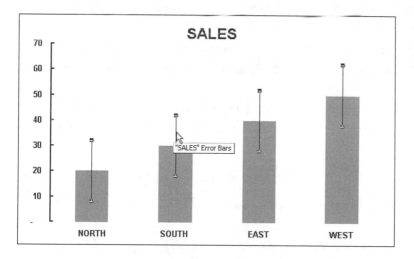

Figure 15.16.
Error bars can help the audience to see by what amount the results may be incorrect.

Figure 15.17.
Formatted error bars.
To format the error
bars, simply select the
error bars and select
Selected Error Bars
from the Format
menu.

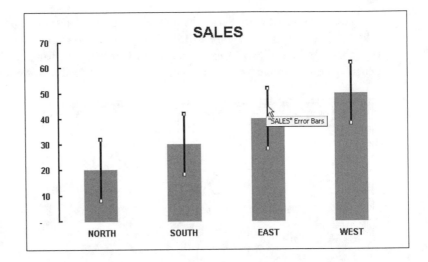

As with any element on the chart, by selecting the error bars, you can format them. The following list describes the options available on the Y Error Bars tab in the Format Data Series dialog box:

- **Both**. Displays both plus and minus error bars on the selected data series.
- **Plus**. Displays plus error bars.
- **Minus**. Displays minus error bars.
- **None**. Removes error bars from the selected data series.
- **Fixed Value**. Uses the value you input as the error amount.
- **Percentage**. Uses the percentage of each data point as the error amount.
- **Standard Deviation(s)**. Uses a fixed number of deviations from the mean of plotted values for the error amount.
- **Standard Error**. Uses the error of the values as the error amount for each data point.
- **Custom**. By typing a value in the plus (+) or minus (–) box or both, you set the error amount for each data point.

FORMATTING TEXT: DATA LABELS, TITLES, LEGENDS, AND TEXT BOXES

As mentioned earlier, all chart elements that can be selected also can be formatted. You can change the font, style, and color of the text as you would any other text in Excel. Simply select the text, title, legend, text box, and so on, and use the appropriate command on the Format menu, Formatting or Chart toolbar, etc.

For details on the techniques for formatting worksheets, see Chapter 6, "Formatting Worksheets."

The following sections provide some details on additional options for formatting the text in a chart.

ADDING AND FORMATTING DATA LABELS

Excel enables you to add information to a chart even after the chart is created. (I seldom get it right the first time.) You can add data labels to a series of data, or you can add data to a single data point.

Tip #205 from 	In many cases, you'll want to point out a certain figure or data point in your chart. In this case, you can add a data label or value to a single data point. To do this, select only the data point.

To add data labels to a chart, follow these steps:

1. Select the data series.

2. Choose Selected Data Series from the Format menu, or right-click the series and choose Format Data Series.

3. In the Format Data Series dialog box, click the Data Labels tab (see Figure 15.18).

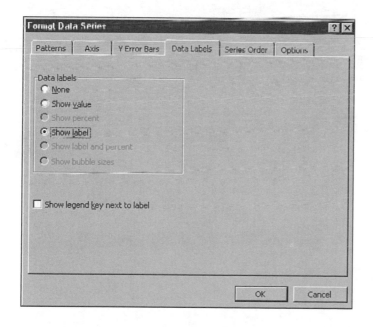

Figure 15.18.
To add labels or values to the desired data series, simply check the appropriate option under Data Labels.

4. Under Data Labels, select Show Label.

5. Click OK.

Tip #206 from

> To add data labels to all data series at once, select Chart Options from the Chart menu to open the Chart Options dialog box. Click the Data Labels tab, select Show Label, and click OK.

After creating data labels, you may want to change the location and appearance of the labels to match the rest of the chart. You can format the data labels by selecting the data label as you would a data value. After the data label is selected, choose Selected Data Labels from the Format menu (or right-click the label and choose Format Data Labels); the Format Data Labels dialog box appears.

 If you want to add space between category labels and the axis line, see "Offsetting the Categories" in the Troubleshooting section at the end of this chapter.

As with other text options, you can use the settings on the Alignment tab to change the alignment and orientation of the labels; you also can adjust the label position in relation to the data series (see Figure 15.19). As shown in Figure 15.20, you can use the Font settings to apply particular font styles, change the color and background, and add effects. In this example, the labels will be formatted with a transparent (invisible) background and a white font, and then placed against dark columns in the data series (see Figure 15.21). Aligning the labels within the data series can give you more room on the chart to call out other points of interest.

Figure 15.19.
Excel enables you to align the data labels in several ways. Here, the label position is set to the inside end of the column and the orientation is at 90 degrees.

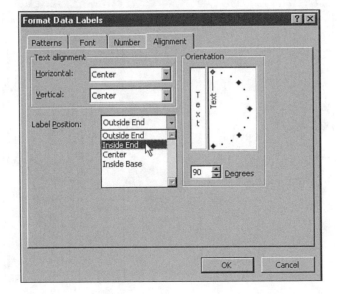

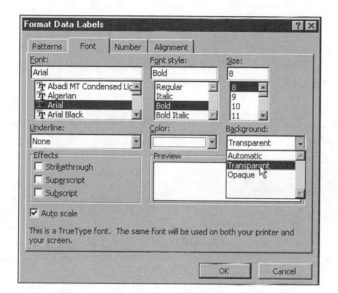

Figure 15.20.
When a label is placed in a dark filled column, create a white font and a transparent background to highlight the label.

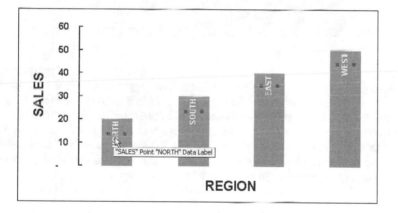

Figure 15.21.
By placing the data labels inside the columns, you can create more landscape on the chart.

Note

In most cases, you should stay away from getting too creative with your data labels. Remember, simple, clear, and concise is usually the best practice.

 If you want to remove the data label backgrounds, see "Eliminating Data Label Backgrounds" in the Troubleshooting section at the end of this chapter.

Moving or formatting a single data label is just as simple; after selecting the whole set of data labels, click the individual label you want to adjust. Then move the label as desired, or use the Format menu to make changes to that specific label.

ADDING AND FORMATTING CHART TITLES

Chart titles consist of the title of the chart, the title of the Y- or Z-axis, and the title of the X-axis. You can enter into a chart and add titles and elements using the Chart Options command on the Chart menu (see Figure 15.22).

Figure 15.22.
You can add chart titles from the Titles tab in the Chart Options dialog box.

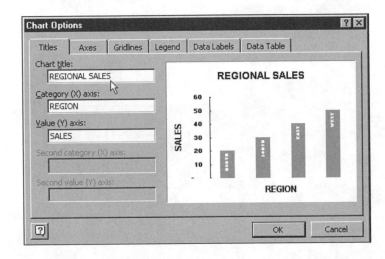

Tip #207 from

A very fast method to add a "title" is to select the chart, type the title text, and then press Enter. A text box will show up on the chart. You can select it and change the font style and size, and then place it in the desired location. Note that the text box doesn't contain the real title of the chart—for example, it doesn't show up in the Chart Options dialog box. This is just a quick way of creating text boxes in charts. This method also won't automatically resize the chart to accommodate the text. See the later section "Inserting and Formatting Text on a Chart" for details on working with text boxes.

When you have all the chart titles on the chart that you want, you'll probably want to change the size, font, style, or some other feature of the titles to fit your chart's appearance. Just select the title element and then choose Selected Chart Title from the Format menu, or right-click the title and choose Format Chart Title. The Format Chart Title dialog box opens, as shown in Figure 15.23. Select the font settings, effects, and alignment you want, and click OK.

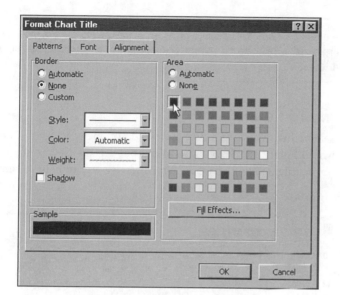

Figure 15.23.
Formatting the chart title. This example will show a black background and white text.

Figure 15.24.
Applying formats to the chart title can make it stand out from the other chart elements.

FORMATTING THE LEGEND

In most cases, you'll notice a legend takes up too much space in the chart. To move the legend, just select it and drag it to any location on the chart. Resizing is just as simple; click the legend and drag one of the handles toward the center of the legend.

INSERTING AND FORMATTING TEXT ON A CHART

Adding text to a chart is something you'll probably want to do on many occasions, not only for visual appeal (as shown in Figure 15.25), but also to call out certain aspects of your presentation. With proper formatting, adding text can be an effective way to help communicate your point.

Figure 15.25.
By adding text to a chart, you can call out certain aspects of the chart or just add a creative touch.

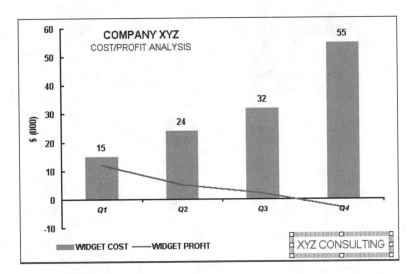

To add text to a chart, follow these steps:

1. Select the chart so the selection handles are showing.

2. Type in the Formula Bar the text you want to display.

3. Press Enter.

You format the text as you would any other chart element. Select the text box, and from the Format menu, choose Selected Object. The Format Text Box dialog box will appear with the font-formatting options available.

ENHANCING CHARTS WITH DRAWING OBJECTS

Adding drawing objects (generally called *shapes*) to a chart enables you to provide additional visual interest and clarify data within the chart. Figure 15.26 shows how you can effectively use some of the drawing tools in a chart. In this example, I've added the season across the charted time and applied the fiscal quarter names between the X-axis and its labels. For more information, see Chapter 16, "Professional Charting Techniques" and Chapter 24, "Professional Formatting Techniques."

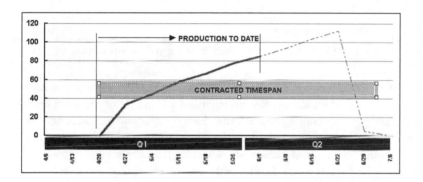

Figure 15.26.
You can add shapes to give several dimensions to your charts, including timelines and time spans that further tell the story of the chart.

Drawing objects are found on the Drawing toolbar, shown as shapes and AutoShapes. Table 15.1 describes some uses for the drawing tools available (see Figure 15.27).

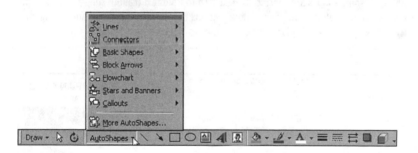

Figure 15.27.
AutoShapes enable you to further enhance charts, tables, and spreadsheets.

TABLE 15.1.   SHAPES ON THE DRAWING TOOLBAR

Shape	Use
Lines	Used to point at or create specific cutoff points on a chart.
Connectors	Generally used for connecting shapes within flowcharts and can be used in Excel charts.
Basic Shapes	You can apply basic shapes (triangles, circles, squares, and so on) for creating visuals.

continues

TABLE 15.1. CONTINUED

Shape	Use
Block Arrows	Used to point at relevant information in a presentation, or to indicate a rise or decline in numbers by connecting one data point to another.
Flow Chart	Can be added to graphic charts to further explain information plotted on the chart.
Stars and Banners	Used to create visual impact with a burst.
Callouts	Used to express ideas or call out points of interest. Points to specific information on the chart with a text message.
Boxes and Ovals	Used for creating legends, keys, and titles.
Lines and Arrows	Points to different elements on a chart in order to draw attention.

Applying shapes to a chart enables you to call out elements of the chart to create direct focus, or apply shapes to tell additional stories directly on the chart. After the chart is created, you can begin adding your drawing tools to the chart by selecting the chart and then selecting the drawing object you want to place on the chart. You can format the drawing objects as you would other elements of a chart—by selecting the element and choosing the desired option(s) from the Format menu. In Figure 15.28, for example, the organizational chart was created with text boxes and connectors. Figure 15.29 shows the individual drawing objects, selected to make them more visible.

Tip #210 from

Although some shapes are specifically designed to hold text (callout shapes, for example), you can convert almost any shape into a text box by selecting the shape and typing, or right-clicking the shape and choosing Add Text from the context menu.

Figure 15.28.
Understanding how to use shapes with charts can establish visual impact, as well as tell the story behind the picture.

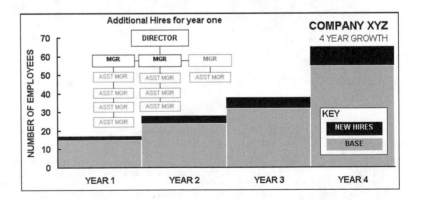

For details on working with the drawing objects, see Chapter 8, "Enhancing Your Worksheet with Excel's Drawing Tools." Chapter 16, "Professional Charting Techniques," also provides some helpful suggestions on ways to use shapes in charts.

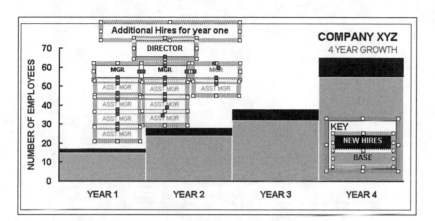

Figure 15.29.
The highlighted shapes placed on the chart were boxes with text typed in the boxes.

FORMATTING DATA SERIES

Probably one of the most important aspects of formatting a chart is the formatting of the data series. You either call attention to or away from a series by how it's formatted. In addition to using the chart options provided specifically for formatting data series, you can add colors, fill effects, patterns, and even pictures, as described in the later section "Changing the Border, Color, or Fill of a Chart Item."

By changing the overlap and gap-width settings for the data series in Figure 15.30, a "stacked column" step chart was created. For this chart, set the Overlap setting on the Options tab in the Format Data Series dialog box to 100 and the Gap Width setting to 0. What is the gap width and overlap? The *gap width* is the gap or space between the categories (for example, the sets of columns on a column chart). The *overlap* is the amount of overlap of the individual data series (the individual columns in a column chart, for example). You can lay the columns of one data series slightly over the next column data series by changing the gap width.

Note

If data series are stacked—for example, in a stacked column chart—there is technically only one column per category, so you would adjust gap width rather than overlap in this case. For charts with multiple series plotted separately, increasing the gap just changes the space between each category's group of columns.

Figure 15.30.
The Overlap and Gap Width settings can be a powerful tool for creating step charts.

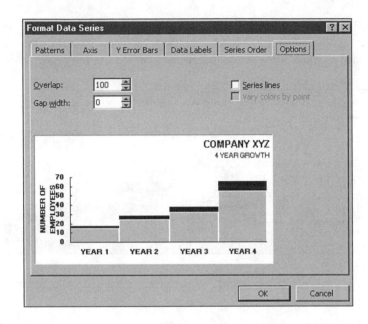

CHANGING THE SERIES ORDER

You can change the series order in the Format Data Series dialog box. Click the Series Order tab and specify how you want the series to move by clicking the appropriate button. In nonstacked charts, you can move data series left and right, forward or backward; stacked charts move series up and down. The preview in the dialog box shows the result you'll get. This feature is particularly useful with area charts, where a smaller set of data might be hidden when a larger set of data is positioned in front of it.

PLOTTING DATA ON THE SECONDARY AXIS

Use a *secondary axis (page 391)* when comparing two sets of information that have totally different measurements, such as units sold for the year versus the revenue generated by those sales. If plotted on the same Y-axis, the chart could effectively diminish one set of values visually. For example, suppose that units sold for the year is 300, with revenue totaling $4 million. In this case, you might plot the dollars on the secondary axis. To add a secondary axis, use the Axis tab in the Format Data Series dialog box.

EXPLODING PIE SLICES

Quite often, you'll see pie charts that have *exploded (page 367)* slices of the pie to make them more noticeable. For example, your pie chart shows the quarterly sales for the year, but each pie slice consists of seven products that make up that quarter's sales. By exploding the pie slice, you can display the values of the sales by product that create the total for the quarter.

To explode a slice, click the individual slice to display the selection handles; then drag it away from the center of the pie.

CHANGING THE DATA SERIES ANGLE IN PIE OR DOUGHNUT CHARTS

Sometimes you may want to rotate a pie or doughnut chart to place particular data series at specific positions in the chart. You can rotate the chart with the Angle of First Slice option on the Options tab in the Format Data Series or Format Data Point dialog box. Specify the setting for Degrees, watching the preview, until the chart is positioned as you want it.

FORMATTING A DATA POINT

Formatting an individual data point can be a great benefit in creating a focus. For example, if you have cost-to-date information in the form of a line chart as well as your projected future costs all in the same data series, you'll want to split the formatting of the line (see Figure 15.31). Notice the cost to date appears in bold, and the projected cost is a dotted line. When you receive the cost for the next week, you'll change the format from projected to actual by selecting the single data point and adjusting the format.

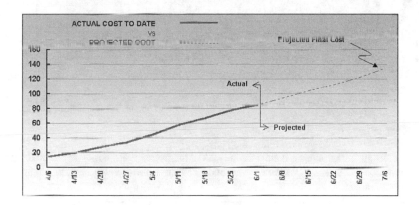

Figure 15.31.
By knowing how to format a single data series, you can create two stories on the same series.

To adjust the format of a single data point, perform the following steps:

1. Select the data series.
2. Select the data point.
3. Choose Selected Data Point from the Format menu.
4. Adjust the format as you would a series.
5. Click OK.

CHANGING THE BORDER, COLOR, OR FILL OF A CHART ITEM

You can format the backgrounds of the chart's data series, individual data points, plot area, chart area, and so on, by adding, altering, or removing borders and changing the color or fill effect used for the item. For example, a standard practice in formatting the background of the chart area is to create a black background with a white plot area. All the titles are converted to white with transparent backgrounds, as shown in Figure 15.32. You'll notice this standard approach to formatting in many publications and magazines.

Figure 15.32.
You can format the plot area in any shade available in Excel. This example uses a sharp contrast to the black chart area color.

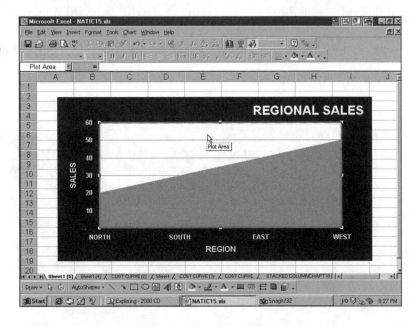

> **Caution**
>
> Formatting backgrounds can enhance the look of the overall chart; however, be careful not to overdo it. It's easy to get carried away and lose focus on what you actually want the picture to show.

> **Tip #211 from**
>
> *Patrick*
>
> One good practice for data series is to remove the standard borders on the series—unless the chart is a line chart, in which case this isn't an option.

To change the border or background of any chart item, select the item and use the F̲ormat menu to access the Format dialog box for that particular item. The options on the Patterns tab provide choices for borders, color, fill effects, and so on, as shown in Figure 15.33.

If you want to create a chart without the chart borders, see "Eliminating Borders and Backgrounds" in the Troubleshooting section at the end of this chapter.

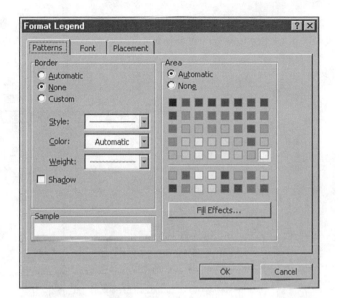

Figure 15.33.
The Patterns tab pro-
vides plenty of options
for selecting just the
right border, color,
pattern, and so on.

FILL EFFECTS

Fill effects (page 207) enable you to use shading, gradients, patterns, and pictures within a
data series, plot area, drawing object, and so on. Fill-effect options enable you to get creative with every element on the chart. Figure 15.34 shows just a few of the different fill
options you can use.

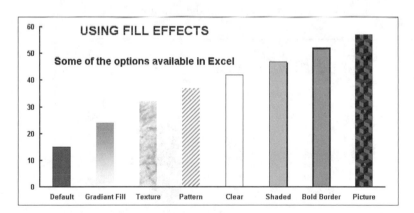

Figure 15.34.
Shown are some of
the different fill effects
you can use to give a
custom look to your
charts.

The fill in the Picture column is actually a picture, stacked and scaled, as shown in Figure 15.35. The following section describes how to use this feature.

Figure 15.35.
Using a picture as a fill effect.

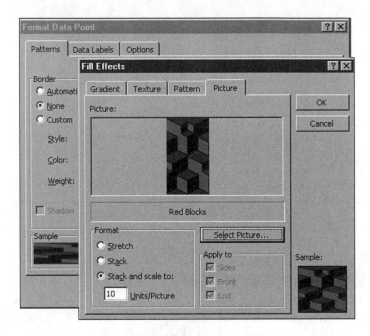

Now, notice the different fill on one column in Figure 15.36. This strong format draws the audience's eyes to the specific chart element you want them to notice.

Figure 15.36.
By applying a different format to one element, you call the attention of the audience to that element.

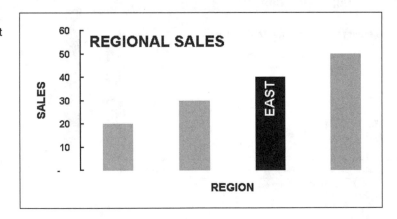

Caution

Be careful with fill effects! If you apply fills to too many elements of a chart, you can create confusion with all the colors and shades. One handy strategy is to apply fills only to every other series, with the remaining series using a solid background color.

To add a fill effect, click the Fill Effects button in the Area section of the Patterns tab. You can choose from four different types of fill effects: gradients, textures, patterns, or pictures.

→ To learn more about fill effects, **see** "Applying Solid Colors and Fill Effects," **p. 207**

> **Note**
>
> Gradient shades can be utilized to draw attention to or from a specified piece of data on the chart. As the gradient shade gets lighter, that's generally where the attention is drawn.

USING PICTURES AS BACKGROUNDS

The Picture tab in the Fill Effects dialog box enables you to apply a picture as a background (see Figure 15.37). You can use pictures in any of the standard picture formats: PCX, WMF, JPEG, GIF, and so on. Click the Select Picture button on the Picture tab, select the desired picture, and then adjust it as necessary, using the following options (see Figure 15.38). Note that some of the options may be disabled for certain picture formats.

- **Stretch**. Applies the picture and stretches it throughout the selected chart item.
- **Stack**. Stacks copies of the picture vertically and horizontally to fill the chart item.
- **Stack and Scale to**. Enables you to stack and scale the picture and adjust it to the size or units you select in the Units/Picture box.
- **Sides**. Used for 3D charts, this option applies the picture to the sides of the data series.
- **Front**. Used for 3D charts, this option applies the picture to the front of the data series.
- **End**. Used for 3D charts, this option applies the picture to the top end of the data series.

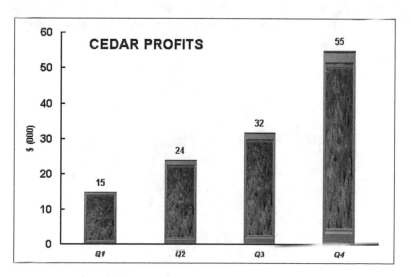

Figure 15.37.
The chart shows the selected picture stretched in the columns.

Figure 15.38.
The Picture tab enables you to insert a picture and scale or stack the picture based on the settings you determine.

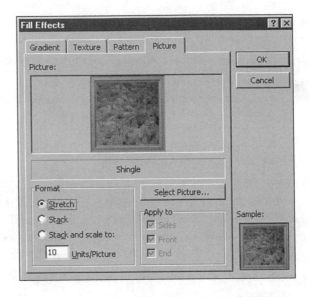

 Does a chart seem to take forever redrawing when you change the underlying data? See "Reducing the Number of Units in a Picture" in the Troubleshooting section at the end of this chapter.

FORMATTING 3D CHARTS

Formatting 3D charts offers a few different options from 2D charts. On a 3D column chart, for example, you can format the front, side, and top of the column because Excel allows you to fill flat surfaces. Figure 15.39 shows the default format of a clustered column with a 3D effect. We'll use this as the starting point and walk through some of the important elements in formatting a 3D chart in the following sections. (For more information, see Chapter 16.)

Figure 15.39.
A 3D clustered column chart in default format.

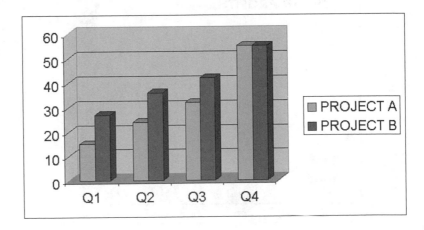

FORMATTING THE WALLS OF A 3D CHART

The walls of a 3D chart can be formatted in several ways, from erasing the walls completely, to applying fill effects. As usual with fill effects, you can apply gradients, textures, patterns, and pictures. As with all cautions on overdoing it, keep it simple and clean on these options. To format the walls of a 3D chart, follow these steps:

1. Select the walls of the 3D chart so the selection handles are showing at each corner of the wall.

2. Right-click and choose Format Walls, or choose Selected Walls from the Format menu.

3. The Patterns tab in the Format Walls dialog box enables you to apply fills to the area as well as outline the walls with border styles. To erase the walls, choose None under Area.

4. To get rid of the remaining gridlines, right-click the gridlines and choose Clear from the context menu, or select the gridlines and press Del.

You'll notice only the floor and axis are left. Many times, you'll find 3D charts work well as standalone charts, and you can get rid of a lot of the fluff that makes up the standard default chart.

FORMATTING THE FLOOR OF A 3D CHART

You format the floor of a 3D chart in a manner similar to that for formatting the other elements of the chart: Right-click and choose Format Floor, or select it and choose Selected Floor from the Format menu. The Format Floor dialog box appears, and the standard options on the Patterns tab become available.

Tip #212 from	In most cases, the floor of a chart isn't an area of focus, so sometimes it's helpful to eliminate the floor.

Fill effects work well on 3D chart floors because you can use a gradient fill to create a light-to-dark effect—for example, placing light colors closer to the audience and gradually darkening to very dark colors at the back.

FORMATTING THE DATA SERIES OF A 3D CHART

More options are available when formatting a data series in a 3D chart. For example, you can apply different column shapes to a column chart and adjust the depth to which the series reaches back into the chart. To use these 3D formatting features, follow these steps:

1. Select a data series on the 3D chart.

2. Choose Selected Data Series from the Format menu.

3. In the Format Data Series dialog box, select the Shapes tab (see Figure 15.40).

4. Select the desired column shape.

Figure 15.40.
The shapes available enable you to format the data series in the picture shape you select.

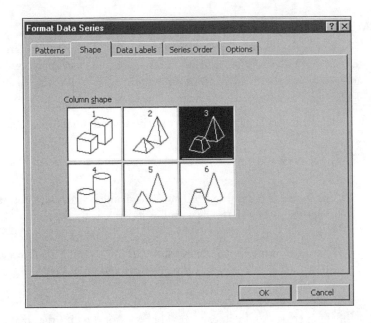

For a dramatic change in a column chart, choose a cone shape for one of the data series. Then, on the Options tab in the same dialog box, set the Gap Depth at 0, the Gap Width at 270, and the Chart Depth at 600, as shown in Figure 15.41.

Figure 15.41.
You can set the width and depth to create a dramatic effect for a 3D chart.

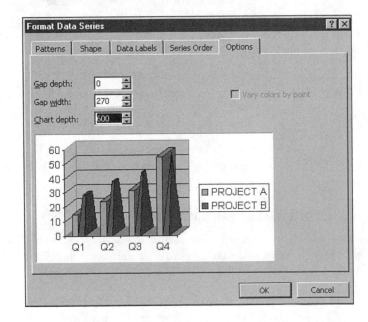

FORMATTING THE 3D VIEW

Now that you have the fundamentals of formatting the different elements of a chart, you can take the chart and create a view from any angle. By selecting the walls of a 3D chart, you can right-click to access the 3D view, or choose 3-D View from the Chart menu to access the 3-D View dialog box (see Figure 15.42).

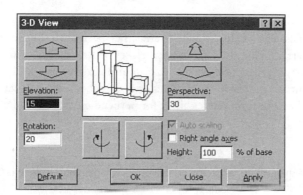

Figure 15.42.
The 3-D View options enable you to adjust the angle of the 3D chart as needed.

Options in this dialog box vary, of course, depending on the type of chart and the items in it, but the following list describes the major options:

- **Elevation**. Enables you to view the chart from a top-down manner, looking at the chart from above.

- **Rotation**. Changes the view in degrees, spinning the chart around the Z-axis.

> **Note**
>
> The arrows for elevation and rotation change the view from top down and right and left views of the 3D chart. Simply click on the appropriate arrow and see the chart angle in the preview window change.

- **Auto Scaling**. Available only when the Right Angle Axes box is checked, this option creates a right-angle proportion. Often, when charts are created in 3D, depending on how you're elevating and rotating the chart, the chart size is reduced.

- **Height % of Base**. Controls the Z-axis height relative to the length of the X-axis.

- **Right Angle Axes**. Independent of the chart rotation, this option sets right angles as opposed to seeing the chart in perspective view. Making sure the Right Angle Axes box is checked usually creates a more uniform look to your chart, because the lines are only displayed in a vertical manner.

- **Default**. Use this button when your adjustments to the chart view have left it a hope loss mess. Excel restores the default settings.

Tip #213 from

You also can adjust the plot view of a 3D chart with the mouse. Click the floor or wall of the chart to display the *sizing handles (page 382)*. Click on one of the corner handles at the corner of the floor (the ScreenTip displays Corners) and drag. You may need to click twice (not double-click) before you can drag successfully. The plot is replaced with a wire-frame image that you can drag to adjust the angle.

- **Perspective.** This option is available only when the chart includes two or more sets of data that compare values across categories and series. Perspective view changes the horizontal view of the chart, making the chart appear closer or farther away. You can specify a particular Perspective setting, or use the arrow buttons above the option to make incremental adjustments. If the Right Angle Axes option is checked, perspective view becomes unavailable, because right angles allow for perpendicular lines and right angles only.

Caution

Charts in perspective view often take on a cluttered, unprofessional look, so use care when using angles other than right angles for 3D charts.

TROUBLESHOOTING

ELIMINATING THE AXIS WHILE KEEPING AXIS LABELS

Excel won't let me eliminate the axis line and keep the axis labels.

Select the axis and choose Format, Selected Axis to open the Format Axis dialog box. Click the Patterns tab, and choose None in the Lines section.

ELIMINATING BORDERS AND BACKGROUNDS

Why can't I chart information without the chart borders?

Select the chart and choose Format, Selected Chart Area. In the Format Chart Area dialog box, click the Patterns tab and choose None in the Border section. You also can choose None in the Area section to eliminate the area.

FORMATTING A SINGLE DATA POINT

Why does Excel make me format all of my data series at once?

You can format just one data point by selecting the data series and then clicking on the individual data point until handles are displayed around the single point. Then format this data point as you would format a series, using the Format options.

OFFSETTING THE CATEGORIES

I need to add space between category labels and the axis line.

The Offset feature enables you to move data labels away from the axis line. Select the axis and choose Selected Axis from the Format menu to open the Format Axis dialog box. Then adjust the Offset setting on the Alignment tab.

ELIMINATING DATA LABEL BACKGROUNDS

The colored background on my chart conflicts with Excel's data label colors.

Select the axis with the labels and choose Selected Axis from the Format menu. Select the Font tab in the Format Axis dialog box and choose Transparent under Background.

REDUCING THE NUMBER OF UNITS IN A PICTURE

Excel seems to take an eternity to redraw a chart that uses fill effects.

If you're using a picture with stacked units as a fill effect, and the number of units is fairly large, Excel may require additional memory and time to redraw the chart if you change the underlying data. You might be able to get away with a reduced number of repetitions, without changing the fill effect noticeably. Select the data point or series and open the Format Data Point or Format Data Series dialog box. Click the Fill Effects button, click the Picture tab, reduce the number in the Units/Picture box, and click OK.

EXCEL IN PRACTICE

By adding a few key titles and callouts to the standard chart in Figure 15.43, the chart can begin to speak for itself. Combining shapes, fill effects, and text boxes can create charts that not only look professional, but also tell a story without discussion, as shown in Figure 15.44.

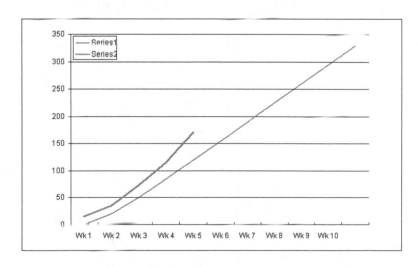

Figure 15.43.
This chart can get the point across.

Figure 15.44.
This chart provides more information in the same space, while simultaneously creating a positive impression on the audience.

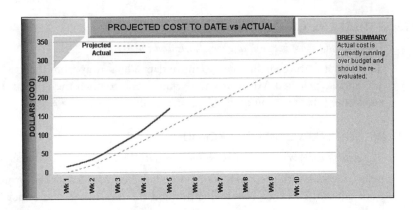

CHAPTER 16

PROFESSIONAL CHARTING TECHNIQUES

by Patrick D. Blattner
Patrick@BlattnerBooks.com

In this chapter

FORMATTING CHARTS FOR A PROFESSIONAL LOOK

What are "professional" chart techniques? And who's to dictate what "professional" is? In my experience, professional techniques separate those who achieve and create impact from those who don't. To be able to say a thousand words with a single chart or a series of charts can be of extreme importance. There's a certain standard in the business world, as you may have noticed, but no one ever says what that standard is. Well, in this chapter, you'll learn some of those basic "professional" elements that can help you achieve greater impact with your charts. In addition, you'll learn some new ways to combine charts with their source worksheets.

This chapter reviews several distinctly different chart types. Learning ways to mix and match information will help you become more creative in utilizing the charting capabilities in Excel. I discuss such techniques as erasing borders and backgrounds, which is one of the key elements in being able to combine and manipulate information on worksheets with charts. Another way to combine tools in Excel is to use form controls. The best way I've found to use form controls with charts is when you have to continually extract cost-to-date information or production-to-date information. This technique is also described.

The key is understanding the tools in Excel—not only how to combine them, but combine them effectively. Because Excel offers more tools with each new edition, the learning curve never stops.

KEY ELEMENTS IN PROFESSIONAL FORMATTING

In Figure 16.1, some of the key elements in professional techniques are pointed out. Table 16.1 describes professional standard formats that will help you create more effective charts in the future. The cleaner, the better, in most cases.

Figure 16.1.
Standard professional formats can create clean, effective presentations without clutter.

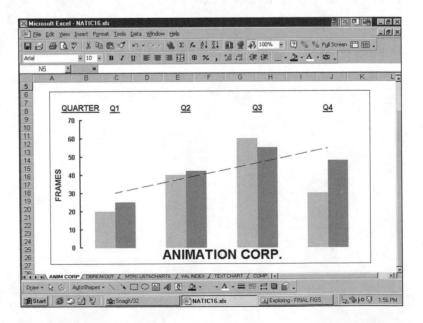

TABLE 16.1.   SUGGESTED FORMATS FOR STANDARD CHART ELEMENTS

Chart Element	Suggested Format
Chart title size	Standard chart title, 16 points
Chart title style	Bold
Y-axis title size	Standard Y-axis title, 12 points
Y-axis title style	Bold
Y-axis tick marks	Inside
Y-axis line style	Bold
X-axis title size	Standard X-axis title, 12 points
X-axis title style	Bold
X-axis tick marks	None
X-axis line style	Bold
Data series border	None
Data series (no emphasis)	Light fill
Data series (emphasis)	Dark fill
Trendlines	Same fill as the data series on which the trendline is based
Trendline style	Thin dotted
Legend border	None
Legend font style	Bold
Legend font size	Standard legend, 8 points
Legend placement	Bottom of chart

Tip #214 from

After you have a group of chart types that are formatted with the proper font sizes, axis thickness, and data series formats, save them as custom chart types to save future time and effort in reformatting.

Whenever possible, it's good practice to differentiate the data series with light and dark shades and create a spectrum of emphasis from light (least emphasis) to dark (most emphasis). The audience's attention is drawn toward bold and dark.

Tip #215 from

Excel offers so many options with callouts and drawing objects that it's easy to add elements and forget the focus. Objects such as bursts and stars can have appeal at times, but use restraint with fancy objects in charts. Don't use different font styles—keeping things constant creates a clean effect. Use consistent axis formatting; if you've created a bold Y-axis, also create a bold X-axis. A constant line size is a good practice.

ADDING PICTURES AND SHAPES TO CHARTS

You can enhance your charts with pictures, *AutoShapes* and *WordArt (page 451)*. Figure 16.2 shows a column chart that could be improved by adding a picture to the background of the chart. To insert a picture, choose Insert, Picture, From File to display the Insert Picture dialog box, in which you can browse and select the desired picture (see Figure 16.3).

Figure 16.2.
From the Insert menu, Excel enables you to insert shapes, pictures, and WordArt.

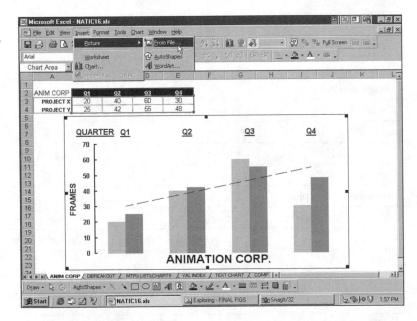

Figure 16.3.
Select the stored picture you want to embed in the chart, and then click Insert.

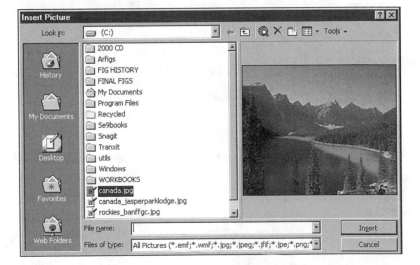

Tip #216 from

For increased flexibility, insert a picture into the worksheet, outside the chart. Outside inserts give you access to clip art and scanner images, which can still appear "in" a chart if you drag them onto the chart.

Note

Even with the chart selected, clip art can be inserted by using the ClipArt button on the Drawing toolbar.

After you select the picture and click Insert in the Insert Picture dialog box, the image appears with the Picture toolbar. This allows you to manipulate the picture's brightness, shading, and so on (see Figure 16.4).

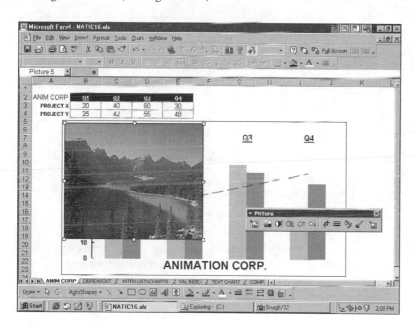

Figure 16.4.
By selecting the chart, you can insert a picture onto a chart and adjust the chart's characteristics with the Picture toolbar.

Table 16.2 describes the buttons on the Picture toolbar.

TABLE 16.2.   BUTTONS ON THE PICTURE TOOLBAR

Button	Name	Description
	Insert Picture from File	Displays the Insert Picture dialog box
	Image Control	Enables the image to be displayed as grayscale, black and white, or watermark

continues

TABLE 16.2.   CONTINUED

Button	Name	Description
	More Contrast	Increases the distinction between light and dark areas of the picture, sharpening the image
	Less Contrast	Decreases the distinction between light and dark areas of the picture, reducing the sharpness of the image
	More Brightness	Lightens the image
	Less Brightness	Darkens the image
	Crop	Hides the edges of the selected picture (but doesn't remove them)
	Line Style	Changes the style of the lines or borders to make them heavier, lighter, and so on
	Format Object	Displays the Format Picture dialog box
	Set Transparent Color	Sets a pixel color within an inserted picture to transparent
	Reset Picture	Resets the picture to its original state

COMBINING CHARTS, PICTURES, AND DRAWING OBJECTS

Because Excel enables you to manipulate the backgrounds and styles of charts and their elements, you can combine charts with graphics, shapes, and worksheet elements. If you're in marketing or you plan to display your company's information in a presentation, for example, an image in the background of the chart can give it a certain look or feel. Figure 16.5 shows a chart/picture overlay. The chart in this figure doesn't have borders or backgrounds, and the line elements, numbers, and text have been formatted white with transparent backgrounds.

Tip #217 from

If you insert a picture into a chart and then drag the picture and size it to the chart, it covers the plot area that contains the data. Insert a picture onto a worksheet, and then size the chart and picture to the same size. Drag the chart over the picture and bring it to the front (right-click and select Bring to Front). Last, select the chart and remove the borders and backgrounds to make the chart transparent so that the picture shows through.

A faster (but less flexible) method is to select the chart area and access the Fill Effects feature. There you can insert a picture and have it appear as a background image without changing any other part of the chart. The drawback is that you can't format the inserted picture.

Figure 16.5.
Rather than inserting a picture into a chart, lay a chart on a picture and size the chart to the size of the picture. Select the chart and choose none for borders and backgrounds to make the chart transparent.

PART

V

CH

16

Chart has no background.

The Star Yacht Sales chart includes several drawing objects used to attain this professional look. Rectangles placed on the data point of Q3 allow for calling out previous years' performance without upsetting the original chart. Tricks like this create a nontraditional look. By using drawing objects over the column of Q3, it's easy to place emphasis in certain areas of the chart. Figure 16.6 shows all the drawing objects selected so that you can see the number of shapes involved in making this chart.

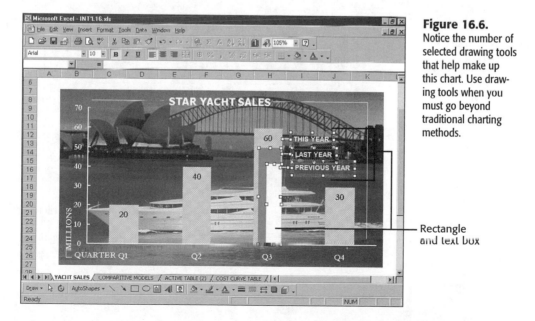

Figure 16.6.
Notice the number of selected drawing tools that help make up this chart. Use drawing tools when you must go beyond traditional charting methods.

Rectangle and text box

Drawing lines reversed to white create a border around the plot area, as well as an elbow connecting the X- and Y-axis titles. Inserting text to differentiate the Q3 performance difference in years calls the attention to Q3 as the high point.

To lay a chart over a picture, perform the following steps:

1. Paste a picture on a worksheet.
2. Place the chart over the picture.
3. Size the chart so that the chart completely covers the picture.
4. Choose Selected Chart Area from the Format menu.
5. Select the Patterns tab in the Format Chart Area dialog box.
6. Choose None in the Border area.
7. Choose None in the Area section of the dialog box.
8. Click OK.

   The chart appears with the picture in the background.

To format the text on the axis, follow these steps:

1. Select the axis.
2. Choose Selected Axis from the Format menu.
3. Choose the Font tab in the Format Axis dialog box.
4. Choose White from the Color drop-down list box.
5. Select Transparent from the Background drop-down list box (see Figure 16.7).
6. Click OK.

Figure 16.7.
To erase the background of fonts on the axis, select Transparent for the background.

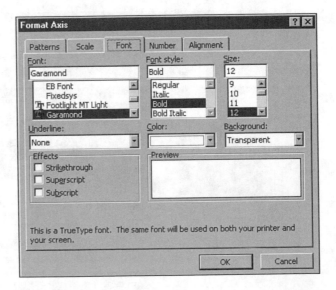

When using several layers of objects, charts, and text, you'll need to become familiar with such tools as the Bring to Front and Send to Back buttons. By selecting an object and choosing Bring to Front, the object is placed on top of all the objects layered. You can add toolbar buttons for the Bring to Front and Send to Back commands (see the following Tip), or you can select these commands from the context menu. For charts, right-click the chart and select Bring to Front or Send to Back. For drawing objects, right-click the object, select Order, and then select Bring to Front or Send to Back. If you have multiple layers of objects, you can use the Bring Forward or Send Backward command on the Order submenu to move the selected object forward or backward one layer at a time.

Tip #218 from

Patrick

If you use the Bring to Front and Send to Back buttons often, add them to your Drawing toolbar. Right-click on the toolbar and select Customize to open the Customize dialog box. In the Categories list on the Commands tab, choose Drawing, and then scroll the Commands list to find the Bring to Front and Send to Back commands and drag them to the toolbar. Close the Customize dialog box when you're finished.

Another method is to open the Draw menu on the Drawing toolbar, select the Order option, and "tear off" the Order submenu as a floating toolbar with the Order buttons. You can use this toolbar as needed, or drag the buttons from the Order toolbar (hold down the Ctrl and Alt keys while dragging) to the desired position on any other toolbar.

ADDING A DRAFT STAMP OR WATERMARK WITH WORDART

You can create draft stamps or *watermarks* that you can place on charts or worksheets with WordArt. This is more of an aesthetic and formatting trick; however, it can add a nice touch for presentations. Figure 16.8 shows an example of a chart with a DRAFT stamp created with WordArt.

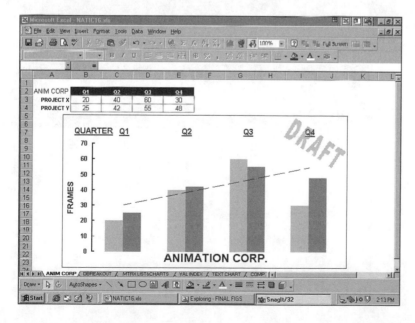

Figure 16.8.
A draft stamp can be used as an "onscreen stamp," as opposed to stamping a chart or document after printing.

Tip #219 from

With Excel's formatting capabilities, you can group objects with lines, creating stamps that show lines for signatures.

To create a transparent stamp, perform the following steps:

1. Click the WordArt button on the Drawing toolbar. Select the desired style for the text, as shown in Figure 16.9, and then click OK.

2. Type **DRAFT** in the Edit WordArt Text dialog box, as shown in Figure 16.10. Add boldface and/or italic, if desired, by clicking the Bold and/or Italic button.

Figure 16.9.
To create a transparent stamp, begin by selecting the WordArt style in the WordArt Gallery.

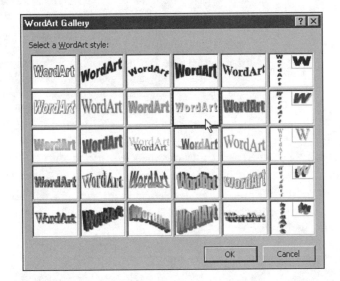

Figure 16.10.
Type the draft text in the Edit WordArt Text dialog box. You can capitalize it or use a combination of cases.

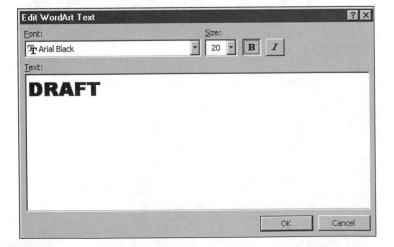

3. Click OK to close the dialog box and display the WordArt object in the chart.

4. On the Drawing toolbar, click the Shadow button and choose No Shadow (see Figure 16.11).

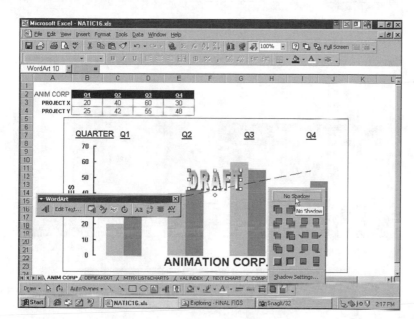

Figure 16.11.
To eliminate the shadow on WordArt, select the Shadow button on the Drawing toolbar and choose No Shadow.

5. With the WordArt image still selected, choose WordArt from the Format menu.

6. In the Format WordArt dialog box, select the Colors and Lines tab.

7. Under Fill, choose Gray-25%.

8. Check Semitransparent.

9. Click OK.

10. Rotate the text as desired by clicking the Free Rotate button on the WordArt toolbar and then dragging the green rotate handles on the WordArt (see Figure 16.12).

ADDING CHARTS TO SHAPES

Not only can you place charts over pictures, but you can also place charts over drawing objects as shown in Figure 16.13. By creating a shape such as the 3D box shown, you can place a chart over the top of the box. Choose None for borders and areas as discussed in the previous example of Star Yacht Sales.

The arrows shown in this example are drawn from AutoShapes on the Drawing toolbar. The up arrow emphasizes the corrugate sales increase, and the down arrow emphasizes the chipboard decrease over the previous period. The arrow objects provide additional information that otherwise wouldn't be included in the chart.

Figure 16.12.
Rotate the text with the Free Rotate command from the WordArt toolbar.

Drag a rotate handle to change the position of the WordArt image.

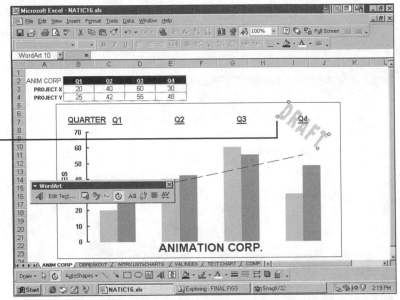

Figure 16.13.
By using fill effects, you can even create a gradient from the center of the pie to the edges.

Drawing tools

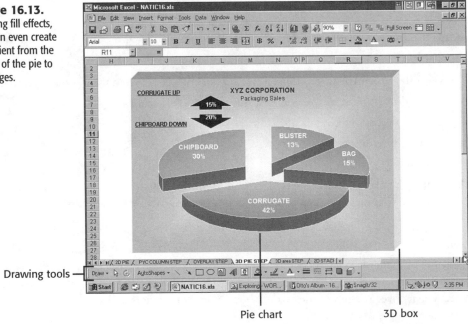

Pie chart   3D box

CREATING COLUMN DEPTH

After creating a default 3D column chart, you can either leave the chart in default format, or you can take advantage of Excel's depth options. By understanding the value of 3D elevation and rotation in Excel's 3D charts, you'll be able to add the right perspective to a chart and create emphasis on certain areas.

Caution

Unless you have specific reasons to plot a chart in a 3D format, I suggest staying with 2D charts. A 3D chart may be more aesthetically pleasing, but remember that the audience should be able to determine what the chart says in seconds. If possible, use 2D charts.

By adding depth to a 3D column chart, you can dramatically change the shapes of the original columns, as shown in Figure 16.14. Applying gradient fills, drawing objects, and WordArt can further enhance the look of the chart.

3D box

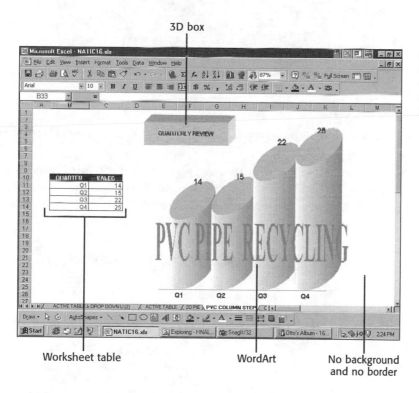

Worksheet table   WordArt   No background
and no border

Figure 16.14.
Utilizing Excel's depth capabilities with 3D charts can give charts more appeal.

The following paragraphs highlight the important steps in creating a chart with depth and perspective similar to the chart shown in Figure 16.14. First, create a simple table like that in the figure. Then create an embedded 3D column chart from the table, using the Cylinder chart type instead of the standard 3D column to give the data series the oval shape.

To add the perspective and depth, follow these steps:

1. Right-click on the plot area of the chart.

2. Select 3-D View from the context menu to display the 3-D View dialog box.

3. Set the Elevation to 6 and the Rotation to 4. Be sure the Right Angle Axes option is checked (see Figure 16.15).

4. Click OK.

Figure 16.15.
Setting the elevation, rotation, and right angles of the 3D column chart.

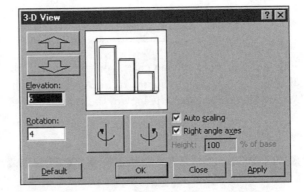

5. Select the data series.

6. From the Format menu, choose Selected Data Series to open the Format Data Series dialog box. Click the Options tab.

7. Set the Gap Depth at 0, Gap Width at 10, and Chart Depth at 960 (see Figure 16.16). These settings change the width of the columns, the depth to which the columns reach "back" into the chart, and the distance between the columns.

8. Click OK.

Figure 16.16.
The Options tab in the Format Data Series dialog box enables you to change the width and depth of the data series.

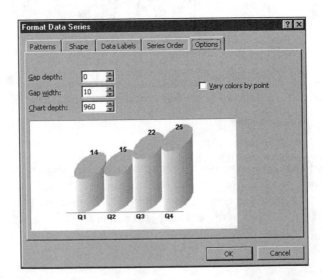

To add a 3D object as shown in the chart title (refer to Figure 16.14), select a drawing shape, draw the shape you want, and then select the 3-D button from the Drawing toolbar. Then apply the 3D perspective and depth you want.

To add the text, select the object and type the text you want. Excel automatically creates a text box that allows for text to be typed on the face of the 3D object.

 To add the WordArt, click the WordArt button on the Drawing toolbar and type the desired text. Place the WordArt over the chart. Right-click and select Bring to Front.

EXPLOITING THE SECONDARY AXIS, OVERLAP, AND GAP WIDTH

Occasionally, you may need to measure two sets of data in a chart. By understanding how to create an overlay, you can compare data more effectively. A simple column chart with overlays (such as the one in Figure 16.17) can compare this year versus last year, but what if you need to show the status on multiple projects for your weekly production meetings? This same approach in the form of a bar chart instead of the column chart could be used to show projected completion versus actual completion by this point in time (see Figure 16.18). The key elements in creating charts like this are to select one of the data series and give it a secondary axis. Then set the gap width and overlap, and set one of the data series fills to None.

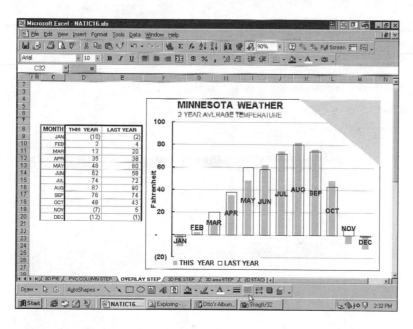

Figure 16.17.
By using the secondary axis and changing the overlap and gap width, you can create overlays.

Excel enables you to align the data series one over another. By eliminating the background of one of the data series, you can create this "thermometer" effect. To create a column chart with a thermometer effect as shown in Figure 16.17, follow these steps:

1. Start with a clustered *column chart*.
2. Select one of the data series.

Figure 16.18.
Using the same overlay approach, you can show projected versus actual on the same line.

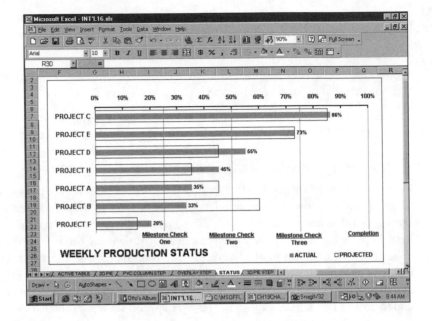

3. From the Format menu, choose Selected Data Series to open the Format Data Series dialog box.

4. Select the Patterns tab.

5. Under Area, choose None.

6. Select the Axis tab (see Figure 16.19).

7. Choose Secondary Axis.

Figure 16.19.
Create separation of the data series by plotting one of the series on a secondary axis.

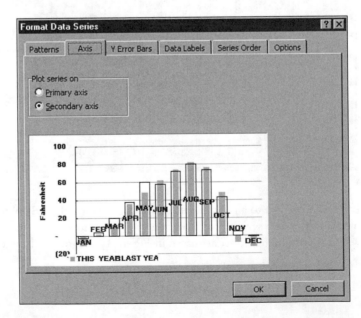

8. Select the Options tab (see Figure 16.20).

9. Set the Overlap to 0.

10. Set the Gap Width to 50.

11. Click OK.

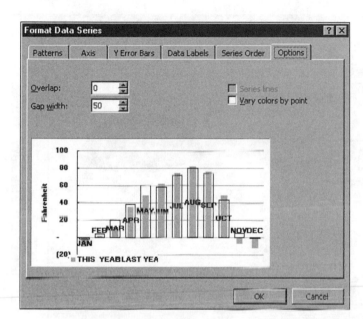

Figure 16.20.
Setting the overlap and gap width.

Tip #220 from

To add the gray corner shown in Figure 16.17, select AutoShapes from the Drawing toolbar, and then select Basic Shapes. Select a triangle and draw it on your chart to the desired size. While the triangle is still selected, *flip* and position it to match the corner of the chart. Choose Draw from the Drawing toolbar, then Rotate or Flip, and last Flip Horizontal or Flip Vertical as needed to position the triangle to match the corner. Place the triangle in the corner and fill with a desired fill.

PIE CHART TECHNIQUES

When creating pie charts, you'll want to bring focus to a certain category. You can focus the audience's attention on a certain pie slice in several ways. One is by formatting the slice to stand out. Another is by changing the angle of the first slice. The following sections describe these techniques.

→ To make a particular slice of the pie chart really noticeable, you can explode the slice. For details, **see** "Exploding Pie Slices," **p. 430**

SPINNING THE PIE CHART

Notice that Q4 in Figure 16.21 is angled to the top. This wasn't the default version of the chart. You can angle the first pie slice to make a particular slice appear on the top, side, and so on.

Figure 16.21.
You can "spin" a chart by changing the angle of the first slice.

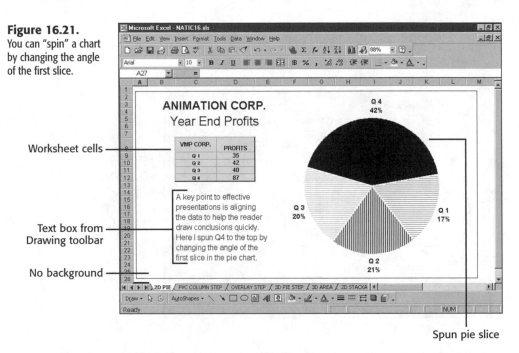

Worksheet cells

Text box from Drawing toolbar

No background

Spun pie slice

To change the angle of the first slice, follow these steps:

1. Select the data series that you want to adjust in the first slice of the pie.
2. From the Format menu, choose Selected Data Series to open the Format Data Series dialog box.
3. Choose the Options tab.
4. Using the spinner, select the desired angle.
5. Click OK.

To create a table on a chart as shown in Figure 16.21, select the chart and choose None under Area in the Format Chart Area dialog box. Drag the chart over a table and then deselect the chart. The table shows through the transparent chart area. You'll have to move and format the different elements of the chart to get the exact appearance you're looking for. It also helps to have the data behind the percentages on the pie.

ORGANIZING PIE CHARTS TO TELL A STORY

The organization of charts is extremely critical when it comes to helping the audience understand the point. Figures 16.22 and 16.23 show two versions of a pie chart showing expenses for a physician. In both cases, sorting the underlying data in ascending order gives the chart structure. In the second version, custom formats and titles are key elements in getting the point across, and the angle of the first slice is adjusted to create further structure. An additional table to the right of the pie chart provides related details.

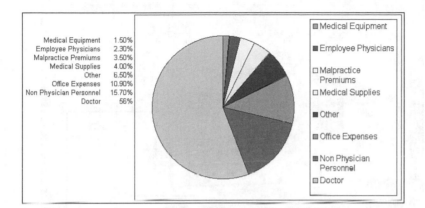

Figure 16.22.
With the data series sorted in order, this pie chart is clear and informative.

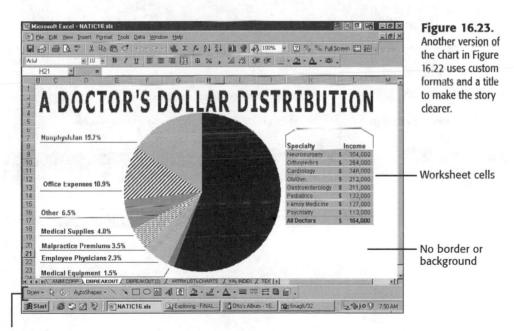

Drawing tools

Figure 16.23.
Another version of the chart in Figure 16.22 uses custom formats and a title to make the story clearer.

Worksheet cells

No border or background

USING FILL EFFECTS TO SHOW VARIANCE IN 3D CHARTS

One way to distinguish levels of data series is to apply a grade that reflects a series with colors or shades. Notice in Figure 16.24 that the different grades of stock are reflected by the gradient fills of the data series. Subtle visual tricks like these can work on the subconscious of the audience to help get the point across.

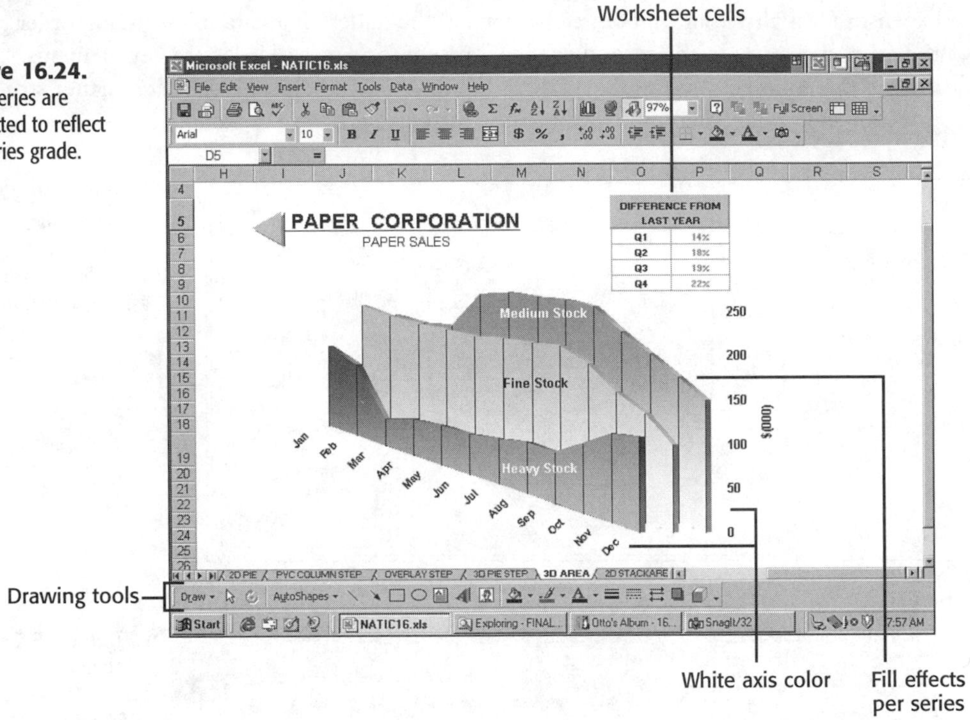

Figure 16.24.
Data series are formatted to reflect the series grade.

To create a 3D area chart with gradient fills that separate products, follow these steps:

1. Create a table that distributes the sets of data, as shown in Figure 16.25.

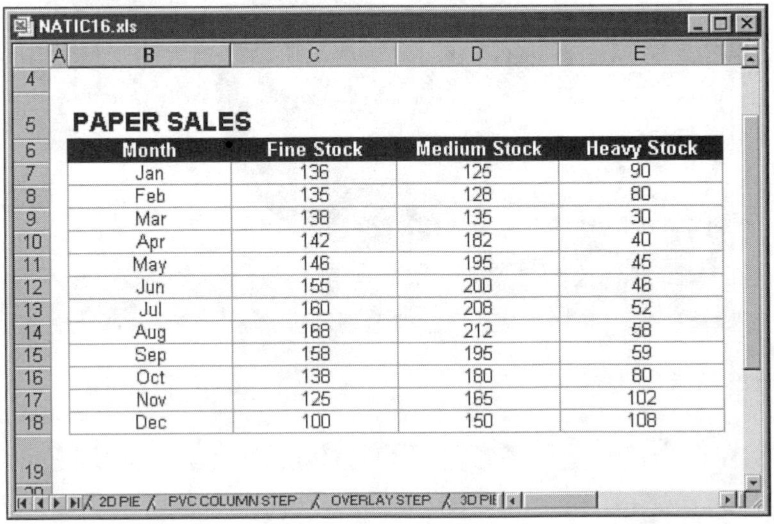

Figure 16.25.
This table distributes three sets of data over a period of time.

PAPER SALES

Month	Fine Stock	Medium Stock	Heavy Stock
Jan	136	125	90
Feb	135	128	80
Mar	138	135	30
Apr	142	182	40
May	146	195	45
Jun	155	200	46
Jul	160	208	52
Aug	168	212	58
Sep	158	195	59
Oct	138	180	80
Nov	125	165	102
Dec	100	150	108

2. Create an area chart with a 3D effect.

3. Right-click over the chart area and choose 3-D View.

4. Set the Elevation to 10 and the Rotation to 60.

5. Check the Right Angle Axes option.

6. Select the data series that you want to look heavy or dark. From the Format menu, choose Selected Data Series to display the Format Data Series dialog box.

7. Select the Options tab. Set the Gap Depth to 500 and the Chart Depth to 60. Select the Drop Lines option.

8. From the Patterns tab, choose Fill Effects to open the Fill Effects dialog box. Choose Two Colors (see Figure 16.26).

PART

V

CH

16

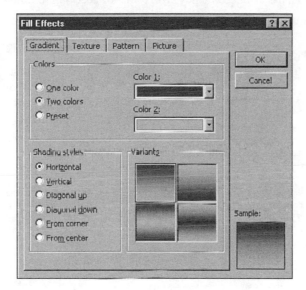

Figure 16.26.
Set the two-color gradients to reflect the grade of paper weight.

9. Choose Black for Color 1 and choose Gray-25% for Color 2.

10. Be sure that the shading style is Horizontal with the upper-left variant selected. Click OK twice.

11. Repeat the fill effect steps with each data series, selecting settings for medium and light shading.

12. Delete the chart wall, gridlines, and chart area.

To incorporate a table in the chart corner as shown, select the chart and be sure that Area is set to None on the Patterns tab in the Format Chart Area dialog box.

USING FORM CONTROLS WITH CHARTS

You might combine *form controls (page 624)* and charts for several reasons. Based on a database from which the information is generated, you can use form controls to combine data into a single chart and make the chart active. (To learn more about combining charts with active tables, see Chapter 20, "Using PivotTables and PivotCharts," and Chapter 21, "Managing Data with Formulas and Form Controls.")

Figure 16.27 shows an example of a chart that uses option buttons to display the desired data. The user clicks the Wichita Plant button or the Middelton Plant button to change the displayed data in the chart. This combination of chart, tables, and form controls uses a formula to extract information from a large database and condense and display it in a small space. Form controls with charts can become powerful tools for accessing multiple data sets with just one click.

Figure 16.27.
Form controls can be a great way to access and view information that must be continually regenerated.

Option buttons

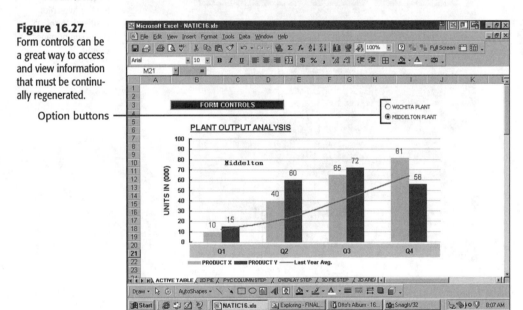

For this example, you create an active table that's derived from two separate tables. Using a simple IF statement, you then create the chart from the active table. Finally, the form control toggles the set cell referenced by the IF statement.

To access the form controls, right-click any toolbar and choose Forms, or select View, Toolbars, Forms.

To create an active chart with an option button, begin by setting up the information as described in the following steps:

1. Set up tables 1 and 2 as shown in Figure 16.28. These are the origin tables that the source table will reference.

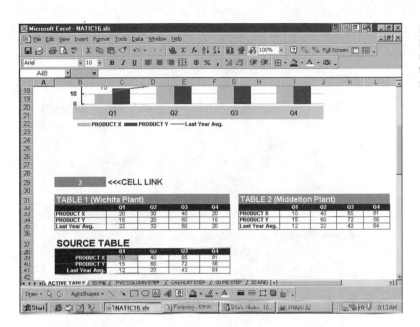

Figure 16.28.
It's important to set up the tables with the proper relative referencing.

2. Set up the source table, formatted identically to the origin tables.

3. Create the chart from the source table, and select it. (If you create the option buttons before selecting the chart, the buttons will be attached to the worksheet rather than the chart. Consequently, the buttons won't move with the chart.)

4. Draw an option button, right-click it, and then choose Format Control from the pop-up menu (see Figure 16.29).

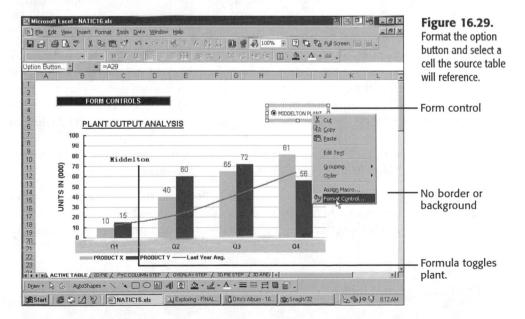

Figure 16.29.
Format the option button and select a cell the source table will reference.

Form control

No border or background

Formula toggles plant.

5. Select the Control tab in the Format Control dialog box (see Figure 16.30).

6. Type the address for the cell link (for this example, in cell B29).

7. Click OK.

Figure 16.30.
Format the control and set the cell link to the desired cell.

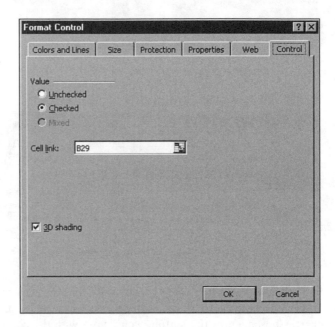

8. Select the option button and title the button.

9. Repeat steps 4 through 8 with the same cell link, but give the second option button a different name. To save time with the cell link and formatting, you can use Ctrl+D to duplicate the option button control. You still need to rename it, of course.

10. Now enter the formula. In this example, in cell C39 of the source table is the following formula: `=IF($B$29=1,C33,I33)`. Drag and fill to the right and then down. The statement will fill to the right and down to mirror that of the two tables. This statement reads from the cell to which the option button is linked. If it's 1, the result is that of the first origin table (Wichita, in this example) or the second origin table (Middelton) if 2.

Notice in Figure 16.31 that when Middelton is selected, the source table values equal that of the origin table Middelton Plant. The chart changes to match.

To create a toggle name (such as Wichita or Middelton) that sits in the plot area, be sure you choose None for Area on the chart. Next, in a cell that won't get in the way of the data series, type a formula that references the cell link again. The formula in this example would reference the cell link B29 and reads as follows:

`=If(B29=1,"Wichita","Middelton")`

This basically says, if B29=1 then Wichita, else Middelton.

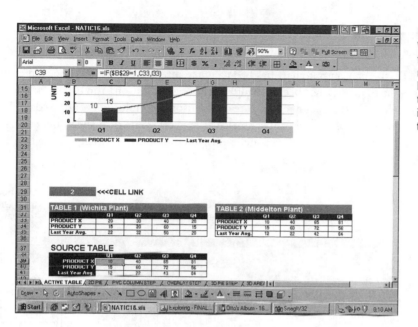

Figure 16.31.
When the formula from the source table references the cell link, the option buttons become actively integrated with the tables.

Tip #221 from

If you expect the chart to move at some point, don't use a cell in the background to represent the label. (Should the chart be moved or resized, a new cell would have to be used.) Chart titles and labels as well as text boxes (or any shape) can contain a reference to any cell on your worksheet. Place the preceding formula in any cell outside the chart area (maybe near the source table). Then select the chart and click on the Formula bar. Type an equal sign; then click or type the cell address containing the preceding formula, and press Enter. A text box will appear in the center of the chart. You can then move, size, and format the text box to your liking. Unlike using a cell directly, this text box will move and size with the chart.

Tip #222 from

You can add as many option buttons as you want and reference the same cell link. The number of the option button will continually increase, based on the number of option buttons you select and link.

If you don't anticipate moving or resizing a chart, you can create the option buttons on the worksheet behind the chart. Then eliminate the borders and the backgrounds in the chart by selecting None under Area on the Patterns tab in the Format Chart Area dialog box.

STACKING MULTIPLE CHARTS

If you have several bits of information to chart and are wondering how to effectively present it all together, the answer may be to separate the data into multiple charts and stack the charts. Because charts often are used to show historical information or projections over time, you can create multiple charts based on time frames, aligning the charts so each period of time appears directly above the next.

In Figure 16.32, the unit output chart has been aligned directly above the associated cost chart, and the fourth quarter has been highlighted to draw attention. You can stack two, three, or more charts in this manner to create comparisons of multiple groups of data. Why not place them on separate sheets? You can place each chart on its own sheet, but seeing how all the data correlates can provide conclusions you might not normally derive by reviewing the data separately.

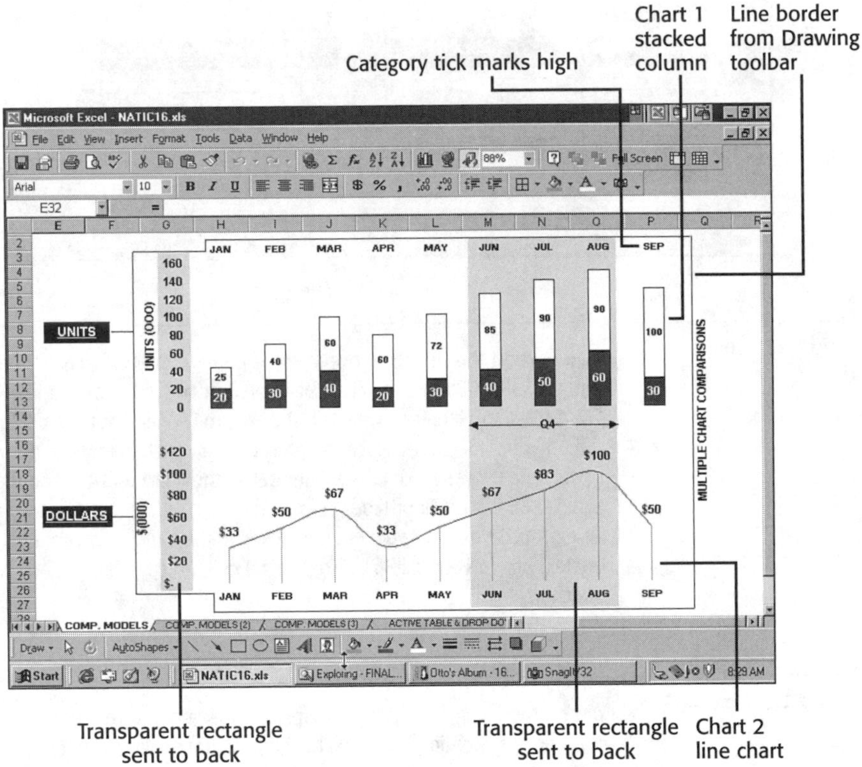

Figure 16.32.
Stacking charts can combine several bits of information on the same sheet, while still showing all the data at the same time.

After the charts are aligned, you can add drawing objects, such as lines and semitransparent boxes. The semitransparent box highlights the quarter and is sent to the back with the Send to Back command. Be sure you've selected None for chart fills so that the charts are transparent. Otherwise, the shape sent to the back will be covered by the chart's fill color.

CREATING COST AND PRODUCTION CURVES WITH CHARTS FOR VARIANCE

What is a *cost curve* or *production curve*? As process happens over time, cost accumulates over time, as do production, percentages, widgets, and so on. All too often, people have difficulty measuring and understanding how to view information over time, and especially being able to draw some relevant conclusion from the data. This section begins by establishing a table that provides projected weekly costs, and then, as the costs are incurred, applies that information as well (see Figure 16.33). By knowing how to lay out the underlying data, you can create charts that have meaning, instead of just graphic appeal. (You can find more information in Chapter 23, "Innovative Ways to Use Excel.")

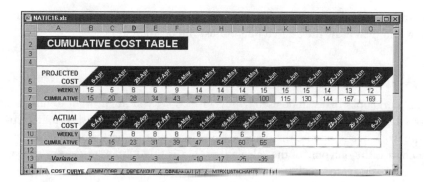

Figure 16.33.
By setting up a cost curve table in this fashion, you can establish a usable measuring tool in the form of a line chart that gives a visual of what has occurred over time.

As costs are incurred, you add that data to the actual weekly cost row. To automate the cumulative cost, sum the previous cumulative week plus the current week. (By doing this, you won't have to add up the cumulative every time a week's cost is input.) To display the data in chart format, select the date range and the cumulative projected/cumulative actual cost range, and then create the chart. Figure 16.34 shows a cost-curve line chart, displaying the variance between projected and actual costs. It's quick-hitting and easy to understand.

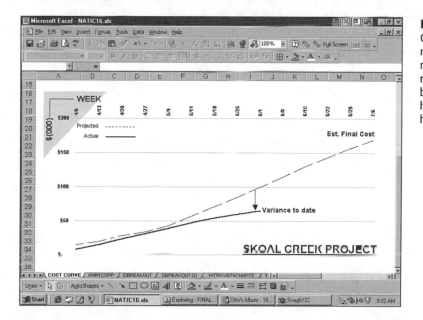

Figure 16.34.
Cost curves not only make for great measuring tools with regard to variance, but also show historically what has happened.

Production curves are created in similar fashion. Because production occurs over time as well, you can cumulate widgets, time, and so on. The key here is to understand that everything is measurable. If it isn't, either you're not accomplishing anything, or you're not creating anything.

To add the text as shown, select the chart, select the text box from the Drawing toolbar, and type the desired text.

To add lines or arrows for callouts, select the chart, select the Line or Arrow tool from the Drawing toolbar, and then draw the desired line. Adjust the position as necessary.

LINKING CHART TEXT TO WORKSHEET CELLS

When setting up workbooks that will be used by several people, you might want to link text or numbers from a cell in the workbook to a chart, so that when the chart is shown, it's representative of the worksheet. Suppose that you have a worksheet that performs many calculations and the chart is the outcome of the calculations, but is titled differently every time a calculation is done. In this case, you'll want to see a different title for each scenario or calculation. To link a cell to a chart, just select the chart and, in the Formula bar, type the formula =cell, substituting the cell reference for cell. When text or a number is generated in the cell, it shows up on the chart as well.

CHARTING HIDDEN DATA

You can maintain a chart's integrity even if you *hide (page 521)* the data that the chart references. By default, Excel hides the information in a chart when the underlying data is hidden. Suppose that you created an outline that sums up the quarters under the months, as shown in Figure 16.35. If you hide the monthly data, as shown in Figure 16.36, the chart displays only the quarterly totals.

To plot nonvisible cells on the chart, perform the following steps:

1. Select the chart.
2. Choose Options from the Tools menu.
3. Select the Chart tab in the Options dialog box (see Figure 16.37).
4. Uncheck Plot Visible Cells Only.
5. Click OK.

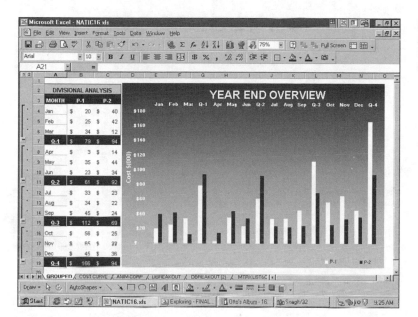

PART

V

CH

16

Figure 16.35.
A chart and its under-
lying monthly and
quarterly data.

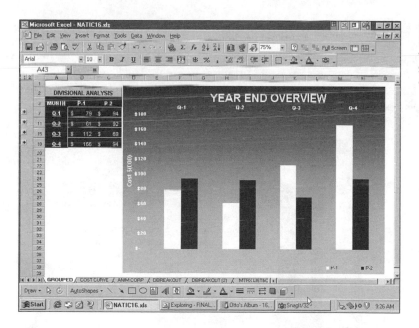

Figure 16.36.
Notice that only the
visible cells are
shown on the
corresponding chart.

Figure 16.37.
Hidden cells remain plotted on the chart when the Plot Visible Cells Only option is unchecked.

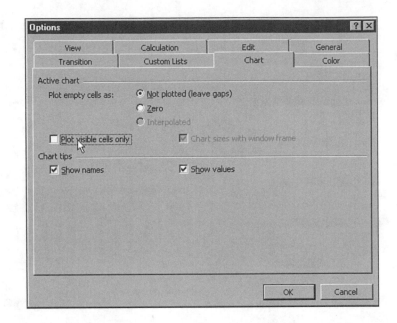

CREATING EFFECTIVE MULTIPLE-COMBINATION CHARTS

Multiple-combination charts are good for comparing two or more sets of data. Figure 16.38 shows the three sets of data used to create the chart in Figure 16.39. This example looks at the total contracted amount minus the monthly completed totals against the prior year's output. Charts can be a great way of showing depletion of total reserves.

Figure 16.38.
You can create multiple sets of data to establish a multiple-combination chart.

GOLD MINING CORP

	CONTRACTED ORE TO MINE	ORE MINED	LAST YEAR
Jan	150	0	0
Feb	148	2	0
Mar	142	6	5
Apr	130	12	15
May	107	23	26
Jun	83	24	34
Jul	59	24	26
Aug	24	35	23
Sep	12	12	12
Oct	5	7	12
Nov	1	4	0
Dec	0	1	0

For this example, you start by establishing three sets of data as shown in Figure 16.39. The Contracted Ore to Mine data series reduces total quantity remaining from the monthly ore amounts mined. The third column represents last year's monthly output as a comparison to this year's quantities.

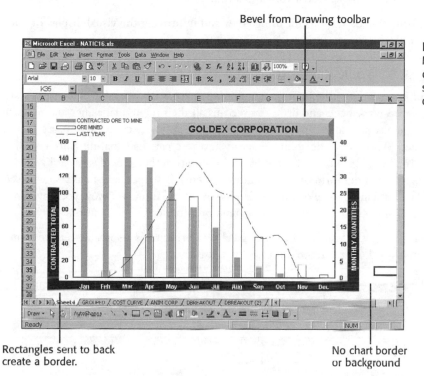

Bevel from Drawing toolbar

Rectangles sent to back create a border.

No chart border or background

Figure 16.39.
Multiple-combination charts can separate several data series on the same chart.

You can create multiple-combination charts in more than one way:

- Select the entire table and create a chart with the Chart Wizard, and then select each data series and change them independently by choosing Chart, Chart Type.

- Paste the data separately.

After formatting a multiple-combination chart, save the chart as a custom chart type to avoid having to reformat each new multiple-combination chart you create.

VISUAL DISPLAY IN EXCEL

Visual display isn't limited to charts. Visual display can include words, objects, lists, or a combination thereof. Take sounds, for example. Although sounds aren't visual, audible sounds can create a sense of calm or urgency. Remember the theme from *Jaws* and how it created a sense of urgency? The same is true when thinking in terms of visual display. Soft pastel colors evoke a calm feeling, while bright or fluorescent colors can evoke urgency or attention.

You see this all the time in finance—illustrations shown in the red or in the black. We all know red is bad and black is good in finance, but because it's second nature, we don't think of it in terms of visual display. The same colors used in a different arena can have quite the opposite effect. Because I'm limited to displaying grayscale in this book, the visual display must be created primarily with structure and layout.

For more information on options for using color and improving the visual display of your Excel charts and worksheets, see Chapters 23 and 24.

COMBINING CHARTS, WORKSHEETS, TEXT, AND TIME

Now that you have some of the basics in combining charts with worksheets, you can start to embed charts into worksheets and lists. You see this all the time in magazines and newspapers; however, many people use graphic programs to create these charts and marry them to the spreadsheet. With Excel's flexibility, you can start to create lists that measure visually. Take Figure 16.40, for example. This is a list of information that provides several vehicles of measure or value in the form of a chart, drawing tools or shapes, and finally words (see Figure 16.41). Combine these elements with a list of information, and now you have one line in a list that provides multiple angles or views on product or competition.

Start to think outside the box. Just because Excel is referred to as a spreadsheet program, don't allow that word *spreadsheet* to limit how you use Excel.

Figure 16.40.
By combining charts, drawing tools, and words with line-item information, you provide the audience with multiple views of the product or company.

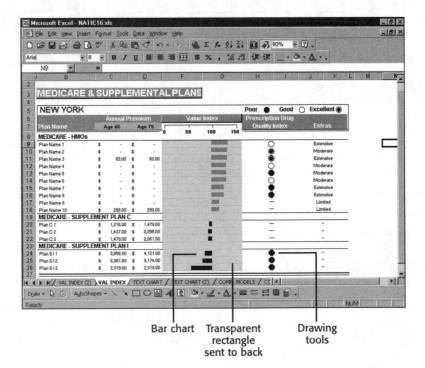

Bar chart   Transparent rectangle sent to back   Drawing tools

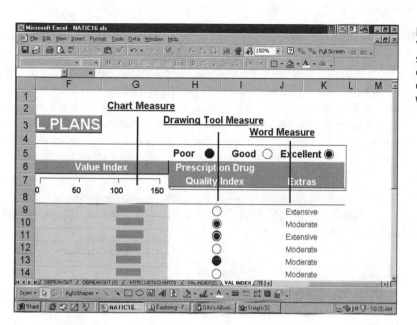

Figure 16.41.
You can create measuring tools from charts, drawing objects, and even words.

In Figure 16.42, I've removed the formatting to show how a bar chart was positioned on top of the grid. (Remove the borders and background fills to make the chart transparent.) In this example, I've constructed the chart to cross the X-axis at 100, so that the value index appears negative or less than average if the bar is to the left of 100.

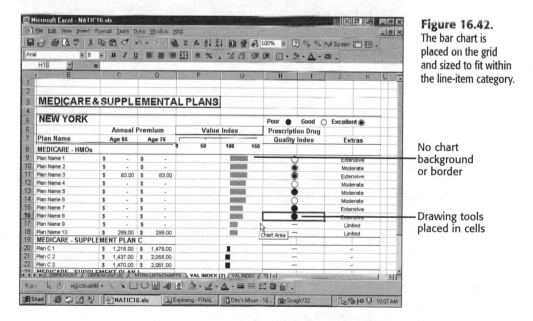

Figure 16.42.
The bar chart is placed on the grid and sized to fit within the line-item category.

No chart background or border

Drawing tools placed in cells

To learn more about measuring with drawing tools and using matrices, see Chapter 23.

CREATING "CHARTS" WITHOUT CHARTS

Sometimes you run into situations where you have to represent data graphically, but a standard chart won't achieve what you need. You can visually display words, numbers, and time without using Excel's charting capabilities, but still creating the visual appeal of a chart with the proper layout and format. Figure 16.43 combines grid structure, fill colors, and text boxes to simulate a chart, visually demonstrating the profit/loss scenario per division over time. (The quality of this chart suffers a bit when the figure is reduced to fit within book margins. To see how the Divisional Analysis chart really works, review the file on the book's CD.)

This chart is created by setting up the grid to accommodate years from right to left. Then you align text boxes above or below the appropriate year in which the event or scenario takes place (see Figure 16.44).

Figure 16.43.
With the proper grid layout, fill colors, and text box placement, you can create charts without using Excel's charting capabilities, but rather tapping into its versatility of drawing tools and grid options.

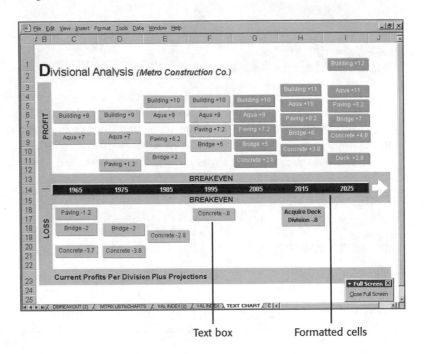

Text box   Formatted cells

EMBEDDING MULTIPLE CHARTS IN A MATRIX LIST

What is a matrix list? A *matrix* can be a table, a list, or anything that provides multiple values or scenarios that can intersect or create units of measure against the whole. In the example in Figure 16.45, each company has line items organized under its heading. The list reflects the four headings in cell B3. The embedded charts are placed within the line-item slot, next to the percentage of minority representation within the organization (see Figure 16.46). After you create the first one, copy and paste it to another location, and change the source data to reflect the line item it represents.

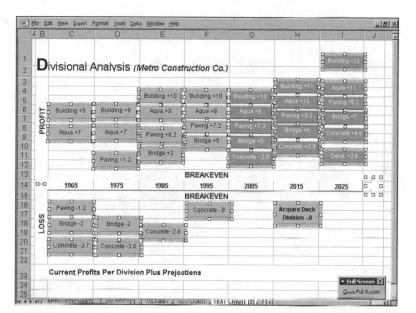

Figure 16.44.
The same chart, showing the drawing objects selected.

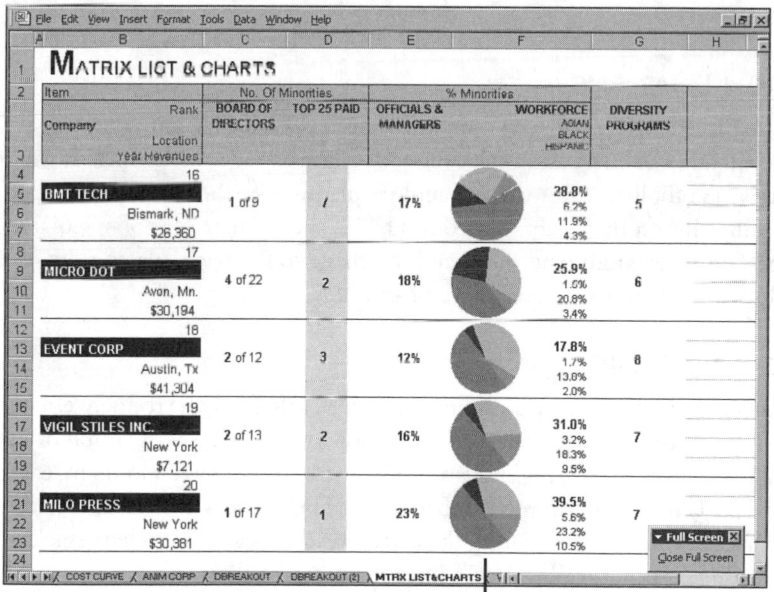

Figure 16.45.
You can combine a matrix list with multiple units of measure with charts to further explain the story.

Multiple pies sized and placed

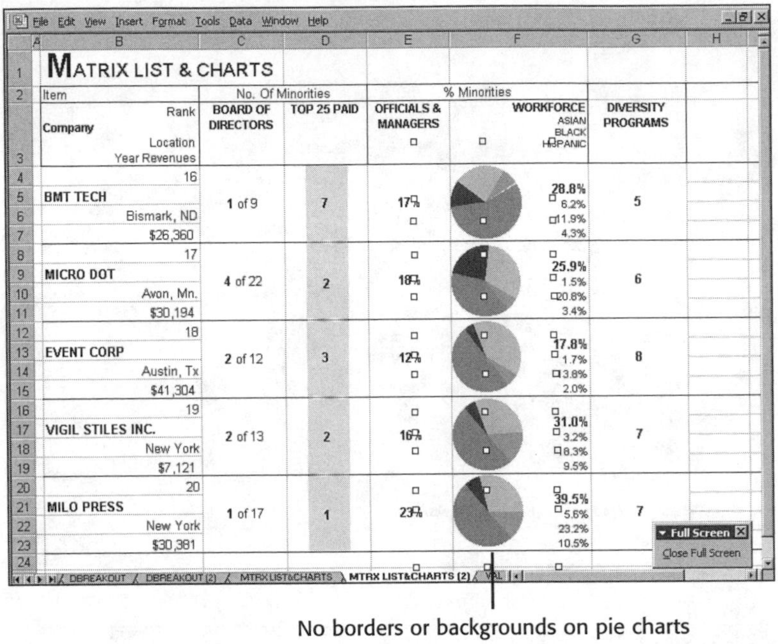

Figure 16.46.
Notice the list struc-
ture when formats
are removed. The pie
charts are sized and
positioned along the
left of column F for
consistency.

No borders or backgrounds on pie charts

CREATING A CUSTOM L-BAR AXIS

Excel enables you to create custom axes, as shown in Figure 16.47. Eliminate the original
axis and background of the chart and replace it with a transparent shape, such as the rectangle from the Drawing toolbar. After the rectangle is placed over the corresponding X and Y
values, select a fill color on the Colors and Lines tab in the Format AutoShape dialog box,
make the shape semitransparent, and then send the shape to the back, placing the object
behind the values of the chart, and creating an *L-bar axis*.

BUILDING SINGLE-STACK CHARTS

Single-stack charts designed with text boxes and drawing tools can be extremely effective
when showing percentages between categories, as shown in Figure 16.48. You'll often see
charts of this nature when comparing industry categories. (If you have too many categories,
however, the stacked chart can become cumbersome.) The borders and backgrounds were
eliminated in this example. By eliminating these features, you can make chart stacks stand
alone, and then use text boxes, callouts, and lines to finish the chart.

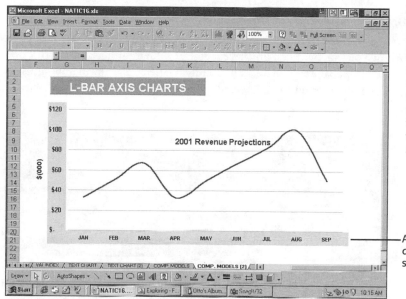

Figure 16.47.
By eliminating the background and the axis of the chart, you can place a drawing object such as a rectangle over the values and send the object to the back, giving it the appearance of an axis.

Axis created with drawing tools and sent to back

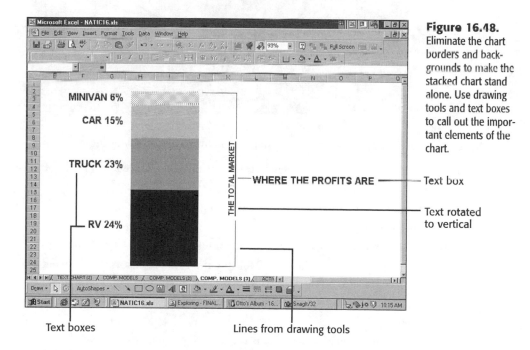

Figure 16.48.
Eliminate the chart borders and backgrounds to make the stacked chart stand alone. Use drawing tools and text boxes to call out the important elements of the chart.

Text box

Text rotated to vertical

Text boxes

Lines from drawing tools

CREATING LIFETIME PROFITABILITY/BREAKEVEN CHARTS

Lifetime charts are great for showing the profitability of a product over time. Notice in Figure 16.49 how you can view loss, breakeven, and profit, all in the same chart. For simplicity, you could also separate these items into individual charts, showing net units, total profits, and so on. It's important to understand the audience and intent of the chart when making those decisions.

Figure 16.49.
Use the line chart to establish lifetime profitability and break-even analysis charts.

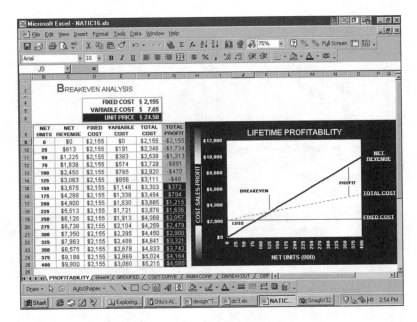

To set up a lifetime profitability chart, establish the table by following these steps:

1. Establish the net units in increments. In the example, the increments are set every 25,000 units in column B.

2. Set up the net revenue in column C, multiplying the net units by the unit price to calculate the net revenue.

3. Establish the fixed cost in column D. The example shows fixed cost of $2,155.

4. Apply the variable cost in column E. Multiply the variable cost rate by the net units in column B to calculate the variable cost in column E.

5. The total cost column in column F combines the fixed cost and variable cost to reach the total cost.

6. To create the chart, select the net units, net revenue, fixed cost, and total cost data from the table. (Select just these columns by holding down the Ctrl key as you click.)

7. Use the Chart Wizard to create a line chart.

8. In Step 2 of the Chart Wizard dialog box, select the Series tab and supply the Net Units range for the Category (X) Axis Labels setting.

9. Click Finish.

10. Select the net units data series in the chart and delete it. The net units is now the category (X) axis.

Tip #223 from

[signature]

> You can automate the Net Units column with a formula. For example, in another cell (let's say B6), type the increment number. In cell B10, type the following formula: **=$B9+$B$6**. Copy the formula down the column. This will enable you to quickly view interval changes in both the table and the chart by changing only cell B6.

TROUBLESHOOTING

MOVING CATEGORY LABELS

Excel won't let me place my category labels in a different location.

You can move the X-axis on a column chart to the top of the chart. Select the axis and choose Format, Selected Axis to open the Format Axis dialog box. On the Patterns tab, choose High under Tick Mark Labels.

INVISIBLE DATA SERIES

When I create a secondary axis for the second data series of my column chart, the columns are hidden behind the first data set.

Select the data series in front of the other data series, and choose Format, Selected Data Series to open the Format Data Series dialog box. On the Patterns tab, choose None under Area.

MOVING A CHART WITH OBJECTS

When I move or resize a chart, the drawing objects don't move with the chart and I have to move and realign them.

There are two ways to fix this problem. You can select all the objects (including the chart) and *group (page 529)* them. Or select the chart before you create an object, which makes Excel treat the object as part of the chart.

ALIGNING CHART LABELS WITH GRIDLINES

Excel doesn't allow me to align my chart labels to match the gridlines on the spreadsheet.

This can be tricky. Align the chart labels to match the gridlines as closely as you can. Then select the range of columns over the width of the chart and adjust the width to a larger size. Readjust the columns to a smaller size, and the category labels on the chart should then match.

EXCEL IN PRACTICE

Good spreadsheet design and chart skills enable you to combine Excel's chart elements to solve problems. Notice how the *Gantt chart (page 642)* and column chart in Figure 16.50 really don't give clear conclusions with regard to demand and capacity over time. The same information in Figure 16.51, applied with good alignment and design, produces a clear picture of the overall demand associated with the projects over time.

Figure 16.50.
The design here is clean, but you have to draw your own conclusions.

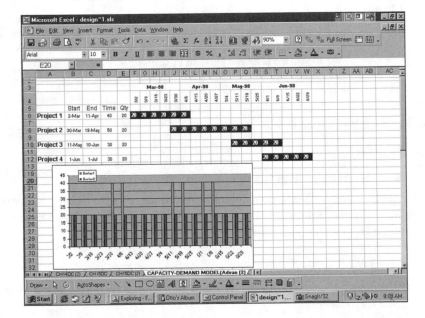

Figure 16.51.
This version provides a real picture of demand over time.

Column chart shows demand.

Place chart over Gantt for resource loading.

For more on dynamic Gantt charts, see Chapter 23.

Chart reference table

Line chart shows capacity.

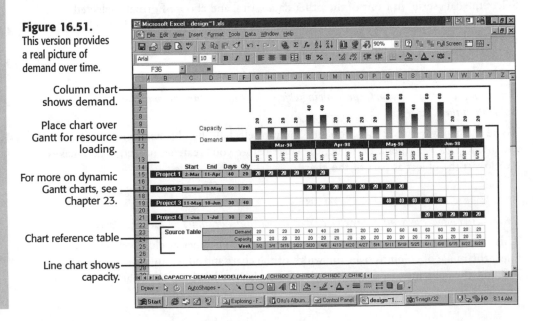

ANALYZING AND MANAGING YOUR DATA

CHAPTER 17

SETTING UP A LIST OR DATABASE IN EXCEL

In this chapter

by Patrick D. Blattner
Patrick@BlattnerBooks.com

USING EXCEL AS A DATABASE PROGRAM

Although "number crunching" is Excel's primary purpose, the row-and-column format lends itself to creating and storing databases (called *lists* in Excel). Generally, a good rule of thumb is that if your list grows to more than 2,000 rows, you should store the information in a data warehouse or relational database. Whether you need to store a product catalog for quick lookups or employee information for use with your accounting software, you can create, edit, sort, analyze, and filter your data with the options on the Data menu.

This chapter begins discussion of data storage and analysis in Excel, with discussions of various methods of data entry and options for viewing, printing, and reporting on the list data. The following chapters explore additional options for sorting, filtering, grouping, consolidating, outlining, and auditing lists and tables; using tools and form controls to analyze data; and PivotTables, an important and useful feature of Excel for use in summarizing and manipulating the structure of your lists.

BUILDING AN EFFECTIVE LIST

Structuring a list is the most important part of the creation process because it ultimately determines what you'll be able to extract from the list and how effectively you can manage the list after it's created. Too much time is wasted in business today restructuring lists that were improperly set up.

Before you start to lay out a list, ask yourself the question, "What data will I need to compile after the list is created?" If you know what information you'll need to extract, laying out the list will become quite simple. In the list in Figure 17.1, for example, each category has its own heading—Date, Product, Process, and so on—and this data can be extracted as a whole or by individual categories.

When building the list, you can look at the list structure in terms of an outline—classify the outline from most important "topics" to least important. This provides a guideline in structuring the information. In Figure 17.1, the most important topic is product; the second is process.

In building the list, keeping things constant is extremely important. When you start to filter lists or extract information from lists with *functions (page 254)* as discussed in later chapters, spelling and text case are critical.

Tip #224 from

Patrick

How can you tell whether your list is structured effectively? As you check it over, ask yourself whether someone else could take over managing the list and understand its logic without assistance.

Field names in header row

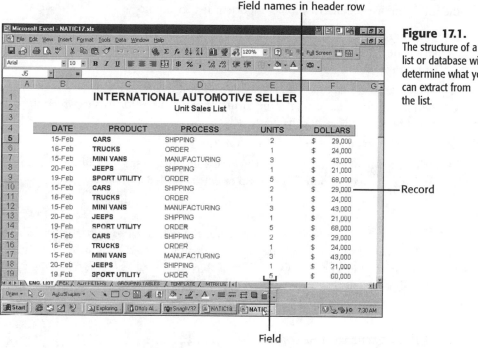

Figure 17.1.
The structure of a list or database will determine what you can extract from the list.

Record

Field

Excel lists are generally made up of a hierarchical structure. What does this mean? Well, think in terms of the lowest common denominator in your database or list. If you're setting up a list to track quantities or dollar amounts for the year by code, for example, the lowest-level item might be the actual cost or quantity, then the code, and finally the week or other timeline. The field names (headings) would be placed at the top of each field's column (working from right to left in this example), and beneath this header row would be the body of the list—the actual list data. The first field would be the week; second, the code; third, the cost or quantity. If you understand how to use PivotTables, you know the importance of information leveling.

Tip #225 from

Don't separate your list with blank columns or rows! Blanks create a mess when you try to manipulate data. Every level of information should have its own column, and there's no need to apply spacing between the rows. If you must add space between rows, use the row height feature to adjust the vertical size of each row.

Caution

Don't combine the names of employees, users, clients, and so on into a single cell. Separate first and last names so that each name has its own column for use in sorting the list by name or creating a PivotTable.

The following list summarizes some important list terminology:

- A *header row* at or near the top of the worksheet contains the field names for the list. This is not a requirement, but many list features won't work correctly (or at all) if the list isn't set up this way.
- *Field names* describe each category of data. These headings usually are positioned as column headings, but can take the form of row headings for lists in which the data is stored horizontally rather than vertically.
- Each cell containing data is called a *field*.
- Fields are combined into a single row or column that comprises all the data for that particular item or person. This group of fields is called a *record*.
- All the records in a database combine to form the *body* of the list.

Table 17.1 describes some suggested formats for the individual parts of the list. These formats will help create a clean, uncluttered list. When uppercase, lowercase, and initial caps are all used in the same list, the list is difficult to read. I would suggest following a standard format in all your lists. It's also good practice to create clean, short headings; the longer the heading, the more difficult the list is for others to review.

TABLE 17.1. STANDARD LIST LAYOUT

Item	Suggested Format
Horizontal field names	Bold type, uppercase, and 12-point font
Left column vertical field names	Bold type, uppercase, and 12-point font
Body text	Uppercase or initial caps and 10-point font, regular style
Font style	Arial, Tahoma, Courier, Garamond

By default, Excel 2000 extends the formatting of the list to any new list entries typed at the end of the list, including any formulas that are part of previous entries (assuming that at least three of the previous five entries used that formatting and/or formula, to establish a pattern for Excel to use). To turn off this feature—for example, if you want to customize certain types of entries within an individual list—choose Tools, Options, click the Edit tab, and deselect the option Extend List Formats and Formulas.

Tip #226 from

Maintain consistency in font style, upper- and lowercase, and initial caps. If you begin the body of your list with one initial style, maintain the same style throughout the list.

Don't enter multiple names and categories in one cell. If there's no consistency, rhyme, or reason to the body of a list, it becomes useless. If lists are set up properly, Excel can become a tool that solves problems for your business, not just a place to store numbers.

It's important to establish field names that match the category. Lists usually grow with time, and new field names are created as the list grows, so try to break down the description of

the field name to its most detailed level from the beginning. Notice the headings in
Figure 17.2.

Figure 17.2.
Create field names
that break down the
description of the
contents to the most
detailed level.

The format for the body of the list (the actual data) is the most critical part of your stan-
dardization process. The data should maintain consistency with like or similar text formats
and case. Consistency here will determine the manageability of the list.

In many cases, you'll inherit someone else's list and have to manipulate some of the current
structure. Figure 17.3 demonstrates changing an existing list from lowercase to uppercase
for consistency in this particular list. (You can change from uppercase to lowercase with the
LOWER function.)

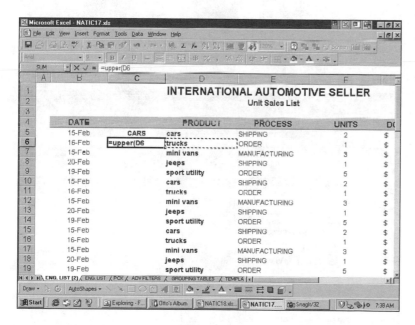

Figure 17.3.
You can use the
UPPER function to
convert lowercase text
to uppercase, and the
LOWER function to
convert uppercase
text to lowercase.

For a complete list of Excel functions, see Appendix A, "Excel Function Reference."

After you convert the lowercase entries to uppercase with formulas for this example, you'll
want to return the converted—now uppercase—text to its original column. To do this, follow these steps:

1. Select the converted range (column of formulas).

2. Choose Edit, Copy.

3. Select the first cell in the range to paste.

4. Choose Edit, Paste Special.

5. In the Paste Special dialog box, select Values (see Figure 17.4). This option converts all the formulas to their resulting values.

6. Click OK. The values are copied to the target cells, as shown in Figure 17.5.

7. Delete the formula column.

Figure 17.4.
The Paste Special dialog box enables you to paste ranges of formulas as values.

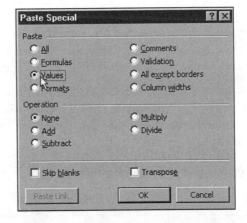

Figure 17.5.
After you convert the text from lowercase to uppercase and paste the converted text in the original column, you can delete the formula column.

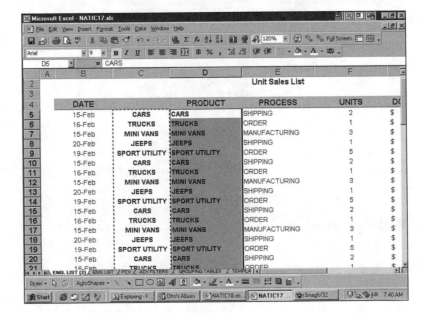

WORKING WITH THE DATA FORM

People who work with Excel on a regular basis usually are comfortable with the row-and-column structure and have no difficulty entering list data directly into the appropriate cells. However, the ongoing data entry and maintenance of a list might be handled by someone who is less familiar with Excel. For those users—and even experienced Excel users who prefer a simpler data-entry method—Excel provides the *data form*. The data form works like a dialog box; it floats over the worksheet and includes buttons and other form controls to enable the user to enter one record at a time into the list.

You also can use the data form to search for specific records in the list, using specified criteria, or even to delete records. *Filters (page 623)* (covered in Chapter 18, "Using Excel's Data-Management Features") are more effective in scrolling for information, but if your list is quite long and you're searching for a specific element in the list, the data form works well in assisting you to find that particular line of information.

To use the data form, click anywhere in the list and choose <u>D</u>ata, <u>F</u>orm. Excel displays a data form, customized with the headings in the worksheet (see Figure 17.6). The data form displays the record count of the list and the scrollbar enables you to scroll the list, record by record, or many records at a time.

PART

VI

CH

17

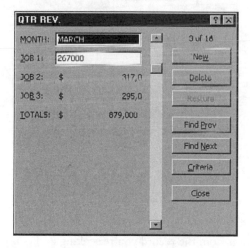

Figure 17.6.
Use the data form to enter or find records in a list.

To enter new records, click the Ne<u>w</u> button and type the information in the appropriate text boxes. (Notice that the record indicator in the upper-right corner of the dialog box changes to display the words New Record. The data form works as a multipurpose form for data entry, searching, and viewing the list; the message in the upper-right corner indicates how the form is currently being used.) Use the Tab and Shift+Tab keys, the underlined hotkeys, or the mouse to move from one text box to another. When the record is complete, press Enter or click the Ne<u>w</u> button to enter the new record at the end of the list and start another new record.

Tip #227 from

Unless the list is sorted chronologically or by a customized account or part number, you probably will want new records to be sorted from the end of the list to their appropriate positions alphabetically or numerically. See Chapter 18 for details on sorting and filtering lists.

Although the data form simplifies the process of entering list data, it doesn't offer the advantage of auto-repeating information you have already typed once. If your list includes the same information in multiple records—for example, each new employee record will list one of a set of five orientation and training classes—you probably won't want to type that information repeatedly when entering data. Enter the data directly into the cells—where you can take advantage of the copy and AutoComplete features—instead of using the data form, or skip those fields and enter that information later.

To find a specific record in a list, follow these steps:

1. Select the <u>C</u>riteria button (see Figure 17.7).

   Notice that the record indicator in the upper-right corner of the dialog box changes to display the word Criteria.

Figure 17.7.
Search for specific information within a list by typing the description in the corresponding text box.

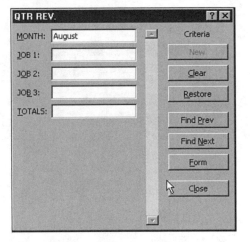

2. Enter any known information from the record you're seeking and choose Find <u>N</u>ext or press Enter.

   The search function works like that in the Find dialog box; you can search for just the first few characters of an entry or type the whole entry.

Note

Typing the first few characters works only on nonnumeric data. To search for salaries, dates entered as dates, and so on, you must include the entire number or date.

Excel searches the list and finds the first record that matches the specified criteria. Note that searches are not case sensitive.

3. To continue searching, click Find Next again. To search in the reverse direction, click Find Prev. Note that either method continues searching from the previous record found, rather than starting at the top of the list.

   When you reach the last record to match the specified criteria, Excel beeps if you try to continue searching in that direction.

4. To enter another set of criteria, click the Clear button and type the new criteria. To return to data entry, click the Form button.

VIEWING AND PRINTING THE LIST

PART

VI

CH

17

The following sections provide a number of helpful suggestions for organizing the view of your list. Aesthetics aside, making your list worksheets attractive and readable can actually help with the data-entry process and make the list easier to use. And it's important that a list be understandable, especially when someone else has to use the list.

Caution

Don't get too carried away with these viewing options. As your data list grows, simple backgrounds and views become more desirable. The more complex the view, the less data you can see or comprehend onscreen.

KEEPING THE FIELD NAMES FROM SCROLLING

When scrolling lists in Excel, you'll notice that when you scroll down or across the list, headings and field names scroll off the screen. To keep the heading or field name onscreen as you scroll the body of the list, you can *freeze (page 64)* the headings onscreen. Select the range below the heading or to the right of the headings and choose Window, Freeze Panes, as shown in Figure 17.8. In this example, rows 2 through 4 will remain onscreen as you work with the list. To unfreeze the panes, choose Window, Unfreeze Panes.

→ To learn more about freezing panes in Excel, **see** "Freezing Columns and Rows," **p. 64**

Splitting (page 67) the window is much like freezing the panes, but the difference is the capability to intersect a row or column. For example, Figure 17.9 shows the same worksheet as in Figure 17.8, but with the window split, intersecting column D, meaning that the *split bar (page 66)* splits right through the cell. Freezing panes freezes to the right or left, top or bottom of a cell. When panes are frozen, you can't move the frozen sections; you have to unfreeze the panes to adjust them. Split bars, on the other hand, can be dragged anywhere you like on the screen, which makes them more useful when working with lists.

Figure 17.8.
Freezing the pane
enables you to scroll
the body of the list
while keeping head-
ings or field names
visible.

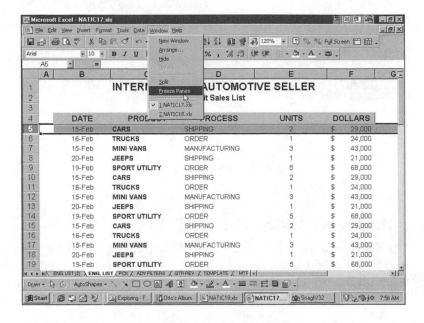

Figure 17.9.
Splitting the window
is similar to freezing
panes; however, with
the split window, you
can intersect a col-
umn or row, and also
adjust it with your
mouse.

You can split the window by selecting a row or column and choosing Window, Split. To
adjust the split, simply drag the split bar to the desired location. Another way to split the
window is to drag one of the split boxes by the scrollbars to the desired location. You can

split the window both horizontally and vertically. To remove a split, double-click the split bar or drag it to the edge of the window.

→ For more details on working with split windows, **see** "Splitting the Screen," **p. 65**

ARRANGING MULTIPLE WINDOWS

When creating lists to store your data, you may need to work with several workbooks at the same time or multiple sheets within the same workbook. I often find myself doing this when I copy and paste information from one list to another, or when I write formulas that correspond from one workbook or worksheet to another.

> **Note**
>
> When establishing multiple lists within a workbook, if possible, start your lists on the same line and cell. This helps in creating efficiencies in managing your workbook. Also try to make the lists as similar in type and style as possible for consistency within the workbook.

To view multiple windows or sheets at one time within the same workbook, perform the following steps:

1. Select one of the sheets in the workbook you want to view.

2. Select <u>W</u>indow, <u>N</u>ew Window. Excel adds a colon and the number 2 to the workbook title in the title bar of the second window and the number 1 to the title bar in the first window.

3. In the new window, select another sheet in the workbook.

4. Choose <u>W</u>indow, <u>A</u>rrange.

5. In the Arrange Windows dialog box, select the desired window arrangement. If you want to arrange only the windows showing the currently active workbook, be sure the <u>W</u>indows of Active Workbook option is checked (see Figure 17.10).

6. Click OK.

Figure 17.10.

PART **VI** CH **17**

Although Figure 17.11 seems to show two workbooks open, you actually are seeing two sheets within the same workbook. Any changes to either workbook are saved to the original workbook. In this example, the upper window and the lower window show two different worksheets in the same workbook.

Using the same method, you can view multiple workbooks or multiple windows showing the active workbook. When arranging multiple workbooks, be sure that the <u>W</u>indows of Active Workbook option in the Arrange Windows dialog box is not checked.

Figure 17.11.
By creating a new window in a workbook, you can view several pages of the same workbook at the same time.

A number after the workbook title indicates that you're viewing the same workbook in multiple windows.

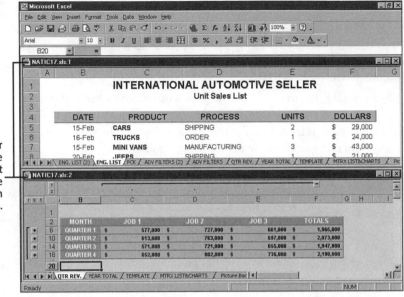

INSERTING DATA RANGES INTO A LIST

You probably are quite accomplished at cutting or copying a range and pasting it to an empty range. When working with lists, however, you may often need to paste cut or copied records between existing records. Rather than using a simple paste operation, use the Insert menu.

Tip #228 from

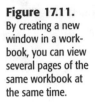

You can select multiple *noncontiguous (page 78)* columns or rows and insert columns or rows between them. For example, you can select row 6 and row 8 at the same time and insert a row by selecting Cells or Rows under the Insert menu.

Figure 17.12 shows a selected group of records. In this example, the intention is to move the North Dakota records above the Minnesota records (assume that this list is not intended to be sorted alphabetically by project). To move these records, you would cut them from their current location and insert them above the Minnesota records. After cutting the North Dakota records, select the target range and choose Insert, Cut Cells. Excel repositions the existing data and inserts the cut cells (see Figure 17.13).

If you are inserting copied rather than cut cells, choose Insert, Copied Cells. The Insert Paste dialog box appears, as shown in Figure 17.14. Choose Shift Cells Down or Shift Cells Right to move the existing data in the target range out of the way of the incoming data.

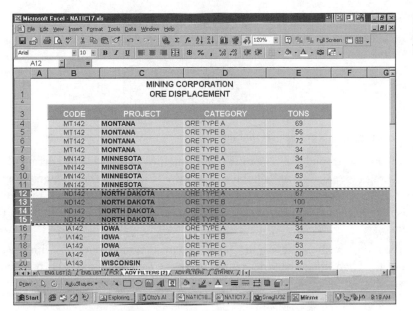

Figure 17.12.
Select and copy or cut the source records.

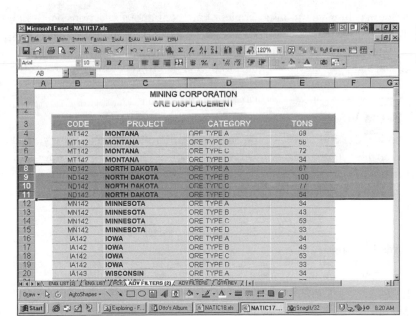

Figure 17.13.
The cut range is pasted into place.

Figure 17.14.
In the Insert Paste dialog box, specify how you want the existing data to move.

Two drag-and-drop methods are also available:

- Position the mouse around the edge of the selection (just like the normal drag and drop), and drag the selection while holding down the Shift key. When the gray single-line-insert indicator appears in the desired location between rows/columns, release the mouse. The existing data is automatically shifted down/to the right, depending on the drag direction.

- Position the mouse in the same manner as the previous method, but drag with the right mouse button. When the gray border representing the data being moved is positioned in the desired location, release the mouse and choose Shift Down and Move (or Copy) from the shortcut menu.

Because Excel doesn't allow you to insert copies of noncontiguous selections, you can use this feature only for a contiguous selection. To enter list data from noncontiguous areas, use Edit, Paste. In Figure 17.12, for example, you could select all the ore type A projects, copy them from the list, and paste them in a new location. The projects would appear in the order copied, with no additional spaces between them.

ESTABLISHING CUSTOM VIEWS

Because lists grow in size and only a certain amount of information needs to be viewed at one time, Excel enables you to create *custom views* to look at just the relevant information defined by the user. You can even name the views to fit the situation. For example, Figure 17.15 shows a breakout by job and month, but you may be interested in only the high-level totals by quarter.

To hide the supporting information and show only the quarter totals, you can create a custom view. Follow these steps:

1. Establish the view you want saved as a custom view. In this example, you would hide rows 3 through 5, 7 through 9, and so on, until only the quarter totals are visible.

2. Choose View, Custom Views to open the Custom Views dialog box (see Figure 17.16).

3. Choose Add to open the Add View dialog box (see Figure 17.17).

4. Type a name for the new custom view.

5. Click OK.

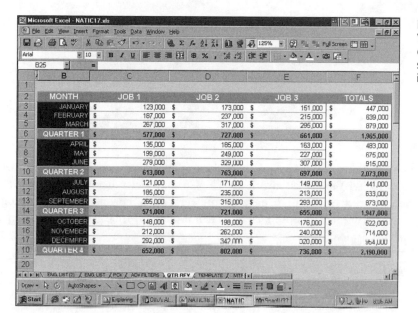

Figure 17.15.
You can create custom views to show only relevant information.

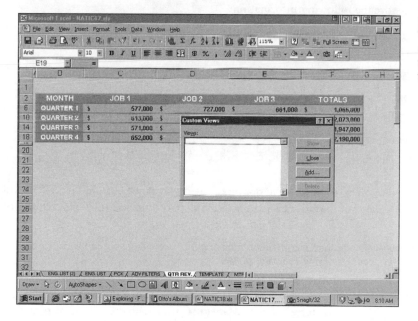

Figure 17.16.
The Custom Views dialog box enables you to add custom views.

Figure 17.17.
Provide a name for
the view. Keep it
as simple and
descriptive as
possible.

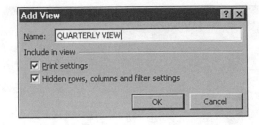

Custom views are saved with the workbook. To show your custom view at any time, open the workbook and select View, Custom Views. The Custom Views dialog box opens. Select the desired view and click Show. To delete a custom view, open the Custom Views dialog box, select the view name, and choose Delete. When prompted, select Yes to confirm that you want to delete the view.

Tip #229 from

Set up custom views in workbooks that are shared among multiple users. Each user can store his or her favorite view and print settings.

Custom views store the following information:

- Window size/position, including splits or frozen panes
- Hidden columns, rows, and sheets in the workbook
- Column-width settings
- Display options
- Selected cells, if any
- Filtered list criteria
- Page Setup settings

The Add View dialog box gives you the option of saving print settings, hidden rows, and filter settings. The last is an important issue for working with lists; see the next chapter for details.

→ If you switch views often, add the Custom Views toolbar button to one of your toolbars. For details on customizing toolbars, **see** "Modifying Toolbars" **p. 869**

CREATING CUSTOM REPORTS

Creating custom reports with Excel's *Report Manager* is similar to creating a custom view (discussed in the preceding section). Because the Report Manager basically consolidates all your named reports in one place, it's helpful when you create reports from different areas of a worksheet or even multiple worksheets in the same workbook. If you hide areas of the worksheet with a custom view for reporting purposes, for example, Excel remembers how that report was structured.

Note

You must define custom views before you can print multiple sets of data from the same worksheet; that is, sets that involve hiding rows/columns manually or via outlining and filtering. (The Report Manager doesn't store these settings directly.)

Report Manager is an add-in program that comes with Excel. If the Report Manager option doesn't appear on the View menu (you may need to wait a few seconds to see the full menu if you're using the personal menu feature), choose Tools, Add-Ins, select the Report Manager in the Add-Ins dialog box, and click OK. If prompted, indicate that you want to install the Report Manager immediately, and insert the Excel or Office CD used to install your software.

To add a report, follow these steps:

1. Choose View, Report Manager. In the Report Manager dialog box, click Add.

2. In the Add Report dialog box, provide a name for your custom report (see Figure 17.18).

3. Create a report by filling in the information in the dialog box. The following list describes the options:

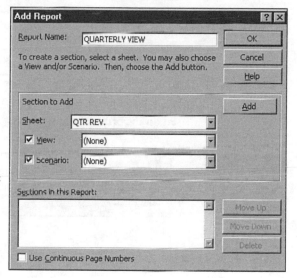

PART

VI

CH

17

   - **Report Name.** Creates a name for the custom report.

   - **Section to Add.** Enables you to select a section to add from the workbook to the report being created.

Figure 17.18.

   - **Sheet.** Enables you to select the sheet containing the data you want included in the section.

   - **View.** Selects a custom view from the selected sheet for the section that you want to add.

   - **Scenario.** Adds a named scenario to the report.

→ For details on using scenarios, **see** "Using Solver," **p. 646**

   - **Add.** After you select your criteria, click Add to add it to the Sections in this Report list.

- **Sections in This Report.** Shows the sections in the report in the order that they will be printed (see Figure 17.19).

- **Move Up.** Adjusts the section order by moving the selected section up.

- **Move Down.** Adjusts the section order by moving the selected section down.

- **Delete.** Deletes the selected section.

- **Use Continuous Page Numbers.** When checked, uses continuous page numbers on printed reports, based on the order of the sections.

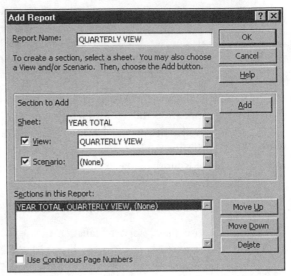

Figure 17.19.

EXCEL IN PRACTICE

There are proper and improper ways to structure a list. Figure 17.20 shows a list with some problems:

- Mixed lowercase and uppercase text, which makes the list difficult to read and draws the audience's attention from the field names to the body of the list.

- The codes shouldn't be placed in separate rows; they should have their own field column and be associated with each record item in the list.

- First and last names are combined into one field, which means that you couldn't sort this list in order by last name.

A good test is to make sure that each line item can stand on its own, giving complete and accurate information per row.

Week	Name	Project	Reg Hours	OT Hours	DT Hours
CODE 22					
2/10/98	Andy Fisher	SKOAL CREEK	40	0	0
2/10/98	Ralph Solvang	SKOAL CREEK	16	0	0
CODE 30					
2/10/98	John Steven	SKOAL CREEK	40	0	0
2/19/98	Bill Cole	SKOAL CREEK	32	0	0
2/10/98	Jim Miller	SKOAL CREEK	38.5	0	0
2/10/98	Tim Valcon	SKOAL CREEK	24	0	0
2/10/98	Steve Witmar	SKOAL CREEK	16	0	0
2/10/98	Will Kiddlestein	SKOAL CREEK	40	5	0
CODE 40					
2/10/98	Scott Villmar	SKOAL CREEK	11	0	0
2/10/98	Chris Heisberg	SKOAL CREEK	38	0	0
CODE 50					
2/10/98	Dave Grust	SKOAL CREEK	28	0	0
2/10/98	Dustin Wilmberg	SKOAL CREEK	1	0	0

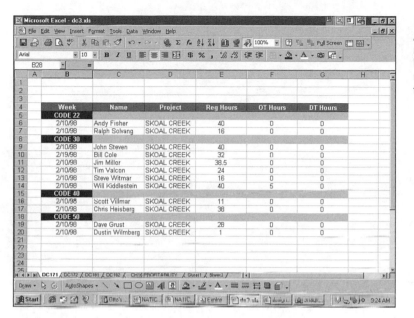

Figure 17.20.
At first glance, this list may seem adequate, but the setup will make it difficult to use.

Figure 17.21 shows a revised version of the list. The field divisions and formatting are consistent, and each record is complete—with date, code, first name, last name, project, and hours. You can now convert this list into a PivotTable for summation, or easily extract information with formulas.

WEEK OF	CODE	FIRST	LAST	PROJECT	REG HOURS	OT HOURS	DT HOURS
2/10/98	30	JOHN	STEVEN	SKOAL CREEK	40	0	0
2/19/98	30	BILL	COLE	SKOAL CREEK	32	0	0
2/10/98	40	SCOTT	VILLMAR	SKOAL CREEK	11	0	0
2/10/98	40	CHRIS	HEISBERG	SKOAL CREEK	38	0	0
2/10/98	30	JIM	MILLER	SKOAL CREEK	38.5	0	0
2/10/98	30	TIM	VALCON	SKOAL CREEK	24	0	0
2/10/98	50	DAVE	GRUST	SKOAL CREEK	28	0	0
2/10/98	50	DUSTIN	WILMBERG	SKOAL CREEK	1	0	0
2/10/98	22	ANDY	FISHER	SKOAL CREEK	40	0	0
2/10/98	22	RALPH	SOLVANG	SKOAL CREEK	16	0	0
2/10/98	30	STEVE	WITMAR	SKOAL CREEK	16	0	0
2/10/98	30	WILL	KIDLESTEIN	SKOAL CREEK	40	5	0

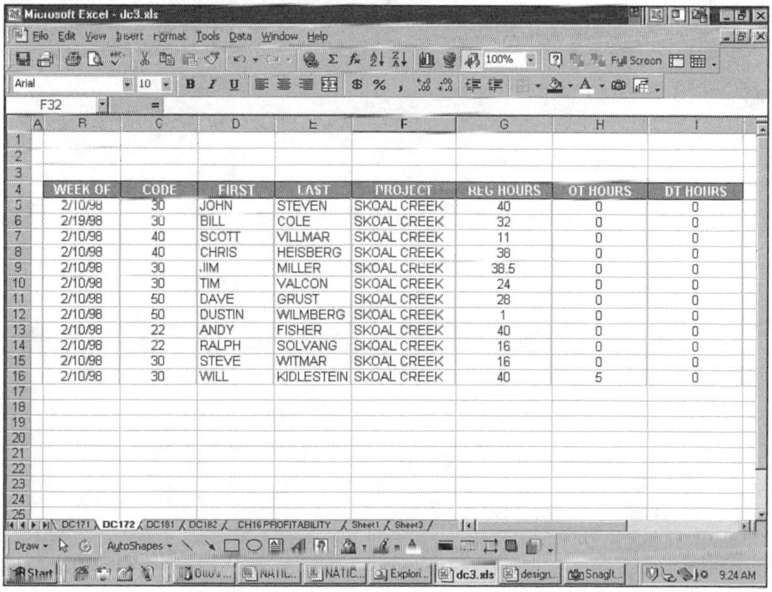

Figure 17.21.
A clean, well-organized list improves the processes of both input and output.

CHAPTER 18

USING EXCEL'S DATA-MANAGEMENT FEATURES

In this chapter

by Patrick D. Blattner
Patrick@BlattnerBooks.com

DATA MANAGEMENT IN EXCEL

Management of data in an Excel workbook shouldn't be time-consuming. This chapter discusses tools available within Excel that will enable you to manage both your time and data efficiently. From extracting information with formulas, to using built-in sorting and filtering tools created specifically for managing worksheet data and lists, to tracking changes in worksheets shared among multiple users, Excel gives you every option necessary to effectively use your time and get the most out of your Excel data. The last section in this chapter also covers a topic close to the heart of any information manager—preventing the loss of important data by protecting workbook contents.

USING CONDITIONAL FORMATTING WITH LISTS

Conditional formatting (page 550) can be a great way to call out specific information within a list, or plot out timelines (discussed in Chapter 23, "Innovative Ways to Use Excel"). The key when using conditional formats is to use a format to call out specific bits of information; for example, you can use it to call out "not to exceed" information or negative numbers.

The example in Figure 18.1 uses an interactive conditional format; when a state is entered in cell D3, the conditional format highlights the cells in the list that match the entry. When you enter a project name in this cell, the conditional formatting highlights the cells referring to that project within the list. Cell E3 contains a formula that then adds the numbers in column E (the Tons column) for the highlighted list entries. The key is to use the Excel tools in innovative ways to make your everyday tasks easier. By combining conditional formatting with a formula, a single entry in cell D3 yields two results: The specified project entries are highlighted in the list, and the tonnage for that project is totaled in cell E3. You can use up to three conditional formats within a list.

Figure 18.1.
By knowing how to use conditional formats, you can call out all references to the information entered in one cell.

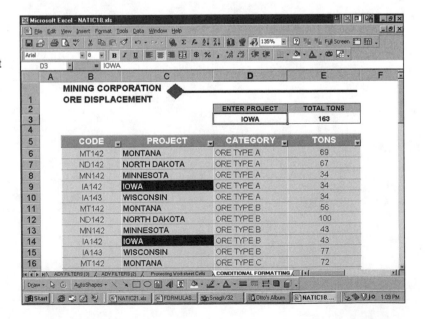

To create an interactive conditional format, follow these steps:

1. Select the list range to which you want to apply the conditional format.

2. Choose Format, Conditional Formatting.

3. In the Conditional Formatting dialog box, choose the first condition you want. For this example, you would choose Equal To from the middle drop-down list in the dialog box, as shown in Figure 18.2.

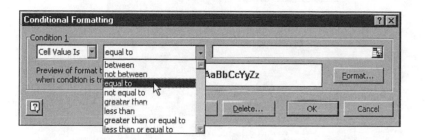

Figure 18.2.
Setting the condition.

4. In the remaining condition box, select the cell to which you want to link your condition (see Figure 18.3).

Figure 18.3.
To set a link for creating an interactive conditional format, enter the cell you want linked to your list.

5. Click the Format button in the Conditional Formatting dialog box.

6. Select the desired format from the three tabs in the Format Cells dialog box. For this example, I selected black shading on the Patterns tab, and made the text bold and white on the Font tab (see Figure 18.4).

7. Click OK. The format is shown in the preview window.

8. If desired, add more criteria by clicking the Add button to add another condition.

9. Make any desired changes and then click OK.

In the sample list, when you enter a project state, the condition applies itself to the list. Any entry in the Project column that matches the value entered in cell D3 will get the conditional formatting set in the Conditional Formatting dialog box (see Figure 18.5).

Figure 18.4.
Format the cells in the
list that meet the
conditional-formatting
criteria.

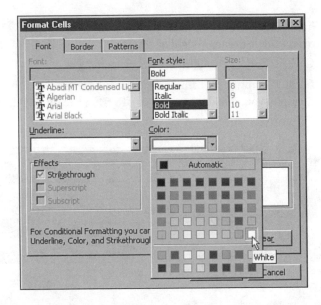

Figure 18.5.
When a project state
is entered, the condi-
tional format operates
based on the trigger
cell D3.

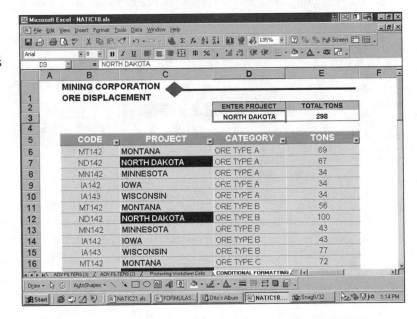

To understand how the formula in cell E3 works, look at the SUM(IF formula in the
Formula bar in Figure 18.6.

Figure 18.6.
With a simple SUM(IF formula, you can add the entries that meet the condition.

The formula sums entries in the range E6:E25 only if the nested IF statement conditions are met. The conditions are that C6:C25 is equal to D3 (that is, the project name matches the entry in cell D3). Notice that the formula appears in braces ({}), indicating that it's an array formula. You enter array formulas by pressing Ctrl+Shift+Enter to activate the array.

Note

An *array formula* performs multiple calculations. The result can be a single result (as in this example) or multiple results. Because the values in the array formula (the *array arguments*) must refer to the same number of rows and columns, this type of formula works well for list data, in which each record has the same number of fields.

SORTING A LIST

After you create your list, you'll want to view your information in different ways. Excel enables you to sort information in multiple ways and even create custom sorts. To sort a list or database, select the information and choose Data, Sort to open the Sort dialog box and specify your sort preferences (see Figure 18.7).

If you don't select anything before opening the Sort dialog box, Excel selects what it assumes is the list—all data contiguous to the active cell, minus the first row, which Excel assumes to be the header row. If your list contains possible blank lines or cells, select the list yourself before starting the sort process, or parts of the list may be excluded from the sort.

If the cell pointer is in a list with no (apparent) header row, Excel selects the No Header Row option. If the list appears to include labels, Excel chooses Header Row and uses the labels as column indicators in the Sort By drop-down lists. When you manually select the data, the sensing feature is disabled. If the automatic selection includes your header row, specify the Header Row option in the Sort dialog box to avoid sorting your field names with the rest of the list (refer to Figure 18.7). If you accidentally end up sorting the field names into the list, use Undo immediately after the sort process to restore the list.

Note

You can sort data in any column or row—it doesn't have to be a list. If you're just beginning a new worksheet, for example, you may start by entering a list of contact names, projects, inventory or catalog numbers, and so on. You can enter this information in random order and then sort it in the same way that you sort a list.

PART
VI
CH
18

Figure 18.7.
Use the Sort dialog box to specify the way you want to sort the list or selection.

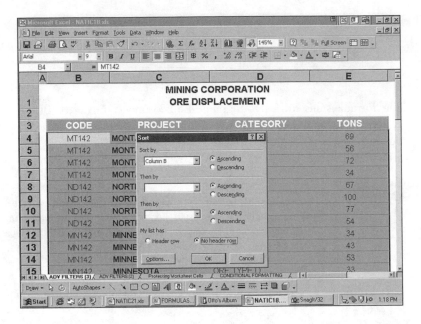

You can sort the list by up to three fields, in *ascending order* (0–9 and A–Z) or *descending order* (9–0 and Z–A). Excel can sort alphabetically, numerically, or by date. By selecting the Options button in the Sort dialog box, you can choose to sort left-to-right rather than the default top-to-bottom sort, in case your list has a horizontal rather than vertical orientation (see Figure 18.8). You can also make the sort case-sensitive—that is, sort such entries as *Oak* and *oak* separately because one is capitalized and the other isn't. In a case-sensitive sort, *Oak* would come before *oak* because capital letters are sorted above lowercase letters. (For details, see the later sidebar "Understanding Excel Sort Sequences.")

Figure 18.8.
The Sort Options dialog box enables you to sort a list from top to bottom or left to right, depending on your list setup.

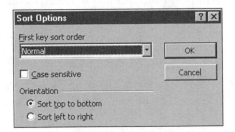

If your list is located contiguous to other data that isn't part of the list, or if you're sorting selected data that isn't part of a list at all, Excel may warn you that you may not have selected the entire list and ask whether you meant to include all the contiguous data (see Figure 18.9). The assumption is that the entire list is contiguous, and that nothing else is located next to the list.

Note

Excel does not always warn you about this, particularly if the list isn't the only data on the sheet.

Figure 18.9.
This dialog box indicates that the selection may not include the entire list.

If you meant to include all the contiguous data, accept the default setting, Expand the Selection; otherwise, choose Continue with the Current Selection.

Understanding Excel Sort Sequences

If you're unfamiliar with how computers "think," you may be surprised by the way in which Excel sorts your data. Excel sorts left-to-right, character-by-character, beginning with numbers first, then spaces, symbols, and finally letters. If your list contains names that include spaces, Excel may not sort them the way you would expect (or prefer). For example, consider the following list of names:

List	Sorted
McArdle	Mc Ardle
Mc Ardle	Mc Lean
McCandle	McArdle
Mc Lean	McCandle

Because Mc Lean includes a space, it falls before any names beginning with Mc that don't include a space. When sorting, Excel ignores apostrophes (in names such as H'ailea, for example), but sorts words with hyphens (–) to last position after the same word with no hyphen. For example, consider the following list of names that differ only in that one includes a space and one includes a hyphen.

List	Sorted
Barkley-North	Barkley North
Barkley North	BarkleyNorth
BarkleyNorth	Barkley-North

The name with the space comes first, followed by the one with no space, and last of all the name containing a hyphen.

You also may be baffled by sorts that include numbers with letters. If your part numbers run from B1 through B102, for example, this is how Excel sorts them:

```
B1
B10
B100
B101
```

continues

continued

```
B102
B11
B12
B13
B14
B15
B16
B17
B18
B19
B2
B20
B21
. . .
```

If you want the part numbers to sort correctly, insert zeros when numbering: B001, B002, and so on.

Excel uses the following sort sequence: 0–9 (space) ! " # $ % & ( ) *, . / : ; ? @ [\ ] ^ _ ` { | } ~ + < = > A–Z.

Blank cells or rows (depending on the sort selection) are sorted to the bottom of the list, whether you sort in descending or ascending order. When sorting values, note that FALSE comes before TRUE, and error values are all equal (but note that they appear in the original order in which they occurred). Ascending sorts place errors at the bottom; descending sorts place them at the top.

Based on custom lists you may have created, you also can define the first key sort order from the drop-down menu in the Sort Options dialog box.

Figure 18.10 shows the list sorted in ascending order by column D, CATEGORY.

Figure 18.10.
Based on the sort defined, Excel sorted the corresponding list by category in ascending order.

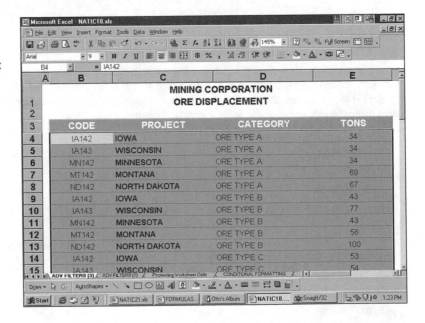

You can combine sorts to get the information the way you want it. For example, a common scenario would be sorting a customer list numerically by purchase, and then alphabetically by name, and perhaps including a third sort by contact name.

The Sort Ascending and Sort Descending buttons on the Standard toolbar sort by the first column in any selection. If you select the whole list and want to sort based on the first column, this is a quick method. But don't select a single column (field) of your data for sorting without selecting the rest of the fields. Excel will sort that field only, separating those entries from the rest of the data in each record.

Because the Sort Ascending and Sort Descending buttons sort based on the position of the active cell, if you don't select any data—perhaps you merely clicked somewhere in the column by which you want the list sorted—the column containing the active cell becomes the sort key.

Reusing Sort Ascending and Sort Descending repeats any sorting options used previously.

FILTERING A LIST

Lists grow quickly, and soon locating a particular record in the list may take more time than you like. When you just want to view a particular record or records, *filtering* the list enables you to display only the selected information you want to see. The list itself is unchanged; you use the filter to specify exactly which data you want to see at that particular moment, and hide the remaining records. You can change the filter at any time to display a different set of records. The filtered records can be formatted, edited, and even charted. The active filter is saved with the workbook. (Note, however, that Excel allows only one list at a time to be filtered on a worksheet.)

Excel offers two types of filtering. An *AutoFilter* applies an automatic (simple) selection filter to the list, which you then can customize. An *advanced filter* enables you to specify more elaborate criteria for filtering.

> **Note**
>
> Filtering demonstrates a major reason for consistent data entry. Entries that are typed inconsistently (for example, *Evans' Plumbing* and *Evans Plumbing*) are treated as two different items by the filter. Excel will not treat them as one and the same.

> **Tip #230 from**
>
> *Patrick*
>
> The fastest method of filtering a list is to use the AutoFilter button. You can add this button to any toolbar, as described in Chapter 28, "Customizing Excel to Fit Your Working Style."

MANAGING THE LIST WITH AUTOFILTERS

To apply an AutoFilter to a list, select a cell in the list and choose <u>D</u>ata, <u>F</u>ilter, Auto<u>F</u>ilter (see Figure 18.11). This command is a toggle; repeat it to turn off the AutoFilter at any time.

In a list with an AutoFilter, Excel displays arrow buttons for each entry in the header row (see Figure 18.12). These buttons activate pull-down menus that allow you to show individual records for viewing one at time or multiple records with the same entry in that particular field—for example, all records that list Minnesota as the project name or all records with ore type D as the category.

When you first set up an AutoFilter, Excel displays the AutoFilter buttons on the column headings but leaves the entire list displayed. To display a filtered list of records, use a button or combination of buttons. To display the records just mentioned, you would click the AutoFilter button in the PROJECT field name cell and select MINNESOTA, or use the CATEGORY button and select ORE TYPE D.

Figure 18.11.
AutoFiltering a list.

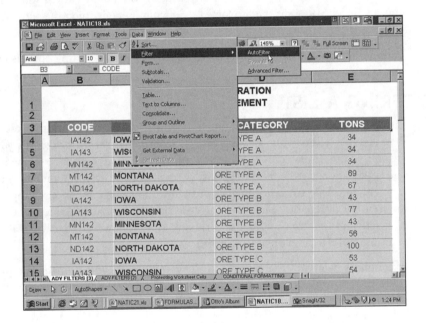

Using more than one AutoFilter button creates a combined filter. In the Mining Corporation example, selecting MINNESOTA in the PROJECT column narrows the displayed records to just those referring to the Minnesota project. If you then use the CATEGORY button to select ORE TYPE D, Excel displays only MINNESOTA records that list ORE TYPE D in the CATEGORY column, as shown in Figure 18.13. The arrows change color on the AutoFilter buttons that are currently in use—from black to blue.

The items at the top and bottom of the AutoFilter drop-down list provide special filtering options, as described in the following list:

- **(All).** Lists all the records in that category. Use this option to redisplay the entire list after filtering for selected records.

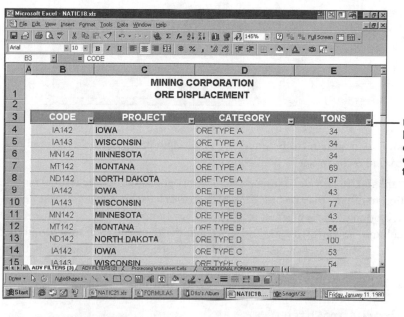

Figure 18.12.
By placing filters on a list, you can narrow the list to any level.

Use the AutoFilter button to open a drop-down list of choices for filtering that column.

Figure 18.13.
This AutoFilter combination displays only the single ORE TYPE D record for the MINNESOTA project.

■ **(Top 10…).** Applies only to columns containing numbers or dates. Displays the Top 10 AutoFilter dialog box, in which you can specify that you want to see the records at the top or bottom of the list numerically (see Figure 18.14). You aren't limited to 10 records; you can specify that you want to see just the top or bottom (1) record, 50 records, or any number you prefer. To display the top or bottom 10% (or 15%, 50%, and so on) of your records, change the setting in the third combo box from Items to Percent.

Note

The Top 10 AutoFilter doesn't sort the displayed records, but you can select and sort them with the Data, Sort command if you want to see them in numeric order—for example, to list former employees in order by termination date.

■ **(Custom…).** Displays the Custom AutoFilter dialog box, in which you can specify a more detailed filtering option. (See the next section for details.)

Figure 18.14.
Use the Top 10 AutoFilter dialog box to display a selected number of records.

- **(Blanks).** Displays the records containing blanks in a particular field (column). Use this option to find records that have missing entries.

- **(NonBlanks).** Displays all records containing any entries in that field (nonblanks). Use this option to display only records for which entries have been made in that field—for example, a nonprofit organization may enter contributions for the current year in a particular column. Records with such listings could then be displayed, sorted, and merged with an end-of-year letter to donors regarding tax deductibility of contributions.

The (Blanks) and (NonBlanks) entries appear only if the column contains empty cells.

CREATING A CUSTOM AUTOFILTER

If the default AutoFilter doesn't provide enough options, you can create a *custom AutoFilter*. Follow these steps:

1. From the drop-down AutoFilter list, choose (Custom...), as shown in Figure 18.15.

Figure 18.15.
To create a custom AutoFilter, select the (Custom...) option.

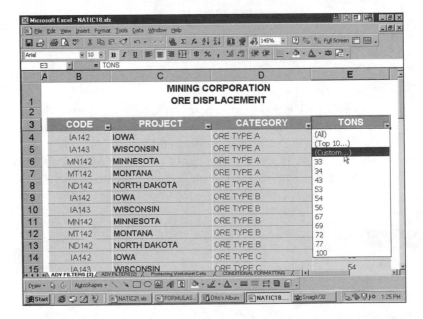

2. In the Custom AutoFilter dialog box, specify the custom criteria to use for filtering your list. Figure 18.16 shows the criteria for selecting records with values between two specified points—greater than 34 and less than 56.

3. Click OK.

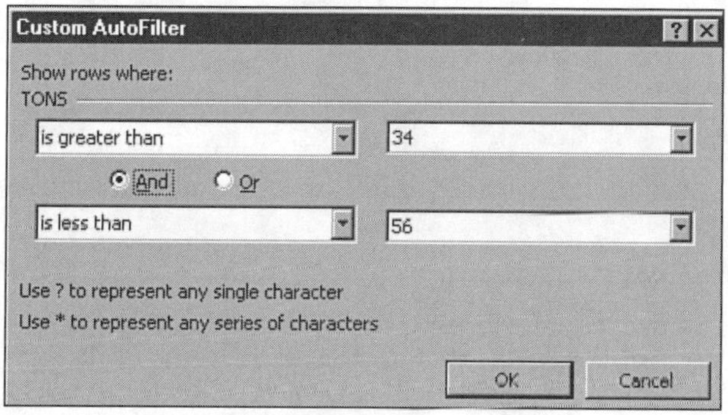

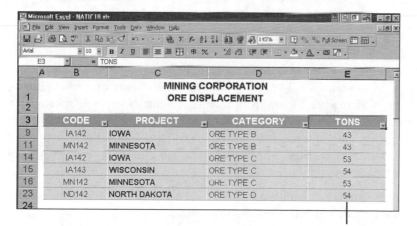

Figure 18.16.
The Custom AutoFilter dialog box enables you to display only records that meet the specified criteria.

Only records within the specified range show up in the filtered list (see Figure 18.17). You can customize the filtering even more by creating additional custom AutoFilters for other fields in the list.

Figure 18.17.
Only records matching the custom AutoFilter criteria are displayed.

Only records of the specified tonnage are shown.

To display more than one type of entry in a particular field—for example, to display entries for two different projects in the Mining Corporation list—enter the first criterion (the *comparison operator*) in the first set of boxes in the Custom AutoFilter dialog box; then enter the value criterion in the second set of boxes. Select the And button if you want the selected row(s) to meet both sets of criteria; select Or if you want records that meet either of the criteria. Figure 18.18 shows how to set the custom AutoFilter to display both the Minnesota and Wisconsin projects. For this example, you could use either contains or equals as the operator (see the following tip).

Figure 18.18.
Use the Or button if you want Excel to display records that meet either of the criteria in this dialog box.

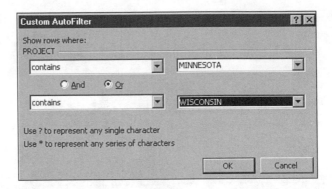

Tip #231 from

You can use wildcard characters to select records in which the entries vary by a single character (?) or multiple characters (*). To find entries that begin with the same character(s)—for example, anyone named *Smith, Smithe, Smythe,* and so on—search for records that contain *Sm**. To find records in which the apostrophe is missing from *Evans' Plumbing,* search for *Evans?Plumbing,* which would display the incorrect *Evans Plumbing* but not the correct *Evans' Plumbing.*

Be careful when using `equals` versus `contains` as the comparison operator. Using `equals` in the previous example will restrict the filter to names starting with *Sm*. Using `contains` will also filter *Desmond* and *Chism*, both of which contain the letters *sm*.

USING THE ADVANCED FILTER

An *advanced filter* is similar to a custom AutoFilter. The difference is that you create a *criteria range* outside the list—using the field names in the header row—and then specify the criteria on which you want to filter. Figure 18.19 shows the Mining Corporation list with a criteria range set up in D3:E4. Notice that the criteria range includes the column heading (field name) above the specified criteria. To use an advanced filter, your list must include field names for use in the criteria range. The worksheet also must include at least one blank row between the criteria range and the list.

The field names in the criteria range must match the field names in the list exactly, except for case (*Category* and *category* will both work, for example).

Tip #232 from

Copy the field names to the criteria range rather than typing them, to prevent errors.

Figure 18.19.
The criteria range determines the displayed entries in the list.

Tip #233 from

Prior to starting the advanced filter, select the list and assign it the range name Database. If you plan to extract filtered records to a different area of the worksheet, select that area also and give it the range name Extract. Excel automatically uses these named ranges in the Advanced Filter dialog box. The Criteria range name is automatically created/redefined each time you specify a criteria range, so there's no need to name this range yourself.

To create an advanced filter, follow these steps:

1. Create the criteria range, specifying the field names in one row and the desired criteria directly below. If possible, place the criteria range above the corresponding columns that you plan to filter for easy viewing of both.

2. To specify multiple criteria, add more rows to the criteria range.

3. When the criteria range is complete, click in the list and choose Data, Filter, Advanced Filter to open the Advanced Filter dialog box (see Figure 18.20).

4. Excel selects the list automatically if it's bounded by blank rows and columns. If the range in the List Range box is incorrect, specify the correct range.

5. Specify the criteria range.

6. Click OK to run the filter. Figure 18.21 shows the result in the Mining Corporation example.

Figure 18.20.
The Advanced Filter dialog box enables you to select the list range and criteria range.

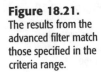

Figure 18.21.
The results from the advanced filter match those specified in the criteria range.

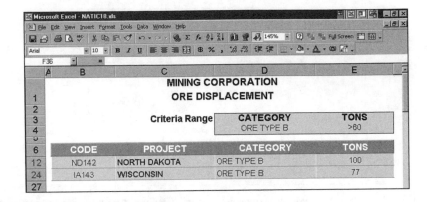

To show the entire list again, select <u>D</u>ata, <u>F</u>ilter, Show All.

Use the Advanced Filter when you need to do any of the following:

- Perform an Or condition across multiple fields.
- Specify more than two criteria in one field.
- Handle extremely complex criteria, requiring the use of functions/formulas, as well as multiple And/Or criteria in one filter.

You can change the entries in the criteria range at any point to display a different set of filtered records. The list responds automatically to the new specifications.

COPYING RECORDS TO A NEW LOCATION

When you use an advanced filter, you can specify a separate location where you want the filtered records copied; for example, to create a separate list of former clients. Select the C<u>o</u>py to Another Location option in the Advanced Filter dialog box and specify the target cell or range in the Copy <u>T</u>o box. Excel will copy just the filtered records to the new location.

SELECTING UNIQUE RECORDS

If your list contains names or records that appear repeatedly, you may want to extract just the unique records. For example, in a list that includes state information, you might want to know how many states are represented in the list. To display only the unique records (a single record of each type), select the Unique <u>R</u>ecords Only option in the Advanced Filter dialog box. Excel hides all the duplicates.

PROTECTING YOUR DATA

Putting together an efficient worksheet—whether it contains simple tables, database lists, charts, or elaborate formulas and functions—requires some time and effort. All this work can be undone with a few keystrokes, however, by an inexperienced or inattentive user.

To prevent data disasters, Excel enables you to protect the workbook, worksheet, ranges, formulas, or single cells in a workbook. Note the following caution, however!

Caution

> Although you can protect cells within a workbook, if you have vital information hidden or protected, advanced Excel users can unprotect and disclose the hidden information. The only way to protect vital information is to protect the workbook, so a password is needed before a workbook is ever opened.

Excel provides multiple levels of protection to keep your data protected:

- The simplest method is to hide rows, columns, or even the whole worksheet or workbook. Of course, because Excel users learn quickly how to *hide (page 470)* and *unhide (page 583)* cells, hiding provides very little real protection.

- Locking cells prevents accidental or deliberate alteration or deletion of the locked cells. This technique is helpful for worksheets that will be used by one person or shared among only trusted users; unlocking cells is very easy (as described in the following section).

- Protecting the workbook with a password is the best method, but of course you must remember the password. Others should know the password as well, in case something happens to you.

The following sections provide details on these protection methods.

PROTECTING SELECTED WORKBOOK CELLS

The most common reason for protecting cells in a workbook is to prevent accidental deletion or alteration of information such as formulas, which provide vital calculations to the worksheet, workbook, or even other workbooks or documents.

Suppose you have a workbook like the one shown in Figure 18.22. As you can see from the [Shared] indicator in the title bar, this workbook is shared among multiple users, which makes it a prime candidate for unintentional changes. In this example, you might want to protect the formula cells in the range F4:F12, so that no one can edit or clear these cells accidentally.

Follow these steps:

1. Select the whole worksheet.
2. Choose Format, Cells to open the Format Cells dialog box.
3. Click the Protection tab and deselect the Locked option. (This option has no effect unless the worksheet is protected.) Deselecting the Locked option enables you to select a specific range or cell and then lock it.
4. If desired, hide the cell content or formula by checking the Hidden option at this time as well.

Figure 18.22.
To protect cells in a worksheet, unlock the worksheet and then lock the range containing the formulas.

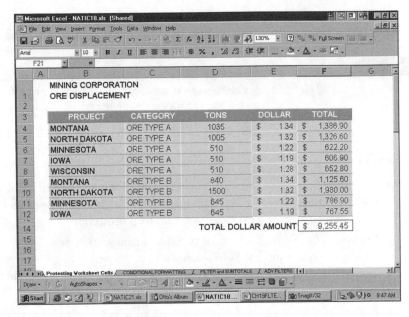

5. After making your selections, click OK.

6. Select the range you want to protect.

7. Choose Format, Cells to reopen the Format Cells dialog box.

8. Select the Locked option on the Protection tab (see Figure 18.23).

Figure 18.23.
To protect the range of cells that contain the formulas, select the range and check the Locked option on the Protection tab in the Format Cells dialog box.

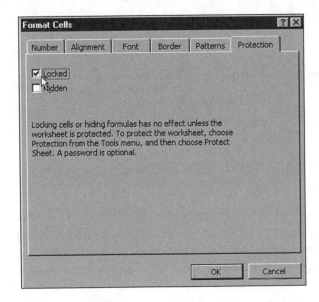

9. Choose Tools, Protection, Protect Sheet. The Protect Sheet dialog box appears and allows you to enter a password; however, the password entry is optional (see Figure 18.24).

Figure 18.24.
With password protection, you can make changes to the protected cells only if the worksheet password is entered and the cells are then unprotected.

HIDING FORMULAS

You can hide formulas within a workbook. To hide formulas, repeat the steps previously discussed; however, choose the Hidden option on the Protection tab in the Format Cells dialog box. Then reprotect the workbook with a password by choosing Tools, Protection.

PASSWORD-PROTECTING A WORKBOOK

You can apply a password to a workbook that will allow only users with the password to open and view the workbook. Password-protecting the workbook is the only fail-proof way of protecting vital information within a workbook. As mentioned previously in this chapter, advanced users can unprotect all other protection devices within Excel (very advanced users can even get past the workbook password, but this feature will provide enough coverage for most situations).

To protect the workbook so that a password is needed before the workbook is opened, follow these steps:

1. With the workbook that you want to password-protect onscreen and active, choose File, Save As.

2. In the Save As dialog box, click the Tools button to display the drop-down menu, and choose General Options.

3. In the Save Options dialog box, enter the password in the Password to Open box (see Figure 18.25). Without the password, the user will be unable to open the file at all.

4. If you want a separate password to be required for editing the file, enter that password in the Password to Modify box. With this option, the user may be able to open the file, but can't change workbook contents unless the password is entered.

   For additional protection, you can enter passwords in both the Password to Open and Password to Modify boxes.

PART

VI

CH

18

Figure 18.25.
The Save Options dialog box enables you to apply a password to a workbook so that the workbook can be opened only after the password is entered.

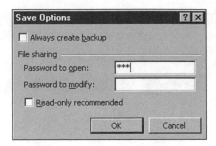

5. In addition to the password options, you can select the following settings:

   ■ **Always Create Backup**. Creates a backup copy of the file every time the file is saved. This is primarily a backup device in case a file is deleted or becomes corrupt.

   ■ **Read-Only Recommended**. When opening the file, the user is asked whether he or she wants to open the file as read-only. If Yes is selected, changes made to the file must be saved under a different name.

6. When the settings are complete, click OK.

7. In the Confirm Password dialog box, reenter the password to verify the correct password.

8. Click OK to close the Confirm Password dialog box and return to the Save As dialog box.

9. Specify a filename and path for the file, if necessary, and click Save.

10. Click Yes to replace the old version of the file with the new password-protected version (unless this is a first-time save or you're saving the file with a different name).

PROTECTING A SHARED WORKBOOK

If you have a workbook that's shared by many people, you'll find it helpful to use the *Track Changes* feature for tracking edits from the other users that occur within the workbook. Excel also enables you to share a workbook and track changes where the tracked changes can't be removed because a password is entered. If the workbook is shared, you first must remove the shared status of the workbook in order to proceed.

To protect and share a workbook with tracked changes, select Tools, Protection, Protect and Share Workbook to display the Protect Shared Workbook dialog box. Check the Sharing with Track Changes option, and enter a password if desired.

TROUBLESHOOTING

SELECTING A RECORD THAT APPEARS MULTIPLE TIMES IN A LIST

How can I filter a record that appears multiple times within a list?

Select the column range with the multiple records you want to filter. Then choose Data, Filter, Advanced Filter. In the Advanced Filter dialog box, check Unique Records Only. This will filter the list with the unique records that appear in the list.

PASTING CONDITIONAL FORMATS OVER MULTIPLE ROWS

When I create a conditional format in a row that equals a cell in that same row, how do I copy the conditional format down, equaling the corresponding cell in the same row pasted?

From the Conditional Formatting dialog box, select Cell Value Is, equal to, and then the cell in the corresponding row. Remove the dollar sign ($) in front of the row number to make it relative instead of absolute. Now the format will copy down, equaling a cell in the corresponding row.

PROTECTING VITAL INFORMATION

What's the best way to protect my data in Excel?

Save the workbook with a password! Choose File, Save As to open the Save As dialog box. Then open the Tools drop-down menu and choose General Options. From here, you have the option of protecting the workbook with a password.

EXCEL IN PRACTICE

Excel offers multiple ways to manage information and add up information in a list. Consider the two methods used here. The first, shown in Figure 18.26, sums up individual cells by selecting the cells. This technique is inefficient and time-consuming. Now look at the formula in Figure 18.27. By using a SUM(IF formula, you can type the project state in cell D3, and the total tonnage will be extracted automatically.

Figure 18.26.
This SUM formula will work, but it's inefficient and time-consuming to create.

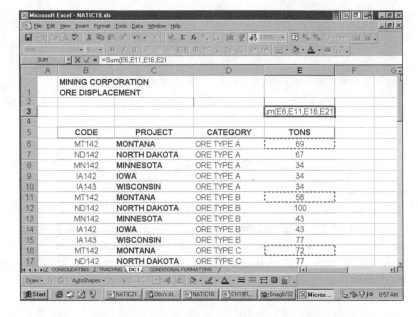

Figure 18.27.
The SUM(IF formula in cell E3 (shown in the Formula bar) efficiently reviews the data in the list to find data matching the entry in cell D3, and sums the results.

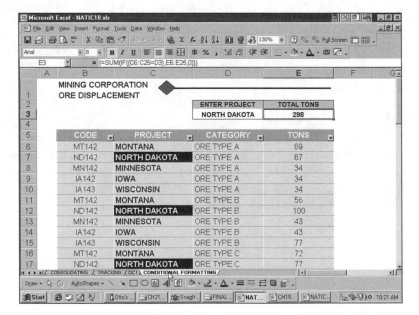

CHAPTER 19

OUTLINING, SUBTOTALING, AND AUDITING WORKSHEET DATA

by Patrick D. Blattner
Patrick@BlattnerBooks.com

In this chapter

ORGANIZING AND AUDITING YOUR DATA

As mentioned often in other chapters of this book, structuring the data in your workbooks is essential to using them effectively. Structure is particularly crucial if you plan to extract, chart, pivot, or create reports from the data. If the worksheet is put together randomly, without good planning, reorganizing it later can cost a lot of time and frustration. When a worksheet is well structured, on the other hand, you can take full advantage of Excel's data-management features to display, print, and report precisely what you want.

Chapter 18 describes the Excel options for *sorting (page 513)*, *filtering (page 513)*, and *protecting (page 521)* your data. This chapter continues with data-management features by providing details on outlining and grouping, consolidating, and using data validation and auditing to help prevent, locate, and correct data errors.

GROUPING AND OUTLINING DATA

Outlining and *grouping* are two of Excel's data-management features. They're very similar. You can use grouping to effectively manage columns and rows with multiple levels of groups that display and hide information. Grouping data is different from outlining in that groups are defined to any depth, level, and location you want. An outline, on the other hand, is based on a structured list or table that has totals and subsets already built in.

Note

When structuring a workbook or database, don't move forward with the intention of just starting to create, and planning to incorporate the functionality as your needs grow. Outlines and groups are created from structure. If your list has no structure, your outline has little or no meaning for the user.

To outline a list or table, I always work backward from the list and ask the question, "What information do I need to extract from the list?" If possible, write down the information and even how it's presented. This will help you work backward in planning the structure of the list.

Before launching into using the grouping and outlining features, you may want to create a custom toolbar for use with these features. Excel offers several very useful outlining and grouping toolbar buttons that can be added to any toolbar or used as a separate custom toolbar. The custom toolbar shown in Figure 19.1 includes buttons for creating, showing, and selecting visible cells in an outline or group. These buttons all come from the Data category on the Commands tab in the Customize dialog box. Another helpful item that you could include is the Group and Outline menu from the Built-in Menus category on the same tab.

Table 19.1 describes the buttons on this custom toolbar. (You can include the buttons on any toolbar, of course, but I've found it helpful to combine these functions in one place.)

Figure 19.1.
This custom toolbar shows tools in Excel useful for establishing outlines and managing the group and outline symbols.

TABLE 19.1. OUTLINING/GROUPING TOOLBAR BUTTONS

Button	Name	Description
	Show Outline Symbols	Shows the outline symbols along the rows and columns
	Group	Groups the selected rows or columns
	Ungroup	Ungroups the selected rows or columns
	Show Detail	Shows the detail by unhiding the hidden groups for the selected row or column
	Hide Detail	Hides the detail of the selected row or column
	Select Visible Cells	Selects or highlights only the visible cells

→ For details on customizing the Excel toolbars, **see** "Modifying Toolbars," **p. 869**

GROUPING DATA

If Excel data contains common attributes, you can *group* the data to make it more readable. In the table in Figure 19.2, for example, the common groups are the months and then the quarters. This *hierarchical grouping* can be done with days, weeks, months, quarters, and years. You also can reduce the list to lower levels, even minutes or seconds.

By creating a group, you can combine multiple rows or columns of information, enabling you to hide and show information with one click. To create a group, select the rows or columns you want to group and then choose Data, Group and Outline, Group. In the Group dialog box, specify whether you want to group Rows or Columns. (If you select the entire row/column, you won't get the Group dialog box; the grouping will occur automatically.) *Outline symbols* appear on the left side of the worksheet, as shown in Figure 19.3. By clicking the *outline buttons*, you can hide or display the selected information, as shown in Figure 19.4. Excel calls these techniques *collapsing* and *expanding* the group. An outline button with a plus sign (+) indicates that the group is collapsed to show only the totals. A minus sign (–) indicates that the group is fully expanded.

Figure 19.2.
The table shown is known as a *hierarchical table*. The months are grouped by their respective quarters.

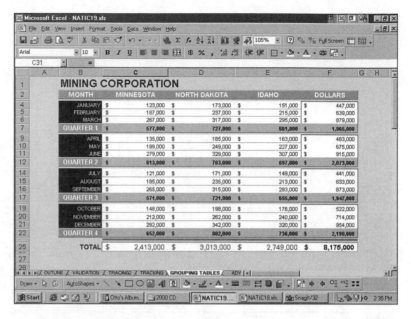

Figure 19.3.
After you create a group, you can hide the group by clicking on the outline buttons shown on the left side of the worksheet.

Clicking a button with a minus sign collapses the group.

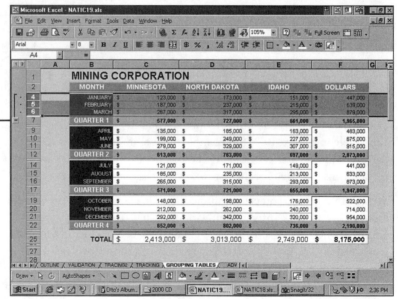

If you group the additional months (refer to Figure 19.2), you can show the quarters or the months by clicking the outline buttons. In addition, you can use the 1 and 2 buttons at the top of the outline area (to the left of the column headings) to control the level of the grouping displayed on the whole list. Click 1 to collapse the entire grouping to show only totals; click 2 to expand the list to show all the supporting rows. Your list may contain additional levels, in which case the buttons would be numbered 3, 4, and so on.

Clicking a button with a plus sign expands the group.   Rows 4–6 are collapsed to show only the total in row 7.

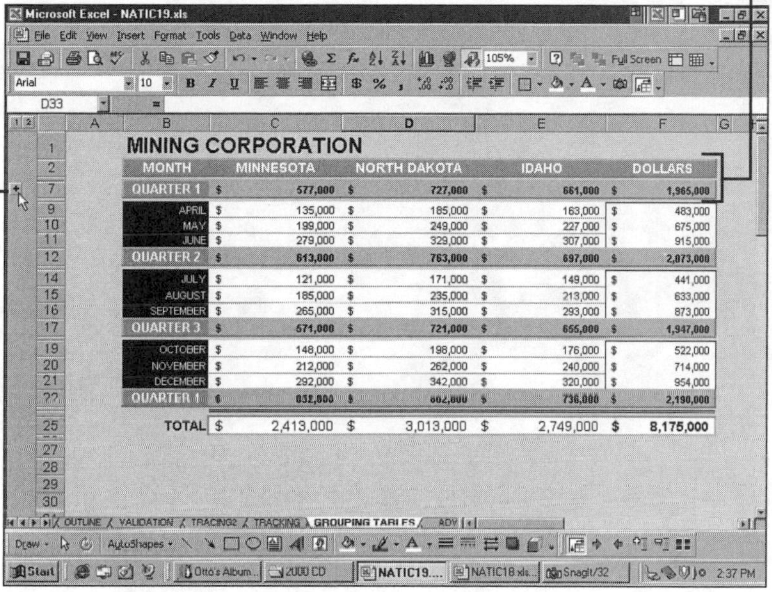

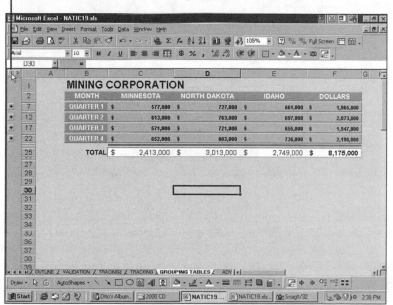

Figure 19.4.
By creating a group, you can collapse (hide) the information so that the quarter is visible and the monthly information above it is hidden.

Notice how effective grouping can be after the groups have been created (see Figure 19.5).

Not only can you group the rows but also the columns, as shown in Figure 19.6. By grouping the columns, you can collapse a view to the maximum—showing only totals—as in Figure 19.7.

Use these buttons to control the level of the grouping on the whole list.

Figure 19.5.
Grouping the quarters enables you to view the summary of quarters, or the months if the groups are expanded.

PART

VI

CH

19

Figure 19.6.
By grouping both rows and columns, you can collapse a list to show only totals.

The outline buttons for columns work in the same way as the buttons for rows, except that they collapse and expand columns.

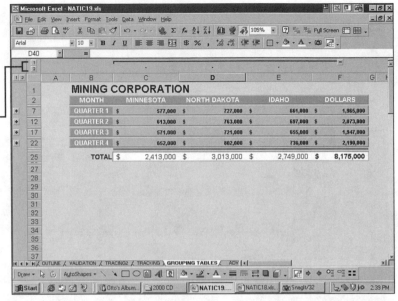

Figure 19.7.
The group now shows the lowest level of detail.

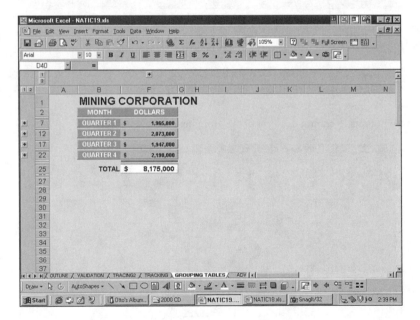

 Excel enables you to add layers of groupings as well. This further enhances the capacity to create hierarchical groups. Notice the additional outline button added to the rows in Figure 19.8. To add an additional layer to the group, select the rows you want to hide, and choose Data, Group and Outline, Group (or click the Group button). Excel applies the group symbols and buttons for the additional layer.

Another level of grouping has been added.

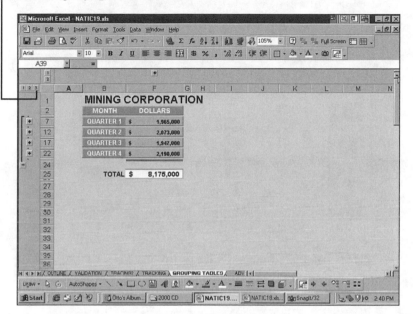

Figure 19.8.
Excel enables you to create groups of groups for multiple-grouping scenarios.

 After your list and groups are in place, you may want to restore the screen space lost to the outline symbols, while still keeping the grouping in place. Use the Show Outline Symbols toolbar button (refer to Table 19.1 in the preceding section) or press Ctrl+8 to hide and show the outline symbols. You also can turn the view of outline symbols off or on by choosing Tools, Options to open the Options dialog box, clicking the View tab, and selecting or deselecting Outline Symbols.

PART
VI

CH

19

GROUPING SUMMARY TABLES

Now that you understand the basic logic of grouping, you can establish multiple summary tables on a single worksheet within a workbook and apply grouping symbols that apply to all the tables. If you have a workbook with several lists, for example, you might want to create one sheet that holds all your summary information. With this technique, you also can create custom views and reports easily and effectively. The key in creating summary tables on one worksheet with combined grouping is to establish similar setups for all the lists you plan to group. In Figure 19.9, for example, the geographic area tables are set up in similar fashion and the outline buttons apply to all.

The groups summarize the information in an effective manner, as shown in Figure 19.10, and can be managed on a single screen at the highest level (see Figure 19.11).

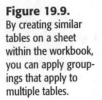

Figure 19.9.
By creating similar tables on a sheet within the workbook, you can apply groupings that apply to multiple tables.

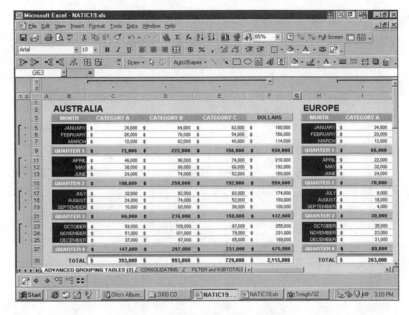

Multiple columns are collapsed.

Figure 19.10.
The groups are collapsed by column.

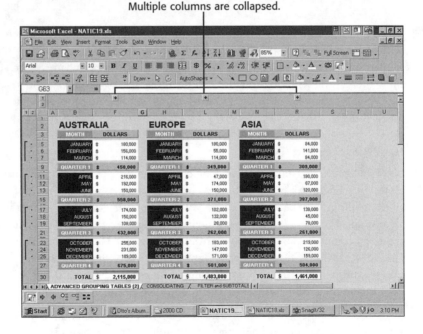

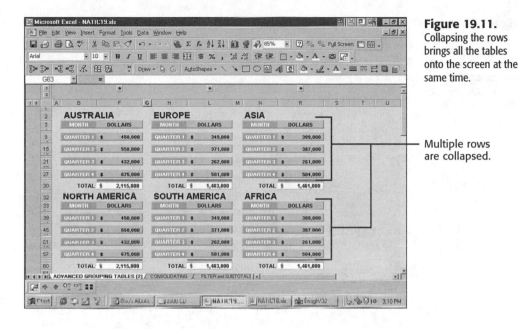

Figure 19.11.
Collapsing the rows
brings all the tables
onto the screen at the
same time.

— Multiple rows
are collapsed.

GROUPING DATA WITH FORMATS

Not only is it important to create consistent structure within an Excel worksheet, it's also important to create formats that visibly tell the story of the worksheet. The lists in Figures 19.12 and 19.13 prove this point. Figure 19.12 is a sea of numbers. In Figure 19.13, the information is identical, but the story becomes clear. If you use structure and formatting well, the numbers can tell a story.

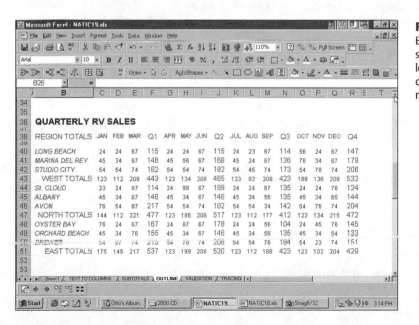

Figure 19.12.
Because this list has
structure but no
logical formatting,
deciphering the infor-
mation is difficult.

Figure 19.13.
The information is the same here as in Figure 19.12; however, the formatted list creates a story, and the structure of the list becomes visible.

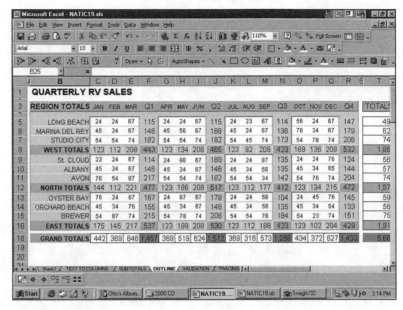

The structure of the list in Figure 19.13 follows simple guidelines. The timeline across the top of the worksheet shows column headings for months and quarter breaks. The city and region breaks are named vertically in the first column of the list. Notice that the spacing is minimized, but this layout still maintains a simple-to-follow grid by using formatting. The interior data has a white background; the remainder of the list is shaded, with the totals and their headings distinguished by boldfacing or a larger font.

→ To learn more about using formatting to distinguish parts of the worksheet, **see** "Combining Excel's Tools for Innovative Formatting," **p. 720**

OUTLINING DATA

Worksheet outlines use the same symbols as groups, but differ in that they're derived from a structured list, with no additional columns or rows. Based on the structure of the list in Figure 19.14, for example, it's easy to see where you can place outlining along the rows and columns. The list's critical information points are highlighted in the figure, with the first group symbol placed to group the first quarter.

 To group selected columns or rows, choose <u>D</u>ata, Group and Outline, <u>G</u>roup, or click the Group toolbar button. The final result of the first level of groups is shown in Figure 19.15. Notice the second-level group in Figure 19.16—it groups the row's regions to roll up a grand total. Excel applies the level buttons to the highest roll-up level; the lower the outline level, the higher the button number.

Tip #234 from

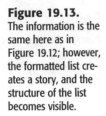

You can group and ungroup a selection, respectively, by pressing Shift+Alt+right arrow and Shift+Alt+left arrow.

The first quarter is grouped.

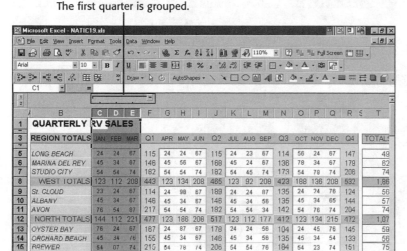

Figure 19.14.
The critical group points to keep visible here are highlighted (columns C through E). The groups are formatted to show the different levels of importance.

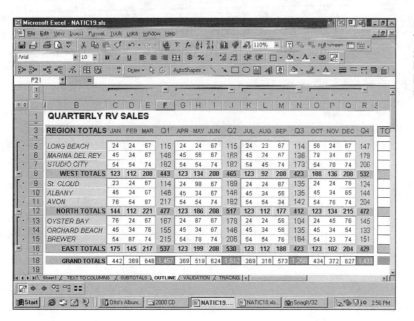

Figure 19.15.
The first level of groups applied in hierarchical fashion by quarters and regions.

PART

VI

CH

19

Figure 19.16.
The second level group applied rolls up the list by regions. Notice the additional level button.

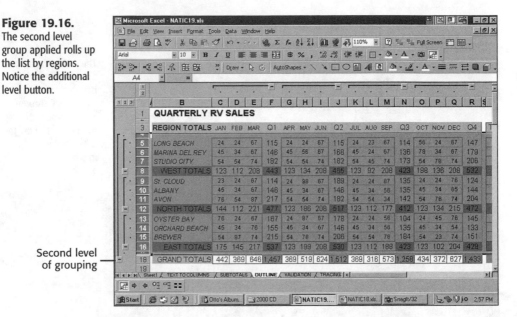

Second level of grouping

CREATING AN AUTO OUTLINE

Another way to outline a list is to use the *Auto Outline* feature. Auto Outline is a quick way to create an outline, but Excel first must understand the hierarchy of your list or database. You can apply all the groupings with one step if the list is structured in a manner that Excel understands. The information must be structured consistently throughout—for example, January, February, March, and then Q1 with no blank columns or rows as separators; then April, May, June, and Q2.

To create a multilevel Auto Outline, select Data, Group and Outline, Auto Outline. Excel applies outline symbols (see Figure 19.17). The active cell doesn't even need to be in the table/data set. You need only select the data if the worksheet includes more than one data set.

The Auto Outline feature depends on Excel's being able to detect the structure of your data automatically. If you get the error message Cannot create an outline, this means Excel doesn't see a logical structure to the data you're trying to outline. But you can place the outline symbols manually—to speed up the process, create the first outline, select the next range of data, and press F4 to repeat the last action.

CLEARING THE OUTLINE

To clear outline symbols, select the range of a single group or outline and use any of the following techniques:

- Choose Data, Group and Outline, Ungroup.
- Click the Ungroup button.

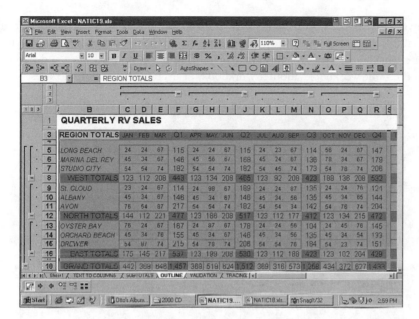

Figure 19.17.
The Auto Outline feature applies outline symbols to the list or table down to the lowest level defined by your list structure.

- Press Shift+Alt+left arrow.
- To eliminate all outlines at once, choose Data, Group and Outline, Clear Outline.

CHANGING THE OUTLINE SETTINGS

You can change the positioning of summary rows in the group or outline and apply Excel's built-in outline styles. Choose Data, Group and Outline, Settings to open the Settings dialog box. Specify whether you want summary rows placed below the detail and columns to the right of the detail (these are the default settings).

To apply Excel's built-in outline cell styles (RowLevel_1, ColLevel_1, and so on), select Automatic Styles in the Settings dialog box.

Clicking Create in the dialog box creates a new outline from the selected data with the settings you have specified in the dialog box. Clicking Apply Styles applies the settings to the existing outline.

CONSOLIDATING DATA

If you establish several lists or tables that have similar setups, you'll probably want to combine certain sets of data from these separate lists or tables into one consolidated list or table. Excel enables you to consolidate tables with the Consolidate command on the Data menu. Consolidation allows for analysis of the tables or lists with functions provided in the Consolidate dialog box.

The best way to consolidate a list or table is to set up a table that represents the format of the original tables, like the example shown in Figure 19.18. Consolidation isn't limited to a worksheet or a workbook—you can consolidate data from the same worksheet, a different worksheet in the same workbook, another workbook, or even from Lotus 1-2-3 files.

Figure 19.18.
When consolidating a list or table (as shown here in the range B21:F28), it's best to set up the consolidation destination with formats similar to those in the source tables.

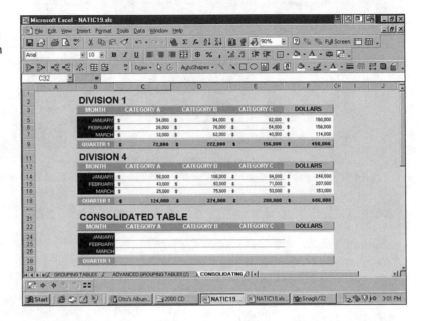

To create a consolidation table, follow these steps:

1. Select the destination for the consolidated data. In the example, the destination cell is C24.

Note

> Don't select multiple cells as the destination unless you're positive that the consolidated data will fit within the selected area; although other existing cells won't necessarily be overwritten, Excel simply may fail to consolidate parts of the source tables.

2. Select Consolidate from the Data menu to open the Consolidate dialog box.
3. Select the type of analysis you want to perform from the Function menu.
4. Under Reference, select the first range you want to include for consolidation. To select the range in the worksheet itself, use the Collapse Dialog button or just drag the dialog box out of the way and click in the worksheet. If the worksheet uses named ranges, you can type the range names in the dialog box, which saves time in selecting.

Consolidation ranges are often found outside the active sheet. You can easily activate another sheet in the current workbook to get to a range there. If the ranges are located in one or more other workbooks, however, open the workbook(s) before starting the consolidation command, and then use the <u>W</u>indow menu to switch to the desired workbook in order to access its ranges.

5. After you establish the range, click the <u>A</u>dd button to add the range to the All References box (see Figure 19.19).

6. If you want the consolidation table to be updated automatically when its source data is changed, select Create Links to <u>S</u>ource Data.

7. Click OK.

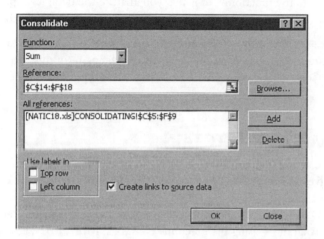

Figure 19.19.
This example uses the SUM function to total the figures for January through March and the quarterly total for Divisions 1 and 4.

The consolidated numbers in the example now reflect the addition of Division 1 and Division 4, as shown in Figure 19.20.

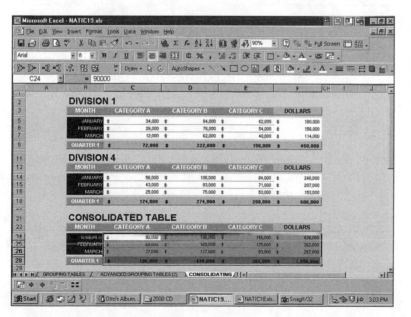

Figure 19.20.
The result of the con-solidated divisions is the addition of the tables because the SUM function was used for analysis.

Tip #235 from

Although matching labels must be identical for the data to consolidate properly, sources that contain different column/row headings can easily be consolidated by using the Use Labels In options in the Consolidate dialog box. Let's say your sources have different row and column headings. You simply include those labels when selecting each source range, turn on both Top Row and Left Column in the dialog box, and both the labels and consolidated data appear in the destination range.

Excel enables you to change the function with which you analyze the data; just open the Consolidate dialog box again, change the setting in the Function box, and click OK.

Consolidation ranges are saved with the workbook, making the refresh process really easy. To refresh the consolidated table, just select the destination cell again (in this example, cell C24) and choose Data, Consolidate again. Verify or change the ranges to consolidate and click OK.

CREATING AUTOMATIC SUBTOTALS

Excel provides automatic subtotaling capability for use with any suitably organized data. Lists often lend themselves to subtotals because the most common question asked after filtering a list is, "How do I total just the visible cells?" In a *filtered (page 491)* list, the Subtotals command on the Data menu subtotals only the visible cells in the list. You can also use subtotaling for other calculations—using the functions COUNT, MAX, MIN, and so on.

Note

To subtotal a filtered list, begin by filtering the list, if desired. For any other kind of subtotaling, simply skip this step. The procedure is the same otherwise.

Tip #236 from

Because a list can vary in size and scope, create the subtotal for use as a quick reference in a place where it won't move and can remain visible at all times—for example, at the top of a list. When you filter the list, the subtotal remains in the same location, which enables you to view the subtotal without scrolling to the bottom of the list.

To add a subtotal to a list, follow these steps:

1. Sort the list (and filter it, if desired), and then select the records. The first sort key you use should be the one you plan to select in the At Each Change In drop-down list in the Subtotal dialog box (see step 3).

Tip #237 from

If your list is surrounded by blank rows and columns, Excel will select the data to subtotal automatically; you don't need to select it before beginning the subtotaling process. The active cell must be somewhere in the list when you start this process.

2. Choose Data, Subtotals.

3. In the Subtotal dialog box, specify the subtotal criteria, function, and other settings you want to apply (see Figure 19.21):

- In the At Each Change In box, select the heading that indicates when you want Excel to perform a subtotal—for example, at each change in state, employee name, client, and so on. If you want to subtotal grouped items, sort the list on the column you select here *before* you subtotal the list.

- In the Use Function box, select the function you want Excel to use for the subtotals.

- In the Add Subtotal To list, select the column(s) that you want to subtotal.

- If you're performing a new subtotal function and want to replace the existing subtotals in the list, select Replace Current Subtotals.

- Select Page Break Between Groups if you want Excel to start each new sub-totaled group at the top of a clean page.

- If you want the subtotals and grand totals to appear below the data, select Summary Below Data. If this option is deselected, Excel places the subtotals above the first entry subtotaled in each group and places the grand total (or grand average, grand min, and so on, depending on the function you selected) at the top of the column, just below the row of headings.

4. Click OK to run the totals.

The SUBTOTAL function uses the following syntax:

```
SUBTOTAL(function_num,ref1,ref2,...)
```

where $ref1$, $ref2$, and so on refer to the range(s) being calculated (up to 29 ranges), and $function\_num$ refers to a number from 1 to 11, with the following values:

Figure 19.21.

Reference No.	Function
1	AVERAGE
2	COUNT
3	COUNTA
4	MAX
5	MIN
6	PRODUCT
7	STDEV
8	STDEVP
9	SUM
10	VAR
11	VARP

PART

VI

CH

19

To learn how to enter functions, see Chapter 11, "Using Excel's Built-In Functions." For a list of available Excel functions and their descriptions, see Appendix A, "Excel Function Reference."

Tip #238 from

You can build multiple layers of subtotals—using different functions and subtotaling different fields—by running the Subtotals feature multiple times and deselecting the Replace Current Subtotals option each time.

Notice that the original data is visible when the subtotal of the category is selected and the grand total of the subtotaled categories shown. You may want to delete the subtotaled records and place the Grand Total row above the category heading as shown in Figure 19.22. You probably will also want to change one aspect of the formula—subtotaling any record pulled from the range.

Figure 19.22.
By placing the sub-total above the row headings, you can view the grand total of the category filtered above the list. Change the subtotal formula's range to equal the full range of the list.

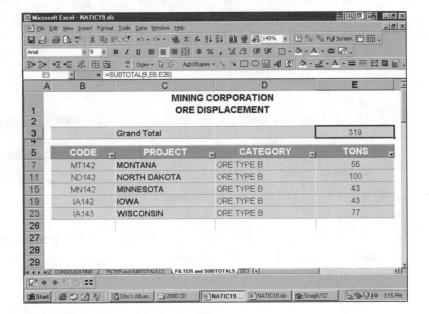

Follow these steps:

1. Select the subtotal cell with the formula in it. In the example in Figure 19.22, the formula cell is E3.

2. The specified range in the formula extracts to the end of the records selected. Change the maximum range to equal the last record in your list. (The last range in the Mining Corporation list is row 26.)

3. Press Enter after the formula has been modified. For this formula, notice that the function number in the subtotal formula is 9, which refers to the SUM function.

Excel ignores any nested subtotals in the list, along with any hidden rows.

The Grand Total now reflects the displayed records only, in a physical location that remains unchanged. This works well when dealing with large amounts of information that must be called up and summed up at a moment's notice.

VALIDATING AND AUDITING DATA ENTRY

Somewhere along the line, the data in every Excel workbook came from a human being. The process may have included typing data directly, downloading from a network or the Internet, importing from a database or data warehouse, and so on, but every bit of data can eventually be traced back to someone "filling in the blanks." Everyone makes mistakes at least occasionally, and the most complex formula is useless if its source data is wrong. On the other hand, accurate source data isn't very helpful if the formulas aren't constructed in a way that returns appropriate results. How can you prevent data errors and incorrect formulas from creeping into your Excel workbooks?

Excel offers some special features for dealing with the possibility of error within a workbook:

- To prevent errors from being typed into a worksheet, the *data validation* feature enables you to provide some guidance for the person entering the data (that may even be you!). You can tell Excel to accept only certain kinds of entries within a cell—for example, numbers or dates within a certain range—and specify a message for the user with instructions on filling in the information. With this feature, you also decide how you want Excel to respond to noncompliance: Display an error message and refuse the entry? Accept the incorrect entry but warn the user that it's problematic?

- If invalid data already exists in the workbook, Excel can locate and circle those entries, using the same data-validation logic.

- To trace relationships between cells and formulas, you can use Excel's auditing feature to display the connection between formulas and their source cells (precedents) or between cells and their dependent formulas. You also can find the sources of error results in formulas.

The following sections describe these features.

As you might expect, Excel provides a special Auditing toolbar for these functions. You can turn on the toolbar from the Toolbars list on the Toolbars tab in the Customize dialog box. Table 19.2 describes the buttons on the Auditing toolbar.

PART

VI

CH

19

TABLE 19.2. AUDITING TOOLBAR

Button	Name	Description
	Trace Precedents	Shows the preceding formulas or cell references that contribute to the cell
	Remove Precedent Arrows	Removes the precedent auditing arrows
	Trace Dependents	Shows the cell references to which the current cell points
	Remove Dependent Arrows	Removes the dependent auditing arrows
	Remove All Arrows	Removes all auditing arrows
	Trace Error	Traces cells with error values
	New Comment	Applies a comment to a cell
	Circle Invalid Data	Circles data outside the parameters set by validation
	Clear Validation Circles	Clears the invalid data circles

DATA VALIDATION

For those who occasionally find that they have entered improper data, Excel has addressed this problem with data validation. Validation enables you to apply parameters to ranges or cells, keeping information within certain boundaries. For example, if your list applies to dates within a certain month only, you can specify parameters from the first of the month until month-end that allow the user to input only dates within that specified period of time. These parameters can be set up to prevent incorrect information completely, warn the user but allow the entry, and so on. (The next section describes how to come back and mark invalid data later.)

To apply validation parameters to a list, cell, or range, follow these steps:

1. Select the area where you want to apply validation. For a range in which you want date validation, for example, select the months, range of dates, and so on.

2. Choose Data, Validation.

3. If necessary, select the Settings tab in the Data Validation dialog box. In the Validation Criteria options, specify the parameters that will be acceptable when the user is entering data (see Figure 19.23).

This example shows dates applied between two specified date ranges; the Ignore Blank option is selected so that the user can either enter an acceptable date or simply skip specifying a date in the input range.

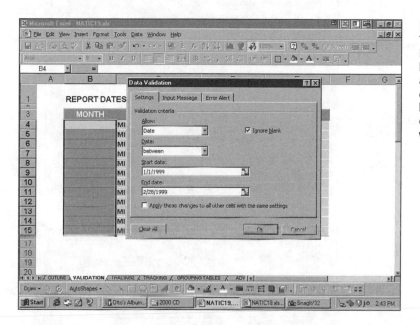

Figure 19.23.
The Settings tab in the Data Validation dialog box enables you to apply validation to dates, times, numbers, text, or even create a custom validation.

Note

Similar to customizing options for filters in lists, you can specify several characteristics on the Settings tab. Under the Data option, you can make the dates equal to, greater than, less than, and so on. Excel allows for flexibility to fit your specific requirements, and the options on the Settings tab change to reflect the selected data.

4. (Optional) You can provide an input message to help the user to enter the correct data. Click the Input Message tab in the Data Validation dialog box, as shown in Figure 19.24. Whatever you specify in the Title box will appear in the title bar for the dialog box, and the Input message will be displayed in the box itself.

5. Next, specify what you want to happen if the user enters invalid data. Click the Error Alert tab (see Figure 19.25). Select a warning Style (the icon changes to match the style you select) and specify the Title you want the title bar of the message box to display. Finally, enter an Error Message to be displayed in the box.

6. After you enter all the information, click OK.

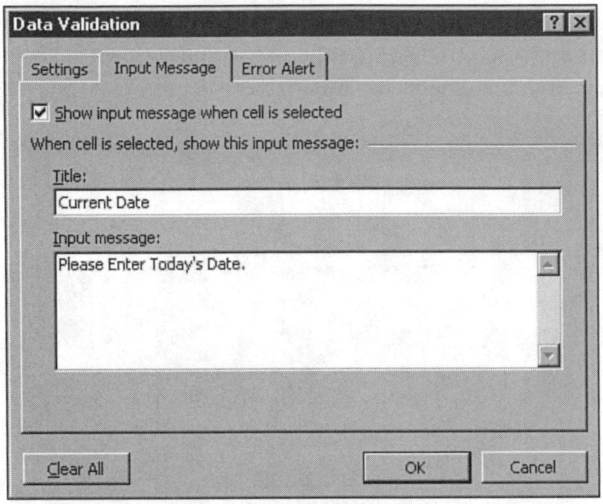

Figure 19.24.
Providing clues can
help the user avoid
making mistakes.

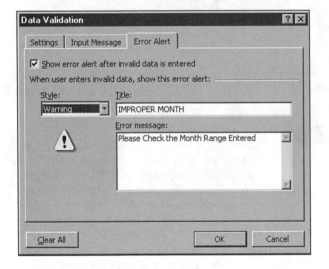

Figure 19.25.
The Error Alert tab
lets you specify
among three types of
errors: Warning, Stop,
and Information. You
also can apply titles
and text to the dialog
box being created.

Figure 19.26 shows what happens when I apply a date that's outside the specified parameters for this example. I have the option of choosing Yes to accept the current date, No to correct the error, or Cancel to void the entry.

Note

Using the Stop style prevents users from entering invalid data.

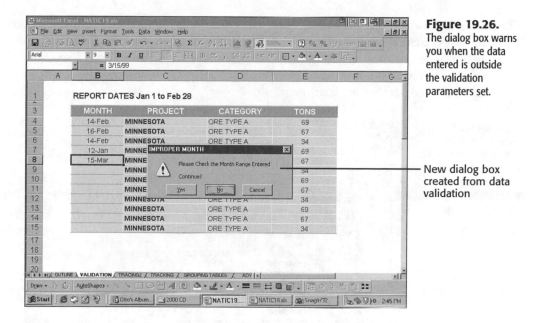

Figure 19.26.
The dialog box warns you when the data entered is outside the validation parameters set.

New dialog box created from data validation

You can change or remove the validation settings at any time by returning to the Data Validation dialog box. In most cases, you will just want to correct the settings, change the input or error messages, and so on. However, if you want to remove all the settings at once—all messages, alerts, and validation criteria, use the Clear All button at the bottom of the Data Validation box. (If you change your mind about this before closing the dialog box, clicking Cancel restores the settings.)

PART
VI

CH
19

Tip #239 from

> You can make one set of changes on the Settings tab and tell Excel to apply those new settings to other comparable validated cells. Select the option at the bottom of the tab, Apply These Changes to All Other Cells with the Same Settings.

CIRCLING INVALID DATA

Excel includes a special validation feature to find and mark invalid data that was previously entered. You might use this feature for a number of reasons:

- Data was entered before you instituted validation, and you want to go back and fix existing errors.

- The validation you have in place allows the user to enter invalid data after displaying a warning. (Sometimes you want to be able to enter invalid information, but have it verified, corrected, or approved later.)

- You want to change the validation conditions.

To audit the worksheet and quickly display a circle around information that doesn't meet the data validation conditions (up to 255 errors), click the Circle Invalid Data button on the Auditing toolbar. Excel circles the invalid data, as shown in Figure 19.27. If Excel finds 255 errors, you'll need to correct some of them and click the Circle Invalid Data button again before the program can mark any more.

Figure 19.27.
Excel circles all information that doesn't fall within the specified validation parameters.

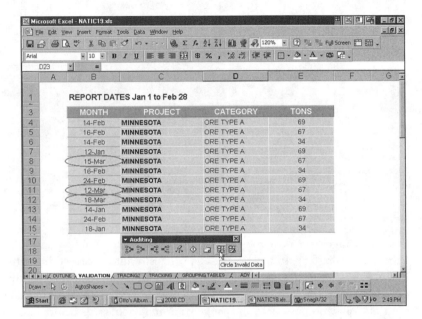

 To remove the displayed circles, click the Clear Validation Circles button on the Auditing toolbar.

Tip #240 from

If validation wasn't applied to your list and you now want to highlight information that falls outside specified ranges, use *conditional formatting (page 506)* and point to ranges and cells that establish parameters to meet your specifications.

AUDITING PRECEDENTS, DEPENDENTS, AND ERRORS

When inheriting a list of information or a workbook created by other users, the first thing you'll want to do is "check the wiring" of the workbook—how all the formulas and their data are connected. Excel's *auditing* feature can trace this information for you, as well as help you locate sources of errors returned by your formulas.

For each cell, auditing can trace the following information:

- If the cell contains a formula, auditing can trace its source cell(s), called *precedents*.
- If the cell contains data or formulas, auditing can trace any formulas that use the information from that cell, called its *dependents*.

- If the cell contains an error, auditing can trace the source of the error. For example, if a formula with a division operation returns #DIV/0, auditing can trace the source cell that either has no entry or contains a zero.

In each case, the relationships are pointed out with colored *tracer arrows*.

 If the auditing menu commands or buttons are disabled, the tracer arrows may be hidden. See "Displaying Tracer Arrows" in the Troubleshooting section at the end of this chapter.

Tip #241 from	You can't audit a protected worksheet. To remove protection, choose Tools, Protection, Unprotect Sheet. If your workbook has more layers of protection, however, you'll have to get through those layers before you can even access the worksheet. Chapter 18, "Using Excel's Data-Management Features," describes the various levels of protection available in Excel.

For example, if a cell contains a formula that sums a column of numbers, the formula's precedents would be the individual numbers being added. Each of those precedent cells would have the formula cell as one of its dependents. If that formula cell is itself included in a grand total somewhere else, the grand total would be a dependent of that formula cell.

The example in Figure 19.28 illustrates a simple scenario with a division formula. The formula divides the selling amount in column D by the number of units in column C for each row, as shown in cell E2. In this case, the worksheet shows several audits (the audited cells are shaded in the figure):

- Tracing the precedents for the formula in cell E4, Excel displays a blue arrow with origins in cells C4 and D4.
- Tracing the dependents of cell C8, Excel displays a blue arrow with the arrowhead in the single dependent formula cell E8.
- Cell D11 also has a single dependent, the formula in cell E11.
- The error in cell E14 is traced with a red arrow to its source, the empty cell C14.

If the information originates from or points to a different workbook or worksheet, the tracer arrow is black and the icon resembles a small worksheet.

To run or remove audits, you can use menu commands or the buttons on the Auditing toolbar, as described in the following list:

- **Trace a formula's precedents.** Select the cell containing the formula and choose Tools, Auditing, Trace Precedents or click the Trace Precedents button.
- **Trace a cell's dependents.** Select the cell and choose Tools, Auditing, Trace Dependents or click the Trace Dependents button.
- **Show multiple levels of precedents/dependents.** Repeatedly click the Trace Precedents or Trace Dependents button. If Excel beeps when you click one of these buttons, you have traced all levels of the formula, or you're trying to trace something untraceable (such as a graphic).

Figure 19.28.
By displaying precedents, dependents, and errors, you can quickly see relationships between cells.

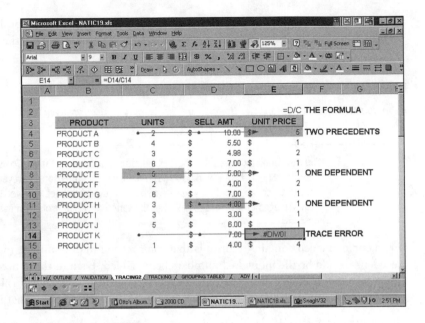

- **Track down the culprit cell leading to an error result.** Select the cell containing the formula with the error result and click the Trace Errors button or choose Tools, Auditing, Trace Errors. You may need to trace repeatedly to find all the errors involved.

- **Jump between dependents and precedents.** Double-click the tracer arrow. If the formula connects different workbooks, the workbook must be open to jump to it. If you jump to a different worksheet or workbook, Excel displays the Go To list; double-click the reference you want.

- **Remove tracer arrows.** To remove the tracer arrow from a cell to its dependents or precedents, select the cell and click the Remove Dependent Arrows or Remove Precedent Arrows button, respectively. To remove all tracer arrows, click the Remove All Arrows button on the Auditing toolbar or choose Tools, Auditing, Remove All Arrows.

Tracer arrows disappear when you save or close the workbook; you can't save an audit from one session to the next. Arrows also disappear if you insert or delete rows or columns, delete or move the cells involved in the formula, or change the formula itself.

→ Use comments to make notations as you explore the worksheet. For details, **see** "Using Comments to Explain Cell Content," **p. 111**

Troubleshooting

Displaying Tracer Arrows

The Auditing toolbar buttons or menu options are unavailable.

If the worksheet isn't protected (you can't audit a protected worksheet), and the auditing features are unavailable, your Excel options are set up to hide graphical objects (which include tracer arrows). The auditing feature relies on tracer arrows to indicate errors, precedents, and dependents. To display the tracer arrows, choose Tools, Options to open the Options dialog box. Click the View tab, and select either Show All or Show Placeholders in the Objects section.

Auto Outline Doesn't Work

Why do I get the error message "Cannot create an outline"?

Excel understands only outlines that are set up consistently. Be sure you don't have inconsistent spaces between categories and totals, and that the rest of the list is organized in a consistent manner.

Excel in Practice

Figures 19.29 and 19.30 show two ways to structure a yearly list with quarters. Both worksheets use good overall structures with consistent titles and no extra spaces, but Excel can use the worksheet in Figure 19.30 to create an Auto Outline. With the grouping in this worksheet, you can roll up the data by quarter and then by year, and you can view grand totals by row and column. The worksheet in Figure 19.29 also can be summarized by quarter and then total, with two levels of grouping applied, but Excel can't understand the worksheet's layout automatically.

Figure 19.29.
You can group this worksheet manually, but Excel can't apply an Auto Outline because the quarter totals all appear at the bottom of the columns rather than after their respective months.

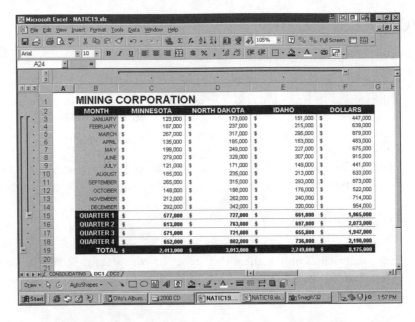

Figure 19.30.
This worksheet uses the same data as the one in Figure 19.29, except that it uses a different layout to make it easier for Excel to understand and different formatting to make it easier for the user to understand.

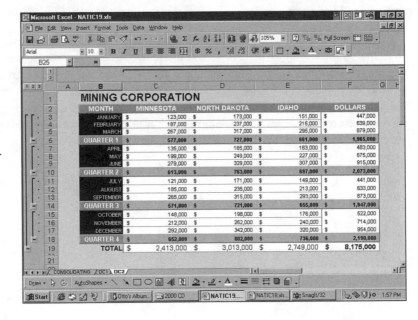

CHAPTER 20

USING PIVOTTABLES AND PIVOTCHARTS

In this chapter

by Patrick D. Blattner
Patrick@BlattnerBooks.com

UNDERSTANDING PIVOTTABLES

A *PivotTable* uses two-dimensional data to create a three-dimensional table—in essence, a summary table based on multiple conditions that have intersecting points. PivotTables are a great way to summarize large amounts of information in a small amount of space, with just a few short steps. They're interactive in that, after the PivotTable is created, you can drag a field to another location, thus *pivoting* the structure of the table with a single step.

PivotTables are often viewed as too complex to understand, but they're not that complicated if you think in terms of an automated summary table. You could write a formula to sum a quantity with multiple conditions, or you could use a PivotTable to summarize the data. Both are effective tools, but the advantage of the PivotTable is its flexibility to view the detail that makes up the total number.

PivotTables enable you to audit your data as well. If you must manage costs on a weekly basis—for example, costs of your employees and the hours they're generating—I'd strongly suggest using PivotTables. (See the later section "Managing Employee Hours and Costs with PivotTables" for specific details.)

It's important to note the new flexibility of PivotTables in Excel 2000. A PivotTable was a great way to summarize information in previous versions; however, it was so difficult to format and manipulate that it was easier to create your own tables and write formulas to extract the information. PivotTables are now a lot easier to format and can be utilized to their full potential. Your data sources for PivotTables can be queried through Microsoft Query if you're using a database or other data source.

→ For details on using Excel with database programs, **see** "Using Excel with Access and Other Databases," **p. 781**

The Excel list in Figure 20.1 shows the data for one division of a corporation. The structure of the list is important. In the example, there are three levels of information. The highest level of information being summarized is the mine site; the PivotTable will be based on the mine site. The next level is the code; the data will be organized and summarized by the code. The third level is the ore grade; the data will be structured and sorted based on the grade of the ore. To summarize this information, you could create a table manually and use formulas, or you could create a PivotTable that summarizes the information for you. The PivotTable in Figure 20.2 was created from this list. When you change the information in the list, you can use the Refresh Data command from the PivotTable toolbar to update the PivotTable.

In its typical form, a PivotTable is the intersection of two columns of data in your list, with one column of information listed down the left side of the table and the other column's information "pivoted" to list its elements across the top of the table. The intersection of the two becomes the summary data.

What's unique about PivotTables is the capacity to move fields by drag and drop. Excel summarizes the data in the new arrangement instantly. Figure 20.3 shows the same PivotTable as in Figure 20.2, but with the MINE SITE field dragged to the inside. When you move a field, the PivotTable *pivots* the data to accommodate the field's new location. You don't need to write new formulas or refilter the data because the PivotTable recalculates automatically when you rearrange the fields.

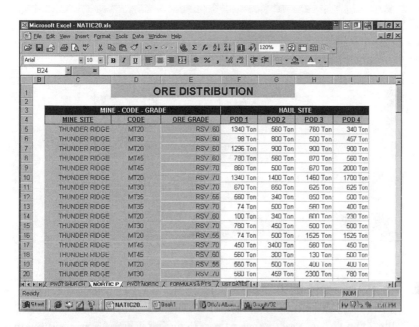

Figure 20.1.
A typical list of data organized by several categories.

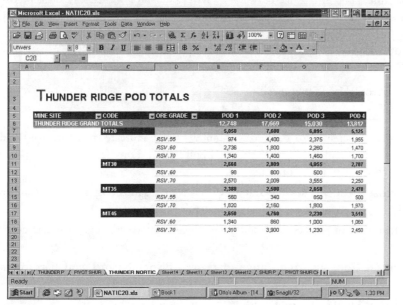

Figure 20.2.
A PivotTable quickly summarizes information in an interactive table.

Figure 20.3.
When you drag a field to a new location, the PivotTable pivots the information to reflect the data's new location.

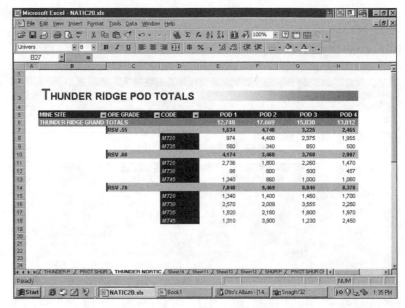

USING THE PIVOTTABLE AND PIVOTCHART WIZARD

You can use the PivotTable Wizard to create a new PivotTable or PivotChart, or to edit an existing PivotTable. (The difference between a PivotTable and a *PivotChart* is simply that one summarizes the data in the form of a table and the other in the form of a chart.) Like other wizards in Excel, the PivotTable Wizard walks you step by step through the process. The new PivotChart feature is also wizard-driven (see the later section "Creating PivotCharts").

To construct a PivotTable, follow these steps:

1. From the Data menu, select PivotTable and PivotChart Report.

2. In the Step 1 of 3 dialog box of the PivotTable Wizard, indicate the source of the data that you want to use in the PivotTable (see Figure 20.4). For the data source to be analyzed, you choose from four options:

   - **Microsoft Excel List or Database.** Uses data organized by row labels and columns on a worksheet. This is the default setting.

   - **External Data Source.** Created from a file or database outside the current workbook.

   - **Multiple Consolidation Ranges.** Creates a PivotTable or PivotChart from multiple Excel worksheets.

   - **Another PivotTable or PivotChart.** Creates a PivotTable or PivotChart from another PivotReport in the same workbook.

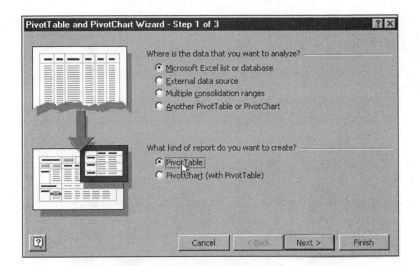

Figure 20.4.
Step 1 of 3 of the PivotTable Wizard enables you to choose from several data source options, as well as pivoting in the form of a table or chart.

3. Specify the type of PivotTable you want to create: a table or a chart. Then select Next.

4. In Step 2 of the PivotTable Wizard, select a data source if none is selected, or if the data is in a different workbook or range than the one shown in the dialog box (see Figure 20.5). Figure 20.6 shows the selected list I'm using for this example.

Caution
If you didn't select the data to be pivoted before starting the PivotTable Wizard, be sure to check the default range that Excel selects for accuracy.

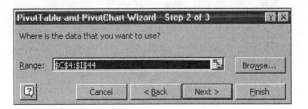

Figure 20.5.
Step 2 of 3 of the PivotTable Wizard enables you to select a range and browse to a different document.

5. Step 3 of 3 of the PivotTable Wizard gives you multiple options to place and format your PivotTable (see Figure 20.7).

The PivotTable can be placed on a new worksheet or on the existing worksheet next to the list; specify the location if you choose to place the PivotTable on the existing worksheet. You also can use the Layout and Options buttons to further specify the desired settings for the new PivotTable (see the following sections for details), or change these settings later, after creating the PivotTable or PivotChart.

6. When you're finished selecting the options you want, click Finish to create the table.

PART
VI

CH
20

Figure 20.6.
This list will be summarized into a PivotTable.

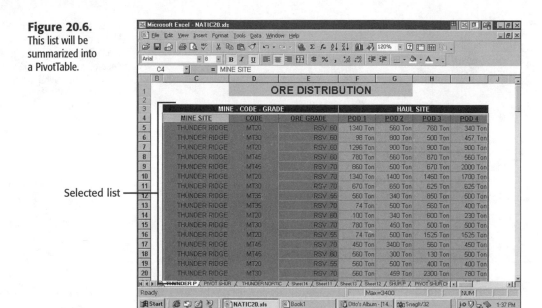

Selected list

Figure 20.7.
Step 3 of 3 of the PivotTable Wizard enables you to establish the location of the PivotTable and also customize the format and other settings.

Note

If the active workbook contains at least one PivotTable, Excel enables you to create another PivotTable from that PivotTable by selecting Another PivotTable or PivotChart in Step 1 of the PivotTable Wizard. This saves on memory when creating large workbooks with multiple PivotTable reports.

LAYING OUT THE PIVOTTABLE

Clicking the Layout button in the Step 3 of 3 PivotTable Wizard dialog box displays the PivotTable and PivotChart Wizard - Layout dialog box shown in Figure 20.8. You can use this dialog box to control the view of data displayed in a PivotTable. The fields from the selected data appear on the right side of the dialog box. Select and drag the desired fields into the area in the center of the dialog box and drop them in the <u>R</u>OW, <u>C</u>OLUMN, <u>P</u>AGE, and <u>D</u>ATA sections of the dialog box to create the desired layout.

Note	The Layout dialog box is the way PivotTables were built in earlier versions. Microsoft kept this method in case users didn't like the new construction method, although usability studies rated the new method superior to the old layout design.

Tip #242 from	After a field is applied to a <u>R</u>ow, <u>P</u>age, <u>C</u>olumn, or <u>D</u>ata section, you can double-click the field to access and change the type of summary information, such as count, average, or sum. You can also customize the field name.

The following list describes the four areas that are available to apply fields:

- <u>P</u>age. Creates a drop-down menu above the table, enabling you to pull up a specified option, such as a selected division or country.
- <u>R</u>ow. Applies a vertical format to the table, summarizing data from top down. The row drop area lists each item in the field down the left side of the PivotTable.
- <u>C</u>olumn. Applies a horizontal format to the table, summarizing the data from left to right; the column drop area lists each item in the field across the top of the PivotTable.
- <u>D</u>ata. The data drop area is the summary of the numbers. This area adds, counts, or creates other analytical functions against the data dropped here. Double-click the field to access the desired function or summary type.

The following figures show the same data or list being summarized with different fields and layouts, to illustrate the change in PivotTable structure and analytical functions.

In Figure 20.8, the MINE SITE field is dropped into the page drop area. Figure 20.9 shows the resulting PivotTable.

PART

VI

CH

20

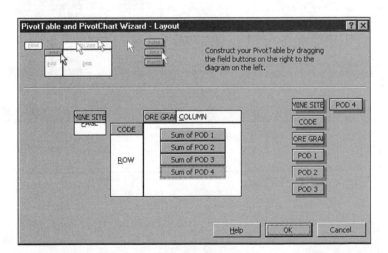

Figure 20.8.
Specifying the PivotTable layout with the wizard. In this example, I dropped the MINE SITE field into the page drop area.

Figure 20.9.
The PivotTable created from the layout in Figure 20.8.

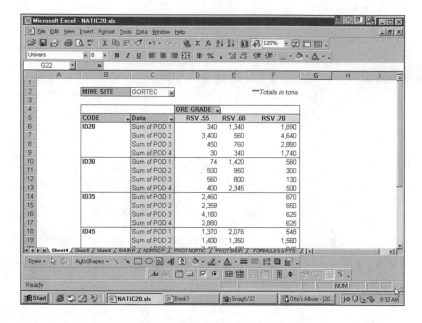

In Figure 20.10, the MINE SITE field is dropped into the row drop area. The result is a summary of the total tonnage for the pods in each mine site (see Figure 20.11).

Figure 20.10.
In this table, the MINE SITE field is dropped into the row drop area and will summarize the total tons for all the pods for each mine site.

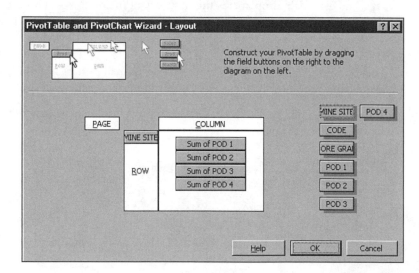

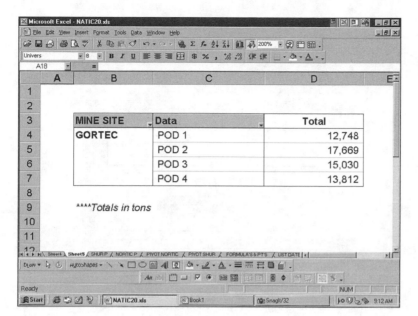

Figure 20.11.
The PivotTable created from the layout in Figure 20.10.

In Figure 20.12, fields are stacked in the row drop area, and the PivotTable will summarize the grades of ore by code. Notice the COUNT function applied to the CODE field in the data drop area. Figure 20.13 shows the result. The order of the ROW fields (from top to bottom) evaluates left to right in the PivotTable. The top ROW field in the Layout dialog box will be the leftmost field in the PivotTable.

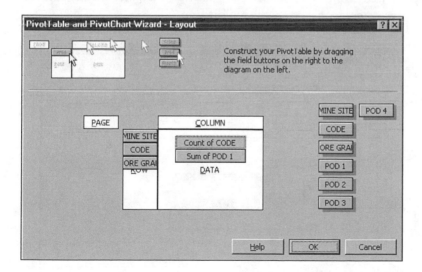

Figure 20.12.
With fields stacked in the row drop area, the PivotTable will summarize the grades of ore by code.

PART

VI

CH

20

Figure 20.13.
The stacked field result summarizes by priority of the field dropped into the row drop area.

COUNT function ——

SUM function ——

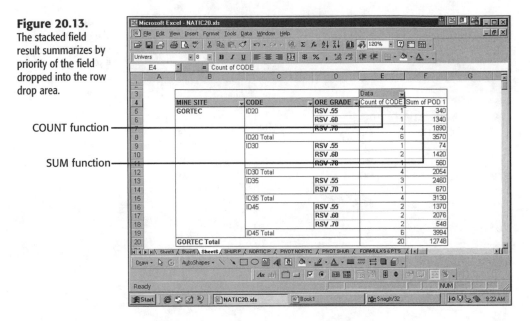

You can click Finish at any point in the PivotTable Wizard to create the PivotTable, and then use the new PivotTable toolbar to drag the fields to the drop zone areas on the PivotTable, as shown in Figures 20.14 and 20.15. This powerful new feature (which also can be used with PivotCharts) enables you to view fields in the drop area as soon as you add them to the PivotTable. In essence, it's an interactive PivotTable builder, with onscreen viewing as it happens (see Figure 20.16). If you don't like the result, drag the field off the table and replace it with another field from the toolbar.

Figure 20.14.
Start with an essentially blank PivotTable and then use the PivotTable toolbar to build the PivotTable.

Select a field and drag it off the toolbar onto the PivotTable.

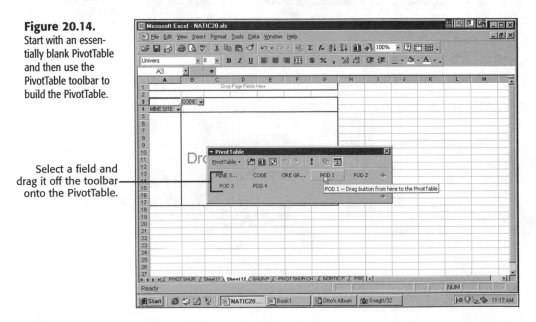

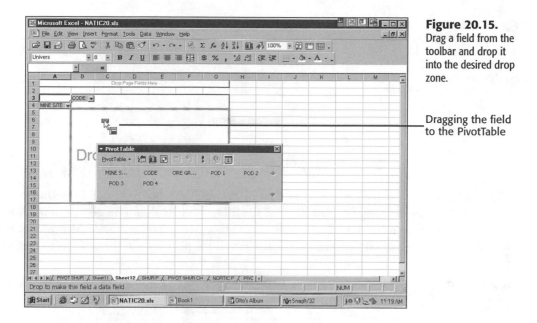

Figure 20.15.
Drag a field from the toolbar and drop it into the desired drop zone.

Dragging the field to the PivotTable

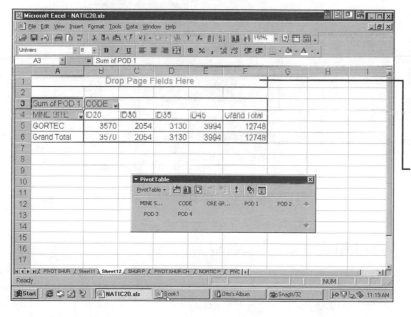

Figure 20.16.
The result of dropping the Pod 1 field in the data drop zone. Note the message in the status bar at the bottom of the Excel window.

Drop indicator

The function Excel chooses (COUNT, SUM, and so on) depends on the nature of the field you dropped. You can choose to apply different functions, such as averaging, showing the maximum or minimum, and so on. To change the function that Excel uses to summarize the data, double-click the field whose function you want to change in the <u>D</u>ATA section of the PivotTable and PivotChart Wizard - Layout dialog box. The PivotTable Field dialog box opens; select the function you want to use (see Figure 20.17).

Figure 20.17.
The PivotTable Field
dialog box enables
you to change how
the data is analyzed.

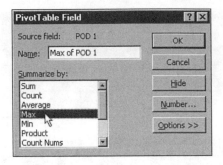

You can customize the summary functions by clicking the Options button to expand the PivotTable Field dialog box (see Figure 20.18). The additional options allow you to analyze data as percents of the total based on fields and base items. The *base field* is the comparison field in the custom calculation, and the *base item* is the field item in the custom calculation.

Figure 20.18.
Click the Options but-
ton in the PivotTable
Field dialog box to
further analyze fields
by base field and
item.

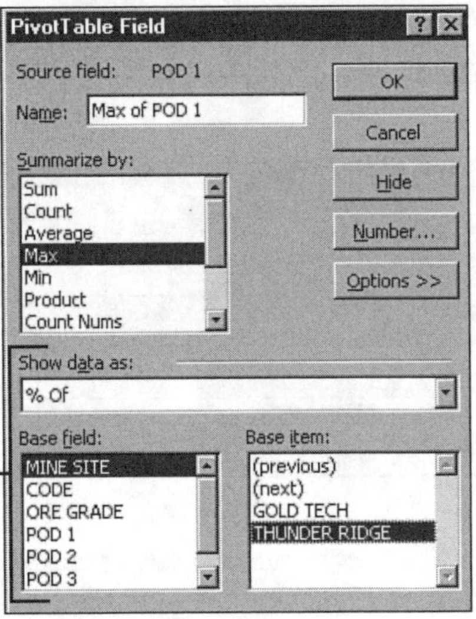

Extended options for analysis ⎯

SETTING PIVOTTABLE OPTIONS

Clicking the Options button in the Step 3 of 3 dialog box for the PivotTable Wizard opens the PivotTable Options dialog box, in which you can further specify formats and data source options (see Figure 20.19). You can access this dialog box after completing the wizard by either clicking the PivotTable button on the PivotTable toolbar and selecting Table Options from the drop-down list, or by right-clicking a completed PivotTable and selecting Table Options from the context menu.

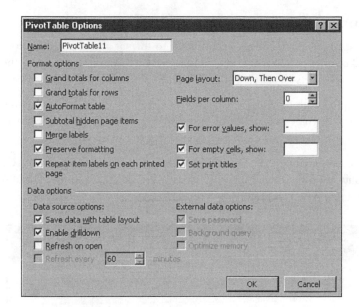

Figure 20.19.
You can customize
the PivotTable format
and data options.

The following sections describe the options.

NAMING THE PIVOTTABLE

The Name option in the PivotTable Options dialog box enables you to specify a name for the PivotTable. By default, Excel names new tables PivotTable1, PivotTable2, and so on, but you can type a different name. It's important to name the PivotTable something identifiable in case you have to start creating PivotTables from other PivotTables to save memory. If you haven't named your PivotTable, you'll find it hard to go back in and identify which PivotTable you want to re-create the PivotTable from. In a PivotChart, the name is still associated with the PivotTable report; changing it changes only the name of the PivotTable the chart is derived from.

ADDING TOTALS

The Grand Totals for Columns option in the PivotTable Options dialog box performs the analysis function and provides the grand totals for each column in the PivotTable. The Grand Totals for Rows option does the same for each row in the PivotTable. The default option selects the grand totals; however, I always deselect these two options because they clutter the PivotTable with too many totals.

If your PivotTable contains hidden fields, you may want those fields subtotaled, but without displaying the field contents. If so, select the Subtotal Hidden Page Items option in the PivotTable options dialog box.

PART
VI

CH

20

APPLYING AUTOFORMATS

In previous versions of Excel, PivotTables were difficult to format and didn't allow for visual flexibility. Excel 2000 enables you to manipulate and format a PivotTable similar to the way in which you format worksheets—changing the font, point size, colors, and so on.

Excel automatically applies a preset *AutoFormat (page 161)* to new PivotTables. If you prefer to select a different format, you can turn off the AutoFormat Table option in the PivotTable Options dialog box, or just change the format after creating the PivotTable.

 To change the AutoFormat applied to a PivotTable, choose Format, AutoFormat or click the Format Report button on the PivotTable toolbar (see Figure 20.20). In the AutoFormat dialog box, select the table style you prefer (see Figure 20.21).

Figure 20.20.
Rather than keeping the default format, you can apply a new AutoFormat to your PivotTable.

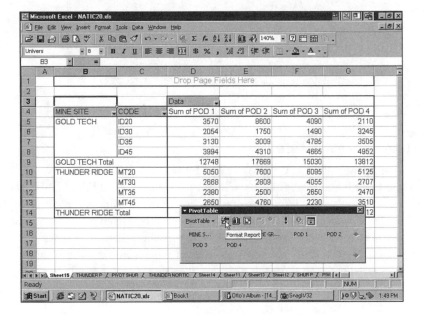

AutoFormats do more than apply the formats for color, font, and so on; they also adjust the fields and can pivot your information to display the information more effectively. After applying the new AutoFormat, if you don't like the result, just undo the change and try a different format. You can also manually reposition the fields after applying the AutoFormat, or repivot the fields.

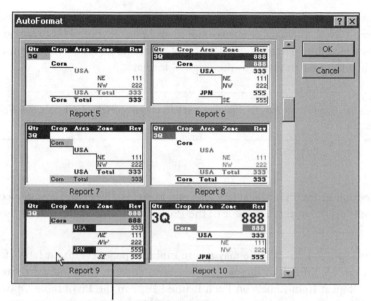

Figure 20.21.
In Excel, you can select from a variety of preset formats that can format and repivot the PivotTable.

Reports 1–10 also change field locations.

Figure 20.22 shows a PivotTable with a new AutoFormat applied. Notice the difference between the PivotTable in this figure and the one shown earlier (refer to Figure 20.20).

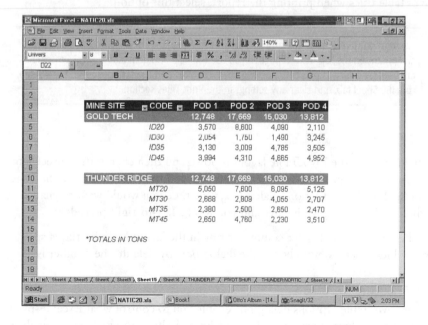

Figure 20.22.
With the right AutoFormat, the table format helps tell the story of the data.

An important improvement in Excel 2000 is Excel's capacity to preserve the formatting of a PivotTable when you refresh the data or change the PivotTable's layout. The Preserve Formatting option is selected by default in the PivotTable Options dialog box, but you can turn off this option if you prefer to revert to the original format.

Note

Manually applied inside borders (on right and left) are not preserved when the PivotTable is refreshed.

DISPLAYING LABELS

The Merge Labels option in the PivotTable Options dialog box enables you to merge column cells and row cells on the outer perimeter of the PivotTable. This is generally a formatting feature.

As with other printed reports, a PivotTable may run to multiple pages. Without labels for columns and rows, it can be difficult or impossible to determine what each individual item refers to. The option Repeat Item Labels on Each Printed Page in the PivotTable Options dialog box is set by default to repeat the item labels on each printed page. To print item labels on the first page only, deselect this option.

Another option in the PivotTable Options dialog box that relates to printing the labels is Set Print Titles. By default, this option is turned off. If you want to use the field and item labels in the PivotTable titles when printing the report, select this option.

Note

For most printed reports, you probably use the first few rows of the worksheet as the title and print it on the top of each page. If you use the field and item labels of a PivotTable as print titles, be sure to prevent repeating other columns and rows. Choose File, Page Setup, click the Sheet tab, and clear any settings in the Print Titles section.

CONTROLLING THE LAYOUT

By default, the field order in the PivotTable layout is down and then over, setting precedent for the vertical format. If you prefer that the order be over and then down, change the Page Layout setting in the PivotTable Options dialog box. One time you would want to change this format is when you're dealing with dates and you want a left-to-right precedent.

You can change the number of fields per column or row in the layout by indicating a specific number in the Fields per Column box in the dialog box. By default, the number is 0.

HANDLING ERRORS AND EMPTY CELLS

Two options in the PivotTable Options dialog box enable you to control what Excel displays in cells that don't display values as expected. The For Error Values, Show __ option enables you to specify a character or a blank in place of the error values; the For Empty Cells, Show __ option enables you to specify a character or a blank in place of the empty cells. For example, if you have a report that shows an #ERR message, you might find it helpful to point your attention to the errors by typing the phrase **missing name** in the box next to the For Error Values, Show __ option. This setup will display that phrase in every cell containing an error. In addition, you can apply *conditional formats (page 506)* in order to apply colors to highlight the cells containing the phrase.

Leaving both options enabled with nothing in their text boxes will display the cells as blank in the PivotTable. Disabling the For Empty Cells, Show __ option will display a zero for empty cells in the PivotTable.

Tip #243 from

fih.k

When enabled, this setting overrides the Zero Values option on the View tab in the general options dialog box for Excel (choose Tools, Options) for PivotTable cells only.

SOURCE DATA OPTIONS

The Data Options section of the PivotTable Options dialog box provides a number of helpful features. The following list describes these options:

- **Save Data with Table Layout.** Saves a copy of the data used from an external data source. Selected by default.

    This option isn't only for external data sources. Deselecting this option saves on the workbook's size but also forces you to manually refresh the PivotTable(s) when opening the workbook (unless the Refresh on Open option is enabled). With this option disabled, you can't work with PivotTables until they've been refreshed.

- **Enable Drilldown.** Shows the detail when a field is double-clicked. Selected by default.

- **Refresh on Open.** Refreshes the PivotTable when the workbook is opened. By default, this option isn't selected; I suggest selecting it for most cases.

- **Refresh Every __ Minutes.** Allows for automatic refreshing based on the minutes set. By default, this option isn't selected. This option is only available for PivotTables based on external data sources. (It really should appear under the External Data Options section of the dialog box.)

- **Save Password.** Saves the password associated with the external data source where the information is derived. This option is deselected by default; enabling this option compromises database security.

- **Background Query.** Runs the query in the background while allowing you to continue to work. Turned off by default.

- **Optimize Memory.** Optimizes and manages the memory when using PivotTables; however, this option slows down performance. By default, this option is not selected.

Creating PivotCharts

Figures 20.23 and 20.24 show data that's structured with the same criteria as a PivotTable versus a PivotChart. When a PivotChart is created, Excel creates both a chart sheet and a PivotTable sheet within the workbook; because the chart information must be derived from a table, Excel automatically creates the table. The default action of the PivotChart feature is to create a chart as a worksheet, but you also can create an embedded chart on a worksheet in the last step of the PivotTable wizard or by selecting Location from the Chart menu and selecting the As Object In option after creating the PivotChart.

Figure 20.25 shows the difference between a PivotTable and a PivotChart: An embedded PivotChart has been formatted and placed on the same sheet as a formatted PivotTable. (Figure 20.26 shows the same worksheet, posted to a Web page. See the later section "Saving and Editing PivotTables in HTML Format" for details.)

PivotCharts can be formatted with worksheets to plot and show data in chart format and combined with other worksheet data, making this new feature flexible and powerful.

Figure 20.23.
A PivotTable based on a structured list.

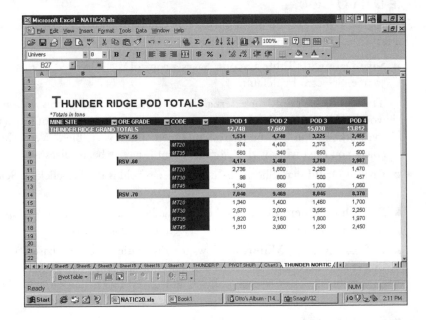

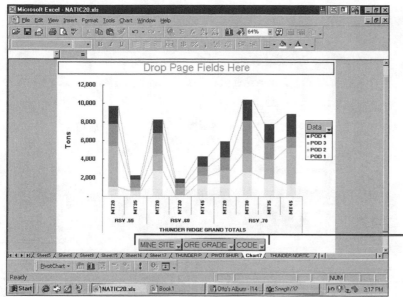

Figure 20.24.
A PivotChart based on the same structured list used in Figure 20.23.

These fields can be dragged.

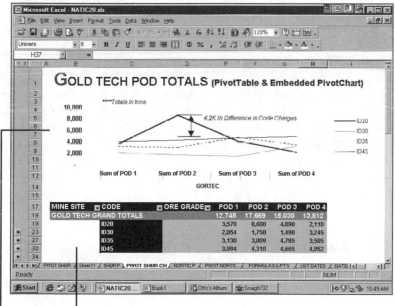

Figure 20.25.
PivotTable and PivotChart shown together in the worksheet. The field options on the PivotChart are turned off.

Embedded PivotChart   PivotTable

Figure 20.26.
With the Web Page Preview option, you can save the worksheet for Internet or intranet posting, keeping the formatting of the PivotTable and PivotChart intact.

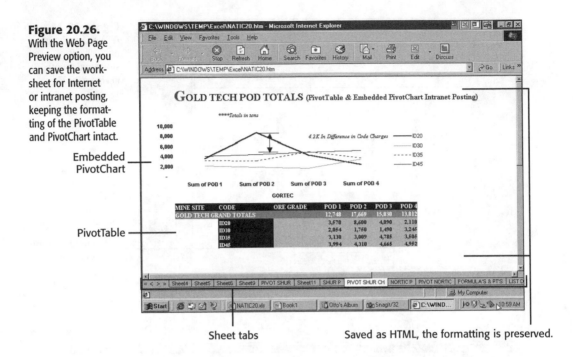

Embedded PivotChart

PivotTable

Sheet tabs

Saved as HTML, the formatting is preserved.

MODIFYING PIVOTTABLES AND PIVOTCHARTS

After you create a PivotTable or PivotChart, you can restructure the PivotTable or the PivotChart to look a different way by dragging and dropping fields, or by using the options on the menus or the PivotTable toolbar. You also can change the look or structure of the PivotTable with formatting options (see the earlier section "Applying AutoFormats"). Because of the new options available with PivotTables in Excel 2000, you can adjust and manipulate just about all aspects of the PivotTable or PivotChart. You can apply colored fills, borders, and font colors just as you would a regular table on a worksheet. PivotCharts are a bit more difficult to format because of sizing limitations on the plot area and legend locations, but for the most part, they're as flexible as charts created with the standard charting features.

USING THE PIVOTTABLE TOOLBAR

The PivotTable toolbar enables you to create a PivotTable layout by dragging the fields from the toolbar to the drop zones of the PivotTable. Table 20.1 describes the options available on the toolbar.

TABLE 20.1.	PIVOTTABLE TOOLBAR	
Button	**Name**	**Description**
PivotTable ▾	PivotTable	Drop-down menu with options for further PivotTable or PivotChart enhancement.
	Format Report	Opens the AutoFormat dialog box for use in formatting the PivotTable.
	Chart Wizard	Opens the Chart Wizard dialog box for use in formatting the PivotChart.
	PivotTable Wizard	Activates the PivotTable and PivotChart Wizard.
	Hide Detail	Hides the detail of a grouped range in a PivotTable.
	Show Detail	Displays the detail behind grouped ranges in the PivotTable.
	Refresh Data	Refreshes the data in the selected PivotTable.
	Field Settings	Allows for adjusting the summarization of the data in the field selected.
	Hide Fields/Display Fields	Hides/displays the field buttons on the toolbar or the outlines and labels in the PivotTable layout.

DRAGGING FIELDS IN A PIVOTCHART

PivotCharts offer the power of PivotTables and charts combined in one interactive surface. You can select and drag fields to new locations on the chart, and Excel will pivot the chart to correspond to the new field location. For example, dragging the field out of the drop zone in the PivotChart in Figure 20.27 eliminates the field and changes the chart to correspond to the new pivoted information, shown in Figure 20.28. Changes to the fields in the PivotChart also are reflected on the corresponding PivotTable.

ELIMINATING FIELD DATA

Clicking the arrow button shown on a field in the PivotChart or PivotTable displays a drop-down list from which you can select or deselect items (see Figure 20.29). The information will be removed from or added to the PivotChart or PivotTable (see Figure 20.30).

Figure 20.27.
You can select and
move the fields in a
PivotChart, just as
in a PivotTable.

PivotChart sheet ——

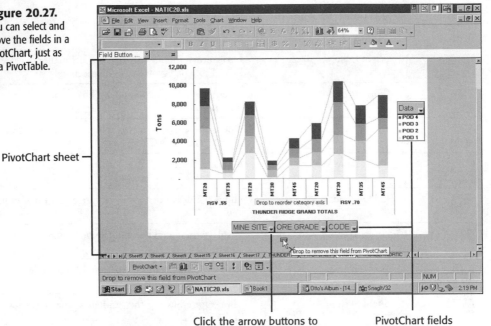

Click the arrow buttons to
display drop-down field lists.

PivotChart fields

Moved field location

Figure 20.28.
By dragging the field
to a new location or
the drop zone, you
can restructure the
chart with one move.

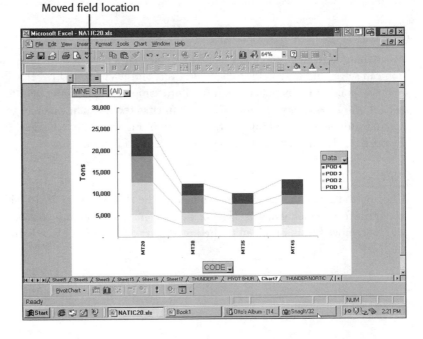

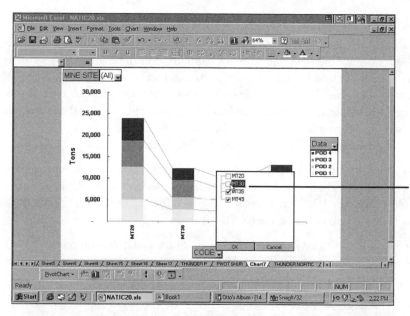

Figure 20.29.
Select or deselect items from fields by using the drop-down list on the field.

Deselecting items from the field list

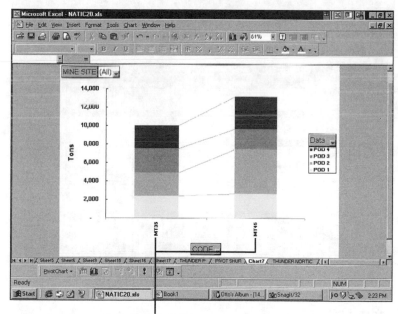

Figure 20.30.
By deselecting categories from fields, you can eliminate data sets with one click.

Only these two items are still selected.

SHOWING AND HIDING DETAIL

You can show detail behind a field by double-clicking the data of the field. If lower-level information exists behind the field, the Show Detail button on the PivotTable toolbar is enabled (see Figure 20.31). Select the category for which you want to show the detail; Excel will drill down (to show the detail that makes up the total number). For example, if you have employees' hours summed for the week and you double-click the total number, Excel shows all the weekly information that creates the total number (see Figure 20.32). In this case, I double-clicked the RSV .55 line to show the detail behind it.

After detail is added, double-clicking RSV .55 again will hide the detail, and another double-click will show it again (without the dialog box appearing a second time). Along the same line, if I double-clicked the ID20, code Excel would hide the ore grades for that item (again, no dialog box would appear) because the CODE field already has ore grade details showing.

If I clicked the field label ORE GRADE and used the Show Detail button on the PivotTable toolbar (double-click won't work here), I could add details for all of the ore grades at once.

Figure 20.31.
Excel enables you to drill down to show the detail that makes up the summary information in the PivotTable.

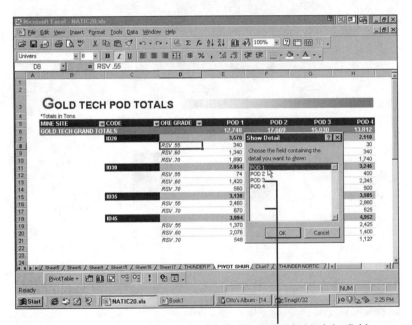

Detailed information behind the field

GROUPING PIVOTTABLE LEVELS

You can manage information in a PivotTable—much like that in a list—by *grouping (page 528)* to roll up different levels of the PivotTable for various reports and views. (Notice the two levels of groups applied to the PivotTable in Figure 20.33.) This strategy is useful if you have quantities of material grouped per week and then per month, for example. You can collapse or expand the groups just like when grouping a list on a worksheet (notice the collapsed example in Figure 20.34).

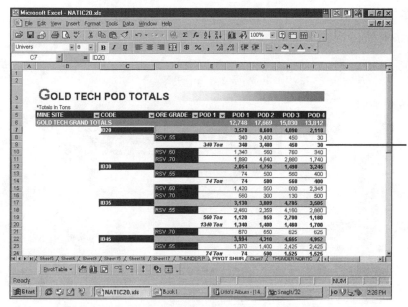

Figure 20.32.
The detail behind the selected region. In this case, I double-clicked RSV .55 and chose to view POD 1 detail.

— Detail

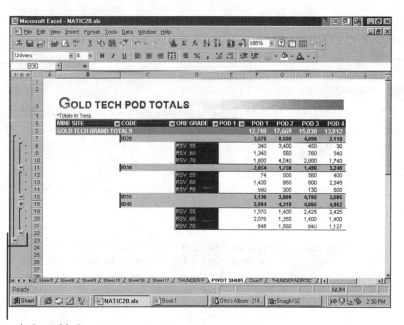

Figure 20.33.
By grouping the PivotTable levels, you can show detail and then roll up the detail as you would a database or list.

PART

VI

CH

20

Grouped PivotTable items

Figure 20.34.
After the groups are applied, you can roll up the PivotTable to the highest level of information.

Collapsed PivotTable group

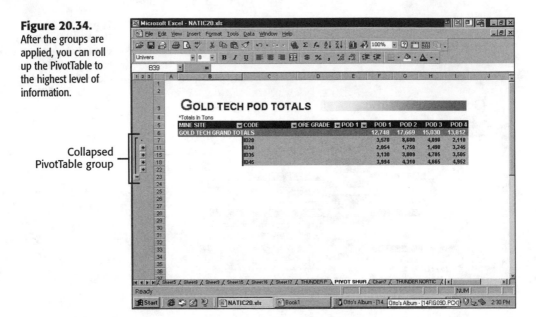

PivotTables have become seamless in that you have the flexibility to move, manage, group, and format just as you would a table, but they summarize more quickly and more efficiently than functions.

PERFORMING CALCULATIONS ON A PIVOTTABLE

You can perform calculations on a field or multiple fields within a PivotTable. Click the PivotTable button on the PivotTable toolbar. Then choose Formulas, Calculated Field from the drop-down menu.

In Figure 20.35, the name of the calculated field to be added represents the overhead for the region. The formula =sum('POD 4')*.12 calculates the percentage of overhead for the region, calculated against the current field amount ('POD 4').

Tip #244 from

You also can create these calculations on the worksheet and reference them to the cells in the PivotTable. Just create a simple function that references the field column and row. Please note that such calculations can't appear inside the PivotTable, but can appear just outside it (although applying AutoFormats might delete such data if the format manipulates the fields).

Notice the results in Figure 20.36 of the new calculated field in the PivotTable. It shows the percentage attributed to overhead for the region. Each time the table is refreshed, the calculations automatically update.

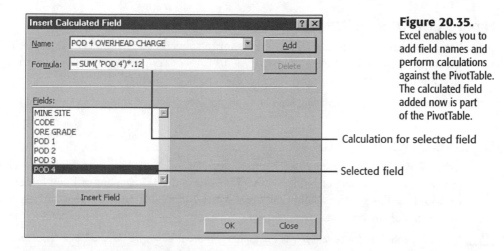

Figure 20.35.
Excel enables you to add field names and perform calculations against the PivotTable. The calculated field added now is part of the PivotTable.

Calculation for selected field

Selected field

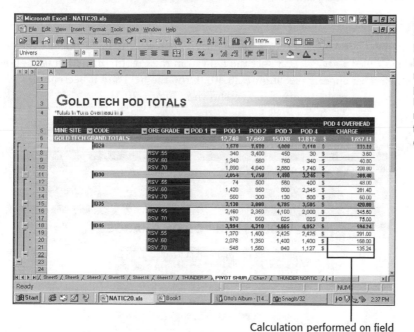

Figure 20.36.
By adding a calculated field to the PivotTable, Excel makes the addition part of the PivotTable. Each time the data is refreshed, the calculations are automatically updated.

Calculation performed on field

HIDING COLUMNS OR ROWS

For presentations or printouts, you may want to show only certain bits of information within the PivotTable. You can *hide (page 470)* rows or columns that you don't want to show (see Figure 20.37) or *unhide (page 521)* hidden rows or columns.

→ For details on hiding and unhiding rows and columns, **see** "Hiding and Unhiding Rows and Columns," **p. 67**

DRILLING DOWN IN A FIELD

In the PivotTable in Figure 20.38, all the information is rolled up to its highest level, without the use of grouping or hidden rows. This shows the 3D element of PivotTables. To drill up and drill down, select a field that has a subset and double-click. It's that simple. Notice the results of the product type in Figure 20.39 after you double-click the product field.

 If double-clicking doesn't allow you to drill down, this feature may be disabled. See "Enabling Drilldown" in the Troubleshooting section at the end of this chapter.

DRAGGING A FIELD FOR A PAGE VIEW

The flexibility of dragging fields in PivotTables enables you to drag fields outside the table and create what's called a *page view*. Select the field from the PivotTable and drag it above the table; the insert bar appears (see Figure 20.40). Drop the field and it becomes a drop-down list to manage the information, as shown in Figure 20.41.

Columns D through I are hidden.

Figure 20.37.
By hiding columns or rows, you can focus on newly calculated fields that point out certain pieces of information that might get lost in the original table with all data showing.

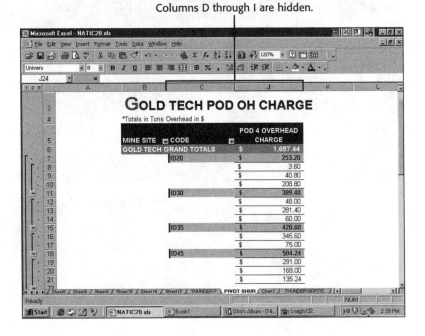

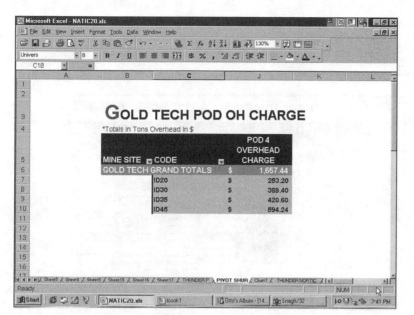

Figure 20.38.
You can hide information by using the drilldown technique on PivotTables. Just double-click the field name.

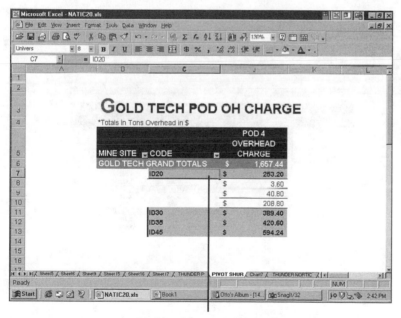

Figure 20.39.
The results of managing the view of the PivotTable by drilling down or double-clicking. Notice how the information acts as though it's collapsed or expanded, similar to grouping.

Double-click to expand detail.

Figure 20.40.
You can drag the field outside the table to create a page view. You're not limited to one field outside the table; you can drag and create multiple drop-downs.

Select and move fields.

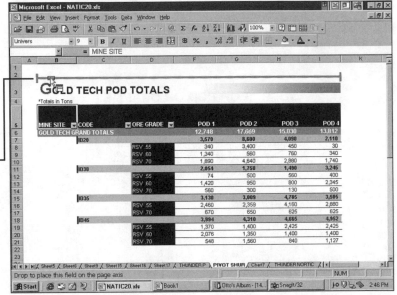

Figure 20.41.
By creating a page view with a PivotTable, you can manage the information from the PivotTable with a drop-down list.

Page drop zone

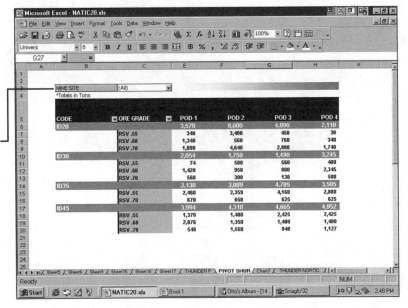

CREATING A QUICK SUMMARY

If you want a quick summary breakout of a data set, simply double-click the grand total, as shown in Figure 20.42, and Excel automatically creates an independent breakout on a separate sheet. The detail from double-clicking the grand total is shown in Figure 20.43. By double-clicking the data set, the subset of data that appears in that set will be displayed or hidden.

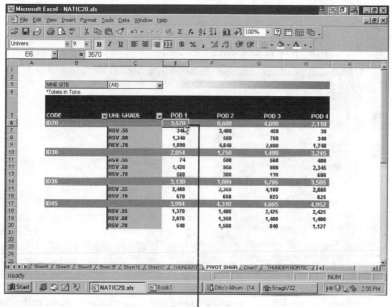

Figure 20.42.
To create an automatic summary, just double-click the grand total.

Double-click to audit.

Figure 20.43.
The result of double-clicking the grand total of a set in a PivotTable is the individual records that make up the total.

	MINE SITE	CODE	ORE GRADE	POD 1	POD 2	POD 3	POD 4
1	MINE SITE	CODE	ORE GRADE	POD 1	POD 2	POD 3	POD 4
2	GOLD TECH	ID20	RSV .70	100	340	600	230
3	GOLD TECH	ID20	RSV .55	340	3400	450	30
4	GOLD TECH	ID20	RSV .70	450	3400	560	450
5	GOLD TECH	ID20	RSV .70	560	340	850	500
6	GOLD TECH	ID20	RSV .70	780	560	870	560
7	GOLD TECH	ID20	RSV .60	1340	560	760	340
8							
9							

Audit data behind code ID20.

PART

VI

CH

20

WORKING WITH DATES IN PIVOTTABLES

Quite often, you'll have information from lists that contain dates. To transpose it into an understandable PivotTable, follow a few simple steps and you can create an effective summary of the information. Again, start with your list or database, like that shown in Figure 20.44.

Figure 20.44.
When working with dates, you can combine the dates to summarize by days, weeks, months, and so on.

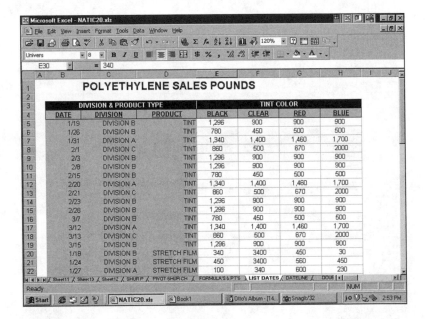

When working with dates, many times it's easier to see the information left to right rather than up and down, because most timelines are generated in this manner. Make sure to set the Page Layout setting in the PivotTable Options dialog box to Over, Then Down (see Figure 20.45).

To group dates together, select the first date field in the PivotTable and choose Data, Group and Outline, Group. The Grouping dialog box appears, enabling you to set parameters on the dates to be grouped (see Figure 20.46). Figure 20.47 shows the PivotTable grouped on a weekly basis (every seven days). You can do the same with numbers—for example, if you have average scores in a PivotTable and you want them grouped in ranges.

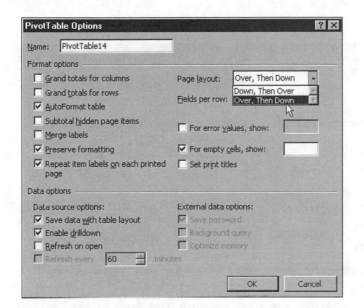

Figure 20.45.
When working with dates, many times it works well to view the information left to right rather than up and down.

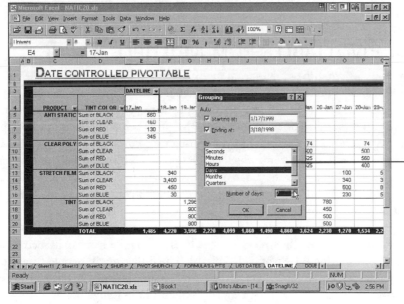

Figure 20.46.
You can set the parameters on date ranges by using the Group option. This works well with summarizing data weekly and monthly.

Set dates to group and sum data.

PART

VI

CH

20

Dates grouped in seven-day increments

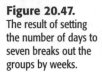

Figure 20.47.
The result of setting the number of days to seven breaks out the groups by weeks.

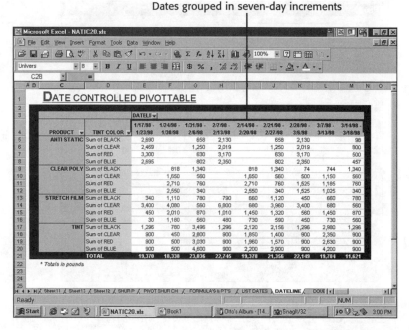

CREATING A PIVOTTABLE FROM MULTIPLE RANGES

Excel enables you to create PivotTables from multiple consolidation ranges by selecting the multiple consolidation control from Step 1 of the PivotTable Wizard. For example, if you have two companies with product sales or two divisions with product sales, you can establish separate worksheets or databases to control the list and then combine into a multiple consolidated PivotTable. (The wizard walks you through step by step.) Figure 20.48 shows Step 2b of 3 of the PivotTable Wizard, which enables you to browse through documents to find the lists or ranges. Drag over the range of data you want to consolidate and click the Add button to add it to the All Ranges section of the dialog box. If your consolidation ranges are coming from multiple files (as opposed to sheets), you can use the Browse button to select unopened files. The problem is that the Browse button doesn't actually open the files. Unless you've memorized the data ranges (addresses or range names), it's better to open the files before starting the PivotTable Wizard. The only time this could be a problem is if you have numerous files to open and restricted computer memory. In such a case, name each consolidation range so that you can manually type it in the Range box.

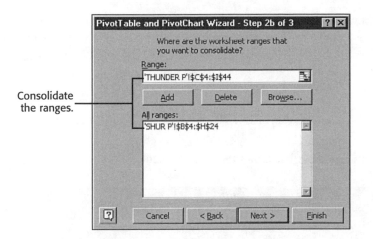

Figure 20.48.
To consolidate lists into a PivotTable, select the consolidation ranges in Step 1 of the PivotTable Wizard and add the ranges together.

Consolidate the ranges.

MANAGING EMPLOYEE HOURS AND COSTS WITH PIVOTTABLES

You can use PivotTables to manage employee hours and costs. After observing several attempts to manage employee hours and costs, I've found the easiest solution to be a combination of a table, list, VLOOKUP, and then a PivotTable. Once set up, such a table requires minimal effort to manage. If you have employee hours in one database or list, and in another area have a table that has the employee rates, use the VLOOKUP function to combine the two and then pivot the list. To build an employee cost-tracking PivotTable, first set up the information. Figure 20.49 shows a table that contains the employee base rate and overtime rate.

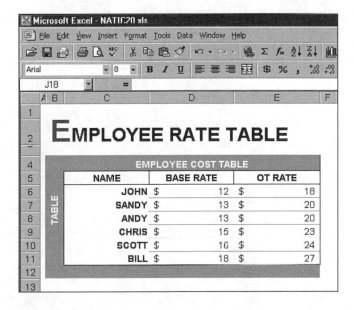

Figure 20.49.
The first step in creating an employee cost-tracking PivotTable is to create the table with rates.

PART

VI

CH

20

Combine the employee cost table with the list of hours an employee worked by using the VLOOKUP function. In the formula in cell G16 in Figure 20.50, the VLOOKUP function looks up the employee in the list in cell D16, refers to the table range $C$5:$E$10, and then the column number of the base rate. In this case, the column number of the base rate in the cost table is in column 2. Make sure the range referring to the cost table has absolute values, because you're going to be dragging the formula down and you want the table range to remain the same. Figure 20.51 shows the VLOOKUP referring to column 3, overtime rate for the employee in cell D16.

→ For details on VLOOKUP, **see** "Using VLOOKUP to Extract Line Items," **p. 619**

Figure 20.50.
Use a VLOOKUP function to refer to the employee in the list and the cost associated with the employee from the cost table.

Match the base rate from the table to the list with VLOOKUP.

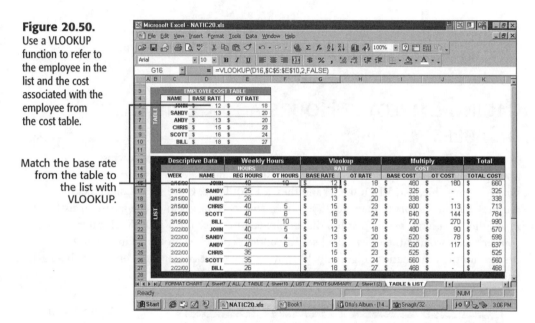

Multiply the regular hours times the base rate to find the base cost for the week for that particular employee. In Figure 20.52, cell I16, the formula reads =E16*G16. Drag the formula to the right to cell J16 to calculate the overtime costs. The total column in cell K16 adds the base cost and overtime cost in cells I16 and J16. Drag cells G16:K16 down the length of the list.

Now that you have the base of information set up, you'll want to pivot the information to summarize the employee cost for the week. In addition, if you have codes and/or projects the employee is working on, you can include that information and break out the summaries in PivotTables by employee, project, week, and so on.

There is a trick to making this PivotTable effortless. In Step 2 of the PivotTable Wizard, the range selected is C16:E2000 (see Figure 20.53). Although the current range of the list only goes down to row 27, I've selected a range that the PivotTable will never actually reach; thus, the PivotTable range will always include all the new rows of information added.

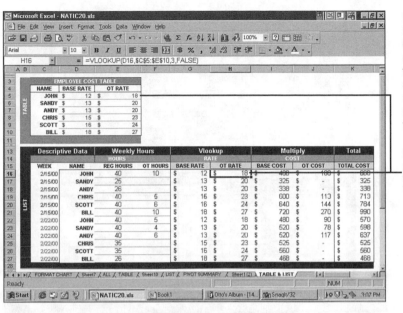

Figure 20.51.
Notice the difference in this VLOOKUP formula. It still refers to the same employee and table; but the column number from the range is 3, referring to the overtime rate.

Match the overtime rate from the table to the list with VLOOKUP.

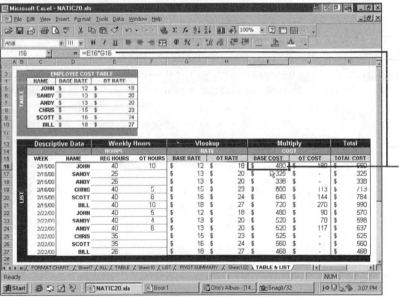

Figure 20.52.
Multiply the base rate and the regular hours to get the base cost for the employee for that week.

Multiply the base rate times the regular hours.

> **Note**
>
> Although highlighting extra blank rows keeps the range updated, they are nevertheless included in the PivotTable calculations, which adds to the calculation effort and the PivotTable cache (memory). It also adds a blank listing to the PivotTable, which can be hidden by using the name field drop-down list.

PivotTable list to manage hours and costs

Figure 20.53.
Select a range that the list will never grow to. This will ensure that when the PivotTable is refreshed, it's always selecting all the information in the list.

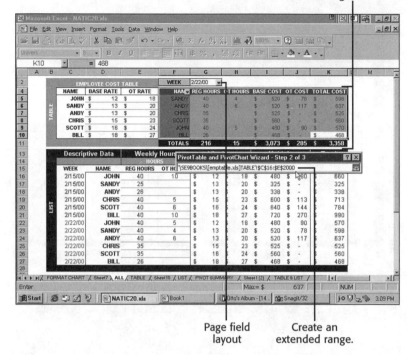

Page field
layout

Create an
extended range.

To arrange the PivotTable in a logical fashion, set the fields in order (see Figure 20.54): the WEEK field in the PAGE section of the diagram and the NAME field in the ROW section. Place the regular hours, overtime hours, base cost, overtime cost, and total cost in the DATA section.

In the final step of the PivotTable Wizard, click the Options button and deselect Grand Totals for Columns and Grand Totals for Rows (see Figure 20.55).

The final setup of the PivotTable shows the Week pull-down at the top and the employees listed down the left column (in F6:F11), with the corresponding totals to the right. I've placed the tables on the same sheet so that you can get an understanding of how they work together (see Figure 20.56).

Week   Employee Name   Hours

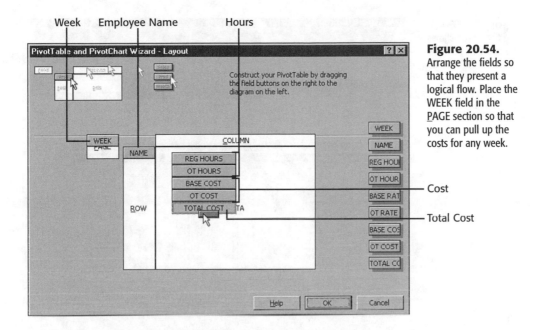

Figure 20.54.
Arrange the fields so that they present a logical flow. Place the WEEK field in the PAGE section so that you can pull up the costs for any week.

Cost

Total Cost

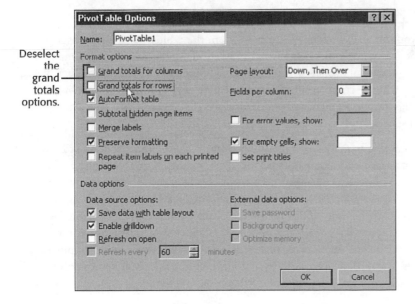

Deselect the grand totals options.

Figure 20.55.
Deselect the grand totals options to help create an easy-to-read PivotTable.

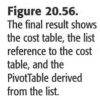

Figure 20.56.
The final result shows the cost table, the list reference to the cost table, and the PivotTable derived from the list.

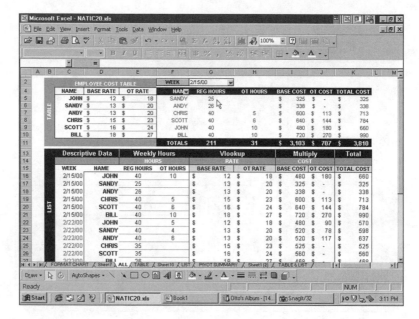

ANALYZING COSTS WITH PIVOTCHARTS

With PivotCharts, you can analyze your information from the table of employee costs. The two important characteristics to look at when analyzing costs are the base costs versus overtime costs, and the regular hours versus overtime hours. These are due to specific variables in the workplace as to why overtime occurs (but you may be able to minimize cost by implementing a checkpoint with a signoff sheet before overtime occurs, and also with proper planning and scheduling).

The PivotChart enables you to get a quick picture of your situation and also look at ratios. If you have a way to measure your company's performance in output, for example, you'll want to look at the ratio of overtime against output and see the trends that occur over time. Soon you'll be able to focus on inefficiencies that result from specific occurrences in the workplace or business environment. Notice the field placement in the PivotChart in Figure 20.57, which includes a secondary axis for the overtime. Look at your information in ratio form—how and where overtime stacks up against regular time, and why certain employees have massive amounts of overtime versus others who have minimal amounts of overtime. This is generally because of improper workload distribution and planning.

The reason for the secondary axis is to get a quick view of how the overtime stacks up against the regular time. By setting both axes to the same constraints, such as the maximum value being $800 and the minimum being $0, you can get a quick comparison of the two. Another way to compare items over weeks is to place the fields WEEK and Data at the bottom and eliminate all other fields (see Figure 20.58).

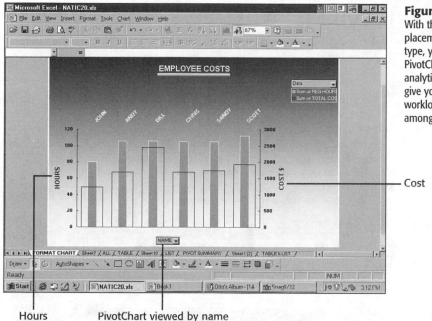

Figure 20.57.
With the proper field placement and chart type, you can make PivotCharts powerful analytical tools that give you pictures of workload distribution among employees.

Cost

Hours   PivotChart viewed by name

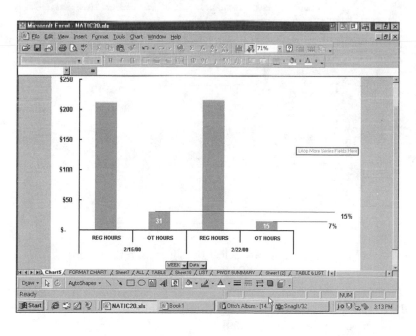

Figure 20.58.
Another way to view the information is to lay out the week and data fields at the bottom and eliminate all others. This PivotChart is viewed by week.

PART

VI

CH

20

SAVING AND EDITING PIVOTTABLES IN HTML FORMAT

New features in Excel 2000 enable you to save a PivotTable as an HTML document and modify HTML documents posted on an Internet or intranet site.

Note

The benefit of this feature is that you can manipulate the data fields while the document is posted and then print the changes. The drawback is that you can't save the changes in Excel format; changes made to the HTML document revert to the format in which the document was posted (HTML). The data can be refreshed, but formatting changes saved must come from the source document, thus making this feature a bit cumbersome.

To save a PivotTable as a Web page, follow these steps.

1. Choose File, Save as Web Page.

2. Specify whether you want to save the whole workbook or the selected worksheet, as shown in Figure 20.59. If you select Selection: Sheet, the Add Interactivity option becomes available. Select Add Interactivity and click Publish.

Figure 20.59.
Add interactivity to your Web PivotTable by selecting Selection: Sheet and checking Add Interactivity.

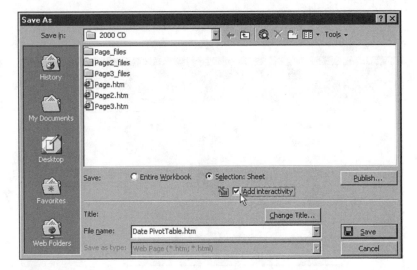

3. In the Publish As Web Page dialog box, select the sheet from the Choose list. Then select the entire sheet or just the PivotTable region.

4. The Add Interactivity With option enables you to create spreadsheet functionality (formulas and so on) or PivotTable functionality (which enables you to move fields). Select PivotTable Functionality (see Figure 20.60).

5. Specify a filename for the Web page and click Publish.

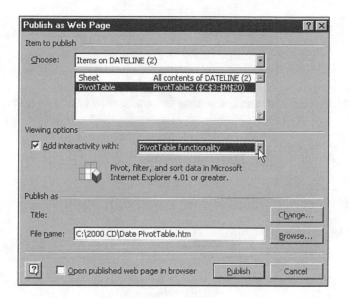

Figure 20.60.
You can choose spreadsheet functionality or PivotTable functionality from the Add Interactivity With option.

6. Select and open the HTML document from the folder where it was saved (see Figure 20.61). You can deselect field items with the drop-down list from the field just as you would in a normal PivotTable. You can also expand and collapse fields (see Figure 20.62), drag and drop fields (see Figures 20.63 and 20.64), and add or remove fields (see Figures 20.65 and 20.66).

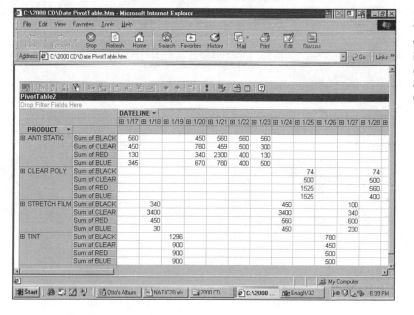

Figure 20.61.
The PivotTable saved with Web functionality enables you to drag and drop fields, and expand and collapse fields.

Figure 20.62.
Week 1/17 expanded, with the colors broken out. From here, you can use the drop-down lists to deselect line items.

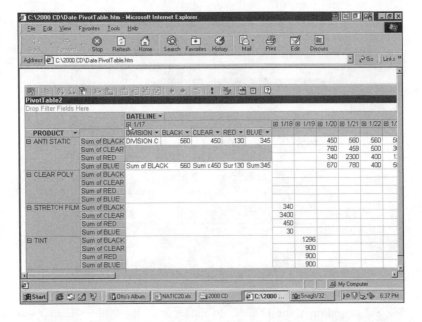

Figure 20.63.
Dragging the field item to a new drop area on the PivotTable.

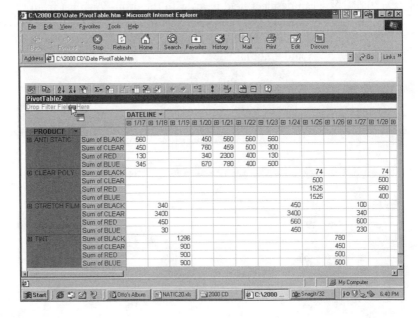

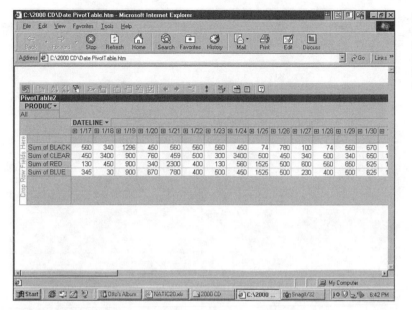

Figure 20.64.
By dropping the major field item to a page view, you can summarize line-item data for your report.

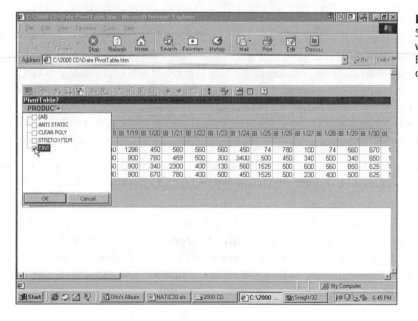

Figure 20.65.
Select the item you want to summarize. Excel will filter the data.

Figure 20.66.
The final filtered data.

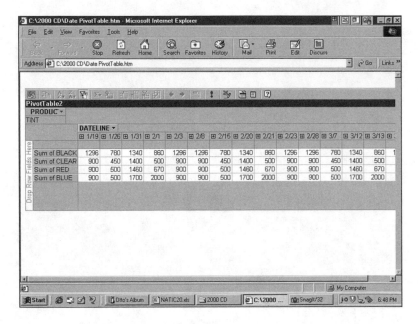

USING THE PROPERTY TOOLBOX AND FIELD LIST

When working with PivotTables in Internet Explorer, you have two special tools available. The *PivotTable Property Toolbox* allows for greater flexibility when manipulating and controlling data while on an intranet or Internet site (see Figure 20.67). From here you can modify text, display and hide the title bar or toolbar, expand and collapse indicators and drop areas, and so on. The most useful option here is the ability to change the field list. To access the Property Toolbox, click the Property Toolbox button on the PivotTable toolbar in Internet Explorer. The toolbox varies depending on what's selected when you click the button.

By clicking the Field List button on the PivotTable toolbar, you can display the *PivotTable Field List* (see Figure 20.68), from which you can add data to the PivotTable from the source document.

Formats and additions to the PivotTable Web page are interactive only while it's open; the document changes can be saved only as HTML. However, the ability to change, move, format, and print data while the PivotTable is posted to the Web is still a powerful feature. One of the most powerful features of all, of course, is that users don't need to have Excel to gain these manipulation features; they need only Internet Explorer.

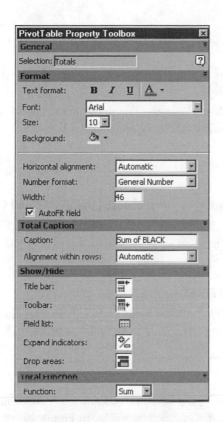

Figure 20.67.
The PivotTable Property Toolbox.

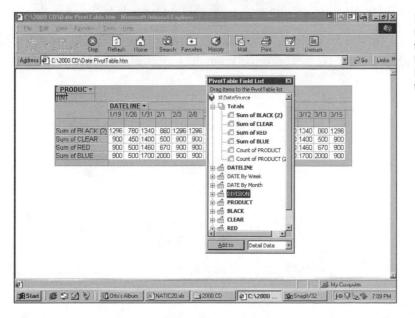

Figure 20.68.
Drag the item from the PivotTable Field List to the HTML PivotTable to add it to the PivotTable.

PART
VI

CH
20

TROUBLESHOOTING

ENABLING DRILLDOWN

Why can't I drill down in my PivotTable?

To be able to drill down by double-clicking, the Enable Drilldown option must be selected in the Data Options section of the PivotTable Options dialog box.

GROUPING PIVOTTABLE DATES

How do I group PivotTable dates?

Select the first date cell in the PivotTable; then choose Data, Group and Outline, Group. Enter the Starting At and Ending At date. Select the time measurement under By, and adjust the Number of Days setting if necessary.

VIEWING THE DATA BEHIND PIVOTTABLE SUMMARIES

How do I see the information behind PivotTable totals?

Double-click on the total of the selected field item. Excel creates a separate sheet that lists the information that makes up the totals on the PivotTable—a powerful auditing device.

EXCEL IN PRACTICE

You can use PivotTables to summarize and control quantities by dates. Figure 20.69 shows a date-controlled PivotTable with dates grouped by weeks. In Figure 20.70, the PivotTable summarizes monthly quantities by using a conditional sum formula as shown in the Formula bar. The formula references the month cell and the date range, then sums the specified column. In this example, the column is C or BLACK. By typing a different month number in cell I20, you can make the formula sum the quantities only for that month.

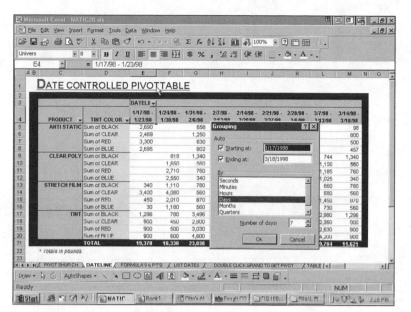

Figure 20.69.
Manage data in
PivotTables by
grouping.

Month reference

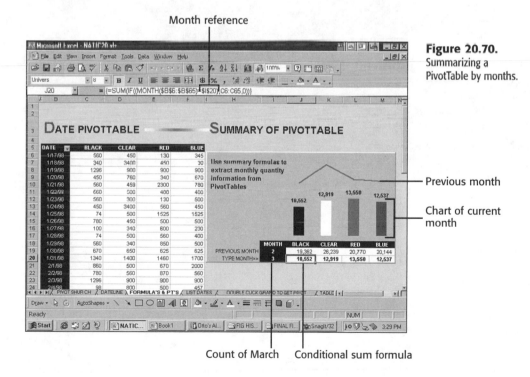

Figure 20.70.
Summarizing a
PivotTable by months.

Previous month

Chart of current
month

Count of March   Conditional sum formula

CHAPTER 21

Managing Data with Formulas and Form Controls

by Patrick D. Blattner
Patrick@BlattnerBooks.com

In this chapter

COMBINING EXCEL FEATURES TO MANAGE YOUR DATA

This chapter provides a number of suggestions for creating worksheets that help you manage your data. Some features may be familiar from other chapters. The point here is to use feature *combinations* that automate worksheets and save time and effort for the user. Although the chapter begins with some simple solutions, the particular focus of this chapter is on building more complex formulas, using database functions, and adding form controls to help the whole process work more efficiently.

Excel offers a variety of features that stand alone to accomplish specific tasks but when combined can be powerful tools to extract information from your worksheets seamlessly and almost effortlessly. Suppose that one of your job functions is to track week-to-date, month-to-date, and year-to-date costs for your company's hourly employees. With the right worksheet setup and formulas, you don't have to manually calculate this information—the worksheet will do it for you, based on the daily entries. The same principle applies whether you're tracking production quantities, inventory, sales, or any other type of information that requires some kind of consistent calculation.

Note

If you manage employee hours and costs, try a PivotTable for analyzing your data. For details on using PivotTables, see Chapter 20, "Using PivotTables and PivotCharts."

EXTRACTING DATE-BASED TOTALS FROM LISTS

When maintaining controls on a business, you'll need proper reporting procedures, and with nearly every business weekly, monthly, and yearly costs to date are standard reporting. You probably also need to know whether the business is on track with projections for the year. After extracting the totals, you'll want to show variances to analyze projections versus actual results. The following sections describe how to set up formulas for all these types of calculations.

Tip #245 from

Patrick

The key element in extracting information effectively is consistency of the data. Formulas or functions can be case sensitive if you set them up that way; they won't return the desired results if the list isn't set up appropriately.

USING NAMED RANGES IN LONG OR COMPLEX FORMULAS

By defining *named ranges (page 258)*, you can avoid certain problems that are inherent when building complex formulas. A range name works as an absolute reference in a formula. In Figure 21.1, for example, the formula in cell F9 references the TOTAL HOURS column above the formula. Dragging that formula elsewhere would change the reference. If you gave the name TOTAL_HOURS to the range F3:F7, however, you could use the formula =SUM(TOTAL_HOURS) to get the same result, as shown in Figure 21.2. You can apply named ranges to any formula by selecting the name from the Paste Name dialog box (choose Insert, Name, Paste or press F3).

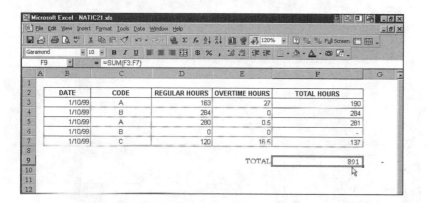

Figure 21.1.
A formula with relative references will be adjusted automatically when copied or moved.

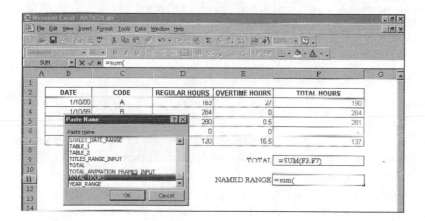

Figure 21.2.
Using a named range in a formula.

You can copy or drag formulas with range names anywhere you want, and Excel will always refer to that particular defined location when totaling the formula.

Tip #246 from

fwh.k

When creating worksheets for use by other people, remember that range names can be much easier to comprehend than row-and-column references. To understand the range F3:F7, you must look at the column and row headings and scan through the worksheet to find the referenced range, and then determine exactly what the range refers to. The range TOTAL_HOURS, on the other hand, indicates exactly what it refers to within the range name itself.

EXTRACTING WEEKLY INFORMATION

Figure 21.3 shows a simple list of weeks with employee hours broken out, including regular time, overtime, and corresponding totals. We'll use this list in this section to extract for the totals by week over a period of time.

Figure 21.3.
This week-by-week
list will be used
to extract totals.

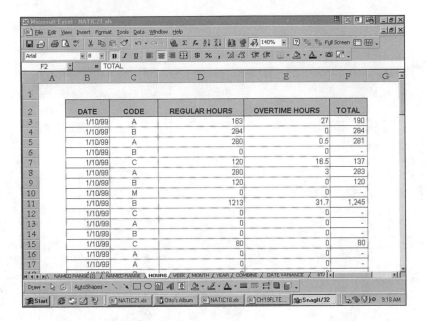

To create an extraction setup, perform the following steps:

1. Set up your worksheet with appropriate column headings, as shown in the preceding example.

2. On a separate sheet, set up a table that represents the columns in the list you want to track (see Figure 21.4). In this example, each row calculates a particular product from the HOURS sheet.

3. Create a SUM(IF formula as shown in the example, using the following syntax:

   `=SUM(IF((sheet!range=criteria)*(sheet!range=criteria),sheet!sum_range,0))`

4. Press Ctrl+Shift+Enter to enter this formula as an array.

The following table shows the ranges used in the formula in Figure 21.4.

Sheet	Range Name	Range
HOURS	DATE	B3:B93
HOURS	PRODUCT	C3:C93
HOURS	REGULAR_HOURS	D3:D93
HOURS	OVERTIME_HOURS	E3:E93
HOURS	TOTAL	F3:F93
WEEK	CODE	D5
WEEK	WEEK	G2

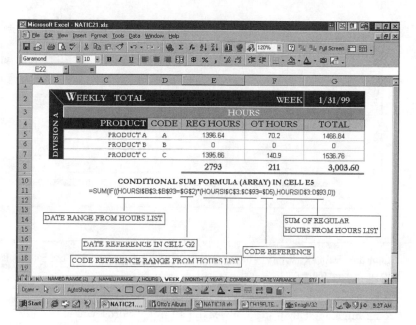

Figure 21.4.
The array formula in cell E5 extracts the total regular hours from the HOURS sheet for the week entered in cell G2.

The formula works from the following two trigger points:

- Cell D5 dictates the product or the product code.
- Cell G2 indicates the week to be used in calculations.

In essence, the conditional sum formula says, "If the date in the range B3:B93 from the HOURS sheet is equal to the date value in cell G2, and the product range C3:C93 from the HOURS sheet is equal to the product code in cell D5, then sum the total hours in the range D3:D93 from the HOURS sheet." Note the use of *mixed references* ($D5 and D$3:D$93), which allow you to properly copy the first formula to the other cells.

Please note that the IF function isn't required in the array formula. The following formula also could accomplish the goal:

`=SUM((HOURS!$B$3:$B$93=$G$2)*(HOURS!$C$3:$C$93=$D5)*(HOURS!D$3:D$93))`

The advantage of using IF is that you can specify text that you want to display for the ELSE portion of the IF (for example, displaying "N/A").

Caution

> Be careful when entering ranges; the ranges must match exactly or the formula will return an error. Also, you must have exact date matches.

If the date or product code changes, the formula automatically changes to accommodate the new references. This problem is solved by using range names, as shown in Figure 21.5. It certainly is easier to understand the formula when using the defined names!

PART

VI

CH

21

Figure 21.5.
Inserting named ranges in conditional formulas with several references can effectively communicate where each of the reference points are coming from.

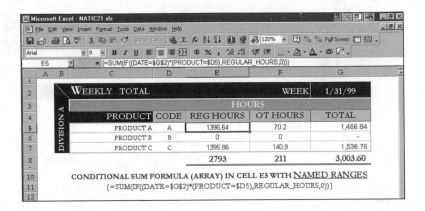

Tip #247 from

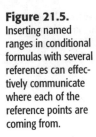

Copy the REGULAR_HOURS formula to the OT HOURS column, and then use <u>E</u>dit, <u>R</u>eplace to change the range name.

What if you're compiling data daily instead of weekly? In other words, you have daily amounts but you want to calculate based on weeks, and the trigger cell G2 needs to indicate the week range (for example, the week of 1/10 through 1/16).

The information still falls within a specified week indicated in cell G2. The date-indicator cell should contain the week-ending date, and your list should include two columns: one with the week-ending date from which the formula will extract, and the other a date-entered column for the actual date the information was entered.

EXTRACTING MONTHLY INFORMATION

When you're tracking costs, widgets, and so on, you probably want to view your information not only by week, but also cumulative month to date. Excel lets you "roll up" the weeks into months by adding a month condition to the conditional sum formula in cell E5, as shown in Figure 21.6. (The number 1 in cell G2 is the month indicator—for example, 1 = January, 2 = February, and so on.)

To set up this table, follow these steps:

1. Set up the table similar to the weeks table in the preceding section, but change the headings in row 2 (MONTHLY TOTAL in B2 and MONTH in F2) and specify in cell G2 the number value of the month you want to track (1 through 12).

2. In cell E5, type the formula, using the following syntax:
   ```
   =SUM(IF((month(sheet!range=criteria)=month_criteria)*(sheet!range=criteria),
   ➥sheet!sum_range,0))
   ```

3. Press Ctrl+Shift+Enter to enter the formula as an array.

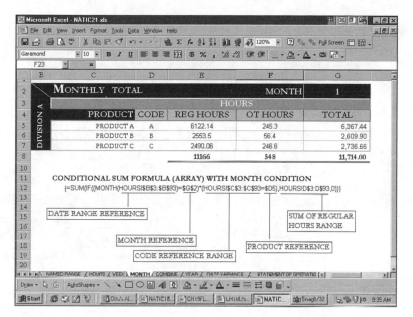

Figure 21.6.
By adding the month condition to the conditional sum formula, you can extract monthly quantity or cost data from a list.

As in the previous example, the trigger points are in cells D5 and G2. In essence, this conditional sum formula says, "If the month in the range B3:B93 from the HOURS sheet is equal to the month value in cell G2, and the product range C3:C93 from the HOURS sheet is equal to the product code in cell D5, then sum the total hours in the range D3:D93 from the HOURS sheet."

EXTRACTING YEARLY INFORMATION

To roll up the months into years, you add a year condition to the conditional sum formula, as shown in Figure 21.7.

To add a year condition to the conditional sum formula, follow these steps:

1. In the calculation worksheet, change the headings in row 2 (YEARLY TOTAL in B2 and YEAR in F2), and indicate in cell G2 the year you want to track. If you're entering the year 2000, simply enter 1/1/00, 1/1/2000, or just 2000.

Tip #248 from

Patrick

If possible, enter dates with four-digit years to prevent Excel from using its internal algorithm to apply the century. For example, entering 1/1/29 results in the year 2029; 1/1/30 yields 1930. Two-digit years between 00 and 29 become 2000–2029; numbers between 29–99 convert to the 20th century (1929–1999).

2. Change the formula in cell E5 to use the following syntax:
   ```
   =SUM(IF((year(sheet!range=criteria)=year_criteria)*(sheet!range=criteria),
   ➥sheet!sum_range,0))
   ```

3. Press Ctrl+Shift+Enter to enter the formula as an array.

Figure 21.7.
By adding the year condition to the conditional sum formula, you can extract yearly quantity or cost data from a list.

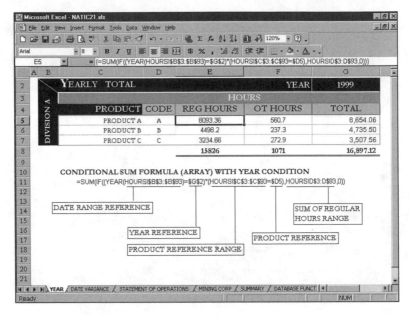

In essence, the conditional sum formula now says, "If the year in the range B3:B93 from the HOURS sheet is equal to the year value in cell G2, and the product range C3:C93 from the HOURS sheet is equal to the product code in cell D5, then sum the total hours in the range D3:D93 from the HOURS sheet."

The previous examples show the calculations being performed on separate worksheets, but you may prefer a consolidated sheet, as shown in Figure 21.8.

Figure 21.8.
Displaying the tables in hierarchical fashion enables you to get the total picture either from top down or left to right.

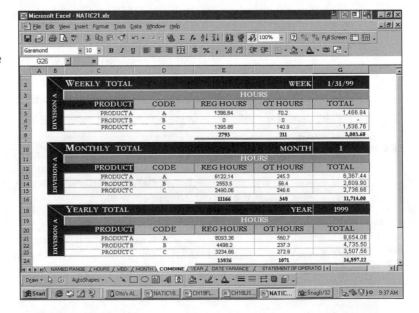

USING THE CONDITIONAL SUM WIZARD AND LOOKUP WIZARD

Not familiar with looking up or summing information with formulas? Excel makes it easy for you with the Conditional Sum Wizard and Lookup Wizard. These wizards assist you in the process of writing formulas with conditions.

Note

To use these wizards, they must be listed on the Wizard submenu of the Tools menu. To add the wizards to the menu, choose Tools, Add-Ins, select Conditional Sum Wizard and Lookup Wizard in the add-ins list, click OK, and confirm that you want to install the add-ins.

USING THE CONDITIONAL SUM WIZARD

A *conditional sum* is used when a list has several columns of data, each of which contains critical criteria for summing up information. For example, if a list has columns that specify quarter, product, sales totals, and so on, you might want to total the sales for a certain product type in a certain quarter.

Figure 21.9 shows a typical worksheet. In the following steps, I'll use the *Conditional Sum Wizard* to sum all totals for the Gold product in Q1 in this worksheet.

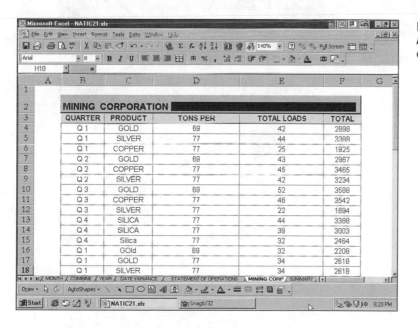

Figure 21.9.
A list containing two conditions to sum.

To use the Conditional Sum Wizard to sum values based on two or more conditions, follow these steps:

1. Select a cell somewhere in the list you want to use.

2. Choose Tools, Wizard, Conditional Sum.

3. The first dialog box of the Conditional Sum Wizard specifies the range of the list (see Figure 21.10). When the list range is defined correctly, click Next.

4. In step 2, use the first drop-down list to select the column you want to sum—in this case, the TOTAL column (see Figure 21.11).

Figure 21.10.
The first step is defining the range you want to use.

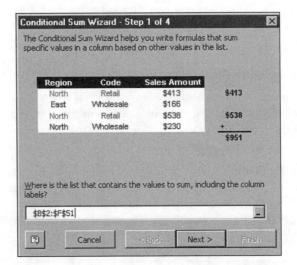

Figure 21.11.
In step 2, specify the conditions you want the formula to apply.

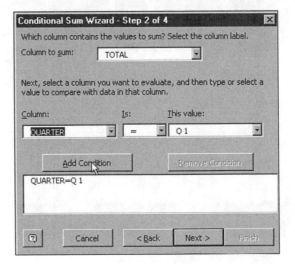

5. Now add the conditions. For this example, the first condition under Column is QUARTER. I selected = in the Is box, and under This Value selected Q1 (in other words, the value in the QUARTER column is equal to Q1). After specifying the first condition, click Add Condition. Then add the second condition—for this example, PRODUCT = GOLD.

6. Choose Next.

7. In step 3, you have two choices (see Figure 21.12):

   ■ Copy the formula you have created to your worksheet.

   ■ Copy the formula and its conditional values. This option creates automation in the formula—that is, when you change a condition, the formula reflects the conditional change. Use this option when you think you will want to sum different values in the same column later on.

   Make your choice and click Next.

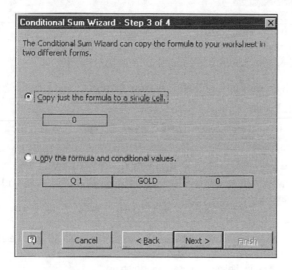

Figure 21.12.
Now that the wizard knows how to create your formula, you just need to indicate where you want it.

8. If you specified copying just the formula in the preceding step, type or select the cell address for the formula. If you're copying formula and conditions, specify the cell for the first value, click Next, specify the location of the second value, click Next, and so on until you have positioned all the conditions and the formula.

   As you click Next, the wizard positions the formula or condition in the specified cell.

9. Click Finish to place the newly created formula in the specified location.

USING THE LOOKUP WIZARD

The *Lookup Wizard* finds the point where two conditions intersect. Let's say you have different points of interest for your global business. You want to be able to pull up data for a global business sector and find out whether the different deals in progress are complete for your business strategies. You could use the Lookup Wizard to find the intersecting points. For this example, look at Figure 21.13. I'll use the Lookup Wizard to find out whether the North America contract for bundled items is complete.

Figure 21.13.
I'll use the Lookup Wizard to look up values and text where two specified points in this worksheet intersect.

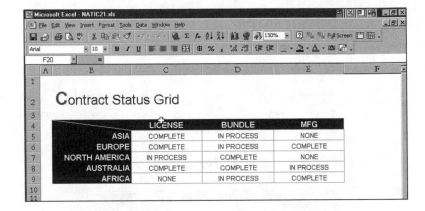

To find the text or value where two points intersect, follow these steps:

1. Click anywhere in the list you want included in your formula.

2. Choose Tools, Wizard, Lookup.

3. Confirm the range you want to use (see Figure 21.14). Be sure that the range includes the row and column headings.

4. In step 2, you indicate which row and column labels identify the value you're looking up (see Figure 21.15). In this example, the lookup column is BUNDLE, and the lookup row is NORTH AMERICA.

Tip #249 from

If the data doesn't include labels, or the labels in the drop-down lists don't exactly match what you want, select No row label matches exactly or No column label matches exactly in the appropriate drop-down list.

5. In the next step, you have two options (see Figure 21.16):

   ■ Copy the formula you have created to your worksheet.

   ■ Copy the formula and its lookup parameters, thus making the formula conditionally interactive. For example, if you change the cell containing the row heading to reflect a new region, the formula automatically updates to reflect the cell change.

Make your choice and click Next.

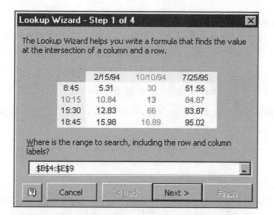

Figure 21.14.
Specify or confirm the range of the list.

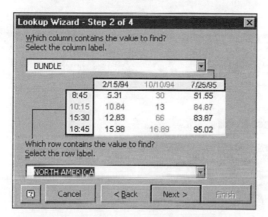

Figure 21.15.
Indicate the headings that will contain the intersecting point.

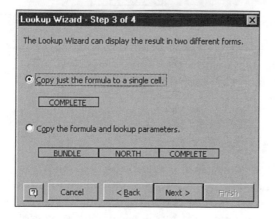

Figure 21.16.
Specify whether you want just the formula, or formula and parameters.

6. If you specified copying just the formula in the preceding step, type or select the cell address for the formula. If you're copying formula and lookup parameters, specify the cell for the first parameter, click Next, specify the location of the second parameter, click Next, and so on until you have positioned all the parameters and the formula.

As you click Next, the wizard positions the formula or parameter in the specified cell.

For this example, I'll place the row heading parameter in cell B12, the column heading parameter in cell C12, and the formula in cell D12.

7. Click Finish to place the newly created formula in the specified location.

The final result for this simple example is shown in Figure 21.17. The formula in the Formula bar reflects cell B12 in MATCH case 1 and cell C12 in MATCH case 2. If the value in cell D12 is changed from NORTH AMERICA to ASIA, the result in cell D12 would be IN PROCESS.

Figure 21.17.
The result of the Lookup Wizard process is an INDEX MATCH formula that matches two conditions to the Index range.

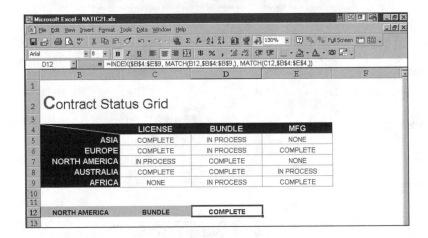

Tip #250 from

Unlike manually using the VLOOKUP or HLOOKUP function, the lookup row or column doesn't have to be sorted A–Z in the Lookup Wizard.

USING FUNCTIONS WITH TABLES

One of the most difficult things for people in business to understand is how to measure data. Whether you're writing a book, creating widgets, dealing with creative factors, or managing finances, each element of the process can be measured. Being able to create a variance analysis is one of the most critical factors in gauging the success of your project or process. Knowing where you are at any given point enables you to both manage your business and peer over the horizon to see potential problems before they occur.

Figure 21.18 shows a simple table that explains the critical components in measuring variance. This particular table is an *active variance table*, which responds to something in process or occurring. A *static* or *final variance table* deals with final analysis—after the fact, when the project or process is complete.

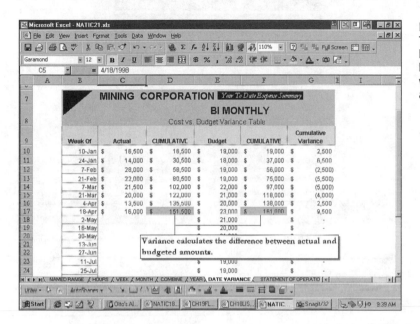

Figure 21.18.
The variance is calculated from the cumulative projected data versus the cumulative actual data.

Tip #251 from

Patrick

Variance can be pulled from any time factor, such as seconds, minutes, weeks, months, quarters, and years. The key is to maintain the projected and actual figures.

In this example, cell G17 shows that the amount budgeted to date exceeds the amount spent to date by $9,500. The critical components for the variance table in this example are the cumulative columns for actual and budgeted dollars.

USING VLOOKUP TO EXTRACT LINE ITEMS

After you establish a variance table or list, you can use Excel's lookup functions to extract line items for variance analysis. The table in Figure 21.19 uses a formula with the VLOOKUP function (in cell D5). In this example, the formula is triggered by the week specified in cell C5. Excel looks for that week within the first column of the data table (in the range B9:B22). When it finds that week, Excel displays in the formula cell (D5) the corresponding amount in the third column of the data table (the cumulative actual amount).

If the source cell in the worksheet doesn't yet contain a cumulative amount—the number hasn't been entered yet—Excel displays a zero in the formula cell.

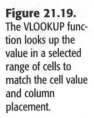

Figure 21.19.
The VLOOKUP function looks up the value in a selected range of cells to match the cell value and column placement.

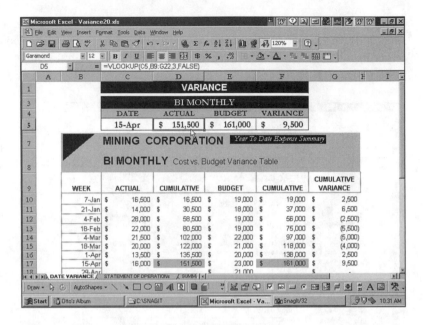

Note

Excel lookup functions count columns or rows only within the data table.

Caution

The lookup column (the Week column, in this example) must be sorted in ascending order (A–Z).

Figure 21.20 shows the VLOOKUP formula (in cell E5) that finds and displays the cumulative budgeted amount. It's identical to the formula in cell D5 except for the column number, which has been changed to indicate that the fifth column in the data table contains the value we're looking up.

LAYING OUT A VARIANCE TABLE REPORT

After you set up a list with the variance of the different categories you want to track, you can automatically extract the information with SUM(IF formulas, as discussed earlier in the chapter, or you could use the VLOOKUP function to extract data for a particular line item.

You can combine multiple variance calculations into a single worksheet, as Figure 21.21 shows. This worksheet uses the date values in cells B3, F3, and J3 to trigger the formula sum variances over time. You also can reference the text in column A to make your table completely automated. After you enter the formula, you can improve the look of the report by hiding the date reference cells in row 3 (see Figure 21.22).

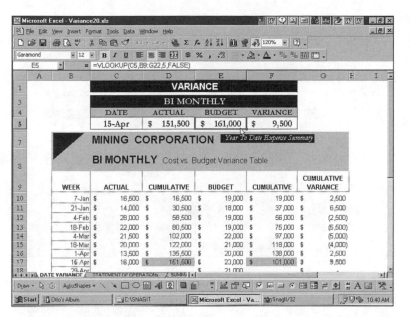

Figure 21.20.
Although you can scan by eye for totals with a simple table like this, most businesses accumulate far more data. Using lookup functions can simplify the process of finding targeted information.

This example references a list that contains the date range in column P, the project range in column Q, and the actual cost in column R. You can reference any list or sheet; in this example, the list is to the right of the summary table, on the same sheet.

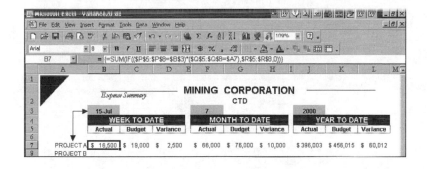

Figure 21.21.
Using absolute values means that you would need to generate this formula only once. If this formula is dragged down one row, the $A7 reference would change to refer to $A8 (Project B), because the row number is relative.

EXTRACTING DATA WITH THE DATABASE FUNCTIONS

Database functions are great for analyzing data with changing criteria. In Figure 21.23, for example, a set of database functions provides a variety of information from the data in the range B3:G9. Notice that in place of the field or cell reference, these formulas use the column heading in quotations. This is just an easier way to understand where the information is coming from. As the example shows, database functions can extract both numbers and text.

Figure 21.22.
Hide the date reference row to finish the variance report for a clear, concise presentation.

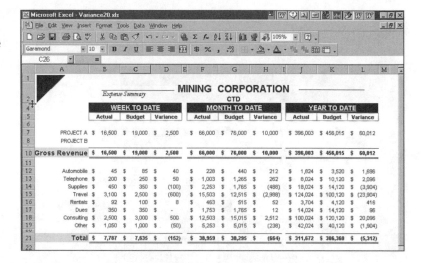

Figure 21.23.
Database functions can be powerful tools for extracting and managing information that meets specific criteria.

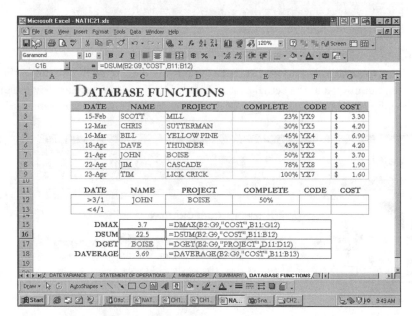

Table 21.1 describes several commonly used database functions.

TABLE 21.1.	COMMON DATABASE FUNCTIONS
Function	**Definition**
DCOUNT	Counts the number of records that meet the specified criteria.
DMAX	Extracts the maximum value within a specified range.

Function	Definition
DSUM	Sums the values within the specified range.
DGET	Extracts a single value from the database, based on the specified criteria.
DAVERAGE	Returns the average of the values within a specified range.

You use the following syntax for database functions:

`=Dfunction(database,field,criteria)`

- The *database* argument refers to the range encompassing the entire list or database.

- The *field* argument refers to a particular column in the list. If you omit the *field* argument, the function operates on the entire list. This argument can consist of either the column heading in quotes (""), or the cell address containing that column heading.

- The *criteria* argument specifies the basis on which you want the function to select particular cells. A criteria range must include column headings, just like the criteria range in a list *filter (page 542)*.

For additional information on functions, see Appendix A.

CLEANING UP DATA WITH TEXT FUNCTIONS

In an environment with multiple lists generated by several people, it's common to inherit lists that weren't set up properly and need to change the format of the list for use in extracting and manipulating data. Figure 21.24 shows several text functions used to account for many variations of text situations.

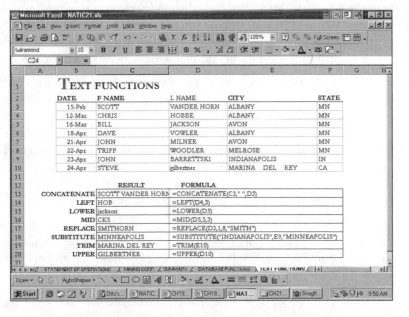

Figure 21.24.
Text functions are great tools for cleaning lists of information that have little or no consistency.

Table 21.2 describes a number of common text functions.

TABLE 21.2.   TEXT FUNCTIONS

Function	Definition
CONCATENATE	Adjoins text from independent cells into one cell.
LEFT	Extracts the left character(s) of text to the number specified.
LOWER	Returns text to lowercase.
MID	Extracts the middle characters of text.
REPLACE	Replaces a portion of a text string with a different string that you specify. Use REPLACE when you want to replace any text string in a specific location.
SUBSTITUTE	Replaces specific text with other text.
TRIM	Removes extra spaces in a cell.
UPPER	Returns text to uppercase.

For additional information on functions, see Appendix A.

ADDING FORM CONTROLS TO YOUR WORKSHEETS

Form controls in Excel include check boxes, drop-down lists, spinners, and so on that you can add to charts, lists, and other areas of your worksheets to create custom forms for use in data entry and data management. There are multiple ways to use form controls, but the underlying premise is to use form controls in conjunction with formulas. Form controls link to a cell, and then you apply a formula that addresses the link to look up the information or calculate from the information. For example, suppose you're creating a standard bid sheet for different types of construction equipment. A check box on the form could be set up so that if you check the box, it automatically includes and calculates the type of equipment and rate.

You can use form controls with tables, lists, charts, and even PivotTables. The controls actually are quite simple to create and use. After you set up your worksheet, you then apply the controls from the Forms toolbar as needed to fit your situation. The form shown in Figure 21.25, for example, uses a simple drop-down list to extract an equipment number. Formulas tied to the cell link then extract the corresponding values. Some form controls can be tied to Excel macros or VBA programs to perform tasks. For information on writing Excel macros and simple VBA applications, see Chapter 29, "Recording and Editing a Macro," and Chapter 30, "Creating Interactive Excel Applications with VBA."

Note

If you have some experience writing Visual Basic code or Web scripts, you can use ActiveX controls from the Control toolbox in Excel to create custom applications for Excel. These topics are beyond the scope of this book, but Macmillan Computer Publishing offers a wide variety of other books that specifically cover Visual Basic and ActiveX. You also can consult the Excel Help system for limited guidance on using the ActiveX controls with Excel.

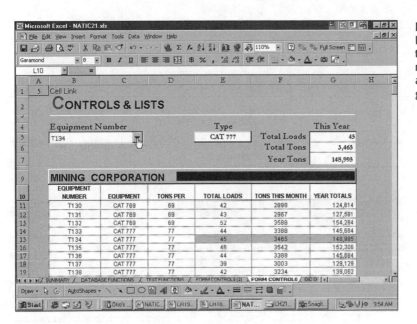

Figure 21.25.
Form controls applied to lists allow for minimal formula writing and can serve as a great analytical tool.

Table 21.3 describes the form controls available from the Forms toolbar.

TABLE 21.3. CONTROLS ON THE FORMS TOOLBAR

Button	Name	Description
Aα	Label	Places a label in the worksheet for use in naming other controls.
abl	Edit Box	Creates a data-entry box for forms. (This control doesn't work on regular worksheets.)
xvz,	Group Box	Groups the selected option buttons. Using two groups allows for additional cell links.
▭	Button	Runs a macro.
☑	Check Box	Produces a TRUE or FALSE response when selected or deselected.
◉	Option Button	Creates the number of the option button in a single group. You can add additional groups for generating a new cell link.
🗏	List Box	Returns the number of the item selected.
🗏	Combo Box	Combines a list box and an edit box.
🗏	Combination List-Edit	A combined list and text box. This feature is not available on a worksheet.

PART
VI

CH
21

continues

TABLE 21.3. CONTINUED

Button	Name	Description
	Combination Drop-Down Edit	A drop-down list with an edit box. This feature is not available on a worksheet.
	Scroll Bar	A draggable scrollbar that allows for high and low limits, as well as incremental change.
	Spinner	A counter that allows for high and low limits, as well as incremental change.
	Control Properties	Displays a dialog box of options for the selected control.
	Edit Code	Enables you to edit code associated with the control selected.
	Toggle Grid	Turns the grid lines of a worksheet on or off.
	Run Dialog	Displays the dialog box on the active dialog sheet. Used as a test or preview of the dialog box drawn. This feature is unavailable on a worksheet.

To apply form controls to a list or form, display the Forms toolbar (choose View, Toolbars, Forms), click the desired tool, and draw the control on the worksheet. After you create the control, you can format it and set its properties as desired.

The following steps describe the process of creating the Equipment Number drop-down list shown earlier (refer to Figure 21.25):

1. On the Forms toolbar, click the Combo Box tool (see Figure 21.26).

2. Draw the control on the worksheet by holding down the left mouse button and dragging the crosshair to the desired size (see Figure 21.27). To create a default-size control, just click in the worksheet.

3. Right-click the form control, and select Format Control from the context menu (see Figure 21.28). The Format Object dialog box appears.

4. In the Format Object dialog box, select the Control tab. In the Input Range box, specify the range of the data you want to display in the drop-down list in the combo box. In Figure 21.29, the range is the Equipment Number column from the list.

5. Input the cell link your formulas will reference. In the example, the cell link is in cell A1. The cell link displays the item number of the chosen value on the list. A link value of 2, for example, would refer to the second item on the drop-down list.

6. Establish the number of drop-down lines you want to display in the combo box. If the number of items in the list exceeds the number of drop-down lines displayed, Excel displays a scrollbar that the user can click to scroll the list and display the rest of the

entries. You need to use this option only if you want to restrict the number of lines shown in the drop-down list. By default, Excel automatically displays as many or as few lines as needed.

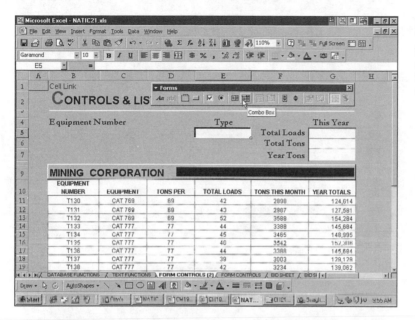

Figure 21.26.
The combo box control creates a drop-down list of entries from which you can choose.

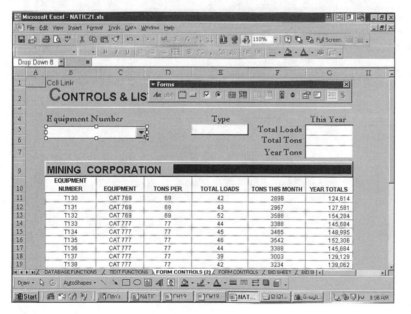

Figure 21.27.
Draw the form control to the desired size above the list. You can resize the control later, if necessary.

Figure 21.28.
Select Format Control from the context menu to establish the range and cell link for the control.

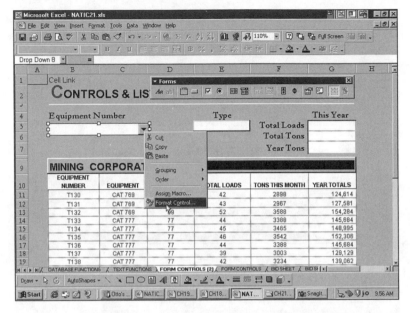

Figure 21.29.
In the Format Object dialog box, format the control and establish the cell link and list range.

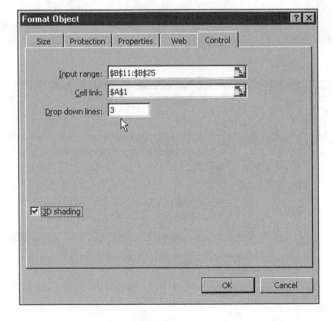

7. If desired, check the 3D Shading option to give the control a three-dimensional look.

8. Set additional options for the control as desired on other tabs in the dialog box. The following list describes some of the options:

- **Colors and Lines (option and check boxes only)**. Determines the color, line, and arrow styles used for the control.

- **Size**. Sets the control's size, scale, and so on.

- **Protection**. Locks the object or its text to prevent changes by users when the worksheet is protected.

- **Properties**. Manipulates the control's reaction to sizing of cells, as well as printing of the object with the worksheet.

- **Web**. Specifies the alternative text you want to display on Web browsers when loading the object or when pictures are not displayed.

9. Click OK when the settings are complete.

10. Click anywhere on the worksheet to deselect the control.

11. To test the control, click the down arrow and select a record so that the cell link is activated (see Figure 21.30).

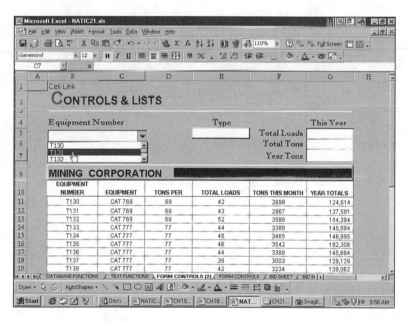

Figure 21.30.
Select a record from the new control to activate the cell link.

Now that you have created the control, reference a formula to the link to activate this model. To do this, use an index formula (see Figure 21.31). In this example, the formula is =INDEX(C11:C25,A1,1). C11:C25 is the list range, the link cell is the form control's record count cell (A1), and 1 is the column number in the range.

Figure 21.31.
Attach or reference formulas to the link and the list. The control then activates the cell link and the formula extracts the values.

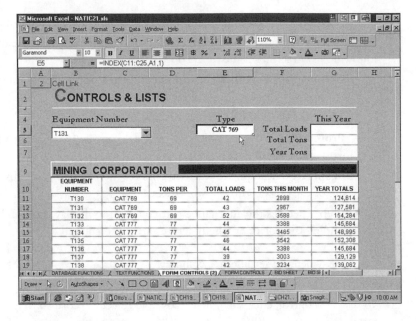

Tip #252 from

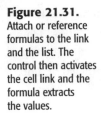

You also can use =INDEX($C$11:$G$25,$A$1,2). Specifying the entire table (minus the equipment column) for the Reference argument and making the first two arguments absolute enables you to copy the formula to the other cells (G5:G7). All you'd need to do then would be to change the Column argument in the pasted formulas.

For each item you want to pull up, select a cell and create the index formula.

USING CONTROLS WITH CALCULATION TABLES

At this point, you may find yourself thinking, "Form controls are a nice feature, but how can I really use them?" Think of it in terms of a formula that's triggered by a result. The result sets off a chain reaction that's determined by how creative you are with the formula and worksheet setup.

Figure 21.32 shows a worksheet that uses check boxes, spinners, and text boxes to create a *calculation table* that determines whether certain criteria are met. In this case, the user fills in a check box to specify the equipment to be used; the client will be charged by the number of weeks using that equipment. A spinner is applied to the number of weeks for each of the different breakouts.

In this example, the check boxes are selected by default, as shown in Figure 21.33. Thus, the check box control establishes a TRUE value in the cell link cell. Using the Unchecked option results in FALSE, and Mixed results in #NA.

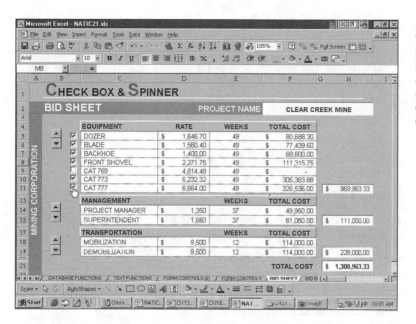

Figure 21.32.
You can use check boxes and spinners in conjunction with calculation tables to automate bid sheets or calculation tables of any kind.

Mixed isn't a value that the user can select when clicking the control. It's the shading effect that appears in the check box when #NA appears in the linked cell. It's normally used to change the appearance of the control by changing the cell link value via programming. Formulas can't directly alter the contents of other cells, so there's no way to change the value of the linked cell (to #NA) unless you manually type it in or change it using VBA code.

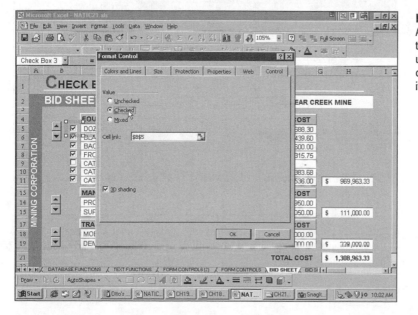

Figure 21.33.
A check box returns the result FALSE if unchecked, TRUE if checked, and #NA if mixed.

PART

VI

CH

21

You can use a check box as an indicator only by placing a formula in the linked cell itself. For example, you can enter a nested IF formula in the linked cell that evaluates to TRUE, FALSE, or #NA. The formula's result then changes the look of the check box. To prevent users from using the check box (and thereby eliminating the cell link's formula), simply lock it (and its associated linked cell); then protect the worksheet.

The cell link for the row 5 check box is in cell B5, as shown in Figure 21.34. When checked, the check box returns the value TRUE, which is used by the IF statement in cell F5. Following is the syntax:

```
=IF(link_cell,true_result,false_result)
```

- **link_cell.** The link cell in B5 returns the result TRUE if checked, FALSE if not. The IF statement refers to the link cell looking for a match.

- **true_result.** The TRUE result is the result of the box being checked. The result returns the text in the link cell.

- **false_result.** The FALSE result in the formula is 0. So if there's no match between the statement and the link cell, the result posted is 0.

Figure 21.34.
Use an IF statement to perform a calculation if the cell link is true.

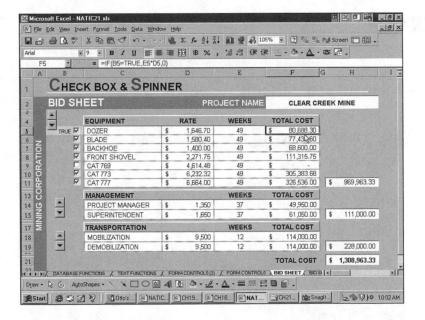

To hide the cell link value, format the cell so that the text color is identical to the background color. If the background is white, the text should be white. Alternatively, you can hide the column or row.

A spinner applies a number in a cell that incrementally increases or decreases, based on the specifications you provide on the Control tab in the Format Control dialog box (shown in Figure 21.35). Setting the minimum value of the spinner controls the lowest value the spinner will spin down to, and vice versa for the maximum value. The range is 0 to 30,000. Specifying an incremental change setting tells Excel to move the values up or down by the specified increment with each click of the spin arrows.

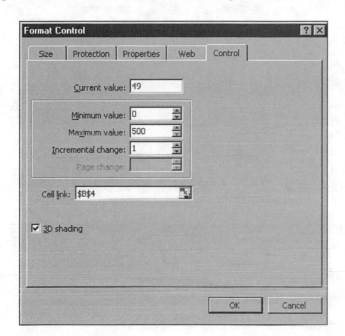

Figure 21.35.
The spinner control enables you to apply maximum and minimum values and also apply an incremental change by which the spinner will increase or decrease the linked cell value.

Setting the weeks in the example equal to the value of the link cell for the spinner changes the weeks to match the spinner (see Figure 21.36). For example, if the cell link to the spinner is in cell B1, apply **=B1** to all the cells that you want to refer to the cell link.

USING CONTROLS WITH CHARTS

You may never have thought of adding form controls to your charts, but the example in Figure 21.37 shows another way that form controls can be helpful. Here, a scrollbar controls the values displayed in the chart. The user can drag the scroll box, click in the scrollbar, or click the scroll arrows to change the quarter values displayed on the chart. The changes are incremental jumps you set when formatting the control. A drop-down list control also would work for switching between quarters.

When drawing a scrollbar control, draw from left to right for a horizontal scrollbar or top to bottom for a vertical scrollbar. Set the value options to a desired high, low, incremental, and page change (see Figure 21.38). A *page change* is just an incremental jump when you click on the scroll track.

Figure 21.36.
Make the weeks equal to the spinner cell link, so that the weeks change when the spinner is activated.

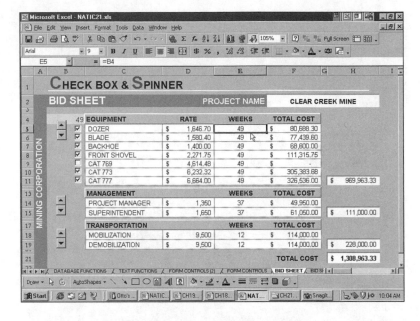

Figure 21.37.
You most often use scrollbars when you have large differences from the lowest value to the highest value. This example demonstrates scrolling through quarters.

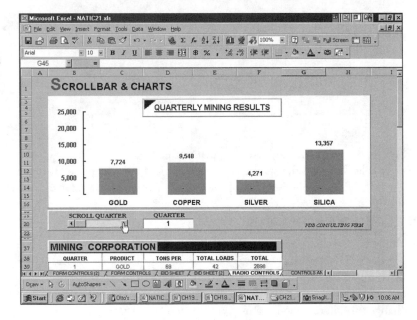

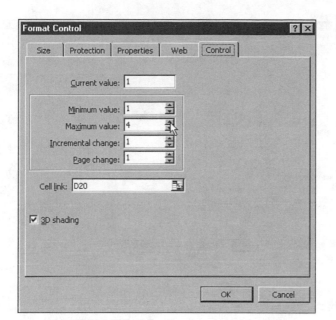

Figure 21.38.
Set the ceiling and
floor to which the
scroll will reach up
and drop down.

To create a chart that responds to the control, you'll need to create a table that references the cell link. Following is one way to do this:

1. Create a SUM(IF formula that extracts the product by quarter from the list (see Figure 21.39). The formula shown here looks up the quarter in column B from the list against cell C$24, which is the quarter indicator 1. Then it looks up the product in column C from the list against the product indicator in cell $B25, Gold. If these conditions are met, then the sum of column F—which is the total quantity for that quarter and product—is applied to the formula cell.

   Figure 21.40 shows the formula that references the cell link in cell D20. The IF statement just states that if the cell link equals 1, apply the value in cell C25, else FALSE (0). Notice the absolute referencing. When the formula is dragged to the right, it references Q2, then Q3, and so on. This way, you have to apply the formula only one time. When it's filled to the right, the referencing corresponds accordingly.

Tip #255 from

Patrick

If you prefer, you could compress this formula with the SUM(IF array into one nested array formula, thereby eliminating the need for the SUM table.

Figure 21.39.
Create a SUM(IF table that extracts the product and quarter. You also could use a PivotTable for this.

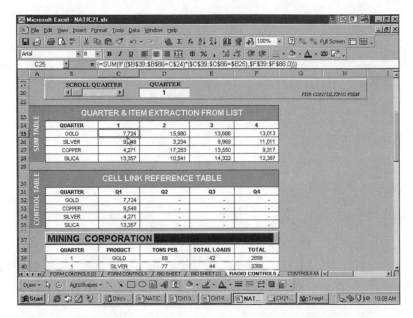

Figure 21.40.
Mirror your SUM(IF table with a table that references the cell link and equals the criteria or zero.

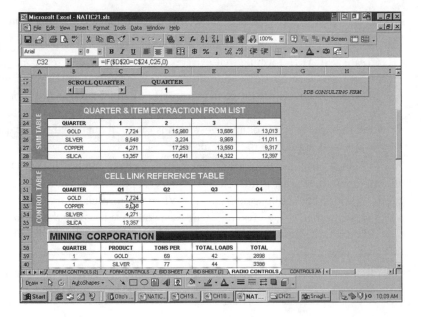

2. Create a column chart from the cell link reference table, setting the series in columns (see Figure 21.41).

You set the series in columns to display the product rather than quarters on the category (X) axis. The product will be displayed all the time, and the quarters respond to the selected quarter from the scrollbar.

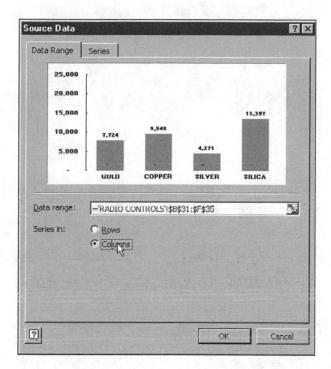

Figure 21.41.
Set the series in columns.

3. Select the data series in the chart, and choose Format, Selected Data Series.

4. Select the Options tab in the Format Data Series dialog box.

5. Set the overlap to 100 and the gap width to 80 (see Figure 21.42). This will place the columns over each other so that they don't move along the axis.

6. Click OK.

CONTROL CHARACTERISTICS

Figure 21.43 shows a variety of controls:

- The list box applies a cell link in the form of the number of the chosen record.
- The combo box does the same, but uses a drop-down list instead of a scrolling list.
- The scrollbar and spinner are similar controls, but the scrollbar allows for horizontal orientation, as well as page change scrolling—an incremental jump when the scroll track is clicked. You can also grab the scroll box and slide it along the scroll track.

- The check box applies the cell link result of TRUE, FALSE, or #NA.

- The option buttons create stacked numbers associated with the number of option buttons. For example, option button number 2 is stacked number 2 in the cell link. If you create a new group of option buttons, that group's cell link numbers start from 1 again.

Figure 21.42.
Set the overlap and gap width so the columns display in the same location rather than jogging on the X-axis.

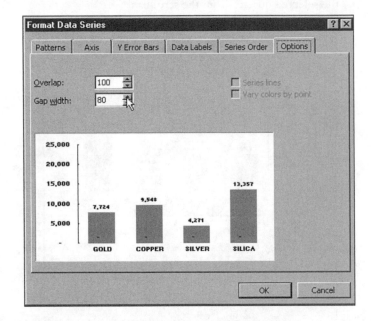

Figure 21.43.
Controls and their characteristics.

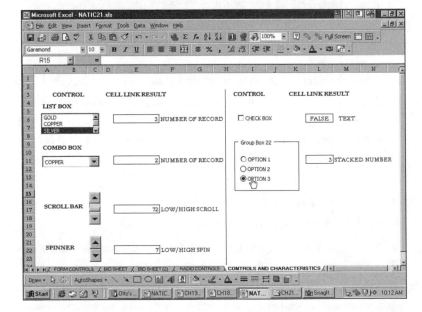

TROUBLESHOOTING

INTERSECTING POINTS IN LISTS OR TABLES

My index formula doesn't work when trying to pull up two intersecting points within a list.

Use the Lookup Wizard to help you rewrite formulas with complex INDEX(MATCH cases. (I suggest using this tool as a way to learn indexing and matching formulas as well.)

COMPLEX FORMULAS

The formula has become too long to understand.

Use named ranges to simplify formulas. (But do this only for ranges that generally don't change.) You also can apply a range that's much longer than the list; as the list grows, the new cells with data will be included in the range.

FORMULAS ARE SLOWING DOWN THE WORKBOOK

How can I increase the performance of a workbook that seems lethargic?

One option is to turn off automatic recalculation. Choose Tools, Options, click the Calculation tab in the Options dialog box, and select Manual. To then calculate the work-book, press F9. Another way to increase efficiency is to use form controls for looking up information. Finally, if possible, use *PivotTables (page 556)*—the most efficient way to sum-marize large amounts of data in a workbook.

PARSING A LIST OF NAMES

I've inherited a list with first and last names combined and random capitalization. What's the best way to fix this problem?

To separate the combined names in a list, use the Text to Columns feature on the Data menu. To fix random capitalization, use the text function UPPER() or LOWER() in an adjacent row or column and then paste the final result back in the list as values (use Paste Special).

EXCEL IN PRACTICE

Formulas can be used alone or combined with form controls to become powerful extraction devices. Figure 21.44 shows a conditional sum formula that extracts the year totals for equipment number T133. However, by using a combo box form control, you can tie several index formulas to one cell link, as shown in cell A1 of Figure 21.45. This setup can pull up multiple bits of information at once. The worksheet is easier to use, and it's more efficient to hook formulas into a cell link and pull up line-item data with index formulas. (You could also use PivotTables to summarize this information.)

Figure 21.44.
This SUM(IF works efficiently to total the amounts for a particular piece of equipment, but you have to revise the formula to look at different equipment.

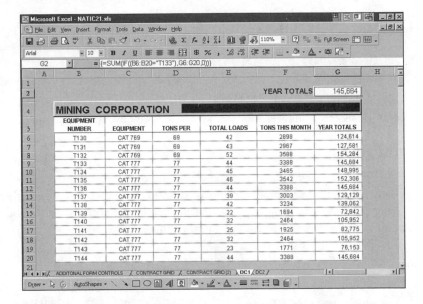

Figure 21.45.
Form controls make lookups really easy.

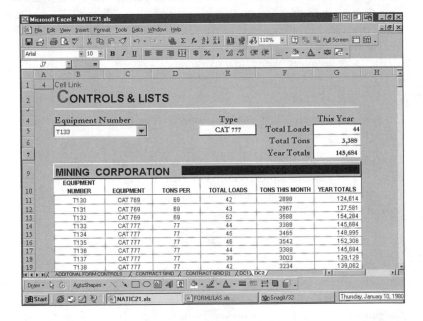

CHAPTER 22

USING EXCEL'S ANALYSIS TOOLS

by Patrick D. Blattner
Patrick@BlattnerBooks.com

In this chapter

USING EXCEL TO ANALYZE YOUR DATA

Many Excel users input data into a worksheet, use simple functions or formulas to calculate results, and then report those results to someone else. Although this is a perfectly legitimate use of Excel, it basically turns Excel into a calculator.

When you need to do more than just type data into a worksheet, you can use special Excel features to analyze your data and solve complex problems by employing variables and constraints. Goal Seek and Solver are two great tools included with Excel that you can use to analyze data and provide answers to simple or even fairly complex problems. Goal Seek is primarily used when there is one unknown variable, and Solver when there are many variables and multiple constraints. Although you may have used Solver in the past, primarily with complex tables for financial analysis, this chapter also shows you how to combine Solver with *Gantt charts (page 482)*. Solver isn't just for financial analysis; it can be used against production, financial, marketing, and accounting models. Solver should be used when you're searching for a result and you have multiple variables that change (constraints). The more complex the constraints, the more you need to use Solver, as shown later in this chapter for resource loading.

Both Goal Seek and Solver enable you to play "what if" with the result of a formula when you know what result you're shooting for, without manually changing the cells that are being referenced in the formula.

→ For more on Gantt charts and Excel, **see** "Creating Gantt Charts in Excel," **p. 686**

The data tables in Excel provide a very important function: creating one- and two-variable tables for use in amortization and other tasks—allowing you to create a series of results based on one formula (such as cash flows). This chapter includes the details on how to set up your tables and shows a few tricks for these kinds of tables that can save you time and effort.

Whether you're manufacturing plastic cups, hauling quantities of material or dirt, or manufacturing digital assets in software development, Excel's powerful analytical tools combined with structured worksheet design can make your life easier and help you to manage your time more effectively.

USING GOAL SEEK

The *Goal Seek* feature in Excel uses a single variable to find a desired result. To understand Goal Seek, let's start with a simple scenario. Suppose that you're a sales representative for a packaging business. You must achieve $100,000 in sales this year to receive a bonus. Figure 22.1 shows a table that displays the current situation—you have sold 2,000 units of a product with a per-unit sales price of $3.46. How many units must you sell to achieve your $100,000 goal?

> **Note**
>
> The goal amount ($100,000 in this case) must be the result of a formula, not just plain data.

At this point, you've probably already set up the formula in your head: (100000 6920)/ 3.46=26901.73 units remaining to be sold. What would be the advantage of using a special Excel feature to calculate something so simple? Wouldn't you just create a formula in a cell and be done with it? The advantage of Goal Seek is that you can set up your formula just once, and then substitute different amounts to get quick alternative routes to your goal.

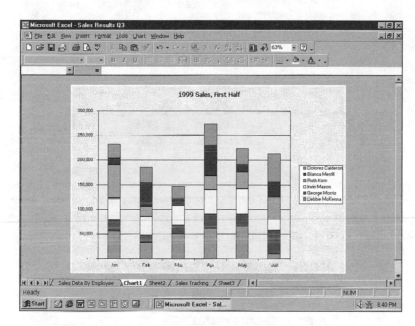

Figure 22.1.
Use Goal Seek to find the unknown variable—such as how many boxes must be sold at a unit price of $3.46 to reach $100,000 in sales.

To use Goal Seek, select the formula cell (D7 in this example) and then choose <u>T</u>ools, <u>G</u>oal Seek to display the Goal Seek dialog box (see Figure 22.2). The following list describes the entries for each of the items in the dialog box:

- <u>S</u>et cell specifies the location of the formula you use to get the end result. In this case, the formula is in cell D7, and simply multiplies the number of units sold by the unit price.

- Type the target value in the To <u>V</u>alue box.

- In the By <u>C</u>hanging Cell box, specify the cell location of the variable that you want to change to reach your goal—in this case, $100,000 in sales.

Figure 22.2.
Specify the settings in the dialog box to begin the Goal Seek process.

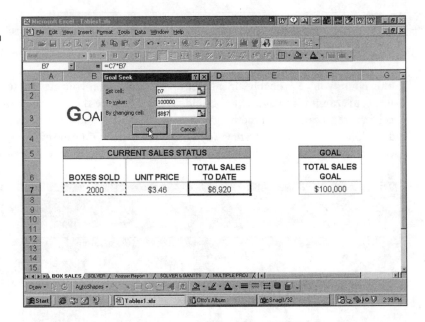

As soon as you click OK or press Enter, Excel begins seeking the specified goal. In this case, the solution indicated is 28901.7341 total units at the current price of $3.46 (see Figure 22.3). In this case, you probably would need to round the solution to the nearest integer (28,902), because units aren't generally sold in fractional amounts.

Figure 22.3.
Goal Seek found the desired result.

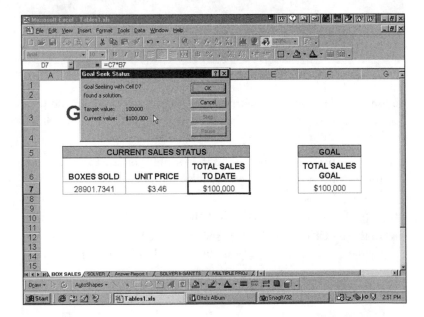

Now suppose you need to determine the unit price—the other variable in the total-sales-to-date formula. If you want to sell only 2,000 units of something, how high would the price need to be for you to reach the $100,000 target? To find out, you change the By Changing Cell setting in the Goal Seek dialog box to specify cell C7, the unit price (see Figure 22.4). Here, Goal Seek will raise the price of the boxes to a dollar value that will equal $100,000 in sales but keep the units sold at 2,000. Figure 22.5 shows the outcome: To reach $100,000 by selling only 2,000 units, each unit must cost $50.

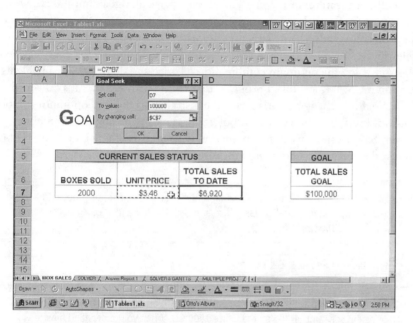

Figure 22.4.
In this case, Goal Seek is adjusting the unit price to reach the target.

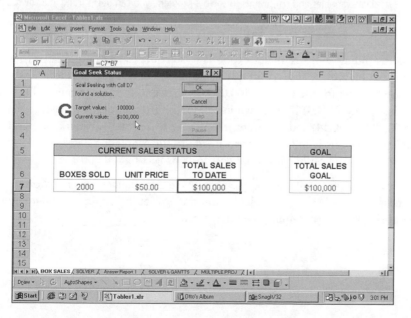

Figure 22.5.
Finding a unit price to meet the target.

Tip #256 from

You can use Goal Seek with complex financial models as well as with a simple solution. Link the final result cell to other cells within the model to drive the changes.

USING SOLVER

Goal Seek is an efficient feature for helping you reach a particular goal, but it deals with only a single variable. For most businesses, the variables are much more complex. How can you reach the profit goal if advertising expenses increase? What's the best mix of products to increase sales in the first quarter, when revenues traditionally decline for your business? Which suppliers give you the optimum combination of price and delivery? For problems like these, you can use *Solver*, an add-in program that comes with Excel. This powerful analysis tool uses multiple changing variables and constraints to find the optimum solution to solve a problem. Previously, Solver was a tool used primarily for financial modeling analysis; however, Solver can be used in conjunction with models of any kind that you build in Excel. Later in this section is a discussion of using Solver with Gantt charts.

Note

Solver isn't enabled by default. To add it to the Tools menu, choose Tools, Add-Ins, select Solver Add-in in the Add-Ins dialog box, and click OK. If asked to confirm, choose Yes. (You'll need the Office 2000 CD.)

→ For details on creating Gantt charts in Excel, **see** "Creating Gantt Charts in Excel," **p. 686**

Tip #257 from

The best way to learn how to work with Solver is to experiment with simple problems, using the Solvsamp.xls file on the Office 2000 CD. When you understand how to work with multiple variables and constraints to solve a problem, you can begin using your own data and solving real business problems.

The key to understanding complex analysis tools is to start with something relatively simple. The example in Figure 22.6 uses several variables to calculate a project's total cost. What if your total budget for the year is $500,000 (as shown in the constraints cell G20) and you were using only $375,351 (as shown in cell G16)? You want each project to have a total cost of $50,000 (G5:G14) and you want to optimize or add to your marketing and advertising dollars (columns E and F). Solver will add to the Marketing cost and Advertising cost for you, adjusting your total cost for a project to $50,000.

Quite often, companies must deal with projects that have total budget caps for the year. For this, Solver works well in adjusting variables within the projects to maximize dollar amounts in certain categories, while maintaining the budget cap.

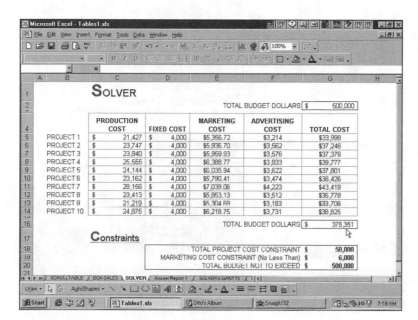

Figure 22.6.
A Solver scenario where you want all projects' total costs to equal $50,000, while optimizing marketing and advertising costs.

To set up this Solver scenario, follow these steps:

1. Set up the table. In the example, the production costs are in C5:C14, the fixed costs in D5:D14, the marketing costs in E5:E14, the advertising costs in F5:F14, and the totals in G5:G14.

2. Set up the constraints. In cell G18 in the example, the constraint is $50,000 for the maximum cost per project. In cell G19, the constraint is marketing costs of no less than $6,000 per project, and the total maximum budget in cell G20 is set at $500,000.

3. Select the target cell, G16, and choose Tools, Solver.

4. In the Solver Parameters dialog box, set the parameters you want to use for the problem (see Figure 22.7). For this example, you want the target cell to be the total dollars spent (cell G16), which you want to equal the budget maximum, $500,000 (specified in the Value of box). Solver will calculate the best dispersion to achieve the optimum result by adjusting the amounts in the range E5:F14 (the changing cells).

Tip #258 from

For many problems, the Guess button does a great job of selecting the cells needed to effect the result. It uses the auditing feature to locate the appropriate cells.

5. Next, you add constraints to the problem. Select Add to specify the first constraint. In this example, you want to spend exactly $50,000 total on any project. The constraint cell is G18, as shown in Figure 22.8.

Figure 22.7.
Establish the target cell, the target value, and the cells that can be changed.

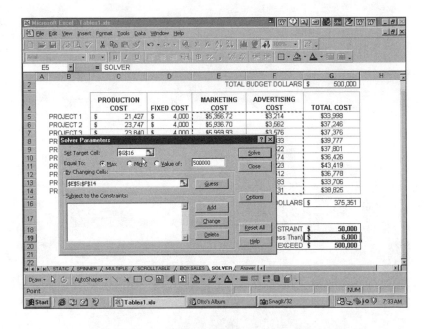

Figure 22.8.
Add variable constraints you want Solver to adhere to.

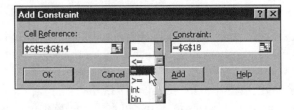

6. To add more constraints, click <u>A</u>dd and specify the constraint. In this example, add another constraint, as shown in Figure 22.9. The marketing costs in the range E5:E14 will be greater than or equal to the constraint set in cell G19, $6,000.

Figure 22.9.
The second constraint ensures that the marketing dollars allocated to each project are greater than or equal to $6,000.

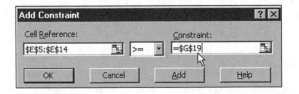

7. The last constraint is the total budget, $500,000, in cell G20 (see Figure 22.10). Don't click Add for the last constraint. Instead, when the constraints are complete, click OK to go back to the Solver Parameters dialog box. Notice that all the constraints added appear in the Su<u>b</u>ject to the Constraints list (see Figure 22.11).

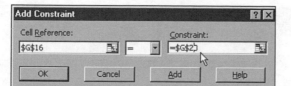

Figure 22.10.
The last constraint
equals $500,000,
or the sum of total
projects.

Figure 22.11.
All the constraints
appear in the Subject
to the Constraints list.
You can add more,
change, or delete any
of the constraints.

8. Click Solve or press Enter to start Solver on the problem. As Solver works, it displays a message in the status bar, as shown in Figure 22.12.

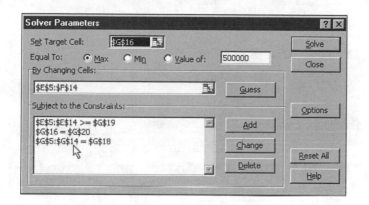

Figure 22.12.
The calculations
appear in the lower
left while Excel runs
through all the con-
straints set.

At this point, Solver has tried 12 possible combinations.

9. When Solver reaches a conclusion, it displays a dialog box that indicates the result and changes the specified values in the worksheet to reach the target. In Figure 22.13, notice the changed cells when Solver has created the optimum solution for the problem. The total costs now equal $500,000 and the projects all equal $50,000.

10. From here, you can save the Solver results and create an answer report that shows the original scenario of costs and the final result. Select Answer under Reports in the Solver Results dialog box, and click the Save Scenario button to display the dialog box shown in Figure 22.14.

11. If you want to reset the worksheet to return to the original values, select the Restore Original Values option to start with the original values again.

Figure 22.13.
Solver enables you to
create reports and
save scenarios so that
you can later view
and recall scenarios
you've run.

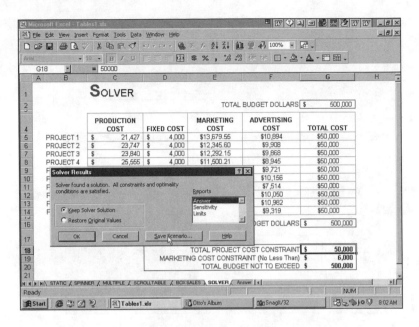

Figure 22.14.
Name the scenario.

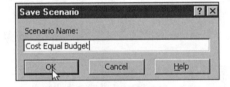

Caution

Excel automatically changes the data in the constraint cells referenced by the formula
(clearing the original data). If the finished scenario isn't what you were looking for, revert
to the worksheet's original state to restore the data.

---

12. Click OK and Excel will restore the values and create the answer report (see Figure
22.15). The answer report compares the original values with the changed values and
indicates the cells that were changed. This way, you can compare scenarios.

Tip #259 from

Patrick

The answer report is created on a separate sheet. If you have multiple reports and scenarios, you may want to hide the report sheet(s).

The constraints are saved with the workbook, so you don't have to retype them each time
the workbook is opened.

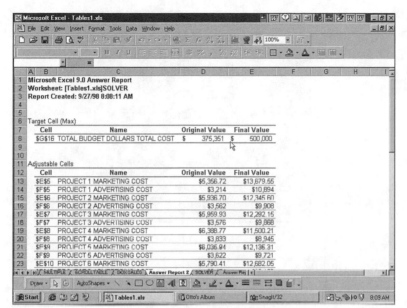

Figure 22.15.
The answer report shows original values against final values, along with the category name and the adjusted cell. The target cell is called out, separated at the top.

If Solver can't reach a satisfactory conclusion with the data provided, a message box will appear. Adjust constraints or variables as needed to continue attempting to solve the problem.

> **Note**
>
> Some problems are too complex even for Solver. For problems with too many variables or constraints, try breaking the problem into segments, solving each segment separately, and then using those solutions together in Solver to reach a final conclusion.

Solver's solution for a complex problem may be correct but unrealistic. Be skeptical; check the appropriateness of any adjusted amounts before reporting or implementing any suggestion from Solver.

Solver can be very useful, but you don't want it to run forever attempting to solve an unsolvable problem. You can change the Solver settings before starting on the problem if you suspect that the solution may take a long time or require too much computing power. Clicking the Options button in the Solver Parameters dialog box displays the Solver Options dialog box, in which you can set the number of iterations of the problem that Solver will run to search for an answer or the amount of time it will spend searching before giving up. Figure 22.16 shows the options available, and Table 22.1 provides descriptions of each option.

Figure 22.16.
The Solver Options dialog box enables you to set parameters for Solver.

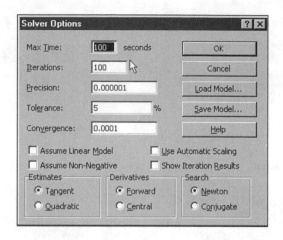

TABLE 22.1. SOLVER OPTIONS

Option	Description
Max Time	Determines the maximum amount of time Solver will search for a solution, in seconds, up to approximately nine hours.
Iterations	Determines the number of times Solver will run the parameters in search of a solution.
Precision	Determines the accuracy of the solution. The lower the number, the more accurate the solution.
Tolerance	When integer constraints are used, it's more difficult for Solver to solve the problem. Here, you can provide more tolerance and give up accuracy.
Convergence	For all nonlinear problems. Indicates the minimum amount of change Solver will use in each iteration. If the target cell is below the convergence setting, Solver will offer the best solution and stop.
Assume Linear Model	When checked, Solver will find a quicker solution, providing that the model is linear (using simple addition or subtraction). Nonlinear models would use growth factor and exponential smoothing or nonlinear worksheet functions.
Assume Non-Negative	Stops Solver from placing negative values in changing cells. (You also can apply constraints that indicate the value must be greater than or equal to zero.) The preceding example would use this option to prevent Solver from using negative amounts.
Use Automatic Scaling	Used when the changing cells and the target cell differ by very large amounts.
Show Iteration Results	Stops and enables you to view the results of each iteration in the Solver sequence.
Load Model	Loads the model to use from a stored set of parameters on the worksheet.

Option	Description
Save Model	Saves a model to a cell or set of cells and allows you to recall the model again.
Tangent	Select when the model is linear.
Quadratic	Select when the model is nonlinear.
Forward	When cells controlled by constraints change slowly for each iteration, check this box to potentially speed up the Solver.
Central	To ensure accuracy when constraint cells change rapidly and by large amounts, use this option.
Newton	Uses more memory but requires fewer iterations to provide the solution.
Conjugate	Use with large models because it requires less memory; however, it will use more iterations to provide a solution for the model.

USING SOLVER WITH GANTT CHARTS

Understanding the simple Solver scenario with constraints described in the preceding section can help you think in terms of combining Excel's powerful tools to solve real-world problems.

Although I've worked extensively with project-management programs, I've found that with the proper construction of workbooks in Excel, Solver can do the following:

- Forecast future costs
- Track actual costs against projected costs
- Forecast production plans
- Track actual production against projected production
- Forecast head count against production loads
- Run resource-loading models for maximum efficiency

Using Gantt charts in Excel, PivotTables, Solver, and formulas to manage production plans is the most efficient mechanism available on the market. The key here is proper worksheet format and workbook construction. If done correctly, the workbook can be completely automated to manage the most complex productions—from managing a construction site, where quantities and haul times are a factor, to the manufacture of digital assets in software development.

Figure 22.17 shows a production model, with constraints indicated on the worksheet under the project's Gantt chart. In this example, a project must start on a certain day (cell O9) and be completed by a certain day (P11), and there is an average number of units or quantities not to exceed per week (Q9:Q11). The target cell is the maximum number of units on the project (Q7), or any quantity you specify. Figure 22.18 shows the parameters for the first problem in the constraints box beneath the Gantt chart setup.

Note

This workbook includes special color formatting to help make the model easier to follow. You may want to open the file from the CD while reading the description in this section.

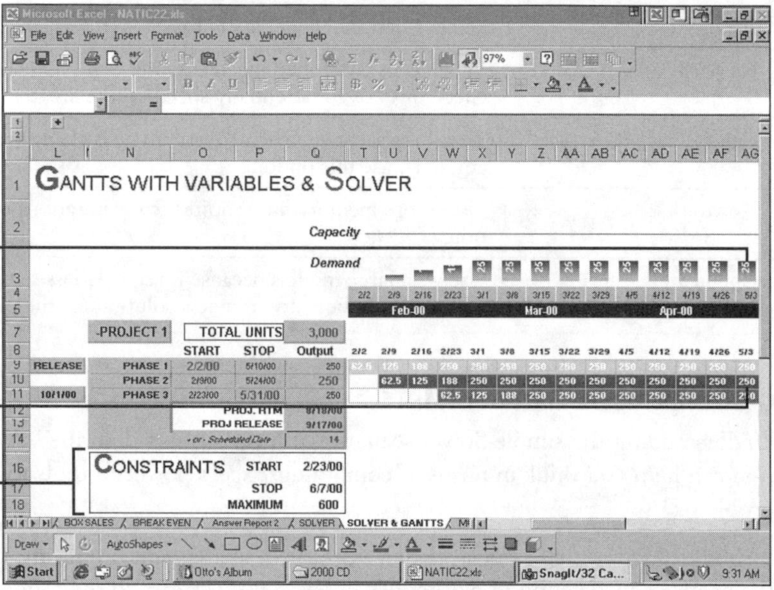

Figure 22.17.
Using Solver to optimize production models can answer questions in seconds rather than running the scenarios manually.

Current demand

Demand based on Phase 2

Constraints used with Solver parameters

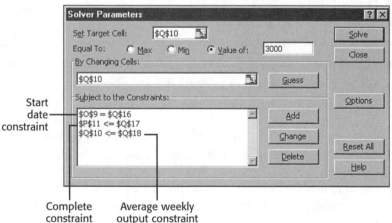

Figure 22.18.
The Solver constraints give the project a start date, stop date (or at least completed by), total quantity of units to produce, and a maximum average weekly output.

Start date constraint

Complete constraint   Average weekly output constraint

The following list describes the issues affecting the problem:

- The original planned start date was 2/2/00, but the constraint start date is 2/23/00, indicating that the project is starting later than planned.

- The original stop date was 5/10/00, but the project must be completed by the constraint set at 5/31/00.

■ The current weekly output is 250 units per week per phase, and the constraint is set not to exceed 600.

Figure 22.19 shows the solution.

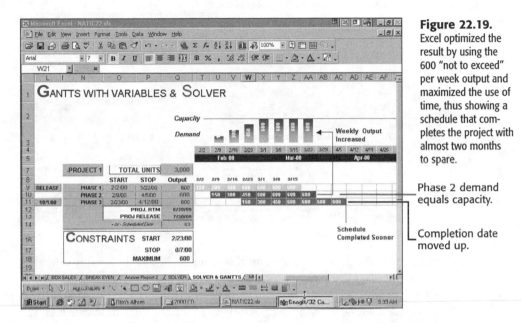

Figure 22.19.
Excel optimized the result by using the 600 "not to exceed" per week output and maximized the use of time, thus showing a schedule that completes the project with almost two months to spare.

Phase 2 demand equals capacity.

Completion date moved up.

A Multiple-Project Solver Scenario

Based on the previous example and understanding how to apply constraints to production models, suppose that you have teams that have to be managed and quantities and dates you must adhere to. Solver can take multiple projects and multiple constraints and determine the optimum solution to the problem. In the example in Figure 22.20, the multiple projects overlap, and Phase 2 of each project is the critical path in the production of the project. The total units of Phase 2 are summed at the bottom, starting in cell T22.

The constraints are called out at the bottom as Start and Stop dates for each project and a maximum total output per week. On any given week, your total capacity to produce equals 600 units, but the example shows several weeks in excess of 1,000 units output in row 22. By applying the constraint to the total at the bottom, it will also take into account your capacity to produce, and find a solution. If the example isn't possible, Excel will still find the optimum solution, given the parameters of the constraints.

→ For details on how to use Excel as a project manager, **see** "Event Management," **p. 696**

Figure 22.20.
Excel can analyze critical-path production and cycle teams, phases, or machines by applying the right constraints with the production model.

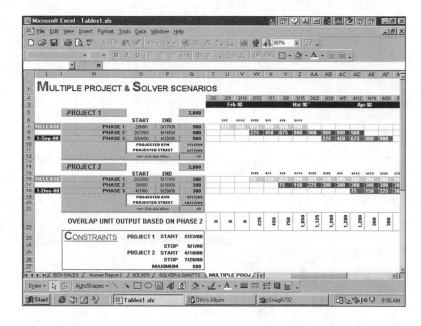

Figure 22.21 shows the parameters used for this example. Notice how many cells are going to be changed based on the parameters or constraints supplied. I've established all the start and stop dates, as well as the maximum quantity per week not to exceed—not only per project, but also based on the overlap range starting in cell T22. This means the total capacity to output cannot exceed 600 per week for the company as a whole, so the projects' time and output will have to be modified to fit all these variables into the Solver parameters.

Figure 22.21.
You can place multiple constraints of start and stop dates and quantities not to exceed, and Excel will find the optimum solution, taking all the variables into account.

The settings are as follows:

- The original start date for project 1 is set at 2/9/00 and, based on the constraints, will start on 2/23 in cell Q23. The original stop date from 4/30/00 will be constrained to 5/1/00. The maximum not to exceed per week currently is 900 and will be constrained to 600 in cell Q27.

- The original start date for project 2 is set at 2/23/00 and will be constrained to 4/10/00. The stop date from 6/30/00 will move to the constraint date of 7/28/00. The weekly not to exceed is constrained at no more than 600 per week in cell Q27.

- The last constraint placed on the model will ensure that each weekly overlap unit output for Phase 2 (row 22) will not exceed the maximum output of 600 in cell Q27.

- The change range is from T22:BB22, which is the sum of Phase 2 of both projects carried out through the length of the timeline.

Figure 22.22 shows overlap per week exceeding the weekly capacity to output in row 22. Figure 22.23 shows all the constraints placed on the project. Excel found the optimum solution.

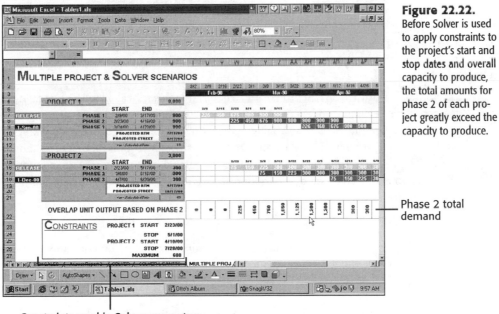

Figure 22.22.
Before Solver is used to apply constraints to the project's start and stop dates and overall capacity to produce, the total amounts for phase 2 of each project greatly exceed the capacity to produce.

Phase 2 total demand

Constraints used in Solver parameters

Figure 22.23.
After Solver applies the constraints to the production model, Excel provides the optimum solution, solving the problem and maintaining efficient project production flow.

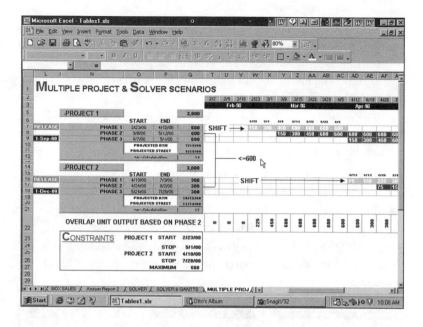

CREATING AMORTIZATION TABLES TO CALCULATE MORTGAGE PAYMENTS

Excel's Table feature helps you to create structured tables for calculating mortgage and lease payments, depreciation, and so on. Suppose that you want to purchase a house; you need to see the mortgage rate based on variable percentages and mortgage amounts. Here, you would use the PMT function to create a table to provide the mortgage rate, as shown in Figure 22.24. The schedule in cells F5:F19 is calculated based on a total loan amount of $100,000 on a 30-year mortgage, with percentage rates starting at 5 percent and increasing in .5 percent increments.

Following is the syntax for the PMT function used to create the table:

The PMT function calculates the loan payment for a loan based on constant payments and constant interest rates. This is the syntax:

```
=PMT(rate,nper,pv,fv,type)
```

- *rate*. The interest rate on the borrowed money. The percentage rate per payment period.

- *nper*. The number of payment periods of the loan. One year has 12 periods. Technically, PMT can be used to calculate a yearly payment instead of the typical monthly payment scenario. That having been said, one year could be one period.

- *pv*. The amount of money borrowed or loaned at the beginning of the transaction. A positive *pv* results in a negative payment and vice versa. (Add a negative sign to this argument to display the result as a positive number.)

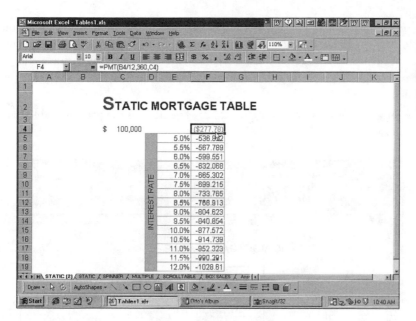

Figure 22.24.
A simple mortgage table calculates the mortgage payments based on the interest rate and the total mortgage.

- *fv.* The future value defines the amount of value remaining at the end of the loan. This might be used for a balloon payment at the end of a loan. The *fv* argument is optional; if not provided, Excel assumes it's zero.

- *type.* The *type* argument is also optional, and determines whether payments on the loan are made at the beginning of the pay period or the end of the pay period. Providing a 0 (or leaving it blank) means the payments are at the end of each period, and providing a 1 means they're at the beginning of each pay period.

To set up a single-variable table, follow these steps:

1. In the first cell in the table, type the first interest rate percentage—for this example, you would type **5%** in cell E5.

2. In the next cell down, type a formula to increase the first percentage by the increment amount. In this example, the increment is .5%, so the formula in cell E6 is =E5+0.005. This will add .5 percent to the previous percentage. Then drag the formula down to the bottom row of the table (cell E19 in this case, which will equal 12 percent, which is the maximum interest rate you're willing to pay).

3. In the trigger cell (cell C4 in this case), type the mortgage amount—for this example, $100,000.

4. In the target cell (cell F4 in this case), type the payment function. Here, the formula is =PMT(B4/12,360,C4) where B4/12 is the monthly interest rate, 360 is the term (30 years is 360 months), and C4 equals the total mortgage. Where cell B4 is a placeholder of zero (Excel assigns a value of zero to a blank cell referenced in a numeric formula), Excel uses the placeholder to calculate the payment needed to amortize the loan at zero percent.

The reason you place the mortgage in a cell rather than in the formula is that all you have to do then is change the mortgage amount. The formula references the cell and the table automatically changes, instead of your having to go into the formula and change the mortgage every time. To maximize the flexibility, you could also place the period value in a cell.

5. Select the range you want to fill. In Figure 22.25, I've deleted the previous table to rebuild the example.

Figure 22.25.
Select the total range to build the table.

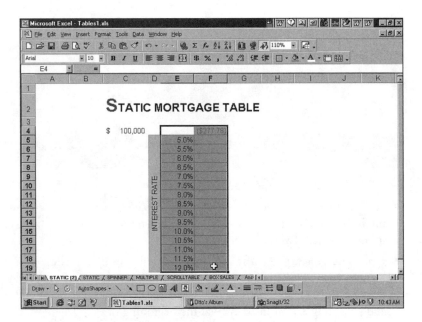

6. Choose Data, Table. Excel displays the Table dialog box shown in Figure 22.26. Because the interest rates in this example are listed down a column, we use the Column Input Cell box to look for the interest rate used in the PMT function.

7. Click OK to build the table (see Figure 22.27).

   Notice that by changing the mortgage amount from $100,000 to $600,000, the table automatically responds (see Figure 22.28).

Figure 22.26.
The input cell is the payment needed to amortize a loan, at zero percent in this case.

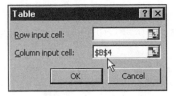

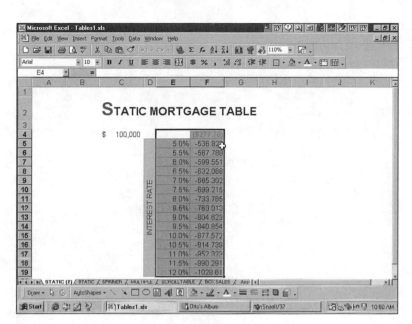

Figure 22.27.
The final result shows the mortgage payments in the body of the table, based on the corresponding percentage and mortgage amount.

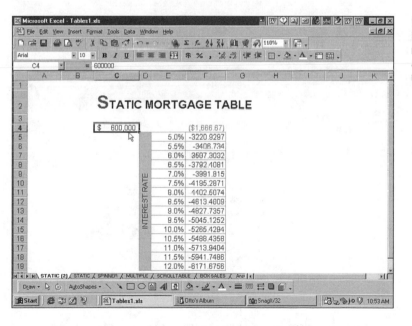

Figure 22.28.
By changing the mortgage, the table automatically responds.

The new table is in the form of an array, which means that you can't change the table, although you can move or delete the table (notice the entry in the Formula bar in Figure 22.29). You can apply tricks to get around this limitation, however. You could copy the table and paste it as values using Paste Special, or you could simply re-create the table with a mirrored table using =. Figure 22.30 shows a mirrored table. Using a simple formula that repeats the entries in the first table (starting with cell E5), you can drag the formula to pick up all the entries in the table, which you then can manipulate.

Figure 22.29.
The table formula.

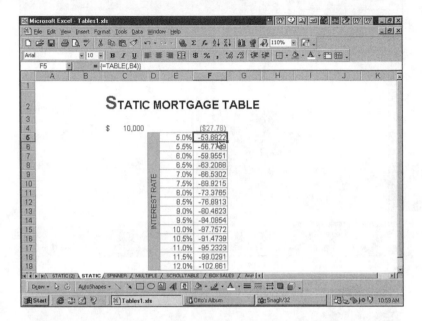

Figure 22.30.
Create a mirrored table to get around the array formula, thus allowing you to manipulate the formula.

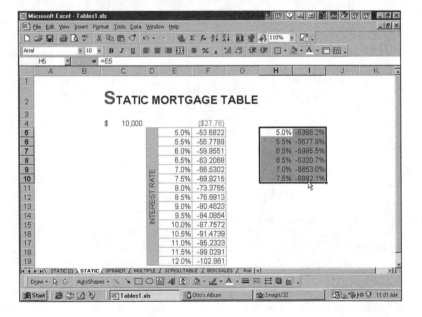

CREATING ACTIVE TABLES WITH SPINNERS AND CHARTS

If your data tables are large, you can add special features such as *form controls (page 464)* to make the tables easier to read and use. I've applied a *spinner (page 664)* to the mortgage table in Figure 22.31. However, because the spinner control allows for a maximum value of 30,000, I use a multiplier in a different cell (cell C4 in this example) that multiplies the cell link in cell A1 times 50, so with every incremental change to the spinner control, it multiplies the cell link by 50.

→ For details on creating form controls, **see** "Adding Form Controls to Your Worksheets," **p. 624**

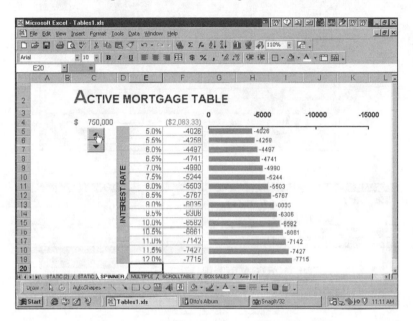

Figure 22.31.
Use spinners with multipliers to drive tables.

Tip #260 from

The chart could actually be used in place of the table column F by hiding column F. If you do this, be sure to plot all cells, not just visible cells.

When creating the spinner, set the cell link to cell A1 in the Format Control dialog box (see Figure 22.32). Set the maximum value to 30,000 and the minimum to 0, and the incremental change to 1000. This means the maximum value the spinner will go up to is 30,000, and the lowest value is 0. By adding the multiplier, we can make the mortgage table more flexible; with each click on the spin arrow, the mortgage change will be 1,000.

Type the multiplier formula in the table reference cell (cell C4 in this example), as shown in Figure 22.33. The formula references the cell link—the current value of the spinner—and multiplies it by 50 to give you the current principal.

Figure 22.32.
Set the cell link, minimum and maximum values, as well as the incremental change as shown.

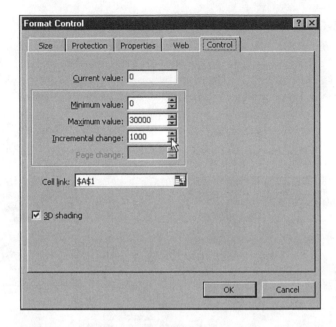

Figure 22.33.
Type the multiplier formula in cell C4, the table reference cell.

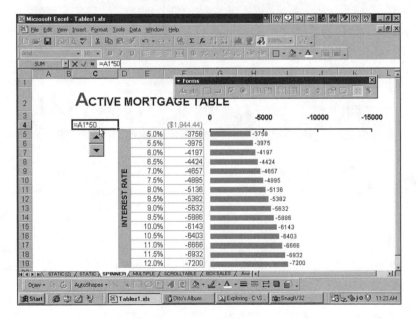

Clicking the spinner increases or decreases the mortgage amount, as shown in Figure 22.34.

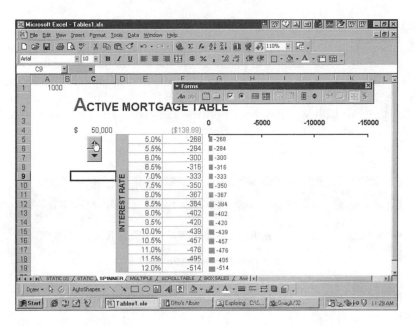

PART

VI

CH

22

Figure 22.34.
Activate the control by pressing the up or down arrow to make the table more interactive.

MULTIPLE-VARIABLE TABLES

After learning the basic one-variable table, you can apply multiple variables to make an expanded table, referenced to different mortgage amounts (see Figure 22.35). In the previous examples, you typed in the new mortgage amounts. In this instance, you reference the different cells across columns in the formula to create a broader-based table.

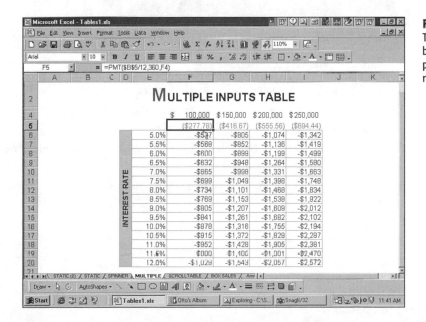

Figure 22.35.
To create a broad-based table, the payment formula references cell F4.

ADDING SCROLLBARS TO THE MORTGAGE TABLE

By adding scrollbars to a table, you can span hundreds of rows and columns in a window of a few rows and columns. In the example in Figure 22.36, the interest is scrolled down to zero percent and the loan amount is scrolled back to 0 in the first column (cell F6). When you scroll up, the maximum interest rate in this example is 13.7% and the maximum mortgage is $1,150,000. It normally would take multiple rows and columns of information to span this list; however, with the proper use of scrollbars, you can create a window in which the table will scroll.

Figure 22.36.
You can span the range of hundreds of rows and columns.

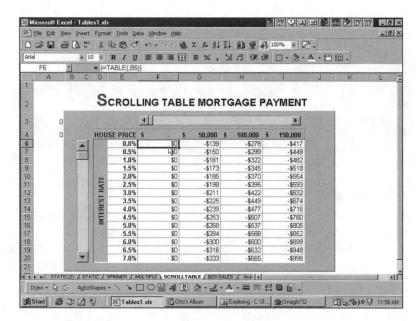

To create a scrolling window, follow these steps:

1. Create the same table setup as in the multiple-variable tables shown previously.

2. In cell E6, the beginning of the interest rate column, type the formula =A4/150, where A4 will equal the cell link for the vertical scrollbar form control.

3. In cell F4, type the formula =$A$3*10,000, where A3 is the cell link (note the absolute reference). Drag the formula to the right to I4.

4. Draw the scrollbar next to the interest rates, right-click it, and select Format Control (see Figure 22.37).

5. Format the control as follows:

    Current Value = 0

    Minimum Value = 0

    Maximum Value = 10

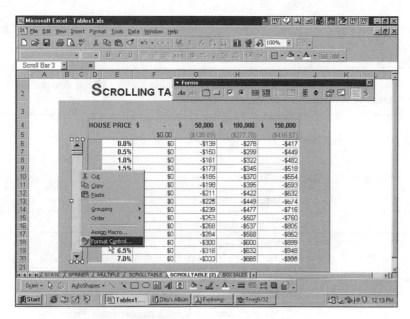

Figure 22.37.
Draw the control and
then right-click and
select Format Control.

Incremental Change = 1

Page Change = 10

Cell Link = A4

These settings mean that the maximum value the scrollbar will reach is 10 and the lowest value is 0; each click will change the value by 1.

6. Click OK.

7. Draw the horizontal scrollbar above the house price. Right-click it and choose Format Control. Set the format control as follows:

Current Value = 0

Minimum Value = 0

Maximum Value = 100

Incremental Change = 10

Page Change = 10

Cell Link = A3

8. Click OK to finish formatting the scrollbar.

USING THE ANALYSIS TOOLPAK ADD-IN

Excel's *Analysis ToolPak* (accessed by choosing Tools, Data Analysis) enables you to perform complex and sophisticated statistical analyses, with 17 statistical commands and 47 mathematical functions. From creating a random distribution of numbers to performing regression analysis, the tools can provide the essential calculations to solve just about any problem.

Note You may need to enable the add-in before you can use it (choose Tools, Add-Ins, and select the Analysis ToolPak in the list of add-ins).

Table 22.2 describes the various tools.

TABLE 22.2. TOOLS IN THE ANALYSIS TOOLPAK

Tool	What It Does
ANOVA: Single Factor	Simple variance analysis
ANOVA: Two-Factor	Variance analysis that includes more than one sample of data for each group
ANOVA: Two-Factor Without Replication	Variance analysis that doesn't include more than one sample of data for each group
Correlation	Measurement—independent correlation between data sets
Covariance	Measurement—dependent covariance between data sets
Descriptive Statistics	Report of univariate statistics for sample
Exponential Smoothing	Smooths data, weighting more recent data heavier
F-Test: Two-Sample for Variance	Two-sample F-Test to compare population variances
Histogram	Counts occurrences in each of several data bins
Moving Average	Smooths data series by averaging the last few periods
Random number generation	Creates any of several types of random numbers: Uniform: Uniform random numbers between upper and lower bounds Normal: Normally distributed numbers based on the mean and the standard deviation Bernoulli: Ones and zeros with a specified probability of success Poisson: A distribution of random numbers given a desired lambda Patterned: A sequence of numbers at a specific interval Discrete: Probabilities based on the predefined percents of total
Rank and Percentile	Creates a report of ranking and percentile distribution
Regression	Creates a table of statistics that result from least-squares regression
t-Test: Paired Two Sample for Means	Paired two-sample students t-test
t-Test: Two Sample Assuming Equal Variances	Paired two-sample t-test assuming equal means

Tool	What It Does
t-Test: Two Sample Assuming Unequal Variances	Heteroscedastic t-test
z-Test: Two-Sample for Means	Two-sample z-test for means with known variances
Fourier Analysis	DFT or FFT method, including reverse transforms
Sampling	Samples a population randomly or periodically

The analysis tools all work in basically the same way. Choose Tools, Data Analysis to display the Data Analysis dialog box (see Figure 22.38). Select the tool you want to use, and click OK to display a separate dialog box for that particular tool.

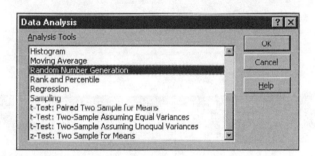

Figure 22.38.
The Data Analysis dialog box.

For example, suppose you want to generate random data sets to perform analysis of calls at your company's call center, based on historical data. By far the simplest method to achieve a random sampling is using the Random Number Generation tool, which creates realistic sample data sets between ranges that you specify.

To create a random sampling, select the Random Number Generation tool in the Data Analysis dialog box. When you click OK, Excel displays the Random Number Generation dialog box, in which you can specify the parameters for the data set you want. For the example in Figure 22.39, I want two columns of variables, each of which contains 15 random numbers in uniform distribution, between 50 and 100. (Seven different distribution generators are available; refer to Table 22.2 for descriptions.)

If you don't specify a particular number for variables or random numbers, Excel fills the cells in the output range.

Figure 22.40 shows the result. Figure 22.41 shows how you can use this data set for multiple analyses—just tie the analysis results to formulas, charts, and PivotTables.

Figure 22.39.
Use the Random
Number Generation
dialog box to set
parameters for
your data.

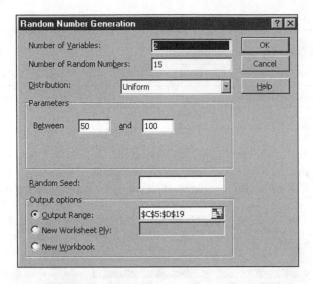

Figure 22.40.
Two sets of random
numbers between
50 and 100.

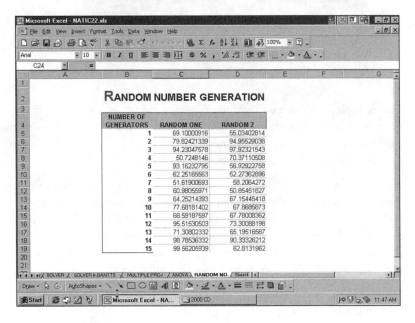

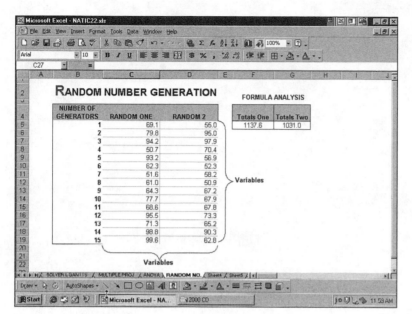

Figure 22.41.
Set up the desired range so you can create the analysis over and over, and tie the analysis to formulas, charts, and PivotTables.

TAKING EXCEL TO THE NEXT LEVEL

CHAPTER 23

INNOVATIVE WAYS TO USE EXCEL

by Patrick D. Blattner
Patrick@BlattnerBooks.com

In this chapter

THINKING "OUT OF THE BOX" WITH EXCEL

Excel's flexibility enables you to go above and beyond the conventional wisdom in which the program was originally designed. By understanding formatting, formulas, form controls, and charts, you can start to use Excel's flexibility to solve just about any problem. This chapter taps into utilizing Excel in interesting and unusual ways. From strategic planning to conventional techniques in business, you can start to visualize the application's sheer strength and understand the power of Excel.

VALUE CHAINS

Value chains measure the value of process or products over a range of variables, such as steps in process or capabilities. You can use value chains to measure product coverage in the marketplace against competitors, or as a strategic business measure to understand the most logical approach in weighing risk factors.

CREATING A MARKET OPPORTUNITY VALUE CHAIN

A *market opportunity value chain* measures market coverage either internally—within an organization—or against competitors. Notice in Figure 23.1 that the market opportunity value chain for a small publisher measures the coverage of their books' accomplishment level and the company's coverage against it. By utilizing Excel's formatting and drawing tools, you can create value chains for presentations or strategic initiatives for future approaches to the marketplace.

Figure 23.1.
By utilizing drawing tools, you can create value chains to indicate market opportunity.

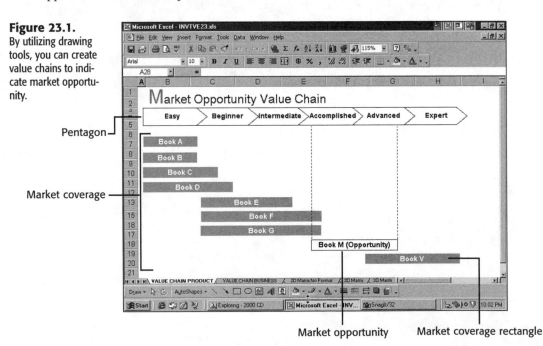

Pentagon

Market coverage

Market opportunity

Market coverage rectangle

When creating a value chain, think in terms of the market or process as a whole with the different sections broken out from least to most, lowest to highest, easiest to hardest, and so on. Use the rectangle as the measurement tool that plots against the value chain.

To create the value chain shown in Figure 23.1, use the pentagon shape for the process or market analysis across the top of the sheet. The pentagon shape in the form of a chain represents the steps in the process, or the sectors in the marketplace. (Click the AutoShapes button and choose Block Arrows from the pop-up list; then click the Pentagon button as shown in Figure 23.2.)

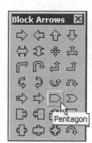

Figure 23.2.
The pentagon shape is used to create the value chain.

Tip #261 from

You can duplicate the first pentagon by holding down the Ctrl key and dragging, or by pressing Ctrl+D. Pressing Ctrl+Shift and dragging creates a duplicate while keeping the horizontal alignment intact.

Use the Bring to Front or Send to Back buttons to create the overlap between the pentagons (the point of one pentagon placed on top of the next pentagon). To add text inside the shape, simply select the shape and type; then press Esc twice when you're done typing.

Tip #262 from

When adding drawn shapes to your charts and worksheets, you're likely to need four toolbar buttons quite often: Bring to Front, Send to Back, Bring Forward, and Send Backward. You can place these buttons on a toolbar within easy access by using one of these methods:

- **Add the buttons to the Drawing toolbar.** Right-click on the toolbar and select Customize to open the Customize dialog box. In the Categories list on the Commands tab, choose Drawing; then scroll the Commands list to find the commands for Bring to Front, Send to Back, and so on, and drag them to the toolbar. Close the Customize dialog box when you're finished.

- **Tear off the Order toolbar.** Click the Draw button on the Drawing toolbar to open the pop-up menu. Click the Order option to display the submenu, and then drag the submenu's title bar away from the Draw menu to create a floating Order toolbar.

To create the product bars, use the Rectangle AutoShape from the Drawing toolbar. To create a white background, select the worksheet and use a white fill color (or just turn off the gridlines by choosing Tools, Options, clicking the View tab, and deselecting the Gridlines option in the Window Options section of the dialog box).

To create the dotted vertical lines shown on the sides of the opportunity block, click the Line button on the Drawing toolbar, draw the line, and then click the Dash Style button and select a style. You can draw an identical line on the other side, or Ctrl+Shift+drag to create the line and position it exactly parallel to the first line.

CREATING A STRATEGIC RISK FACTOR VALUE CHAIN

A *strategic risk factor value chain* enables you to measure business risk against different strategy approaches. In Figure 23.3, the solutions take a multiple-vendor approach against a single-source solution—the value chain measures the different steps in creating the product. Two approaches to producing the product are shown:

- Corporate Solution I shows multiple processes divided among several companies. This strategy creates dependencies on the other companies, thus creating greater risk, but lower cost in the short term; however, it ultimately will cost more in time and delivery risk.

- Corporate Solution II creates a single-source dependency with one company. The short-term cost may be a bit higher, but risk is minimized with sole control and single-source dependencies.

This example may seem a bit complex, but think in terms of your business and the different steps required to produce a service or product. Then look at the opportunities available to create the same product or process, and the risks and cost associated with that opportunity.

Figure 23.3.
A strategic risk factor value chain measures strategic approaches in order to arrive at a logical conclusion.

Multiple vendor approach

Single-source approach

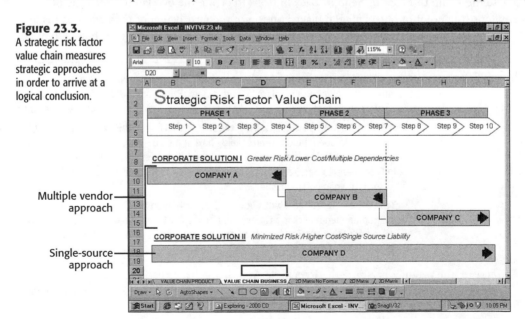

By utilizing the pentagon shape, lines or connectors, arrows, and text, you can create strategic approaches to arrive at business conclusions.

VALUE MATRICES

You use a *value matrix* to measure multiple components of processes or products. They're created with two forms: two-dimensional and three-dimensional. Value chains are created primarily with drawing programs for presentations; however, considering that most number decisions are based in Excel, you also can create matrices and metrics in Excel for presentations or strategic cross sections of a market or business.

CREATING A 2D MATRIX

A *two-dimensional matrix* is a cross section between components where the equal components or intersections are checked. Figures 23.4 and 23.5 show two matrices: one to show the structure on the worksheet, and the second to illustrate a final form with formatting. In Figure 23.4, the two-dimensional matrix measures the product and the components within the product. It provides a cross section overview of the product's components as a whole. Figure 23.5 shows the matrix in final formatted form.

→ For details on creating professional-looking formats for your matrices, **see** "Professional Tables," **p. 726**

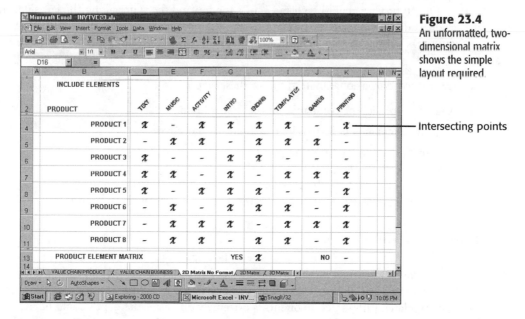

Figure 23.4
An unformatted, two-dimensional matrix shows the simple layout required.

Intersecting points

Note

Obviously, the grayscale used for printing this book can only distantly represent the colors used in charts and other graphics. To see the actual worksheets, refer to the CD accompanying this book.

Figure 23.5.
The final formatted two-dimensional matrix.

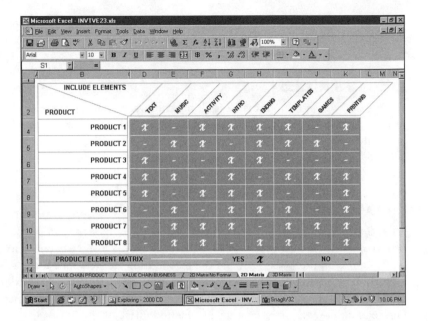

Suppose that your business distributes 10 different types of products throughout the United States. The 10 products could be listed across the top and the states along the left side, and the products distributed within the states would then be checked at the intersections. A matrix creates a simple intersecting picture that helps visualize complex cross sections of data.

To create a two-dimensional matrix, follow these steps:

1. Align the products or companies in the first column.

2. Align the components across the top in one or more rows.

3. Add an X, check mark, or other graphic where categories cross.

By adjusting column and row heights and centering text horizontally and vertically, you can establish a balanced matrix that resembles one created in a drawing program.

CREATING A 3D MATRIX

A *three-dimensional matrix* is used when levels of complexity are involved, adding a depth measure to the 2D matrix. Depth can include performance, perceived value, cost associated with like items, and so on. For example, if you have three cars with like components, but the cost associated with the components is extremely different, the depth could be measured in cost as inexpensive, moderate, and expensive. In Figure 23.6, the three-dimensional matrix measures several components, as well as the value of items associated with the vehicle type. The structure of the matrix is the same as the two-dimensional matrix covered previously; however, the three-dimensional component is created with shapes from the Drawing toolbar to display depth: the level of performance.

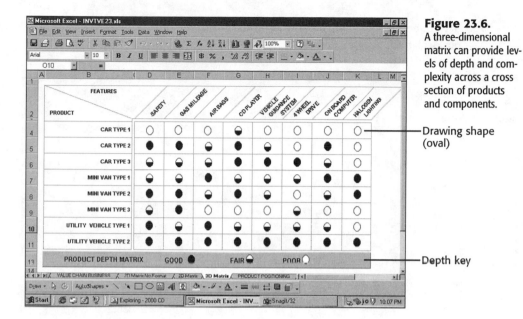

Figure 23.6.
A three-dimensional matrix can provide levels of depth and complexity across a cross section of products and components.

To create the ovals as measuring tools for the matrix, perform the following steps:

1. Create an empty oval, as shown in Figure 23.7.
2. Copy and paste the empty oval and fill it with black to create a full oval.
3. Copy and paste the empty oval again for use as the half oval (I'll describe how to make it a half shortly).
4. Copy and paste the half oval, filling it with black so that you have one full and one empty oval for use as half ovals.
5. From the Drawing toolbar, select the Rectangle AutoShape and drag it over half the oval, as shown in step 3 in Figure 23.7.
6. Keeping the rectangle selected, choose Format, AutoShape to open the Format AutoShape dialog box. Select the Colors and Lines tab. In the Line section of the dialog box, choose No Line for the Color option.

   Step 4 in Figure 23.7 illustrates the result.
7. Place the empty oval from step 1 in Figure 23.8 over step 5, making sure the oval has no fill color.
8. Bring the empty oval to the front, if necessary, and the final result is shown as step 6 in the figure.
9. Select each of the shapes in step 6 in the figure (the filled oval, the empty oval, and the "invisible" rectangle). Click the Draw button on the Drawing toolbar and select Group to group the pieces of the new shape together so that you can copy or move them as one unit.

10. Select and place the individual ovals in the cross section of the matrix that best suits the performance level.

Figure 23.7.
Create the shapes for the three-dimensional matrix with drawing tools.

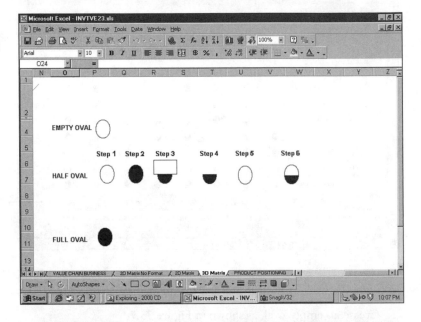

Figure 23.8.
By using multiple shapes, you can create the half-full effect.

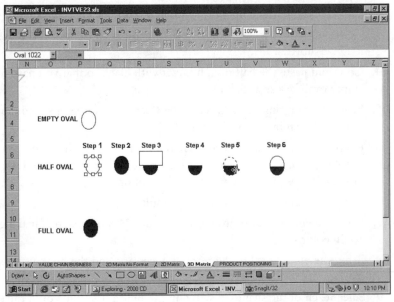

Tip #263 from

When the "half oval" is complete, you can resize it by dragging. To move the filled half of the oval to the top, click the Draw button, select Rotate or Flip, select the Free Rotate option, and drag one of the handles until the shape is positioned as desired.

USING DRAWING TOOLS TO CREATE QUADRANTS

Quadrants are used to measure market penetration in several forms. You can use quadrants to understand your product mix in the marketplace and compare your strategy to that of other businesses in the same market. You also can measure your market share and penetration per quadrant. Another way to use quadrants is in conjunction with comparative analysis for two market factors, such as market penetration and consumer dollar spending. The quadrant examples in the following sections show effective solutions for business strategies and fully utilize Excel's drawing tools to solve problems—not just to place boxes on the worksheet—thus using Excel the way it was meant to be used.

For details on using Excel's drawing tools, see Chapter 8, "Using Excel's Drawing Tools."

PART

VII

CH

23

MEASURING PRODUCT PLACEMENT WITH PRODUCT POSITIONING QUADRANTS

A *product positioning quadrant* helps you visualize your market coverage per product. Combinations of drawing tools create visual presentations that can help your company make effective decisions. The quadrant in Figure 23.9, for example, measures the market categories by using arrows from the Drawing toolbar. Insert the quadrants with the rectangle on the Drawing toolbar, and use shapes, letters, or names to call out the product.

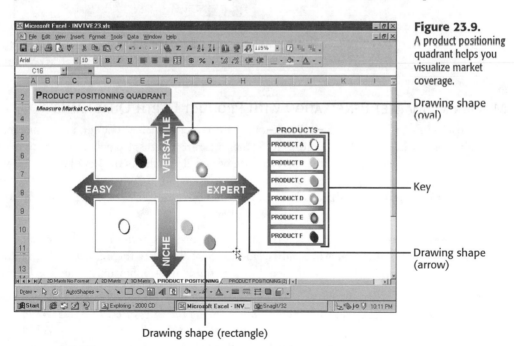

Figure 23.9.
A product positioning quadrant helps you visualize market coverage.

Drawing shape (oval)

Key

Drawing shape (arrow)

Drawing shape (rectangle)

Notice that the ovals in this example tend toward different locations in the quadrant. This is due to the product's coverage. For example, product C's location in the lower-right quadrant indicates that this product reaches the extreme edge of the niche market and the mid-expert level.

To create the quadrant arrows, simply use one of the Drawing toolbar's block arrows. Then click the D<u>r</u>aw button and use the Rotate and Fli<u>p</u> option to place the arrows facing opposite directions. Figure 23.10 shows all the individual drawing objects selected, to show the extended use of drawing tools to create the quadrant.

Figure 23.10.
Notice the extended use of Excel's drawing tools to create the quadrant.

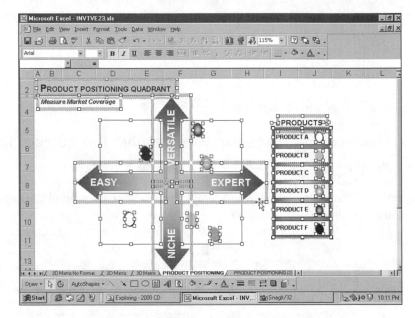

MEASURING MARKET PENETRATION WITH PRODUCT DEPTH QUADRANTS

Quadrants can reflect product or positioning focus in a particular market, or the marketplace as a whole. Use drawing tools to further measure and display penetration into market categories. In Figure 23.11, the market share per quadrant shows the depth and areas of coverage into the marketplace. Use the Freeform tool on the Drawing toolbar to draw the market penetration into the quadrant and then fill the new freeform shape with a fill color. Use text to apply the percentages to the quadrant.

To measure your company's market penetration in comparison to the consumer dollar distribution, use drawing tools in quadrant form to visually create the market. By using drawing tools effectively, you can understand where your market opportunities lie (see Figure 23.12).

Notice the "perfect world" dollar distribution among the categories. Business would be simpler if we could segment the world this way, in even amounts, wouldn't it? In real life, of course, the consumer determines the profitable market, and this example clearly indicates that more opportunities and dollars are available in the easy/versatile quadrant for this publishing company.

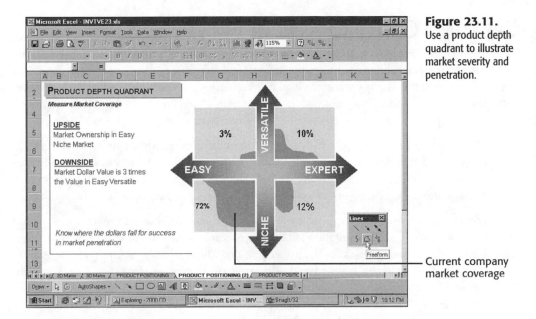

Figure 23.11.
Use a product depth quadrant to illustrate market severity and penetration.

Current company market coverage

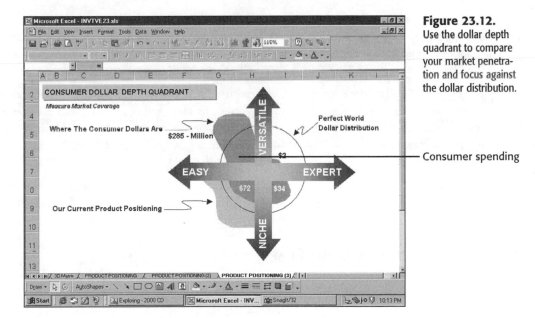

Figure 23.12.
Use the dollar depth quadrant to compare your market penetration and focus against the dollar distribution.

Consumer spending

As another example, suppose your particular industry is construction. You want to determine where your focus should be in current and future markets. If you do state work, you could look at the dollars being let for bridges, roads, dams, and tunnels, and compare your focus against the distribution of the total dollars being allocated by the state over the next few years.

CREATING GANTT CHARTS IN EXCEL

You may be surprised to learn that you can use Excel for project management, resource loading, forecasting, marketing management, and any process that occurs over time. You can create static Gantt charts for visual representation, or dynamic Gantt charts that calculate durations and automatically plot, coupled with charts and formulas. With the proper approach, Excel can be used to tackle just about any problem.

It's likely that project management for your business is currently a combination of using project management software coupled with Excel to calculate durations. But the illustrations and examples in the following sections show how Excel can handle all your project and scheduling needs, without requiring the use of project management software.

Here's a question. What happens if you have a thousand lines of information in a project and you have to put in a duration (an "educated guess") for each line? That's right, after a thousand educated guesses for the project, you're still in trouble, because durations should really take into account several factors that are a calculation of some type (hours per day minus 15 percent times 6 days a week, and so on). Now what if you have several release dates for different projects and you need to know when you have to start each project to get it completed by the scheduled release date?

These are examples of one of the biggest headaches in business today—whether you're writing a book, managing multiple projects, or building software. By understanding spreadsheet design and layout, coupled with formulas and proper referencing, you'll soon discover how Excel can work effectively for you to solve these kinds of problems.

Because all processes occur over time, you can use Excel to calculate dollars over time and process over time for marketing, production, sales, finance, and accounting, as well as any other function of business. By setting up timelines appropriately, down to the level of tracking and forecasting required by your situation, you can tie or reference formulas to the timeline to shift events, move money, forecast widgets, and so on, as shown in Figure 23.13.

From marketing to finance to production, Excel is the most flexible tool on the market, and can cover and manage any sector in business today. The following sections show you how to get started using Excel for project management in your business.

CREATING A BASIC STATIC GANTT CHART

Figure 23.14 illustrates a simple multiple-project Gantt chart. In this example, the output levels per week are directly aligned with the week and project. Figure 23.15 illustrates formats applied to the Gantt chart. You can see the value of formatting in this comparison. Based on this principle, you can apply charts for resource loading, create employee allocation charts for understanding future needs, and apply formulas and form controls to automate the Gantt chart, as described later in the chapter.

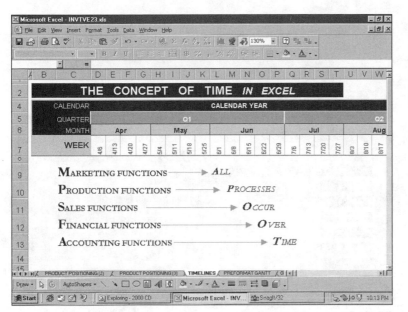

Figure 23.13.
By utilizing timelines appropriately, you can start to make Excel into a powerful forecasting and process program.

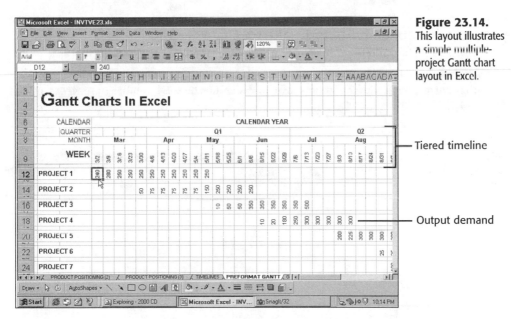

Figure 23.14.
This layout illustrates a simple multiple-project Gantt chart layout in Excel.

Tiered timeline

Output demand

Note

The best way to learn how to create and use Gantt charts in Excel is to experiment with a working Gantt chart. All the worksheets in this chapter are included on the CD in the back of this book.

Figure 23.15.
By utilizing Excel's formatting tools, you can provide clear, concise pictures of your production process.

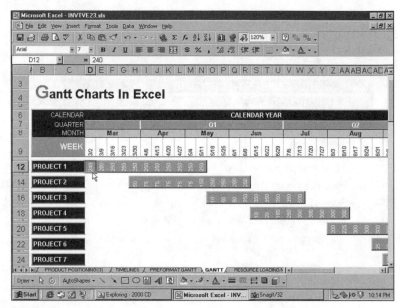

ADDING A RESOURCE LOADING CHART TO A GANTT CHART

With a basic Gantt layout in place, you can apply a demand/capacity chart for resource loading, people utilization, and so on. To do this, simply create a row under the projects that corresponds with the week above, and sum up the total number of project rows, as illustrated in Figure 23.16. Drag the formula to the right to carry out the SUM formula through the weeks.

Figure 23.16.
Sum the total number of projects below the Gantt chart and create a demand/capacity chart aligned with the corresponding weeks.

Line chart capacity —

Column chart — demand

Weekly demand —

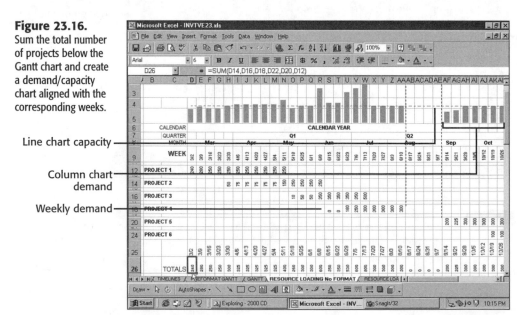

You also can apply a capacity row directly under the SUM formula. Select the entire range summed (including the date range) to create the chart. Then align the chart above the Gantt chart and eliminate the borders and background of the new chart. Now, whenever a project moves from its original production window, the chart automatically reflects the change. This works well with dynamic Gantt charts to run scenarios in production. Notice in Figure 23.17 that June and July are running over the current capacity of the resource or production facilities. There's also a period of time in August and early September where no demand appears. By setting up a resource-loading chart above the Gantt grid as shown, you can smooth out your production plan and optimize your resources. This principle could also apply to cash flow. Because costs are associated with each event, you can lay out cash flow against the production plan as well, and even track actual costs associated with the plan.

PART

VII

CH

23

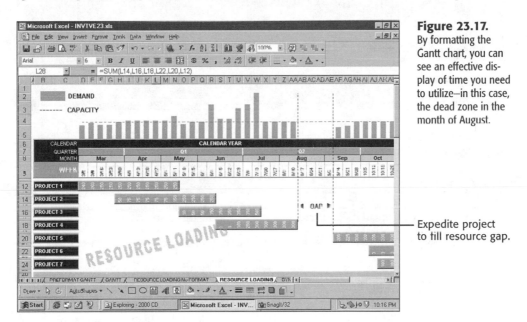

Figure 23.17.
By formatting the Gantt chart, you can see an effective display of time you need to utilize—in this case, the dead zone in the month of August.

Expedite project to till resource gap.

CREATING DYNAMIC GANTT CHARTS

Dynamic Gantt charts are driven by timelines and start-and-stop dates. The duration drives the period between the start date and stop date and the week value plots the output per week. The week value also can be a percentage, a unit, a person, and so on. (For more information, see the later section "Advanced Gantt Chart Principles.") The key is that the Gantt bar is a dynamic moving timeline based on a simple formula that references the weeks and the week value. The week value can be a name, letter, or number (see cell G9 of Figure 23.18). Notice in the figure how the formula is tied to four key cells: the timeline in cell H5, the start date in cell D9, the stop date in cell E9, and the plotted week value in cell G9. The duration drives the time between the start and stop dates and can be derived with calculations—a key difference between project management programs and Excel.

Figure 23.18.
With the right layout approach, a simple formula can be created to automate Excel into a production tool to drive processes.

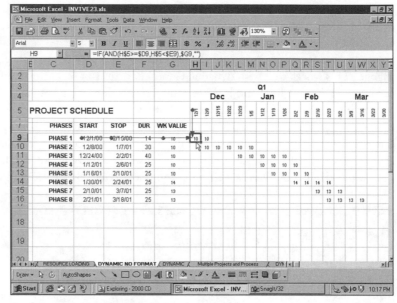

Tip #264 from

Patrick

Review this worksheet on the CD as you follow the steps, so that you can see the formulas and scroll all rows and columns into view as needed.

To create an automated Gantt chart in Excel, follow these steps:

1. Set up the timeline or weeks. This example starts in cell H5 of the worksheet with the date 12/1/2000.

2. Create a seven-day increment of the original timeline date. For this example, the formula in cell I5 is =H5+7, filled to the right to the desired end date of the timeline.

3. Set up the key information to prepare your Gantt references. In Figure 23.18, row 7 contains the titles.

4. Enter the start date for phase 1 (cell D9, 12/1/2000 in this example). The start date will drive all phases in this example because you'll establish links between the phases.

5. Type a formula to provide the end result once a duration is entered. In the example, cell E9 contains this formula: =D9+F9. This example uses a static duration. This means that you'll just enter a number. You can get creative with formulas to drive the duration as well, however, and even use Goal Seek. (See Chapter 22, "Using Excel's Analysis Tools," for more details on using Goal Seek.)

6. Enter the duration for phase 1. In the example, cell F9 contains the duration 14, which adds 14 days to the start date, and the stop date is therefore 12/15/00.

7. Enter a value for the week. This is optional, depending on what you want to track. You also could enter a percent. For this example, 10 was entered in cell G9.

   The value for the week can represent unit output, percent of total, or even a name. This is one of the key values in Excel and building Gantt charts, and helps you visually understand complex timing issues associated with multiple productions.

8. Type the formula for the calculation (in cell H9 in the example.) Be sure to use absolute references in the right place in order to be able to drag the formula to the right and down.

   In cell H9 of the example, the formula is =IF(AND(H$5>=$D9,H$5<$E9),$G9,""). The formula reads: If the timeline is greater than or equal to the start date and the timeline is less than the stop date, plot the value in cell G9.

9. Drag and fill the formula to the right and the Gantt automatically plots the week value to the start and stop dates (see Figure 23.19).

PART

VII

CH

23

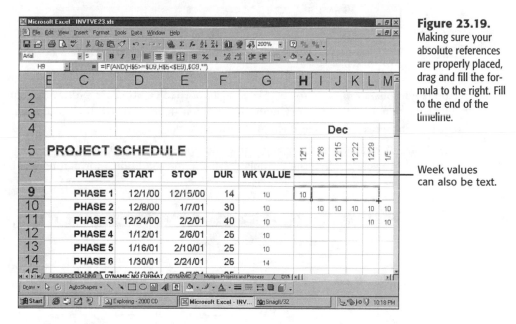

Figure 23.19.
Making sure your absolute references are properly placed, drag and fill the formula to the right. Fill to the end of the timeline.

Week values can also be text.

10. Link another phase under the first phase by following the previous steps; however, in the first cell (cell D10 in the example), enter a formula to link to the first phase. In Figure 23.20, the formula entered is =D9+7. Whenever the start date of the project changes, phase 2 automatically responds.

Figure 23.20.
To add another phase and link it to the project, simply establish a formula that responds to the start date or stop date of the previous phase.

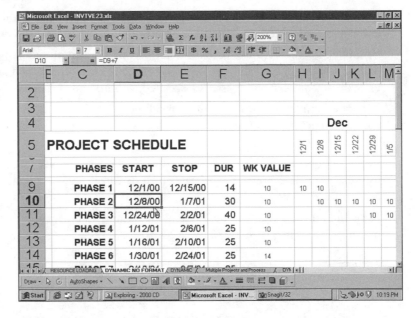

11. Add conditional formatting to complete the automated Gantt chart. Notice in Figure 23.21 the first condition in the Conditional Formatting dialog box. If the cell value is equal to the week value, then Excel will format the cell.

    Make sure that the formula is mixed—absolute column reference and relative row reference—so you can drag the formula down and the conditional formatting will be applied to the week value for each phase.

Figure 23.21.
When applying a conditional format to the Gantt, make the row reference relative so that you can drag the formula down and it will reference the week value in the corresponding row.

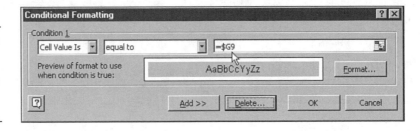

Note

It's important to establish the absolute references in the right places when using formulas in both cells and conditional formatting commands, so that you have to create them only once.

Now that you have the basic structure of the Gantt chart set up, you can apply formats to complete the Gantt. The chart in Figure 23.22 uses a start date of 12/1/2000. With the proper links in place, if I shift the start date to 1/1/2001, the whole project automatically shifts, as shown in Figure 23.23.

To see this example with all the formulas and links in place, open the file from the CD. You also will get a better understanding of how the conditional formatting was applied.

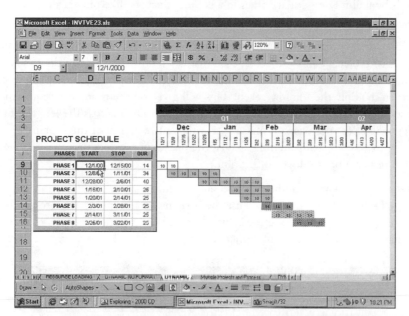

Figure 23.22.
A simple project with phases linked to each other and durations for each phase. The week value that plots the number in the timeline is hidden (refer to Column G in Figure 23.20 to see the column).

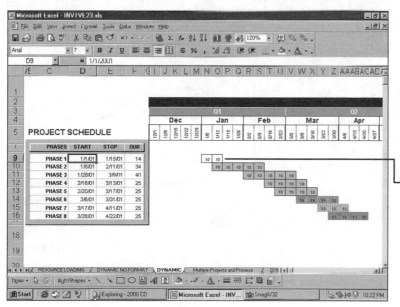

Figure 23.23.
By changing the start date in cell D9 to 1/1/2001, the project dates automatically shift and the automated Gantt chart "walks" (plots) to correspond with the timeline.

Project automatically shifts based on new start date.

STACKING PROJECTS

When you understand the fundamentals of setting up a Gantt chart in Excel, you can go on to establish multiple projects that overlap, and begin to extract by phases of production, according to your needs. You can add the like phases of multiple projects to discern future monetary needs by multiplying dollar values in a table against the like phases added together. When projects shift, the dollars automatically reflect the change in time.

Suppose you know that every phase 2 unit costs seven dollars. You have two projects going on during the year, Project A and Project B, each one listed down the side of the timeline, and stacked one on top of the other. You sum up all phase 2 values for the first week in the timeline and then multiply the total by seven. This will give you the monetary requirement (cost) for phase 2 for the first week. You then can drag the formula across the length of the timeline to determine cost per week of phase 2 over the entire length of the timeline. (Another use might be comparing staffing against the phases of production to project head-count needs for resource or employee utilization.)

Figure 23.24 shows this chart. In addition, this Gantt includes a baseline that shows the original projected start and stop dates. Because the baseline isn't linked to the project, when a project shifts its schedule you can see the actual dates versus projected dates. I've also grouped the phases so that I can roll the project up to baseline, as shown in Figure 23.25.

Figure 23.24.
By stacking projects and processes, you can see your needs over time from a global perspective. The baseline enables you to see the project's actual result versus the original projected window.

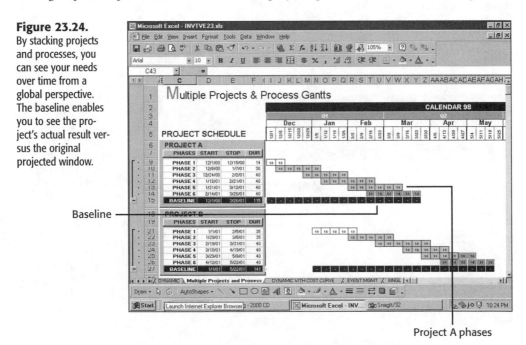

Baseline

Project A phases

→ For details on using Excel's outlining and grouping capabilities, **see** "Grouping and Outlining Data," **p. 528**

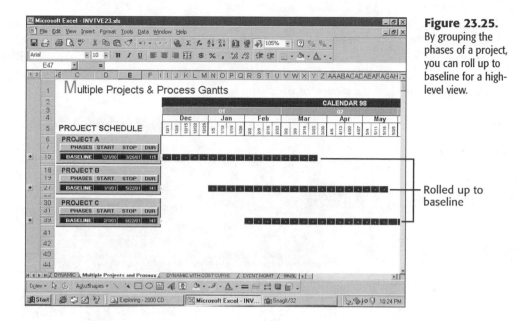

Figure 23.25.
By grouping the phases of a project, you can roll up to baseline for a high-level view.

ILLUSTRATING TIME COMPLETED

Use Excel's drawing tools to illustrate the time completed or passed for a project, or even the percentage complete. In Figure 23.26, a shaded rectangle helps the worksheet's audience to picture the time passed.

→ If you really want to get fancy, you can use conditional formatting to automate the time passed. For details on using conditional formatting, **see** "Conditional Formatting," **p. 176**

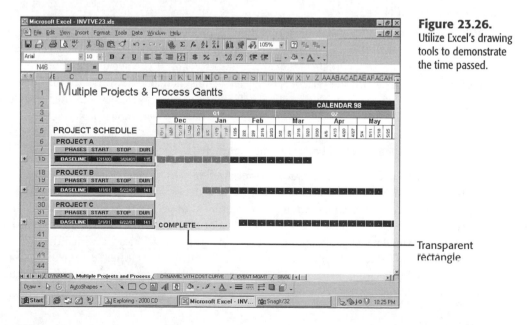

Figure 23.26.
Utilize Excel's drawing tools to demonstrate the time passed.

To create the "curtain" (the semitransparent covered area), simply use a rectangle from the Drawing toolbar. After creating the shape, right-click it and choose Format AutoShape from the context menu to open the Format AutoShape dialog box. On the Colors and Lines tab, select a light gray fill and check the Semitransparent option. Select No Line for the Color setting in the Line section of the dialog box, as shown in Figure 23.27.

Figure 23.27.
Create a semitranspar-
ent curtain with the
Format AutoShapes
dialog box.

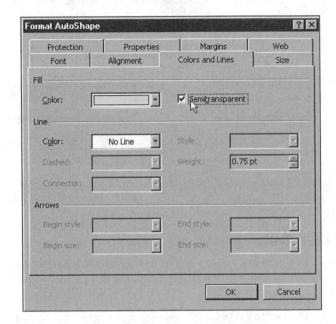

EVENT MANAGEMENT

Whether you're creating timelines for marketing, production, sales, or other departments, the basic principle is that you incur cost over time for every week. When you accumulate the costs, you can see the total cost for the project to date. If you accumulate the projected cost, you could establish the variance, projected against actual. The worksheet in Figure 23.28 illustrates this point with two visual references: the cost table beneath the body of the Gantt chart; and a line chart, created from the cost table, which shows projected cumulative and actual cumulative costs. The chart visibly shows the variance in actual cost over time against the projected cost laid out over the Gantt chart.

When you understand how to create dynamic schedules that refer to timelines and start-and-stop dates, you can use Excel to manage events in ways you may never before have tried. In Figure 23.29, the marketing events that need to occur are grouped together, and the dates on which the events occur are to the right of the event. The dynamic Gantt that refers to the timeline, kick off, and date due event, plots the window in which the event is to occur. Using the same formula and setup as described in the earlier section "Creating Dynamic Gantt Charts," conditional formatting is applied to refer to the cell right of the Date Due column.

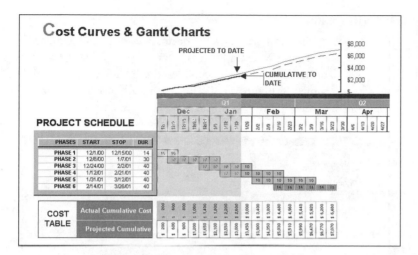

Figure 23.28.
With cost occurring over time, you can use Excel to cumulate the cost and provide a visible analysis of the project's current state in time.

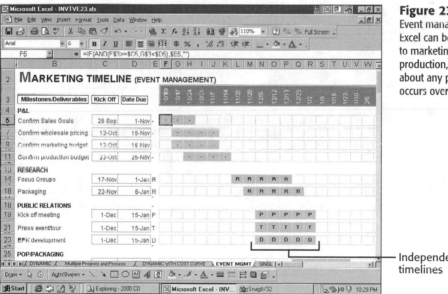

Figure 23.29.
Event management in Excel can be applied to marketing, finance, production, or just about any process that occurs over time.

Independent task timelines

Note

Remember to adjust the absolute reference in the conditional formatting equal to the cell with the plotted value: =$(Column)Row. Now when you copy the formula, the conditional format always refers to the line item.

You also could apply projected dates and insert actual occurrences beneath the projected date.

MILESTONE MANAGEMENT (SINGLE EVENT)

Milestone management is used when important events occur. *Milestone* is a term used to describe a point in time in the future. For example, if your project requires certain deliveries or achievements by key dates in the future, you could establish a milestone schedule as a reminder of the key dates, as shown in Figure 23.30. The events are just occurrences tied to one date—in this case, the date due.

Figure 23.30.
Manage key dates with a milestone Gantt chart. By tying the formula to the timeline and date due, Excel creates a dynamic model.

Single event week value as day from timeline

Single event week value as text

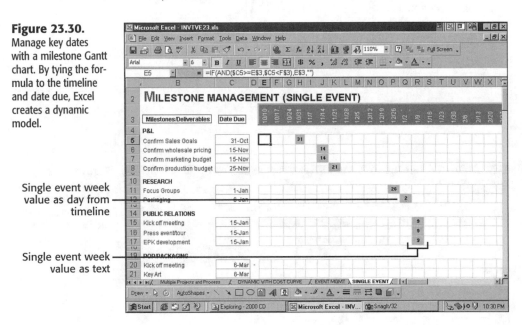

The formula is different from the start-and-stop date formula previously described. The timeline reference is pointing to the date due cell per event only, and the plot text or result cell refers to the timeline plotting the day of the event. To establish a milestone management schedule, follow these steps:

1. Create your timeline. In Figure 23.30, the timeline is every seven days starting in cell E3.

2. Create the Date Due column (in the example, starting in cell C5).

3. Type the formula. In the example, cell E5 contains this formula:
   `=IF(AND($C5>=E$3,$C5<F$3),E$3,"")`

4. Apply the conditional formatting (Format, Conditional Formatting). For this example, the condition is Cell Value Is equal to =E$3 (the date from the timeline), and a fill color is applied if the condition is met.

Tip #265 from

Patrick

Notice that the conditional formula uses an absolute row reference ($3), which enables you to copy the conditional formatting so that all the pasted conditional formulas still look to row 3 for its timeline date.

5. To display the day from the timeline, open the Format Cells dialog box. On the Number tab, choose Custom in the Category list. In the Type box, enter **d** to display the day.

6. Drag the formula to the right, as well as filling the formula down.

Now, when you drag the formula to the right, references to the date due stay intact. When you drag the formula down, the new formulas still refer to the timeline dates.

MILESTONE MANAGEMENT (MULTIPLE EVENT)

You can manage Gantt charts and milestones with multiple events occurring on the same line. Suppose that you have a product that has three milestone completion dates and the dates are quantified with a percentage completion. Broken out evenly, you would see milestone completions of 33.33 percent per milestone. If you have 30 or 40 projects to view, this is a good way to manage the view from a high level. Notice the example in Figure 23.31. By adding conditional IF(AND) statements, as shown in Figure 23.32, you can tie multiple dates to the same row or line. Use the conditional formatting tool to fill the cells when a number occurs.

PART

VII

CH

23

> **Note**
>
> The example shows numbers; however, you can apply names, percentages, dates, or any other type of grid information that would be applicable to the elements scheduled.

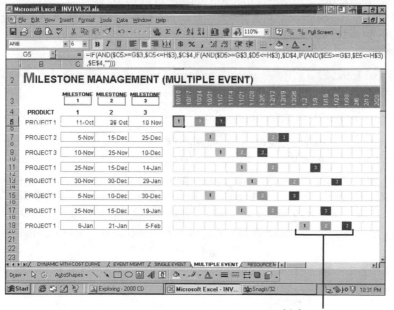

Figure 23.31.
By applying IF(AND) statements, you can track multiple milestone events.

Multiple events moving along the same timeline

Figure 23.32.
Apply conditional formats to the line of information so that when a date or number falls on the timeline, it's highlighted with a format.

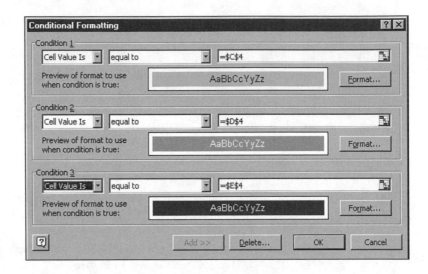

BUILDING A RESOURCE CHART

A resource chart can be placed under a Gantt chart to automatically tie the automated Gantt chart to the total number of machines, people, or resources of any kind. This approach can be used for marketing, finance, accounting, and other divisions, as well as production, to take the guesswork out of future needs. This is the last element in creating a fully dynamic system on one worksheet that will allow you to load resources, account for costs, forecast for future resource needs, and compute just about anything—all on one worksheet within one workbook. Why have multiple systems when the right approach the first time can actually automate your environment?

Figures 23.33, 23.34, and 23.35 show three of the formulas used for driving the resource chart. (The formulas are displayed in the Formula bar.)

To create this dynamic resource chart, follow these steps:

1. The resource chart is based on weekly demand, so establish the weekly demand in F10:W10. Demand can be static or based on a weekly demand Gantt chart.

2. Set up the person, machine, or whatever you're tracking, and the associated output capacity per week. In Figures 23.33, 23.34, and 23.35, the cells populated are C13:D22. Enter the names in the C column and the weekly output in the D column from D13:D22.

3. In cell F13, type the formula `=IF(F$10>$D13,$D13,F$10)`. (Figure 23.33 shows the example.)

4. In cell F14, type the formula `=IF(F$10-F13>$D14,$D14,IF(F$10-F13>0,F$10-F13,0))`. (Figure 23.34 shows the example.)

5. In cell F15, type the formula `=IF(F$10-SUM(F$13:F14)>$D15,$D15,IF(F$10-SUM(F$13:F14)>0,F$10-SUM(F$13:F14),0))`. (Figure 23.35 shows the example.)

6. Drag the formula in cell F15 down to cell F22, and then select F13:F22 and drag the formulas to the right through to column W.

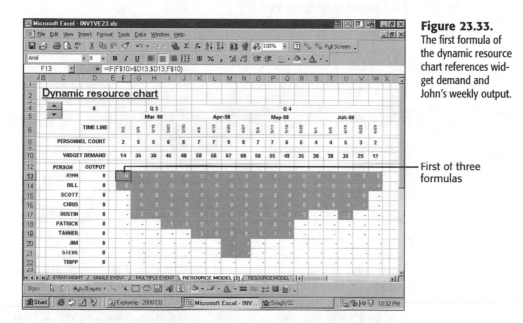

Figure 23.33.
The first formula of
the dynamic resource
chart references wid-
get demand and
John's weekly output.

First of three
formulas

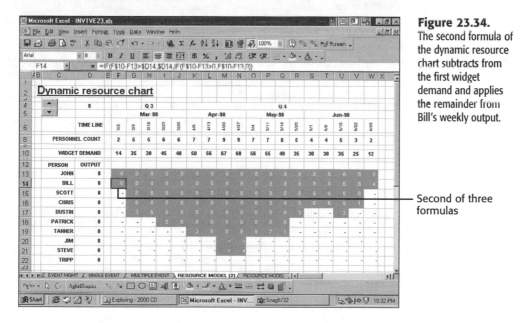

Figure 23.34.
The second formula of
the dynamic resource
chart subtracts from
the first widget
demand and applies
the remainder from
Bill's weekly output.

Second of three
formulas

Figure 23.35.
The third formula of
the dynamic resource
chart subtracts from
the widget demand
and sums up the pre-
vious cells and applies
the remainder from
Scott's weekly output.

Third of three
formulas

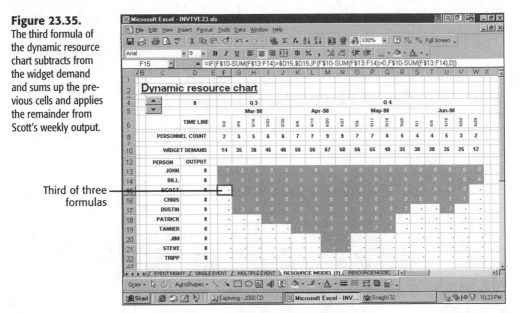

Tip #266 from

> Add a spinner to the output cells to toggle the output levels if all are constant. You also
> could apply a counter in F8:W8 with the formula that counts the weekly personnel or
> machine needs. The formula starting in cell F8 is =COUNTIF(F13:F22,">1"). For details
> on using spinners, counters, and so on, see Chapter 21, "Managing Data with Formulas and
> Form Controls."

Figure 23.36 shows the final formatted example (including the optional form controls mentioned in the Tip). As capacity increases to from 8 to 18 units per week, and the demand is
the same, fewer resources are needed to complete the tasks.

To further illustrate the point, look at Figure 23.37. If Bill's capacity is increased to an
extreme level of 70, Bill can handle the overflow of demand and the resources (personnel
count) needed throughout the period drops to 2. Of course, humans as well as machines
have unit output limits.

TYING GANTT CHARTS TOGETHER

By applying the principles discussed in this chapter, you can create a dynamic Gantt
chart—with a resource-loading demand/capacity chart above the Gantt chart and a
resource needs chart below the Gantt chart—for a fully dynamic project management
spreadsheet. Of course, there are ways to create a more "micro" approach, but the examples show a high-level approach on how you can start to use Excel as a fully functional
project management tool.

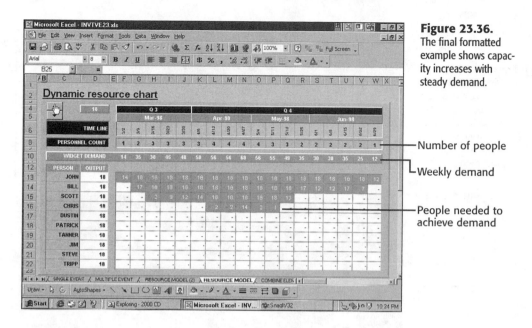

Figure 23.36.
The final formatted example shows capacity increases with steady demand.

—Number of people

└Weekly demand

—People needed to achieve demand

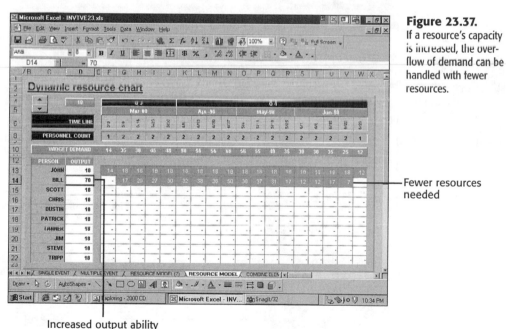

Figure 23.37.
If a resource's capacity is increased, the overflow of demand can be handled with fewer resources.

—Fewer resources needed

Increased output ability

As the Gantt chart in Figure 23.38 moves, the resource charts above and below the Gantt chart react accordingly. Now look at the example in Figure 23.39. If the projects are stacked, the charts again respond to the Gantt chart.

Figure 23.38.
By tying Gantt charts to resource charts, you can manage resource loading and resource needs, based on the Gantt chart's windows of production.

Column chart represents demand.

Line chart represents capacity.

Dynamic worksheet Gantt chart

Staggered projects

Dynamic resource needs chart

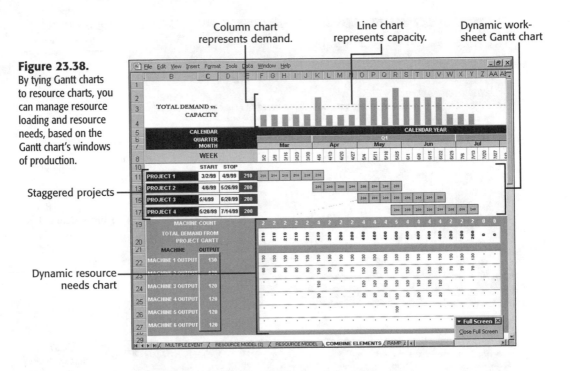

Figure 23.39.
If the projects are stacked over one another in the Gantt chart, the resource charts respond accordingly.

Demand exceeds capacity.

Projects stacked

Resources needed to achieve demand

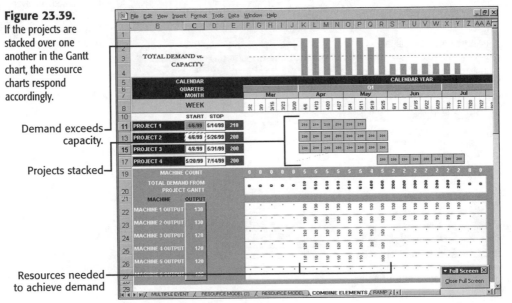

ADVANCED GANTT CHART PRINCIPLES

Earlier in the chapter, some basic techniques were discussed for dealing with time and process with Gantt charts. Now, take a situation in which you have multiple variables to deal with. What if you need to know when you have to start a certain project to complete it on time, or by a certain release date? This probably is the biggest question in business today. Or what if you have a required total unit output for a project, or tons of material to produce or mine? You can expect to produce a certain amount per week—the delivered average—and you have start and stop dates per phase. These issues are why project programs fall short—because you can't play with multiple scenarios, such as in the examples in the following sections.

Tip #267 from	Most of the examples are on the CD, so that you can see how they work with your particular situation.

GANTT CHARTS DRIVEN BY TOTAL UNITS AND WEEKLY OUTPUT CAPACITY

One powerful approach to event management is a Gantt chart driven by total number of units to produce and capacity to produce (on a units-per-week basis). Look at the example in Figure 23.40. The total number of units for the project is 2,000 and the weekly output is 900. Also included is a ramp up (the startup period before the phase reaches optimum production) for each phase before it reaches its optimum capacity or output. The demand chart is based above the timeline on phase 2.

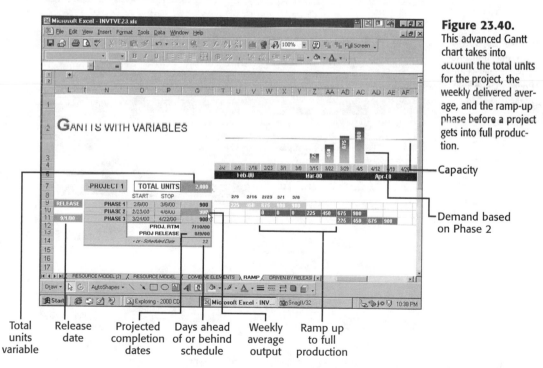

Figure 23.40.
This advanced Gantt chart takes into account the total units for the project, the weekly delivered average, and the ramp-up phase before a project gets into full production.

Total units variable — Release date — Projected completion dates — Days ahead of or behind schedule — Weekly average output — Ramp up to full production

Now, watch what happens when the weekly output is changed to 500. The Gantt chart adds two additional weeks to complete the project (see Figure 23.41). If you reduce the total units for the project to 1,000 but leave the weekly output at 500, the Gantt chart automatically accounts for the change and reduces the time frame of production by two weeks (see Figure 23.42). This approach can be tied to units, elements, tonnage, or any other type of occurrence over time.

Figure 23.41.
By changing the weekly output from 900 to 500 a week, this Gantt chart automatically adds two more weeks to complete the project.

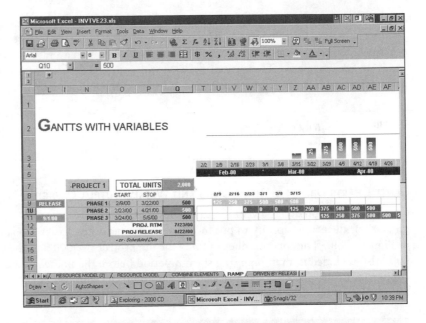

Figure 23.42.
The Gantt chart automatically adjusts for a change in total units.

Reduction in total units from 2,000 to 1,000

Shortened timeline

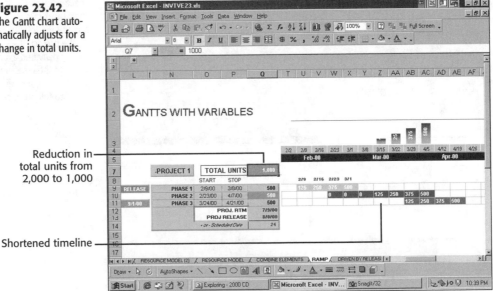

GANTT CHARTS DRIVEN BY RELEASE OR COMPLETION DATES

A Gantt chart can tell you when to start a project in order to complete it on time. This type of chart helps you manage resource needs, forecast production schedules—even manage inventory needs based on replenishment cycles. The following example uses three phases within a production cycle; the other variables are known time frames. The example takes into account the following variables: release date, output per week, and total quantity to produce. I show the setup a bit later in the chapter; meanwhile, look at Figure 23.43 to see the behind-the-scenes calculations that make up the phase time frames to the release date.

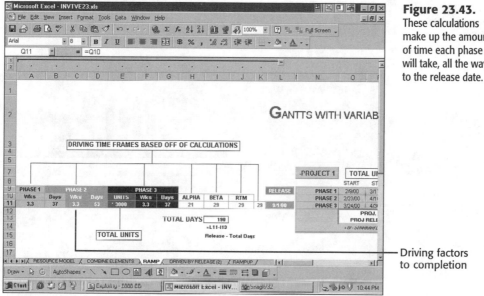

Figure 23.43.
These calculations make up the amount of time each phase will take, all the way to the release date.

Driving factors to completion

Figure 23.44 subtracts the release date from the total days to give you the start date of the project. Changing the variables, such as weekly output and total quantity, is just part of the equation. If the weekly output decreases, the Gantt chart moves the project to start earlier.

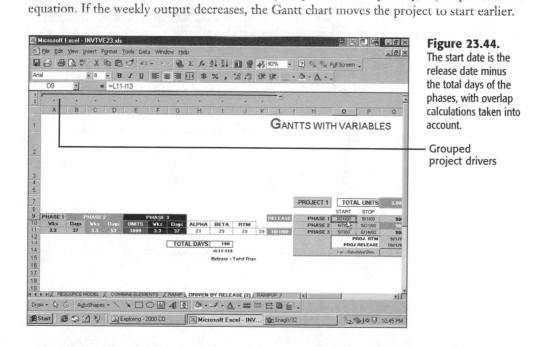

Figure 23.44.
The start date is the release date minus the total days of the phases, with overlap calculations taken into account.

Grouped project drivers

Watch what happens when you change the release date from 8/1/00 to 10/1/00 (see Figure 23.45). The time frame shifts out two months, given that the total units and weekly output remain the same (see Figure 23.46).

Figure 23.45.
The release date of 8/1/00.

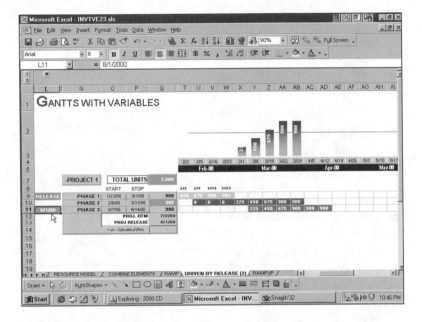

Figure 23.46.
By changing the release date to 10/1/00 (two months later), the project start date automatically shifts to a later date.

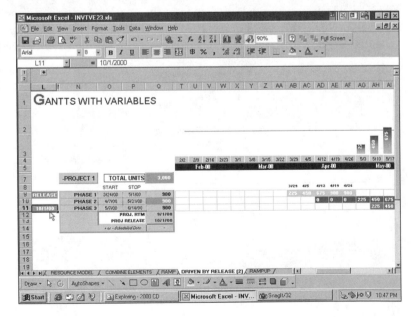

If the weekly output changes to 300, however, and the total quantity remains the same, the Gantt takes into account the additional time needed, based on a reduced weekly output, and then plots to start sooner because the cycle of the project will last longer (see Figure 23.47). Last, if the total units for the project changes from 3,000 down to 2,000, the weekly output remains at 300, and the release date remains at 10/1/00, the Gantt chart automatically takes all these factors into account and plots the start date to start later (see Figure 23.48).

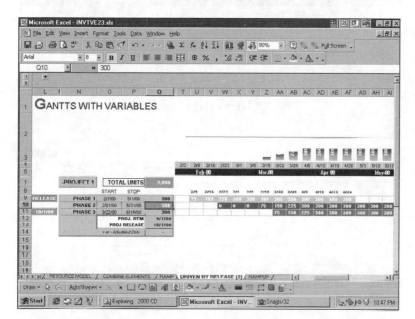

Figure 23.47.
The Gantt chart automatically plots out the additional time needed to complete the project based on a reduction in output, and starts the project sooner.

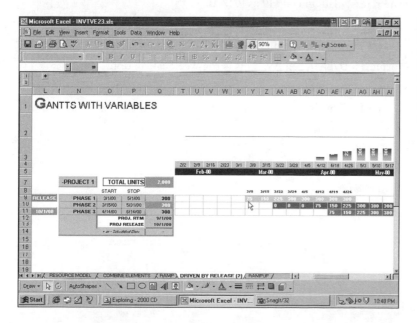

Figure 23.48.
Reducing the total quantity while maintaining the release date and weekly output causes the Gantt chart to plot a new start date.

To build a Gantt chart with multiple variables, we'll use one phase of the previous examples (notice the setup behind the scenes in Figure 23.49). Perform the following steps:

1. Set up the timeline with seven-day intervals, starting with 2/2/2000 in P4:AX4.
2. Place the total units of 3000 in cell M7.

Figure 23.49.
To build an automated Gantt chart with a ramp-up phase and multiple variables that drive the Gantt chart, you'll need to establish the proper setup.

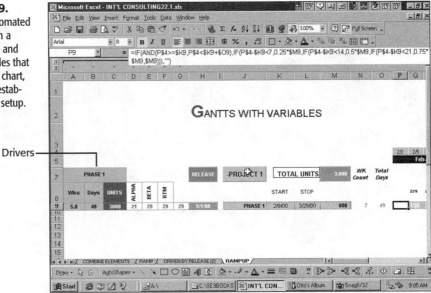

3. Establish the release date in cell H9 as 9/1/00.
4. Type the formula =M7 in cell C9.
5. Type the weekly output average number in cell M9: for this example, type **600**.
6. Type the formula =M7/M9 in cell A9. This is the week calculation.
7. In cell B9, type the formula =A9*7. This converts weeks into days.
8. In cell D9, type **21**. This is a known time frame between the release date and the end of the phase.
9. In cell E9, type **29**.
10. In cell F9, type **29**.
11. In cell G9, type **29**.
12. In cell J9, type **Phase 1**.

13. In cell K9, type the start date of **2/9/00**. (To have the start date driven by the release date, refer to Figure 23.44.)

14. In cell L9, type the formula **=K9+B9**.

15. In cell N9, type the formula **=Count(P9:AX9)**.

16. In cell O9, type the formula **=B9**.

17. And last, in cell P9, type the formula **=IF(AND(P$4>=$K9,P$4<$K9+$O9),IF(P$4-$K9<7,0.25*$M9,If(P$4-$K9<14,0.5*$M9,IF(P$4-$K9<21,0.75*$M9,$M9))),"")**.

18. Drag the formula to the right the length of the timeline from P9:AX9.

The changing variables in this example are the start date, total units, and weekly output. Change the quantities or dates, and the Gantt chart walks along the timeline and plots the phase window of production. With this setup, you can build a hidden table that calculates behind the scenes the different phases of the production (see Figure 23.50). Make sure your weeks and units in the table are absolute references before you drag and copy down the table. Also notice in Figure 23.51 the different outputs associated with each phase.

PART

VII

CH

23

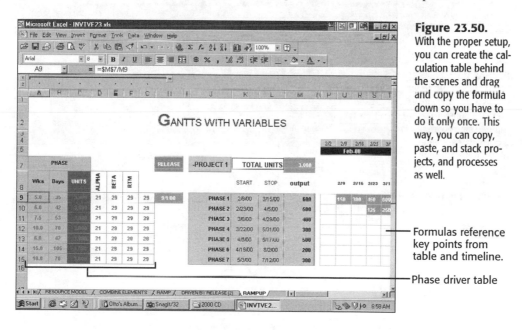

Figure 23.50.
With the proper setup, you can create the calculation table behind the scenes and drag and copy the formula down so you have to do it only once. This way, you can copy, paste, and stack projects, and processes as well.

Formulas reference key points from table and timeline.

Phase driver table

And last, notice the floating timeline in Figure 23.52. To attach a floating timeline to the Gantt chart, type the formula **=IF(ISNUMBER(P9),P$4,"")** beginning in cell P8. Drag the formula the length of the timeline, through AX8.

Figure 23.51.
Hide the table and link the phases, if necessary, as shown with the start date of phase 2 linked to phase 1, plus 14 days.

Linking phases

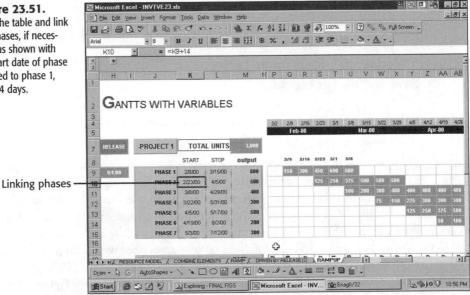

Figure 23.52.
The floating timeline shows a date only if there's a number in the cell, always giving a quick date reference of when the timeline begins.

Timeline formula

Automated floating timeline

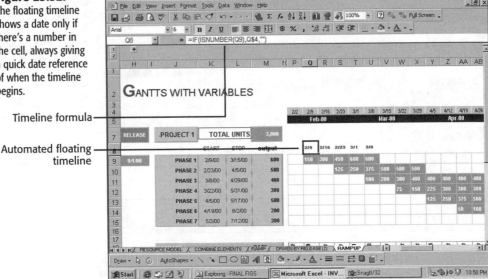

ADVANCED PROCESS PRINCIPLES

Production timelines consist of independent outputs or multiple steps to achieve an output. For example, Figure 23.53 shows a production process in which between step 1 and step 2 are six phases that must be completed before a unit is output. This could be steps in a production line before one unit is complete, for example. In the example, step 2 is the baseline of production units to output; the vertical production process that takes place before one unit is complete is illustrated as phases one through six.

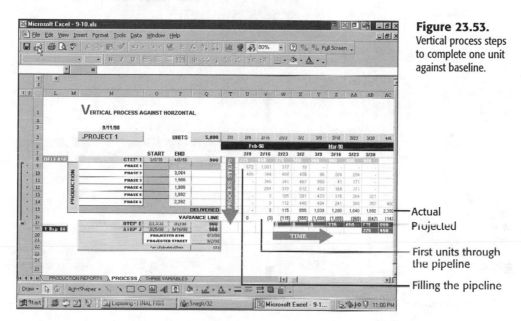

Figure 23.53.
Vertical process steps to complete one unit against baseline.

To create or implement the multiple phases that can occur against the baseline Gantt chart, just insert rows between the Gantt chart lines, and place the steps in vertical process columns from the top down (in the example, column N starting on row 9). Now, notice the formula that extracts the process step from the production log sheet in Figure 23.54. This formula refers to a sheet that logs the steps in the process against the phase (see Figure 23.55).

Use formulas to automate the actual production that occurs against projected baseline. Actual production can have several steps before production of one unit is complete. The formula to extract from the production log sheet syntax reads as follows:

```
{=SUM(IF(Sheet!DateRange=WeekDate)*(Sheet!ProjectRange="Project"),
➥Sheet!PhaseRange,0))}
```

For the italicized variables in the formula, substitute the correct sheet names, date ranges, and so on.

Figure 23.54.
The SUM(IF formula extracts the process step from the production log sheet.

Formula looks up information from production report sheet (as shown in Figure 23.55).

PRODUCTION REPORTS

Product	Week	PHASE 1	PHASE 2	PHASE 3	PHASE 4	PHASE 5	PHASE 6
PROJECT 1	9-Feb-98	672	400				
PROJECT 1	16-Feb-98	1,001	344	340	284	3	
PROJECT 1	23-Feb-98	317	408	391	319	185	11
PROJECT 1	2-Mar-98	10	408	487	612	391	44
PROJECT 1	9-Mar-98	-	96	558	433	473	48
PROJECT 1	16-Mar-98	-	204	41	169	315	24
PROJECT 1	23-Mar-98	-	204	171	171	304	36
PROJECT 1	30-Mar-98		-	-	-	321	35
PROJECT 1	6-Apr-98						40

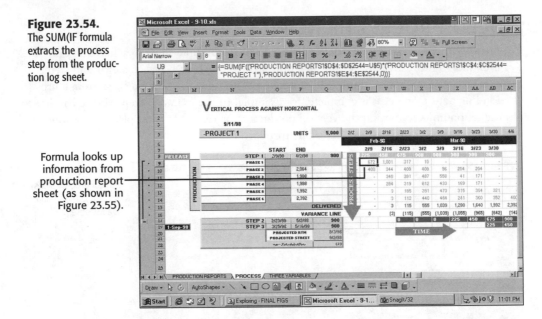

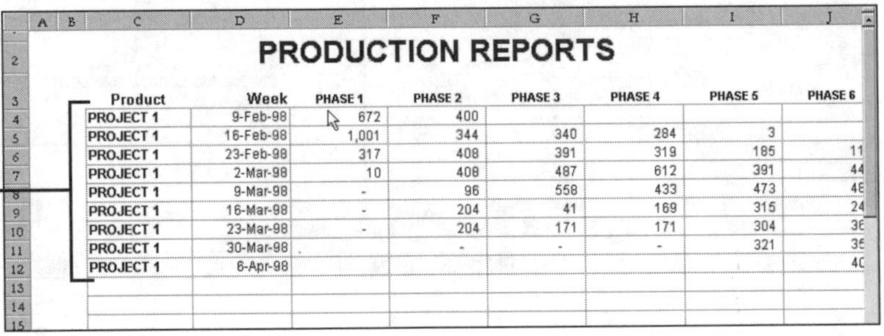

Figure 23.55.
The production log sheet logs the steps in the process to complete one unit in production.

Production report sheet

A Brief Overview of Critical Path

Critical path is the path that cannot be interrupted in production; if interrupted, it throws off all timelines with dependencies. Let's say you're building software and you have multiple teams of engineers. However, you have just one team to animate the 3D or 2D animation; this is the *gating factor* in production. If the gating factor is delayed, it can create a chain-reaction bottleneck that affects other lines of production that follow.

Figure 23.56 shows the staggered approach to three phases of three projects. This is the critical path stage that needs to be closely managed for multiple-product production. Notice in Figure 23.57 how the critical path has multiple-team dependencies that have to ultimately flow off one project to another. If critical path slips on one project, multiple teams are affected. (Be sure to look for this worksheet on the CD to analyze the layout more closely.)

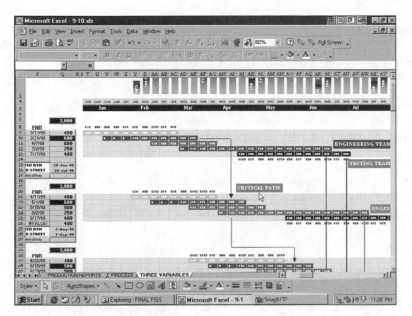

Figure 23.56.
The critical path of production is the gating factor that controls all dependency time frames.

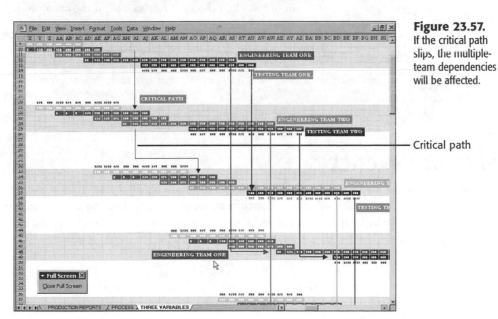

Figure 23.57.
If the critical path slips, the multiple-team dependencies will be affected.

I could go on for several more chapters about project management with Excel, but space doesn't allow for that. However, I hope that this brief overview gives you some ideas on how you can use the flexibility of Excel to fit your project-management environment.

TROUBLESHOOTING

SELECTING A CHART WITH NO BACKGROUND OR BORDERS

Excel won't let me select a chart after I set the background and borders to none.

Use the Select Objects button on the Drawing toolbar to select the chart.

ALIGNING A CHART TO THE GRID ON A WORKSHEET

Is there a way to align a chart with the grid of the worksheet?

It's a bit tricky. Align the chart as best you can to the grid. Then select the columns that span over the range of columns and chart, resize the columns to a larger size, and then resize them back to the smaller size. The chart bars now should align pretty closely.

ABSOLUTE REFERENCING

When I drag my automated Gantt formula down or to the right, it doesn't seem to work.

Several things could be going on here. The most likely problem is your formula referencing. Make sure that you make the right rows or columns absolute with dollar signs ($). If the formula works in one row, it should work in the next row as well, if the absolute references are set up correctly.

PASTING A CONDITIONAL FORMAT

Excel won't let me copy and paste a conditional format without it referencing the original cell reference.

Make sure the column reference is absolute, but not the row reference.

EXCEL IN PRACTICE

Instead of managing by a table of dates as shown in Figure 23.58, create a table and link the table with an IF(AND formula, conditional formatting, and a dateline to plot the milestone dates for you. By looking at dates sorted in order of occurrence, you can grasp vast amounts of information with just a glance, as shown in Figure 23.59.

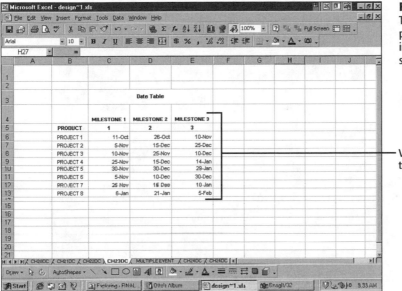

Figure 23.58.
The typical date table provides limited useful information on a single level.

Visually difficult to grasp

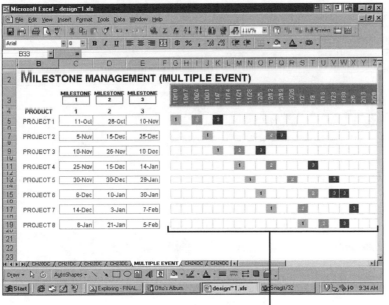

Figure 23.59.
A milestone table creates a visual reference to the date table, making the information understandable.

Automated milestones move along timeline.

CHAPTER 24

PROFESSIONAL FORMATTING TECHNIQUES

by Patrick D. Blattner
Patrick@BlattnerBooks.com

In this chapter

COMBINING EXCEL'S TOOLS FOR INNOVATIVE FORMATTING

The formatting possibilities are becoming endless with every new edition of Excel. Using the tools properly is the key to separating average formatting from professional-looking formatting. Because Excel is used across business environments of all types, think in terms of how you can apply formats from other industries to your current situation or business.

One of the first things I did to learn professional techniques in presenting information was surround myself with articles, magazines, and periodicals from all walks of life. Because there are so many demonstrations in different literature around us every day, I started to apply techniques I was seeing in newspapers, magazines, and just about any other piece of literature I could get my hands on. This chapter presents some of the possibilities I've discovered; however, don't limit yourself to my examples. Take these examples and build from them or apply them in new ways to fit your environment or business.

COMBINING DRAWING TOOLS WITH CHARTS AND WORKSHEETS

Understanding how and when to use tools, as well as how to combine tools to create dramatic effects, can enhance your charts, worksheets, and tables. The difficulty is that no set rule exists to help you decide which tools to combine, or even how to combine them. This chapter attempts to show you some ideas on how to effectively combine tools to enhance your information. Start by picking up magazines, newspapers, and periodicals to get ideas for presentations, and then visualize which tools it would take to re-create the presentation shown in the literature.

For the most part, there are very few presentations that you can't re-create with all of the tools available in Excel. The drawing tools, particularly, offer a wide variety of opportunities for improving your charts and worksheets—making them more understandable and simultaneously more interesting. Chapter 8, "Using Excel's Drawing Tools," provides details on the types of tools available and how to work with them. The following sections of this chapter take off from those basics, combining drawing objects in unique and sometimes unexpected ways to give your worksheets and charts a polished look.

LAYING A CHART ON A BEVEL

You can lay charts on bevels to give them a "raised-off-the-surface" look. The next time you look through one of the top financial publications, chances are you'll see this technique in use. It works especially well for onscreen presentations, but also can look great in print. Notice that in Figure 24.1 the chart is actually lying on the bevel and the chart area is filled with the same fill as the background of the sheet. The plot area is formatted white.

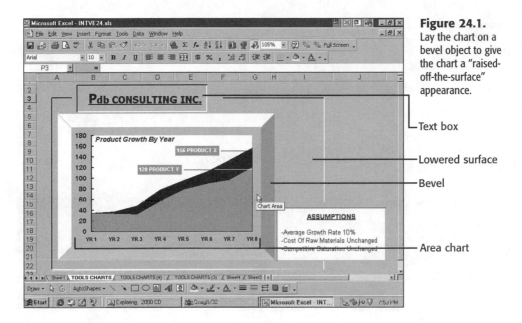

Figure 24.1.
Lay the chart on a bevel object to give the chart a "raised-off-the-surface" appearance.

— Text box

— Lowered surface

— Bevel

— Area chart

To lay a chart on a bevel, perform the following steps:

1. On the Drawing toolbar, click the AutoShapes button, select Basic Shapes, and click the Bevel tool (fourth row, second from the right), as shown in Figure 24.2.

2. Drag the bevel object to size it so that its raised portion approximately matches the height and width of the chart (see Figure 24.3).

Figure 24.2.
The bevel is found on the AutoShapes button under Basic Shapes.

3. Adjust the degree of the beveling (the raised portion of the bevel object), if desired, by dragging the yellow sizing handle.

4. Drag the chart over the surface of the bevel. (If necessary, right-click the bevel and select Order, Send to Back to bring the chart to the front.)

5. Drag the chart to fit the size of the surface of the top of the bevel, as shown in Figure 24.4.

Figure 24.3.
Size the bevel to an adequate size for the chart.

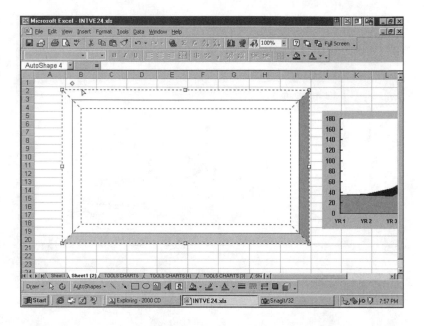

Figure 24.4.
Lay the chart on the bevel and drag the chart size to fit the top surface so that the lines and corners meet.

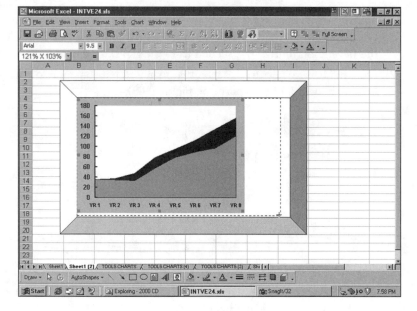

6. Format the chart area as gray.

7. Select and format the plot area as white.

8. Select the entire worksheet by clicking on the Select All button in the upper-left corner of the worksheet frame.

9. Apply a light gray fill.

CREATING A PRESENTATION ON A FILLED BEVEL

You can use Excel's drawing tools to become creative and effective at presenting information other than in chart format. In Figure 24.5, for example, I've filled a bevel object with gray, and used text, rectangles, and lines from the Drawing toolbar. As you can see, visual presentations aren't limited to just charts. In this example, I've created the measuring boxes in conjunction with color or grayscale to show the amount of coverage—white being minimal, gray being average, and black being extended.

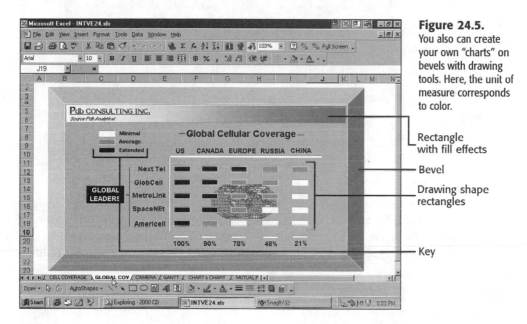

Figure 24.5.
You also can create your own "charts" on bevels with drawing tools. Here, the unit of measure corresponds to color.

Rectangle with fill effects

Bevel

Drawing shape rectangles

Key

PART
VII

CH
24

Tip #268 from

Patrick

After you lay out all the elements of the drawing, select them all, click the D**r**aw button on the Drawing toolbar, and choose **G**roup to group all the pieces into one "picture" that you can move, copy, or resize as desired.

To further prove how this is just simple drawing tools placed on a larger drawing tool, all the objects in Figure 24.6 have been selected. Here you can clearly see how everything is placed in a chart fashion, without actually being a chart. After you create one box and format it to fit the legend, just copy and paste the legend boxes in the intersecting paths of the "chart"—for example, where CANADA and GlobCell intersect. The globe in the background is just a picture pasted on the bevel.

→ To learn more about inserting pictures with charts, **see** "Adding Pictures and Shapes to Charts," **p. 446**

Figure 24.6.
Notice how the three drawing tools—text box, line, and rectangles—are all that's used to create this "chart" on the bevel.

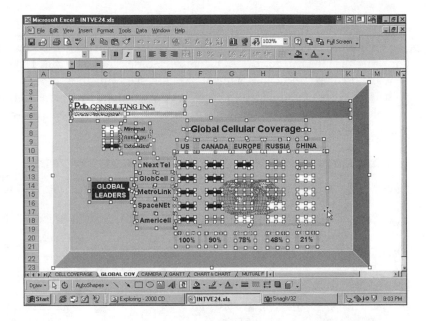

After creating the drawing, make sure that it looks substantial when printed by adding a title, subtitle, and possibly a footer. Often, without a heading of some kind, the presentation can lose impact. In Figure 24.7, the heading has been placed on the left side with a bold Arial font of 26 points, and a CONFIDENTIAL footer on the left side to balance out the printed sheet.

Figure 24.7.
Provide a substantial title to the sheet for an effective presentation that stands out.

Custom heading—

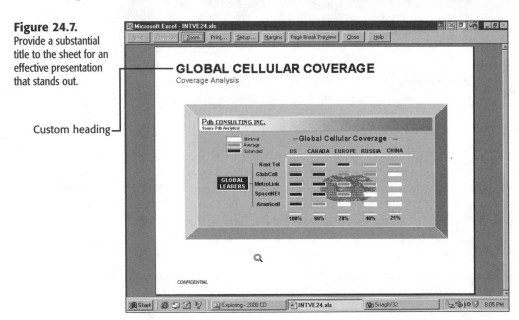

DRAWING TOOL COMBINATIONS

Figure 24.8 shows how you can marry the worksheet, drawing tools (on and off the chart), and text.

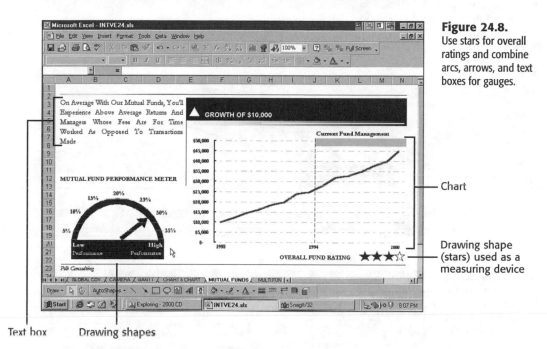

Figure 24.8.
Use stars for overall ratings and combine arcs, arrows, and text boxes for gauges.

Text box   Drawing shapes

The performance meter consists of four drawing tools placed together to create the meter (see Figure 24.9). The tools are a text box formatted with a black fill and white text, an arrow from the block arrows set on the Drawing toolbar, and a block arc (found on the Basic Shapes submenu from the AutoShapes button). Use the yellow sizing handle to size the thickness of the arc.

By utilizing fills appropriately, you can place stars side by side and use the fill as indication of achievement against overall industry standards (see Figure 24.10). In this example, the fund rating is three out of four stars.

Figure 24.9.
Combine several drawing tools to create measuring pictures and devices. Here, a performance meter gives additional information on the fund's performance over time.

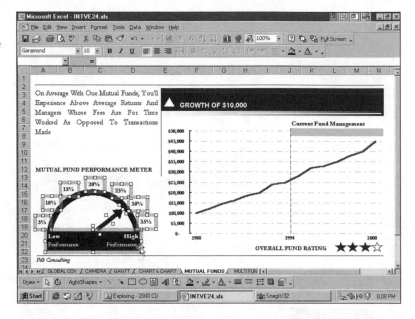

Figure 24.10.
Add drawing tools to the chart to further call out the important aspects of the fund's performance.

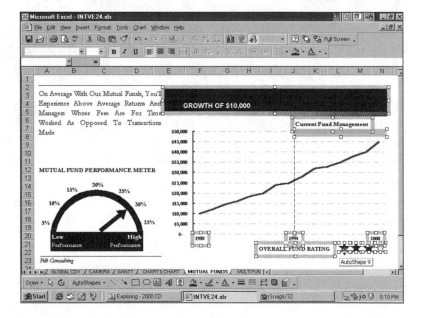

PROFESSIONAL TABLES

Not only can you apply drawing tools to charts to enhance the chart and display additional information, you also can create *multiple-dimension tables* (tables with views that show depth of coverage, or a view that adds a third dimension). These tables can convey massive amounts of information in a small space. If you have multiple bits of information that fall into one category, for example, you could add multiple columns to give the table the appropriate headings, and break out the elements to the lowest level of detail. You also could create a multiple-dimension table that includes all the elements or detail in minimal worksheet space.

The following sections describe how to work with these custom tables.

MULTIPLE-DIMENSION TABLES

A multiple-dimension table uses *inclusion tables* (tables that either include or exclude features on a single line item) to provide another dimension to a list or table. For the example in Figure 24.11, you have cartridge types that are coded and priced at a certain amount. You also want to show the different products across the market that the cartridge works with, as well as the total units sold and sales for the line item. This can be accomplished by using a multiple-dimension table.

PART

VII

CH

24

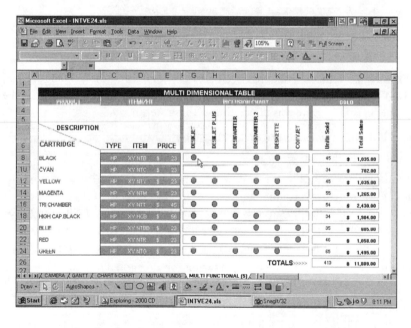

Figure 24.11.
A multiple-dimension table enables you to create lists or tables with the addition of a third dimension—in this case, the inclusion chart. The chart specifies which product works with the different products on the market.

Use the Merge and Center button on the Formatting toolbar to align and center the titles of the different table or list elements, and fill with different colors to separate the title levels (see Figure 24.12).

Figure 24.12.
Merge and center the title across several columns of information.

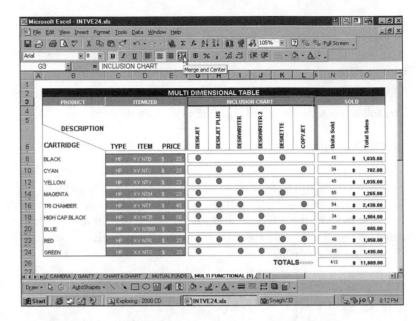

Notice in cell B6 that an "elbow" effect has been created, combining the heading for row 6 (DESCRIPTION) and column B (CARTRIDGE) in a single cell, with a dividing line between the two headings. To create this effect, follow these steps:

1. Select the cell in which you want to create the "elbow" heading.

2. Align the cell text to the left.

3. Type the row heading first. Then hold down the Alt key and press Enter to create blank lines between the row heading and the column heading. Figure 24.13 shows that Alt+Enter was pressed two times to create two blank lines between the headings (look at the Formula bar). Then type the column heading to complete the elbow text.

4. Place the insertion point in front of the row heading and add three or so blank spaces. This moves the row heading to the right, allowing for a diagonal line to fit between the two headings.

5. Adjust the column width and row height as necessary to achieve the effect.

6. Insert the diagonal line, applying a light gray line color (see Figure 24.14).

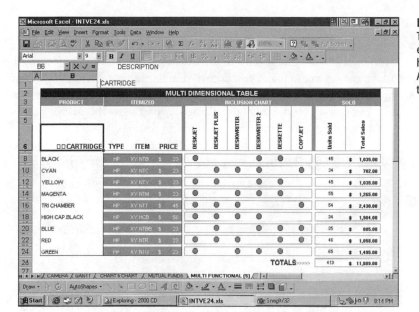

Figure 24.13.
To create the "elbow" effect, type the row heading, press Alt+Enter, and type the column heading.

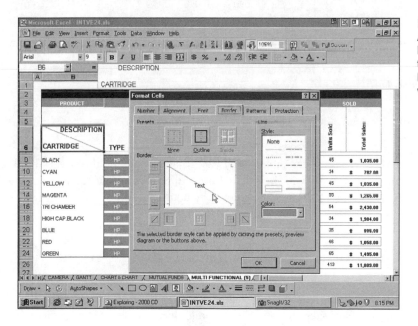

Figure 24.14.
Apply the diagonal line to show separation between the horizontal and vertical headings.

TWO-DIMENSION TABLES

You can add a second dimension to a single cell and give it more than one value or meaning (see Figure 24.15). Notice the use of a legend to call attention to the symbol meanings. By adding the second dimension to the table, you do two things: eliminate countless headings across the columns, and optimize worksheet real estate. You can use this in conjunction with charts or for presentations, optimizing advertising space to show the cost of your current products and how they work with other products in the marketplace.

Figure 24.15.
Add a second dimension to a single cell to give the cell multiple values.

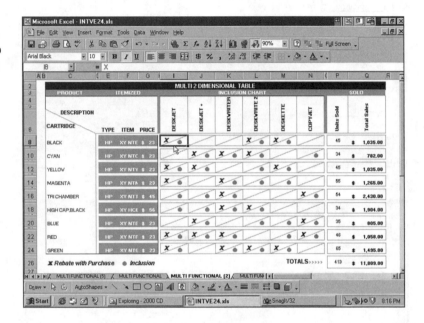

To add the second dimension to the table, simply apply a diagonal line through the cell (see Figure 24.16). You can apply an X in the cell and use a drawing tool such as an ellipse or circle for the second cell value. (You create a circle by holding down the Shift key as you create an ellipse.)

Tip #269 from

Patrick

A top vertical alignment should be used to properly position the X in the cell.

After you have the proper alignment in the cell, copy the cell and paste it into the other cells that apply. Excel pastes the value and the drawing object in the same alignment. To establish the proper alignment the first time, it helps to zoom in on the cell with the Zoom feature and position the object in the most logical place, as shown in Figure 24.17.

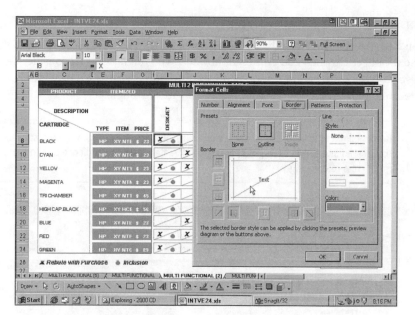

Figure 24.16.
Apply the diagonal line to the cell from the Border tab in the Format Cells dialog box.

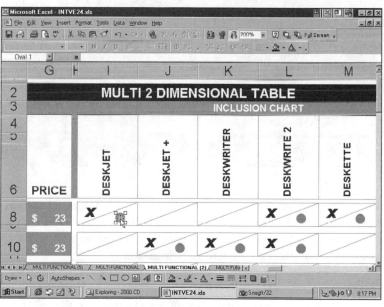

Figure 24.17.
Align the values and objects, then simply copy the cell and paste to a new location. The identical alignments are re-created.

THREE-DIMENSION TABLES

Now that you have the concept from the two-dimension table, take on a three-dimension table. Because it can get crowded and cluttered, however, you might want to consider a new format to the cell. Notice the pyramid approach used in Figure 24.18. This provides a raised 3D effect and separates the multiple dimensions within a single cell.

Caution

Be careful not to get too carried away with using multiple dimensions. I've seen situations using seven and eight drawing shapes, which ultimately loses the audience due to too much cross-referencing.

Figure 24.18.
Create three dimensions in a single cell and apply a pyramid effect to separate the dimensions and raise the cell from the surface.

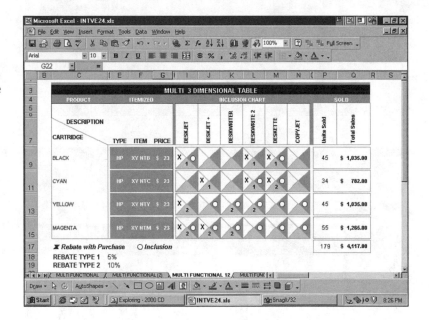

You can create a pyramid effect in several ways. One is to use the bevel tool discussed earlier. Press and hold down the Shift key while drawing the bevel to create a perfect square. Then use the yellow sizing handle and drag it to the center, thus creating the pyramid. Apply the objects to the bevel object's surface to add dimension.

Another way is to use the Isosceles Triangle tool. Follow these steps:

1. Make sure that the cell is rectangular and place an X and borders in the cell. Click the AutoShapes button on the Drawing toolbar, select Basic Shapes, and click the Isosceles Triangle tool (see Figure 24.19).

2. Draw the triangle over the cell so that the edges meet, as shown in Figure 24.20.

3. Format the triangle by selecting Format, AutoShape and give it a fill color of light gray, with no line color (see Figure 24.21).

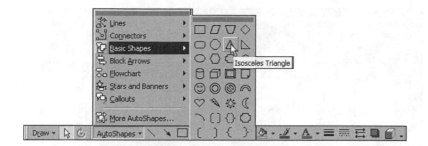

Figure 24.19.
Choose the Isosceles Triangle shape to create the pyramid.

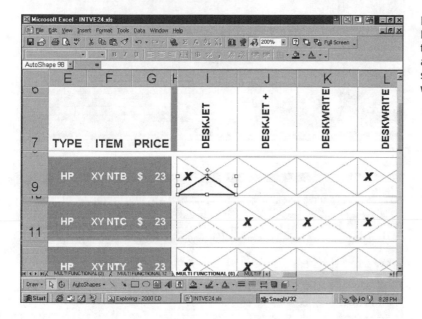

Figure 24.20.
Drag the triangle over the cell so the corners and lines meet. A square bevel also works well.

PART

VII

CH

24

4. Create a copy of the triangle (pressing Ctrl+D when the triangle is selected is a quick method). Then format the copy with a darker shade of gray, flip it to the left, and place it in the right quadrant of the cell (see Figure 24.22).

Note

To flip an object, select it, click the Draw button on the Drawing toolbar to display the pop-up list, select Rotate or Flip, and then select the direction you want to flip from the submenu.

5. Apply circles, triangles, and numbers to the quadrants, along with the legend to illustrate the third dimension. You may need to use the BRING TO FRONT and SEND TO BACK commands to position everything correctly.

Figure 24.21.
Format the triangle with a light gray fill. You also can remove the border by choosing No Line for the Color option in the Line section of the dialog box.

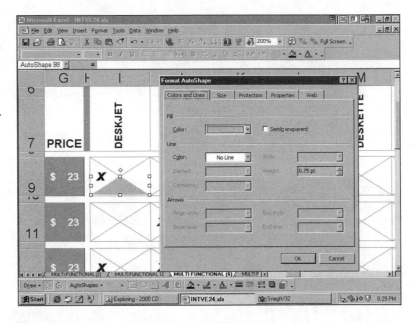

Figure 24.22.
Fill and flip the second triangle and size it to the right quadrant of the cell.

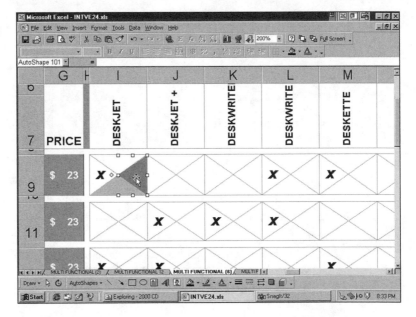

FOUR-DIMENSION TABLES

Add the fourth dimension to "round out" the quadrants. In Figure 24.23, all four quadrants are used to illustrate the products that intersect with the product type, the rebate, the rebate type, and the increase or decrease from previous rebate. Remember that you can apply the objects simply by copying a cell and pasting it into another cell. The units sold are actual numbers in cells, with a circle object copied and pasted in the cell, similar to how the other objects were placed, copied, and pasted.

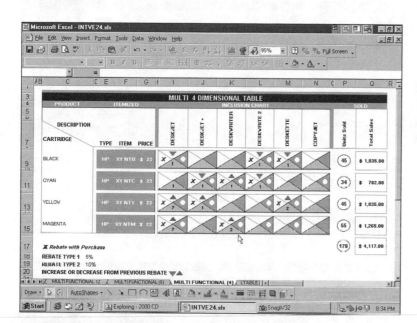

Figure 24.23.
By applying a fourth dimension, you can fully utilize the real estate of the worksheet. This works well for onscreen presentations, when you need to say a lot within a small space.

Caution

To avoid resizing later, all rows and columns that will use the quadrant effect should be sized to match the original, before copying the quadrants into place.

ORDER OF OCCURRENCE TABLES

When selling product in distribution channels, you ultimately will be looking for sales within specified periods of time, as well as lifetime sales. In addition, you probably will want to do comparative analysis among your various products.

Suppose that you have two products in the marketplace for the year and both have sold the same number of units. After further analysis of the products, you see that one product has been in the distribution channel two months longer, thus giving you a different perspective on the sales figure. Being able to create tables in order of occurrence will help give you visual understanding of the performance of your products.

Look at the two examples in Figures 24.24 and 24.25. Figure 24.24 is categorized in a random fashion that provides no real picture of the products' life spans. Figure 24.25 shows how the proper approach to setting up a table can take on a whole new meaning and help you to a better understanding of your products' sales and life spans.

Figure 24.24.
A random table without proper organization gives no real picture of the order of occurrence.

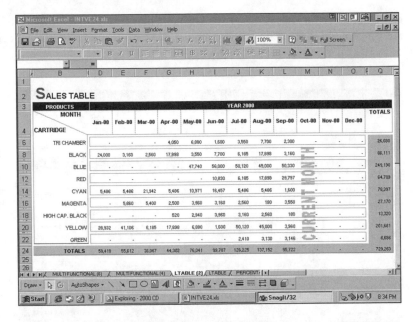

Figure 24.25.
Sales in order of occurrence gives you visual understanding of distribution in the sales channel.

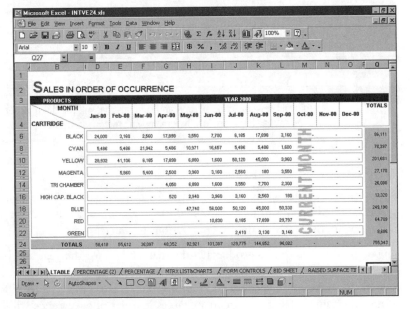

As mentioned before, make sure when setting up to print that you establish a prominent title, and balance the printed sheet with footers, as shown in Figure 24.26.

PERCENTAGE TABLES

Standard grids and tables often can take on a cumbersome, scrunched appearance that's difficult to look at, to say the least. The two tables in Figures 24.27 and 24.28 contain the same information; however, Figure 24.28 is formatted as a percentage table, meaning that the percentage is below the number it represents, and a space is applied between the percentage and the next row of information. To distinguish the percentages, making them easy to find, box the percentage and leave the currency number freestanding above the box. To make the look cleaner and more professional, you can add spaces between the totals at the bottom and the right for separation, and shade the totals.

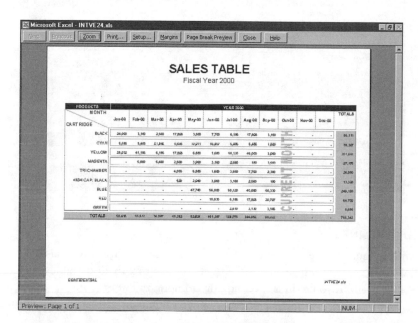

Figure 24.26.
Make sure you add prominent titles to the page and balance the sheet with footers.

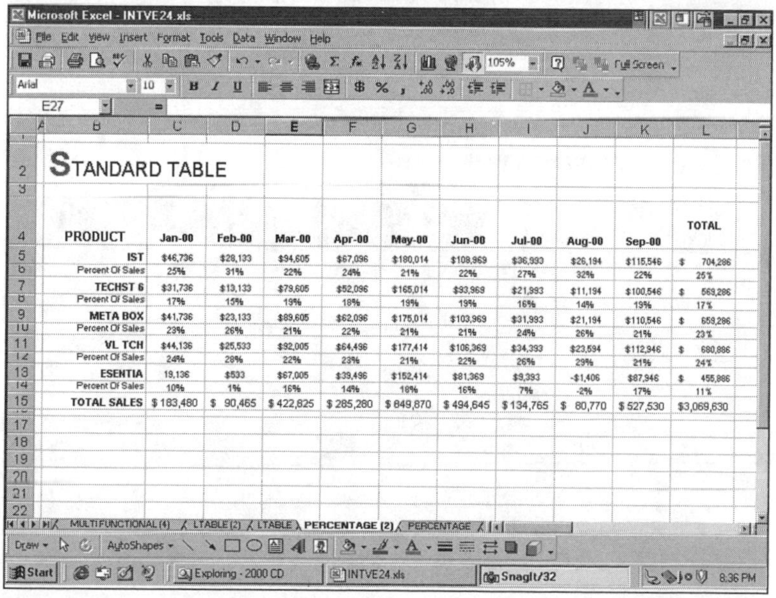

PART

VII

CH

24

Figure 24.27.
A standard table can take on a scrunched look, making it difficult to view and even more difficult to understand.

Figure 24.28.
A formatted percentage table, with the percentage boxed off below the number it represents, helps the audience draw conclusions and ultimately makes the numbers easier to understand.

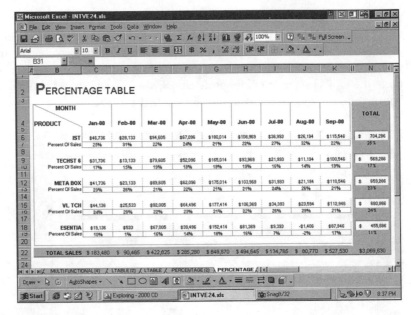

CREATING RAISED TIMELINES

When displaying a sequence of events in which the events continue over time, raised-surface timelines can create an impact and make the timeline instantly discernible (see Figures 24.29 and 24.30). If you're in marketing, for example, and want to create a presentation that displays the marketing sequence of events, a visual timeline can be an effective tool.

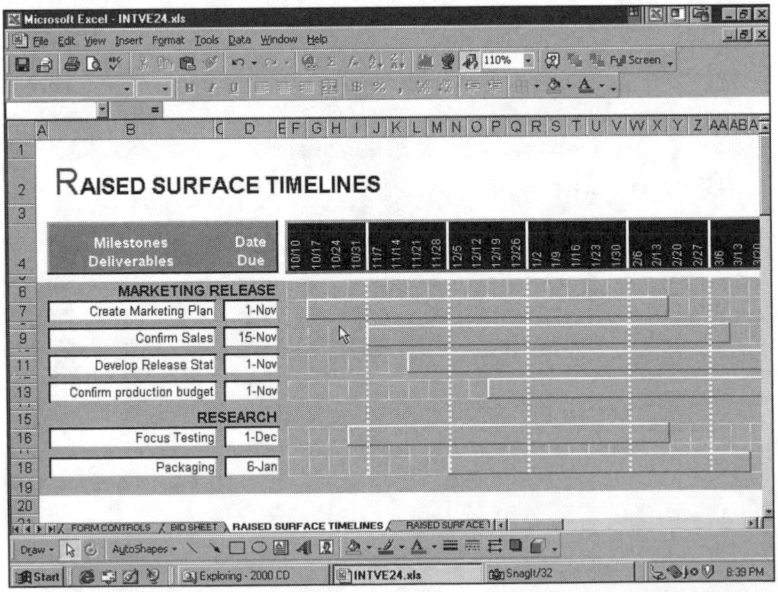

Figure 24.29.
Create raised-surface timelines to show events that occur over time.

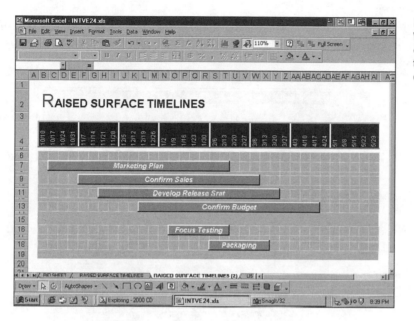

Figure 24.30.
When space is critical, create timelines with the process or name on the timeline.

To create a raised surface, follow these steps:

1. Select a range of cells (see Figure 24.31).

2. Choose Cells from the Format menu or right-click the selection and choose Format Cells from the context menu. The Format Cells dialog box opens.

3. Select the Border tab.

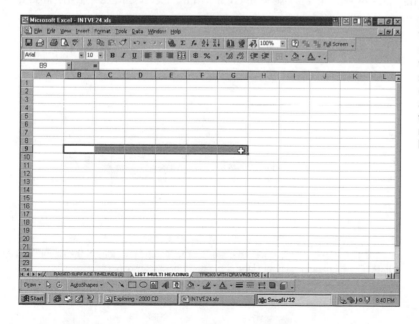

Figure 24.31.
When selecting the range of cells you want to raise from the surface, stay at least one column and row away from the edge of the worksheet, or the raised-surface effect loses impact.

4. Select a semi-bold solid line in the Style box. Make sure the line is a dark color.

5. Place dark lines on the bottom and the right sides of the preview in the Border box (see Figure 24.32).

Figure 24.32.
To create a raised surface, set the bottom and right line styles to dark, and the top and left to light.

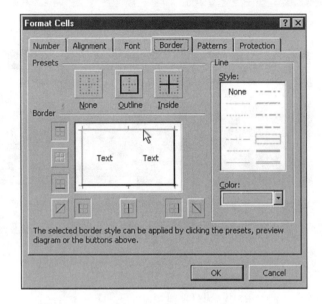

6. Change the color selection in the Color box to a light gray.

7. Place a light gray line on the top and on the left side in the Border box.

8. Select the Patterns tab and choose a fill color. (In most cases, I use gray because it prints better.) The result is shown in Figure 24.33.

Figure 24.33.
The final result of changing the external border styles is this raised effect.

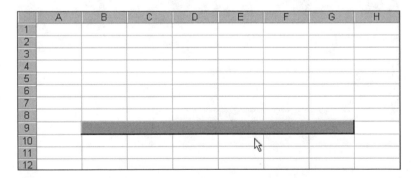

Note

To create a sunken effect, place dark lines on the top and left sides of the region, and light lines on the bottom and right sides of the outer perimeter only.

To apply text to the bar, select the bar, click the Merge and Center button, and then type the text. To move the bar, insert or delete cells to the left or right of the bar.

CAPTURING A DYNAMIC PICTURE FROM ANOTHER WORKSHEET

The *Camera* option in Excel is a unique tool few people know how to use, but I've found that this tool can be priceless. Suppose that you have a worksheet formatted to suit your presentation, and need to include something from another sheet. If you copy and paste, the data from the other sheet would be mixed into the current formatted sheet. The Camera tool can solve this problem by "taking a picture" of the data on the other sheet that you then can place in the target worksheet, without worrying about the data being combined.

In the example in Figure 24.34, notice that the Gantt chart appears to have different formatted columns and headings. That's because it's actually a linked object. It comes from a different sheet and sits on the surface of this sheet, but isn't really part of it. When it's changed on the original sheet, the link causes it to update automatically on the current sheet.

PART

VII

CH

24

Tip #270 from

Patrick

Obviously, you can reproduce this trick with OLE, but using the Camera makes Excel create the linking formula for you and reduces the number of steps involved.

To access the Camera, right-click any toolbar and choose Customize to open the Customize dialog box. Click the Commands tab, if necessary. Under Categories, choose Tools, and then scroll the Commands list until you see the Camera option (see Figure 24.35). Drag the Camera button to the desired toolbar and drop it in place.

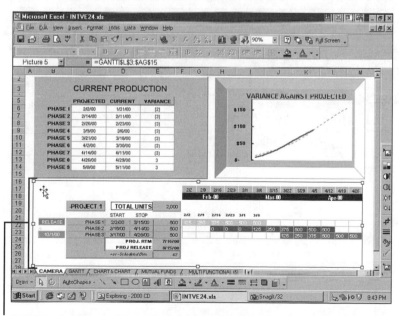

Figure 24.34.
The Camera tool enables you to take pictures of one worksheet and place them on a different sheet. The picture doesn't disturb the target sheet because it's really an object that floats on top of the sheet.

Notice the sizing handles and the mouse pointer. This "chart" is actually a linked object.

Figure 24.35.
Select the Camera icon and drag it to a toolbar.

→ For details on how to create a custom toolbar, **see** "Building Custom Toolbars," **p. 875**

To use the Camera tool, follow these steps:

1. Select the region you want to "photograph," as shown in Figure 24.36.

Figure 24.36.
Select the region for which you want to take a picture.

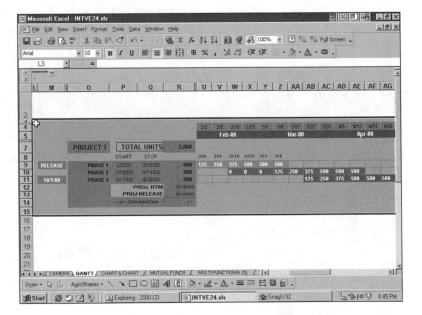

2. Click the Camera button to copy the picture (see Figure 24.37). The mouse pointer changes to display a crosshair.

Figure 24.37.
When you click the Camera button, it copies the selected region.

3. Select the final destination of the picture and place the crosshair where you want the upper-left corner of the picture (see Figure 24.38).

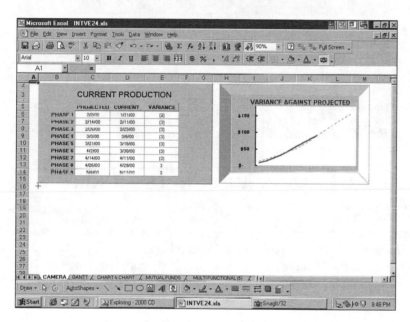

Figure 24.38.
Place the pointer where you want the upper-left corner of the picture.

4. Click to place the picture. Notice that the picture has a formula attached to it in the Formula bar, referencing the source sheet and region of the picture (see Figure 24.39).

Notice the formula for the picture in the Formula bar.

Figure 24.39
By clicking, the picture is placed on the destination worksheet. You can crop the picture to show as little or as much of the linked selection as desired.

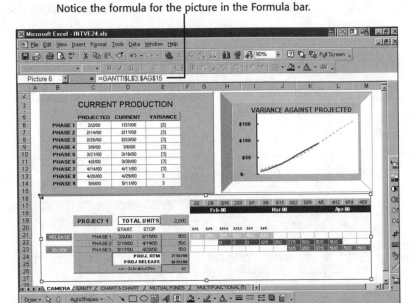

CREATING VISUAL EFFECTS AND PROFESSIONAL POINTING DEVICES

After you create worksheets, tables, presentations, and so on, you are likely to want to draw the reader's attention to an area of significance. What other choices do you have in addition to the (stale) straight arrow? One option is arrows that have more visual interest. If your chart has a breakeven point, for example, you can highlight it with an architectural arrow (see Figure 24.40).

> **Note**
>
> The connector AutoShapes can achieve a similar effect, although not with as dramatic a curve. Connectors aren't required to connect two other shapes; they can be used as stand-alone drawing objects. You also can use the arrows on the Block Arrows submenu of the AutoShapes button, but they're not quite as flexible as arrows you create yourself.

To create curved arrows like this, follow these steps:

1. Click the AutoShapes button, choose Lines, and select the Curve tool from the Lines submenu.

2. Draw the line up and to the right, click once, draw down, click once, and then draw back up and to the right, double-clicking to end the line (see Figure 24.41).

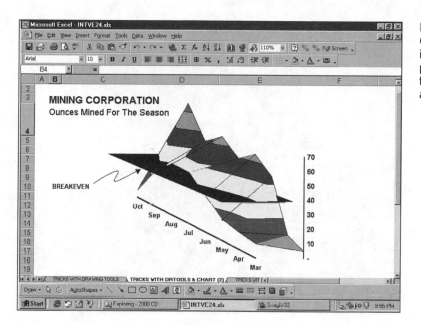

Figure 24.40.
Create arrows with interesting shapes as pointing devices for features of lists, charts, and tables.

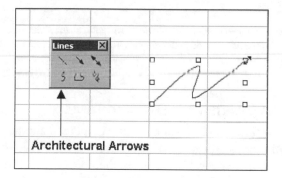

Figure 24.41.
Use the Curve tool to draw the architectural arrow.

Tip #271 from

Patrick

Figure 24.41 shows the Lines palette as a floating toolbar. You can "tear off" any submenu or palette to a floating toolbar if the submenu or palette displays a small title bar at the top.

3. Format the curve to add the arrow by selecting the curved line and then choosing AutoShape from the Format menu or right-clicking the line and choosing Format AutoShape from the context menu. The Format AutoShape dialog box opens.

4. Add an arrowhead as shown in Figure 24.43, click OK, and then position and size the arrow as desired. You also can flip and rotate the line to point the arrow in any direction.

Figure 24.42.
Add the arrow to the
end of the curve.

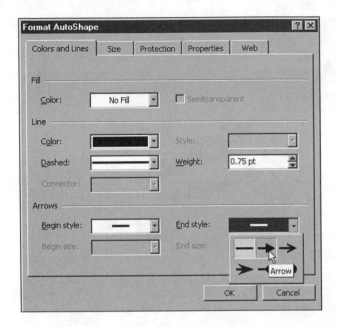

Tip #272 from

Another method for adding or changing arrow styles is to select the arrow and then click the Arrow Style button on the Drawing toolbar. Note that this method doesn't work for the block arrows.

SLICING THROUGH CHARTS WITH DRAWING TOOLS

Occasionally, you may find it useful to take a graphic to another plane. In Figure 24.43, the breakeven point of the 3D area chart was outlined with a freeform shape and then filled with black. To create effects like these, use the Freeform tool from the Lines submenu of the AutoShapes button on the Drawing toolbar.

Figure 24.44 shows the Freeform drawing tool being used to draw against the 3D chart for the slice effect. Click once to start the line, and again at each corner where you want the line to turn. When you reach the beginning corner, click again to close off the freeform object. Then apply a fill color or other formats to make the freeform object stand out.

Tip #273 from

Be sure that the lines of the freeform object are parallel to the chart's angles.

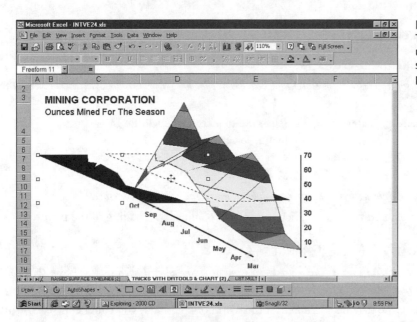

Figure 24.43.
The Freeform tool was used to create the slice through this 3D perspective chart.

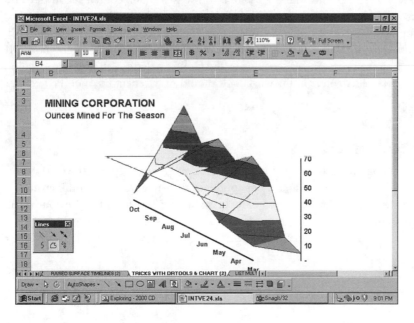

Figure 24.44.
Outline the breakeven points on the 3D chart with the Freeform tool, drawing the slice in perspective to the angle of the chart.

TROUBLESHOOTING

UNGROUPING GROUPED OBJECTS

I've inherited someone else's worksheet and Excel won't let me select a single object in what appears to be a group of objects.

The objects are probably grouped. Select the objects and click the Draw button on the Drawing toolbar. From the pop-up menu, select Ungroup.

CORRECTING THE SHADE OF CAMERA PICTURES

Excel gives the Camera picture a different shade than in the original worksheet.

Use the contrast controls on the Picture toolbar to adjust the shading of the picture.

CORRECTING COLOR PALETTE CHANGES

I have extensive formatting within a workbook, and at times when I open the workbook the colors change. Is there a solution to this problem?

The workbook file may be corrupted. If the workbook is small, you could copy each worksheet and paste it as values into a new workbook. If the workbook contains many sheets, however, that would be pretty complicated. Instead, choose Tools, Options to open the Options dialog box. Click the Color tab, select the color that appears to be wrong on the Standard Colors palette, and click the Modify button to open the Colors dialog box. On the Standard tab, replace the incorrect color in the Colors palette with the correct color, and click OK twice. The colors in the workbook should now reflect the modified color on the palette.

EXCEL IN PRACTICE

By utilizing all potential landscape within a cell, you can create a table that would normally stretch out the span of several columns, but condense the table into a multidimensional table. In Figure 24.45, the rebate types and increase or decrease from the previous rebate span several columns. By creating quadrants within cells as shown in Figure 24.46, you add depth to each cell, allowing for greater information coverage within minimal landscape on the worksheet.

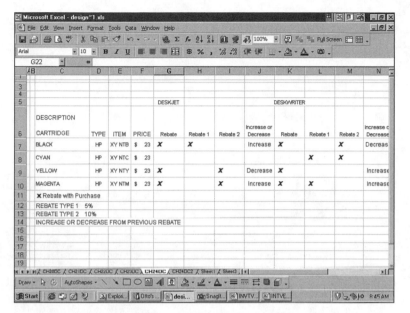

Figure 24.45.
This worksheet shows the typical layout—one cell per bit of data.

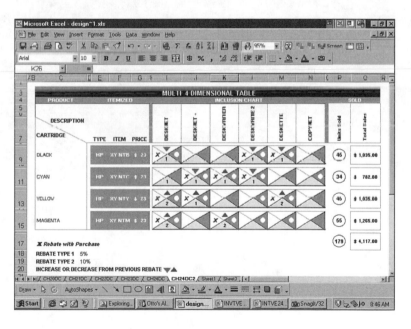

Figure 24.46.
Creating quadrants enables you to quadruple the amount of information within the same amount of space.

PART VIII

INTEGRATING EXCEL WITH OTHER APPLICATIONS

CHAPTER 25

USING EXCEL WITH WORD AND POWERPOINT

by Laurie Ann Ulrich
laurie@limehat.com

In this chapter

USING EXCEL WITH OTHER MICROSOFT OFFICE PROGRAMS

Interoperability is probably the main reason that users purchase a suite of products rather than buying word processing programs, spreadsheet software, and presentation products individually. The pricing of suite software is generally attractive, but the capability to share content between applications easily, with predictable results, is a powerful incentive.

Office 2000's focus on Web-enabled collaboration improves upon previous versions' collaborative tools. Microsoft's vision for the workplace requires that everyone's efforts be shared, and toward that end, HTML becomes the common file format among applications. The result? Through the Clipboard and Insert menu, you can insert as much or as little as you like of one application's content into another application's file quickly and easily, retaining as much or as little as you like of the source application's formatting.

COPYING EXCEL DATA TO A WORD DOCUMENT

Why add Excel content to a Word document? To save time and effort in reentering existing text and/or numbers, and to ensure consistency between files. If your Word document discusses numbers already entered into an Excel worksheet, don't create a Word table and re-enter the numbers—copy them from Excel and paste them into the Word document. The result is an instant table, containing the numbers as they appeared in Excel.

Using Excel for tables that contain numeric data also gives you access to Excel's tools for calculation and numeric formatting, which you don't have to the same extent in Word. Therefore, you should try to create, format, and add formulas to the table in Excel—before you copy the table to a Word document.

Figure 25.1 shows the Word and Excel application windows tiled, with a selection in Excel pasted into a Word document. When Excel data is copied to a Word document, it appears in table format—the worksheet cells become table cells that match the dimensions of the selected range of cells from Excel. All of Word's formatting and table tools are at your disposal—just as though the table were originally created in Word.

Tip #274 from	If you can't see the table's gridlines, choose Table, Show Gridlines in Word. Nonprinting gridlines such as those in Excel will appear.
Laurie	

If you create charts in Excel, you can also copy those charts to a Word document (for instance, to support data presented in a written proposal). Excel provides extensive charting capabilities, whereas Word provides only limited chart features through the use of Microsoft Graph.

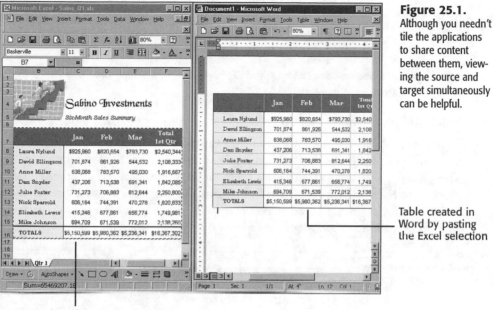

Figure 25.1.
Although you needn't tile the applications to share content between them, viewing the source and target simultaneously can be helpful.

Table created in Word by pasting the Excel selection

Source content selected in the Excel worksheet

You can add Excel content to a Word document in one of two ways:

- Copy the Excel source content (such as a range of cells or a chart) to the Clipboard, and paste it into the Word document.
- Insert an Excel workbook in its entirety or select an individual worksheet to insert.

PASTING EXCEL DATA AS A WORD TABLE

One of the simplest ways to take Excel content and place it in a Word document is to use the Clipboard. In Office 2000, the Clipboard toolbar can hold up to 12 items, making the Clipboard a much more powerful and flexible tool than in previous versions.

To paste Excel data into a Word document, follow these steps:

1. In an Excel worksheet, select the cell or range you want to copy.
2. Choose Edit, Copy, click the Copy button, or press Ctrl+C.
3. Switch to Word, and click in the document to position the insertion point where you want to place the Excel data.
4. In Word, choose Edit, Paste, click the Paste button, or press Ctrl+V.

The Excel content appears as a table, in Arial, 10-point text (or whatever default font you have set in Excel).

Tip #275 from

Laurie

If you want to copy all the data in a worksheet, press Ctrl+A in the Excel worksheet to select all the cells. Only the range of cells that contain data will be pasted in Word.

→ For more information on using the improved Clipboard feature in Office 2000, **see** "Using the Clipboard to Move and Copy Data," **p. 116**

INSERTING AN EXCEL FILE

In many cases, especially in the case of large reports developed in Word, the need arises to paste an entire Excel workbook (or an entire worksheet) into the Word document. Doing so saves you the time of selecting small sections of the worksheets one at a time and pasting them from Excel to Word individually. Inserting the workbook or worksheet saves not only time and effort, but eliminates the possibility of missing a particular section of a worksheet or pasting worksheet sections out of order in the Word document.

Note

When inserting an entire workbook or even an individual worksheet, only the portion of the worksheets that contain data will be inserted—you won't see 256 columns and thousands of rows appear in the Word document.

Also, when you use the Insert, File command, you may need to reformat the data after you insert it in a Word document. For example, if your Excel data uses fill colors or font colors, these colors won't transfer to Word—instead, all the data appears in black and white. You may prefer to use the Clipboard to copy data if you want to retain all your Excel formats, including colors.

INSERTING AN EXCEL WORKBOOK

Before you can insert a workbook into a Word file, you must ensure that you've already saved the workbook. To insert a workbook into a Word document, follow these steps:

1. In the Word document, position the insertion point at the point where you want to insert the workbook.

2. Choose Insert, File.

3. In the resulting Insert File dialog box, change the Files of Type to All Files (*.*).

4. Using the Look In list box and/or the list of files and folders displayed, locate the workbook file you want to use (see Figure 25.2).

5. Double-click the desired file, or click it once and choose the Insert button.

6. In the Open Worksheet dialog box, leave Entire Workbook selected in the Open Document in Workbook list box, and choose OK (see Figure 25.3).

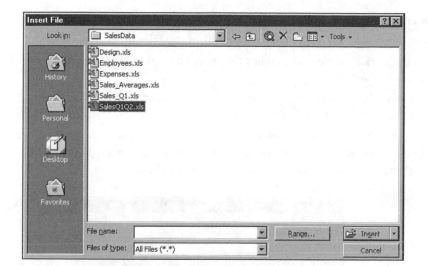

Figure 25.2.
Use the Insert File dialog box to search for the .xls file you want to insert.

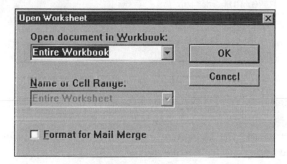

Figure 25.3.
By default, the entire workbook will be inserted into the Word document.

The entire workbook will be inserted into the Word document, appearing as a table. If you want to maintain a connection between the Excel source workbook and the data copied to the target Word document, you can insert the file as a link. To do so, in the Insert File dialog box, click the drop-down arrow beside the Insert button and choose Insert As Link. As long as your source and target files remain in the same locations and retain the same names, the link will remain intact. Each time the target file is opened, you can choose to update the link, and any changes to the source workbook will be updated in the document. You can also preserve the Word document's current content by not updating the linked content.

INSERTING AN INDIVIDUAL WORKSHEET

Perhaps your Word document doesn't require all the data in the entire workbook—maybe one or two specific sheets from a workbook contain the data you need. To insert an individual sheet from a workbook file, follow these steps:

1. In the Word document, position the insertion point where you want the inserted worksheet(s) placed.

2. Choose Insert, File.

3. In the Insert File dialog box, select All Files (*.*) from the Files of Type list box.

4. Navigate to the workbook file that contains the sheet you want to use, and double-click the filename.

5. In the Open Worksheet dialog box, click the Open Document in Workbook list box, and select the name of the sheet that you want to insert.

6. In the Name or Cell Range list box, select Entire Worksheet to insert the whole worksheet, or type a range of cell addresses (B7:F16, for example) or a named range from within the selected worksheet to insert just that range of cells (see Figure 25.4).

Figure 25.4.
If you've named any ranges in the worksheet, you can type the name to select that range of cells for insertion.

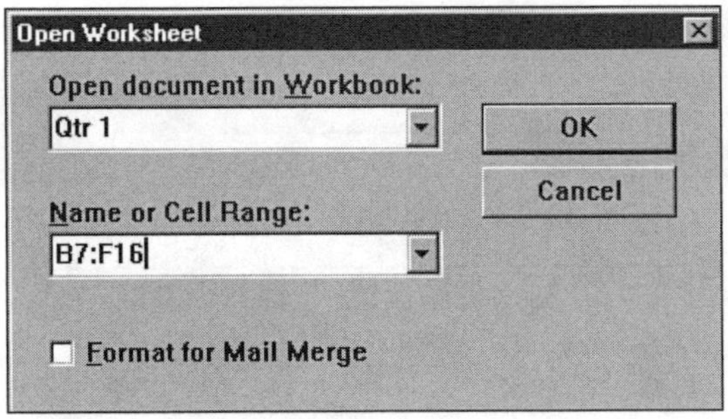

7. Choose OK to close the Open Worksheet dialog box and insert the data.

Once inserted, the data appears and functions as a Word table, and can be formatted by using Word's table, text, and paragraph formatting tools.

INSERTING A WORKSHEET RANGE

In some cases, you may want to insert just a portion of your Excel worksheet—perhaps just a few cells are of use, or you want a large section, but not the entire sheet and the inherent increase in file size for your target Word document. Whereas you could just copy and paste the range, inserting it instead frees you to add the content even if your Clipboard is full.

To insert a worksheet range in a Word document, follow these steps:

1. In the Word document, position the cursor at the point where you want to insert the Excel range.

2. Choose Insert, File.

3. In the Insert File dialog box, select All Files (*.*) from the Files of Type list box.

4. Navigate to the folder containing the workbook from which you want to insert a range, and click on the workbook file once to select it (see Figure 25.5).

5. Choose the Range button in the Insert File dialog box.

6. Enter the range addresses (such as B7:F16) in the Set Range dialog box (see Figure 25.6), and choose OK.

7. In the Insert File dialog box, choose Insert to add the specified range to your Word document.

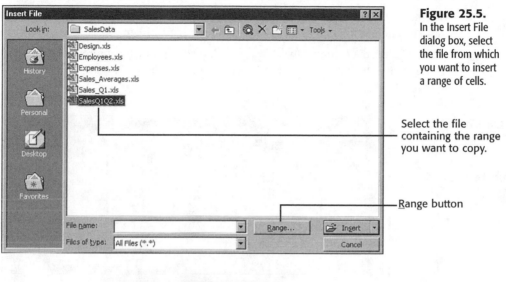

Figure 25.5.
In the Insert File dialog box, select the file from which you want to insert a range of cells.

Select the file containing the range you want to copy.

Range button

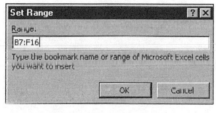

Figure 25.6.
Type your range of cells by entering two cell addresses separated by a colon.

MERGING EXCEL DATA INTO WORD MAIL MERGE DOCUMENTS

An Excel list database can be used as the data source for your Word form letters, labels, and catalogs. When a Mail Merge is performed in Word, a document (such as a letter or sheet of labels) is combined with a table of data, which provides the data called for in the document. For example, in a form letter, *merge codes* are inserted to tell Word where to place the recipient's name. When the document and the data are merged, Word goes to the cited database and extracts data from the field (or column, in Excel) that contains the requested data, such as First Name or Last Name. The data is inserted within the letter's body text, and a form letter is completed.

Your Excel list database must be set up properly. The complete set of rules for proper data entry is described in detail in Chapter 17, "Setting Up a List or Database in Excel." The basic requirements are as follows:

■ Your column labels become your field names, also known as a header row. Choose short, illustrative names such as First Name or Product Number. Each column label should be unique.

- Break down your data into as many fields as possible. For example, break your address data down into Address 1, Address 2, City, State, and Zip. A single "Address" field would be too hard to use for mailings restricted to people in a particular town or state.

- Leave no blank rows between your column labels and the first record (row) in your database. There can be no blank rows within your data, either.

- Each row (after the column labels) is a record, made up of data entered into the fields that are created by your column headings. Figure 25.7 shows an example of an employee database.

Figure 25.7.
The more care you put into the building of your Excel database, the more you'll be able to do with it.

Records   Field names (header row)

After the database has been set up correctly, you can select it as the source for your mail merge data as described in the following steps:

1. In Word, choose Tools, Mail Merge. The Mail Merge Helper dialog box opens, as shown in Figure 25.8.

Figure 25.8.
The Mail Merge Helper dialog box is divided into three sections, or steps, to be followed sequentially.

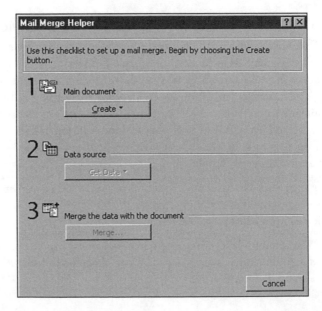

2. In step 1 of the dialog box, choose the Create button, and choose the type of merged document you want to create—Form Letters, Mailing Labels, Envelopes, or Catalog.

3. Choose a new window or the current (Active) window for your new document.

4. Choose the Get Data button, and choose Open Data Source (see Figure 25.9).

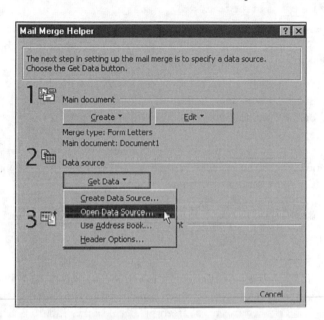

Figure 25.9.
Among other data sources, Word will accept Word documents (containing a table of data), Excel worksheets, and Access tables (.mdb files) as sources of data for your mail merge.

PART

VIII

CH

25

5. In the Open Data Source dialog box, select All Files (*.*) from the Files of Type list box.

6. Navigate to the folder containing the worksheet you want to use, and double-click the filename.

7. In the Microsoft Excel dialog box, select or type the name or cell range in the Named or Cell Range text box, and then choose OK.

8. Complete your mail merge by editing your document, which includes inserting merge codes (instructions for where to place data and which data to use), and merging the document and the selected data source.

To learn more about the complete process of merging a document and a database, consider the book *Special Edition Using Microsoft Word 2000*, published by Que (ISBN: 0-7897-1852-9).

FORMATTING EXCEL DATA IN A WORD DOCUMENT

Excel workbooks, worksheets, or cell ranges appear in Word in the form of a Word table—a collection of columns and rows, forming cells. Word provides a significant set of tools for adjusting the dimensions of table columns and rows, and visually formatting table cells and their content.

You can use Word's formatting tools to format the inserted Excel content in the Word document:

- *Change the width of columns and height of rows.* Click anywhere inside the table and choose T<u>a</u>ble, Table P<u>r</u>operties. Using the <u>R</u>ow and/or Col<u>u</u>mn tabs, adjust the measurement of selected sections of the table.

- *Apply paragraph formatting.* If you want space above or below the cells' text, select the cells and then choose F<u>o</u>rmat, <u>P</u>aragraph. Enter a point measurement in the <u>B</u>efore and/or Aft<u>e</u>r boxes in the Spacing section of the Paragraph dialog box.

- *Format the text.* Select individual cells or columns/rows, and change alignment, fonts, font sizes, and font styles (such as Bold, Italic, and Underline). You can use the Formatting toolbar or the Font dialog box (choose F<u>o</u>rmat, <u>F</u>ont).

Unless you don't need or want any formatting of the data in Excel (perhaps the worksheet requires a plain appearance), it may be easier to format the cell content in Excel and utilize the Paste Special procedure to preserve formatting.

COPYING EXCEL DATA TO A POWERPOINT PRESENTATION

PowerPoint presentations often contain numeric data in the form of tables and charts. Charts are perhaps the more prevalent form in which numeric data is presented—they're highly graphical, and if set up properly, easy to interpret. Because presentations are generally best when they contain more pictures than words, charts are an important component.

PowerPoint presentations can display Excel data as cell blocks (which appear as tables) and as charts. You can build the chart in Excel and then copy it to the presentation slide, or you can use Excel data to build the PowerPoint datasheet, which in turn produces a PowerPoint chart.

Deciding which Excel content to use (cell ranges or an Excel chart) depends on what already exists in Excel—if you have only Excel data and haven't created a chart, you can use the data and create the chart in PowerPoint. However, keep in mind that Excel provides more extensive charting capabilities than PowerPoint. You may prefer to complete the chart in Excel and then transfer it to PowerPoint.

USING EXCEL RANGES IN A POWERPOINT SLIDE

Assuming Excel is your primary tool for storing statistical, financial, and list data, it's very likely that the information you want to use in your PowerPoint presentation already exists in an Excel worksheet. Rather than risk a typo or waste time retyping it into a PowerPoint table, why not use the Clipboard and/or Office's OLE tools for placing the Excel data into your PowerPoint slide?

It's a simple procedure to take a range of cells from your Excel worksheet and paste them into a PowerPoint slide. Somewhat more complex methods can be employed to insert the

Excel content and at the same time create a link between the worksheet and the slide, enabling you to keep the slide updated when changes are made to the worksheet. The approach you take depends on whether or not you need such a relationship between the source file (Excel worksheet) and the target file (PowerPoint slide).

PASTING EXCEL RANGES INTO A POWERPOINT SLIDE

To paste a range of cells from an Excel worksheet into your PowerPoint slide, follow these steps:

1. In your Excel worksheet, select the contiguous range of cells that you want to use in your PowerPoint slide.

2. Choose Edit, Copy or press Ctrl+C.

3. Switch to or open your PowerPoint presentation, and go to the slide to which you want to add the Excel content. Be sure to use Slide View or Normal View.

4. In the PowerPoint window, choose Edit, Paste, or press Ctrl+V. If the Clipboard tool-bar is displayed, click the icon that represents your Excel content.

Your Excel range appears as a table in your PowerPoint slide, and it can be formatted as such by moving, resizing the object as a whole, or by adjusting the dimensions of columns and rows by using PowerPoint's table tools. To find out more about PowerPoint, check out Que's *Special Edition Using Microsoft PowerPoint 2000*, ISBN: 0 7897 1904-5.

LINKING EXCEL DATA TO YOUR POWERPOINT SLIDE

To create a relationship between your Excel source range and the copy of it pasted on a PowerPoint slide, you must link the two files. Once linked, moving or renaming either the Excel workbook or the PowerPoint presentation severs the link. You can update and break links later should you need to. Chapter 5, "Moving, Copying, Linking, and Embedding Information," explains this process in full detail.

To paste Excel content into your PowerPoint slide and establish a link between the source and target files, follow these steps:

1. In your Excel worksheet, select the contiguous range of cells that you want to use in your PowerPoint slide.

2. Choose Edit, Copy, or press Ctrl+C.

3. Open or switch to your PowerPoint presentation, and use Slide View to display the slide into which you want to paste the Excel content.

4. In the PowerPoint window, choose Edit, Paste Special.

5. In the Paste Special dialog box, choose the Paste Link option (see Figure 25.10).

6. Choose Microsoft Excel Worksheet Object from the As box, and choose OK.

Figure 25.10.
Your copied Excel content will now be linked to the PowerPoint presentation, and you can keep the data between source and target in sync as needed.

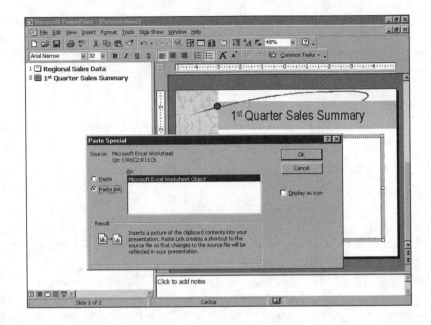

Your linked Excel content appears in the form of a table, and can be moved or resized. To edit its content, double-click it. The Excel worksheet from which it came will open, and any edits you perform there will be updated in the slide. Make your changes, and then switch back to the PowerPoint slide (use the Taskbar or Alt+Tab) and you'll see the changes reflected there.

Tip #276 from

Laurie

Each time you open the target presentation in the future, you can choose whether or not to update the link—if changes have been made to the source Excel content, you can opt to have them reflected in the presentation. If you choose not to, you can always update them later by choosing Edit, Links and choose the Update Now button.

Excel content can also be embedded in your PowerPoint slide, which will give you not only the existing Excel content, but when the Excel object is active, the tools of Excel as well, right within your PowerPoint window.

→ To find out more about embedding content, **see** "Embedding Excel Data in Other Office Applications," **p. 129**

PASTING EXCEL DATA IN A POWERPOINT DATASHEET

In addition to using existing Excel data directly on a PowerPoint slide, you can use it to fill in your PowerPoint datasheet when creating a PowerPoint chart. To use Excel data in a PowerPoint datasheet, follow these steps:

1. With both the PowerPoint presentation and Excel worksheet open, select the Excel content you want to use (see Figure 25.11).

Don't select the
worksheet titles.

Select column headings that will
become category axis labels.

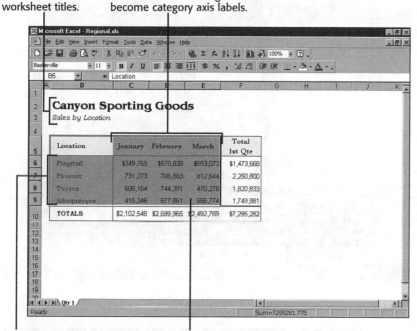

Figure 25.11.
Keep the chart's
content in mind when
selecting the range of
cells to paste into the
PowerPoint datasheet.

Select row headings that
will form the legend.

Select the numeric data that
will be plotted in the chart.

2. Choose Edit, Copy.

3. Switch to the PowerPoint presentation, and go to the slide in which you'll be using the data.

4. Double-click the chart placeholder to display the datasheet. The datasheet appears with sample data inside it.

5. In the PowerPoint datasheet, click the upper-left gray cell to select all the cells in the datasheet (see Figure 25.12).

6. Press Delete to remove the datasheet's sample data.

7. Click in the first cell in the datasheet (above row 1, in the blank column to the left of column A).

8. Choose Edit, Paste. The Excel content appears in the datasheet, and you see a chart form behind the datasheet (see Figure 25.13). Continue the chart-creation process in PowerPoint.

Note

You use the first blank column instead of column A in the datasheet because the first blank column contains the chart's legend data. The row above row 1 contains the category axis information. PowerPoint's charting tools will enable you to switch these two groups of data as needed.

Figure 25.12.
Selecting all cells before deletion enables you to be certain that all the sample data is removed.

Click here to select all the cells in the datasheet.

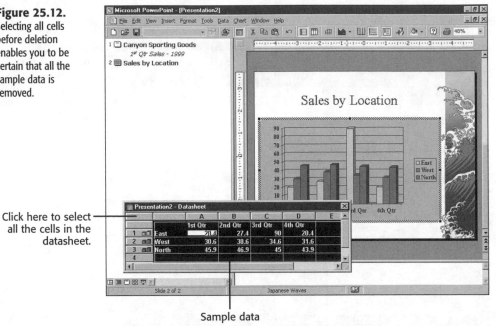

Sample data

Figure 25.13.
The Excel data is immediately used to create a PowerPoint chart.

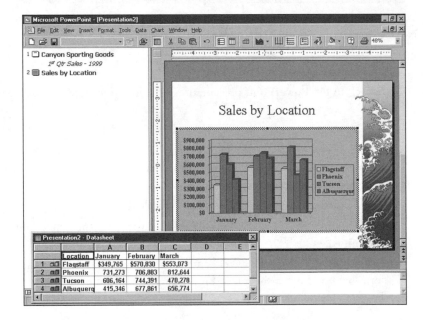

USING EXCEL CHARTS IN A POWERPOINT PRESENTATION

If you've already created a chart in Excel, why go through the process of building it again in PowerPoint? Unless you want to create a different type of chart, it's much easier to use the Excel chart in the PowerPoint presentation.

Follow these steps to paste the Excel chart into the PowerPoint slide:

1. With both the Excel worksheet that contains the chart and the target PowerPoint presentation open, click once on the Excel chart to select it.

2. Choose Edit, Copy.

3. Switch to the PowerPoint presentation, and move to the slide onto which you want to paste the chart.

4. If a chart placeholder appears on the slide, delete it.

5. In PowerPoint, choose Edit, Paste.

The chart appears in the PowerPoint presentation, exactly as it appeared in Excel. You can move and resize the chart as needed, or double-click it to access Excel's charting tools to make any adjustments to the chart's appearance.

Note

If you want the Excel data that was used to create the chart to remain linked to this copy of the chart, use Paste Special and choose to paste link the chart. If the chart is linked and not simply pasted, changes to the Excel data will update the chart.

For more information on using Excel to create a chart, see Chapter 13, "Building Charts with Excel." To learn more about formatting Excel charts, see Chapter 15, "Formatting Charts."

→ You can read more about linking objects from one file to another in "Linking Excel Data," **p. 121**

COPYING WORD AND POWERPOINT DATA TO AN EXCEL WORKSHEET

Whereas Excel data can be a valuable addition to Word documents and PowerPoint presentations, the reverse also is true—you can realize significant savings of time and effort by using existing Word and PowerPoint content in Excel worksheets. Following are some examples of how you can use Word and PowerPoint content:

■ If the data's first appearance is in a PowerPoint datasheet, copy it to an Excel worksheet to avail yourself of Excel's superior formatting and calculation tools. If the data is valuable beyond the scope of the presentation, you'll get much more out of it in Excel.

■ If a table containing a valuable list already exists in Word, bring it into Excel for quick sorting and filtering. Whereas these features are available in Word, their Excel equivalents are much more powerful and easier to use.

- Reuse clip art or drawn objects from PowerPoint or Word in an Excel worksheet. If the graphic images you need already exist in another file, don't reinsert or redraw—paste them!

- Copy an individual PowerPoint slide into your Word document. If you've created a visually pleasing slide that conveys something valuable for your document, don't waste time re-creating it. Using slide content in your Word documents also contributes to an overall visual consistency between your files.

ADDING WORD TEXT TO AN EXCEL WORKSHEET

Word text appears in two formats that you can use in Excel—paragraph text and table text. Obviously, Word tables are a natural for placing in an Excel worksheet—the data is already arranged in cells. Paragraph text is best used when it appears in the form of short phrases or titles. Unless the Excel cells are formatted for text wrapping, a long sentence or paragraph can cause problems fitting into an existing Excel worksheet. If you insert paragraph text as an object into a worksheet, it will appear as a text box, obscuring worksheet cells.

Tip #277 from
Laurie

> Your paragraph text can be parsed (separated) into individual cells through Excel's Data, Text to Columns feature, discussed later in this chapter.

You can add Word content, regardless of form, to an Excel worksheet in one of the two following ways:

- *Use the Clipboard.* Copy the Word text and paste it into the Excel worksheet. You can use this method for tables or paragraph text. When pasting, be sure to click in the cell that should contain the text or that will serve as the first cell in the pasted range.

- *Insert a Word object.* In this case, the text is typed into the object after it's inserted (see Figure 25.14). It will be placed in a floating object window, which, when active, will cause Word's tools to take over the Excel toolbars and menus.

SORTING AND FILTERING TABLE DATA

One of the primary reasons for bringing Word table data into an Excel worksheet is to avail yourself of Excel's sorting and filtering tools. While you can perform simple sorts in Word, Excel's sorting tools are faster and easier to use, and provide additional sort options.

Sorting and filtering commands are found in the Data menu in Excel. Sorting can be performed on up to three fields, and filtering can be performed on as many fields as you desire.

Tip #278 from
Laurie

> If you still need to use the table data in a Word environment, paste it back into the Word document after you've sorted and/or filtered it in Excel.

→ For more information on sorting and filtering Excel lists, **see** "Sorting a List," **p. 509** and "Filtering a List," **p. 513**

Word tools in Excel window

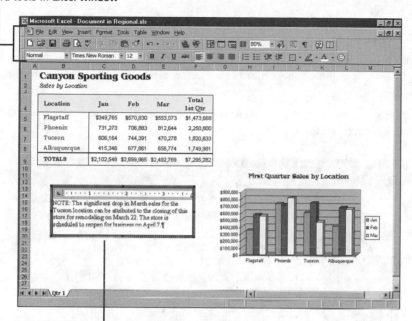

Figure 25.14.
Choose Insert, Object, and choose Microsoft Word Document. Type the text into the Word window that opens on the worksheet.

Word window on top of worksheet

PARSING DATA

Because users don't expect the level of flexibility in their use of Word tables that one finds in Excel, tables designed and completed in Word don't tend to be as well planned in terms of their use as a database as those that are built from the ground up in Excel. For example, in order to have the greatest degree of sorting and filtering capability, tables should be broken down into as many fields as possible—instead of a "Name" field in a name and address list, the name should be divided into two fields, "First Name" and "Last Name." This gives you the capacity to sort the list by last name, and to use it for a mail merge wherein letters contain a salutation such as "Dear Mr. Smith" or "Dear Bob" instead of "Dear Bob Smith." Also, breaking "Address" down into "Street," "City," "State," and "Zip" makes filtering by city or zip code much easier.

So what do you do if the Word-created table isn't currently conducive to effective sorting and filtering? You parse the table in Excel. Parsing takes larger pieces and breaks them down, making more analysis possible.

Note

Parsing isn't only for Word lists. You can parse any list that you can import to Excel—including database information from Access, text-formatted lists from other programs, and so on.

To parse table data, follow these steps:

1. If the column to the right of the column you want to parse contains data, insert columns to make room for the parsed information. For example, if you're parsing a single column into three columns, insert two columns to the right of the column you're parsing. To insert a column, select the column before which to insert the column and choose Insert, Columns.

2. After pasting the table from Word into Excel, select the rightmost column that requires further breakdown (see Figure 25.15).

Figure 25.15.
Working from right to left avoids accidental overwriting of table data with the columns added through parsing. In this example, only the first column needs to be parsed.

The Name column will become two columns—First Name and Last Name.

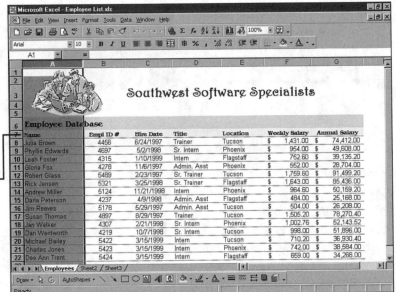

3. Choose Data, Text to Columns.

4. The Convert Text to Columns Wizard opens, as shown in Figure 25.16.

5. In the Original data type box, choose Delimited. Delimiters are characters (such as commas, spaces, or semicolons) or codes (such as tabs or hard returns) that are used to break text content into pieces.

6. Choose Next.

7. Choose the delimiters that you want Excel to use in determining where column breaks should occur (see Figure 25.17).

8. Choose Next.

9. After checking the Data Preview in the wizard's final dialog box, choose Finish to complete the wizard and apply the commands to the selected column.

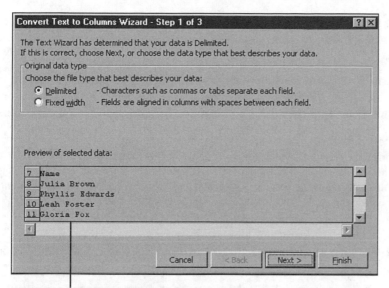

Figure 25.16.
Preview the selected data in Step 1 of 3 of the wizard.

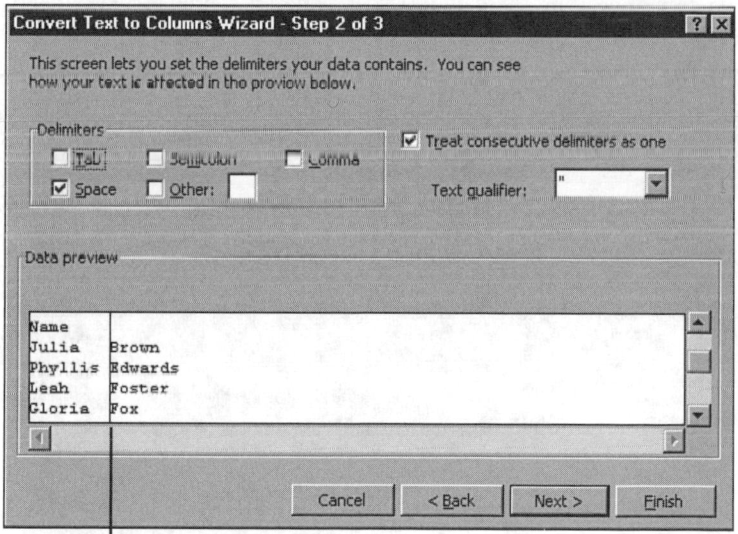

Spaces used between first and last names

Figure 25.17.
After selecting one or more delimiters, view the Data preview to see how the data will be parsed.

Vertical line indicates intended column break.

In the wizard's last step, you can also choose to apply General (the default), Text, or Date formats to the new columns. In addition, you can specify a particular Destination for the parsed cells.

You may notice the need to do subsequent parsing, especially when you've used a combination of delimiters in the text. If you didn't use consistent delimiters, you can always reparse one of the new columns and choose a different delimiter for the second conversion of text to columns.

Tip #279 from	Sometimes you need to combine text into one cell from separate cells, rather than the other way around. In the target cell where you want the combined data, enter the formula =CONCATENATE(cell1,cell2), where cell1 is the first cell whose contents you want to include and cell2 is the second. Excel will combine the text into one cell.
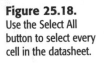	

USING POWERPOINT DATASHEET CONTENT IN EXCEL

There may be times that your initial use of pertinent data occurs first in PowerPoint—for example, when sales figures are entered into the PowerPoint datasheet for the purpose of creating a chart for a presentation. In these cases, the creation of the PowerPoint datasheet can become the first step in later using the data in Excel, where it can be formatted and used in calculations. The datasheet data can be the start of a new worksheet or can be added to an existing worksheet.

To copy the PowerPoint datasheet content to an Excel worksheet, follow these steps:

1. In the PowerPoint slide, display the datasheet and the content you've entered.

2. Drag through the datasheet's cells or click the Select All button on the datasheet (see Figure 25.18).

Figure 25.18.
Use the Select All button to select every cell in the datasheet.

The Select All button

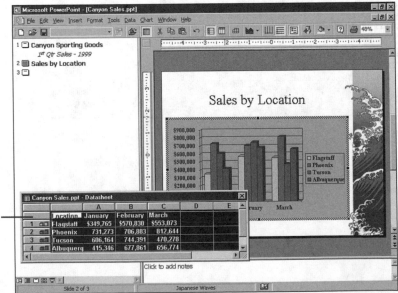

3. Choose Edit, Copy, or press Ctrl+C.

4. Switch to or open the Excel worksheet, and click in the cell where you'd like the pasted content to begin.

5. Choose Edit, Paste, or press Ctrl+V.

After pasting the datasheet content, you might need to move things around or add column/row labels to fit the desired layout for the Excel worksheet. The data is now ready for any formatting or formulas you want to apply.

Note

> While you can paste a chart from PowerPoint to Excel, it's generally not a good idea to do so. It's much better to re-create the chart in Excel so that changes and updates to the data (which are more likely to occur in Excel than PowerPoint) can easily update the chart.

COMBINING WORD, EXCEL, AND POWERPOINT FILES WITH HYPERLINKS

A powerful way to use Office 2000 applications together is to use hyperlinks. A *hyperlink* is a selection of text or a graphic image that is associated with another file, a Web page on the Internet, or your company's intranet. You can link Word, PowerPoint, and Excel files quickly and easily with hyperlinks, making it possible to open a worksheet from within a Word document, a Word document or Excel worksheet from within a PowerPoint presentation, or a PowerPoint presentation from within a Word document or an Excel worksheet. There is no limit to the number of hyperlinks you can insert into a single file, nor is there a limit to the relationships that hyperlinks can create—for example, a hyperlink in a Word document can point to a presentation that contains an Excel chart, thus combining two applications in a single link.

Following are some ideas for using hyperlinks with Office 2000:

- *Access supporting data.* Create a hyperlink in a PowerPoint presentation that opens a worksheet containing the data that a PowerPoint chart reflects. If someone asks to see the supporting data, you can get to it quickly, but you haven't wasted space on the slide displaying the data.

- *Refer to related documents.* If you're sending a memo that refers to an Excel list (database), include a link to that worksheet. This is more efficient for the memo recipients than merely telling them where the database is stored.

- *Display a chart on command.* What if you don't want to waste space on the worksheet with a chart or have a sheet within the workbook used for the chart? Copy the chart data to another workbook, create a chart from it, and then create a hyperlink in the original workbook that points to the chart. If the chart is of interest, it's accessible, but it's not taking up valuable space.

CREATING A HYPERLINK

Hyperlinks can be represented by text or graphics. The procedure you use to create hyperlinks is the same for Word, Excel, and PowerPoint.

To create a hyperlink in Word, Excel, or PowerPoint, follow these steps:

1. In the open file, select a single word, short phrase, or a graphic object that you want to use as a hyperlink.

2. Choose Insert, Hyperlink.

3. In the Insert Hyperlink dialog box, enter a folder and filename (or Web page name) for the file to which the hyperlink should point (see Figure 25.19).

The selected cell

Figure 25.19.
It's a good idea to browse for the file if you're not absolutely sure of the path and filename.

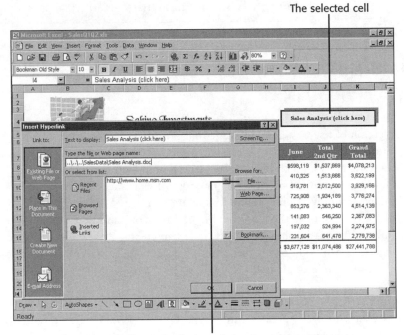

Choose File to simultaneously locate and enter the path and filename to which the hyperlink will point.

4. If you don't know the exact folder path to the file or the full filename, choose the File button on the right.

5. After entering or selecting the file for the hyperlink, choose OK.

In the file that contains the hyperlink, test it by pointing to it with the mouse—the mouse pointer should turn into a pointing hand (see Figure 25.20). The file referenced in the link appears in a ScreenTip beside the pointing hand. Click the hyperlink to verify that the link points to the appropriate file.

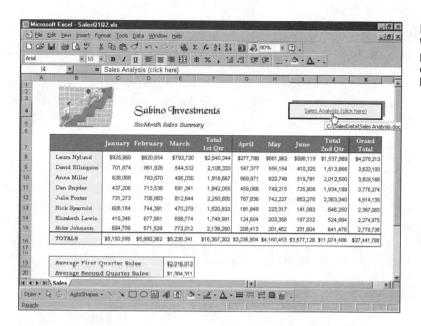

Figure 25.20.
When you see the pointing hand, click once to go to the hyperlinked file.

In the destination file (the file that the hyperlink jumps to), you may choose to include another hyperlink that returns the reader to the previous file (the source file containing the first hyperlink). Use the same procedure detailed previously to add the second hyperlink, and then reference the original file in step 3. You also could instruct readers to click the Back button in the Web toolbar (if it appears onscreen) to return to the previous file.

Caution

If others within your organization will use the file containing hyperlinks, be sure that the files to which the hyperlinks point will be available to those users. The hyperlinked files should be on network drives to which everyone has access. If the hyperlink is for your own use, the linked files can reside on your local hard drive.

If you'd like a different ScreenTip (other than the filename) to appear onscreen when you point to a hyperlink, choose the ScreenTip button in the Insert Hyperlink dialog box. Type the ScreenTip text in the resulting dialog box, and choose OK.

Tip #280 from

Laurie

If you'd like the person reviewing the file to be able to easily email you with comments or questions, add a hyperlink that points to an email address. When the link is clicked, a new message window will open, automatically addressed to the address you specify. Choose the E-mail Address button on the left side of the Insert Hyperlink dialog box and supply all requested information.

USING HYPERLINKS TO ACCESS A RANGE OF CELLS

You also can use hyperlinks to navigate within an open Excel workbook. Working similarly to named ranges, hyperlinks can be established in a worksheet, pointing to other cells within the workbook. This quick navigation/access method eliminates the need to create names for the ranges, and makes it possible to create the look and feel of a Web page within the workbook.

To create a hyperlink to access a specific range of cells, follow these steps:

1. In the open workbook, click on the cell or graphic image that will serve as the hyperlink.

2. Choose Insert, Hyperlink, and choose the Place in This Document button on the left side of the dialog box.

3. Type the cell address. It can be a single cell or a range of cells (see Figure 25.21). You also can select a named range from the Defined Names list.

This graphic will be used for the hyperlink.

Figure 25.21.
Create the feel of a Web site within the workbook by creating hyperlinks to cells within the workbook.

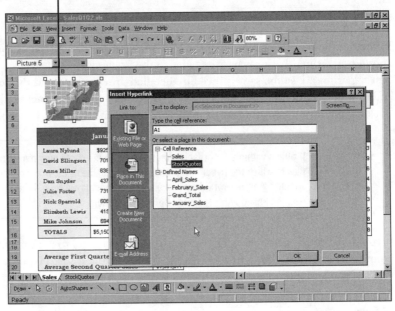

4. Choose the ScreenTip button, then type the pop-up text that will appear when pointing to the link (see Figure 25.22), and choose OK.

5. In the list box, select the worksheet that contains the specified cell or range.

6. Choose OK.

Figure 25.22.
Type the name of the cell range or a description of the information to which the hyperlink points.

Tip #281 from

Laurie

You can nest links by creating a hyperlink in Word or PowerPoint that points to an Excel workbook that contains its own hyperlinks to important locations within its own worksheets.

UPDATING HYPERLINKS

Over time, hyperlinks can become invalid—perhaps the file to which the hyperlink points has been moved or deleted, or the information considered important enough to link to is no longer of interest. For a multitude of reasons, you'll want to update the hyperlinks.

To edit the hyperlink, follow these steps:

1. Right-click the hyperlink you want to edit.
2. From the shortcut menu, choose <u>H</u>yperlink, Edit <u>H</u>yperlink.
3. The Edit Hyperlink dialog box opens, looking very similar to the Insert Hyperlink dialog box (see Figure 25.23). Click the appropriate Link To button (on the left side of the dialog box) to choose the type of link.
4. Make the desired changes to the link, and choose OK.

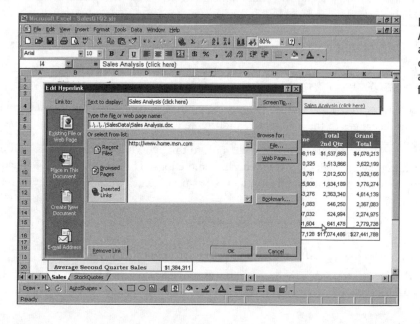

Figure 25.23.
Adjust the folder path and filename, or choose a new sheet and/or range of cells for the hyperlink.

DELETING HYPERLINKS

If a hyperlink is no longer of use, you can delete it. Deleting a hyperlink doesn't delete the text or graphic that currently serves as a hyperlink—deleting the link merely eliminates the text or graphic's role as a pointer to another file or range of cells within the worksheet.

To delete the hyperlink, follow these steps:

1. Right-click the hyperlink text or graphic.
2. From the shortcut menu, choose Hyperlink, Remove Hyperlink.

Tip #282 from

Laurie

You also can delete a hyperlink from within the Edit Hyperlink dialog box by clicking the Remove Link button.

TROUBLESHOOTING

UPDATING LINKS BETWEEN FILES

The Excel data that I linked to a PowerPoint slide seems to be broken. Whenever I change the data in Excel, these edits aren't reflected in PowerPoint. How do I fix the link?

Switch to the application containing the link (PowerPoint, in this example), and choose Edit, Links. Then, select the link you want to reconnect from the Links list box and choose the Change Source button. In the Change Source dialog box, select the file you want the linked object to connect to (select another folder from the Look In list, if necessary). Choose the Open button. The file you chose appears in the Links dialog box; choose Close to close the dialog box. The updated link information appears in the application.

EDITING AN EXISTING HYPERLINK

I need to make changes to an existing hyperlink, but when I try to click the hyperlink to select it, I jump to the file referenced in the hyperlink. How do I edit the hyperlink?

Right-click the hyperlink. Then choose Hyperlink, Edit Hyperlink from the shortcut menu. Make the desired changes in the dialog box, and then choose OK.

If you just want to make simple formatting changes to the hyperlink (such as using a different font or adding italic), right-click the hyperlink and choose Hyperlink, Select Hyperlink. Then use the menus or toolbars to format the text, as usual. Click outside of the hyperlink to deselect it.

FIXING INVALID HYPERLINKS

The hyperlink I created in an Excel workbook no longer works. How do I fix this?

Most likely, the file referenced in the hyperlink was moved or deleted, or you moved the Excel file itself. To update the hyperlink, right-click the hyperlink and choose Hyperlink,

Edit <u>H</u>yperlink. Click the appropriate Link To button, edit the location of the destination file, and choose OK.

If this doesn't seem to be the source of the problem, and the hyperlink references file(s) on a network, ensure that you have access to the files on the network.

EXCEL IN PRACTICE

Creating consistency between data sources as well as visual consistency is essential to the effective distribution and presentation of data in any business. Providing a similar look and feel to your documents, worksheets, and presentations helps your audience see the connection between them. In addition, ensuring that the source of the data is updated in a timely fashion (and updated to all relevant files) helps the audience feel confident in the data's accuracy and reliability.

Figure 25.24 shows a Word report that contains linked Excel data (a linked range) and a pasted PowerPoint slide that connects the report to a PowerPoint presentation which those people reading the report will view. Tying the report and the presentation together enhances the effectiveness of both.

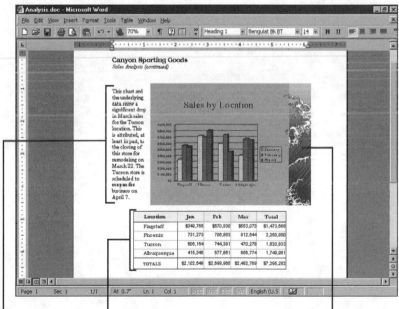

Figure 25.24.
Combine Excel and PowerPoint content in your Word documents to give your reports the combined power of the core Office 2000 applications.

Word text that wraps around the graphic from PowerPoint ties the content together.

Excel content is pasted as a link, so that changes to the worksheet can be updated in the report for future publication.

The PowerPoint slide becomes the visual touchstone for the audience, who will see this same data in a PowerPoint presentation.

CHAPTER 26

USING EXCEL WITH ACCESS AND OTHER DATABASES

by Timothy Dyck
timothy_dyck@dyck.org

In this chapter

USING EXCEL WITH DATABASE SOFTWARE

Excel is no slouch at handling data. With its sophisticated list-handling capabilities (which you can read more about in Part VI, "Analyzing and Managing Your Data"), you can easily sort or filter data to find key values, as well as create subtotals and custom formulas to see the big picture.

However, if you spend much of your time working with lists of data (such as customer lists or product catalogs), or if your lists grow larger than a few hundred items, you'll find Excel starts getting in your way more than getting you on your way. When that happens, it's time to switch to using a database program instead of Excel to manage data.

The obvious choice for Excel users is to use Microsoft's desktop database, Microsoft Access. If you have the Microsoft Office 2000 Professional or Premium edition, you already have Microsoft Access. Excel and Access have been designed specifically to work together, so Access is the natural choice for Excel users.

This chapter discusses when you should make the switch from Excel to Access, and how to move your data seamlessly between the two programs. I also include some pointers on how to move data between Excel and databases other than Access, should you prefer to go that route. Finally, you'll learn how to retrieve financial data directly from the World Wide Web.

Note

While this chapter covers specific techniques for getting Excel data into Access, I won't get into how Access itself works, or how Access databases should be designed. If you need to learn more about Access, see Que's *Special Edition Using Microsoft Access 2000* (ISBN 0-7897-1606-2).

Although you might keep most of your data in Excel, if you work in a business, it's a sure bet most of the business's data is stored in a corporate database somewhere. If you work in a large company, that data is probably stored on a mainframe system running a database such as IBM's DB2, a UNIX system running Oracle Corp.'s Oracle, or a Windows NT-based server with Microsoft's own server database, Microsoft SQL Server. This chapter also shows you how to access the entire world of data outside of your PC without leaving Excel's familiar environment. As you'll see, Excel is a champ at getting at the data you need, wherever it might be stored.

If you work with large amounts of data, you'll also want to check out the next chapter to learn how to use Excel 2000's new analytical data processing features. They'll be a big help on tough data-analysis jobs.

USING ACCESS TO COMPLEMENT EXCEL

Access and Excel do a good job of filling in each other's rough spots. If you need to work with long lists of data, for example, you'll appreciate the built-in Access tools that help make sure your information is entered without mistakes.

The following sections cover how to decide when to stay with Excel and when to use Access. You'll also learn how to move your Excel data over to Access painlessly, and how to create Access forms and reports that work with Excel data.

WHEN TO USE ACCESS INSTEAD OF EXCEL

The single biggest difference between Access and Excel is that Access is a relational database, while Excel's database features are nonrelational. Here's what this means in practical terms. Say you're a sales manager and have built up a list of customer contacts over the years. The list contains information about each contact's name, address, credit limit, and so on. When a contact places an order, you naturally have to track the associated invoice number; you place it in a spare column at the end of your list. So far, so good.

However, because customers were so pleased with their purchases (and because you were doing such a fine job staying on top of each account!), they place a few more orders.

At this point, Excel puts you in a bind. You have to keep all the invoice numbers around for historical order tracking, yet you need to track new orders as they occur. One solution is to keep adding new columns to the table as needed, as shown in Figure 26.1.

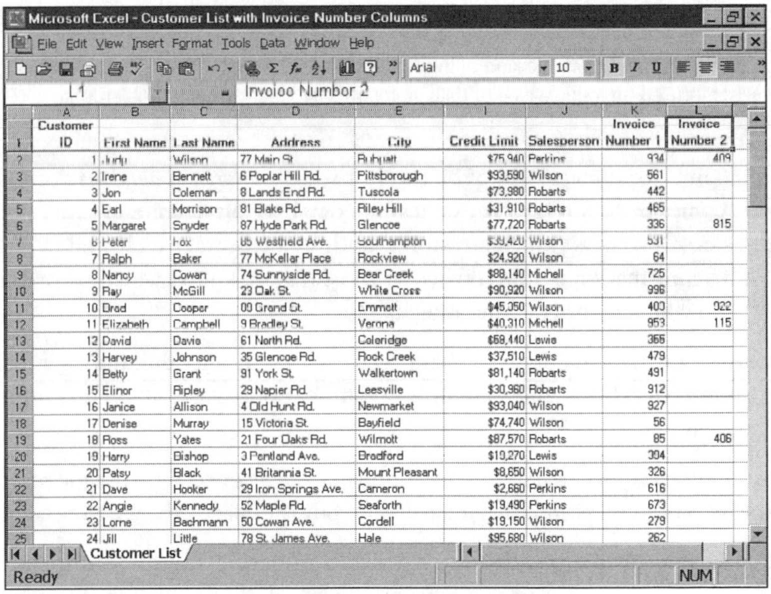

	A	B	C	D	E	I	J	K	L
1	Customer ID	First Name	Last Name	Address	City	Credit Limit	Salesperson	Invoice Number 1	Invoice Number 2
2	1	Judy	Wilson	77 Main St.	Rubyatt	$75,940	Perkins	934	409
3	2	Irene	Bennett	6 Poplar Hill Rd.	Pittsborough	$93,590	Wilson	561	
4	3	Jon	Coleman	8 Lands End Rd.	Tuscola	$73,980	Roberts	442	
5	4	Earl	Morrison	81 Blake Rd.	Riley Hill	$31,910	Roberts	465	
6	5	Margaret	Snyder	87 Hyde Park Rd.	Glencoe	$77,720	Roberts	336	815
7	6	Peter	Fox	85 Westfield Ave.	Southampton	$39,420	Wilson	531	
8	7	Ralph	Baker	77 McKellar Place	Rockview	$24,920	Wilson	64	
9	8	Nancy	Cowan	74 Sunnyside Rd.	Bear Creek	$88,140	Michell	725	
10	9	Ray	McGill	23 Oak St.	White Cross	$90,920	Wilson	996	
11	10	Brad	Cooper	09 Grand Ct.	Emmett	$45,350	Wilson	403	922
12	11	Elizabeth	Campbell	9 Bradley St.	Verona	$40,310	Michell	953	115
13	12	David	Davis	61 North Rd.	Coleridge	$68,440	Lewis	365	
14	13	Harvey	Johnson	35 Glencoe Rd.	Rock Creek	$37,510	Lewis	479	
15	14	Betty	Grant	91 York St.	Walkertown	$81,140	Roberts	491	
16	15	Elinor	Ripley	29 Napier Rd.	Leesville	$30,960	Roberts	912	
17	16	Janice	Allison	4 Old Hunt Rd.	Newmarket	$93,040	Wilson	927	
18	17	Denise	Murray	15 Victoria St.	Bayfield	$74,740	Wilson	56	
19	18	Ross	Yates	21 Four Oaks Rd.	Wilmott	$87,570	Roberts	85	406
20	19	Harry	Bishop	3 Pentland Ave.	Bradford	$10,270	Lewis	394	
21	20	Patsy	Black	41 Britannia St.	Mount Pleasant	$8,650	Wilson	326	
22	21	Dave	Hooker	29 Iron Springs Ave.	Cameron	$2,660	Perkins	616	
23	22	Angie	Kennedy	52 Maple Rd.	Seaforth	$19,490	Perkins	673	
24	23	Lorne	Bachmann	50 Cowan Ave.	Cordell	$19,150	Wilson	279	
25	24	Jill	Little	78 St. James Ave.	Hale	$95,680	Wilson	262	

Figure 26.1.
Bad design alert! Mixing two types of information in the same table (in this case, customer information and invoice information) is a recipe for trouble and a sure sign a relational database is needed.

PART VIII CH 26

Seeing the same column repeated over and over to track the same type of information (such as the Invoice Number columns in this example) is a dead giveaway that Excel's data-handling features have run out of steam.

Tip #283 from

Timothy

> Do you find yourself tacking extra data columns onto the ends of lists because you need to track more information than really fits? Are you continually adding the same information (such as the client's information on each new order)? These are sure signs that you should be switching to a relational database.

The real limitation is the fact that a spreadsheet is a two-dimensional surface. After you've used the horizontal dimension (the columns) to label your fields, only the vertical dimension (the rows) is left for data. As a result, lists can effectively manage only one type of data—customer information, order information, or product information, for example, but not two or more at once.

You could have customer information in a list on one worksheet, and put invoice information in a second list on a separate worksheet. That strategy keeps the information grouped properly, but introduces a new problem: You have to duplicate some customer information in the second list (such as the customer ID number) so you'll know which customers are connected with which invoices. Keeping duplicated information synchronized between the two lists is going to be a painful job. If you add a third list (for example, invoice line items) and then must keep invoice numbers in two places, you'll wish you'd never heard of Excel.

Tip #284 from

Timothy

> Don't mix more than one kind of information in a list at once. Keep the structure of your lists focused on a single type of data, and you'll avoid big growth problems later.

Tracking multiple kinds (or dimensions) of data is just what a *relational database* does. The name "relational" comes from the fact that tables in a database often contain some duplicated data (such as customer IDs, which are stored both in a customer table and in an invoices table). This information is stored twice so the database knows which records in one table are "related" to which records in the other table.

Relational databases can track hundreds of these relationships at once and have sophisticated ways of guaranteeing that if information is updated in one place, all related information is updated as well.

Needing to store multiple types of (still related) information at once is the major reason a database like Access should be used rather than Excel, but there are other reasons as well:

- **You need to have multiple people accessing and updating the same information at once.** If you require more than one person entering data at once (for example, a group of data-entry clerks entering data from a stack of paper invoices), you'll want to use Access. Excel has some simple facilities for tracking multiple users working on the same worksheet, but Access is built from the ground up for this job.

- **You would like to use your own data-entry forms to get more flexibility in how you enter data (as well as use more professional-looking forms).** Unlike the "one size fits all" Excel data-entry form, Access provides a graphical development environment for building completely customizable forms. These forms can contain pictures and other graphic elements to look professional and simplify the data-entry process and can include information from more than one table at the same time on the same form.

■ **You want to be able to automate forms to provide additional information from a single entry.** Access can automate the entry of information in a form (without VBA). For example, picking a client ID number from a drop-down list in an Access form can automatically fill in the rest of that client's info (such as the address and phone number) in other parts of the form. To perform a comparable action in Excel would require programming with VBA.

■ **You need to store more than 65,536 records (Excel's limit).** Access can store much larger data sets than Excel can, while still doing so very quickly. Excel worksheets can have up to 65,536 rows of data, but Access 2000 databases can have an unlimited number of rows, as long as the total database doesn't get larger than 2GB (Access 97 databases can't be larger than 1GB). Access also can build special database structures called *indexes* that make searching through a few hundred thousand rows a quick operation, and Access databases of this size are common.

■ **Your worksheet has grown larger than will fit into your PC's memory.** Excel must be able to hold all data in the list in memory at once. Access doesn't have this requirement. This isn't nearly as big a deal as it once was back in the days of DOS spreadsheets (because Windows can make free disk space act like memory), but it still is an issue for some users.

■ **You need to produce professional reports presenting and summarizing your data.** If you need professionally formatted reports for summarizing and presenting data, Access has much better tools for the job than Excel. Excel has terrific formatting capabilities for one-of-a-kind printouts but has trouble with multiple-page reports (for instance, you can't print out a running page subtotal in Excel).

Access also separates the format of a report from its data—you can use the same data to produce many different kinds of reports. In Excel, you'd have to copy the data to a new sheet or link from the new sheet back to the original each time to get the same result.

When you reach the point where it's necessary to move some of your Excel data over to Access, the following section shows how to do it.

Sending Excel Data to Access for Further Analysis

A number of methods are available for transferring Excel data into Access. As you might expect, the tried-and-true copy-and-paste technique works fine (even better than in previous versions, in fact). You also can choose to use the Import Spreadsheet Wizard in Access if you want more control over the resulting Access database, or you can leave your data in Excel and just link to it from Access by using the Link Spreadsheet Wizard.

A number of features discussed in this section use Excel's Access Links add-in. With this feature installed, you'll these three new commands on the Data menu: MS Access Form, MS Access Report, and Convert to MS Access. They make it easy to send data from Excel to Access.

Before getting into the Access Links add-in, you'll have to add it to your list of available add-ins in Excel. Choose Tools, Add-Ins, select the Access Links check box, and choose OK. If the add-in isn't installed on your system, you'll get a message saying "Microsoft Excel can't run this add-in. This feature is not currently installed. Would you like to install it now?" Choose Yes and the add-in will be installed and activated.

Note

If the Office 2000 CD isn't already inserted in your CD-ROM drive, the installer program will request it.

COPYING DATA USING COPY-AND-PASTE

As you might expect, the simplest way to copy data from Excel to Access is by using the Clipboard and a simple copy-and-paste.

Access understands Excel's row-and-column format and will automatically turn Excel data into a new table when the data is pasted into Access. For a simple transfer of an Excel list into Access, select the entire list; then copy the data to the *Office Clipboard (page 116)* by choosing Edit, Copy or pressing Ctrl+C.

Tip #285 from

Timothy

If you have a long list of data items, let Excel select the list for you. Place the cell pointer somewhere in your list and press Ctrl+Shift+* (asterisk) or choose Edit, Go To, click the Special button, select the Current Region option, and click OK. Excel will highlight the contiguous group of cells containing the active cell (out to the first column and row of blank cells found).

Now start Microsoft Access. When Access starts, it will ask if you want to create an empty Access database or open an existing file (see Figure 26.2). Choose Blank Access Database, choose OK, type a filename for the new database, and choose Create. (If this is the first time you have used Access, the Office Assistant may appear; choose Start Using Microsoft Access from the list of options offered by the Assistant.)

The main database management window opens for the new database. Choose Edit, Paste or press Ctrl+V to paste in the data. Access will then ask whether the first row of your data contains column headings (see Figure 26.3). If you selected column headings in Excel (a smart thing to do), choose Yes. You'll then see Access create a new table containing the pasted data. The table will have the same name as the name of the Excel worksheet you have open.

What you've done here is a straight copy of Excel data into Access. The data isn't linked in any way, and the two files (the Excel file and the Access file) are completely independent. Sometimes (if you'll send the file to someone else, for example), independence is exactly what you want. If not, you can link the data from one program to the other. See the later section "Linking Data Using the Link Spreadsheet Wizard."

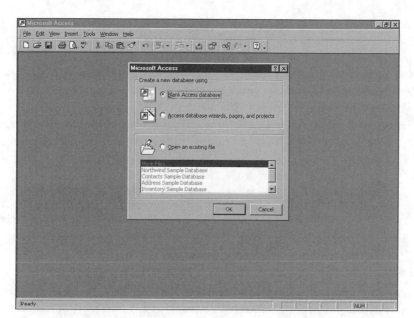

Figure 26.2.
Unless someone sent you an Access database to use (ending with an .mdb extension), you should create a new one by choosing Blank Access Database.

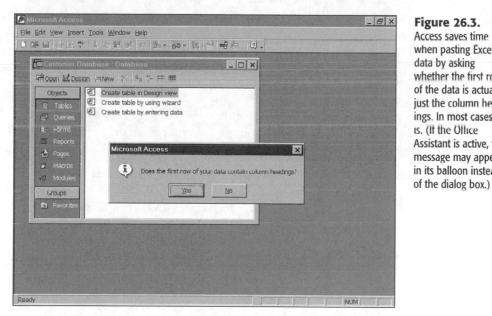

Figure 26.3.
Access saves time when pasting Excel data by asking whether the first row of the data is actually just the column headings. In most cases, it is. (If the Office Assistant is active, the message may appear in its balloon instead of the dialog box.)

PART

VIII

CH

26

Note   Copied columns that contain formulas are converted to values when pasted into Access.

 If the source list is AutoFiltered, you may be surprised to see that the new Access table contains the entire list, rather than the filtered version. For details on solving this problem, see "Copying Visible Cells Only" in the Troubleshooting section at the end of this chapter.

Tip #286 from

Timothy

If you're pasting a whole Excel list into Access, paste it into the main database window, not a blank database table window. You'll preserve the column names that way.

If you already have a table created and are pasting more rows into it, be sure to select the entire final row in Access (by clicking on the asterisk next to the bottom row) before you paste the data. The pasted data will all appear jammed together in one field if you don't select the whole row.

IMPORTING/EXPORTING EXCEL DATA WITH THE IMPORT SPREADSHEET WIZARD

If you plan to move a large set of Excel rows permanently into Access, you're better off using the Import Spreadsheet Wizard in Access instead of a copy-and-paste operation. This technique takes a little more work, but enables you to do more, such as create indexes and a primary key for your new table, and thus produce a better-designed Access database.

On the other hand, if you need to keep the data up to date in Excel, linking the Excel list to an Access database may be a better plan. See the later section "Linking Data Using the Link Spreadsheet Wizard" for details.

To start the Import Spreadsheet Wizard, start Access and create (or open) a database file. Then choose File, Get External Data, Import to open the Import dialog box. Select Microsoft Excel in the Files of Type drop-down list, and choose the Excel workbook you want to import.

The Import Spreadsheet Wizard opens and asks which worksheet or named range you'd like to import. (The wizard can import only one of either at a time.) A preview of the data appears in the lower half of the dialog box, which makes it easier to choose the data you want to import (see Figure 26.4). If the workbook doesn't contain additional sheets or named ranges, this step may be skipped.

Tip #287 from

Timothy

Creating a named range for the list in Excel makes this first step much easier, especially if the worksheet contains more than just the list (such as titles or queried data).

After specifying the worksheet or range you want to import, choose Next to continue.

Step 2 of the wizard just asks if the first row of data you're importing contains column names, or if all the rows are data (see Figure 26.5). Check First Row Contains Column Headings, if appropriate, and choose Next. If the first row contains data that can't be used as field names, Access presents a warning message. Click OK; the wizard will make up valid field names, which you can review and edit later as needed.

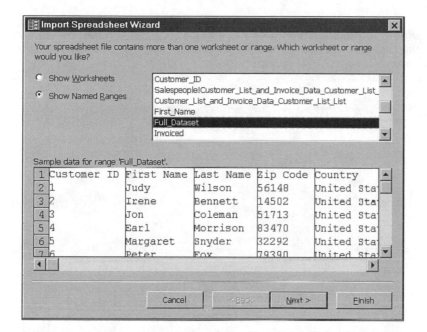

Figure 26.4.
The Import Spreadsheet Wizard can import only one worksheet or named range at a time. Choose which one you want to import in the first step of the wizard.

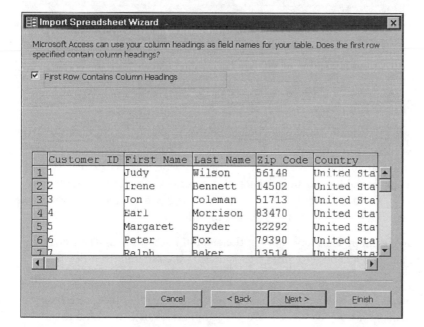

Figure 26.5.
Look in the data preview area to double-check whether the data has column headings. In this example, the data does have column headings.

The wizard next asks whether Access should put your data into a new table by itself—you specify the name later—or add the data to an existing table (see Figure 26.6). If you choose to add data to an existing table, you'll skip right to the last step of the wizard.

Tip #288 from

Timothy

If you don't have column headings in your data, you won't have the option of putting your imported data into an existing table. Access must know column names in order to match new data to columns in an existing table.

Figure 26.6.
In most cases, you'll want to put imported data into its own table.

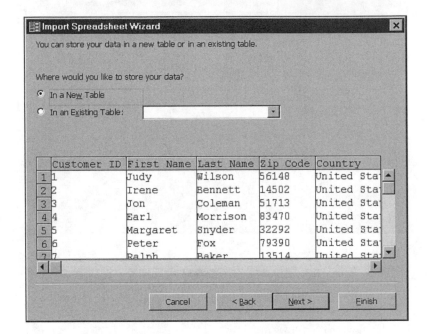

After making your selection, choose Next to keep going.

Step 4 of the wizard asks whether you'd like to add indexes to particular columns as part of the data-import process. Remember that indexes are special database objects that make searching for data in that column very fast. If your database will be larger than a few hundred rows, you definitely should add an index for each column containing key search information. For example, if you'll probably search for customers based on their customer code, zip code, or state, all three of these columns should be indexed.

To add an index to a column, click anywhere in the column in the wizard dialog box to select the column, and then choose to index the data using the Indexed drop-down list (see Figure 26.7).

You can choose two kinds of indexes: those that allow the same data to be entered more than once in the column, for which you choose Yes (Duplicates OK), and those that guarantee that each field entered in the column is unique, for which you choose Yes (No Duplicates). If you don't know for certain that all the records in a given column are in fact unique, pick the Yes (Duplicates OK) option. Unique indexes are faster than indexes that allow duplicates, so use unique indexes when you can.

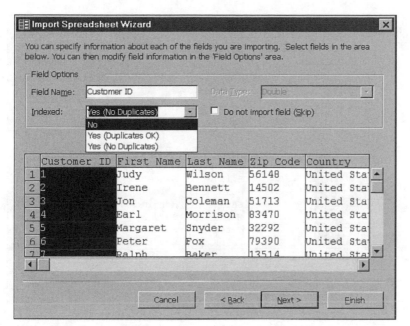

Figure 26.7.
Adding indexes to your data really speeds up database searches. Add an index to each column in your database you will use in later searches.

Caution

Keep in mind that, although indexes speed up searches, they can slow record updates performed with operations such as append queries. Index fields only if necessary.

When you're finished creating indexes, choose Next.

The next to last step of the wizard asks you to define a *primary key* for the table (see Figure 26.8). A primary key isn't anything mysterious; it's just a special name for a selected column that has no duplicates in its data (and has a unique index defined on it).

If you already have such a column in your data—for example, a customer code column—select it as the primary key. If you don't, let Access add a primary key to the table for you. Access will create a new column of ascending numbers (the first data row will be number 1, the next number 2, and so on) as a primary key column.

Each table can have either one primary key or none. When you've selected one (or asked Access to add one), choose Next.

Tip #289 from

Timothy

A primary key isn't required for each table, but the primary key (and other columns with no-duplicate indexes) are really important database building blocks. When the database grows and you begin to combine information from multiple tables, having a primary key for each of your tables will become very important.

Figure 26.8.
Using a primary key index can speed up your database considerably. If you don't have any columns with all unique entries in them, Access can add a special primary key column to your database.

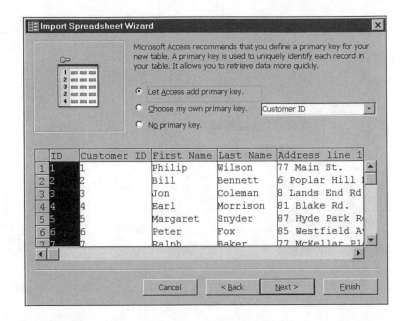

Finally, you'll be asked to name the new table (see Figure 26.9). Access defaults to the name of the worksheet or named range you selected earlier, but you can type in any name you want. Choose Finish, and Access will actually perform the import operation.

 You may get an error if you select a primary key that contains null (empty) values or if duplicates exist in the key column (in which case no key is applied). See "When Access Can't Create an Index" in the Troubleshooting section at the end of this chapter.

Figure 26.9.
To wrap things up, give your new table a name.

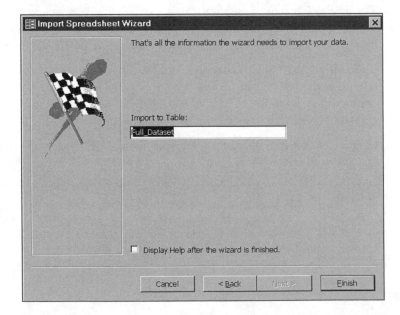

Tip #290 from

Timothy

> There's a handy way to get to the Access Import Spreadsheet Wizard from within Excel. Just click anywhere in the list you want to convert, and choose Data, Convert to MS Access (note that you must have the Access Links add-in installed for this command to appear). You'll be asked if you want to put the Excel data into a new database (which will have the same name as the open Excel file) or into an existing database. When you choose OK, Excel starts Access and its Import Spreadsheet Wizard for you. You then continue through the wizard as described earlier.

LINKING DATA USING THE LINK SPREADSHEET WIZARD

Linking the Access database to the source Excel spreadsheet is a good idea if you want to use the data-entry and reporting capabilities in Access while still keeping the source data in only one place. The easiest way to have Access link its database back to the Excel file is to just open the Excel file in Access! This feature is new in Access 2000. Just choose File, Open (or press Ctrl+O) in Access, select Microsoft Excel in the Files of Type box, and choose Open. Access then launches its Link Spreadsheet Wizard.

Note

> This method automatically creates a new Access database file and places it in the same folder as the Excel file. If you want to place the link in an existing Access database file, open the file and choose File, Get External Data, Link Tables to open the Link dialog box. Specify Microsoft Excel in the Files of Type box, select the workbook you want to link, and click the Link button or press Enter to open the Link Spreadsheet Wizard. After this point, the steps are the same.

Choose which workbook or named range you'd like to link to, as shown in Figure 26.10. Then choose Next to continue. (If you don't have multiple workbooks or named ranges, you won't see this first wizard screen.)

In the next step, Access asks whether the first data row of the workbook contains column headings. The data is conveniently displayed so you can double check (see Figure 26.11).

Choose Next, give the new table a name, and choose Finish. A message box appears, indicating that the database table is linked to the Excel workbook. Click OK. When the wizard closes, you'll see that Access uses a special icon in the database window to indicate that the table has a live link back to the Excel file (see Figure 26.12).

Linked tables are really convenient because you can modify data in either Access or Excel (but not at the same time) and see changes from either program.

Two important drawbacks must be mentioned. First, although you can modify and add records to your Excel data list from Access, you can't delete them! Access displays a message saying that deleting records isn't supported.

Figure 26.10.
If you have multiple worksheets or named ranges in the linked Excel workbook, you'll be asked to choose which worksheet or named range you want to use.

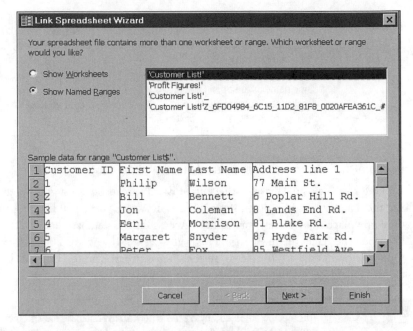

Figure 26.11.
Open an Excel file in Access, specify whether the first data row contains heading names, and choose Finish. You've just linked Access to Excel!

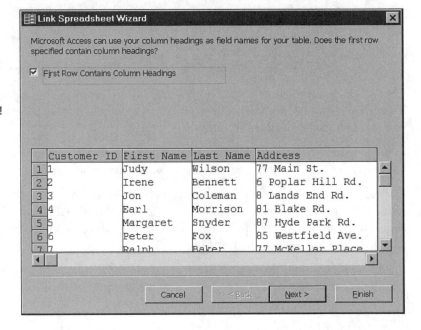

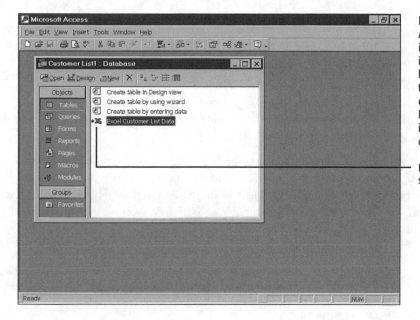

Figure 26.12.
Access uses a special icon (an arrow pointing to the Excel symbol) to indicate that a table is getting its data directly from an Excel workbook instead of storing the data in Access itself.

Linked spreadsheet icon

Also, you shouldn't have both the Excel table and Access database open at the same time. If you have the linked table open in Access, you won't be able to open it in Excel—you'll get a dialog box saying that Excel can't access the file. As long as Access has the table window open, you won't be able to use Excel to open the workbook. This happens even if you've made your workbook multiuser-capable by choosing Tools, Share Workbook.

These negatives also affect Access forms and reports created from Excel data, because they use linked workbooks behind the scenes to get their data.

Caution

If you open the worksheet first in Excel, Access may not protest when you open the linked table and work with it, but I recommend avoiding this practice. You're risking crashes, data corruption, and other mysterious errors. The problems may not occur until the linked table itself is opened from within Access, but this is definitely a risk.

CREATING ACCESS FORMS AND REPORTS FROM EXCEL DATA

Most of the time, just moving or linking raw Excel data to an Access database isn't the point. What you really want to do is take advantage of Access's richer forms and reports using your Excel data. Excel makes it easy to jump right into this step.

If you haven't already installed the Access Links add-in, you'll need to do so for the commands described in this section to appear on your menus.

CREATING ACCESS FORMS FROM EXCEL DATA

Excel's own data form (which you can call up by choosing Data, Form) is a leftover from earlier versions of Excel. Everything you can do with it (viewing, editing, and searching through your data) is much more ably handled by normal Excel worksheet tools, such as data filters.

As an alternative, through Excel's Access Links add-in, you have the option of using Access to build data forms that link to your Excel data.

Access forms are far more capable than the simple data form Excel offers. If you want, you can completely change the layout of an Access form to suit your needs, as well as add controls such as radio buttons or drop-down lists as alternatives to the simple text boxes Excel offers. Access forms are also fully programmable and can have buttons that bring up other forms, as well as calculated elements such as totals and counts.

Note

Because the Access Links add-in uses a data link (instead of a one-way copy of your data), it has the same link limitations as when you use the Link Spreadsheet Wizard described earlier. Namely, you can't delete records using an Access form. You can edit and add records, though.

To create an Access form for entering and editing Excel data, follow these steps:

1. Open the Excel file containing the data you want to edit in Access. Place the cell pointer in the list you want to use, and choose Data, MS Access Form.

2. In the resulting dialog box, specify which database file you want to copy the data into (you can create a new database file if you want) and whether the data list has a header row (see Figure 26.13). Then click OK.

3. Access starts and launches its Form Wizard (see Figure 26.14). Choose which fields you want in the Access form by clicking their names and then the > button. (Or click the >> button to select all the available fields, and then remove any unwanted fields with <.) Choose Next to keep going.

   If some of the fields/columns in the Excel data contain formulas, you may not want to use them in the form. If you do, Access won't let you update them, although you can enter the field and type data (easily changeable by disabling the control in Design view).

4. Access now quickly walks you through how you want the form to look. In this step, you can choose how you want the new form to be laid out (see Figure 26.15).

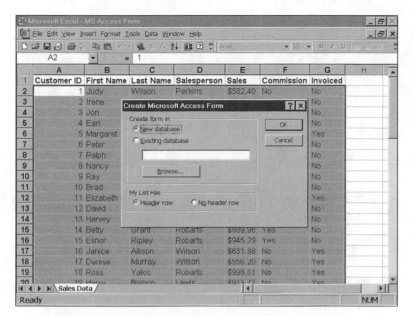

Figure 26.13.
Here's how to kick off the Microsoft Access Form Wizard. Choose to create a new database or use an existing one, specify whether the data list has a header row or not, and choose OK.

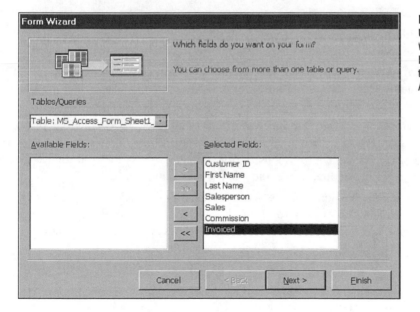

Figure 26.14.
Using the Form Wizard, select which Excel fields you want to see in the new Access form.

Figure 26.15.
You can quickly choose how to arrange the form by selecting an overall style. For data from Excel, it's best to use either Columnar or Datasheet layouts.

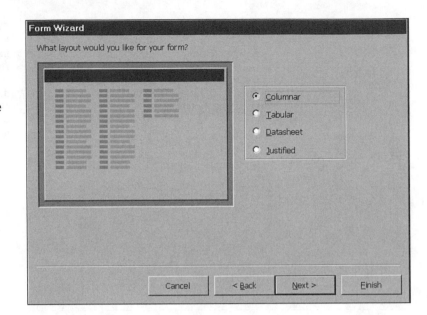

The wizard offers four choices:

- **Columnar.** Fields are arranged from top to bottom and then left to right, with one record per form. It's a good, simple arrangement, and the best overall choice.

- **Tabular.** Fields are arranged in left-to-right order (and squished to fit), with many rows displayed on a single form. If you want a tabular layout, the Datasheet choice is a better option.

- **Datasheet.** Fields are arranged in left-to-right order, with many rows displayed on a single form. Rows are displayed on a spreadsheet-like grid, making this a good quick choice for Excel users. You don't get the ability to customize the form's layout or appearance, though; it's only a simple grid.

- **Justified.** The same as Columnar layout, except that fields are stretched to fill the whole width of the form. It results in an awkward crowded layout and is hard to edit later because the field boundary box lines are all so close together.

Choose the layout and click Next to continue.

5. The next step in the wizard provides some limited choices for the look of the form, including font, color, and background. Pick whatever option you like the best and choose Next to keep going (see Figure 26.16).

6. The final step asks you to give the new form a title (see Figure 26.17). You also can choose to open the form for immediate use (choose Open the Form to View or Enter Information) or start the Access form editor to make further customizations (choose Modify the Form's Design). When you've typed in a title, choose Finish; Access will create and open the form.

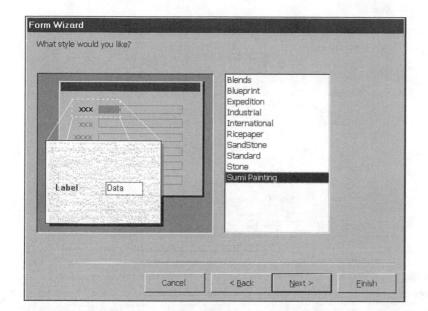

Figure 26.16.
Access forms can have multiple fonts and backgrounds to help you highlight important information.

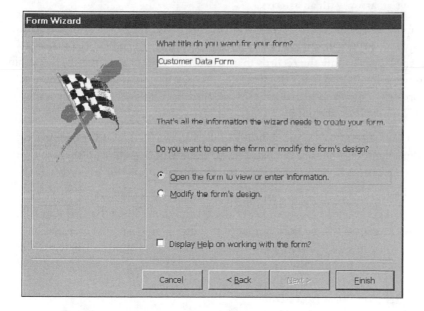

Figure 26.17.
Give your form a title and choose Finish to start using the new form.

The form you're looking at now is a live view of your Excel data (see Figure 26.18). Access creates a link to the original workbook (just as you can do on your own, as described in the earlier section "Linking Data Using the Link Spreadsheet Wizard"), so you don't have to edit the same data in two places.

Figure 26.18.
Here's the Excel data in an Access form. You can use the form as is, or do all kinds of tweaking (see the final section of this chapter for some ideas).

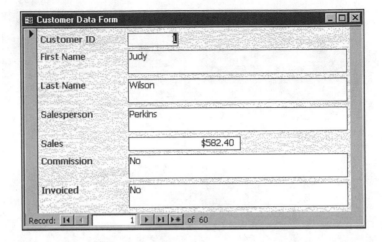

To edit data in the form, you can use the arrow and Tab keys to move, and type just as you do in Excel. You can move between records by pressing the Page Up or Page Down keys or by clicking the arrow buttons at the bottom of the form. To add a new record, click on the button that displays an arrow with an asterisk.

You also can do quick filters and sorts with Access forms that you can't do with Excel data forms. For example, just right-click a field (a last name, for example) and choose Filter by Selection. Access will display only the records that match that field's value. Right-click again and choose Remove Filter/Sort to get rid of the filter. Remember that, unfortunately, you can't delete records from the form because it uses a spreadsheet link behind the scenes (that's a problem Microsoft needs to fix).

Back in the Excel worksheet, you'll notice a button called View MS Access Form above or to the right of the column headings in the data list. This control is saved with the file; when you come back to the file later, you can just click the button to jump right back into the Access form.

On the other hand, if you want to move or delete the button, hold down the Ctrl key, then click once on the button (you'll see a border appear around it). You can now drag the button by its border, or just press the Delete key to remove it. Keep in mind that deleting the button will force you to go through the wizard again (although step 1 will be eliminated).

CREATING ACCESS REPORTS FROM EXCEL DATA

If your needs tend more toward detailed reports than fancy forms, Excel can use Access for that, too. Excel can add multiple subtotals to summarize data lists and allows very customized layouts for printing forms, but doesn't offer much for users wanting to print long lists of data. In particular, if you need to print many pages of information (as opposed to just looking at something onscreen), the flexible multiple-page report printing capabilities in Access make it the way to go.

To create an Access report linked to your Excel data, follow these steps:

1. Open the Excel file containing the data you want to edit in Access, place the cell pointer in the list you want to use, and choose <u>D</u>ata, MS A<u>c</u>cess Report to open the Access Report Wizard.

2. The wizard will start and ask whether you want to create a new Access database to hold the report (which will have the same name as your Excel workbook) or place the report into an existing database (see Figure 26.19). Make your choice, indicate whether your data list has column titles, and choose OK to start Access.

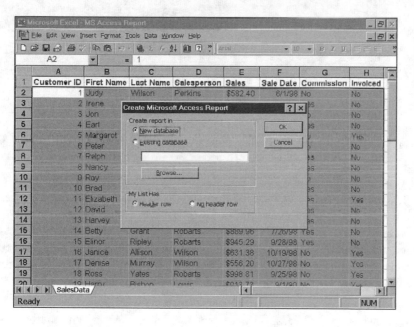

Figure 26.19.
Excel's Data, MS Access Report command makes it easy to turn Excel data into a printed Access report.

3. Access will now start and walk you through its Report Wizard. The Report Wizard asks which fields you want to include in the report (see Figure 26.20). (This process is similar to that for choosing fields for a data form, as described in the preceding section.) Choose the fields you want and choose <u>N</u>ext.

4. The next step is to decide how you want to group report information. By setting grouping levels, you're telling Access where you want to have subtotals—if you don't define any grouping levels, you'll just get information printed out in a big, unbroken list.

Figure 26.20.
The Report Wizard needs to know which fields you want included in the report. Use the > button to copy individual fields or the >> button to select all the fields at once.

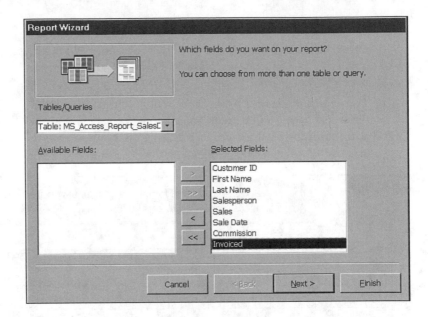

In this example, assume that you'll print a report of each salesperson's sales activities. Under each salesperson, you want a list of his or her sales grouped by month, and you want to end both the monthly and salesperson lists with dollar subtotals showing how much that person has sold.

Because you want to group first by salesperson name, that should be the outside grouping level. Click on the field you want to select and then click on the > button to create a grouping arrangement (see Figure 26.21). You can create multiple levels of groups on any fields. For this example, I used salesperson name and sale date, but geographical groupings such as country, then region, then town are also very common. If you get the order wrong, you can click the blue group section name you want to change, and then click the up- and down-arrow Priority buttons to change grouping order.

If you're grouping by date, read the next step, as it shows you how to handle date grouping problems. Otherwise, specify the grouping levels you want and then choose Next (and go on to step 6).

5. Dates have special grouping problems because you generally don't want to group on each change in day—that would give you a daily subtotal for a list that might include only one or two transactions (depending on your volume, of course).

The Report Wizard has special options for grouping fields—options you can change by clicking on the Grouping Options button to display the Grouping Intervals dialog box (see Figure 26.22). By selecting an option from the Grouping Intervals list, you can group dates by Year, Quarter, Month (the default choice for dates), Week, and so on. If you prefer to group by quarter or year, select that option and then choose OK to get back to the main grouping level dialog box.

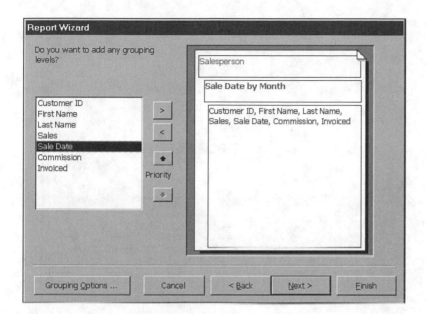

Figure 26.21.
You control how a report will subtotal figures by controlling field grouping levels. This report will sub-total by salesperson name and then by month.

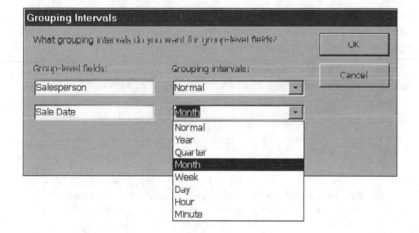

Figure 26.22.
The Grouping Intervals dialog box makes it possible to group dates by year or by quarter, instead of by month. You can also change how text and numeric fields are grouped here.

Tip #291 from

Timothy

> The Grouping Intervals function also comes in handy when you're printing reports containing product codes or zip codes (which are most often handled as text fields). You can change grouping options for text fields based on matches in their first one to five letters. This option would enable you to group all people living in similar zip codes, for example.

6. Now the Report Wizard asks how you want to sort fields that aren't grouped (grouped fields are printed in sorted order automatically). If you want to have detail records sorted within report blocks, just select the field(s) on which you want to sort in the drop-down lists of fields (see Figure 26.23).

Figure 26.23.
Sort within report blocks by selecting the field(s) on which you want to sort. Higher-numbered sort keys have priority over those with lower numbers.

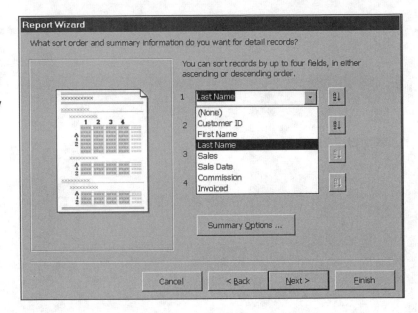

7. This step in the wizard is also where you add subtotals. Choose the Summary Options button and specify whether you want to have a sum, average, minimum, or maximum calculation added to the fields you choose (see Figure 26.24).

You also can choose here to have detail rows printed in the report (this is the default Detail and Summary option, which most people will want), or not have detail rows printed at all, grouping only by rows and totals in the report (the Summary Only option). This option is handy if you only want to see subtotals and grand totals.

Choose OK to return to the Report Wizard sort order dialog box and choose Next to continue.

Tip #292 from

Timothy

The Report Wizard gives you the option of adding calculations only to numeric fields, not text fields. If you want to add a count (rather than a sum or average), you have to do it yourself in the Access report designer. To do that, open the report in Design view and add a blank text box to the footer section of the group you want to count. Then right-click the box, choose Properties from the context menu, and enter =Count([*fieldname*]) in the Control Source box, where *fieldname* is the name of the field you want to count.

8. You can now decide how you want the report to look. Access reports are totally customizable, so if a layout you see in the dialog box is close to what you want, go for it and tweak it later (see Figure 26.25). For example, I find that the Align Left options make the best use of page space.

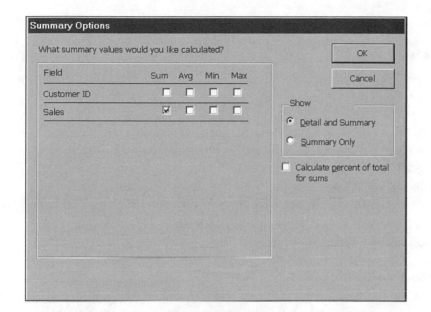

Figure 26.24.
Check off how you want numeric fields to be summarized in your report. You also can choose here to display both subtotals and grand totals, or only grand totals.

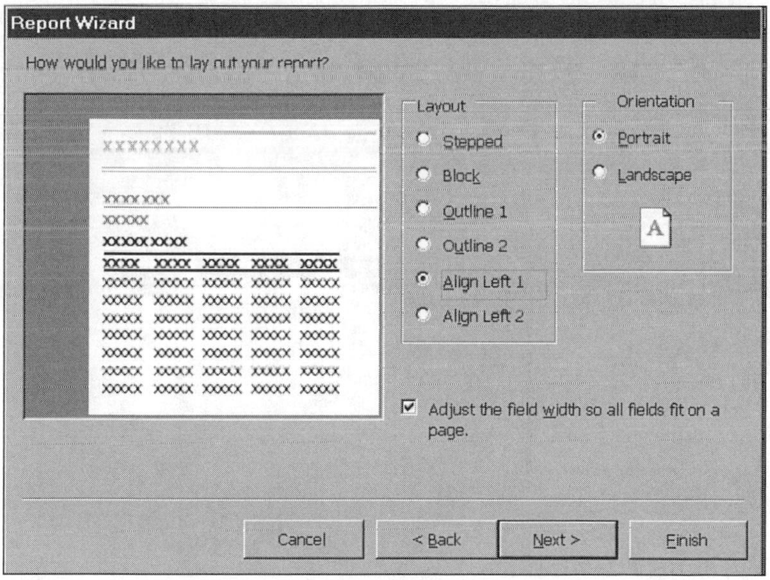

Figure 26.25.
Access provides several layout options for how to handle grouping. The Align Left options provide the most compact printouts, while the Stepped and Block options make your grouping arrangement very prominent.

Your choice of layout here will make sure that the fields you previously selected as grouping fields are clearly separated from other report information. You can choose from the following layout options:

- **Stepped.** Puts each grouping field on a line by itself and indents each subgroup field. This option leaves lots of empty space on the page and will require a landscape layout to show more than a few fields.

- **Block.** Places all grouping and detail fields on the same line, although later lines in the report are indented to show their relationships. Again, landscape orientation works best here.

- **Outline 1 and 2.** Very similar to the Stepped layout, except that the column headings are printed above detail information, not above the first grouping field.

- **Align Left 1 and 2.** All fields are printed flush left, making this layout a compact choice, suitable for portrait printing.

9. After making your selection, choose Next to continue.

   Now you're asked to make a similar formatting choice for how your report's fonts and colors should look (see Figure 26.26). Pick a style you like and click on Next one more time to get to the last step in the wizard.

Figure 26.26.
You can make a quick selection here that will make your report look formal or casual.

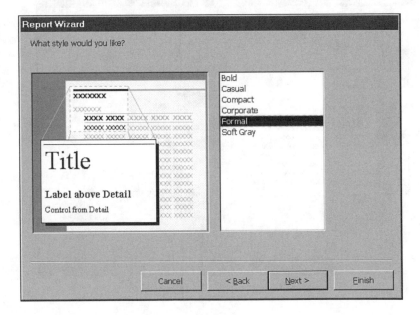

10. Finally, you just have to type a title that will appear at the top of your report (see Figure 26.27). Then choose Finish to see the report in its full glory!

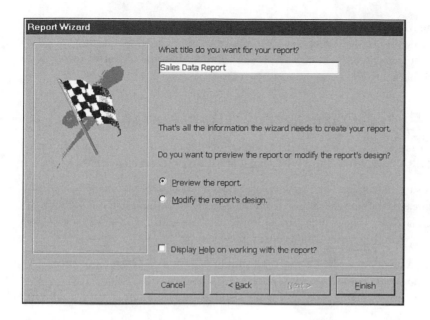

Figure 26.27.
Now type in a title for the first page of your report and choose Finish to see what you've done!

Figure 26.28 shows the final result for my report. You can page through the report by clicking on the arrows at the bottom of the report window and print it by choosing File, Print.

Are words being cut off in some fields in the report? See "Adjusting Text Labels on Access Reports" in the Troubleshooting section at the end of this chapter.

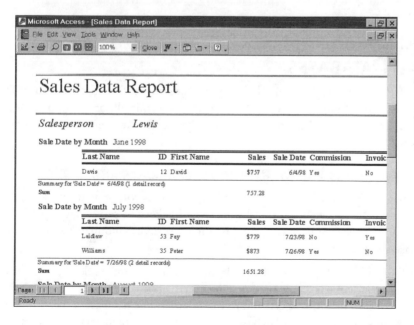

Figure 26.28.
Here's the final Access report, created using Excel data. It provides a slick, polished look you can only get in Excel with a lot of painstaking cell merging and formatting.

Just as with the MS Access Form wizard, you'll notice a button called View MS Access Report added to your original Excel file (it's to the right of or above the headings for the data list). This button is saved with the file; if you come back to the file later, just click the button to jump back into the Access report.

EXPORTING EXCEL DATA INTO OTHER DATABASES

It isn't as easy to move Excel data into databases other than Access (for example, Inprise Corp.'s Visual dBASE or Corel Corp.'s Paradox), but it isn't rocket science either.

The way most sure to work the first time is to save your Excel data as a *comma-delimited file* (a file in which each column is separated from the next by a comma). Comma-delimited format is a standard way to pass data around in the database world, and all the major database products support importing comma-delimited data.

You can create a comma-delimited file by choosing File, Save As and then selecting CSV (which stands for *comma-separated values*, which is what the file will contain) in the Save as Type box in the Save As dialog box. CSV is the standard extension for comma-delimited files.

Tip #293 from	Use comma-delimited files to transfer data to and from databases that don't support cutting-and-pasting the data. Comma-delimited files are understood by every database program.

RETRIEVING DATA FROM ACCESS AND OTHER RELATIONAL DATABASES

Moving data from Excel into Access is obviously the right move if the data started its life in Excel in the first place. But what if you didn't type the data yourself, or if it's not in an Excel workbook? This section describes how to get at database data wherever (and however) it might be stored.

WHERE CORPORATE DATA IS FOUND: RELATIONAL DATABASES AND ODBC

In most companies, the most likely place for important data is corporate databases. These databases might be Access databases, but they're more likely to be server databases, such as Oracle, DB2, or Microsoft SQL Server, running on large servers and managed by professional database administrators.

The standard way Microsoft products access database data is through a database industry standard called *ODBC*, which stands for *Open Database Connectivity*. ODBC allows database clients such as Excel to log into, select, and retrieve data from a database server without having to know how that particular database handles those tasks (and each database program handles them differently).

Microsoft is currently phasing out the ODBC standard in order to move to a new standard called *OLE DB*. [The *OLE (page 122)* standard is a couple of years old now and has been replaced by other standards; OLE DB is just a name by itself.] OLE DB is better suited than ODBC to handle unusual data types such as images and sounds. ODBC is so entrenched in the industry that this may take many years to happen, however.

Office 2000 is the first version of Office that uses OLE DB internally; in fact, Excel actually accesses ODBC through OLE DB. The database drivers included with Excel are also OLE DB drivers, although they're used in exactly the same way as ODBC drivers.

The key piece of magic that makes ODBC or OLE DB work is a *database driver*, which is a bit of software (usually written by the database vendor) that lives on your computer system and translates standard ODBC or OLE DB programming calls into whatever format the particular database is expecting. With an ODBC database driver, any ODBC-enabled software package on your system can access data from that database without having to know all the grimy details involved.

Excel is most definitely a database-enabled software package, and so with the right database drivers installed, a whole new world of data opens up. In fact, Excel includes a set of Microsoft-written drivers for a set of common desktop databases plus two server databases— Microsoft SQL Server and Oracle. You can retrieve data from any of the following databases (drivers are included with Excel), plus any others for which you might have an ODBC driver:

- Corel Paradox
- Inprise Visual dBASE
- Microsoft Access
- Microsoft Excel
- Microsoft FoxPro
- Microsoft SQL Server
- Oracle
- Text files (such as those in comma-delimited format)

PART

VIII

CH

26

Tip #294 from

Timothy

> Notice that Excel includes an ODBC database driver for itself! This enables you to access Excel data lists from any ODBC-enabled software package, even if the application doesn't know how to read Excel files. You can set up an ODBC link to Excel data in the same way you set up ODBC links to other databases. The next section shows how.

QUERYING THE DATABASE WITH THE QUERY WIZARD

The mechanism by which you retrieve data from a database is called a *database query*. Like other multiple-step tasks, Excel walks you through the process of retrieving database data using a wizard: the Query Wizard.

CHOOSING THE DATA SOURCE

To kick off the querying process, choose Data, Get External Data, New Database Query in Excel. The Choose Data Source dialog box opens (see Figure 26.29).

Note

If you don't have the database query components installed on your system, you'll get a message from Excel saying that it can't start Microsoft Query, and asking if you want to install it. If you see this message, go ahead and choose Yes. You'll need the Office 2000 CD.

Figure 26.29.
If you're accessing a database for the first time, choose <New Data Source>; otherwise, choose a data source you've already created.

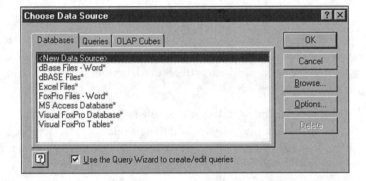

If the data is a dBASE, Excel, Access, or FoxPro database, select one of those types. Otherwise, choose <New Data Source> and click OK. This last approach is more general and will handle any kind of database, so the following sections describe how that procedure works.

The Queries tab is discussed later in this chapter; the *OLAP (page 838)* options are covered in Chapter 27, "Retrieving Data from OLAP Servers."

CREATING AN ODBC DATA SOURCE DEFINITION

For this example, I'll use the sample Access database called Northwind (it's included with Access) as the data source. When you're first working with Excel's query tools, it's a good idea to use a sample database such as Northwind rather than your live data. Any errors in your procedure won't damage the real data, and you can experiment until you get the hang of the querying process.

Type a name for the data source in step 1 of the Create New Data Source dialog box (see Figure 26.30). The name can be anything that makes sense to you and helps you remember which data tables this data source accesses.

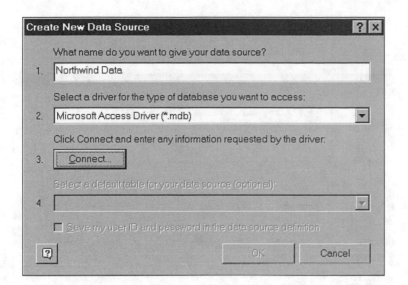

Figure 26.30.
Type a data source name and select the right driver from the drop-down list to start defining a new data source.

Next, select a database driver to use for this data source. It should be a driver that matches the database you're going to use: the Microsoft Access Driver (*.mdb) for Access databases, the SQL Server driver for Microsoft SQL Server, and so on. If you don't see the driver you need in this list, you must install it (or have your database administrator install it) before you can continue.

Click the Connect button to continue the process.

The next screen you see differs according to the specific database driver you selected. In general, all drivers require you to identify which database file or server you want to access, and many drivers request a database username and password. (Get these from your database administrator.)

To complete the dialog box in this example (ODBC Microsoft Access Setup), you need to tell the driver which database to access. Click Select in the Database group of buttons, and browse to find the Access database (see Figure 26.31).

To use the Northwind database, we'll browse to c:\Program Files\Microsoft Office\Office\Samples and select the Northwind database (Northwind.mdb). If you don't see the database there, you'll need to install it from the Office CD-ROM, using the Add/Remove Programs option in the Windows Control Panel.

After you select an .mdb file and click OK, you should return to the ODBC Microsoft Access Setup dialog box and see the path and filename of the database listed there. That's all you need to do here, so click OK to return to the Create New Data Source dialog box.

You're almost finished. The last step is to choose a default table to use when selecting which data to retrieve. You don't have to decide now if you're not sure which table you really want, but if you do know, it will save some time later on. For this example, we'll choose the table Customers.

PART

VIII

CH

26

Figure 26.31.
Click <u>S</u>elect to indicate from which Access database you want to get information.

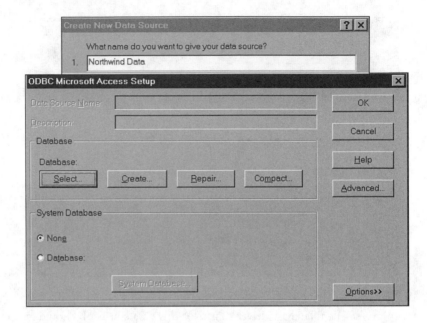

Not selecting a default table forces a prompt each time you access the source using Microsoft Query.

Tip #295 from

Timothy

By this point, some databases already will have asked you to log in with your database username and password. You can choose to save the database user ID and password with the data source definition, which saves you from having to type this information each time to use this data source.

However, note that this option compromises database security. Anyone who can access Excel on your system can then retrieve data using that data source as if they were you! In addition, the password itself is easily visible in the data source definition file.

Excel will warn you about these facts before it lets you save your database ID and password with a data source definition.

When you choose OK in the Create New Data Source window, you'll be returned to the Choose Data Source window. The Northwind Data source is now listed in the Databases tab, and you're finished creating the new source! The good news is you have to create a data source only once, and then you can use it over and over again.

SELECTING THE RIGHT INFORMATION: CHOOSING COLUMNS

After the data source is created, it should be selected in the list. If not, select it by clicking its name (in this case, click Northwind Data). Then choose OK. This will launch the actual Query Wizard (see Figure 26.32).

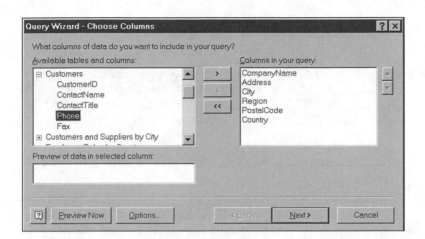

Figure 26.32.
This is the heart of the data-retrieval process. Select which columns from which tables you want to retrieve by clicking selected column names and then clicking the > button to place them into the query.

When the Query Wizard's Choose Columns dialog box appears, it might look like you have the whole world to choose from. In the left pane is a list of all the tables and columns in the source database. On large databases, this might be a very long list.

Tip #296 from

You can sort the list alphabetically by clicking the Options button to open the Table Options dialog box, selecting the option List Tables and Columns in Alphabetical Order, and clicking OK.

You also can jump quickly to a particular table by typing the first few letters in its name.

Select the columns you want to retrieve from the data source by clicking their names. You may need to click the plus (+) symbol in front of the selected table first to expand its column list. Then click the > button to place the selected column in the query. You should select the columns in the order that you want them to appear (left to right) in Excel. If you want to change the order, you can click on a column name you want to move and then click on the up and down arrows on the right side of the Query Wizard dialog box.

If you make a mistake and select something you don't want, just click on the column name in the right pane and click the < button to remove it from the query.

Tip #297 from

To copy all the columns in a table at once, highlight the table name itself and click the > button.

If you aren't sure exactly what information is in a particular table column, highlight the column and click the Preview Now button to display a few rows from the column in the Preview of Data in Selected Column box.

You're free to select columns from more than one table, but remember that Excel must be able to find a relationship between the two tables for this kind of database query to work. If Excel can't do that, you'll get the warning shown in Figure 26.33.

PART
VIII
CH
26

Figure 26.33.
You'll get this warning if Excel can't figure out how to join information from more than one table into a single query. If you really meant to create this query, you must create the join yourself.

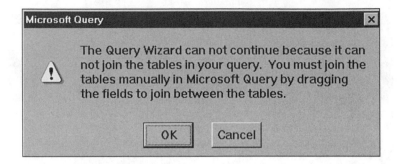

Microsoft Query

The Query Wizard can not continue because it can not join the tables in your query. You must join the tables manually in Microsoft Query by dragging the fields to join between the tables.

OK   Cancel

Note

Queries that involve more than one table use database links called *joins*. Normally joins are created automatically by Excel. If Microsoft Query can't find shared information required to create a join, double-check the query to be sure that it uses columns only from related tables and that these columns contain the same data (a customer ID field in both a customer list table and customer order list table, for example). If a relationship genuinely exists between the two (or more) tables you're using, and Microsoft Query can't detect it, you'll need to manually create the join yourself. See the later section "Creating Joins."

When you're finished selecting the columns you want, click <u>N</u>ext to continue to the next step in the Query Wizard.

SELECTING THE RIGHT INFORMATION: FILTERING DATA

The next step in the Query Wizard is the Filter Data dialog box. Here you can limit how many rows of data you'll retrieve in the final query. It's easy to pull down 10,000 rows of data from a server database unexpectedly; this is where you fix the problem.

The Query Wizard provides a wide range of conditions you can add to restrict the query. To add a rule that limits how much data is returned (*filtering* the data), click one of the columns in the query, select a condition (or, in database terminology, a *constraint*) from the first box, and select or type a data value in the second box. Microsoft Query looks up all the possible values for that field, so you don't have to type a value if you don't want to. The filtering process here should be familiar if you have *filtered (page 542)* Excel database lists.

You can have from zero to three conditions on the query, and they can be combined by AND (in which case, all constraints apply simultaneously) or by OR (in which case, each acts independently of the others). Figure 26.34 shows an example, in which records will be filtered to include only those where Region is either California or Washington.

When you're finished adding conditions, choose <u>N</u>ext.

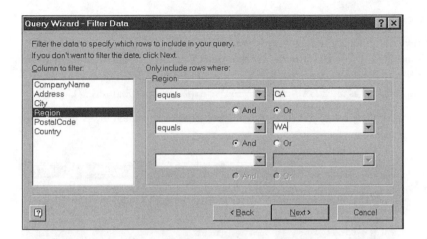

Figure 26.34.
You can limit the number of records you retrieve by adding conditions to the query.

SORTING THE DATA

The last step is quick. You can choose to sort the rows returned by up to six columns, each of which can be sorted in ascending or descending order. You can sort the data later in Excel, if you prefer, but it saves time to do it now (it might also be faster, because the database server instead of your PC will do the sorting). The sort order is saved as part of the query; each time you use the query, your preferred sort will be applied.

To add a sort, select the column(s) you want to sort and then choose Ascending or Descending (see Figure 26.35). When you've got that step out of the way, choose Next.

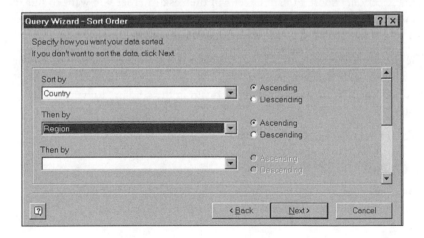

Figure 26.35.
Sorting data from a database query is just like sorting a list in Excel. Click the fields you want to sort; then choose Ascending or Descending.

THE LAST STEP: SAVING THE QUERY FOR REUSE

The query is now complete, and Excel wraps everything up by presenting three final options (see Figure 26.36). You can just return the query's data to Excel (the default option), or send the query to Microsoft Query for further fine-tuning (which I'll discuss shortly). You also can save the data as an OLAP cube (OLAP is explained in Chapter 27).

It's a good idea to save your query at this point. I cover how to run it again, as well as edit it, in the following sections.

Figure 26.36.
After all the work of creating a finished database query, don't forget to save it. You'll then be able to run the saved query from another worksheet.

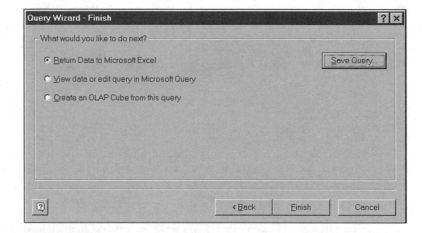

After making your selection, choose Finish. Excel will then ask whether you want to put the returned data in the current worksheet (and if so, starting in what cell), in a new worksheet, or directly into a PivotTable (you can create a PivotTable later, if you prefer).

If you choose the Properties button, you'll be able to set various advanced settings on your query, including whether your database password should be saved with the query and how often it should be refreshed. We'll visit this window again in the section "Refreshing Data," later in this chapter.

Make your choice, choose OK, and you'll see the data appear like magic!

USING MICROSOFT QUERY

As you might expect, the Query Wizard doesn't have the flexibility to deal with special situations, or ones where you want to have complete control. For that, you need to use Microsoft Query.

Microsoft Query is a full-fledged database query tool included with Excel that lets you take advantage of all that your database has to offer. It also lets you use SQL (Structured Query Language) to write queries, if you know how to do that. You don't have to use any SQL if you don't want to, though—Microsoft Query has graphical tools that will write SQL for you behind the scenes.

Note

Structured Query Language (SQL, usually pronounced *sequel*) is a specialized computer language developed just for writing database queries. It's based on mathematical set theory and is an extremely powerful way to specify which records you want and which you don't. As you might expect, many books are available on SQL, and database administrators are expected to live and breathe the stuff.

At the same time, basic SQL isn't hard at all to understand, and you'll get an immediate feel for it by seeing how Microsoft Query writes your SQL query for you.

If you need a more detailed view of SQL, see Que's *Special Edition Using Microsoft SQL Server 7.0*, ISBN #0-7897-1523-6.

SQL You can see (and change) the SQL commands Microsoft Query writes for you by clicking the View SQL button in Microsoft Query.

WHEN TO USE MICROSOFT QUERY

Microsoft Query is a much more powerful interface into a database than the Query Wizard, for the following reasons:

- Although you can retrieve columns from different tables by using the Query Wizard, the process is easier to understand in Microsoft Query because you can see table relationships graphically and preview the data.

- You can add more criteria (and more complex criteria) using Microsoft Query to restrict which rows are returned to Excel.

- With Microsoft Query, you can perform calculations on the query, such as counting or summing the records returned, or retrieving only the largest or smallest values in a column.

- Finally, you can write database queries directly in SQL with Microsoft Query.

The following list describes the circumstances in which you should use Microsoft Query instead of the Query Wizard:

- You want to work with multiple tables.
- You need to create your own joins (table relationships).
- You need to add complex criteria to filter returning records.
- You need to see calculations such as counts or sums.
- You want to write your own database query using SQL.

STARTING MICROSOFT QUERY

You start Microsoft Query the same way you start the Query Wizard: Choose <u>D</u>ata, Get External <u>D</u>ata, <u>N</u>ew Database Query. Select a data source from the Choose Data Source dialog box (if you want, go back to a database you used before), or create a new query.

Before choosing OK, be sure to deselect the option Use the Query Wizard to Create/Edit Queries. Deselecting this option tells Excel that you want to use Microsoft Query, not the Query Wizard (see Figure 26.37). Then choose OK, and Microsoft Query will start.

> **Note**
>
> Microsoft Query does the work, regardless of how the option Use the Query Wizard to Create/Edit Queries is set. Deselecting this option simply gives you full access to the interface/tools of Microsoft Query. Even if you forget to deselect this option, you can still invoke Microsoft Query by clicking Cancel anywhere in the wizard.

Figure 26.37.
Select the data source you want to use, or click <New Data Source> at the top of the list.

Deselect this option to tell Excel you want to start Microsoft Query.

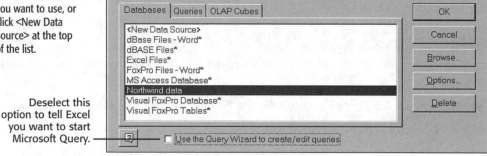

CHOOSING WHICH DATABASE TABLES TO USE

If you didn't select a default table when defining the data source, the first thing you're asked when Microsoft Query starts is which tables you want to use in the query.

Notice that while the Query Wizard jumps immediately to selecting columns within a table, Microsoft Query is designed to work with multiple tables from the beginning. It's part of the difference between the Query Wizard and Microsoft Query—Microsoft Query assumes that you want the bigger picture and will be ranging more widely over the database than possible with the Query Wizard.

To select the additional table(s) you want to access, click on the Add Table(s) button in the middle of the toolbar (the one with the plus sign). The Add Tables dialog box appears. Select the first table you want from the Table list in the dialog box and click the Add button, or just double-click the desired table. Microsoft Query displays a small window in its query pane, listing the name of the table you've just selected, along with the columns in that table (see Figure 26.38).

Tip #298 from

> This table list can be quite long on a large database system. If you know the table name you want, you can jump right to it by starting to type its name.

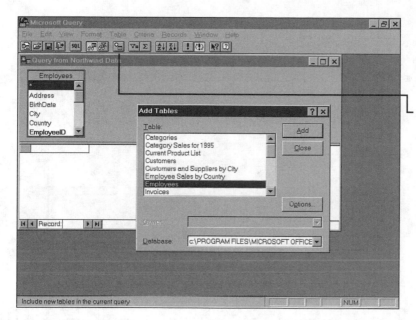

Figure 26.38.
Select the tables you want to use in the Add Tables dialog box.

The Add Table(s) button

Notice that the Add Tables dialog box remains open after you've added the first table. You can close the dialog box, but you can also select more tables to include in the query—and you'll probably want to. Why? Remember that proper database design says that each table should have only one kind of information in it. An Employees table should only have information about the employee that normally doesn't change or accumulate over time. So if you want to just get a list of employee names and addresses, the base Employees table should have that information.

However, if you want to find out which of your customers are handled by which employees, you'll need information from both the Customers and Employees tables. If you're in this kind of situation, select each table you need to include in the query and click Add.

If you accidentally add the wrong table, click the table and press Delete.

Choose Close when you're finished adding tables.

> **Caution**
>
> Although you can do so, I advise against clicking the Options button and making selections in the Table Options dialog box unless you know what you're doing. The default settings in Table Options really shouldn't be changed. It's easy to get really confused by turning System Tables on, for example—there are hundreds of them in server databases.

CREATING JOINS

To combine information from several tables, you need to connect the tables together using relationships called *joins*. (If you just need to access information from one table, you can go straight to the next section, because you won't need any joins.)

Notice in Figure 26.39 how Microsoft Query has connected the tables together using a line between tables? The lines represent joins.

Figure 26.39.
The lines between columns in each table are called *joins* and are needed to retrieve information from more than one table. Create them by dragging a column name from one table and dropping it onto the same column in another table.

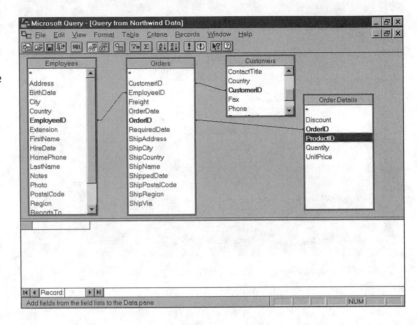

Microsoft Query automatically creates joins between two tables when it notices that one table has a column with the same name as a special index column in another table called a *primary key*. (Microsoft Query marks primary keys in bold.) This is a guess on its part, but it is a pretty safe guess and will be right most of the time.

If Microsoft Query can't find joins between your tables, you'll have to add them yourself. Select a column in one table and drag-and-drop that column name onto the matching column name in another table (in the database world, this column is called a *foreign key*). You'll see a join line appear.

Column names need not have the same names to participate in a join; they just have to contain the same data. It's good database design to give columns containing the same information the same name, because identical names are a good tip-off that the two columns can be joined together. It's not a sure thing, though; your database administrator might have decided to break the same-name rule for some reason.

Tip #299 from

Timothy

Microsoft Query will warn you if you try to join two columns with different data types. This is a sure sign that you shouldn't be joining those two columns together!

You don't need to create more than one join between tables—one is enough. If you accidentally create a join you don't want, double-click the join line to display the Joins dialog box. Correct the join as needed, or select it in the Joins in Query list and click the Remove button.

Tip #300 from

Timothy

If you're having a hard time finding the right columns in a big table, you can make the table windows bigger (I always find they start out too small) and drag the table windows around into more convenient places.

SELECTING WHICH TABLE COLUMNS TO USE

Now that you've selected the right tables (and created relationships between them if you're accessing more than one table), you need to select which actual columns you want to return to Excel.

All you need to do is drag-and-drop the column names you want into the lower half of the Microsoft Query window (see Figure 26.40). You also can select column names by double-clicking them.

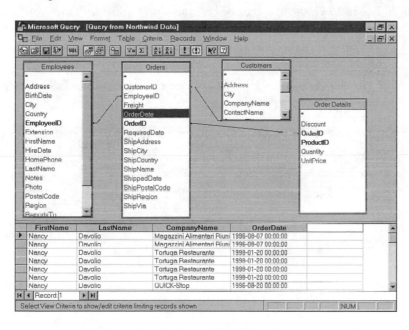

Figure 26.40.
Mark the columns you want to retrieve by double-clicking their names. The first few rows of actual data will show up in the lower half of the Microsoft Query window.

PART

VIII

CH

26

If you want to remove a column from your query, move the mouse pointer over its column name. In the data pane, the pointer will turn into a down arrow if you're in the right area. Click to select the column and then press the Delete key. Be careful not to try to get rid of a column in your query by highlighting its name in the table pane and pressing Delete! You'll actually delete the whole table from the query, which will really set you back.

What we're getting in this example is a list of employees, the customers they handled, and the dates those customers placed their orders.

The column order in Microsoft Query is the same column order that will appear in Excel. You can drag and drop added fields to rearrange the column order. Click the field name to select it; then drag the field name and drop it in the desired position.

If you scroll to the bottom of the list of data and click on the last record, you'll see how many rows will be returned to Excel.

Tip #301 from

Timothy

You can click anywhere in the sample data and press Ctrl+End to jump to the last record.

LIMITING WHICH INFORMATION IS RETURNED

You can restrict the records returned to Excel by adding *criteria* (various restrictions) to the query. Click on the Show/Hide Criteria button (with the eyeglasses and a funnel) to show the criteria grid window.

You add criteria by selecting which field you want to limit in the Criteria Field drop-down list and then adding a value to which you want to limit that field in the Value box under the Criteria Field. In Figure 26.41, the data returned is limited to records with the value Callahan in the LastName field.

Tip #302 from

Timothy

If the Criteria Field drop-down list contains too many field names to scroll through comfortably, drag the desired field from the table above and drop it into the Criteria Field box.

Figure 26.41.
Specify filter criteria to indicate which records you want returned to Microsoft Excel.

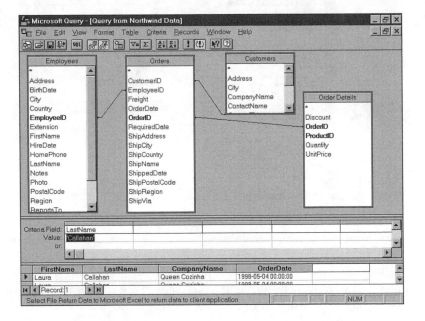

Now you can just type a value or double-click the Value box to display the Edit Criteria dialog box, which presents a long range of conditions you can add, including some very handy conditions such as `"begins with"`, `"contains"`, and `"is between"` (see Figure 26.42). The

Values option enables you to pick one of the values from the field without having to type it (which could lead to spelling errors).

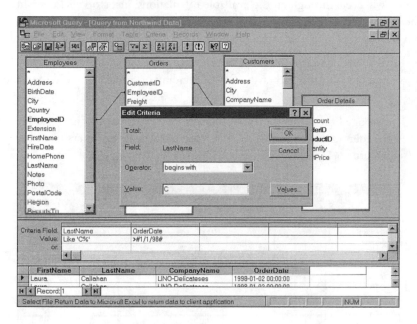

Figure 26.42.
Double-click the Value edit box to display this handy Edit Criteria dialog box, which simplifies handling complex criteria.

Don't worry about the strange characters—the percent and pound (#) signs—that Microsoft Query might put in the Value box when you use the Edit Criteria dialog box; it's all valid SQL syntax and needed by the database.

Tip #303 from

Timothy

If you specify criteria including a phrase surrounded by brackets ([ ]), Excel will ask you to fill in that value when the query is run. For example, if you want to use the same query to get data for different cities, type [What city do you want to use?] in the criteria Value box with the city field in the Criteria Field box. You'll immediately be asked to answer the question (you can type any value or just choose OK at the Enter Parameter Value box for now).

When you return to Excel (and every time you refresh the query later), a box will pop up asking you for a new city name to use as a filter in place of this parameter. This is called a *parameterized query*.

ADDING COUNTS AND TOTALS

Suppose you don't want to see just the raw data, but some "big picture" information, such as the total number of orders per customer, or which salesperson sold more dollars worth of product. Microsoft Query can automatically perform five kinds of calculations on your data: sums, averages, counts, minimums, and maximums.

To add these calculations, click in the data column to which you want to add a calculation, and then click the Cycle Through Totals button—the one with the Greek Sigma (Σ). Microsoft Query will cycle through all the available calculations; just stop clicking when you get to the one you want. You can add a specific field more than once and use a different calculation on each one.

 You also can sort the data before returning it, by clicking anywhere in the column of data you want to sort and then clicking either the Sort Ascending or Sort Descending button in the toolbar.

For example, I've changed the OrderID column in this example to be Count of OrderID and then sorted the column in descending order to find out which customers placed the most orders (see Figure 26.43).

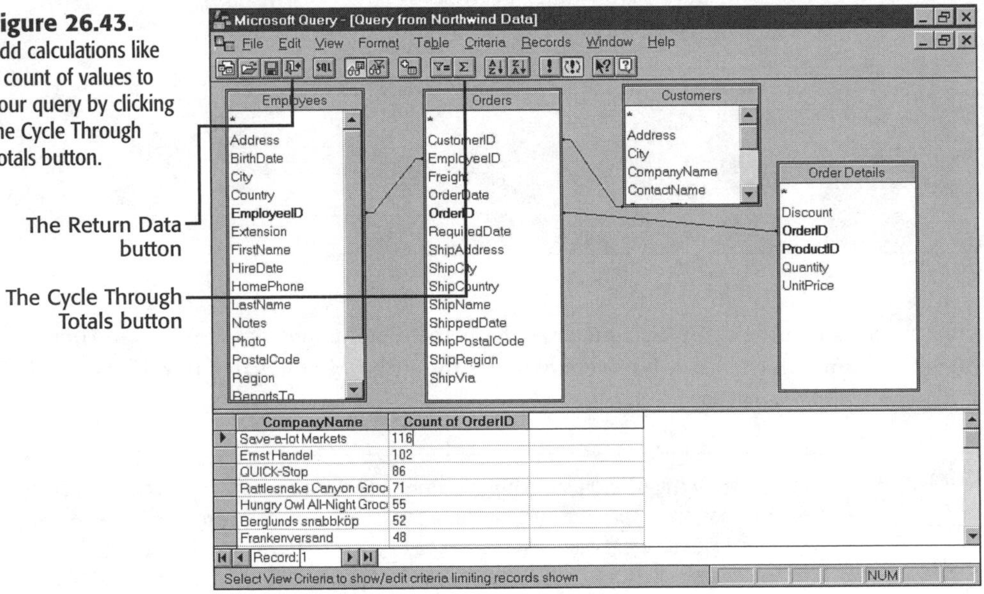

Figure 26.43.
Add calculations like a count of values to your query by clicking the Cycle Through Totals button.

The Return Data button

The Cycle Through Totals button

 When you've got the final query you want, click the Return Data button (the one with the door) to close Microsoft Query and send the data to Excel. Specify where you want to place the data, and once you've clicked OK again, you're done!

MANAGING DATABASE DATA IN EXCEL

Creating a database query is most of the work when accessing database data from Excel, but there are still some tricks to learn that will really make Excel hum.

The following sections cover how to set advanced query properties to make sure your query is always showing the latest data. You'll also learn how to rerun and modify existing queries so you don't have to create a new query from scratch each time you want to see what's changed in the database.

REFRESHING DATA

Now you're looking at the product of your hard work: an Excel worksheet filled with up-to-the-minute data from your corporate database. But what if you come back to the file tomorrow or next week? How will you know if the data is still current? If you queried historical data, there's little reason to think it will change in the database. But if you're looking at operational data—for example, orders this week—the data will be changing hour by hour.

There isn't any way to know if the data in your Excel worksheet matches what's currently in the database, but it's easy to refresh the worksheet so that it has the most recent data. Just choose Data, Refresh Data; right-click anywhere in the returned data set and choose Refresh Data; or click anywhere in the data and click the Refresh Data button on the External Data toolbar.

You can also configure Excel to update a query for you automatically. Choose Data, Get External Data, Data Range Properties while the cursor is in the query data (that's important—the option won't be activated otherwise). The Data Range Properties button on the External Data toolbar runs the same command. You'll see the dialog box shown in Figure 26.44 (External Data Range Properties). You can configure the Refresh Control settings to tell Excel to refresh the query every so many minutes, refresh it each time you open the Excel file, or both.

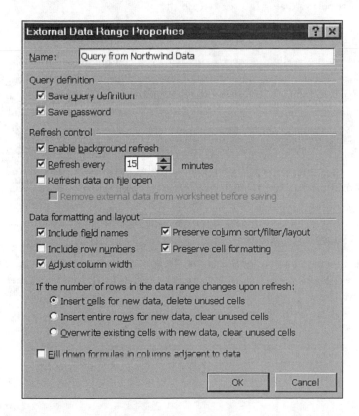

Figure 26.44.
You can configure Excel to automatically refresh the query for you.

RERUNNING AND MODIFYING QUERIES

After working with Excel's query tools for a while, you'll build up a sizable collection of saved queries. You can easily run any of these again from another workbook by choosing Data, Get External Data, Run Saved Query and then selecting the saved query from the file list that appears.

And what if you've gone through all this work and then discovered that there was really one more column you should have included in the query? No problem. You just need to edit the query to make the change.

 Choose Data, Get External Data, Edit Query while the cursor is in the query data set (or click the Edit Query button on the External Data toolbar) and Excel will launch the tool you used to create the query (either the Query Wizard or Microsoft Query) with the query definition ready to be edited.

You can edit a saved query by choosing Data, Get External Data, New Database Query, and then choosing the Queries tab of the Choose Data Source window. You'll see your saved queries listed. Click the one you want to edit and then choose Open, and it will be opened up for editing.

You also can right-click any query data cell and choose to edit the query, bring up the External Data Range Properties dialog box, or refresh the data.

THE TEMPLATE WIZARD: USING EXCEL IN A CLIENT/SERVER WORLD

The Excel Template Wizard is really the reverse of what I've been talking about so far in this chapter. Rather than helping you bring external database data into Excel, the Template Wizard lets you use Excel to input data into an external database. What this does is turn Excel into a front end for the database—rather than using a Visual Basic or PowerBuilder application as a database client application, you use Excel.

You do lose a lot by doing this—the Template Wizard only updates the database when you save the file you're working with, and each worksheet contains only one record, so you end up with many small worksheets all over your hard drive, each containing one data record. You can use the same workbook to enter multiple records, however. When entering subsequent records using the same "form" cells, saving the workbook adds a Create New Record option to the Save to Database dialog box.

In addition, it's very cumbersome to edit information already in the database. You have to find the workbook that contains the record you want to edit, change the data, and then save it again. When you save the workbook, you'll be asked whether you want to update the related record in the database or insert the changed data as a new record. If you want to have separate Excel files for each database record as extra documentation, this is a good option, but otherwise, it's better to use Access or some other option.

Caution

Obviously, I don't recommend using the Template Wizard, but the following paragraphs provide some details just in case you decide to try it anyway.

Should this be the route you want to take, begin the process by designing an input form for your data. You can make the form anything you want, so long as some blank cells are ready to use later for data entry. See Figure 26.45 for an example.

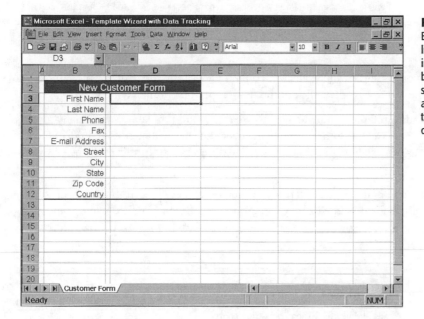

Figure 26.45.
Excel can use a form like this to enter data into an Access database behind the scenes. The label cells are in column B and the data cells are in column D.

Tip #304 from

Timothy

It will save you some time later if you put labels for each cell somewhere left of the cell where users will later enter data. The labels don't have to be next to the data entry cells—you can put in a spacer column if you want.

Now choose <u>D</u>ata, Te<u>m</u>plate Wizard to start the process of connecting the worksheet to an Access database.

Note

If you don't see the option in the <u>D</u>ata menu, you need to activate the Data Template add-in. Choose <u>T</u>ools, Add-<u>I</u>ns and make sure the box next to Template Wizard with Data Tracking is checked.

If the add-in isn't installed on your system, you'll get a message saying "Microsoft Excel can't run this add-in. This feature is not currently installed. Would you like to install it now?" Choose <u>Y</u>es and the add-in will be installed and activated. You'll need the Office 2000 CD, of course.

You'll now see the Template Wizard itself. Step 1 just asks you to confirm the name of the template. Choose Next to keep going.

Step 2 asks what kind of database you want to use to store information entered into the form. You can put it into another Excel workbook if you want, or into an Access or dBASE database. I'll use an Access database for this example.

Note

If you're placing the data in a new file, type a new filename and path in this step. If you're adding records to an existing data source, you need to type it out or use the Browse button to select it.

Step 3 asks you to select which cells will contain data. Type the name of the table or worksheet into the Table box, then click in the first empty box in the Cell column.

You now need to tell the Template Wizard where to find the data it's eventually going to store in the database. Click the empty worksheet cell that will later contain data (moving the Template Wizard dialog box out of the way if necessary). In this case, the cell we want is D3.

Click in the Field Name box. If Excel can find a text label in a cell to the left of the data cell, it fills in the Field Name cell for you. You also can type the field name yourself, or edit what Excel has typed for you. Continue the process with the rest of the data-entry cells in the worksheet.

Note

You can't type a field name in the Field Name column of the Template Wizard dialog box unless you're storing the records in a new database source. The field names are automatically added when using an existing source.

When you're finished, you should have something that looks like Figure 26.46. Click Next to continue.

In Step 4, the wizard asks whether you already have existing worksheets formatted like this one that contain data to be placed into the database. If you do, you'll be asked to select the worksheets containing the data.

Step 5 is just a summary page, so click Finish to wrap up the process. You can now distribute the generated template to a group of users if you want.

To use the template, choose File, New and then select the template you just created. You might see a warning that the template contains macros. This is normal, and it's safe to select Enable Macros to continue. Fill in data into the blank cells in the worksheet and then save the file as normal. You'll be asked as part of the save process whether you want to insert the data into the database as a new record.

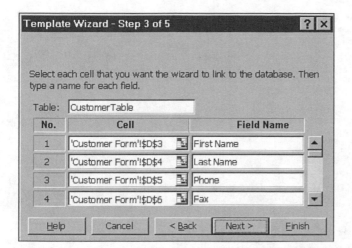

Figure 26.46.
This step in the Template Wizard associates particular worksheet cells with columns in a database. Identify the Excel data cells by address in the Cell column, and place the associated database field name in the Field Name column.

RETRIEVING DATA FROM TEXT FILES OR THE WEB

In addition to database server access, Excel also can access data stored on a Web page somewhere or in plain text files. You probably won't do this as often as you access data on a corporate database, but these are handy options for special circumstances.

ACCESSING DATA ON THE WEB

In keeping with Office 2000's major focus on Web integration, Excel now includes a new feature, *Web Query*, that will go to a particular Web page, read its contents, and then dump the information back into Excel.

If you have certain Web pages you check frequently to get information such as current exchange rates or stock prices, this is the perfect way to get that information into a place where you can actually do something with it—Excel!

Create a new Web query by choosing Data, Get External Data, New Web Query (see Figure 26.47).

Now you need to enter the Web address (URL) of the page you want to scan. You can just type it if you know it or browse for it using your Web browser. This is a much better option; choose Browse Web to launch your browser.

What we'll do with Web Query for this example is retrieve Microsoft's current stock price from the NASDAQ (National Association of Securities Dealers Automated Quotation System) Web site at www.nasdaq.com (see Figure 26.48). The procedure is the same for any Web site, though.

Figure 26.47.
You can choose to retrieve all of a Web page's contents, all the tables, or just a particular table.

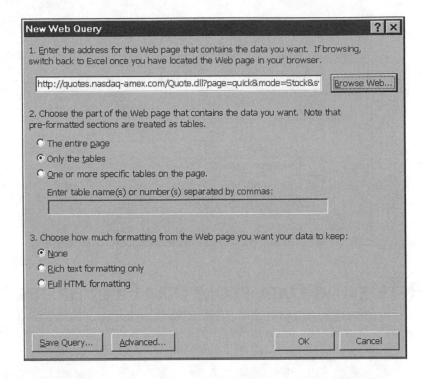

Figure 26.48.
Excel can retrieve information from any Web site, making the wealth of financial information available on the Web easily accessible to Excel.

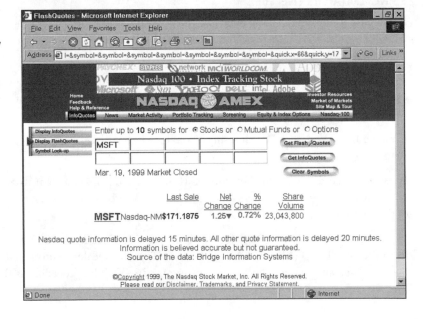

Using your browser, go to the page that actually has the data you want. You might have to fill in some Web forms first to specify the kind of information you want (the process will vary from site to site).

After you've got the magic page, switch back to Excel. The Web page's address appears in the address box of the Edit Web Query dialog box.

Note

The address won't appear in the Web Query dialog box if you launched the browser yourself (as opposed to using the Browse Web button in the New Web Query dialog box). Also, if you switch to Excel before accessing the page, then go back and complete the data search in the browser window, Excel won't display the completed address in the New Web Query dialog box.

Now choose whether you want Excel to retrieve all the information on that page (which will leave you with a lot of text to clean up), just the tables from the page, or one particular table. You can identify the table by name (if it's named in the HTML source for that page—not many are) or by number.

You also can choose to import the data as formatted or unformatted text. Choose OK when you're ready to start the import.

You can refresh the data by right-clicking anywhere in it and choosing Refresh Data or by using the Refresh Data button on the External Data toolbar. You also can use the same automatic refresh settings available to database data by right-clicking in the Web data and choosing Data Range Properties, or clicking the Data Range Properties button on the External Data toolbar. You'll be able to configure the Web query to automatically refresh itself every so many minutes or when you open the worksheet. That way you can be sure the information is always current.

IMPORTING DATA FROM TEXT FILES

If you regularly analyze data from other sources in Excel, it's a sure bet you're going to eventually get a file sent to you in raw text format. Text files are the lowest common denominator for data files because they can be handled by just about any program on any platform. For example, mainframe data is often distributed in text file format.

If you do get a text file from someone, Excel has special tools to help you import successfully. If the file is in Excel's standard text format (comma-delimited format), you can open the file using the standard File, Open command without another thought. However, if it isn't, Excel will notice and you'll see the Text Import Wizard start up (see Figure 26.49).

Figure 26.49.
The Text Import Wizard helps you tell Excel how to interpret text data files. In this case, the file I'm importing is delimited using tab characters.

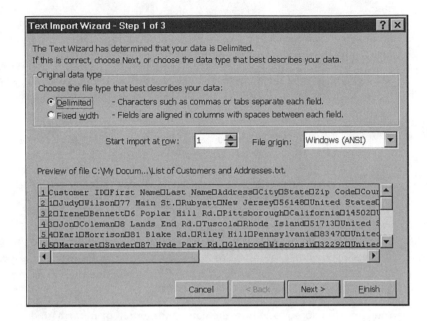

Step 1 of the wizard asks whether the text file is delimited or fixed width. *Delimited* means that data elements in the file are separated by some special character, usually a comma or tab. *Fixed-width files* don't use a separator, they just use spaces to guarantee that every field always starts at the same column number. For example, the first field always starts at column 1 and the second field always starts at column 16. The wizard shows you a preview of the file to help out and sets the default choice to its best guess.

Tip #305 from

Timothy

Here are some rules of thumb to tell the two types apart visually. If the fields in each row of the file are packed together without any space between them, the file is probably delimited. If the fields in the file appear to line up nicely in the preview, it's a fixed-width file. The file in Figure 26.49 is delimited with tabs.

Choose either Delimited or Fixed Width, and then click Next.

If you chose Delimited in step 1, the wizard now asks what character acts as the delimiter (separator) between fields. You can tell by looking in the Data Preview box. Tab characters look like little boxes in the Data Preview. If you see small boxes regularly appearing between fields in each row of text, it's a dead giveaway that the file is delimited with tabs.

Select the delimiter character (or type it into the Other box if Excel doesn't have the right option presented in a check box). You'll see the Data Preview box update itself immediately after you make your choice.

If the file now looks correctly separated into columns, choose Next to continue.

If you chose Fixed Width in step 1, the wizard asks you to confirm its guess as to where each column starts. Check the file over in the Data Preview. The Text Import Wizard might have gotten a column boundary wrong or missed a few (see Figure 26.50).

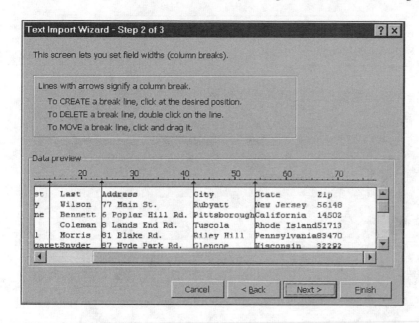

Figure 26.50.
Sometimes you have to help the Text Import Wizard. Here I'm importing a fixed-width text file, and the wizard missed the start of the Zip field.

You can add, delete, or move column boundaries by clicking and dragging in the Data Preview. When the column boundaries look correct, choose Next to continue.

Step 3 of the Text Import Wizard asks you to confirm the data type of each column, that is, which are numbers, which are dates, and so on. The wizard is really good at figuring this out for itself, so you usually can just choose Finish to complete the import.

PART
VIII
CH
26

Tip #306 from
Timothy

If you regularly import the same file, set up a database query definition for the text file. Choose Data, Get External Data, Import Text File, and then choose which file you want to import. The Text Import Wizard starts; import the file the same way you would using File, Open. The difference is after you're finished with the import (and anytime later); you can right-click anywhere in the data and choose Refresh Data, or click the Refresh Data button on the External Data toolbar, to redo the whole import with one click.

USING THE CONVERT TEXT TO COLUMNS WIZARD

The Convert Text to Columns Wizard enables you to use the power of the Text Import Wizard on data that's already in your worksheet. If you paste data by hand from a text file, for example, or retrieve long text fields from a database you'd really rather have broken up into separate columns, you can use the Convert Text to Columns Wizard.

Highlight the cells you want to break apart and choose Data, Text to Columns to start the wizard. The key thing to remember when starting the wizard is that you need to have high-lighted all the text cells you want to break apart into separate columns (see Figure 26.51).

Tip #307 from

Timothy

If you don't have any other data in that column, just highlight the whole column as a shortcut.

Figure 26.51.
Turn nonseparated text values like this into nicely separated columns using the Convert Text to Columns Wizard.

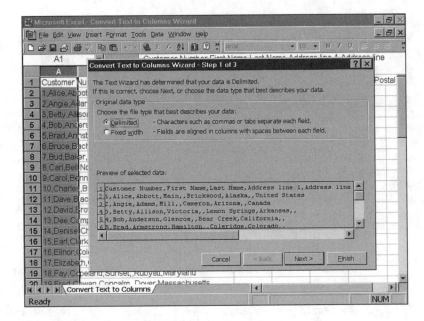

What you see now is basically the Text Import Wizard with a different name. The process is identical: Identify the data as delimited or fixed width and then continue through steps 2 and 3 of the wizard. When you click Finish, your data will be properly separated into columns.

TROUBLESHOOTING

COPYING VISIBLE CELLS ONLY

I copied a filtered Excel list to an Access table and got the entire list rather than the filtered version. How can I copy just the filtered records?

If you want just the filtered data, two methods are available:

- Copy the filtered data to a separate section of the worksheet, and then copy that new section to Access.

- Select and then paste only the visible cells. First create a blank Access table. Then go back to Excel and use Edit, Go To to open the Go To dialog box. Click the Special button, select Visible Cells Only in the Go To Special dialog box, and click OK. Then copy the selection and paste it into the blank Access table.

WHEN ACCESS CAN'T CREATE AN INDEX

I was using the Import Spreadsheet Wizard, and Access says that it can't create an index.

If you get this message, double-check that the data is actually unique in the column you specified for the primary key. Telling Access to build a unique index on a column that actually has a few sneaky duplicate values (which are probably data-entry errors) or extra blank rows is the most common problem when running this wizard.

ADJUSTING TEXT LABELS ON ACCESS REPORTS

When creating a report with the Report Wizard in Access, I found that some of the text labels in the report were initially sized too small and cut off words. If you have the same problem, switch to Design view by choosing View, Design View, and then resize the problem bounding boxes. To get back to the report, choose View, Layout Preview.

EXCEL IN PRACTICE

Excel's data-entry forms are plain and just not very functional. It's difficult to search for data and difficult to check that entered data is correct. By using Excel's Data, MS Access Form command, you can use Access instead of Excel for data entry. Figures 26.52 and 26.53 show data forms in Excel and Access for you to compare.

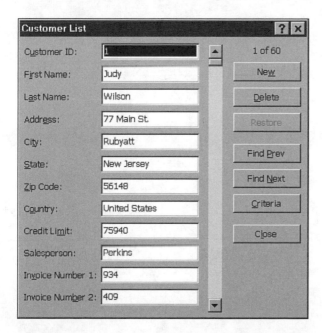

Figure 26.52.
This plain-Jane data form in Excel is functional, but that's it.

Figure 26.53.
With its graphics, formatting, and better organization, this Access form is much easier to read and use.

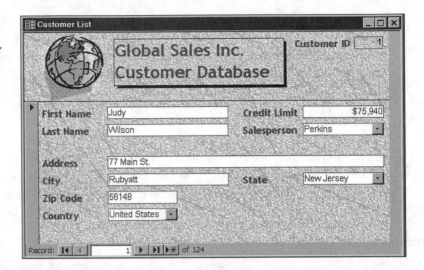

The Access form is a dressed-up version of the Excel data form, adding graphics and formatted text. I've also really made the form more useful by organizing it more logically and by converting some fields to drop-down lists. These fields can be restricted by Access so that users can enter only valid data. For example, with a bit of configuring, I set the State field to show only U.S. states when the Country field is set to United States.

CHAPTER 27

RETRIEVING DATA FROM OLAP SERVERS

by Timothy Dyck
timothy_dyck@dyck.org

WHAT IS OLAP?

Excel 2000 introduces big changes for financial analysts and planners. Excel now has the capability to do *On-Line Analytical Processing* (*OLAP*) analysis, a technique for analyzing very large amounts of information.

For years, OLAP (pronounced OH-lap) has been a specialized analysis technique accessible to only the largest corporations able to spend hundreds of thousands of dollars on it. Now, with OLAP supported directly by Excel, it's accessible to everyone.

Using OLAP techniques, you can analyze much larger sets of information than ever before. OLAP is especially good at helping you see long-term trends, forecasting, and revealing hidden relationships in your data that you wouldn't have found any other way.

Excel can help you perform OLAP-type analysis using a corporate OLAP server (the most common approach), or it can do OLAP analysis itself. The next section explains what OLAP is, and later sections cover how to do either type of analysis.

SERVER VERSUS CLIENT OLAP

OLAP sounds difficult because of its not-very-informative acronym, but if you think about how *PivotTables (page 639)* summarize large sets of information, you've basically got the concept. OLAP is a way of doing "power" PivotTables—PivotTables that summarize an entire year's financial transactions, for example, or maybe even many years of data across multiple business units over several countries. These are PivotTables like you've never seen before, summarizing millions of data points at once with lightning speed! These are PivotTables with huge rippling muscles, and they know how to use them.

OLAP gives you the big, BIG picture. It's an essential tool for doing trend analysis, forecasting, setting manufacturing baselines, performing competitive analyses, and developing executive information systems. The key difference between normal Excel PivotTables (which are still fully supported) and OLAP PivotTables is that OLAP PivotTables normally work with an OLAP server (or get their data from OLAP data you've stored on your PC). After all, it's incredibly difficult to count millions of data points to get the kind of bird's-eye view that OLAP lets you have. There's no way Excel or your PC could handle the task.

What's done to handle this problem is to use dedicated OLAP servers that crunch data for hours (sometimes days) in a back room somewhere so you can have it at your fingertips when you ask. Products such as Hyperion Software Corp.'s Essbase and Oracle Corp.'s Express are leaders in this field, but Microsoft is making a huge effort to get into it, and Excel is the client part of that effort.

The other half—the server half—is handled by the latest release of Microsoft's server database, Microsoft SQL Server 7.0. SQL Server 7.0 includes a new component called *OLAP Services*, which, as its name suggests, is an OLAP server. Excel is able to access any OLAP Server that's accessible through (unsurprisingly) Microsoft's new OLAP access standard, called *OLE DB for OLAP*. At the moment, SQL Server 7.0 is the only product that supports this standard, so it's the only server you can use with Excel. That will probably change as time passes, particularly as millions of users gain the capability to access OLAP servers for the first time from the desktop.

> An OLAP database has a special name: It's called an *OLAP cube*. The name comes from how OLAP servers calculate their data—they assemble all the data columns (*dimensions*) they're summarizing into a multidimensional grid structure, and then calculate every possible total at each intersection point on the grid. It makes for millions and millions of calculations.

Excel can also do limited OLAP analysis by itself. Its new OLAP Cube Wizard can do the same job an OLAP server does, except on much, much smaller sets of data. Its main use, though, is to pull down subsets of data from an OLAP server so that you can use OLAP PivotTables while on the road or otherwise unable to connect to an OLAP server.

OLAP PivotTables Versus Normal PivotTables

OLAP PivotTables (or PivotCharts, which work the same way) behave very similarly to normal PivotTables, but with a few important differences.

OLAP PivotTables receive their data from a server (or from a subset of OLAP data stored on your system); they don't calculate their totals dynamically as normal PivotTables do. This means that OLAP PivotTables don't have to do any calculation at all to get their data—they just retrieve it. That's why OLAP PivotTables are so fast.

However, it also means that you can't do such things as change the type of measurement data displayed from, say, dollar sales totals (a sum) to a count of the number of sales completed (a count) the way you can with a normal PivotTable. What data is returned to you has been decided up front by your database administrator and can be changed only at the OLAP server.

The second major difference is that OLAP PivotTables organize their data hierarchically, while normal PivotTables display all their dimensions (the column headings of an Excel list or database query) on the same level. You can stack dimensions in a normal PivotTable yourself to see a hierarchy, but it's a manual process, and you have to view every detail item in that dimension at once instead of just the specific detail items you wanted to see.

Hierarchical groupings are essential when looking at really large amounts of data and enable you to see just the level of detail you need. You'll immediately see what hierarchical grouping looks like the first time you use an OLAP PivotTable. It means that country figures include region figures, which include state figures, which include city figures. It also means that date data is automatically grouped upward, into weeks, months, quarters, and years (or whatever your database administrator has selected). Excel can group date data by month or quarter in a normal PivotTable, but changing the grouping is a hassle, and Excel won't arrange any other kinds of data (such as geographic data) into hierarchies.

The last major difference is that you can't see the actual source data rows that make up a particular total in an OLAP PivotTable. In a normal PivotTable, this is easy to do: Just double-click on any total, and you'll "drill" through the PivotTable to a new worksheet containing the actual database rows that made up that total. With an OLAP PivotTable, Excel doesn't know a thing about where the OLAP server got its data from, and so can't display that data when requested. When you double-click on a total in an OLAP PivotTable, you just get an Excel error message stating that it can't show details.

CREATING AN OLAP DATA SOURCE DEFINITION

Receiving data from an OLAP server works just like the way you get data from a regular database. Follow these steps:

1. Kick off the process by choosing Data, Get External Data, New Database Query to bring up the familiar Choose Data Source dialog box shown in Figure 27.1.

→ For more information on querying external databases, **see** "Choosing the Data Source," **p. 810**

Figure 27.1.
This is the same dialog box you use to create a query with the Query Wizard or Microsoft Query, as discussed in Chapter 26, "Using Excel with Access and Other Databases."

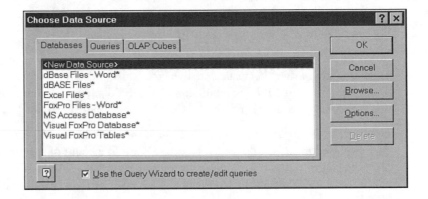

2. Now, instead of building a new *query (page 839)* or accessing a saved query, we're going to obtain data from an OLAP server. Click on the OLAP Cubes tab and then, with <New Data Source> highlighted, choose OK. The Create New Data Source dialog box opens (see Figure 27.2).

3. Type a name for the data source in the step 1 box.

4. Choose an OLAP provider (the type of OLAP server you want to access) in the step 2 box. At the moment, you have only one choice: Microsoft OLE DB Provider for OLAP Services.

5. Click the Connect button to log into the server.

6. Excel asks whether the data will be coming live from an OLAP Server or from a Cube File (a file containing OLAP data stored on your computer or network), as shown in Figure 27.3. Until you copy OLAP information down to your machine using the OLAP Cube Wizard, you must access server data, so choose the OLAP Server option.

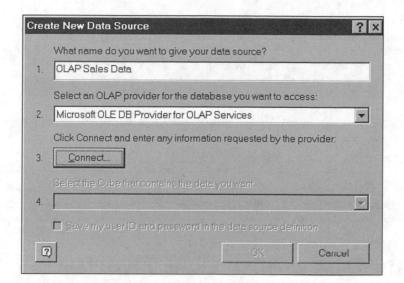

Figure 27.2.
Give your OLAP data source any name you want, and then select which kind of OLAP server you want to use.

7. In the Server box, type the name of the OLAP server you want to access, and then choose Next.

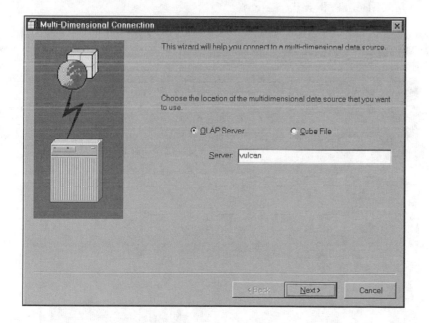

Figure 27.3.
The OLAP Server option accesses data on a remote server; the Cube File option accesses OLAP data stored on disk.

8. You'll now see a list of databases you can use. Select one and then choose Finish to return to the Create New Data Source dialog box, where you have one final task.

9. Select the OLAP cube you want to access from the drop-down list in the step 4 box.

Tip #308 from

Timothy

You can save your user ID and password in the data source definition by selecting the check box at the bottom of the Create New Data Source dialog box. Keep in mind that this action poses some security risks, as described in the section "Creating an ODBC Data Source Definition" in Chapter 26.

10. Click OK to finish creating the OLAP data source definition, and return to the Choose Data Source dialog box.

Tip #309 from

Timothy

To immediately use the new data definition, just select it and choose OK. You'll jump into step 3 of the PivotTable and PivotChart Wizard (described in the following section).

RETRIEVING THE DATA WITH AN OLAP PIVOTTABLE OR PIVOTCHART

To actually retrieve data from an OLAP server, you need to create a PivotTable or PivotChart (you can't use Excel's normal query tools, the Query Wizard and Microsoft Query, to access OLAP data). Follow these steps:

1. Choose <u>D</u>ata, <u>P</u>ivotTable and PivotChart Report to start the PivotTable and PivotChart Wizard (see Figure 27.4).

Figure 27.4.
OLAP data access starts with the PivotTable and PivotChart Wizard. OLAP server data is defined as an external data source.

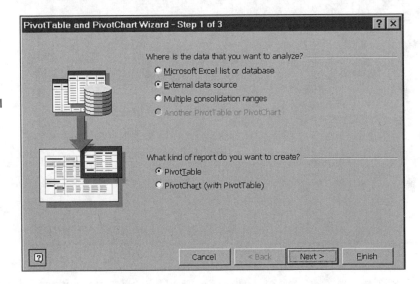

2. Choose <u>E</u>xternal Data Source.
3. Specify whether you want to create a PivotTable or a PivotChart. You can easily convert one to the other later if you want. Then choose <u>N</u>ext.

4. In step 2 of the wizard, you tell Excel where your external data is coming from (see Figure 27.5). Click the Get Data button to open the Choose Data Source dialog box.

Figure 27.5.
Click the Get Data button to specify the location of the external data for the report.

5. This dialog box should be familiar by now (refer to Figure 27.1). Click the OLAP Cubes tab, and select the OLAP data source you created previously.

6. Choose OK to return to the step 2 dialog box for the PivotTable and PivotChart Wizard, and then choose Next to advance to step 3.

7. Step 3 asks where you'd like to put the final PivotTable or PivotChart (see Figure 27.6). Choose to place it in your current worksheet or in a new one the wizard will create for you. Then choose Finish to wrap up the process.

Figure 27.6.
Choose whether you want your new OLAP PivotTable to go into its own worksheet or the one you're currently using. Click Finish to create the PivotTable.

What you'll see now is a blank PivotTable, waiting for you to fill in the table fields (dimensions) and table data (measures), as described in the next section.

USING OLAP PIVOTTABLES AND PIVOTCHARTS

An empty OLAP PivotTable is just potential waiting to be explored. On the floating PivotTable toolbar, you'll see all the fields you can use in the PivotTable. Some fields (the dimension fields) will work only as page, row, or column fields, and the other fields (the measure fields) work only as data fields. Excel won't let you drag a field to the wrong spot; you'll get a dialog box telling you that the field can't be placed in that location.

You can see which fields are which by hovering the mouse pointer over a field in the PivotTable toolbar and waiting for a *ScreenTip (page 383)* (see Figure 27.7). The fields on the toolbar are broken up into separate rows. The icons to the left of the first field name indicate to what area on the PivotTable the fields in that toolbar row can be dragged.

Figure 27.7.
ScreenTips help you know which OLAP fields can act as row and column headings, and which should be used only in the PivotTable data area.

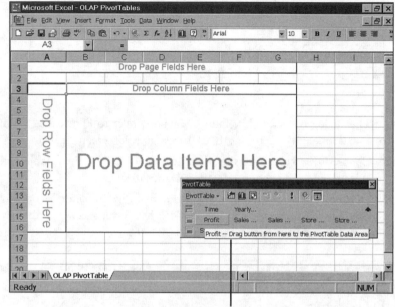

Pointing to the Profit field displays this ScreenTip.

Drag at least one dimension field to the PivotTable row area (marked Drop Row Fields Here) and at least one measure field to the data area (marked Drop Data Items Here). For this example, I'll use product family as the row heading, time of sale as the column heading, and number of unit sales as the data area item (see Figure 27.8). You'll see the PivotTable fill with data as soon as you define your dimension and measure fields.

Initially, you see the highest level of information the OLAP server has to offer, but you can drill down into the information. Double-click on either a row or column item—not the row or column heading, but an actual data item, such as a product name or year name—to see the next level of detail under that item. Figure 27.9 shows how the example looks when expanded along both product and time dimensions.

Tip #310 from

All items in a field can be expanded/collapsed at once by selecting the gray field button and clicking the Hide Detail or Show Detail button on the PivotTable toolbar.

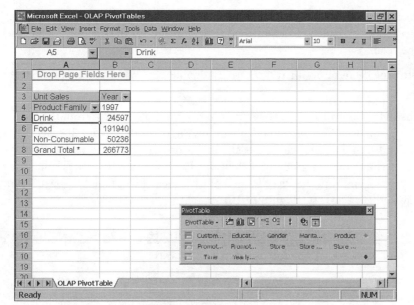

Figure 27.8.
Drag at least one row field or one column field and at least one data item into the PivotTable to see it take shape.

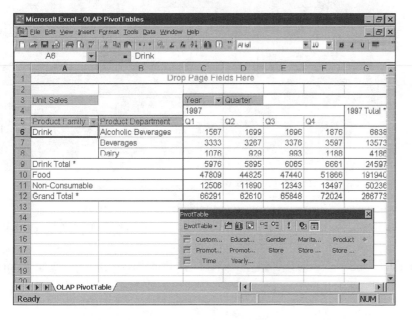

Figure 27.9.
OLAP PivotTables contain an enormous amount of detail hidden behind each row or column data item. Double-click each item to see what lies behind it.

PART

VIII

CH

27

You can keep drilling down until you reach the end of whatever hierarchy you're using. Excel displays a message saying, "Cannot show or hide detail for this section," when you hit the end of the road.

If you want to hide detail rather than show it, just double-click again on an open category item to collapse it.

To change the dimensions or measures you're using, you can drag them from the PivotTable back onto the PivotTable toolbar—or anywhere off the PivotTable, actually—to remove them, and then drag new choices back in. You also can use a special layout dialog box that enables you to make a group of dimension changes at once (which is called a *pivot* in OLAP terminology). From the PivotTable toolbar, choose PivotTable, Wizard, Layout to see the Layout dialog box (see Figure 27.10).

Figure 27.10.
You can make multiple changes to the layout of your OLAP PivotTable at once, using the PivotTable and PivotChart Wizard - Layout dialog box.

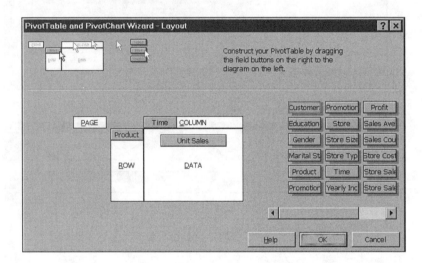

Right-clicking in the PivotTable displays a context menu with several useful options:

- Choose Format Report to format your PivotTable nicely for printing.
- Choose PivotChart to create a PivotChart from the PivotTable. A PivotChart is just a chart displaying the information currently in the PivotTable.
- Choose Table Options to display the PivotTable Options dialog box shown in Figure 27.11, in which you can make a number of settings changes, including turning totals on or off.

Use these options to turn totals on or off.

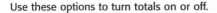

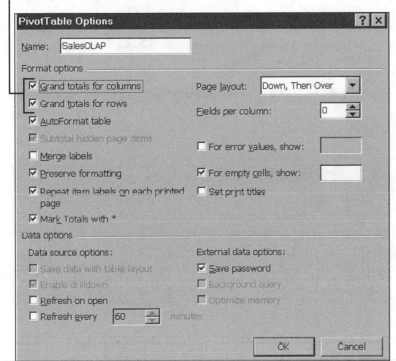

Figure 27.11.
Use the PivotTable Options dialog box to change the PivotTable settings.

PERFORMING OLAP ANALYSIS ON DATABASE DATA

You can use OLAP PivotTables and PivotCharts with data that doesn't come from an OLAP server (that is, data from a regular database such as Access or Oracle). You do this to get the organizational benefits an OLAP hierarchy gives you, or to handle larger data sets than an ordinary PivotTable can handle. If you're running out of memory, or if a regular PivotTable operates just too slowly because of all the calculations it's doing behind the scenes, this is the right option. For this technique, you use the OLAP Cube Wizard, which creates OLAP cubes (or databases) out of regular database data.

STARTING THE OLAP CUBE WIZARD

The procedure for the OLAP Cube Wizard is very similar to that for creating and running a normal database query. Choose Data, Get External Data, New Database Query, and create a new query or edit one that's already saved.

If you used the Query Wizard to create the query, the Query Wizard will start again. Step through it as described in Chapter 26 but stop at the last step. Here you're asked whether you'd like to return data to Microsoft Excel, view data, or edit the query in Microsoft Query or create an OLAP cube from the query (see Figure 27.12). Choose Create an OLAP Cube from This Query, and choose Finish to launch the OLAP Cube Wizard.

Figure 27.12.
You'll get much faster PivotTable performance by creating an OLAP cube from database data.

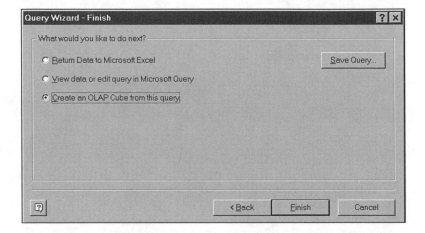

If you're using Microsoft Query, just choose File, Create OLAP Cube to start the OLAP Cube Wizard.

In either case, the wizard starts with a welcome message, which you can disable for future uses by selecting Don't Show This Screen Again, and then go on to selecting the data you want to use, as described in the following section.

SELECTING AND SUMMARIZING DATA

Step 1 of the OLAP Cube Wizard, shown in Figure 27.13, asks which fields in the query are data fields (measures). They should be the fields that actually contain the data you want to measure and must be numbers of some kind. You also decide here how you want to measure them (summing and counting are the most common choices). Choose Next to continue.

Tip #311 from
Timothy

> You can turn nonnumeric fields into numeric data by counting them. For example, counting OrderIDs creates a data field that will represent the number of different orders.

ORGANIZING DATA INTO HIERARCHIES

Step 2 of the wizard requires you to group the remaining fields into one or more hierarchies (dimensions), as shown in Figure 27.14. You should group fields logically according to the type of information they contain. For example, a set of fields that all describe the location of a store should be grouped into a dimension called *location*, and a set of fields describing various product data should be grouped into a product dimension.

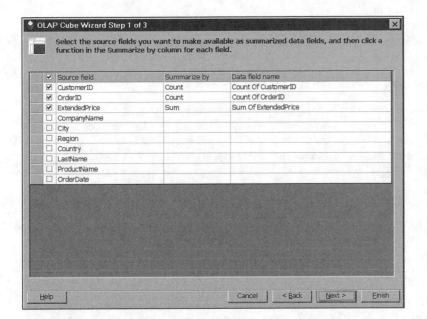

Figure 27.13.
Check off the fields you want summarized by the OLAP Cube Wizard. You also can choose how Excel will summarize this data by changing the contents of the Summarize By column.

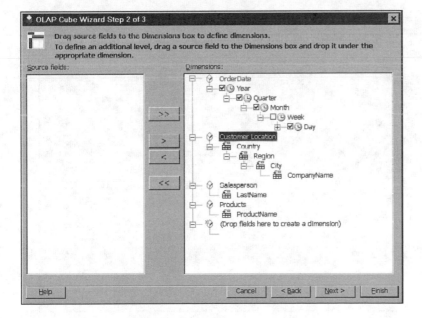

Figure 27.14.
Group all remaining source fields into dimensions by dragging and dropping. Note that date/time fields automatically expand into full-date dimensions.

Drag and drop each field from the Source Fields window into the Dimensions window. If you drop the field onto the (Drop fields here to create a dimension) item, it becomes a new dimension. If you drop it onto an existing dimension, it becomes part of that dimension. Keep going until you've placed all the source fields into a dimension.

You'll notice that date fields are turned automatically into fully realized date dimensions, complete with multiple levels of summarization. You can choose to summarize all the way from a year down to a second!

When you're finished creating dimensions, choose Next.

Tip #312 from *Timothy*	You can rename a dimension element by right-clicking its name and choosing Rename. Naming your dimensions with proper names makes using the cube a lot easier, particularly if you send the cube to someone else to use.

SAVING THE CUBE

Congratulations! You've done pretty much what a database administrator does when setting up an OLAP server database for the first time.

Step 3 of the wizard just asks how you'd like to save the cube (see Figure 27.15). You can choose to rebuild the cube each time you open a worksheet that references it, or you can build it once and then rebuild it as needed (which is important to do when the source database data is updated).

Figure 27.15.
When you've built your new cube database, save it with its data to your local system.

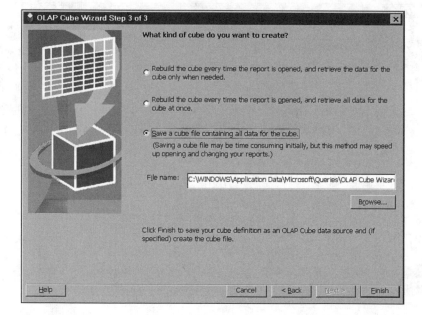

In most cases, you'll want to choose Save a Cube File Containing All Data for the Cube, because this maximizes the speed benefits of using an OLAP cube in the first place.

Type a name for the cube data file (it has a .cub extension), and then choose Finish. You'll then be asked to save the OLAP query definition (.oqy extension). Give it a name and choose Save. You'll need to use this query definition file when you want to use the cube.

Next, you'll see the OLAP Cube Wizard running the query and creating the cube. A status box appears, saying that Excel is creating an offline cube.

Tip #313 from	It's normal for this process to take a few minutes, particularly if you're summarizing a large query.
Timothy	

After the local cube has been created, Excel pops you into Step 3 of the PivotTable and PivotChart Wizard so you can immediately create an OLAP PivotTable based on your new cube (refer to Figure 27.6).

USING THE CUBE

If you chose not to create an OLAP PivotTable as part of the process of creating your local OLAP cube, or if you want to reuse the same cube in another PivotTable, you'll need to tell Excel to use the cube for OLAP data. If you think back to when you first created an OLAP PivotTable, you'll probably remember that the PivotTable and PivotChart Wizard gives you the option of using a local OLAP cube instead of an OLAP server.

To take advantage of this option, follow these steps:

1. Choose Data, PivotTable, and PivotChart Report to start the PivotTable and PivotChart Wizard.

2. In the Step 1 of 3 dialog box, choose External Data Source and click Next.

3. In the Step 2 of 3 dialog box, click the Get Data button.

4. When the Choose Data Source dialog box opens, click the OLAP Cubes tab. There you'll see listed the OLAP query definition you created when you built the cube in the OLAP Cube Wizard. Select it and choose OK. You'll then be back in the PivotTable and PivotChart Wizard, Step 3 of 3.

5. The rest of this should be old hat to you. Click Next; then decide where you want the OLAP PivotTable to go.

Tip #314 from	You can also send the cube file to someone else, who then can create an OLAP data source based on it. This is a handy way to get information to people who don't have access to your OLAP server.
Timothy	

TAKING OLAP SERVER DATA WITH YOU: USING OFFLINE OLAP CUBES

Just as you can turn regular database data into local OLAP cubes, you can copy bits of the big OLAP server cube down to your system. This isn't really any faster than querying directly against the server, but it's handy if you want to access OLAP server data without being connected to the network.

Here's how you do it:

1. Create an OLAP PivotTable or PivotChart as you normally would, using an OLAP server as your data source.

2. In the PivotTable toolbar, open the PivotTable drop-down menu and choose Client-Server Settings to open the Client-Server Settings dialog box. (You won't be able to choose this option if you don't have any data displayed in your PivotTable.)

3. Click the Create Local Data File button to display the Create Cube File Wizard. The first screen just tells you what an offline cube file is; choose Next to continue.

4. Step 2 of the wizard asks you to decide which dimensions you'd like to copy down to your PC, as well as how much detail in each dimension you want (see Figure 27.16). Check off the dimensions you'll need to work with on the road, and choose Next to continue.

Figure 27.16.
Because server OLAP files are huge, you need to be picky about what data you want to store on your local system. Just check off the parts of the server cube you really need.

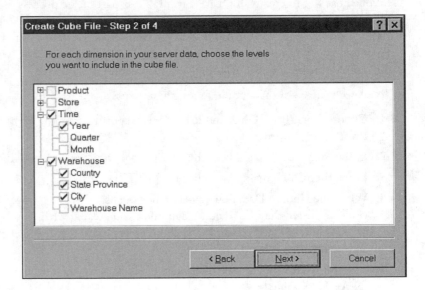

5. Step 3 of the wizard again narrows the data that will be brought down to the PC—remember how big server OLAP databases can be (see Figure 27.17). You've already indicated which dimensions you want to use; now you need to choose which measures you want to bring down.

You also must decide whether you want to bring all dimension data with you or only part of each dimension. For example, you'll probably want to copy down only one or two measures and only current calendar year data from your time dimension, leaving previous years on the server.

6. Choose Next to continue.

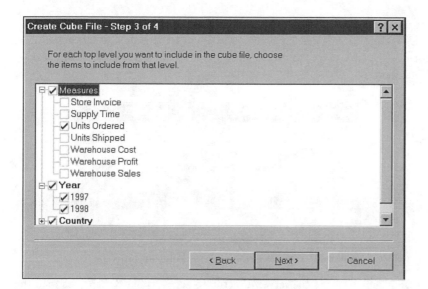

Figure 27.17.
You can limit cube file size by choosing certain measures and only parts of particular dimensions (you might choose to leave older data on the server, for example).

Tip #315 from

Timothy

The wizard defaults to saving the dimensions and level of detail you currently have displayed in your PivotTable. If you expand the PivotTable to show just as much detail as you need (and not more), the wizard will automatically be correct.

7. The last step is to save the data. Type a cube filename and choose Finish (see Figure 27.18). A Create Cube File dialog box appears as the cube file is created (you can click the Stop button if it's taking too long to finish), and then you're returned to the PivotTable's Client-Server Settings dialog box.

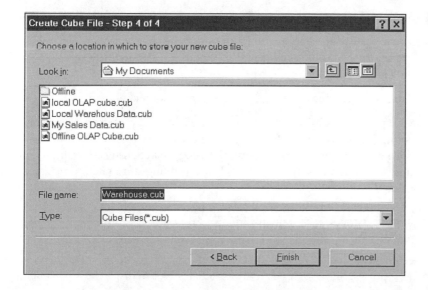

Figure 27.18.
After you've chosen what goes into your local cube, save it onto your hard drive.

PART

VIII

CH

27

Notice that the Local Data File option is now selected in the Client-Server Settings window (see Figure 27.19). That shows that your PivotTable is now using the new local cube file for its data. You're free to disconnect your machine from the network and continue your work.

Figure 27.19.
The Client-Server Settings dialog box lets you switch back and forth between using an OLAP server or a local OLAP data file as your data source.

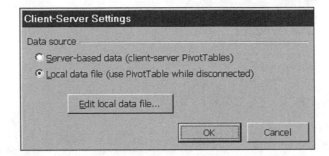

If you want to switch back to using the server directly (to access other dimensions than the ones in your local cube, for example), just go back to the Client-Server Settings dialog box (PivotTable, Client-Server Settings), and choose the Server-Based Data (Client-Server PivotTables) option.

Tip #316 from

After you've created a local cube file once, you'll notice that the button that was labeled Create Local Data File is now called Edit Local Data File. If you click it, you'll be able to rebuild your local cube to change its contents. If you just want to refresh the cube, choose PivotTable, Refresh Data from the PivotTable toolbar, or click the Refresh Data button.

EXCEL IN PRACTICE

OLAP PivotTables can display an enormous amount of detail—sometimes too much. For example, it's hard to see in the promotions analysis in Figure 27.20 what data is really important and what's just background noise.

To turn the raw data into useful information, I'll use a number of techniques:

- Discover the top performers by placing the cell pointer in the Promotion Name column and choosing PivotTable, Field Settings, Advanced from the PivotTable toolbar (or right-clicking anywhere in the column and choosing Field Settings, Advanced), and setting the AutoSort option to sort promotions by descending store sales, using the Field Store Sales Net.

- Cut down on the number of promotions displayed by using the PivotTable, Field Settings, Advanced, AutoShow, Automatic option to limit the list to the top 10 promotions. Now I know which promotions were the top 10 revenue earners.

- Placing the cell pointer in a Store Sales Net data cell, and then choosing PivotTable, Field Settings, Options, Show Data As, I set Store Sales Net to display as a percentage of row value, not an absolute value.

- Finally, I selected the entire PivotTable (PivotTable, Select, Entire Table) and used the Format, Conditional Formatting command to mark values between 50 percent and 99 percent in red. Now, out of the top promotions, I instantly can tell where each worked the best.

For example, it's now easy to see in Figure 27.21 that You Save Days is a promotion to repeat in California, but not worth running again in Oregon or Washington. However, Washington customers responded extremely well to the Super Savers promotion, making it a winner in that state.

Store Sales Net	Store Country / USA CA	OR	WA	USA Total	Grand
Promotion Name	CA	OR	WA		
Bag Stuffers		780.9823	373.091	1154.0733	115
Best Savings	1970.4652		581.2759	2551.7411	255
Big Promo			2195.3673	2195.3673	219
Big Time Discounts		671.899	511.3219	1183.2209	118
Big Time Savings	830.2069		70.3816	900.5885	90
Bye Bye Baby	1215.4033			1215.4033	121
Cash Register Lottery		5865.7519		5865.7519	586
Dimes Off	1562.9593			1562.9593	156
Dollar Cutters	522.4703				
Dollar Days	620.8626				
Double Down Sale	940.5926				
Double Your Savings					
Free For All					
Go For It					

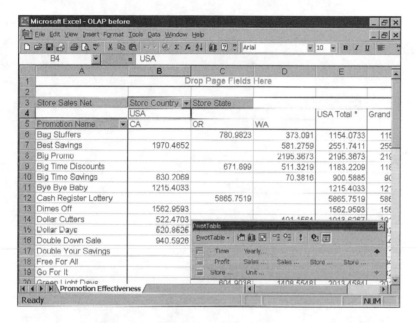

Figure 27.20. This table's immense amount of data makes it too complicated to comprehend.

Store Sales Net	Store Country / USA CA	OR	WA	USA Total	Grand Total
Promotion Name	CA	OR	WA		
No Promotion	26.44%	26.65%	46.91%	100.00%	100.00
Cash Register Lottery	0.00%	100.00%	0.00%	100.00%	100.00
Price Savers	24.92%	26.61%	48.47%	100.00%	100.00
You Save Days	***61.25%***	27.56%	11.19%	100.00%	100.00
Super Duper Savers	0.00%	0.00%	100.00%	100.00%	100.00
High Roller Savings	100.00%	0.00%	0.00%	100.00%	100.00
Sales Galore	33.13%	0.00%	***66.87%***	100.00%	100.00
Super Savers	24.57%	0.00%	***75.43%***	100.00%	100.00
Price Destroyers	43.81%	19.14%	37.05%	100.00%	100.00
Save-It Sale	43.55%	0.00%	***56.45%***	100.00%	100.00
Grand Total	28.16%	25.18%	46.66%	100.00%	100.00

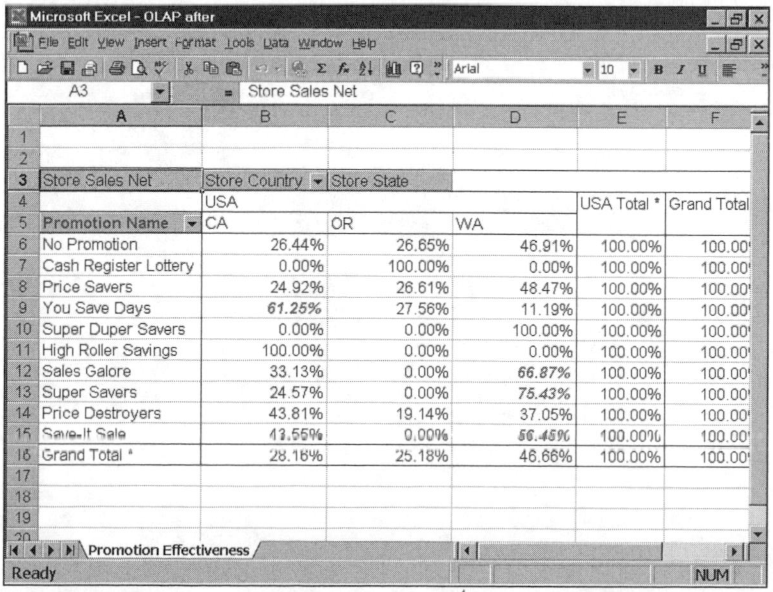

Figure 27.21. Sorting, limiting the list, using conditional formatting, and other techniques produce a much more useful report.

CUSTOMIZING AND AUTOMATING EXCEL

CHAPTER 28

Customizing Excel to Fit Your Working Style

by Patrick D. Blattner
Patrick@BlattnerBooks.com

In this chapter

WHY CUSTOMIZE EXCEL?

Microsoft designed Excel to be powerful and yet easy to use, but every user is different. You may manage a number of small lists in Excel and need frequent access to the data tools on a toolbar. Perhaps your job requires building charts every day, and you want to add options to the Chart menu for this purpose. Maybe you create custom workbooks for other users and need special tools constantly at hand.

You can tailor Excel to look and work the way you want. If you want a certain type of font, worksheet color, and number of sheets within each workbook you open, Excel enables you to adjust such components and tools to fit your style. If you create workbooks that other people will use, you can tailor the workbook environment to protect your original information. You can even create custom toolbars and menus for yourself and your business.

This chapter reviews a number of options for customizing Excel so that it works the way you prefer to work. It's important to note, however, that Excel—particularly in conjunction with the other Microsoft Office products—is nearly infinitely customizable. No single chapter or even a whole book can provide all the details on all the changes you can make. You don't need to feel limited by the features and suggestions of this chapter; the Excel Help system can help you explore a wide range of other options.

CHANGING THE DEFAULT EXCEL SETTINGS

Excel enables you to customize a number of the default settings for the program. Each of these features is controlled by settings in the Options dialog box. To open this dialog box, choose Tools, Options. The following list describes some suggested changes:

- **Move data entry in a different direction.** By default, when you press Enter after typing a cell entry, Excel accepts the entry and moves down to the next cell in that column. In many workbooks, however, moving to the next cell to the right, left, up, or even disabling this option completely would be more useful. You can change the direction that the *cell pointer (page 7)* moves. Click the Edit tab in the Options dialog box. In the Direction box, select the direction you want the cell pointer to move, as shown in Figure 28.1. To prevent the cell pointer from moving, deselect the Move Selection After Enter option.

Tip #317 from

Patrick

> When entering data using the Enter key, you can control direction in a limited area of the worksheet by selecting that area first. As you enter the data, Excel moves down until you reach the bottom of the first column in the selection and then moves to the top of the next column, and so on.

- **Control the default number of sheets in a workbook.** By default, Excel creates new *workbooks (page 862)* with three blank *worksheets (page 862)*. You may prefer to start with fewer sheets or more sheets. To change the default number of worksheets in a new workbook, click the General tab in the Options dialog box. In the Sheets in New Workbook box, type or select the number of sheets you want (see Figure 28.2).

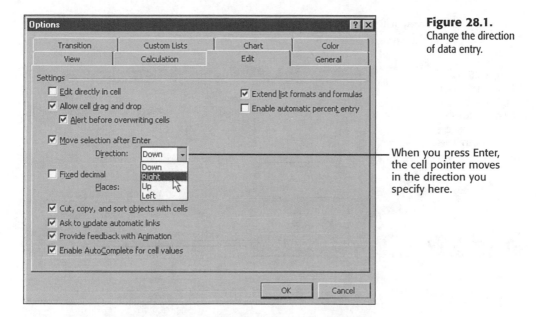

Figure 28.1.
Change the direction
of data entry.

When you press Enter,
the cell pointer moves
in the direction you
specify here.

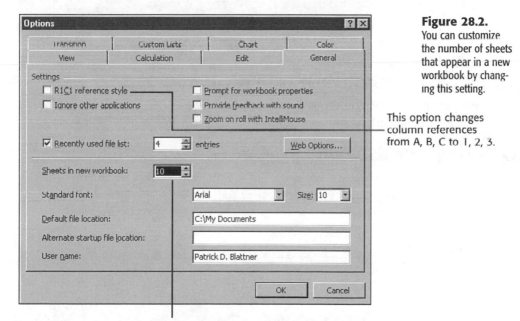

Figure 28.2.
You can customize
the number of sheets
that appear in a new
workbook by chang-
ing this setting.

This option changes
column references
from A, B, C to 1, 2, 3.

Type a new number or use the spin arrows to change this setting.

- **Set the default font and point size.** Excel defaults to a standard Arial font, but you can change the default font settings to something more appropriate. Click the General tab in the Options dialog box, and change the settings for Standard Font and Size, as shown in Figure 28.3. When Excel displays a warning message that this change affects all future workbooks, confirm that you want to use the new setting as the default, or cancel the change.

Figure 28.3.
Change the default font format so that you don't have to change the font every time you start a new workbook.

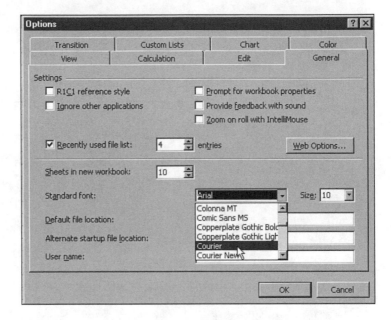

CHANGING WORKBOOK SETTINGS

In addition to changing the overall settings that apply to all new workbooks, you can make changes within specific existing or new workbooks, as described in the following sections.

CHANGING THE COLOR PALETTE

For any open workbook, you can change the colors available on color palettes and customize the default palette by simply selecting and changing the colors on the palette. Note that this change applies only to the active workbook, not to Excel as a whole.

Tip #318 from

Patrick

When you copy or move a sheet to another workbook, the colors on the source sheet change to reflect the color palette in the target workbook. Excel replaces your custom color(s) with the color(s) in the corresponding position(s) on the color palette in the target workbook. To solve this problem, try the following techniques:

- To retain your custom colors when copying worksheets to other workbooks, copy the color palette from the customized workbook to the other workbook before you copy the worksheet. It's important to note that copying the color palette will change all the customized colors used in the target workbook, which may be something you didn't expect (or want).

To copy the color palette, open both the source and the target workbooks. If necessary, switch to the target workbook. Open the Options dialog box (Tools, Options), and click the Color tab. In the Copy Colors From box, specify the source workbook. Then choose OK.

- To use your custom colors in new workbooks, customize the palette for a blank workbook, save the workbook as a template, and use the template to create new workbooks.

To change a color on the palette, follow these steps:

1. Choose Tools, Options. In the Options dialog box, select the Color tab (see Figure 28.4).

2. Select the color you want to change on the Standard Colors, Chart Fills, or Chart Lines palette.

3. Click the Modify button to open the Colors dialog box (see Figure 28.5).

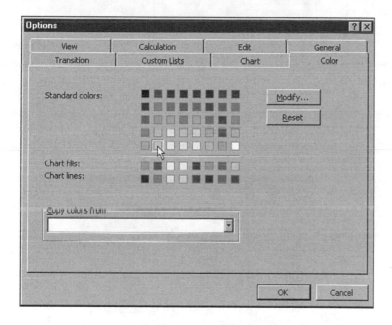

Figure 28.4.
Select the color you want to change.

4. If the color you want to use is shown in the Colors palette, click it. The indicator in the lower-right corner displays a sample of the old and new colors.

5. If you need a custom color, you can modify the existing color or create your own color. Click the Custom tab (see Figure 28.6). Here, you can click the desired color in the Colors box, or drag the slider to the right of the Colors box to modify the existing color visually. You also can adjust the settings at the bottom of the dialog box to change the red/green/blue mix or customize the color to a specific level of luminance, saturation, and hue.

6. When the color is correct (whether you're working on the Standard or Custom tab), click OK.

PART

IX

CH

28

Figure 28.5.
Select the color
you want from the
color palette.

Gradient selections ─

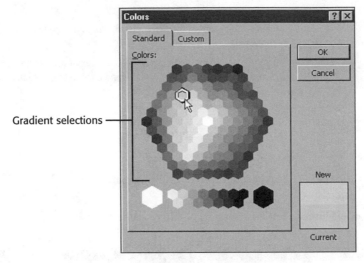

7. Click OK in the Options dialog box. Note that you must save the workbook to save the new color setting(s).

The default colors have ScreenTips that display the color name. Your custom color won't have such a ScreenTip; instead, Excel displays `Color Scheme` when you point to that color on a palette or in a dialog box (see Figure 28.7).

Figure 28.6.
The Custom tab in the
Colors dialog box
enables you to adjust
colors to specific lev-
els of hue, luminance,
saturation, and
red/green/blue (RGB).

Drag in the
Colors box
or...

Specify a
setting or...

...Drag the
arrow.

New color
you're creating

Current color

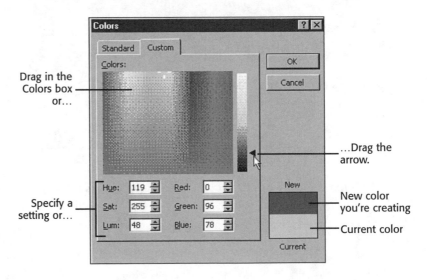

To restore the original factory settings for the colors in a workbook, open the Options dialog box again, click the Color tab, and click the Reset button. Be sure you want to do this, however; Excel doesn't ask you to confirm this change. Note that making this change resets any modified colors in the workbook—wherever those colors were used.

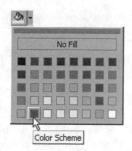

Figure 28.7.
By changing the colors on the palette, you permanently change the colors within the workbook.

HIDING PARTS OF THE WORKBOOK

For various reasons, you may want to *hide (page 470)* parts of a worksheet. You probably are already familiar with hiding and unhiding columns and rows. The following sections provide other options for hiding parts of the worksheet.

→ For details on how to hide and unhide columns and rows, **see** "Hiding and Unhiding Rows and Columns," **p. 67**

HIDING SHEETS

If you send out a report every week that contains summary information, you may want to display the backup data for the summary info only when you need to add more data. When you want to keep information in a workbook but also keep it out of view for the sake of confidentiality, privacy, or simplicity, you can hide the worksheet with that information.

You can hide a single worksheet at a time or hide multiple worksheets simultaneously. To hide a single worksheet, begin by displaying that worksheet. To hide multiple worksheets, hold down the Ctrl key and click the sheet tabs until you have gathered all the applicable worksheets into a group. With the worksheet(s) selected, choose Format, Sheet, Hide. The Unhide command becomes available when sheets are hidden within the workbook; to unhide sheets, choose Format, Sheet, Unhide. Excel displays a dialog box where you can specify which sheet to restore to view. You must unhide each sheet separately.

→ You can prevent hidden worksheets from being unhidden by protecting the workbook with a password. For details, **see** "Password-Protecting a Workbook," **p. 523**

HIDING OR CHANGING THE DISPLAY OF ZERO VALUES

By deselecting the Zero Values option on the View tab in the Options dialog box, you can make all cells containing a zero on the active sheet appear blank. This helps keep spreadsheets from looking cluttered with lots of zero values.

→ To learn how to hide formulas, **see** "Hiding Formulas," **p. 523**

HIDING CELL ENTRIES

You may have cell content that you want to hide—without hiding the whole column or row. Excel offers a trick for this, as described in the following steps:

1. Select the cell(s) you want to hide.

2. Choose Format, Cells to display the Format Cells dialog box.

3. Click the Number tab.

4. Click Custom in the Category list. Type three semicolons (;;;) in the Type box.

> The value disappears from the worksheet and doesn't print. Of course, you can still see the value in the Formula bar when the cell is selected or in the cell if you edit the entry.

This trick works for any kind of entry. To view the cell value again in the worksheet, select the cell and change the format to General, Currency, or some other format. Other ways to hide the values in a cell would be to hide the formula by protecting the cell or to simply format the text to the same color as the background.

CHANGING THE EXCEL WINDOW SETTINGS

You can customize the Excel program window to look a certain way for your own use or to prevent other users from moving to different worksheets or scrolling the worksheet. You can show or hide the horizontal and vertical scrollbars and the status bar, as described in the following sections.

ADDING AND REMOVING SCROLLBARS

Excel enables you to remove the vertical and horizontal scrollbars from the Excel window. If you have a document that contains information in a specific location on a worksheet, for example, and you don't want users to scroll this information off the screen, you may want to eliminate the scrollbars. (Note that they are easily restored by experienced users, however.)

To remove or restore the scrollbars, choose Tools, Options to open the Options dialog box, and click the View tab (see Figure 28.8). To remove the horizontal scrollbar, deselect the Horizontal Scroll Bar option. To remove the vertical scrollbar, deselect the Vertical Scroll Bar option. To restore the scrollbar(s) at any point, open the Options dialog box again and select the option(s). Figure 28.9 shows the Excel window with the scrollbars removed.

> **Note**
>
> Removing just the horizontal scrollbar doesn't restore any usable screen space, but you regain an extra line if you also remove the sheet tabs (see the later section "Hiding the Sheet Tabs" for details).

CUSTOMIZING THE STATUS BAR FOR QUICK ANALYSIS

If you're not currently showing the status bar onscreen, consider adding it. In addition to indicating the edit mode, providing quick instructions, and displaying messages, the status bar offers another quietly efficient feature: *AutoCalculate (page 264)*. This is a great tool for quick analysis. If you have a list of costs associated with months, for example, you can highlight certain months—without summing or subtotaling—and see the total cost for those months. Any time you have a range of numbers for which you want to know the total value, average, count, and so on, just select the individual cells/ranges and look at the AutoCalculate section of the status bar. As the example in Figure 28.10 shows, you can select noncontiguous ranges to be calculated (just hold down Ctrl as you click the cells or select the ranges). In this example, AutoCalculate is showing the sum of February for Minnesota, March for North Dakota, and April for Idaho.

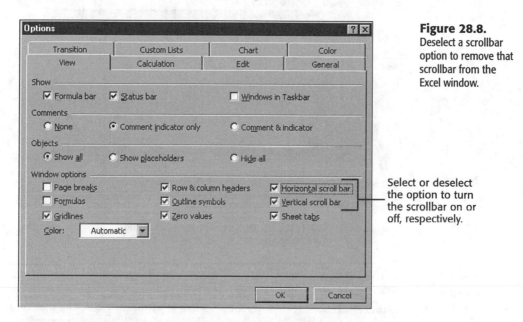

Figure 28.8.
Deselect a scrollbar option to remove that scrollbar from the Excel window.

Select or deselect the option to turn the scrollbar on or off, respectively.

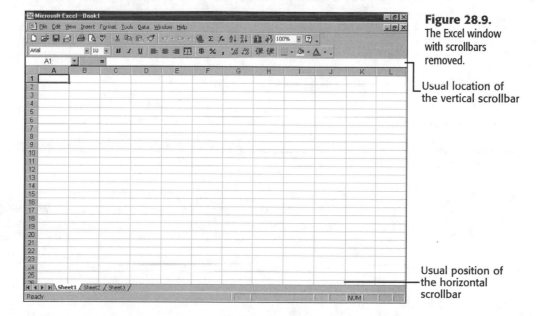

Figure 28.9.
The Excel window with scrollbars removed.

Usual location of the vertical scrollbar

Usual position of the horizontal scrollbar

PART

IX

CH

28

Figure 28.10.
When you drag over the range(s), the status bar displays the total.

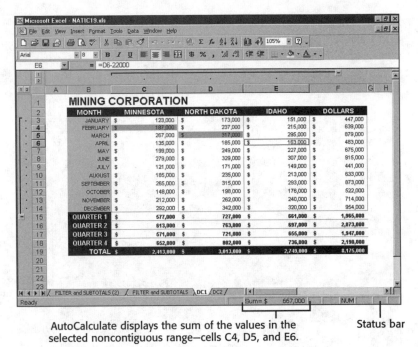

AutoCalculate displays the sum of the values in the selected noncontiguous range—cells C4, D5, and E6.

Status bar

You already may have discovered AutoCalculate, but did you know that you can change the function it uses? To change the AutoCalculate function, right-click anywhere on the status bar and select the desired function from the pop-up list. If you want to see the maximum value, for example, change the AutoCalculate function to Max (see Figure 28.11). Excel then shows the maximum value in the selected range(s), as shown in Figure 28.12. In this example, AutoCalculate is showing that the maximum value in the range D3:D14 is $342,000.

Figure 28.11.
Change the AutoCalculate function on the status bar by right-clicking and selecting a function from the pop-up list.

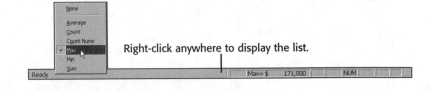

Right-click anywhere to display the list.

Note

If the status bar is turned off, select the Status Bar command from the View menu to toggle it back on.

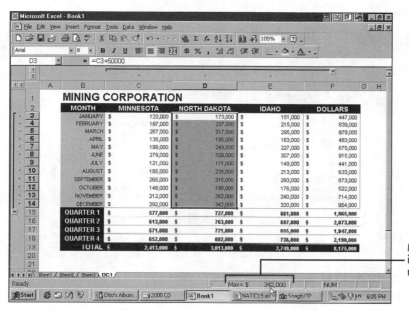

Figure 28.12.
With the Max function on the AutoCalculate list, you can find the highest value in a list of numbers simply by dragging over the numbers.

Maximum value in the selected range D3:D14

MODIFYING TOOLBARS

Many tools are available on the default Excel toolbars, but you're likely to find that you use certain tools repeatedly, and the others rarely or never. You're probably already comfortable with turning the various toolbars on and off with the View, Toolbars command, and have undoubtedly noticed that Excel displays certain toolbars automatically when you work in certain modes—the Chart toolbar appears when you're creating or editing charts, and so on. But you may not have thought about customizing those default toolbars to fit your specific needs. Excel enables you to add and remove buttons on any of the default toolbars, move buttons from one toolbar to another, and even create custom toolbars for various purposes.

To begin customizing toolbars, start by opening the Customize dialog box. Choose View, Toolbars, Customize, or simply right-click any toolbar and select Customize from the pop-up menu to open the Customize dialog box. With this dialog box open, you can right-click any toolbar button to display a special pop-up context menu for customizing that button, as shown in Figure 28.13.

With the options on the pop-up menu, you can copy the images on the button faces and paste them on other buttons, create your own button names, display text on the buttons—even change the images on the button faces completely. The following sections describe how to use these options.

PART

IX

CH

28

Figure 28.13.
Use this context menu to customize toolbar buttons.

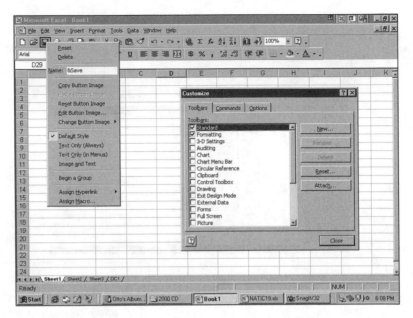

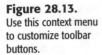

For most of these operations, the Customize dialog box must be open. However, you can move, copy, and delete menus and buttons without the Customize dialog box visible by holding down the Alt key for moving (or Alt+Ctrl key for copying) as you drag the menu/button.

DELETING BUTTONS FROM TOOLBARS

Suppose that you want to delete a toolbar button you never use, just to get it out of the way (and maybe use that space for a different button that might be more helpful to you). To delete an existing button on a toolbar, open the Customize dialog box and then simply drag the button off the toolbar—being careful not to drop it over a menu or another toolbar, in which case Excel would move the button to that menu or toolbar. (It's safe to release the mouse when the pointer displays a large black X attached to the arrow pointer.) Another method is to right-click the button and select Delete (see Figure 28.14).

DISPLAYING TEXT ON BUTTONS

By default, the buttons on the toolbars don't display any text, but you may find it helpful to display text on certain buttons, along with or instead of the button images. Change buttons to display text only, for example, if Excel users are unfamiliar with using toolbar buttons, or if they have a difficult time remembering what command an image represents. To make the Save button more obvious, for example, you can display the word Save on the button instead of or in addition to the button image. Begin by displaying the Customize dialog box as usual. Then right-click the button you want to change and select the appropriate text option (see Figure 28.15).

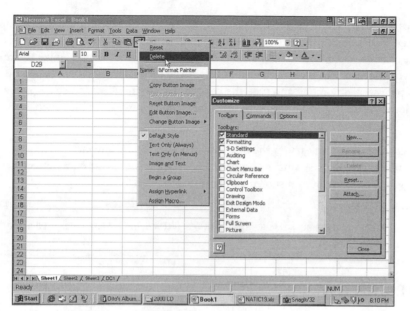

Figure 28.14.
To delete a button on a toolbar, open the Customize dialog box. Then right-click the button and choose Delete, or just drag the button off the toolbar.

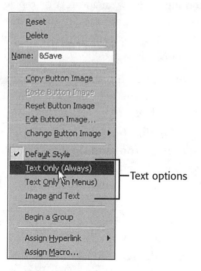

Figure 28.15.
Use the text options to add text to the button image or replace the button image with text.

Figure 28.16 shows buttons customized to show the button image with text, the image alone, the text alone, and customized text.

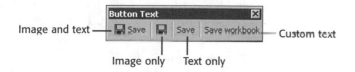

Figure 28.16.
Keep in mind that showing text, or image and text, takes more space than just showing the button image.

Excel supplies text to go with every default button; the text is displayed in the ScreenTip when pointing to that button. Sometimes the button name isn't quite enough information to help the user figure out how or when to use the button, but you can customize the text to say whatever you want. To change the text, click in the text box next to the <u>N</u>ame option on the pop-up customizing menu and type the desired text. If you want to use a hot key (underlined letter) to activate a button, type an ampersand (&) before the letter that you want to underline.

The <u>N</u>ame setting is what appears on the button when you choose any customizing option that includes text. The <u>N</u>ame setting is also how you create custom text on a button face (such as the <u>S</u>ave workbook button shown earlier in Figure 28.16).

Caution

Be sure to use a hot key letter that doesn't conflict with the hot key letters used in the Excel menus.

CHANGING THE BUTTON IMAGES

Sometimes the image on a button doesn't help you to figure out what the button does. If you want to change the button image, you can add text or replace the image with text, as described in the preceding section, or you can modify the button image itself. With the Customize dialog box open, right-click the button you want to change to display the pop-up customizing menu. You have the following choices for changing the button image:

- **Replace the image with one from the set of extra images supplied with Excel.** Select Change <u>B</u>utton Image from the pop-up menu and then click one of the images on the submenu (see Figure 28.17).

- **If an image on an existing toolbar button is close to what you want, copy that image, paste it onto another button, and then edit it.** Display the Customize dialog box, right-click the source button, and choose <u>C</u>opy Button Image. Then right-click the target button and choose <u>P</u>aste Button Image. Finally, edit the image as described in the following item.

- **Edit a default image or one of the extra images.** With the image in place on the button, select <u>E</u>dit Button Image to display the Button Editor, as shown in Figure 28.18. Then edit the button as desired. (To edit one of the extra images, you must display that image on the button before selecting <u>E</u>dit Button Image.)

- **Copy an image from an image file.** Open the image file in Paint, Microsoft Photo Editor, or some other image-management program. Copy the image and switch back to Excel. Right-click the button whose image you want to change and choose <u>P</u>aste Button Image. Excel replaces the original image with the copied image. Note that scaling an image down to button size may cause distortion; start with a simple image or edit the image with the Button Editor.

- **Create your own image, using the Button Editor.** Right-click the button and choose <u>E</u>dit Button Image, and then create the desired image. You also can start from an existing image and edit it in the Button Editor to get the desired effect (see the preceding item).

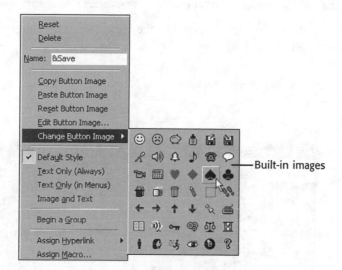

Figure 28.17.
You can apply these predesigned images to buttons on the toolbar.

Built-in images

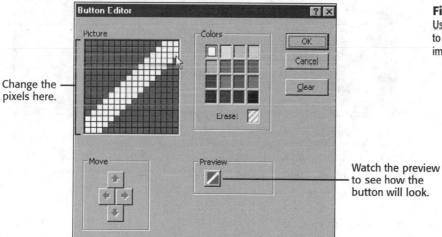

Figure 28.18.
Use the Button Editor to modify or draw an image.

Change the pixels here.

Watch the preview to see how the button will look.

To change an image with the Button Editor, click a color and then click a pixel in the Picture box. The image changes to reflect the new color. The Move buttons adjust the location of the image up, down, left, or right on the button face. The Erase feature sets the image to the background color.

ASSIGNING HYPERLINKS

In addition to being able to insert *hyperlinks (page 773)* directly into worksheets, you can create toolbar buttons that let you jump quickly to other places in the current worksheet, other worksheets, or workbooks, or even hop over to Web sites that you often use in your business. For example, if you often jump to a certain financial Web page or check stocks regularly, you may want to add a link to a custom button that takes you directly to that financial page.

With the Customize dialog box open, right-click the button to which you want to assign a hyperlink. Select Assign Hyperlink, Open to display the Assign Hyperlink: Open dialog box (see Figure 28.19).

→ To learn how to create hyperlinks in your worksheets, **see** "Combining Word, Excel, and PowerPoint Files with Hyperlinks," **p. 773**

Figure 28.19.
Apply or select the Web site you want to assign to a button.

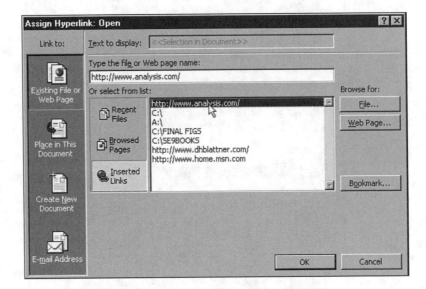

This dialog box enables you to assign a hyperlink to an email address, a new document, an existing file, or a Web page. Select one of the buttons in the Link To list to indicate the target for the new link. The dialog box changes to display options associated with the destination you chose. You then can type the path to the file or Web site, using the text box, or click the appropriate button to select the path from a list (Inserted Links, Browsed Pages, or Recent Files). You also can browse for the file or Web page.

ASSIGNING MACROS

To create efficient toolbar buttons that provide options you use frequently, you can assign macros to toolbar buttons. If you often need to adjust column width to provide room for lengthy text, for example, you can create a button that AutoFits all columns.

To assign a macro to a toolbar button, you first create the macro as described in Chapter 29, "Recording and Editing a Macro." Then create the button you want to use, right-click it, and select Assign Macro from the pop-up customizing menu to open the Assign Macro dialog box (see Figure 28.20). In the Macros In box, specify the location of the macro you want to use. Then select the name of the macro in the list in the center of the dialog box, type its name in the Macro Name box, or click the Collapse Dialog button and select the macro from the open workbook where it's stored.

Note

Macros stored in the *Personal Macro Workbook (page 889)* begin with PERSONAL.XLS! in the list box. See Chapter 29 for details on using the Personal Macro Workbook.

Custom toolbar
with custom button

Specify the name of the
macro you want to assign.

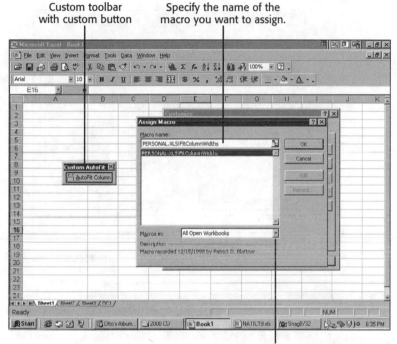

Figure 28.20.
Use the Assign Macro dialog box to apply a macro to a toolbar button.

Specify where the macro is stored.

Tip #319 from

Patrick

If you created the macro and will be the only user of the new toolbar button, the macro name may suffice as the text on the button, and you may not even want an image. For other users, try to assign text that's not as cryptic as the typical macro name, and/or use an appropriate button image to suggest the function of the button.

BUILDING CUSTOM TOOLBARS

Sometimes customizing the default buttons and toolbars isn't quite enough. For those instances, you can build custom toolbars that supply the exact combination of buttons that you need. To create a custom toolbar, open the Customize dialog box and click the New button to display the New Toolbar dialog box (see Figure 28.21). Type a name for the toolbar; this name will appear in the list of toolbars in the Customize dialog box and in the title bar of the toolbar (see Figure 28.22).

PART

IX

CH

28

Tip #320 from

Unfortunately, Excel automatically resizes toolbars to accommodate the exact size of the buttons on the toolbar. You can't widen the toolbar to display the whole toolbar name in the title bar. Unless you have sufficient buttons on the toolbar to widen it, the name will be truncated. You sometimes can solve this problem by changing the toolbar name to use a shorter name, adding separators (described shortly), displaying the button text instead of or in addition to the button images, or reshaping the toolbar (drag the sides or corners as you would to resize a window).

Figure 28.21.
Assign a name to the custom toolbar.

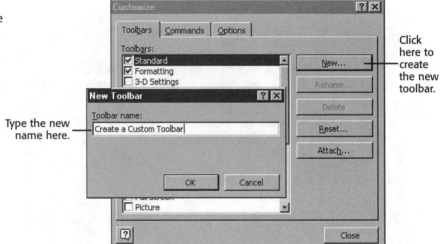

Click here to create the new toolbar.

Type the new name here.

Figure 28.22.
The new toolbar shows up in the list of toolbars.

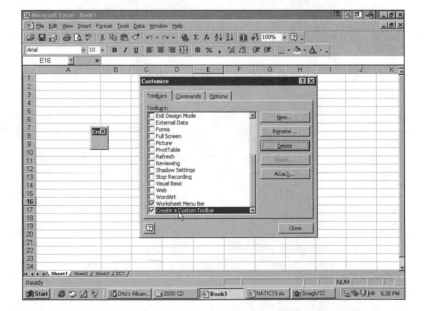

The toolbar appears with no buttons. To add buttons, you can use either of the following methods:

- **Copy buttons from other toolbars.** The source toolbar must be displayed to use this method. To copy a button from an open toolbar, hold down the Ctrl+Alt and drag the button from its original toolbar to the custom toolbar. If the Customize dialog box is open, you can just hold down Ctrl.

- **Add buttons from the Commands tab in the Customize dialog box.** Click a category in the Categories list and then scroll the Commands list until you see the command, macro, shape, and so on, for which you want to add a button. Drag the item from the Commands list to your custom toolbar and drop it into position (see Figure 28.23).

With either method, Excel displays an I-beam on the toolbar to indicate where the button will be placed when you drop it.

Excel displays an I-beam where the button
will be positioned when dropped.

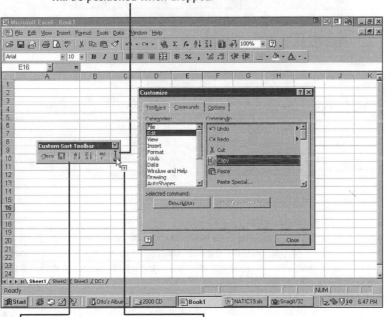

Figure 28.23.
Drag the button to the desired location on your custom toolbar.

Separator bars visually
separate one group of
buttons from another
on a toolbar.

Excel displays special mouse pointers
when dragging buttons around.

PART

IX

CH

28

You may have noticed that toolbars in Windows programs generally are separated into *groups* with vertical markers (called *separator bars* or just *separators*) that group similar toolbar buttons together. You can add separator bars to your custom toolbar or any default toolbar.

Right-click the button that you want to be first (reading from left to right) in the group and select Begin a Group from the pop-up customizing menu. Excel displays a separator bar to the left of the button.

Tip #321 from

To create separators with the mouse, click the first button you want in the group and drag it slightly to the right (or down if the toolbar is vertical). Dragging the button to the left (or up on a vertical toolbar) removes the separator.

To attach custom toolbars to specific workbooks, start by opening the workbook to which you want to attach a toolbar. Open the Customize dialog box and click the Attach button on the Toolbars tab. In the Attach Toolbars dialog box, select the toolbar in the Custom Toolbars list and click the Copy button to copy the toolbar name to the Toolbars in Workbook list (see Figure 28.24). Close the Customize dialog box and save the workbook. Now every time the workbook is opened, the attached toolbars appear in the workbook.

Figure 28.24.
Attach custom tool-
bars to a workbook to
provide specific tools
for that workbook.

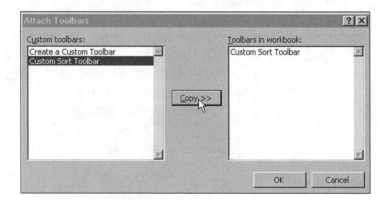

Considerations When Attaching Toolbars

When you attach a toolbar, Excel makes a separate copy of the toolbar just for that workbook. In effect, you now have two copies of the toolbar on your machine: the one you created, which appears on the toolbars list (let's call it the global toolbar for simplicity), and the one attached to the workbook, which we'll call the custom toolbar. The one on the toolbars list (global) takes precedence. If you hide the global toolbar, Excel won't display the attached toolbar when the workbook is opened. If no such toolbar name appears on the toolbars list when the workbook is opened, however, the custom toolbar appears. In the latter case, Excel adds a (global) separate copy of the custom toolbar to the list. If you delete your global custom toolbar, then open the workbook containing the attached toolbar, the toolbar should still appear.

One more point: Because the global and attached toolbars are separate entities, if you customize the global toolbar after adding the attached toolbar, the attached toolbar doesn't update to show the changes. You must delete the old attachment and reattach the new modified toolbar.

In short, attached toolbars can cause havoc, particularly when sharing workbooks with attached toolbars with unsuspecting/inexperienced users. It's perplexing for users to see five or six custom toolbars appear on their list that they never created themselves, but were the result of attached toolbars being added to their global list.

DELETING AND RESETTING TOOLBARS AND BUTTONS

You can delete custom toolbars and buttons or restore customized default toolbars and buttons to their original forms. Start by opening the Customize dialog box as usual. Then use the following options:

- To delete a custom button, drag the button off the toolbar or right-click it and select Delete.

- To delete a custom toolbar, select the toolbar in the Toolbars list on the Toolbars tab in the Customize dialog box and click the Delete button. When Excel asks you to confirm this action, click OK.

- To restore a default toolbar to its original form, select it in the Toolbars list and click the Reset button. When Excel asks you to confirm this action, click OK.

- To restore a default button to its original form, right-click it and select Reset. Be sure that you want to do this, however: Excel doesn't ask you to confirm this change.

CUSTOMIZING THE EXCEL MENUS

With all the options available in Excel, people can get carried away and add or change things in the setup or a workbook. By knowing how to change the environment, you can eliminate this risk by customizing the Excel environment on your computer or those of other users. Changing the menus also can simplify or improve your own use of Excel. Customizing the menus and customizing the toolbars in Excel are closely related operations—both are fairly simple tasks that use the Customize dialog box.

Suppose that you have a worksheet you want someone to use to input information, but you don't want that user to be able to manipulate the file in any way. Figure 28.25 shows a custom setup for this type of situation—providing a single menu item, File, and removing the Standard and Formatting toolbars.

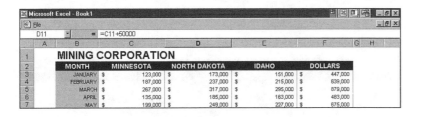

Figure 28.25.
Minimize your risk for error by changing the environment so that a small number of options (if any) are available.

Caution

An experienced user may reset the menus or use shortcut keys to access hidden commands, unless you program Excel to generate and maintain the custom environment. Chapter 30, "Creating Interactive Excel Applications with VBA," explores options for customizing Excel with custom programs.

To change menu names, delete menus, change hotkeys, or change the location of the menus, begin by right-clicking the menu bar or a toolbar and selecting <u>C</u>ustomize from the pop-up menu to open the Customize dialog box. With the Customize dialog box open, you can customize any of the standard menus or create your own menu.

Tip #322 from

> When creating or customizing menus, be sure to assign unique hotkeys (the underlined letters in the menus) for use with the Alt key. If a hotkey is used more than once on a particular menu or submenu, the first use of the hotkey by the user selects the item closest to the top of the menu or dialog box. The user then must press Enter to execute the command. Pressing the hotkey a second time highlights the next command with that underlined letter, and so on.

The following list describes how to customize existing menus. For details on creating custom menus or menu items, see the next section.

- To delete a menu, right-click the menu and select <u>D</u>elete from the pop-up customizing menu, as shown in Figure 28.26.
- To move the menu item to a new location, drag it to the desired location, as shown in Figure 28.27.

Figure 28.26.
Use this menu to change the menu name or location, or to delete the menu.

Figure 28.27.
You can reposition a menu or even drag it onto another menu.

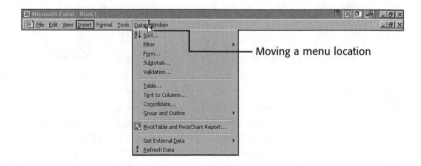

Moving a menu location

Tip #323 from

> Excel's menu bar works like a toolbar in that you can drag it to a different position on the screen. Keep in mind, however, that most users will expect the menu to be at the top of the screen and may find it disconcerting to see it positioned elsewhere.

CREATING A CUSTOM MENU

You can create your own menus in Excel to reflect custom macros and commands. For a workbook with different summary tables, for example, you might create a menu with options to print the specific tables.

Tip #324 from

> If you frequently go to specific Internet sites to download or review information, create a custom menu with submenus hyperlinked to those sites. See the earlier section "Assigning Hyperlinks" for details on hyperlinking.

To create your own custom menu, open the Customize dialog box, click the Commands tab, and select New Menu at the bottom of the Categories list. Click the New Menu item in the Commands list (see Figure 28.28). Drag it to the menu bar or toolbar where you want to place the menu. As you drag, Excel displays a button and a black plus sign (+) with the pointer. Drop the new menu in place, right-click it, and name it with the Name option in the pop-up customizing menu, as shown in Figure 28.29.

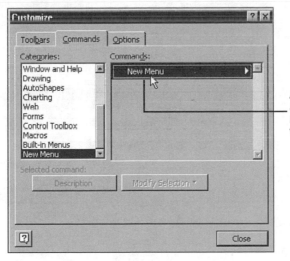

Figure 28.28.
Create your own menu with the New Menu option in the Commands list.

A button will appear as you drag the New Menu item out of the dialog box.

Figure 28.29.
Name the custom
menu to reflect the
submenu items
you plan to place
in the menu.

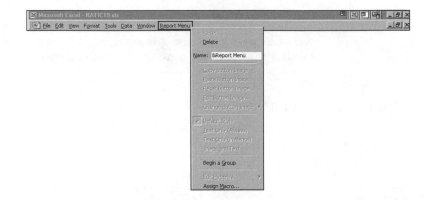

To create the items in your new menu, you can Ctrl+drag existing items from other menus or toolbars, or create new items. To create new items, click Macros in the Categories list on the Commands tab in the Customize dialog box. Then drag the Custom Menu Item from the Commands list to the new menu and drop it in place (see Figure 28.30). When the custom menu is in place, assign a macro to it, as described in the earlier section, "Assigning Macros."

Tip #325 from

There's very little difference between a custom menu item and a custom toolbar button. Dragging a button onto a menu displays both the image and text; a menu item displays only text (and has no image by default). If you want an image on a menu item, just add a custom button with text instead of a custom menu item.

Adding a menu item

Figure 28.30.
Create the custom
menu subitems by
dragging the Custom
Menu Item to the
custom menu.

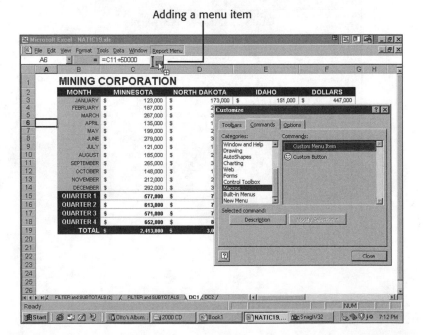

To remove a custom menu or menu item, open the Customize dialog box and then drag the menu or menu item off the menu bar.

TURNING PERSONALIZED MENUS ON AND OFF

Excel 2000 includes a new feature, *personalized menus*, which allows the user to see the most recently used commands first and temporarily hides commands that haven't been used or are used less frequently. Personalized menus are the default menu setup when Excel 2000 is installed. To revert the menus to Excel 97 style (displaying the entire menu when opened), choose Tools, Customize and click the Options tab in the Customize dialog box. Deselect the option Menus Show Recently Used Commands First.

Tip #326 from 	Custom menu items added to the default menu bar (which is actually a toolbar called Worksheet Menu Bar) will always appear. The personalized menu feature never hides them.

TROUBLESHOOTING

RETRIEVING DELETED MENUS

How can I get the menus back after deleting them?

Right-click where the toolbars should be. Choose Customize from the pop-up menu to open the Customize dialog box. Click the Commands tab and select Built-in Menus in the Categories list. Then select and drag the menu you want from the Commands list to the menu bar.

To get all menus back (and, unfortunately, delete any custom menu items added to the default menu bar), you can simply reset the Worksheet Menu Bar. Click the Toolbars tab in the Customize dialog box, select Worksheet Menu Bar in the Toolbars list, click the Reset button, and confirm that you want to reset the menu bar.

RETURNING MENUS TO THE STYLE OF PREVIOUS VERSIONS

How can I get rid of the new personalized menus?

Select Customize from the Tools menu to display the Customize dialog box. Select the Options tab. Deselect the option Menus Show Recently Used Commands First.

EXCEL IN PRACTICE

By utilizing Excel's customizing features, you can eliminate, move, or change the Excel menus to make the best use of a shared workbook, or simply to customize the tools you use most often. In Figure 28.31, the menus and toolbars are in default form. The scrollbars along the side and bottom are visible, and the worksheet tabs are visible as well. Figure 28.32 shows the same worksheet, but with the Excel environment changed. The toolbars

PART

IX

CH

28

are not displayed. Menus have been eliminated except the one in the upper-left corner of the window. Scrollbars and status bar are turned off, and worksheet tabs are hidden.

Figure 28.31.
In the default window format, you can see the Standard and Formatting toolbars, the menu bar, the worksheet tabs, and so on.

Default toolbars and menus

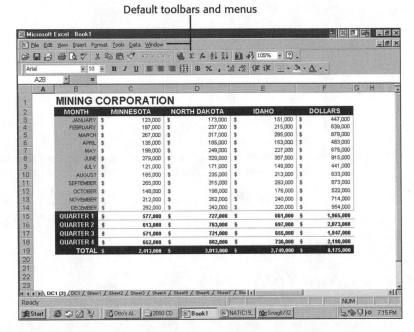

Figure 28.32.
Customizing the Excel environment can dramatically simplify the window for new or inexperienced users.

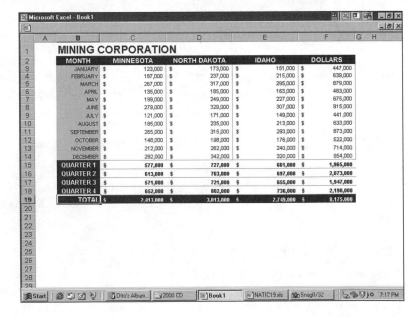

CHAPTER 29

RECORDING AND EDITING A MACRO

In this chapter

by Ken Cook

CREATE YOUR OWN COMMANDS WITH MACROS

Have you ever wished that you could create your own commands in Excel? Perhaps you print the same report every month. To print that report, you must follow the same 10 steps. Wouldn't it be nice to click a button or press a keyboard shortcut and have the report print automatically? For operations like these, you can create a macro—a mini-program that performs a specific task—to repeat the steps perfectly each time. Macros are written in a programming language called *Visual Basic for Applications* or *VBA*.

Fortunately, you don't have to be a programmer to create a macro. Excel provides the *Macro Recorder*. The Macro Recorder works like an audio tape recorder. Rather than recording sound, however, the Macro Recorder records keystrokes and mouse actions. In this chapter, you'll learn how to create macros using the Macro Recorder. You'll also learn how to play and edit macros.

WHAT IS A MACRO?

A macro is a VBA procedure. A *procedure* is a group of VBA statements that either perform a specific task or return a result. There are two types of procedures that you can create in Excel. *Subroutines* are procedures that perform a specific task. The code for subroutines begins with the word Sub and ends with the words End Sub (see Listing 29.1 for an example). A macro is a subroutine-type procedure. For the purposes of this chapter, macro and subroutine are interchangeable terms.

LISTING 29.1. THIS MACRO SELECTS AND PRINTS THE CURRENT REGION

```
Sub PrintRegion()
    Selection.CurrentRegion.Select
    Selection.PrintOut Copies:=1, Collate:=True
End Sub
```

Tip #327 from 	A nice feature of recording macros in Excel is that the program automatically adds some comment information about the recording process: the macro's name and date, who recorded it, and any shortcut key(s) assigned to the macro. (For the sake of space, these comments aren't shown in the examples in this chapter—just the macro code itself appears in the examples.)

Functions are procedures that return a result. You are undoubtedly familiar with Excel's built-in *functions (page 254)*, such as SUM and AVERAGE. VBA gives you the power to create custom functions that can be used like Excel's built-in worksheet functions. Functions begin with the word Function and end with the words End Function (see Listing 29.2 for an example). This chapter covers creating macros; custom functions are addressed in Chapter 30.

LISTING 29.2.   THIS FUNCTION CALCULATES INCOME TAX FOR A GIVEN INCOME, DEDUCTIONS, AND TAX RATE

```
Function INCOMETAX(curIncome As Currency, curDeductions
As Currency, sinRate As Single) As Currency
Dim curNetIncome As Currency
curNetIncome = curIncome - curDeductions
INCOMETAX = curNetIncome * sinRate
End Function
```

Tip #328 from

When you record macros, the Macro Recorder automatically indents procedures for easier readability. If you create rather than record a macro, it's a good idea to add your own indenting (Excel doesn't do it automatically).

WHY CREATE YOUR OWN COMMANDS?

Macros give you the power to create your own commands. Why should you care? Because they can save you time, that's why! Think of some of the tasks that you perform repeatedly in Excel. Macros can do these tasks for you. Following are some typical repetitive tasks that can be automated with macros:

- Format and print a report.
- Assist in the completion of an Excel form, such as an expense report.
- Consolidate data from several workbooks into a master workbook.
- Import and plot data to a chart.
- Assign a keyboard shortcut to a frequently used command.
- Apply your favorite AutoFormat to a range of cells.
- AutoFit all columns on the current worksheet.
- Create your own custom spreadsheet application.

→ Macros also are used to create custom toolbar buttons and shortcut keys. For details, **see** "Modifying Toolbars," **p. 869**

CREATING A MACRO WITH THE MACRO RECORDER

The Macro Recorder records all your keyboard and mouse actions to a VBA macro. You use it like a tape recorder. Turn it on, complete the Excel task that you want to automate, and turn it off.

Tip #329 from

> Before you begin to record a macro, ensure that you are familiar with the steps involved with the task to automate. A good practice is to write them down on a piece of paper, as in the following example, which details the steps required to print two copies of the entire workbook.
>
> 1. Choose File, Print from the menu.
> 2. Type 2 in the Number of Copies box.
> 3. Choose Entire Workbook from the Print What option group.
> 4. Click OK.
>
> Remember that the Macro Recorder records everything you do, whether it's an intended step or an unintended step. Knowing the steps to record before beginning will make the macro easier to record and play back faster.

WHAT YOU SHOULD CONSIDER BEFORE RECORDING

Before you begin recording, you must decide where to store the macro and how to record it. The following sections discuss the options to consider when making these decisions.

MACRO STORAGE OPTIONS

Excel provides the following three options for storing your macro:

- Current workbook
- Personal Macro Workbook
- New workbook

If you choose to store the macro in the current workbook, you can play back that macro when this workbook is open. Suppose that you're recording a chart macro that will create a series of expense analysis charts in a workbook called Expenses.xls. It would make sense to store the macro with the Expenses.xls workbook. You wouldn't want to play back the macro in another workbook that doesn't contain expense data. The charts would be incorrect.

If you store the macro in the Personal Macro Workbook, it will be available to any workbook. Suppose that you frequently must save some of your workbooks as text files for export to another program. You want to automate this process with a macro. If you store the export macro in the Personal Macro Workbook, you can run it regardless of which workbook is open. If you store the macro in another workbook, you have to open that workbook each time you want to run the macro.

Tip #330 from

> If you attach a macro to a workbook and then assign the macro to a toolbar button, clicking that button from a different workbook will (if necessary) automatically open the workbook containing the macro.

The *Personal Macro Workbook* is a hidden workbook that Excel creates the first time you choose this option for storage. It's saved to the XLStart folder—a subfolder of the Excel folder on your hard drive. When you launch Excel, this workbook is opened automatically (although it's hidden, so you're not aware that it's open), thus making its macro content available to any other workbook.

Caution

> The Personal Macro Workbook is a file called Personal.xls, usually located in the folder c:\Windows\Application Data\Microsoft\Excel\XLStart. Be careful not to delete or move this file accidentally. If you record macros frequently, or record complex macros, back this file up occasionally to protect it.
>
> Upgrading from Office 97 or 95? If you had a Personal.xls file (or any workbook) in your XLStart folder, you'll find those files in a second XLStart folder, usually located in c:\Program Files\Microsoft Office\Office\. Any additional globally recorded macros will be stored in your old Personal.xls in the second XLStart folder.

The option to store a macro in a new workbook is the least common storage option. It usually is used when you want to begin recording with no workbooks open. For example, you may want to record creating a new workbook as part of the macro process.

ABSOLUTE VERSUS RELATIVE RECORDING

A macro can be recorded relatively or absolutely. If you choose to record *relatively*, the macro will always play back from the current position of the cell pointer. If you choose to record *absolutely*, the macro will always play back on the range used when you recorded the macro. Depending on the purpose of the macro, this can be important. As a general rule of thumb, if you want the macro to play back on a different range of cells each time, record it relatively. If you want it to play back on the same range of cells each time, record it absolutely. If the macro's purpose does not require modifying or selecting a range of cells, don't worry about relative or absolute recording. The following example illustrates the difference between absolute and relative playback.

A macro recorded absolutely:

1. Start recording in cell A1.
2. Select cell A4.
3. Bold the cell.

Here's the same macro recorded relatively:

1. Start recording in cell A1.
2. Select the cell that's three down from the current cell.
3. Bold the cell.

The absolute macro will always bold cell A4. The relative macro will always bold the cell that's three cells down from the current cell.

RECORDING A MACRO

After you decide what to record, how to record it, and where to store it, you can begin the macro recording process.

Tip #331 from

In most cases, you'll want to select cells or objects that the macro will affect before you begin the recording process. To illustrate the point, suppose that you're recording a macro to freeze panes. If you start recording, select cell B4, and then freeze panes, the macro will always freeze panes at cell B4. If you select cell B4 before you start recording, on the other hand, the macro will freeze panes at the current position of the cell pointer during play-back. This makes the macro more versatile.

The exception to this rule is if you want the macro to affect the same cells or object every time it plays back. For example, if you want a macro to always place the date in cell A1, you should record the process of selecting cell A1 as part of the macro.

To record a macro, follow these steps:

1. Choose Tools, Macro, Record New Macro to open the Record Macro dialog box (see Figure 29.1).

Figure 29.1.
Use the options in this dialog box to set up the new macro's back-ground information.

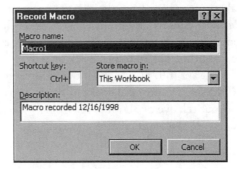

2. Type a name in the Macro Name text box. Macro names can contain letters, numbers, and underscores, but no spaces. They must begin with a letter and be no more than 64 characters in length.

Tip #332 from

Keep macro names short (20 characters or fewer) and make them descriptive of the task they will perform. Separate each word in the name with an underscore or use capitaliza-tion to differentiate each word. Structure the names—for example, Print_Expense_Rpt or PrintExpenseRpt.

3. (Optional) Select the storage location for the macro from the Store Macro In combo box. The default setting stores the new macro in the current workbook.

   If you're recording more than one macro in a session, you'll notice that the Store Macro In option displays whatever choice you made in the previous recording attempt. The setting here returns to This Workbook for each new Excel session.

4. (Optional) If you want to play back the macro by pressing a shortcut key, type the letter that you want to use as part of the shortcut key in the Shortcut Key text box.

Caution

Macro shortcut keys override Excel's built-in shortcut keys. If you choose Ctrl+P as the shortcut key for a macro, for example, Ctrl+P will no longer open the Print dialog box. This isn't a good practice, especially if you're creating macros in a workbook that other people will use. Imagine opening a workbook created for you. You press Ctrl+P to open the Print dialog box and instead a ten-page report prints! Excel already uses most of the Ctrl+<letter> key combinations as keyboard shortcuts. Try using Ctrl+Shift+<letter> key combinations instead.

5. (Optional) Type in the Description text box a brief description of what the macro does. The description can be seen in the Macros dialog box at playback time. Descriptions help you to remember what task each macro performs, especially if you plan to record a lot of macros.

   Figure 29.2 shows the completed Record Macro dialog box.

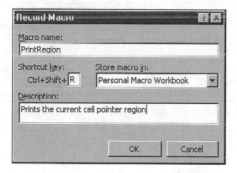

Figure 29.2.
When the Record Macro dialog box is complete, you're ready to begin recording.

6. Choose OK to close the Record Macro dialog box. The status bar displays the word Recording and the Stop Recording toolbar appears (see Figure 29.3).

Caution

Don't hide the Stop Recording toolbar. You'll need it to stop the macro recorder! If you do accidentally hide it, choose Tools, Macro, Stop Recording.

To get the Stop Recording toolbar to reappear after you've hidden it, you must start recording a macro, use the View, Toolbars command, and select the Stop Recording toolbar. Then end the macro recording and delete the macro you just recorded, or edit it to remove the step that redisplays the toolbar.

Stop Recording button   Relative Reference button

Figure 29.3.
Use the Stop
Recording toolbar to
record relatively and
to stop recording.

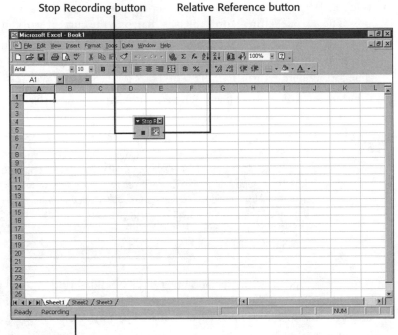

The status bar shows the word Recording when the Macro Recorder is running.

7. To record the macro relatively, click the Relative Reference button on the Stop Recording toolbar.

8. Perform each step that's part of the task you are recording.

9. Click the Stop Recording button on the Stop Recording toolbar.

Caution

It's easy to forget that the Macro Recorder is on. It will keep recording until you tell it to stop, so be sure that you turn it off when the task at hand is recorded, or you'll get unexpected results at playback time! If you do forget to stop the recorder, you don't have to rerecord the entire macro; you can just edit it to remove the extra steps. See the later section "Editing a Macro" for details.

CREATING AN AUTOFIT COLUMN MACRO

A simple and time-saving macro to record is one that will AutoFit every column on the active worksheet. The following macro will select every column on the current sheet, AutoFit each, then select cell A1. (If you prefer your worksheets to have custom column sizes, of course, you can record something else for practice, or just delete this macro—or never use it—after recording.) To record the AutoFit macro, perform the following steps:

1. Be sure that cell A1 is visible onscreen.

2. Display the Record Macro dialog box by choosing Tools, Macro, Record New Macro. Store the macro in the Personal Macro Workbook so that it will be available to any workbook. Name it FitColumnWidths (or some other appropriate name). If desired, assign a keyboard shortcut of Ctrl+Shift+C. Choose OK to start recording.

3. Press Ctrl+A to select all the cells on the current sheet.

4. Choose Format, Column, AutoFit Selection.

5. Select cell A1 on the current sheet.

6. Stop the Macro Recorder.

7. Now test the new macro. Switch to a new sheet or workbook that requires column-width adjustments. Press Ctrl+Shift+C to AutoFit the column widths.

WHERE ARE MACROS SAVED?

A workbook is composed of objects such as worksheets, chart sheets, and modules. A *module* is an object that holds VBA code. Collectively, a workbook's objects are called a *project*. When you save a workbook, you're really saving the project that contains all of the workbook's objects.

→ To learn more about projects, **see** "Understanding the Visual Basic Editor," **p. 925**

If you're storing a macro in the current workbook, save the workbook after recording. If you're storing a macro in the Personal Macro Workbook, you'll be prompted to save it when you exit Excel. Choose Yes when prompted to save the Personal Macro Workbook, or you'll lose any new macros you designated for storage there.

> **Caution**
>
> If you're recording or creating lengthy or complex macros, save the Personal Macro Workbook (Personal.xls) from the Visual Basic Editor immediately after completing each macro. A power loss can condemn unsaved macros to the bit bucket. Chapter 30, "Creating Interactive Excel Applications with VBA," describes the use of the Visual Basic Editor.

OPENING WORKBOOKS THAT CONTAIN MACROS

When you open a workbook that contains a macro, you see the message box shown in Figure 29.4.

Figure 29.4.
This message box appears when opening a workbook that contains macros.

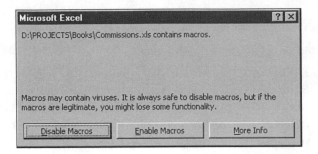

If you know the source of the workbook is reliable, choose Enable Macros. If you don't know who created the workbook, choose Disable Macros. Some macros contain viruses that can corrupt workbooks or Excel itself.

If you know that the source of your macros is always reliable (you open only workbooks that contain macros you have created yourself, for example) you can disable the warning message box. To do so, choose Tools, Macro, Security to open the Security dialog box and select Low from the Security Level tab (see Figure 29.5).

Figure 29.5.
Use the Security dialog box to disable macro warning-message boxes.

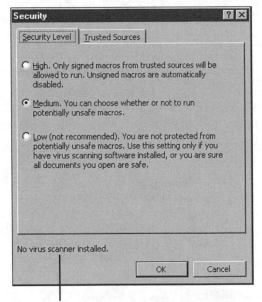

If you see this message, you probably shouldn't choose the Low setting.

Caution

If you download sample workbooks from the Internet or receive them via email from unreliable sources, don't disable the macro security warning. You could expose Excel and your workbooks to potentially damaging macro viruses.

Note

Excel 2000 allows you to digitally sign your macros. By doing so, other users of your macro workbooks can bypass the security message, yet keep security in place for workbooks from less-reliable sources. For more information on digital signatures, search the Help system for "digital signatures" and jump to the help topic "Digitally sign a macro project."

Tip #333 from

Ken

To learn more about Excel macro viruses, go to Microsoft's Excel virus Web page at `http://www.microsoft.com/excel/productinfo/vbavirus/emvolc.htm.` (If the address changes, as is common with Web sites, you may need to search the Microsoft Web site or Knowledge Base for details on Excel macro viruses.)

MACRO PLAYBACK

Excel provides a variety of ways to play back a macro:

- Select the macro from a list in the Macro dialog box.
- Give it a keyboard shortcut.
- Attach it to a toolbar button.
- Assign it to a menu.
- Assign it to a graphic object.

Caution

Always save a workbook that contains a macro before you test the macro. If the macro contains errors, you may lose data when it plays back! If you find that data loss occurs after playback, close the workbook without saving and open it again to restore the lost data.

Table 29.1 lists each method's pros and cons.

TABLE 29.1. MACRO PLAYBACK METHODS

Playback Method	Pro	Con
Macro dialog box	No additional setup for playback required.	Longest method of playback.
Keyboard shortcut	Fast and easy. Can be assigned at the time of recording or by clicking the Options button in the Macros dialog box. Access to the macro from anywhere in the workbook.	Must know the shortcut.

continues

TABLE 29.1. CONTINUED

Playback Method	Pro	Con
Toolbar button	Macros can be grouped by function. Quick access to the command. Access from any part of the workbook.	Buttons are small and sometimes hard to understand.
Menu command	Macros can be grouped by function. More familiar to new and casual users. Easy access to macros from any part of the workbook.	Menus aren't used as often by frequent or power users.
Graphic object	Large surface area to click for playback. Space for typing a longer text description directly on the object. Can be placed directly in a workbook.	Too many objects can clutter the worksheet. Object available to only one sheet in the workbook. Easy to lose the object when scrolling.

How should you decide which method is best? If the workbook that contains the macros is for your own personal use, select the method that you find easiest. Avoid graphic objects if the macro will be used in a large, multiple-sheet workbook.

If you're designing a workbook that other people will use, find out a little about the likes, dislikes, and skill level of the users. If they're casual or inexperienced users, use menus. If they're experienced or power users, assign a toolbar button and a keyboard shortcut to each macro. Give the inexperienced users fewer options to minimize confusion and give the experienced users more options so that they can choose their own method of playback.

Tip #334 from

Menus can't be attached to a workbook as can toolbars, but you can create a custom toolbar that consists of menus, which then can be attached to a workbook, yet looks and works like a menu bar. See Chapter 28, "Customizing Excel to Fit Your Working Style," for details on creating custom toolbars.

USING THE MACRO DIALOG BOX

Playing back a macro using the Macro dialog box requires the least amount of effort on your part; however, it's also the least convenient method of playback. It's used mostly in the testing phase of macro creation. Use the command as follows:

1. Choose Tools, Macro, Macros or press Alt+F8 to open the Macro dialog box (see Figure 29.6).

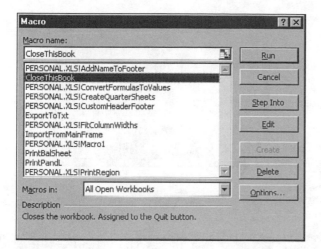

Figure 29.6.
The Macro dialog box displays a list of macros from all open workbooks for playback or editing.

2. Select the macro you want to play back. As you click on a macro name in the Macro Name list, note the description of the macro at the bottom of the dialog box.

3. Click the Run button or press Enter.

ASSIGNING A KEYBOARD SHORTCUT

A keyboard shortcut can be assigned to a macro at the time of recording (see the ealier section "Recording a Macro"). There are times, however, when you will want to assign or change a keyboard shortcut after the macro has been recorded. Keyboard shortcuts are easy to use provided that you can remember them! If your macro is part of a workbook that will be used by others, consider another method of playback, such as a button or menu command. Most users find these methods easier than remembering a keyboard shortcut. (As mentioned earlier, keyboard shortcuts can also surprise the user—even you—if they replace the Excel default shortcuts, or if they use a key combination that can be pressed by accident.)

To assign a shortcut to a macro after recording is complete, follow these steps:

1. Choose Tools, Macro, Macros, or press Alt+F8.

2. From the Macro Name list in the Macro dialog box, select the macro to which you want to assign a keyboard shortcut.

3. Click the Options button to display the Macro Options dialog box.

4. Place the insertion point in the Shortcut Key text box (see Figure 29.7).

Figure 29.7.
Assign a shortcut key to an existing macro with the Macro Options dialog box.

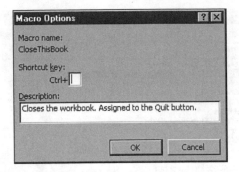

5. Press the desired shortcut-key combination.

Note

You don't have to press the Ctrl key when entering a shortcut-key combination. Instead, press the remaining key or keys. For example, to assign Ctrl+Shift+P to a macro, just press Shift+P.

6. Choose OK, and then close the Macro dialog box.

Tip #335 from

You also can add or change the description of a macro in the Macro Options dialog box.

ASSIGNING A MACRO TO A TOOLBAR OR MENU

In Excel, toolbars and menus are very similar. Both consist of button groupings. The only real difference between the two is the way menus and toolbars appear onscreen. When assigning macros to toolbar buttons or menu commands, the same procedures are followed.

You may want to assign a macro to a menu or toolbar to provide for easier playback, especially if you're mouse-oriented. You also may want to make the commands available to other people in a familiar way if you're designing a workbook that they'll use.

To attach a macro to a toolbar button or menu, follow these steps:

1. Right-click any toolbar button or menu command.
2. Choose Customize from the shortcut menu to open the Customize dialog box.
3. Choose the Commands tab.
4. Select Macros from the Categories list (see Figure 29.8).

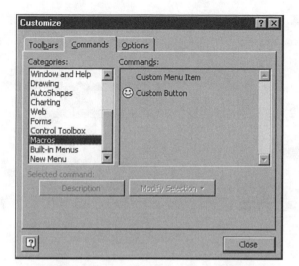

Figure 29.8.
Drag Custom Button
to add a new toolbar
button or Custom
Menu Item to add a
new menu command.

5. To add a new toolbar button, drag Custom Button from the Commands list to the desired location on the existing toolbar and release it.

   To add a new menu command, drag Custom Menu Item to an existing menu. For example, if you want to place the new command on the File menu, drag Custom Menu Item on top of the File menu. Don't let go of the mouse button yet! The entire File menu will appear. Drag down the File menu until you have the new command positioned properly on the menu; then release the mouse button. If you opened the wrong menu by accident, just continue dragging the Custom Menu Item button, placing it over the correct menu, and position it.

6. Right-click the new button or command.

7. Choose Assign Macro from the shortcut menu (see Figure 29.9).

8. Select the macro that you want assigned to the button or command from the Macro Name list in the Assign Macro dialog box (see Figure 29.10).

9. Choose OK.

10. Close the Customize dialog box.

ScreenTips can be assigned to toolbar buttons. The name you assign to the button will appear as its ScreenTip. The name also functions as the button's text if you choose one of the text display options. Here's how to assign a name to a toolbar button or menu command:

1. Right-click any toolbar button or menu.

2. Choose Customize.

Figure 29.9.
Right-click a custom
menu command or
toolbar button, and
choose Assign Macro.

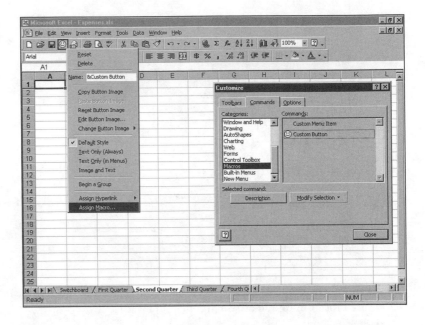

Figure 29.10.
Select a macro from
the Assign Macro dia-
log box to assign to a
toolbar button or
menu command.

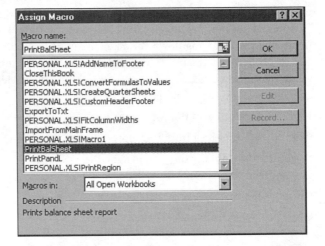

3. Right-click the button or command to which the macro was assigned. From the resulting shortcut menu, type a name for the command in the Name text box. Keep the
name as succinct as possible. Long names don't work well as ScreenTips or button-
display text.

Note

The ampersand (&) in the Name box signifies where the underscore will appear on the menu command. Therefore, if the new command is called Print Region and you want the e to be underscored, you would type **Print R&egion** in the Name box.

As a reminder, menus can be operated from the keyboard by pressing Alt and the underscored letter of the command (as in Alt+F to access the File menu). It's good practice to provide this functionality for consistency with other Excel menu commands.

4. Press Enter to lock in the new name.

5. Close the Customize dialog box.

Caution

Before you assign an underscore to the new command, be sure that the letter you choose doesn't conflict with the letter of any other command on that same menu. If two or more commands on the same menu contain the same letter, Excel will cycle through, selecting the commands that share the same letter. When the desired command is selected, you must press Enter to execute the command.

If you assign the command to the File menu, for example, place it below the Print command, and give it an underscore of P. When you press Alt+F+P on the keyboard, Excel will select the Print command on the menu. Press P a second time, and Excel will select your command. Press P a third time, and Excel will go back to selecting the Print command. Press Enter, and the Print dialog box will appear because Print is the currently selected command. If this happens to you, return to the custom command, and change the underscored character to a unique one for the menu in question.

Excel enables you to control how the button or command will display on the toolbar or menu. You can display an image, text, or both for either a toolbar button or a menu command. To change menu or button display, use the context menu that pops up when you right-click the custom menu item or the button with the Customize dialog box open.

Table 29.2 shows the display commands and their meanings.

TABLE 29.2. TOOLBAR BUTTON AND MENU COMMAND DISPLAY OPTIONS

Display Option	On a toolbar, displays...	On a menu, displays...
Default Style	Image only	Both image and name
Text Only (Always)	Name only	Name only
Text Only (In Menus)	Image only	Name only
Image and Text	Both image and name	Both image and name

Tip #336 from

Assign images to toolbar buttons that will be used for your personal use. If the toolbar is part of a workbook that will be used by other people, consider displaying text on the button instead of or in addition to the image.

To change a button image, follow these steps:

1. Right-click any toolbar button or menu.
2. Choose Customize.

Note

The Customize dialog box must be open when editing a custom button or menu item. Otherwise, right-clicking the custom button or the menu just opens the toolbar list.

3. Choose Change Button Image.
4. Select an image from the cascading menu of images (see Figure 29.11).

Figure 29.11.
Select a new button image with the Change Button Image command.

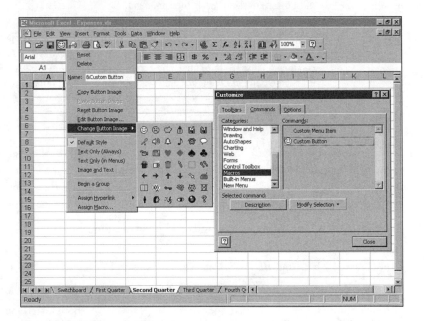

5. Close the Customize dialog box.

→ You can edit the default button images or copy images from other sources for use on button faces. For details, **see** "Changing the Button Images," **p. 872**

To change toolbar button or menu command display options, follow these steps:

1. Right-click any toolbar button.
2. Choose Customize.

3. Right-click the button to which the macro was assigned.

4. Choose one of the display options from the shortcut menu (see Figure 29.12).

5. Close the Customize dialog box.

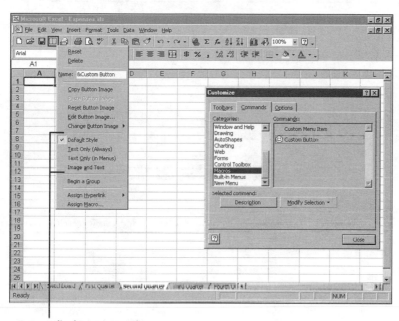

Figure 29.12.
The display commands on the button shortcut menu enable you to control button display.

Button display commands

CREATING A NEW TOOLBAR OR MENU FOR MACROS

Sometimes it's more convenient to have all your macros on a new custom toolbar or menu. You might do this to organize and categorize your macros. It's also wise when you're creating a workbook for other users. Such a workbook can be designed to display custom menus and toolbars upon opening. There are several reasons for this approach:

- **Making the workbook easier to use.** If you're designing a workbook for other people to use, it's likely that the majority of these people don't know much more than the basics of Excel. Your first goal is to make the workbook as easy for them to use as possible.

- **Preventing the user from modifying the workbook.** If you remove commands that allow the user to modify the workbook, you won't have to worry about seeing your workbook in several different versions. Custom toolbars and menus allow you to control the commands to which you want the user to have access and, sometimes more importantly, the commands to which you don't want them to have access.

Tip #337 from

Although this section discusses placing buttons and menu items on custom toolbars and menus, it's important to note that you can edit any of the Excel menus to add, change, or remove items as desired.

To create a custom toolbar, follow these steps:

1. Right-click an existing toolbar.

2. Choose Customize.

3. Click the Toolbars tab, if necessary.

4. Click the New button.

5. Enter a name for the new toolbar in the Toolbar Name text box (see Figure 29.13).

Figure 29.13.
Type a name for the custom toolbar in the New Toolbar dialog box.

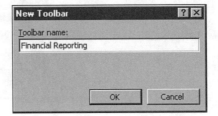

6. Choose OK.

7. Add buttons to the toolbar. For details, see the earlier section "Assigning a Macro to a Toolbar or Menu."

→ You may want to assign built-in Excel tools to your new toolbar as well. To learn how, **see** "Building Custom Toolbars," **p. 875**

To create a custom menu, follow these steps:

1. Right-click an existing toolbar.

2. Choose Customize.

3. Click the Toolbars tab, if necessary.

4. Click the New button.

5. Enter a name for the new menu in the Toolbar Name text box.

6. Choose OK.

7. Click the Commands tab in the Customize dialog box.

8. Select New Menu from the Categories list.

9. Drag New Menu from the Commands list to the new menu (see Figure 29.14).

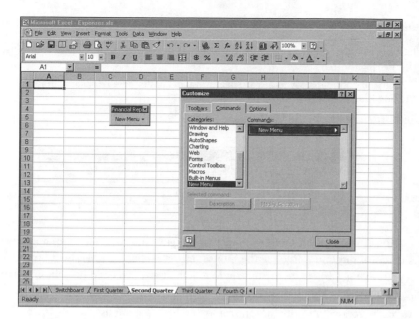

Figure 29.14.
Create a new menu with the New Menu command from the Customize dialog box.

10. Right-click the New Menu button on the new menu.

11. Type a name for the menu in the <u>N</u>ame text box. Keep the name short and descriptive of the type of commands the menu will display. Place an ampersand (&) in front of the letter that you want underscored for keyboard access to the menu (for more on the ampersand and its usage, see the earlier section "Assigning a Macro to a Toolbar or Menu").

12. Press Enter to lock in the new name.

13. To assign commands to the new menu, see the earlier section "Assigning a Macro to a Toolbar or Menu."

ASSIGNING A MACRO TO A GRAPHIC OBJECT

The last method of macro playback is the graphic object. The most common graphic object used is a button, but macros can be assigned to most graphic objects created with the Drawing and Forms toolbars.

Tip #338 from *Ken*	Use a graphic object if you have only a few macros to assign or if you want a large object with a long name. Avoid them in large workbooks. They're hard to access when scrolling great distances and when frequent switching between sheets is required.

To assign a macro to a button on a worksheet, follow these steps:

1. Right-click an existing toolbar and choose Forms from the shortcut menu. This will display the Forms toolbar.

→ You can add a command button directly to a worksheet if you're comfortable working with form controls. **See** "Adding Form Controls to Your Worksheets," **p. 624**

2. Select the Button tool from the toolbar (see Figure 29.15).

Figure 29.15.
Create a worksheet button with the Button tool on the Forms toolbar.

The Button tool

3. Move the mouse to the position on the sheet where you want the button to appear and drag in a diagonal direction. Release the mouse button when the worksheet button is drawn to your liking. (To create the button in a default size, you can just click, rather than drag.) The Assign Macro dialog box appears.

4. Select the macro to assign to the button from the Macro Name list.

5. Choose OK.

6. Drag across the name on the button to select it. Type a name descriptive of the macro the button will play (see Figure 29.16).

Figure 29.16.
Apply a descriptive name to a worksheet button by selecting and typing over the generic name given by Excel.

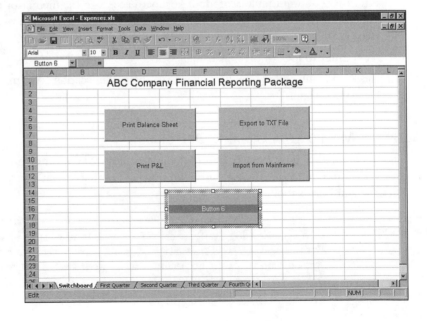

7. Click any cell in the current sheet to deselect the button. After the button has been deselected, it becomes active. An active button plays when it's clicked. Excel changes the mouse pointer into a hand when it's placed over an active button.

Tip #339 from

Ken

You may need to reselect the button to change its name, assign a new macro to it, or delete it. Press and hold down the Ctrl key before you click the button to select it, or right-click the button.

Assigning a macro to a nonbutton graphic object is very similar. The only difference is that the Assign Macro dialog box won't appear after you draw the graphic object. If you want to assign a macro to a rectangle, for example, draw the rectangle, right-click it, and choose Assign Macro from the shortcut menu. Select a macro from the Macro Name list and choose OK.

If you need to assign a macro to a graphic object that contains text, select the object by Ctrl+clicking it, or right-click a selection handle—or anywhere on the border of the object—to access the Assign Macro command (see Figure 29.17).

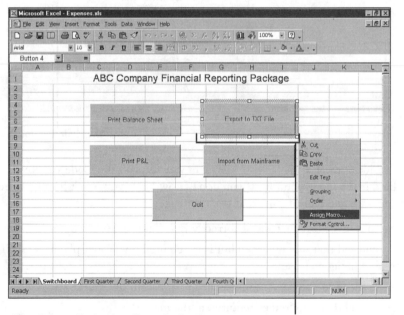

Figure 29.17.
Right-click a graphic object's border or handles to access the Assign Macro command.

Right-click a selection handle or the border to access the Assign Macro command.

EDITING A MACRO

Editing a macro can be intimidating the first few times you try it. Macros are edited in the Visual Basic Editor. The Editor is a very sophisticated program that contains multiple windows (see Figure 29.18). Don't worry! You don't have to know much about the editor to make a simple macro edit. If you decide you want to tackle the Editor and VBA in more detail, see Chapter 30.

Figure 29.18.
Don't let this picture scare you. You don't have to know much about the Visual Basic Editor to edit a macro.

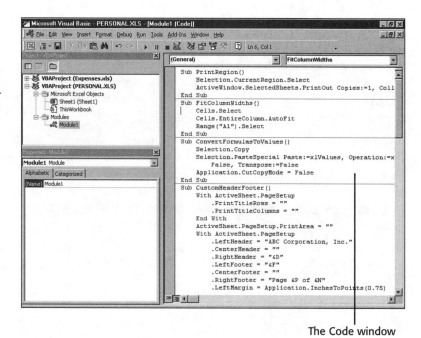

The Code window

Notice the right side of the Editor screen. The right side displays the Code window. Macros are edited in the Code window. If you don't know VBA, you won't be able to edit much. Following are some typical edits that you can make:

- Change the spelling of text that was incorrectly typed during recording.
- Remove a command that was recorded but isn't required for proper playback, such as an accidental scrolling command.
- Correct an erroneously recorded number, such as a margin or column width.
- Delete a command that's no longer required in the macro.

Macros are composed of VBA statements. You can edit these statements just as you would edit text in a word processing document. You can get a sense of what most statements do by looking at them. Following are some sample VBA statements that need editing, followed by a description of the edit that needs to be made:

- .LeftHeader = "ABC Corperation"

  Corporation is misspelled.

- ActiveWindow.SelectedSheets.PrintOut Copies:=1

  The number of copies to print should be 2.

- Range("A1").Select

  A4 is the cell that should be selected.

- .TopMargin = Application.InchesToPoints(1)

  The top margin was supposed to be 1.5 inches, not 1 inch.

Caution

Literal text always appears between quotation marks (" "). If you remove one or both of the quotation marks during editing, the macro will generate an error.

Don't delete a VBA statement if you're not sure what it does. This may result in the macro's not playing back properly.

To edit a macro, follow these steps:

1. If the macro you want to edit is stored in the Personal Macro Workbook, you must unhide the workbook before you can edit the macro. To unhide the Personal Macro Workbook, choose <u>W</u>indow, <u>U</u>nhide from the menu (see Figure 29.19). Choose Personal.xls from the Unhide dialog box and then choose OK.

Note

Remember, the Personal Macro Workbook is just like any other Excel workbook except that it's hidden by default. Therefore, when you unhide it, you won't see macros in the VB Editor but rather Sheet1 of the workbook.

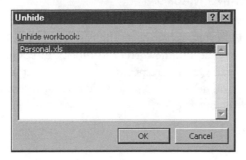

Figure 29.19.
Unhide the Personal Macro Workbook to edit the macros it contains.

2. Choose <u>T</u>ools, <u>M</u>acro, <u>M</u>acros, or press Alt+F8.
3. Select the macro to edit from the <u>M</u>acro Name list (see Figure 29.20).

Figure 29.20.
To edit a macro, select
the macro name and
choose Edit.

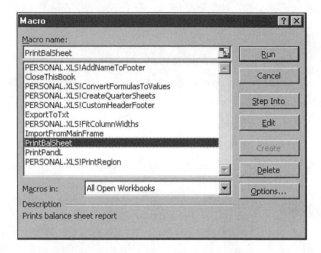

4. Choose Edit. The selected macro will open in the Visual Basic Editor.

5. Edit the macro in the Code window.

6. Close the Visual Basic Editor.

7. Save the workbook.

Note

When you have completed editing a macro in the Personal Macro Workbook, hide the workbook by activating its window and choosing Window, Hide from the menu. If you don't hide the Personal Macro Workbook, it will be the first workbook you see every time you launch Excel.

EXAMPLE: EDITING A SHEET-NAMING MACRO

A typical macro that you might need to edit is one that records the typing of text. The macro in this example is named CreateQuarterSheets and is stored in the Personal Macro Workbook. It names the first four sheets in the current workbook First Quarter, Second Quarter, Third Quarter, and Fourth Quarter, respectively. Suppose that after recording, you found the names were too long. You decide to edit the word Quarter to the abbreviation Qtr. Here's how you would make the change:

1. Unhide the Personal Macro Workbook. Open the macro CreateQuarterSheets in the Visual Basic Editor.

2. Select the first instance of the word Quarter in the Code window (see Figure 29.21).

Select this word.

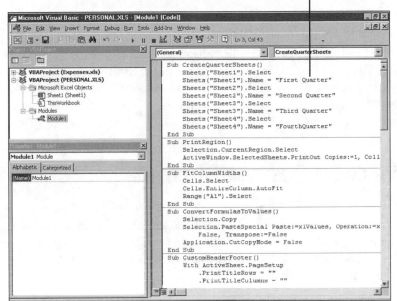

Figure 29.21.
Select the word
Quarter in the Code
window of the Visual
Basic Editor.

3. Type **Qtr** in its place, as shown in Figure 29.22.

The revised text

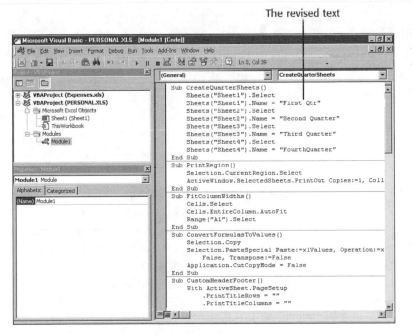

Figure 29.22.
Type over the old text
with the word **Qtr**. Be
sure to leave the quo-
tation marks.

4. Repeat this edit for the other three quarters.

5. Close the Visual Basic Editor.

6. Save and hide the Personal Macro Workbook.

7. Upon exiting Excel, be sure to choose <u>Y</u>es when prompted to save the Personal Macro Workbook. What you're saving here is the setting that the workbook is hidden. You'll always see this prompt after hiding the Personal Macro Workbook and exiting Excel. Always choose <u>Y</u>es, or the Personal Macro Workbook will be the first workbook to appear each time you start Excel.

DELETING MACROS, CUSTOM BUTTONS, AND CUSTOM MENU ITEMS

From time to time, you may need to delete a graphic object, macro, custom toolbar button, or custom menu item, usually because the item is no longer needed or was created in error. The easiest object to delete is a graphic object, such as a worksheet button. Right-click the object, and choose Cu<u>t</u> from the shortcut menu.

Other objects require a little more work to remove.

To delete a macro, follow these steps:

1. Unhide the Personal Macro Workbook (or the workbook containing the macro, if it's hidden), and choose <u>T</u>ools, <u>M</u>acro, <u>M</u>acros from the menu, or press Alt+F8.

2. From the <u>M</u>acro Name list, select the macro that you want to delete.

3. Click the <u>D</u>elete button.

4. Click Cancel to close the Macro dialog box.

5. Save the workbook and hide it again, if necessary.

To delete a custom toolbar button or menu item, follow these steps:

1. Right-click any toolbar button or menu command, and choose <u>C</u>ustomize from the shortcut menu.

2. To remove the button or command, do one of the following:

   • Drag the button or menu command that you want to remove from the toolbar or menu away from the toolbars and menus (so you don't accidentally drop it on a different toolbar or menu). When the mouse symbol shows a black X, release the mouse. The button or command will be deleted.

   • Right-click the toolbar button or menu command that you want to delete. Choose <u>D</u>elete from the context menu.

3. Click Close, and the Customize dialog box closes.

Caution

Be careful what you drag off of a menu or toolbar. All Excel menus and toolbars are completely customizable. This means that you can remove any command or button.

If you remove a menu command or button in error, don't panic! All toolbars and menu commands can be reset to their defaults. Here's how:

1. Right-click any menu command or toolbar button, and choose **C**ustomize.
2. Click the Tool**b**ars tab, if necessary.
3. To reset a toolbar, select the toolbar (such as Standard, for example) from the Tool**b**ars list. To reset the menu bar, select Worksheet Menu Bar from the list.
4. Click the **R**eset button and then the OK button in the resulting message box.
5. Close the Customize dialog box.

MACROS TO HELP YOU WORK FASTER

This section provides some helpful suggestions for macros that can speed up your work. Be sure to store them in the Personal Macro Workbook so that they'll be available for playback in all your workbooks. Consider assigning each a keyboard shortcut or toolbar button for faster playback.

- **Print the current region.** This macro selects all the cells in the current region and prints them. The *current region* is defined as a range of contiguous cells bounded by blank columns and blank rows (or positioned at the edge of the worksheet). When recording this macro, use Edit, Go To, click the Special button, and select Current **R**egion to select the current region.

Tip #340 from

Ken

To take full advantage of the "print current region" macro, don't include any blank spacing rows or columns between titles, subtitles, or within the data. If you need to add spacing, change row heights and column widths instead.

- **AutoFormat.** Record a macro to apply your favorite AutoFormat for quick and professionally formatted worksheets. You can record the macro one of two ways: It can apply an AutoFormat to the current selection or apply it to the current region. As you may know, if a range of cells is selected, the AutoFormat command applies the AutoFormat to the selection. If a single cell is selected, the AutoFormat command applies an AutoFormat to the current region. Regardless of how you choose to record it, select a range or single cell before you turn on the recorder.

TROUBLESHOOTING

INCREASING MACRO PLAYBACK SPEED

My macros play back slower than I like. How can I get them to play back faster?

When played back, any recorded macro will show screen motions such as scrolling. In some instances, this can significantly increase playback time. To turn off screen updating and thereby decrease playback time, open the VB Editor, and add the following line of code directly under the Sub *<macro name>* line of the macro:

```
Application.ScreenUpdating = False
```

RUNTIME ERRORS

I keep getting a runtime error during playback and can't determine why. What should I do?

A *runtime error* indicates that some part of the code no longer makes sense in the current playback environment. For example, perhaps as part of the original macro recording, you selected a sheet called Expenses. Later, after recording, you rename the sheet Current Expenses. A runtime error is generated because the macro is attempting to select a sheet called Expenses that no longer exists.

Of course, finding and correcting runtime errors (known as *debugging*) isn't always easy. So, you have two choices. You can rerecord the macro from the beginning or use the VB Editor's debugging tools to find the bug. If you don't have the time or desire to learn more about macros beyond recording them, rerecording is the fastest solution. However, if you know you'll work with macros often or will have to create complex macros in the future, you should learn more about debugging with the VB Editor.

→ To learn more about debugging, **see** "Debugging," **p. 942**

EXCEL IN PRACTICE

A common task in Excel is applying custom headers and footers to the current sheet or all sheets in a workbook. If you want a macro to apply headers and footers to all sheets, right-click a sheet tab, and choose Select All Sheets from the shortcut menu before you set the headers and footers. It's also a good idea to record deselecting all the sheets as part of the macro so that you don't have all of the sheets grouped when the macro stops playing. A quick way to deselect all sheets is to click the active sheet tab while pressing the Shift key. To record the macro, follow these steps:

1. Turn on the macro recorder. Store this macro in the Personal Macro Workbook, and call it CustomHeaderFooter or something similar.

2. Select all the sheets in the current workbook (see Figure 29.23).

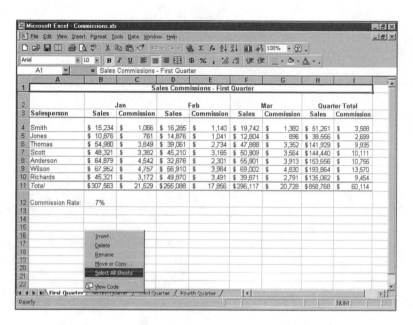

Figure 29.23.
Select all the sheets using the Select All Sheets command from the sheet tab shortcut menu. This will apply the same headers and footers to all sheets in the workbook.

3. Set the headers and footers using the File, Page Setup command from the menu (see Figure 29.24).

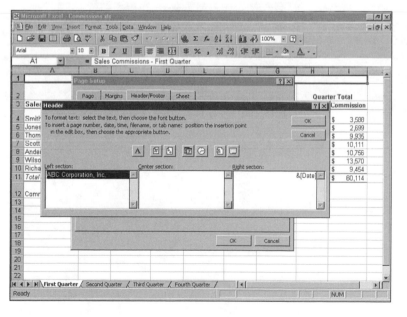

Figure 29.24.
Set the header and footer using the Custom Header and Custom Footer buttons in the Page Setup dialog box.

4. Press and hold down the Shift key as you click the sheet tab for the active sheet.

5. Stop the recorder.

CHAPTER **30**

CREATING INTERACTIVE EXCEL APPLICATIONS WITH VBA

In this chapter *by Ken Cook*

WHY WRITE MACROS RATHER THAN RECORD THEM?

The *Macro Recorder (page 886)* enables you to create your own command macros in Excel by recording menu selections, keystrokes, and mouse movements. Recorded macros have their limitations, however. Following are a few things that can't be recorded:

- **Interaction**. You want the user to have input into how the macro will play back. Suppose that you create a workbook that charts sales data for 20 product segments. Rather than force users to print a chart for each segment (in this case, 20 charts), you would rather have them select which segments they want to print.

- **Decisions**. You want the macro to make decisions on how to play back based on what it encounters when playing back. Suppose that you have a worksheet with one thousand rows of product sales data at the SKU level. Your sales data provider gave you the data in Excel workbook form. The file contains some SKUs with sales amounts equal to zero interspersed among the data rows. You want to eliminate these SKUs.

- **Custom functions**. You continually perform the same complex or lengthy calculation in your spreadsheets. Suppose that you have several worksheets that require you to display the number of year-to-date days. Rather than entering that complex formula every time you need the current number of year-to-date days, you want a simpler way to enter the calculation.

> **Caution**
>
> The Macro Recorder can be inefficient. For example, in most cases you don't have to select a range of cells to do something to it, yet because the Macro Recorder can only record keystrokes, it knows of no other way to refer to a range. For this kind of operation, writing the macro yourself with VBA is much more efficient.

Visual Basic for Applications (VBA), Excel's programming language, provides the tools to create solutions to scenarios that can't be recorded. Through VBA, you can create a solution to virtually any problem that you encounter in Excel. You can make using Excel more efficient for yourself and, sometimes more importantly, for other users who don't know much about the application but are required to use it. You can completely customize Excel through VBA to perform a specific task. You can even change the entire Excel interface.

The goal of this chapter is to provide you with a basic VBA foundation. With that foundation, you can create a simple VBA application. Due to the enormous scope of VBA, of course, this chapter can't possibly provide more than a brief overview of the possibilities for programming Excel procedures with VBA. You'll have to consult other resources to become highly VBA proficient.

The first part of this chapter explains some VBA terms and concepts and shows code samples that help define the concepts. The latter part of the chapter explains how to use the tools that Excel provides to write VBA code. By gaining an understanding of these VBA concepts, your code writing will come easier.

→ For more in-depth information on VBA, see Que's *Special Edition Using Visual Basic 6*, ISBN #0-7897-1542-2.

INTRODUCTION TO OBJECT-ORIENTED PROGRAMMING

VBA is a structured programming language just like English is a structured communication language. English sentences are constructed of building blocks such as nouns, verbs, and adjectives; VBA sentences (called *statements*) are constructed of building blocks such as objects, methods, and properties. English sentences are grouped in larger blocks of related information called paragraphs; similarly, VBA statements are grouped in larger blocks called procedures. A *procedure* is a set of VBA statements that performs a specific task or calculates a specific result. If you want to learn how to construct VBA statements and procedures, you first must learn more about the building blocks. This section provides some background information on VBA's building blocks.

PART

IX

CH

30

OBJECTS

VBA is an object-oriented programming language. Excel is made up of a series of objects that you can manipulate through code. Think of some of the objects that make up your office. You probably have a desk, chair, computer, and telephone. You use these objects to complete the various tasks that your job requires.

Similarly, when using Excel to complete a task, you're manipulating Excel objects to complete the task. For example, when you complete an Excel expense report form, you might open the workbook containing a worksheet with the expense report form, then enter data in a range on that form, and save the workbook. The workbook, worksheet, and range are all Excel objects. VBA can be used to manipulate such objects, making it easier for you to complete the task of submitting an expense report. Emailing the report to the Finance department, for example, is a process that could be automated. (For a complete list of Excel objects, see the Object browser located in the Visual Basic Editor.) To learn more about the Visual Basic Editor, see "Understanding the Visual Basic Editor," later in this chapter.

COLLECTIONS

Some objects are collection objects. A *collection* is a group of similar objects that are treated as one. Suppose that in your office, you have a desk with three drawers. You call them the top, middle, and bottom drawers. Together, you could say that they make up the "drawers collection." You refer to each drawer by its name when completing a task that involves the drawer. You might say to your coworker, "Please get the Murphy account folder from the bottom drawer of my desk."

The Workbooks collection is an example of an Excel collection object. The Workbooks collection consists of each workbook object that you have at your disposal. You refer to a workbook in the Workbooks collection by enclosing its name in parentheses. The following VBA snippet refers to the Expenses workbook:

```
Workbooks("Expenses.xls")
```

Methods

A *method* is an action that can be performed by an object. Think once again of the desk drawers in your office. They can be opened and closed. So, you could say that each has an open method and a close method. When you open a drawer to get a file, you are using the open method of the drawer.

An Excel object has methods as well. Excel's workbook object has an Open method and a Close method. You can use the menu to manually manipulate the workbook object with the Open and Close commands, or you can use VBA to programmatically manipulate the workbook object with the Open and Close methods. Excel objects are separated from their methods by a period. The following VBA snippet uses the Close method to close the Expenses workbook:

```
Workbooks(Expenses.xls").Close
```

Properties

Properties are used to describe an object. You could describe your office desk drawer as brown and made of wood. You could say that these are its color and material properties, respectively.

Some properties are read-only; others are read/write. Read-only properties can't be changed; read/write properties can. Your desk drawer's color property would be read/write. You can always pull out your paintbrush and change the color of the drawer. However, you can't change the material from which it's made without changing the drawer entirely, so the material property would be read-only.

Excel properties describe Excel objects. For example, the workbook object has a Path property. It describes the complete path to the referenced workbook. The Path property is read-only. You can't change the path of a workbook without saving it to a different folder. Just as methods are separated from objects by periods, so are properties. The following code snippet uses the Path property of the workbook object to display the path of a workbook called Expenses.xls in a message box onscreen:

```
Msgbox Workbooks("Expenses.xls").Path
```

> **Note**
>
> Msgbox is a function that displays a small message dialog box onscreen to alert or inform the user of something. For more information on functions, see the next section "Functions."

If you set a read/write property equal to something, it will change the current value. If you don't set a read/write property equal to something, it will tell you (also known as *return*) its current value. The Name property of the Sheet object of the Sheets collection is a read/write property. It can return the name of a sheet or set the name of a sheet.

This code snippet sets the name of Sheet1 to January:

```
Sheets("Sheet1").Name = "January"
```

The following code snippet returns the name of the active sheet (the one with the white sheet tab) in the current workbook in a message box onscreen:

```
Msgbox ActiveSheet.Name
```

FUNCTIONS

A VBA *function* is similar to a workbook function. It performs a calculation and then returns a result. Functions provide information that can assist you in building VBA procedures. Suppose that you want to ask the user of your application a question. The InputBox function displays a dialog box onscreen, with a prompt and text box. Figure 30.1 shows an input box.

Figure 30.1.
This input box prompts the user for a title.

When the user types a response in the input box and closes it with the OK button, the function returns whatever was typed in the box. If you typed **Sales** in the input box displayed in Figure 30.1, it would return the word Sales to your VBA code. You could then write code to place the word in a cell, use it as a header on a report, or make it a title of a chart—just to name a few uses. For a complete list of functions, including what they return and how to use them, see "Functions" under "Visual Basic Language Reference" on the Visual Basic Help Contents tab. For more information on accessing Visual Basic Help, see the section "Getting Help with Visual Basic," later in this chapter.

PUTTING IT ALL TOGETHER

Objects, methods, and properties are the building blocks of VBA code. Understanding what they are and how they're put together will give you a head start when writing VBA code. There will be times, especially in the beginning, when you know what should be done next but you don't know the correct VBA statement you need to complete your task. That's when you should ask yourself the following questions:

- What object am I trying to manipulate?
- Do I want to change the way the object is described?
- Do I want to do something to the object or have it do something?

If you know the answers to these questions, you can search the Help system for the statement you'll need. For example, if you want to use VBA to determine whether the current workbook is saved, start with the workbook object. Whether it's saved or not is descriptive. This tells you to look for a property. Each object's help page provides a link to the methods and properties of that object. Through that link, you can obtain information on various properties and methods of an object, including examples of how to use them.

When you query the Help system for the workbook object and then click on its properties link, you'll see the Saved property.

VARIABLES AND CONSTANTS

During code playback, there are times when information that's gathered from the user, returned by a function, or defined by the programmer must be stored temporarily for use later on. Sometimes, this information will change as the code is running. Other times, it will stay the same the entire time the code is running. Variables and constants are used to store this type of information during code playback.

WHAT IS A VARIABLE?

A *variable* is a temporary storage location in your computer's memory for a piece of information used by a procedure. Certain procedures obtain different data each time they run. Suppose that you've written a procedure that asks the user for his or her name and places it in the footer of the current workbook. If many people use this procedure, the name will be different every time the procedure is run. These are the logical steps such a procedure would follow:

1. Ask the user for his or her name.

2. Store it somewhere temporarily.

3. Place it in the footer.

Because you can't ask the user a question and alter the footer simultaneously through VBA, you must have a place to store the name temporarily—a variable. A variable name can be anything you want it to be; however, you must follow these guidelines when choosing a name:

- The name can be from 1 to 255 characters in length.
- It must begin with a letter.
- It can't contain spaces or periods.
- It must be unique among all other variable names within the same procedure.

Tip #341 from

Ken

Try to keep your variable names to 20 characters or less. For multiple-word variable names, capitalize the first letter of each word for better readability. Following are some sample variable names:

- CompanyName
- ShippingDate
- ReportTitle

The code in Listing 30.1 shows how the variable UserName is employed in a procedure. The procedure uses the InputBox function to query the user for a name, and then places that name in the left section of the footer. It also adds the page number to the right section of the footer and clears all header sections. (Later in the chapter, I will discuss in detail how to create this type of procedure in Excel.)

LISTING 30.1. THIS PROCEDURE UTILIZES THE VARIABLE USERNAME TO STORE A NAME GARNERED FROM THE USER. NOTE THAT THE VARIABLE IS USED TO SET THE LEFT SIDE OF THE FOOTER LATER IN THE PROCEDURE

```
1 Sub AddNameToFooter()
2    UserName = InputBox("What is your name?", "Add Name to Footer")
3    With ActiveSheet.PageSetup
4        .LeftHeader = ""
5        .CenterHeader = ""
6        .RightHeader = ""
7        .LeftFooter = UserName
8        .CenterFooter = ""
9        .RightFooter = "Page &P of &N"
10   End With
11 End Sub
```

Let's look at the procedure line by line. The first and last lines of the procedure define its starting and ending points. In addition, the first line defines the procedure's name, AddNameToFooter. Every command procedure begins with the word Sub followed by the name of the procedure, and ends with the words End Sub.

Line 2 uses the InputBox function to ask the user for his or her name and then stores that name in a variable called UserName. Lines 3 and 10 begin and end a With statement that executes a series of statements (in this case, properties) on an object (in this case, the PageSetup object). This technique saves you the time of having to type the word **PageSetup** in front of each PageSetup property you want to set.

Lines 4-9 use the header and footer properties of the PageSetup object to set the text of the header and footer. In particular, line 7 sets the left section of the footer equal to the value of the UserName variable, and line 9 sets the right section of the footer equal to the current page number and the total number of pages. Lines 4, 5, and 6 clear all three parts of the header, and line 8 clears the center section of the footer by setting those properties equal to "".

Note

An empty set of quotation marks (" ") in VBA represents what's called a *zero-length string*. A zero-length string is equivalent to nothing. Therefore, if you set a property or variable equal to " ", you erase its current value.

WHAT IS A CONSTANT?

Like a variable, a *constant* is a temporary holding area for a piece of information used in a procedure. Unlike a variable, however, a constant, as its name implies, never changes.

Suppose that you have a procedure that uses your company name four times. Further suppose that the company name is a long one, such as Widget Manufacturing & Development, Incorporated. Rather than typing that text in your procedure each time it's needed, you can assign it to a much shorter constant name. That way, when you need your company name, you don't have to type out all that text. Instead, you can type the constant name. Plus, should the value of the constant (in this case, the name of the company) change at some point in the future, you only have to change the definition of the constant and not the multiple lines of code that refer to it.

Constants must be declared. A *declaration statement* in VBA is used to define the value of a constant. Each constant declaration begins with the word Const. Constants should be declared at the top of a procedure, usually right under the Sub or Function statements. They often are designated in all caps for easy identification. Each word of a multiple-word constant usually is separated from the next with the underscore character (_). Listing 30.2 shows what the company name constant might look like in a procedure.

LISTING 30.2. THE DECLARATION AND USE OF A CONSTANT IN A PROCEDURE

```
1 Sub SetCoTitleToPage()

2    Const CO_NAME = "Widget Manufacturing & Development, Incorporated"

3    Range("A1").FormulaR1C1 = CO_NAME
4    With ActiveSheet.PageSetup
5       .LeftHeader = ""
6       .CenterHeader = ""
7       .RightHeader = ""
8       .LeftFooter = CO_NAME
9       .CenterFooter = ""
10      .RightFooter = "Page &P or &N"
11   End With

12 End Sub
```

Notice that the CO_NAME constant on line 2 is used to place the company name in cell A1 and in the left footer (lines 3 and 8, respectively).

Note

The company name is enclosed in quotation marks. All *literal text* (this is what VBA calls a string) placed in a procedure must be surrounded by quotation marks or an error will occur when running the procedure.

A closer look at the procedure in Listing 30.2 reveals that line 2 declares the constant CO_NAME equal to the literal text Widget Manufacturing & Development, Incorporated. Line 3 uses the FormulaR1C1 property of the Range object to set the value of cell A1 equal to the value of the CO_NAME constant. This line is the VBA equivalent of typing text in a cell.

Lines 4 through 11 use With to set the header and footer properties of the PageSetup object. The CO_NAME constant is used in line 8 to set the left footer equal to Widget Manufacturing & Development, Incorporated.

Tip #342 from	Type constant names in all caps and separate each word of a multiple-word constant name with an underscore. This makes it easier to visually distinguish constants from variables in a procedure.
Ken	

UNDERSTANDING THE VISUAL BASIC EDITOR

The Visual Basic Editor is the tool used to display VBA code in Excel. All VBA code is accessed through the Editor.

Before you look at the Editor, here's a little background on what it displays. Every workbook is made up of a series of Visual Basic objects, as mentioned earlier. Each sheet in a workbook is an object, as is the workbook itself. If a workbook contains a VBA procedure, it will have a *module* object. A module looks and acts like a word processing document. It contains the VBA instructions or code that make up procedures. The collection of all objects that make up a workbook is called a *project*. The Editor displays projects and their associated objects.

The Visual Basic Editor can be intimidating when first examined. To view it, choose Tools, Macro, Visual Basic Editor from the menu or press Alt+F11. The Standard toolbar contains tools required to manage your project.

Table 30.1 shows the Editor's Standard toolbar buttons.

TABLE 30.1. VISUAL BASIC EDITOR STANDARD TOOLBAR BUTTONS

Button	Name	Description
	Microsoft Excel	Returns you to Excel.
	Insert Object	Adds a new object to the current project.
	Save	Saves the workbook that contains the current project.
	Cut	Cuts selection so that it can be moved elsewhere.
	Copy	Copies selection so that it can be duplicated elsewhere.
	Paste	Pastes cut or copied selection to the location of the insertion point.

continues

	TABLE 30.1. CONTINUED	
Button	**Name**	**Description**
	Find	Finds a word or phrase within the project.
	Undo	Reverses previous actions.
	Redo	Reverses the Undo command.
	Run	Plays the current macro. Place the insertion point in a macro's code to make it the current macro. It also displays custom forms.
	Break	Pauses macro execution. Continue a paused macro from the breakpoint with the Run button.
	Reset	Stops macro execution.
	Design Mode	Toggles design mode on and off. Macro code doesn't run in design mode.
	Project Explorer	Shows the Project Explorer window if it's hidden. The Project Explorer enables you to browse the objects that make up a project for each open workbook.
	Properties Window	Shows the Properties Window if it's hidden. Properties describe an object. For example, a worksheet object has a Name property.
	Object Browser	Shows the Object Browser. The object browser displays all the objects that can be manipulated through VBA code.
	Toolbox	Shows the Toolbox. The Toolbox is used during the design of a custom form.
	Help	Accesses the help system.

By default, the Editor is divided into three windows (see Figure 30.2). The *Project Explorer* (or simply Project window) displays all open projects and their associated objects. You use this window to browse modules when attempting to locate a particular procedure.

The *Properties window* displays the properties of the selected object in the Project window. If a module is selected in the Project window, for example, the Properties window will display the only property of a module—its Name property. Read/Write properties of selected objects can be changed directly in the Properties window.

The *Code window* displays the code that is associated with the object selected in the Project Explorer. Because all procedures appear in the Code window, this is the window that you will use most often in the Editor.

Project Explorer · Code window

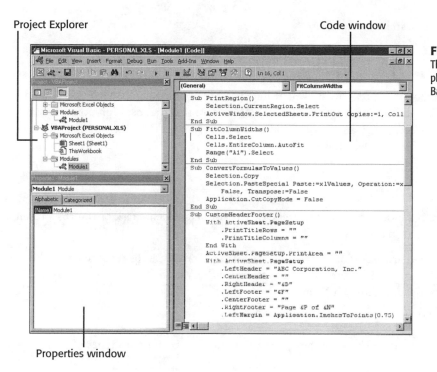

Figure 30.2.
Three windows displayed by the Visual Basic Editor.

Properties window

Tip #343 from

Ken

If you inadvertently close any of these windows, you can reopen them in the Editor by using the View menu.

GETTING HELP WITH VISUAL BASIC

The fastest and cheapest VBA help resource is Excel's online Help system. It contains the entire VBA language reference. Even experienced programmers find themselves using the Help system on a regular basis.

There are several ways to access the Help system. The most common, logically, is to use the Help menu. Follow these steps:

1. While in the Editor, choose Help, Microsoft Visual Basic Help from the menu or press F1. The Office Assistant appears.

2. Formulate a question for the topic for which you need help and type it in the Office Assistant's text box.

3. Click the Search button.

4. Choose a topic from the resulting list to display a help screen about the topic you selected.

Another method is to press the F1 key. While working on a module in the Editor, select or type the VBA word for which you want help. Make sure that the insertion point is somewhere in the word or that the word is selected. Then press F1. The Help system displays the help topic for the selected word.

VBA PROCEDURES

A procedure is a block of VBA code that either performs a specific task or returns a result. Procedures come in two flavors:

■ Subroutines are procedures that perform a specific task. Macros recorded with the Macro Recorder are subroutines. (For more on the Macro Recorder, see Chapter 29, "Recording and Editing a Macro.")

■ Functions are procedures that return a result.

The following sections show you how to use the Editor to create both types of procedures.

CREATING A NONRECORDED PROCEDURE

Whether you're creating a subroutine or a function, you can follow these general guidelines to get started:

1. Open the workbook to which you want to add the new procedure.

2. Choose Tools, Macro, Macros from the menu or press Alt+F8 (see Figure 30.3).

Figure 30.3.
Use the Macro dialog box to create a new nonrecorded procedure.

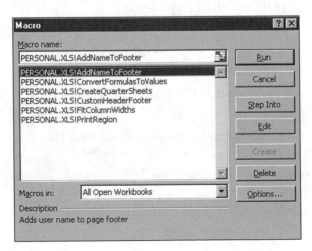

3. Type a name for the procedure in the Macro Name box.

Procedure names must begin with a letter and can contain letters, numbers, and the underscore character. They can't contain spaces.

4. Click the <u>C</u>reate button. The Visual Basic Editor opens with the new procedure displayed in the Code window (see Figure 30.4). The Sub statement is followed by the procedure name and the End Sub statement.

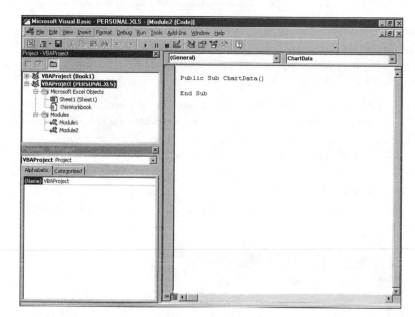

Figure 30.4.
A new procedure named ChartData() is displayed in the Code window of the Visual Basic Editor.

5. If you want to create a function, change the word Sub to Function on the first line of the new procedure. The last line will change automatically from End Sub to End Function.

6. Type the VBA statements required to create the new procedure.

Type all VBA statements (objects, methods, properties, built-in functions) in lowercase. By doing so, you can catch your mistakes as you type. When you move off the current line, the Editor capitalizes at least one letter in each word if you have typed the word correctly. The Editor also appropriately capitalizes the names of the variables and constants. If no capitalization takes place, check the word in question. Is it spelled correctly? Is it an actual Excel object, method, property, or VBA function?

Suppose that you type the following line:

```
range("A1").formular1c1 = CO_NAME
```

continues

continued

> When you move off it to the next line, the Editor changes it to this:
>
> `Range("A1").FormulaR1C1 = CO_NAME`
>
> So far, so good. Now what if the Editor displays this?
>
> `rane("A1").FormulaR1C1 = CO_NAME`
>
> The first word has no capital letters, so you know that you made some kind of typing error that must be corrected. In this case, *range* is misspelled at the beginning of the line.

After you create your first procedure in the Editor, you might need to add more procedures. You can use the Macros command on the Tools menu of the Editor; however, it's easier to add the new procedure using another command in the Editor window, especially if you're adding a function. Here's how:

1. Make sure that the module to which you want to add the new procedure is selected in the Project Explorer. If it isn't, look for an entry such as VBAProject (*<filename.xls>*). Expand the project (if necessary) to reveal its Microsoft Excel Objects and Modules folders. Expand the Modules folder if necessary to reveal the modules for the selected workbook. Then double-click the module name (most likely Module1) in the Modules folder to open the module in the Code window.

2. Choose Insert, Procedure from the menu. The Add Procedure dialog box appears (see Figure 30.5).

Figure 30.5.
Use the Add Procedure dialog box to add a new procedure to the currently displayed module in the Code window.

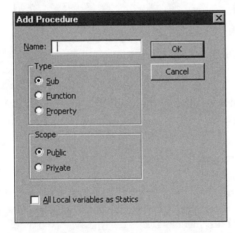

3. Type a name for the procedure in the Name text box.

4. To create a new subroutine, select Sub from the Type section of the dialog box. To create a function, select Function.

5. Leave the default scope of Public. *Scope* refers to the availability of the procedure to other procedures in the current project that aren't in the same module. Public procedures can be accessed by any other procedure in a project. For more information on scope, search the Help system for the word *scope*.

Caution

You can't have two public procedures with the same name in the same project. To be on the safe side, always use a unique name for each procedure within the same project.

6. Choose OK to add the new procedure to the selected module.

7. Type the VBA code required of the new procedure in the Code window.

PART
IX
CH
30

Tip #346 from

A faster way to create a new procedure is to type **Sub** or **Function** directly in the Code window, followed by the name of the procedure. When you press Enter, the Editor automatically adds the End Sub or End Function statement to the end of the new procedure.

There may be times when you need to add a new module to a VBA project. Usually this is done to organize procedures in some way. Perhaps you want to place all your functions in one module and your subroutines in another. This makes individual procedures easier to find when browsing for them in the Editor. To add a new module, use the following steps:

1. Choose Tools, Macro, Visual Basic Editor from the menu or press Alt+F11.

2. Select Insert, Module from the menu.

Similar to sheets in a workbook, after you have several modules in a project, you may want to name each module with a more meaningful name than the default for easier identification of the type of procedures the module contains. Here's how to name a module in the Editor:

1. Select the module to name in the Project Explorer. It will be in the Modules folder under the project that contains it.

2. Click the (Name) property heading or double-click the default name next to the Name property in the Properties window.

3. Type the new name and press Enter.

If you added a module in error or want to delete it for some other reason, perform the following steps:

1. Right-click the module to delete in the Project Explorer window.

2. Choose Remove <module name> from the shortcut menu.

3. Select No when asked whether you want to export the module before removing it (see Figure 30.6).

Note

The Editor allows you to export a module. This means that you're saving the module and all of its code. By doing so, you can import the module to another workbook. In effect, by exporting and importing, you're copying a set of procedures between workbooks.

Figure 30.6.
Choose No in this
message box when
deleting a module.

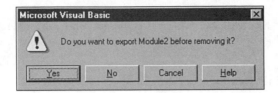

CREATING A FUNCTION PROCEDURE

As mentioned previously, a function is a type of procedure that returns a result. For example, the built-in Excel SUM function returns the total of a range of numbers that you supply to it. There may be times when you want to create your own custom functions, usually when the calculation you're attempting is complex or lengthy and you would like to simplify its entry. This section details some scenarios for creating a custom function and explains how to create one.

CREATING A FUNCTION TO CALCULATE THE NUMBER OF DAYS IN A MONTH

You can use custom functions to automate the process of entering a complex or frequent calculation in Excel. Suppose that you often must calculate the number of days in a given month. Listing 30.3 shows a formula that supplies this number.

> **LISTING 30.3.   ENTER A DATE IN CELL A2 AND THIS FORMULA IN ANOTHER CELL (SUCH AS A3). THE FORMULA RETURNS THE TOTAL NUMBER OF DAYS IN THE MONTH OF THE DATE YOU ENTERED**

```
=DAY(DATE(YEAR(A2),IF(MONTH(A2)=12,1,MONTH(A2)+1),1)-1)
```

It might be difficult to remember this calculation or too time-consuming to enter it repeatedly in each new worksheet that requires it. So, as an alternative, you can create a function. The function requires you to enter the formula one more time. In the future, however, when you need your calculation, all you have to enter is the name of the function, just as you would any other Excel function (plus any required arguments).

Most functions require at least one argument. An *argument* is a piece of information that the function needs so that it can perform its calculation correctly. In this case, the information the function needs is a date so that it can determine the number of days in the month referenced by the date.

Here's how to create and use this function:

1. Unhide the Personal Macro Workbook. If you don't have a Personal Macro Workbook to unhide, start a new workbook.

→ For more information on the Personal Macro Workbook, **see** "Macro Storage Options," **p. 888**

2. Navigate to a module in the Personal Macro Workbook or insert a new module.

3. Type the code in Listing 30.4 at the end of the module.

LISTING 30.4. ENTER THIS FUNCTION IN A MODULE TO CALCULATE THE NUMBER OF DAYS IN A GIVEN MONTH

```
Function NoDays(FullDate)
    NoDays = Day(DateSerial(Year(FullDate), IIf(Month(FullDate) = 12, 1,
➥   Month(FullDate) + 1), 1) - 1)
End Function
```

> **Note**
>
> Some worksheet functions have VBA equivalents with slightly different names. The VBA function equivalent of the worksheet function DATE is DATESERIAL. The VBA equivalent of the worksheet function IF is IIf.

4. Click the Save button on the Editor's Standard toolbar.

5. In a new workbook, type **2/15/00** in cell A1.

6. Select cell A2 and choose Insert, Function from the menu.

7. From the Function Category list, select User Defined.

8. Choose PERSONAL.XLS!NoDays from the Function Name list.

> **Note**
>
> The function name includes the workbook name PERSONAL.XLS! only if the Personal.xls workbook is hidden when you insert the function.

9. Type **A1** in the FullDate text box.

10. Choose OK. The custom function returns 29—the year 2000 is a leap year, so February contains 29 days. Figure 30.7 displays the function in use in a simple worksheet.

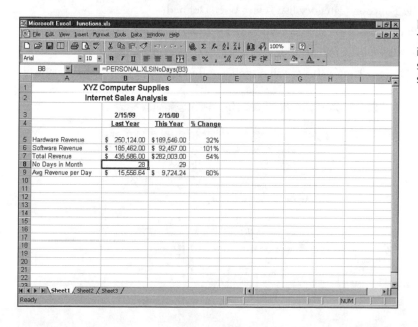

Figure 30.7.
The NoDays function in use in a simple sales analysis worksheet.

CREATING A PERCENT CHANGE FUNCTION

A difficult calculation for some to remember is the percentage change between two numbers. Do you divide by the first number or the second? A custom function can help here as well. Although this is a simple calculation, you only have to remember it once if you make it into a custom function.

Here's how to create the function:

1. Open the Visual Basic Editor and activate the Personal Macro Workbook (Personal.xls).
2. Choose Insert, Procedure from the menu. The Add Procedure dialog box opens.
3. Type **PerChange** in the Name box.
4. Select Function from the Type list.
5. Choose OK.
6. Modify the new function so that it matches Listing 30.5.

LISTING 30.5. THE COMPLETED PERCHANGE FUNCTION

```
Function PERCHANGE(Current, Prior)
    PERCHANGE = (Current - Prior) / Prior
End Function
```

To use the function, follow these steps.

1. Place the cell pointer in the cell where you want the answer to appear.
2. Choose Insert, Function from the menu.
3. From the Function Category list, select User Defined.
4. Select Personal.xls!PerChange from the Function Name list.
5. Select a cell for the Current value and a cell for the Prior value.
6. Choose OK. See Figure 30.8 for an example of the function in use in an actual worksheet.

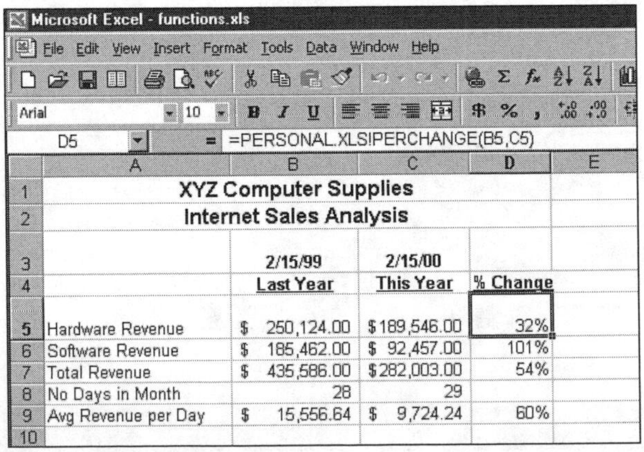

Figure 30.8.
The PerChange function in use in a simple sales analysis worksheet.

Caution

> If you plan to type out the entry of a custom function that's stored in another open workbook (such as the Personal Macro Workbook), you must precede the name of the function with the name of the workbook in quotation marks and followed by an exclamation point, like this: `"Personal.xls!"`.

CONTROL STRUCTURES

Control structures give your procedures more power and efficiency by allowing them to make decisions or perform repetitive tasks. Think of how powerful your VBA procedures could be if they could make decisions. If the user chose hardware from a product list, for example, you could show a graph of hardware sales. If the user chose software, you could show a software sales graph. Without a decision structure, providing for and acting on user choices wouldn't be possible.

Repetition is another common scenario in VBA procedures. If you record enough VBA procedures, you'll eventually encounter repetition. It will be in the form of a lengthy procedure that repeats the same several lines of code over and over again. Loops help you make this type of procedure much more efficient.

DECISION-MAKING STRUCTURES

Decision structures are commonly used to check user-supplied data entry. In Listing 30.1, earlier in this chapter, the InputBox function was used to gather the user name so that it could be placed in the footer of the current workbook. One of the problems with this procedure is that, regardless of which button the user chooses from the InputBox, the same thing will happen. A footer will be inserted into the current sheet of the current workbook.

Usually, when you choose OK you want the procedure to continue, and when you choose Cancel you want it to stop. Decision structures can test for which button was chosen and act accordingly. The most common decision structure is the If-Then structure. Listing 30.6 shows the syntax used for the If-Then structure.

LISTING 30.6.   THE IF-THEN DECISION-MAKING STRUCTURE

```
If <condition1> Then
    <code if condition1 is true>
ElseIF <condition2> Then
    <code if condition2 is true>
Else
    <code if all other conditions are false>
End If
```

Note

> The InputBox function returns nothing, indicated by an empty set of quotation marks (" "), if the Cancel button is chosen.

Listing 30.7 shows how to use If-Then in the footer procedure to make it cancel properly. The condition is indicated by the test for the value of the variable UserName. If the variable is equal to nothing, then exit the procedure. Otherwise, set the footer equal to the value of the variable UserName.

LISTING 30.7.   THE REVISED ADDNAMETOFOOTER PROCEDURE

```
Sub AddNameToFooter()

    UserName = InputBox("What is your name?", "Add Name to Footer")
    If UserName <> "" Then
        With ActiveSheet.PageSetup
            .LeftHeader = ""
            .CenterHeader = ""
            .RightHeader = ""
            .LeftFooter = UserName
            .CenterFooter = ""
            .RightFooter = "Page &P of &N"
        End With
    End If

End Sub
```

> **Note**
>
> Comparison operators are used quite often in VB decision-making structures. Not all operators are represented in computer programs the way they are on paper. All computer programs use >= to represent greater than or equal to, <= to represent less than or equal to, and <> to represent not equal to.

As mentioned earlier, the With control structure applies a number of statements to the same object, thus saving you from having to type the name of the object repetitively. The Macro Recorder often uses the With control structure as you record a procedure. In the AddNameToFooter procedure, the With control structure is used to set several properties of the PageSetup object.

LOOPS

Suppose that you have a list containing 1,000 rows of data and you want every other row to have a border under it. This process would use the same lines of code over and over. A *loop* would allow you to run those same lines of code multiple times. This dramatically cuts down on the length of your procedures and improves their readability and playback speed.

If you were to record this process, you would have quite a long macro. Listing 30.8 shows just a small part of what such a macro would look like. Notice the same general pattern to the macro:

- Select four cells in a row.
- Place a thin border across the bottom of the selection.
- Move down two rows and start all over again.

LISTING 30.8. PART OF A PROCEDURE TO PLACE A BOTTOM BORDER UNDER EVERY OTHER ROW IN A LIST OF DATA. NOTE THE REPETITION IN THE CODE

```
1 Sub AddBorders()

2     ActiveCell.Range("A1:D1").Select
3     With Selection.Borders(xlEdgeBottom)
4         .LineStyle = xlContinuous
5         .Weight = xlThin
6         .ColorIndex = xlAutomatic
7     End With
8     ActiveCell.Offset(2, 0).Range("A1:D1").Select
9     With Selection.Borders(xlEdgeBottom)
10        .LineStyle = xlContinuous
11        .Weight = xlThin
12        .ColorIndex = xlAutomatic
13    End With
14    ActiveCell.Offset(2, 0).Range("A1:D1").Select
15    With Selection.Borders(xlEdgeBottom)
16        .LineStyle = xlContinuous
17        .Weight = xlThin
18        .ColorIndex = xlAutomatic
19    End With

20 End Sub
```

A closer look at Listing 30.8 reveals that the procedure is divided into three sections of repetitive code: lines 2–7, 8–13, and 14–19. The first line of each section (2, 8, and 14) uses the Select method to select a range of cells. So, in effect, these lines are selecting a certain number of cells from the current position of the cell pointer (the active cell).

Line 2 selects the active cell plus the three cells directly to its right. Lines 8 and 14 are slightly different in that they use the Offset property to select a range of cells that's a designated number of rows and columns from the active cell. In this case, the Offset property is used to designate a range of cells that's two rows down and zero columns over from the active cell. Both of these lines then use the Select method to actually select the new range of cells. So lines 8 and 14 select four cells in the row that's two cells directly below the active cell.

The code in lines 3–7, 9–13, and 15–19 actually draws the border under the range of cells that the corresponding previous line of code selects. The Borders object is a collection object. It refers to all four borders surrounding a cell. The constant xlEdgeBottom designates which border in the collection to change (in this case, the bottom border). LineStyle, Weight, and ColorIndex are properties of the Border object. They describe the type of border that the code will create.

There are two problems with this procedure. First, if it were to run for 1,000 rows, its length would be somewhere around 6,000 lines of code! Imagine trying to edit or modify that procedure. Second, it can only be used on a listing of 1,000 rows. Wouldn't it be nice if it ran on any number of rows, not just 1,000?

This is where looping can help. The most commonly used looping structure in VBA is the Do loop. Do loops repeat the same lines of code until a particular condition occurs that you define as part of the loop. For example, you may want the loop to continue on a list until it encounters a blank cell (a blank cell would indicate the end of the list).

Tip #347 from	To test a cell for a value of nothing (an empty cell) in VBA, use an empty set of quotation marks (" ").
Ken	

The AddBorders procedure can be written more efficiently with a loop, as shown in Listing 30.9. The loop will continue until the active cell is empty, indicating the end of the list. This new procedure places a border under every other row, regardless of the length of the list. So not only is the procedure more efficient, it's also more flexible.

LISTING 30.9.   THE ADDBORDERS PROCEDURE REWRITTEN USING A DO LOOP

```
Sub AddBorders()

    ActiveCell.Range("A1:D1").Select
    Do Until ActiveCell.Value = ""
        With Selection.Borders(xlEdgeBottom)
            .LineStyle = xlContinuous
            .Weight = xlThin
            .ColorIndex = xlAutomatic
        End With
        ActiveCell.Offset(2, 0).Range("A1:D1").Select
    Loop

End Sub
```

To make this procedure even more efficient, you can have it determine the number of cells in each row to select. Listing 30.10 shows how.

LISTING 30.10.   THE ADDBORDERS PROCEDURE MODIFIED TO SELECT TO THE END OF THE DATA IN EACH ROW. COMPARE IT TO THE ORIGINAL PROCEDURE IN LISTING 30.9 THAT SELECTED FOUR CELLS IN EACH ROW

```
Sub AddBorders()

    Range(Selection, Selection.End(xlToRight)).Select
    Do Until ActiveCell.Value = ""
        With Selection.Borders(xlEdgeBottom)
            .LineStyle = xlContinuous
            .Weight = xlThin
            .ColorIndex = xlAutomatic
        End With
        ActiveCell.Offset(2, 0).Select
        Range(Selection, Selection.End(xlToRight)).Select
    Loop

End Sub
```

> **Caution**
>
> It's possible—even easy—to create an infinite loop. If you've done so, you'll know it; your code won't stop running after a lengthy period of time and an hourglass remains onscreen. To stop any code during its execution, press Ctrl+Break.

CODE-WRITING TIPS

There are some general rules to follow when writing code that make the code easier to read and understand. The Editor has some options that you can use to your advantage in this area.

USING THE AUTO LIST MEMBERS AND AUTO QUICK INFO

As you type statements in the Editor, you may notice a pop-up list box will appear after you type an object name followed by a period. This is called the *List Members list* (see Figure 30.9). It normally displays a list of methods and properties appropriate for the object that preceded the period. This list can help you complete the VBA statement you're typing. Select a method or property from the list, using the mouse or by typing the first few letters of the method or property name. Press the spacebar to have the Editor place the selection in your statement.

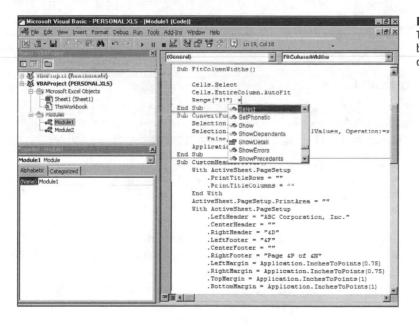

Figure 30.9.
The List Members list box for the Range object.

When typing a function, Auto Quick Info will display the arguments required by that function in a ScreenTip box (see Figure 30.10). This helps cut down on errors with function syntax. To display a Quick Info ScreenTip, type the desired function name and an opening (left) parenthesis.

Figure 30.10.
The Quick Info box for
the VBA DateSerial
function.

Quick Info box

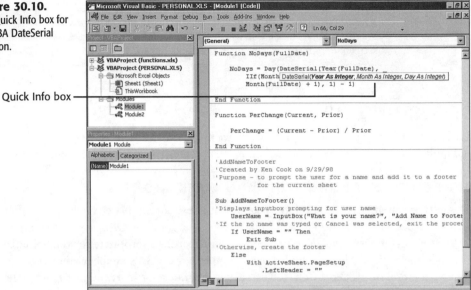

Tip #348 from

Ken

Use the Tools, Options menu command in the Editor to enable or disable Auto List Members and Auto Quick Info. By default, each feature is enabled.

WRITING EASY-TO-READ CODE

When writing code, adding indents in the proper areas makes the code easier to read. Indents are usually added to control structures to indicate that they go together. All the previous code listings in this chapter contain indents to group control structures.

Note

While indents make code easier to read and understand, they aren't required. Excel ignores indents when running code that contains them.

Listing 30.11 shows the AddNameToFooter macro without indents. Notice how hard it is to see where the If-Then and With control structures begin and end. Listing 30.12 contains the same procedure with indents. Notice how much easier it is to read and understand. Use the Tab key to add an indent to a line of code and Shift+Tab to remove an indent. Be sure to position the cursor just in front of the first character in the code line before you press the key.

LISTING 30.11. THE ADDNAMETOFOOTER MACRO BEFORE INTENTS HAVE BEEN ADDED. NOTICE THE DIFFICULTY INVOLVED IN FINDING WHERE THE CONTROL STRUCTURES BEGIN AND END

```
Sub AddNameToFooter()

UserName = InputBox("What is your name?", "Add Name to Footer")
If UserName <> "" Then
With ActiveSheet.PageSetup
LeftHeader = ""
CenterHeader = ""
RightHeader = ""
LeftFooter = UserName
CenterFooter = ""
RightFooter = "Page &P of &N"
End With
End If

End Sub
```

LISTING 30.12. THE ADDNAMETOFOOTER MACRO AFTER INDENTS HAVE BEEN ADDED. NOTICE THE IMPROVED READABILITY OF THE PROCEDURE

```
Sub AddNameToFooter()

    UserName = InputBox("What is your name?", "Add Name to Footer")
    If UserName <> "" Then
        With ActiveSheet.PageSetup
            .LeftHeader = ""
            .CenterHeader = ""
            .RightHeader = ""
            .LeftFooter = UserName
            .CenterFooter = ""
            .RightFooter = "Page &P of &N"
        End With
    End If

End Sub
```

Tip #349 from

The length of the indent (measured in spaces) can be changed using the Tools, Options menu command of the Editor.

COMMENTING CODE

You've probably noticed by now that the Macro Recorder places green text at the beginning of each procedure it records. This text is called a *comment*. You can add comments to your code so that you and others can better understand it in the future.

Here's a common scenario. You wrote a procedure eight months ago. It needs to be updated. You view it in the Editor, ready to make the change, look at it for a few minutes, and can't remember how it works. You spend the next several minutes or even hours reviewing the procedure before you can make your changes.

Procedures that are commented are easier to understand, and therefore easier to change. Excel ignores comments when playing back a procedure.

Placing an apostrophe in front of a line of text in the Code window of the Editor creates a comment. When you move the cursor off a commented line, the Editor changes the color of that line to green. Listing 30.13 shows the AddNameToFooter procedure with comments.

LISTING 30.13.   THE AddNameToFooter PROCEDURE WITH COMMENTS ADDED FOR A BETTER UNDERSTANDING OF THE PROCEDURE

```
'Procedure - AddNameToFooter
'Created By - Ken Cook on 9/29
'Purpose - Prompt the user for a name and add it to the footer
'          for the current sheet

Sub AddNameToFooter()
'Displays input box prompting for user name
    UserName = InputBox("What is your name?", "Add Name to Footer")
'If no name was typed or Cancel was selected, exit the procedure
    If UserName <> "" Then
'Otherwise, create the footer
        With ActiveSheet.PageSetup
            .LeftHeader = ""
            .CenterHeader = ""
            .RightHeader = ""
            .LeftFooter = UserName
            .CenterFooter = ""
            .RightFooter = "Page &P of &N"
        End With
    End If

End Sub
```

Tip #350 from

When writing code for other people, always comment your code. This can help them understand your code should they need to make a change.

You also can add comments at the end of code lines by typing an apostrophe followed by the desired comment text. This technique is good for adding brief comments without taking up extra lines.

DEBUGGING

The process of finding and correcting errors in code is called *debugging*. There are several types of errors that can occur in code. The first is a *syntax* error. Syntax errors occur when you misspell a word or don't follow the proper word sequence when writing a VBA statement or series of statements. An If statement without the word Then at the end is an example of incorrect word sequence. The Editor has a feature called Auto Syntax Check that checks a line of code for syntax errors when you move off the line. If an error is detected, it's displayed in a message box, and the Editor applies a red color to the line of code containing the error. Then it's up to you to correct the error.

The second type of error is a *runtime* error. As the name suggests, runtime errors occur when the code is running. Even if the syntax is correct, the code may be attempting to perform a task that's impossible, such as saving a file to a folder that doesn't exist. When a runtime error occurs, the code stops running, and a message box displays the nature of the error (see Figure 30.11). This message box gives you the option of stopping the code from running with an End button or viewing the line of code causing the error with the Debug button.

PART

IX

CH

30

An error in the sheet name causes a runtime error.

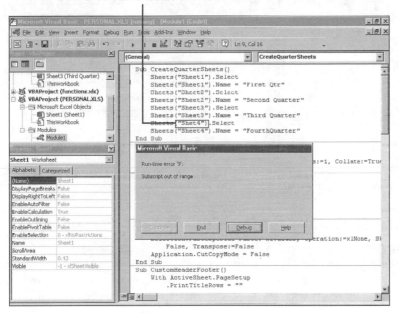

Figure 30.11.
This message box is displayed when a runtime error occurs. This particular error occurred because an incorrect sheet name was referenced (Shet4 instead of Sheet4).

The third type of error that can occur is a *logic* error. Logic errors occur when the code runs properly but doesn't do what you intended it to do. It may select the wrong cells to delete or chart the wrong data.

Excel provides tools to help you correct all these types of errors.

COMPILING A PROJECT

VBA's compiler checks code for syntax errors. Auto Syntax Check detects single-line syntax errors as they occur. However, some syntax errors occur across multiple lines of code. These types of syntax errors often involve control structures; for example, a Do without a Loop or an If-Then without an End If. To have the Editor check for these types of syntax errors, choose Debug, Compile VBAProject. If an error is found, a message box displays the type of error that occurred and the line containing the error is colored red (see Figure 30.12). After you correct an error found by the compiler, you must compile the project repeatedly until all errors are corrected.

Figure 30.12.
This message box appears when a compile error occurs. This particular error occurred because an End If statement was omitted from the end of the procedure.

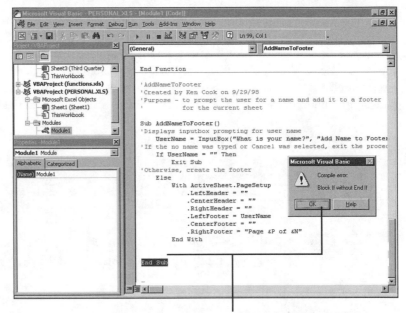

An error occurs due to a missing End If statement.

STEPPING THROUGH CODE USING THE STEP COMMAND AND BREAKPOINTS

The process of running VBA code one line at a time is called *stepping*. Stepping is used to correct logic and runtime errors. It's not always possible to look at a procedure and determine how to fix what's wrong with it. Sometimes you have to slow down the procedure as it plays back so that you can see what it's doing step by step. This strategy often sheds light on how to correct the problem. You can step through the procedure from its very first line or by using a *breakpoint*.

Here's how to step through a procedure from the very beginning:

1. Choose Tools, Macro, Macros from the menu or press Alt+F8.

2. In the Macro Name list, select the macro that you want to step through.

3. Click the Step Into button. The Editor appears with the first line of the procedure colored in yellow.

4. (Optional) Minimize all application windows except the Excel and Editor windows. Then tile the two windows.

5. Press the F8 key to step through each subsequent line of the procedure. The F8 key works as long as the insertion point is anywhere in the routine.

Tip #351 from

Watch what the procedure is doing in the Excel window as you step through each line of code in the Editor window. When the procedure does something incorrectly, take note of the line of code that's executing. This will pinpoint the area of your procedure that needs correcting.

If you have a lengthy procedure that contains errors, you can waste plenty of time stepping through lines of code, waiting to reach the point in the procedure that requires scrutiny. This is where a breakpoint can help. A breakpoint is used to mark a specific line of code as a stopping point during playback. After you reach the stopping point, you can step through the remaining lines of code.

Here's how to step through a procedure using a breakpoint:

1. Place the insertion point on the line at which the procedure should pause.

2. Choose <u>D</u>ebug, <u>T</u>oggle Breakpoint from the menu or press F9. The Editor will enclose the line in a dark red rectangle and place a dark red circle on the Margin Indicator Bar (see Figure 30.13).

Margin Indicator Bar

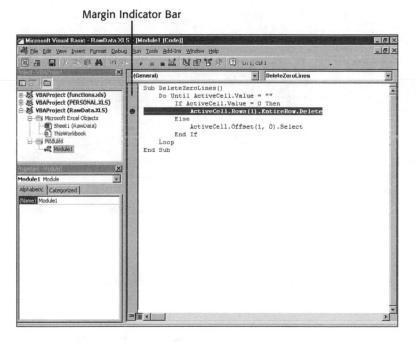

Figure 30.13.
The DeleteZeroLines() procedure with a breakpoint on the delete row code line.

3. Return to the Excel window (optional) and run the procedure. The procedure will run until it reaches the breakpoint, and the Editor will open displaying the procedure.

4. Press F8 to step through the rest of the procedure.

The breakpoint command is a toggle between on and off. To remove a breakpoint, follow the same steps that you used to add it.

Tip #352 from	You can add a breakpoint using the mouse by clicking on the Margin Indicator Bar in front of the line for which you would like to add a break.
Ken	

When you close a workbook that contains procedures with breakpoints, the breakpoints are automatically removed.

THE IMMEDIATE WINDOW

The *Immediate window* displays the result of a function or property. To display the Immediate window in the Editor, choose View, Immediate Window, or press Ctrl+G. To display a function result or property result in the Immediate window, perform the following steps:

1. Type the function or property name, preceded by a question mark. Be sure to use the proper syntax for the function or property.

2. Press Enter. The current value of the function or property appears below the line of text that you typed (see Figure 30.14).

Figure 30.14.
The Immediate window displays the results of the custom NoDays function and the application path property.

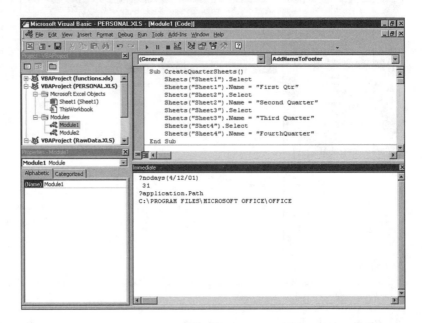

So how can the Immediate window help you? You can use it to test custom functions. For example, you can test the NoDays function created earlier in this chapter (see "Creating a Function to Calculate the Number of Days in a Month") by typing **?NoDays(4/12/01)** in the

Immediate window. If you get the correct answer (30), you know the function was written properly. If you get the wrong answer, you know that more work needs to be done.

You also can use the Immediate window to experiment with properties. If you type **?Activeworkbook.Path** in the Immediate window, you'll see the path of the active workbook in the Excel window. This type of experimentation can help you become more familiar with objects and their properties. The more familiar you become with objects and properties, the easier it will be to write code.

WATCHING VARIABLES AND EXPRESSIONS

Sometimes, during the debugging process, you need to know the value of a variable or property. Suppose that you wrote the procedure in Listing 30.14. You run it and it doesn't stop when it passes the last row of your list. The loop is supposed to stop the procedure when the value of the active cell equals zero. To help you determine the problem, you can place a watch on the ActiveCell.Value statement to see what the value property of the active cell is as the procedure loops through the rows of data.

LISTING 30.14.   USE THIS PROCEDURE TO EXPERIMENT WITH WATCHES. PLACE A WATCH ON THE VALUE PROPERTY OF THE ACTIVECELL AND THE NEWHEIGHT VARIABLE

```
'****************************************************************
' SUB: AddRowSpacing()
' PURPOSE:
'    Add double spacing to every fifth row in a list
' ARGUMENTS:
'    None
'****************************************************************

Sub AddRowSpacing()

    Do Until ActiveCell.Value = 0
        X = X + 1
        If X = 5 Then
            CurrentHeight = ActiveCell.RowHeight
            NewHeight = CurrentHeight * 2
            ActiveCell.RowHeight = NewHeight
            X = 0
        End If
        ActiveCell.Offset(1, 0).Select
    Loop

End Sub
```

To place a watch on a statement or variable, perform the following steps:

1. In the Editor's Code window, select the variable or property statement whose value you want to watch.

Caution

When testing a property, you must select the object name and its property before invoking the Quick Watch command. If you don't, the command won't work properly.

2. Choose Debug, Quick Watch from the menu or press Shift+F9. The Quick Watch dialog box appears (see Figure 30.15).

Figure 30.15.
Choose Add from the Quick Watch dialog box to watch the value of the currently selected statement or variable.

3. Choose Add.

4. The Watches window appears (see Figure 30.16). Note the Expression and Value columns in the Watches window. The Expression column shows the name of the statement or variable being watched. The Value column shows the value of the statement or variable as you step through the procedure.

Figure 30.16.
Use the Watches window to display and track the value of a VBA property or variable.

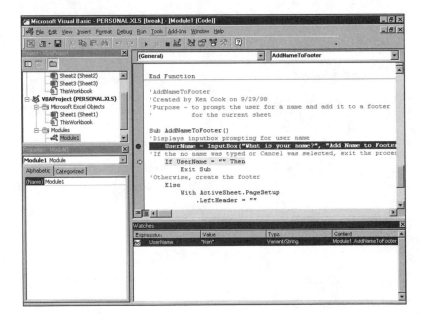

5. Step through the procedure that contains the watch.

6. Note the value of the property or variable after you step past it in the Code window.

To display the value of a property statement or variable temporarily, roll the mouse over the statement or variable after you have stepped past it (see Figure 30.17). A ScreenTip appears, displaying the value of the statement or variable. This trick works only if you're stepping through a procedure.

PART

IX

CH

30

> **Note**
>
> The content of the Watches window is cleared when you exit Excel.

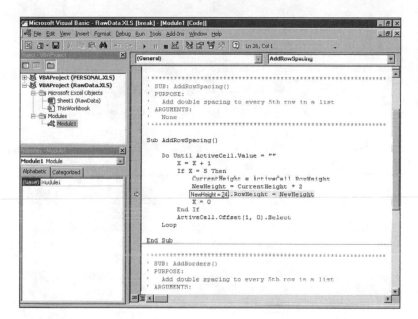

Figure 30.17.
The mouse was placed over the variable NewHeight to display a ScreenTip of its current value as the procedure is running.

AUTOMATIC EXECUTION OF VBA CODE

In some instances, you may want Excel to start your code when you open the workbook that contains it. Perhaps the workbook is an expense report form that contains some VBA code to help the user complete the form. When the workbook opens, you may want the code to start so that the user doesn't have to start it separately.

Some procedures can run automatically through the use of events. An *event* is a predetermined occurrence to which you can attach code that will run when that occurrence takes place. For example, each workbook has an Open event. Code that's attached to the Open event will run when the workbook is opened. Here's how to make your code run automatically using the Open event:

1. Open the Visual Basic Editor. In the Project Explorer window, expand the desired workbook's VBA Project object by clicking the plus sign (+) next to the object's icon.

2. Right-click the ThisWorkbook object and select View Code (see Figure 30.18). Each object has an associated module. This step opens the module of the ThisWorkbook object.

Figure 30.18.
Access the ThisWorkbook object's module to add your Open event procedure.

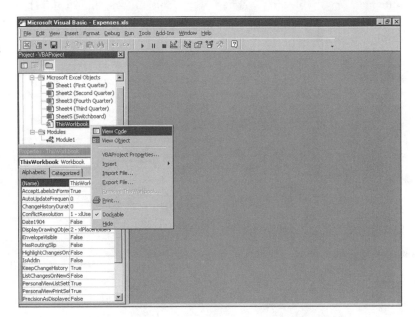

3. Insert a new procedure and name it Workbook_Open (see Figure 30.19).

Figure 30.19.
Insert a procedure in the ThisWorkbook module called Workbook_Open.

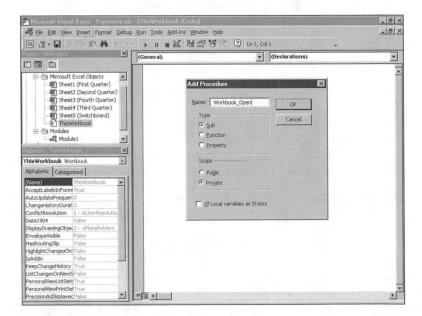

Caution

It is important that you place the Open event code in the ThisWorkbook object's module and that you name the procedure Workbook_Open. If you don't, your procedure won't run automatically when the workbook is opened.

4. Enter the code that you would like to execute automatically when the workbook is opened.

5. Save and close the workbook.

6. Reopen the workbook to test. Your code in the Workbook_Open procedure should run automatically.

PART

IX

CH

30

Note

To disable the Workbook_Open event, press and hold down the Shift key as you open the workbook that contains the event.

Tip #353 from

Ken

You can use the Object drop-down list in the upper-left corner of the code window to access all the Workbook events (including Workbook_Open). The Procedure drop-down list in the upper-right corner can be used to access many other automatic events.

EXCEL IN PRACTICE

A common spreadsheet problem that relates to macros and VBA is having to loop through a variable number of rows of data and do something to rows that meet certain criteria. For instance, the worksheet in Figure 30.20 (Sales.xls) contains sales data for more than 400 products. Notice that some of the products in the current year have zero sales values. These are discontinued products.

Suppose that you're going to export this data to another program and you only want to export viable products, not discontinued ones. You could work your way through the list and manually delete the rows that contain discontinued products. With more than 400 products, though, this could take quite some time! So as an alternative, you can use VBA to remove the unwanted rows. Here's how:

1. Open the workbook that contains the rows to be deleted. You can try this on one of your existing worksheets or enter the data that you see in Figure 30.20 into a new worksheet.

Caution

If you're going to try this on one of your existing worksheets, make a backup copy of it before you continue

2. Choose Tools, Macro, Macros from the menu or press Alt+F8.

Figure 30.20.
The first few rows of the Sales.xls worksheet. Notice the zero values in the Current YTD column.

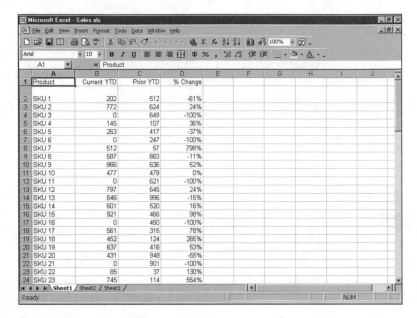

3. Type **RemoveDiscontinuedSkus** (or something similar) in the Macro Name box.

4. Click the Create button. The Visual Basic Editor opens with your new procedure displayed in the Code window.

5. Type the code that you see in Listing 30.15 into the new procedure. When finished, your procedure should look exactly like the one in Figure 30.21.

Figure 30.21.
Compare your Removal procedure to this one.

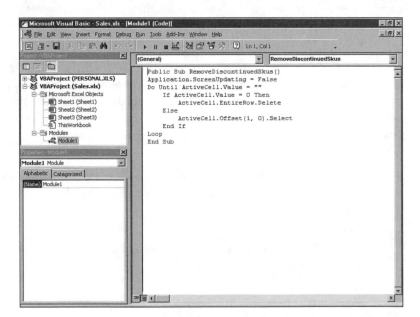

LISTING 30.15. TYPE THIS TEXT INTO THE NEW PROCEDURE REMOVEDISCONTINUEDSKUS (OMIT THE LINE NUMBERS)

```
1 Application.ScreenUpdating = False
2 Do Until ActiveCell.Value = ""
3     If ActiveCell.Value = 0 Then
4         ActiveCell.EntireRow.Delete
5     Else
6         ActiveCell.Offset(1, 0).Select
7     End If
8 Loop
```

6. Close the Editor and save the file.

7. Place the cell pointer on the first number in the column that contains the zero values (in the Sales.xls example, use cell B2).

8. Run the RemoveDiscontinuedSkus procedure. Verify that the rows with the zero values have been removed.

Line 1 of the code in Listing 30.15 turns off the updating of the screen display. This makes the code play back faster because Excel doesn't have to refresh the screen during playback. Line 2 of the code initiates a loop that runs until a cell with a value equal to nothing is encountered (in other words, an empty cell). Line 3 tests whether the value of the active cell is equal to zero. If so, line 4 deletes the row that contains the zero. If not, as indicated by the Else in line 5, line 6 moves to the next cell. Line 7 marks the end of the VBA decision-making structure. Line 8 loops back to line 1.

CHAPTER 31

Using Excel on the Web

In this chapter

by Laurie Ann Ulrich
laurie@limehat.com

EXPLORING EXCEL'S WEB CAPABILITIES

Hypertext markup language (*HTML*) format and Web compatibility are a major focus for Office 2000. One of the ways that this is demonstrated is in the improvement of Excel's tools for saving a worksheet as HTML—not only can the worksheet be posted to or used as a Web page, it can be reedited as an .xls-format worksheet in Excel, even after being saved in HTML. This is because HTML is now a companion file format to the standard .xls spreadsheet format, enabling the user to go from viewing a worksheet as a Web page to editing it as a worksheet, and back again. You don't even need to have Excel installed to edit Excel Web pages that are saved in HTML format—all you need is browser software, such as Internet Explorer.

Note
> Changes to the data from the browser program can be saved only with the Save As command. Even then, each time you make changes that you want to save, you'll need to perform another Save As operation. (If you have Excel, of course, you can open the file in Excel and perform a regular save.)

Excel has simplified the Web publishing process significantly—gone is the Internet Assistant wizard, replaced by an extra step in the saving process. This simplification is yet another sign that Office 2000's applications offer complete integration with the Internet—from creating Web pages to retrieving content from the Web for use in local documents.

PUBLISHING YOUR WORKSHEET AS A WEB PAGE

Whether you or your organization have a Web site on the Internet and/or on an intranet, you'll find that Excel 2000 makes it easy to turn a workbook, worksheet, or *range (page 258)* of worksheet cells into a Web page. Office 2000 has streamlined the process of saving Excel content as HTML and gives you new options for how that data will be viewed and used by those who visit your Web site:

- **Add Interactivity**. Available when publishing a range of cells, this option means that the user on the Web can actually work with the workbook—total, sort, filter, and use the Clipboard to manipulate the content. You even can view and manipulate the selection in *PivotTable (page 556)* format.

- **After Saving, Open Published Web Page in Browser**. This option enables you to quickly view a new page in browser format, immediately upon saving the file as HTML.

SAVING YOUR WORKSHEET AS HTML

To begin, decide which part of your workbook will be saved as HTML—the entire workbook, a sheet within it, or cells within a single sheet. If a single sheet or cells within it are to be saved as HTML, select them before invoking the Save as Web Page command.

After selecting your desired cells (if necessary), follow these steps to save your Excel content as HTML:

1. Choose File, Save as Web Page.

2. In the Save As dialog box, type a name for your HTML file (see Figure 31.1). You don't need to type the .htm extension (Excel will insert it for you), but if you need an .html or other extension specifically, type it after the filename.

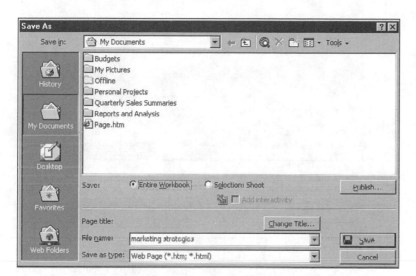

Figure 31.1.
Choose a filename for the Web page, remembering that if viewed online, the filename will be part of the address, visible to the user.

3. Choose a folder into which the file should be saved (if you want it to be saved to your local or a network drive).

4. The Save section of the dialog box indicates whether you're saving the Entire Workbook or a Selection (followed by the word Sheet, or a specific range if you highlighted a range before beginning this procedure). Change this setting if necessary.

5. Click the Publish button. This opens the Publish As Web Page dialog box (see Figure 31.2).

6. Confirm the item to publish in the Choose list box (see Figure 31.3). If you selected a range before starting the procedure, Range of cells will be selected in the Choose box. You can edit the range manually, or click the Collapse Dialog button to expose the worksheet. You can then select the desired cells and reexpand the dialog box to continue.

7. If publishing a range or single sheet, select the Add Interactivity With option, and choose Spreadsheet Functionality or PivotTable Functionality from the drop-down list.

→ For details on converting Excel PivotTables to Web pages, **see** "Saving and Editing PivotTables in HTML Format," **p. 596**

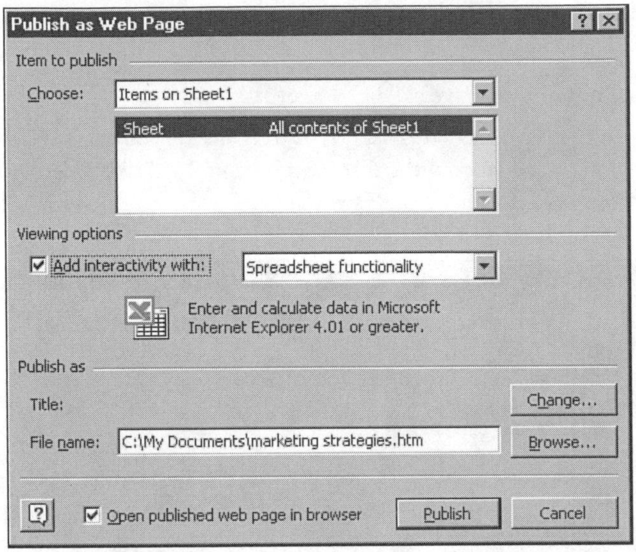

Figure 31.2.
If you choose to publish the page (in addition to simply saving it in HTML), the options for how the page will be viewed and used are offered in the Publish As Web Page dialog box.

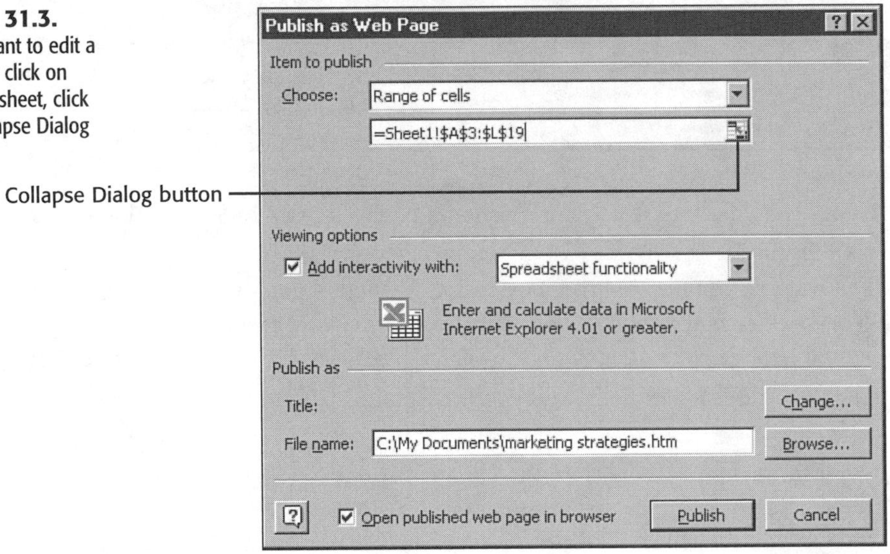

Figure 31.3.
If you want to edit a range or click on another sheet, click the Collapse Dialog button.

Collapse Dialog button ——

8. In the Publish as section, enter a File Name and path for the file. You can enter an HTTP or FTP address.

9. If your browser program is open, select the Open Published Web Page in Browser option. (This step is optional, but useful.)

10. If you want to add a title centered over the published selection, click the <u>C</u>hange button. The Set Title dialog box opens, as shown in Figure 31.4; type a title in the text box and then click OK to return to the Publish as Web Page dialog box.

11. Click <u>P</u>ublish.

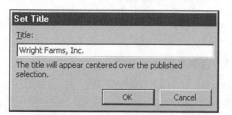

Figure 31.4.
Type a title that you want to display over the published Web content.

PART

IX

CH

31

Note

At this point, you might receive a warning message indicating that certain Excel features included in your workbook won't be supported in the browser.

If the browser isn't open and you've turned on the <u>O</u>pen Published Web Page in Browser option, your Web browser will open automatically and display the page.

The workbook, worksheet, or specified section is now published as a Web page, saved in HTML format. Figure 31.5 shows a worksheet section published with interactivity, viewed in an Internet Explorer window.

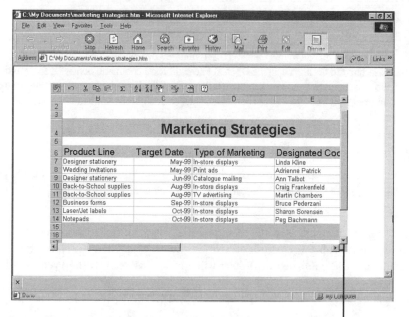

Figure 31.5.
A set of tools appropriate for the interactivity setting you choose will be displayed with the cells that you published.

Use the scrollbars to see the portions of the published worksheet that don't fit in the view.

Caution

If the workbook, worksheet, or range of cells contains hyperlinks, be sure that the files to which the hyperlinks point are available to online viewers—in other words, consider publishing these files to the Web as well. If this isn't possible, delete the hyperlinks before publishing the Web page. If the hyperlinks point to Web sites, it's a good idea to check that they're still valid sites before publishing (and check them later on, too, to ensure that the hyperlinks stay updated).

VIEWING YOUR WORKSHEET AS A WEB PAGE

You can view the Excel Web page with Excel, Word, or Web browser software (Internet Explorer, Netscape, or other comparable programs). To open a previously published Web page, follow these steps:

1. In Excel, choose File, Open.
2. In the Files of type list box, select Web Pages, so that you see only HTML-formatted files.
3. Locate the folder that contains the Web page file, and double-click the Web page to open it.

The Web page will open in Microsoft FrontPage if you have that program installed. Otherwise, the file will open in Word. The display will include a toolbar if the page was saved with interactivity added. Depending on the size of your range of cells, there may also be scrollbars around the Web content, in addition to the scrollbars found in the Word window (see Figure 31.6).

Tip #354 from

Laurie

You can force Excel to open the Web page (thereby bypassing FrontPage and Word) by selecting the file and using the Open in Microsoft Excel command on the Open drop-down list. This leads to a drawback in the HTML feature: Even though you can open the Web file in Excel, you don't gain all of Excel's functionality. You get the same functionality you had in the browser.

Opening a Web page in Internet Explorer (while offline) is very similar—choose File, Open, and from within the Open dialog box, click the Browse button to locate the file you want to open (see Figure 31.7). After selecting the file, click OK to close the Open dialog box and view the Web page.

To preview a Web page as it will actually be seen online, type the full path to the file (such as **c:\My Documents\Web Pages\budget.htm**) in the address/URL list box in the browser's window, and the published worksheet will appear onscreen. If the Web page has already been posted to your Web site, you can use Internet Explorer's address bar to enter the Web address, such as www.yourcompany.com/travel.htm (see Figure 31.8). An address such as this will take you to your Web site, and, additionally, go to the .htm file posted at the site.

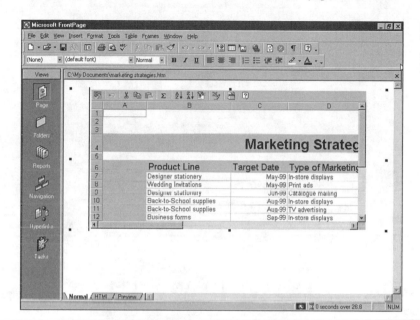

Figure 31.6.
The Web page is displayed within a FrontPage window.

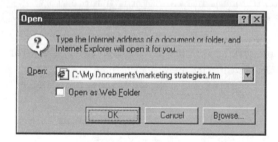

Figure 31.7.
Type the path and file-name, if you know it, or click Browse to look for an HTML file.

Tip #355 from	If you'll be using or updating this particular page often, add it to your Favorites list in Internet Explorer.
Laurie	

Figure 31.8.
Type the URL (Web
address) of your
posted Web page into
Internet Explorer's
address box.

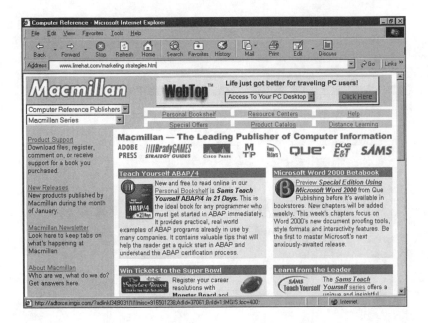

COPYING TABULAR WEB DATA TO AN EXCEL WORKSHEET

You can copy Web page content—viewed in Excel, Word, or through a browser—to an Excel worksheet by way of the *Clipboard (page 116)* or drag and drop. This capability is a significant benefit to organizations and workgroups: One person can post a worksheet on the Web and other people can not only view but also copy portions of the worksheet to their local Excel workbook, and use the data there.

To copy Excel Web content to another worksheet, follow these steps:

1. With both the Web page (in a Word or browser window) and the target Excel worksheet open, switch to the Web page.

2. Select the source cells within the Web page, and copy them to the Clipboard with your favorite copying method.

3. Switch back to the target worksheet, select the target cell, and paste the data from the Clipboard.

It can be very helpful to tile the two application windows when you're copying Web content—right-click a blank space on the taskbar and choose Tile Ve̲rtically (or H̲orizontally). As shown in Figure 31.9, this allows you to see both the source (Web page) and target (local worksheet).

Pasted Web content in the worksheet

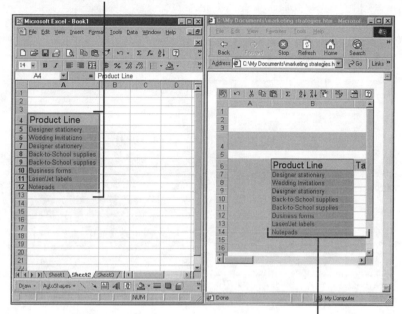

Figure 31.9.
Tile the browser and Excel windows to facilitate copying from the Web page to the worksheet.

Web content selected and copied

Using drag and drop is possible only if the application windows are tiled, as you must be able to see both the source and target locations simultaneously.

Tip #356 from

Laurie

You may be able to drag data from the browser to Word, Excel, and PowerPoint without having to tile the windows. Drag the data from the browser down to the Office program's taskbar button. You'll see a "no drag allowed" symbol, but leave the mouse over the taskbar button for a second or two. If this feature is going to work, the program you're pointing to should activate, at which time you can drag the data up into the newly activated window and release it. (This method doesn't seem to work in all cases.)

When using drag and drop between an online view of the Web content and the local worksheet, a copy will be made by default. If you're using drag and drop between the Web page in Word and an offline view through the browser, you must press the Ctrl key while dragging in order to make a copy. If you forget to use Ctrl in this situation, you risk editing the offline Web content by removing the content that's dragged and dropped onto the worksheet. Figure 31.10 shows content being dragged from the Web page to a worksheet.

Plus sign on the mouse pointer indicates a copy is being dragged.

Figure 31.10.
In lieu of the Clipboard, use drag and drop to copy content from the Web page to a worksheet on a local or network drive.

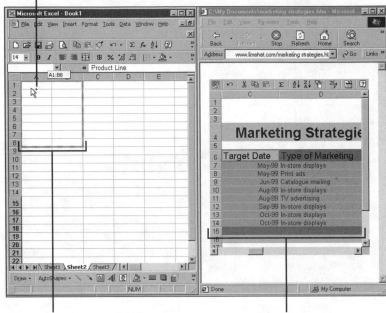

Target location on the worksheet

Web page content

COLLABORATING ONLINE WITH EXCEL

Publishing a worksheet to the Web, placing Excel content on a Web page, and using Web content in worksheets on your local drive are significant uses of the Web in relation to Excel. These features truly expand your distribution capabilities and access to Excel data. However, in each of these situations, you're operating alone in that you're not discussing or sharing information interactively. Publishing a Web page and copying Web content to a local workbook are solitary activities, and any questions or ideas that other users might have would need to be shared through an external vehicle such as email or a phone call.

To remedy this situation, Excel 2000's online tools include *online collaboration*, enabling you to communicate live with other users—people within your organization or in the outside world—via the Internet or an intranet. Meetings can be set up for immediate collaboration or scheduled for a future date, and Web discussions can be held to share ideas and information.

Note

Microsoft NetMeeting, the software used for collaborating "live" online, is beyond the scope of this book, but the following section provides a brief discussion of how it's used.

MEETING WITH COWORKERS ONLINE

To set up an immediate meeting, choose Tools, Online Collaboration, Meet Now. The Meeting dialog box opens as shown in Figure 31.11, allowing you to set up your user information—first and last name, email address, and the server to which you'll be attached for the online meeting.

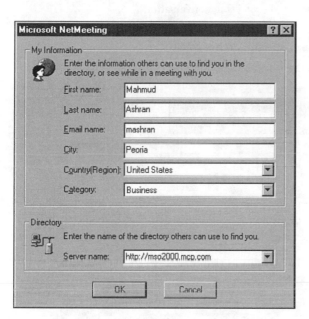

Figure 31.11.
Identify yourself and the server to which you and your collaborators will be attached for the meeting.

If you've already provided this information on a previous collaboration, this dialog box will not appear when Meet Now is selected. Rather, the Place a Call dialog box will appear, enabling you to select from a list those people with whom you'd like to have an online meeting.

Tip #357 from

All the people you call must be running NetMeeting at the time you call them—otherwise, you'll just get an error message. It's a good idea to call your intended collaborators before setting up the meeting, to be sure they're on their computers, logged onto the server, and running NetMeeting.

After your meeting begins, you can use the Online Meeting toolbar to access meeting tools, as described in the following list (see Figure 31.12):

- **Participant List**. Displays a list of the people currently involved in the online collaboration.
- **Call Participant**. Reopens the Place a Call dialog box, in case you need to add a new participant.

- **Remove Participant**. If a participant logs off or exits NetMeeting, it removes him or her from the participant list.

- **Allow Others to Edit**. Gives the other participants the rights to contribute to the meeting and edit the content of the Chat and Whiteboard windows.

- **Display Chat Window**. Opens a chat-room window into which each participant can type text contributions to the meeting conversation.

- **Display Whiteboard**. Displays a window in which you can write, type, and draw, such as a whiteboard or easel in a conference room.

- **End Meeting**. Ends the online collaboration.

Figure 31.12.
Control the list of meeting members or access a chat window from the Online Meeting toolbar.

In some cases, the people with whom you'd like to collaborate aren't available right away, and you have to pick a future time to meet online. Excel gives you the ability to set up a meeting in the future, selecting the time and date for the meeting, as well as the names of the people who will be included in the meeting.

To schedule an online meeting, follow these steps:

1. Choose Tools, Online Collaboration, Schedule Meeting.

2. In the resulting Outlook Meeting dialog box shown in Figure 31.13, enter the names of the people you want in the meeting, and choose the time and date for the online collaboration.

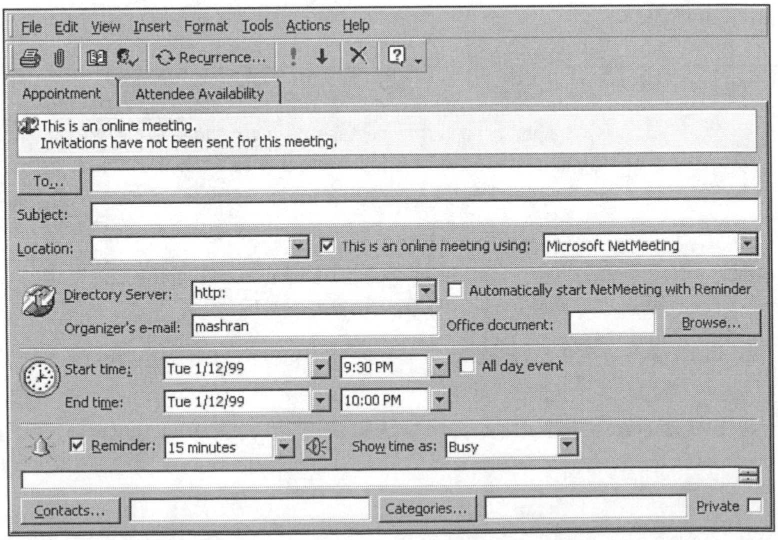

Figure 31.13.
Select the date, time, and planned duration of your online meeting.

3. If you and those whom you've invited are on a network and can view each other's schedules through Outlook, click the Attendee Availability tab (see Figure 31.14) to select a time at which everyone will be free to participate.

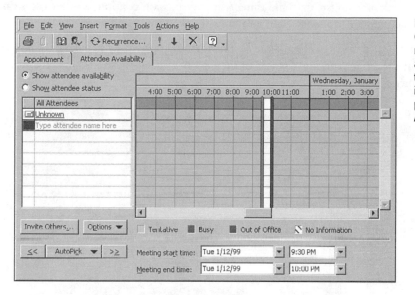

Figure 31.14.
Coworkers' schedules need to be up-to-date and available to you through your network in order to make proper use of Attendee Availability.

4. Click Send to send the invitations to your attendee list.

Note

If you're not a Microsoft Outlook user or you haven't yet set up Outlook as part of Office 2000, starting the process of scheduling an online meeting will generate a wizard that takes you through the process of setting up Outlook so that you can schedule the meeting.

DISCUSSING DOCUMENTS ONLINE

By placing Excel documents in HTML format at a central server location, you can collaborate on the design and use of those documents with other users—and no one is required to have Excel for this purpose. This feature is useful for creating new workbooks that will be used by more than one department, redesigning existing worksheets (especially if they're shared cross-country or cross-division), posting proposals or quarterly results, and so on.

Each person who logs onto the server can open the shared document(s) and provide discussion about the document as needed, replying to existing comments and creating new comments. The discussion works like that of a newsgroup, where you post a comment and other people reply to it, or you reply to other people's comments—no one else has to be online while you are commenting or replying to other users' comments.

To enter or initiate a discussion about a document, log on to the server and open the document. Click the Discussions button on the Discussions toolbar. (If the Discussions pane or toolbar isn't visible in the Internet Explorer window, choose View, Explorer Bar, Discuss.)

Then choose <u>In</u>sert about the Document to place a comment about the document in the discussion pane, or <u>I</u>nsert in the Document to place a comment within the document itself. The discussion pane displays the comments made by each person, his or her user name, and the comments, along with the date and time. As the discussion continues, other users can add comments, reply to comments, add questions for the group, and so forth.

Figure 31.15 shows the Enter Discussion Text dialog box (opened by choosing to insert discussion about the document) and the text of the next comment/question that will appear in the discussion.

Figure 31.15.
Type your comment or question in the Discussion <u>T</u>ext box, and click OK to insert it into the discussion pane.

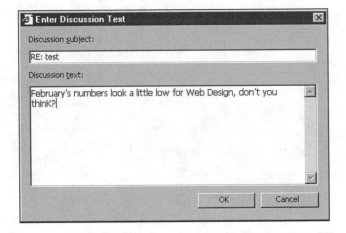

As the attendees' comments accumulate, you see them stack up in the discussion pane. Figure 31.16 shows a discussion of marketing tactics underway. To reply to a comment, edit it, or delete it, click the down arrow next to the note icon and select <u>R</u>eply, <u>E</u>dit, or <u>D</u>elete, as appropriate. You may be asked for additional confirmation, depending on the network setup.

Note

Changes like this undoubtedly will require you to have certain permissions or rights on the network. If you get error messages when trying to save, edit, or delete discussion comments, consult the network administrator.

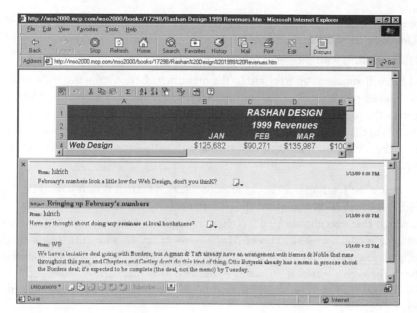

Figure 31.16.
Each comment/
question appears with
a small note icon,
helping to keep each
one visually separate.

SENDING YOUR EXCEL WORKBOOK VIA EMAIL

Excel enables you to share Excel workbooks via email by turning a single worksheet into the body of a message or by attaching your workbook file to an email message. When sending a workbook as an attachment, the recipient should also have Excel, and it's a good idea to find out which version she's running, to make sure you save the file in a format that will be compatible with that installed version. If the recipient will be receiving the worksheet as the body of the message, she doesn't need to have Excel unless she wants to take the message content and paste it into a worksheet of her own on her local drive.

Tip #358 from	
Laurie	If the recipient is a Lotus 1-2-3 user, save the Excel worksheet to a Lotus 1-2-3 format that matches that version. When in doubt, check with the recipient before sending. If that's not possible, choose the oldest version that supports all of your worksheet's content and formatting.

The exact procedure for attaching the file to the message will vary slightly with different software programs (CompuServe, America Online, Outlook, Netscape, Internet Explorer, among others) but the basic procedure consists of the following steps:

1. In the email message window, click the Attachments button. It may appear as a paper-clip button on the toolbar or as a button with the word Attach or Attachments on it.

2. In the resulting dialog box, navigate to the folder that contains the file you want to attach. Double-click the worksheet file.

3. Click OK to confirm your intention to attach the file.

The attached file will appear as an icon within the message (wherever the insertion point was when you clicked the Attach button) or listed somewhere in the window. When the recipient receives the message, double-clicking the icon in the message or clicking a Download button in the message window opens a dialog box. From there, she can choose a location to save the file or merely opt to view it onscreen without saving it to her local or network drive.

Another easy option for sending workbooks to other users via email is to use the File, Send To command from Excel. This command allows for attaching the active workbook as either body text, in which case you choose Mail Recipient from the submenu, or as an attachment to a mail message, in which case you choose Mail Recipient (as Attachment). The submenu also offers an underused but very effective Routing Recipient command, which sends the active workbook through a series of recipients either one at a time (in any order you choose) or all at once. You can even send the workbook to someone in an online meeting you're currently attending.

APPENDIXES

EXCEL FUNCTION REFERENCE

by Patrick D. Blattner
Patrick@BlattnerBooks.com

In this appendix

How to Use This Guide

This appendix provides a quick reference summary of the functions available in Excel 2000. For further information and complete details on using the functions, please refer to the Excel Help feature.

Database Management and List Management Functions

General Syntax

In the following sections, a separate syntax line is included for each database or list function that doesn't conform to the following general syntax:

`=Dfunction(database,field,criteria)`

- The `database` argument refers to the range encompassing the list or database.
- The `field` argument refers to a particular column in the list. If you omit the `field` argument, the function operates on the entire list. You can refer to the column number within the list, the name of the column heading (in quotes), or a cell reference referring to either the label or the column number.
- The `criteria` argument specifies the basis on which you want the function to select particular cells. The criteria include a duplicate list of column headings from the list, with words, phrases, numeric values, or formulas listed underneath those headings.

DAVERAGE

Indicates the average of the values that meet the specified criteria.

DCOUNT

Counts the number of cells that contain numbers that meet the specified criteria.

DCOUNTA

Counts nonblank cells containing numbers or text that meet the specified criteria.

DGET

Returns a single value that meets the specified criteria. If duplicates are found, DGET returns #NUM.

DMAX

Extracts the highest value that meets the specified criteria.

DMIN

Extracts the lowest value that meets the specified criteria.

DPRODUCT

Returns the product of multiplying the values that meet the specified criteria.

DSTDEV

Returns the calculation of the standard deviation of a population, based on the sum of the whole population.

DSUM

Returns the total of the values that meet the specified criteria.

DVAR

Estimates the variance of a sample population, based on the values that meet the specified criteria.

DVARP

Returns the calculation of the variance of an entire population, based on the values that meet the specified criteria.

GETPIVOTDATA

Returns a value of data stored in a PivotTable. The syntax is as follows:

```
=GETPIVOTDATA(PivotTable,name)
```

DATE AND TIME FUNCTIONS

DATE

Returns the DATEVALUE serial number.

```
=DATE(year,month,day)
```

DATEVALUE

Converts date text to a DATEVALUE serial number.

```
=DATEVALUE(date_text)
```

DAY

Returns the corresponding day of the month serial number, from 1 to 31.

```
=DAY(serial_number)
```

PART

X

APP

A

DAYS360

Returns the number of days between dates that you specify, based on a 360-day year (twelve 30-day months).

=DAYS360(*start_date*,*end_date*)

EDATE

Returns the value or serial number of the date specified by you and the number of months before or after the specified date. Use EDATE to calculate the maturity date or date due that falls on the same day of the month as the date of issue.

=EDATE(*start_date*,*months*)

EOMONTH

Returns the serial number for the last day of the month (as specified by *months*) before or after *start_date*. Used to calculate maturity dates or dates due that fall on the last day of the month.

=EOMonth(*start_date*,*months*)

HOUR

Returns the hour as a serial number integer between 0 (12:00 a.m.) and 23 (11:00 p.m.).

=HOUR(*serial_number*)

MINUTE

Returns the serial number integer from 0 to 59 that corresponds to the minute.

=MINUTE(*serial_number*)

MONTH

Returns the corresponding serial number of the month between 1 and 12.

=MONTH(*serial_number*)

NETWORKDAYS

Returns the number of working days between two dates. Excludes weekends and specified holidays.

=NETWORKDAYS(*start_date*,*end_date*,*holidays*)

NOW

Returns the current date and time in the form of a serial number. When entered in a cell, Excel formats the number as a date and time. There are no arguments for this function.

=NOW()

SECOND

Returns the corresponding serial number of seconds as an integer between 0 and 59.

=SECOND(*serial_number*)

TIME

Returns the corresponding serial number of time as a decimal between 0 and 0.99999999.

=TIME(*hour*,*minute*,*second*)

TIMEVALUE

Returns the serial number represented by text as time.

=TIMEVALUE(*time_text*)

TODAY

Returns the current date as a serial number. When entered in a cell, Excel formats the number as a date. There are no arguments for this function.

=TODAY()

WEEKDAY

Returns the corresponding day of the week (from 1 to 7) as a serial number.

=WEEKDAY(*serial_number*,*return_type*)

WORKDAY

Returns a number representing the date that is the number of days (specified by *days*) before or after *start_date*. You can exclude dates with the *holidays* argument.

=WORKDAY(*start_date*,*days*,*holidays*)

YEAR

Returns the corresponding year as a serial number in the form of an integer from 1900–9999.

=YEAR(*serial_number*)

YEARFRAC

Returns the calculated fraction of the year represented by whole numbers between two dates.

=YEARFRAC(*start_date*,*end_date*,*basis*)

DDE AND EXTERNAL DATA FUNCTIONS

CALL

Calls up the procedure in a dynamic link library or code resource.

Syntax 1, with register:

`=CALL(register_ID,argument1,...)`

Syntax 2, used alone:

`=CALL(module_text,procedure,type_text,argument1,...)`

REGISTER.ID

Supplies the registered ID of the dynamic link library or code resource.

`=REGISTER.ID(module_text,procedure,type_text)`

SQL.REQUEST

Runs a query from a worksheet and connects an external data source.

`=SQL.REQUEST(connection_string,output_ref,driver_prompt,query_text,`
`➥col_names_logical)`

ENGINEERING FUNCTIONS

> **Note**   You must have the Analysis ToolPak installed and enabled to use (see) these functions.

BESSELI

Returns the Bessel function in modified form for imaginary arguments.

`=BESSELI(x,n)`

BESSELJ

Returns the actual Bessel function, where x is the value at which to evaluate the function, and n is the order of the Bessel function.

`=BESSELJ(x,n)`

BESSELK

Returns the Bessel function in modified form for imaginary arguments.

`=BESSELK(x,n)`

BESSELY

Returns the Bessel function, also known as the Weber or Neumann function, where x is the value at which to evaluate the function, and n is the order of the function.

=BESSELY(*x*,*n*)

BIN2DEC

Converts a binary number to decimal form.

=BIN2DEC(*number*)

BIN2HEX

Converts a binary number to hexadecimal.

=BIN2HEX(*number*,*places*)

BIN2OCT

Converts a binary number to octal.

=BIN2OCT(*number*,*places*)

COMPLEX

Converts real and imaginary coefficients into a complex number of the form x+yi or x+yj.

=COMPLEX(*real_num*,*I_num*,*suffix*)

CONVERT

Converts from one measurement system to another.

=CONVERT(*number*,*from_unit*,*to_unit*)

DEC2BIN

Converts decimal numbers to binary.

=DEC2BIN(*number*,*places*)

DEC2HEX

Converts decimal numbers to hexadecimal.

=DEC2HEX(*number*,*places*)

DEC2OCT

Converts decimal numbers to octal.

=DEC2OCT(*number*,*places*)

DELTA

Tests whether numbers or values are equal.

=DELTA(*number1*,*number2*)

ERF

Returns the integrated error function between *lower_limit* and *upper_limit*.

=ERF(*lower_limit*,*upper_limit*)

ERFC

Returns a complementary ERF function integrated between x and infinity, where x is the lower bound for integrating ERF.

=ERF(*x*)

GESTEP

Returns 1 if *number* is greater than or equal to a specified *step* or threshold, otherwise returns 0.

=GESTEP(*number*,*step*)

HEX2BIN

Converts hexadecimal numbers to binary.

=HEX2BIN(*number*,*places*)

HEX2DEC

Converts hexadecimal numbers to decimal.

=HEX2DEC(*number*)

HEX2OCT

Converts hexadecimal numbers to octal.

=HEX2OCT(*number*)

IMABS

Returns the absolute value (modulus) of a complex number in x+yi or x+yj text format. The formula takes the square root of (x^2+y^2).

=IMABS(*inumber*)

IMAGINARY

Returns the coefficient of a complex number in x+yi or x+yj in text format.

=IMAGINARY(*inumber*)

IMARGUMENT

Returns the theta argument and angle expressed in radians.

=IMARGUMENT(*inumber*)

IMCONJUGATE

Returns the complex conjugate of a complex number in x+yi or x+yj text format.

=IMCONJUGATE(*inumber*)

IMCOS

Returns the cosine of a complex number x+yi or x+yj in text format.

=IMCOS(*numbers*)

IMDIV

Returns the quotient of complex numbers x+yi or x+yj in text format.

=IMDIV(*number1*,*number2*)

IMEXP

Returns the exponential of complex numbers x+yi or x+yj in text format.

-IMEXP(*inumber*)

IMLN

Returns the natural logarithm of complex numbers x+yi or x+yj in text format.

=IMLN(*inumber*)

IMLOG10

Returns the common logarithm (base 10) of complex numbers x+yi or x+yj in text format.

=IMLOG10(*inumber*)

IMLOG2

Returns the base 2 logarithm of complex numbers in x+yi or x+yj in text format.

=IMLOG2(*inumber*)

IMPOWER

Returns a complex number raised to a power in x+yi or x+yj text format.

=IMPOWER(*inumber*,*number*)

PART

X

APP

A

IMPRODUCT

Returns the product from 2 to 29 in complex numbers x+yi or x+yj text format.

`=IMPRODUCT(inumber1,inumber2,...)`

IMREAL

Returns real coefficients of complex numbers x+yi or x+yj in text format.

`=IMREAL(inumber)`

IMSIN

Returns the sine of complex numbers x+yi or x+yj in text format.

`=IMSIN(inumber)`

IMSQRT

Returns the square root of complex numbers x+yi or x+yj in text format.

`=IMSQRT(inumber)`

IMSUB

Returns the difference of two complex numbers x+yi or x+yj in text format.

`=IMSUB(inumber1,inumber2)`

IMSUM

Returns the sum of two complex numbers x+yi or x+yj in text format.

`=IMSUM(inumber1,inumber2,...)`

OCT2BIN

Converts an octal number to binary.

`=OCT2BIN(number,places)`

OCT2DEC

Converts an octal number to decimal.

`=OCT2DEC(number)`

OCT2HEX

Converts an octal number to hexadecimal.

`=OCT2HEX(number,places)`

SQRTPI

Returns the square root of a positive number multiplied by pi. This value cannot be less than zero. (Also found under "Math and Trigonometry Functions.")

=SQRTPI(*number**pi)

FINANCIAL FUNCTIONS

ACCRINT

Returns accrued interest for security that pays periodic interest.

=ACCRINT(*issue*,*first_interest*,*settlement*,*rate*,*par*,*frequency*,*basis*)

ACCRINTM

Returns accrued interest for security that pays interest at maturity.

=ACCRINTM(*issue*,*maturity*,*rate*,*par*,*basis*)

AMORDEGRC

Returns appreciation for each accounting period.

=AMORDEGRC(*cost*,*date_purchased*,*first period*,*salvage*,*period*,*rate*,*basis*)

AMORLINC

Returns depreciation for each accounting period.

=AMORLINC(*cost*,*date_purchased*,*first_period*,*salvage*,*period*,*rate*,*basis*)

COUPDAYBS

Returns the number of days from start date of the coupon period to the settlement.

=COUPDAYBS(*settlement*,*maturity*,*frequency*,*basis*)

COUPDAYS

Returns the number of days in the coupon period that includes the settlement date.

=COUPDAYS(*settlement*,*maturity*,*frequency*,*basis*)

COUPDAYSNC

Returns the number of days from the settlement date to the next coupon date.

=COUPDAYSNC(*settlement*,*maturity*,*frequency*,*basis*)

COUPNCD

Returns the number of the next coupon date after the settlement date.

=COUPNCD(*settlement*,*maturity*,*frequency*,*basis*)

COUPNUM

Returns the total number of coupons payable between the settlement and maturity date, rounded up to the nearest whole coupon.

=COUPNUM(*settlement,maturity,frequency,basis*)

COUPPCD

Returns the number of the previous coupon date before the settlement date.

=COUPPCD(*settlement,maturity,frequency,basis*)

CUMIPMT

Returns the cumulative interest on a loan between start and stop dates.

=CUMIPMT(*rate,nper,pv,start_period,end_period,type*)

CUMPRINC

Returns the cumulative principal amount between start and stop dates.

=CUMPRINC(*rate,nper,pv,start_period,end_period,type*)

DB

Returns the asset depreciation for a period using the fixed declining balance method.

=DB(*cost,salvage,life,period,month*)

DDB

Returns the asset depreciation for a specified period using the double-declining balance method, or another method you specify.

=DDB(*cost,salvage,life,period,factor*)

DISC

Returns the security discount rate.

=DISC(*settlement,maturity,pr,redemption,basis*)

DOLLARDE

Converts a fraction dollar price into a decimal dollar price.

=DOLLARDE(*fractional_dollar,fraction*)

DOLLARFR

Converts a decimal dollar price into a fraction dollar price.

=DOLLARFR(*decimal_dollar,fraction*)

DURATION

Returns the duration for an assumed par value of $100 using the Macauley method.

=DURATION(*settlement*,*maturity*,*coupon*,*yield*,*frequency*,*basis*)

EFFECT

Returns the effective interest rate annually, give the nominal annual interest rate and the number of compounding periods per year.

EFFECT(*nominal_rate*,*npery*)

FV

Returns the future value of periodic payments and a constant interest rate.

=FV(*rate*,*nper*,*pmt*,*pv*,*type*)

FVSCHEDULE

Returns the future value of the initial principal after applying several compound interest rates.

=FVSCHEDULE(*principal*,*schedule*)

INTRATE

Returns the interest rate of a fully invested security.

=INTRATE(*settlement*,*maturity*,*investment*,*redemption*,*basis*)

IPMT

Returns the interest payment for a period of time based on an investment with periodic constant payments and a constant interest rate.

=IPMT(*rate*,*per*,*nper*,*pv*,*fv*,*type*)

IRR

Returns the internal rate of return for a series of cash flows represented by numbers in the form of values.

=IRR(*values*,*guess*)

MDURATION

Returns a modified duration of a security with an assumed par value of $100.

=MDURATION(*settlement*,*maturity*,*coupon*,*yield*,*frequency*,*basis*)

MIRR

Returns a modified internal rate of return for several periodic cash flows.

=MIRR(*values*,*finance_rate*,*reinvest_rate*)

PART

X

APP

A

NOMINAL

Returns the nominal annual interest rate given an effective rate and a number of compounding periods per year.

=NOMINAL(*effective_rate*,*npery*)

NPER

Returns the number of periods for an investment based on periodic constant payments and a constant interest rate.

=NPER(*rate*,*pmt*,*pv*,*fv*,*type*)

NPV

Calculates the net present value of an investment with the discount rate and several future payments and income.

=NPV(*rate*,*value1*,*value2*,...)

ODDFPRICE

Returns the value of a security based on a per $100 face value and an odd first period.

=ODDFPRICE(*settlement*,*maturity*,*issue*,*first_coupon*,*rate*,*yield*,*redemption*,*frequency*,
➥*basis*)

ODDFYIELD

Returns the security yield with an odd first period.

=ODDFYIELD(*settlement*,*maturity*,*issue*,*first_coupon*,*rate*,*pr*,*redemption*,*frequency*,
➥*basis*)

ODDLPRICE

Returns the per $100 face value of a security having an odd last coupon period.

=ODDLPRICE(*settlement*,*maturity*,*last_interest*,*rate*,*yield*,*redemption*,*frequency*,
➥*basis*)

ODDLYIELD

Returns the security yield that has an odd last period.

=ODDLYIELD(*settlement*,*maturity*,*last_interest*,*rate*,*pr*,*redemption*,*frequency*,*basis*)

PMT

Calculates the loan payment for a loan based on constant payments and constant interest rates.

=PMT(*rate*,*nper*,*pv*,*fv*,*type*)

PPMT

Returns the principal payment for a specific period of an investment based on periodic constant payments and a constant interest rate.

=PPMT(*rate*,*per*,*nper*,*pv*,*fv*,*type*)

PRICE

Returns the value of a security based on price per $100 face value and periodic payments.

=PRICE(*settlement*,*maturity*,*rate*,*yield*,*redemption*,*frequency*,*basis*)

PRICEDISC

Returns the value of a discounted security based on a price per $100 face value.

=PRICEDISC(*settlement*,*maturity*,*discount*,*redemption*,*basis*)

PRICEMAT

Returns the value of a security that pays interest at maturity and price per $100 face value.

=PRICEMAT(*settlement*,*maturity*,*issue*,*rate*,*yield*,*basis*)

PV

Based on an investment, returns the present value.

=PV(*rate*,*nper*,*pmt*,*fv*,*type*)

PART

X

APP

A

RATE

Returns per period the interest of an annuity.

=RATE(*nper*,*pmt*,*pv*,*fv*,*type*,*guess*)

RECEIVED

Based on a fully invested security, returns the amount received at maturity.

=RECEIVED(*settlement*,*maturity*,*investment*,*discount*,*basis*)

SLN

Based on one period, returns the straight-line depreciation on an asset.

=SLN(*cost*,*salvage*,*life*)

SYD

Based on a specified period, returns the sum-of-years-digits depreciation of an asset.

=SYD(*cost*,*salvage*,*life*,*per*)

TBILLEQ

For a treasury bill, returns the bond equivalent yield.

`=TBILLEQ(settlement,maturity,discount)`

TBILLPRICE

For a treasury bill, returns the price per $100 face value.

`=TBILLPRICE(settlement,maturity,discount)`

TBILLYIELD

For a treasury bill, returns the yield.

`=TBILLYIELD(settlement,maturity,pr)`

VDB

For a period you specify, returns the depreciation of an asset.

`=VDB(cost,salvage,life,start_period,end_period,factor,no_switch)`

XIRR

For a schedule of cash flows that are not necessarily periodic, returns the internal rate of return.

`=XIRR(values,dates,guess)`

XNPV

For a schedule of cash flows that are not necessarily periodic, returns the present value.

`=XNPV(rate,values,dates)`

YIELD

Based on a yield that pays periodic interest, returns the yield of the security.

`=YIELD(settlement,maturity,rate,pr,redemption,frequency,basis)`

YIELDDISC

For a discounted security, returns the annual yield.

`=YIELDDISC(settlement,maturity,pr,redemption,basis)`

YIELDMAT

Based on a security that pays interest at maturity, returns the annual yield.

`=YIELDMAT(settlement,maturity,issue,rate,pr,basis)`

INFORMATION FUNCTIONS

CELL

Returns information about a cell's location, formatting, or contents in the upper-left cell in a reference.

`=CELL(info_type,reference)`

COUNTBLANK

Counts the number of empty cells in a specified range.

`=COUNTBLANK(range)`

ERROR.TYPE

Returns the corresponding number value associated with an error type in Microsoft Excel. Returns #NA if no error exists.

`=ERROR.TYPE(error_val)`

INFO

Returns operating environment information.

`=INFO(type_text)`

PART

X

APP

A

ISBLANK

Returns TRUE if *value* refers to an empty cell.

`=ISBLANK(value)`

ISERR

Returns TRUE if *value* refers to any error value in Microsoft Excel except #NA.

`=ISERR(value)`

ISERROR

Returns TRUE if *value* refers to any error value in Microsoft Excel.

`=ISERROR(value)`

ISEVEN

Returns TRUE or FALSE if the number is even or odd, TRUE being even and FALSE being odd.

`=ISEVEN(number)`

ISLOGICAL

Returns TRUE if the value is logical.

`=ISLOGICAL(value)`

ISNA

Returns TRUE if *value* is associated with the error type #NA.

`=ISNA(value)`

ISNONTEXT

Returns TRUE if *value* refers to any item that isn't text. Returns TRUE if value refers to a blank cell.

`=ISNONTEXT(value)`

ISNUMBER

Returns TRUE if *value* refers to a number.

`=ISNUMBER(value)`

ISODD

Returns TRUE if *number* is odd and FALSE if *number* is even.

`=ISODD(number)`

ISREF

Returns TRUE if *value* refers to a reference.

`=ISREF(value)`

ISTEXT

Returns TRUE if *value* refers to text.

`=ISTEXT(value)`

N

Returns *value* converted to a number.

`=N(value)`

NA

Returns the error value associated with #NA.

`=NA()`

TYPE

Returns the type of value—for example, number = 1, text = 2, logical value = 4, error value = 16, and array = 64. Use TYPE when the behavior of another function depends on the type of value in a particular cell.

`=TYPE(value)`

LOGICAL FUNCTIONS

AND

Returns TRUE if all arguments in the formula are true and FALSE if any one argument is false.

`=AND(logical1,logical2,...)`

FALSE

Returns the value FALSE. There are no arguments associated with this function.

`=FALSE()`

IF

Returns a value if one condition is true and returns another value if the condition is false.

`=IF(logical_test,value_if_true,value_if_false)`

NOT

Returns the reverse value of its arguments.

`=NOT(logical)`

OR

Returns TRUE if any one argument is true. Returns FALSE if all arguments are false.

`=OR(logical1,logical2,...)`

TRUE

Returns the value TRUE. There are no arguments associated with this function.

`=TRUE()`

LOOKUP AND REFERENCE FUNCTIONS

ADDRESS

Given specified row and column numbers, creates a cell address as text.

`=ADDRESS(row_num,column_num,abs_num,A1,sheet_text)`

AREAS

Returns the number of areas in *reference*.

=AREAS(*reference*)

CHOOSE

Returns the index number from a list of arguments.

=CHOOSE(*index_num*,*value1*,*value2*,...)

COLUMN

Based on a given reference, returns the column number.

=COLUMN(*reference*)

COLUMNS

Based on an array or reference, returns the number of columns.

=COLUMNS(*array*)

HLOOKUP

Searches for a specified value in an array or tables, based on the value found in the first row.

=HLOOKUP(*lookup_value*,*table_array*,*row_index_number*,*range_lookup*)

HYPERLINK

Creates a shortcut or jump that switches to another location within the workbook or opens a document stored on a local drive, a network server, an intranet, or the Internet.

=HYPERLINK(*link_location*,*cell_contents*)

INDEX (ARRAY FORM)

Based on a table or array, returns the value of an element selected by the row number and column letter indexes.

=INDEX(*array*,*row_num*,*column_num*)

INDEX (REFERENCE FORM)

Based on the intersection of a particular row and column, returns the reference of the cell.

=INDEX(*reference*,*row_num*,*column_num*,*area_num*)

INDIRECT

Returns the reference based on a text string.

=INDIRECT(*ref_text*,*A1*)

LOOKUP (VECTOR FORM)

Based on a range of one row or one column, returns the value from the same position in a second row or column.

`=LOOKUP(lookup_value,lookup_vector,result_vector)`

LOOKUP (ARRAY FORM)

Looks in the first row or column of an array, and returns the specified value from the same position in the last row or column of the array.

`=LOOKUP(lookup_value,array)`

MATCH

Returns the position of an item in an array that matches a specified value and order.

`=MATCH(lookup_value,lookup_array,match_type)`

OFFSET

Returns a reference to a range that is a specific number of rows and columns from a cell or range of cells.

`=OFFSET(reference,rows,columns,height,width)`

ROW

Based on a reference, returns the row number.

`=ROW(reference)`

ROWS

Based on a reference or array, returns the number of rows.

`=ROWS(array)`

TRANSPOSE

Returns a horizontal range of cells as vertical or vice versa.

`=TRANSPOSE(array)`

VLOOKUP

Looks for a value in the leftmost column of a table and returns a value from the column number you specify.

`=VLOOKUP(lookup_value,table_array,column_index_num,range_lookup)`

PART

X

APP

A

MATH AND TRIGONOMETRY FUNCTIONS

ABS

Returns the absolute value of *number*.

`=ABS(number)`

ACOS

Returns the arc cosine of *number*. The arc cosine is the angle whose cosine is *number*.

`=ACOS(number)`

ACOSH

Returns the inverse hyperbolic cosine of *number*.

`=ACOSH(number)`

ASIN

Returns the arc sine of *number*.

`=ASIN(number)`

ASINH

Returns the inverse hyperbolic sine of *number*.

`=ASINH(number)`

ATAN

Returns the arc tangent of *number*.

`=ATAN(number)`

ATAN2

Returns the arc tangent of the specified x- and y-coordinates.

`=ATAN2(x_num,y_num)`

ATANH

Returns the inverse hyperbolic tangent of a number.

`=ATANH(number)`

CEILING

Returns *number* rounded up to the nearest integer, or to the nearest multiple of significance (for example, to the nearest nickel).

`=CEILING(number,significance)`

COMBIN

Returns the number of combinations for a given number of items.

=COMBIN(*number*,*number_chosen*)

COS

Returns the cosine of a given angle.

=COS(*number*)

COSH

Returns the hyperbolic cosine of *number*.

=COSH(*number*)

COUNTIF

Counts the number of cells in a specified range that meet the criteria you specify.

=COUNTIF(*range*,*criteria*)

DEGREES

Converts radians into degrees.

=DEGREES(*angle*)

EVEN

Returns *number* rounded up to the nearest integer.

=EVEN(*number*)

EXP

Returns e raised to the power of *number*.

=EXP(*number*)

FACT

Returns the factorial of *number*.

=FACT(*number*)

FACTDOUBLE

Returns the double factorial of *number*.

=FACTDOUBLE(*number*)

FLOOR

Rounds *number* down, toward zero, to the nearest multiple of significance.

`=FLOOR(number,significance)`

GCD

Returns the greatest common divisor of two or more integers.

`=GCD(number1,number2,...)`

INT

Rounds *number* down to the nearest integer.

`=INT(number)`

LCM

Returns the least common multiple of integers.

`=LCM(number1,number2,...)`

LN

Returns the natural logarithm of a number.

`=LN(number)`

LOG

Returns the logarithm of a number to the base you specify.

`=LOG(number,base)`

LOG10

Returns the base 10 logarithm of a number.

`=LOG10(number)`

MDETERM

Returns the matrix determinant of an array.

`=MDETERM(array)`

MINVERSE

Returns the inverse matrix for the matrix stored in an array.

`=MINVERSE(array)`

MMULT

Returns the matrix product of two arrays.

`=MMULT(array1,array2)`

MOD

Returns the remainder after *number* is divided by *divisor*.

`=MOD(number,divisor)`

MROUND

Returns a number rounded to the desired multiple.

`=MROUND(number,multiple)`

MULTINOMIAL

Returns the ratio of the factorial of a sum of values to the product of factorials.

`=MULTINOMIAL(number1,number2,...)`

ODD

Returns *number* rounded to the nearest odd integer.

`=ODD(number)`

PI

Returns the number 3.14159265358979, the mathematical constant pi, accurate to 15 digits. There are no arguments associated with this function.

`=PI()`

POWER

Returns the result of a number raised to a power.

`=POWER(number,power)`

PRODUCT

Multiplies all the numbers given as arguments and returns the product.

`=PRODUCT(number1,number2,...)`

QUOTIENT

Returns the integer portion of a division. Use this function to discard the remainder of a division.

`=QUOTIENT(numerator,denominator)`

PART

X

APP

A

RADIANS

Converts degrees to radians.

`=RADIANS(angle)`

RAND

Returns an evenly distributed number greater than or equal to 0 and less than 1. There are no arguments associated with this function.

`=RAND()`

RANDBETWEEN

Returns a random number between the numbers you specify.

`=RANDBETWEEN(bottom,top)`

ROMAN

Converts an Arabic numeral to Roman, as text.

`=ROMAN(number,form)`

ROUND

Rounds a number to a specified number of digits.

`=ROUND(number,num_digits)`

ROUNDDOWN

Rounds a number down toward 0.

`=ROUNDDOWN(number,num_digits)`

ROUNDUP

Rounds a number up away from 0.

`=ROUNDUP(number,num_digits)`

SERIESSUM

Returns the sum of a power series based on the formula.

`=SERIESSUM(x,n,m,coefficients)`

SIGN

Determines the sign (positive or negative) of number.

`=SIGN(number)`

SIN

Returns the sine of the given angle.

=SIN(*number*)

SINH

Returns the hyperbolic sine of *number*.

=SINH(*number*)

SQRT

Returns the positive square root of *number*.

=SQRT(*number*)

SQRTPI

Returns the square root of (*number**pi).

-SQRTPI(*number*)

SUBTOTAL

Returns a subtotal from a list or database.

=SUBTOTAL(*function_num*,*ref1*,*ref2*,...)

SUM

Adds the numbers in a range of cells.

=Sum(*number1*,*number2*,...)

SUMIF

Adds the cells specified by *criteria*.

=SUMIF(*range*,*criteria*,*sum_range*)

SUMPRODUCT

Multiplies corresponding components in the given array, and returns the sum of those products.

=SUMPRODUCT(*array1*,*array2*,*array3*,...)

SUMSQ

Returns the sum of the squares of the arguments.

=SUMSQ(*number1*,*number2*,...)

PART

X

APP

A

SUMX2MY2

Returns the sum of the difference of squares of corresponding values in two arrays.

=SUMX2MY2(*array_x*,*array_y*)

SUMX2PY2

Returns the sum of the sum of squares in corresponding values in two arrays.

=SUMX2PY2(*array_x*,*array_y*)

SUMXMY2

Returns the sum of squares of differences of corresponding values in two arrays.

=SUMXMY2(*array_x*,*array_y*)

TAN

Returns the tangent of the given angle.

=TAN(*number*)

TANH

Returns the hyperbolic tangent of *number*.

=TANH(*number*)

TRUNC

Truncates *number* to an integer, removing the fractional part of the number. Note that this function does not round *number*.

=TRUNC(*number*,*num_digits*)

STATISTICAL FUNCTIONS

AVEDEV

Returns the average of the absolute deviations of data points from their mean.

=AVEDEV(*number1*,*number2*,...)

AVERAGE

Returns the average of the arguments.

=AVERAGE(*number1*,*number2*,...)

AVERAGEA

Calculates the average of the values in the list of arguments.

=AVERAGEA(*value1*,*value2*,...)

BETADIST

Returns the cumulative beta probability density function.

`=BETADIST(x,alpha,beta,A,B)`

BETAINV

Returns the inverse of the cumulative beta probability density function.

`=BETAINV(probability,alpha,beta,A,B)`

BINOMDIST

Returns the individual term binomial distribution probability.

`=BINOMDIST(number_s,trials,probability_s,cumulative)`

CHIDIST

Returns the one-tailed probability of the chi-squared distribution.

`=CHIDIST(x,degrees_freedom)`

CHINV

Returns the inverse of the one-tailed probability of the chi-squared distribution.

`-CHINV(probability,degrees_freedom)`

CHITEST

Returns the test for independence.

`=CHITEST(actual_range,expected_range)`

CONFIDENCE

Returns the confidence interval—the range on each side of a sample mean—for the population mean.

`=CONFIDENCE(alpha,standard_dev,size)`

CORREL

Returns the correlation coefficient of *array1* and *array2* cell ranges.

`=CORREL(array1,array2)`

COUNT

Counts the number of cells that contain numbers within the list of arguments.

`=COUNT(value1,value2,...)`

PART

X

APP

A

COUNTA

Counts the number of cells that are not empty within the list of arguments.

=COUNTA(*value1*,*value2*,...)

COVAR

Returns covariance, the average of the products of deviations for each data point pair.

=COVAR(*array1*,*array2*)

CRITBINOM

Returns the smallest value for which the cumulative binomial distribution is greater than or equal to a criterion value.

=CRITBINOM(*trials*,*probability_s*,*alpha*)

DEVSQ

Returns the sum of squares of deviations of data points from their sample mean.

=DEVSQ(*number1*,*number2*,...)

EXPONDIST

Returns the exponential distribution.

=EXPONDIST(*x*,*lambda*,*cumulative*)

FDIST

Returns the F probability distribution.

=FDIST(*x*,*degrees_freedom1*,*degrees_freedom2*)

FINV

Returns the inverse of the F probability distribution.

=FINV(*probability*,*degrees_freedom1*,*degrees_freedom2*)

FISHER

Returns the Fisher transformation at *x*.

=FISHER(*x*)

FISHERINV

Returns the inverse of the Fisher transformation.

=FISHERINV(*y*)

FORECAST

Calculates or predicts a future value by using existing values.

=FORECAST(*x*,*known_y's*,*known_x's*)

FREQUENCY

Calculates how often values occur within a range of values, and then returns a vertical array of numbers. This function returns an array of values and therefore must be entered as an array formula (using Ctrl+Shift+Enter).

=FREQUENCY(*data_array*,*bins_array*)

FTEST

Returns the result of an Ftest.

=FTEST(*array1*,*array2*)

GAMMADIST

Returns the gamma distribution.

=GAMMADIST(*x*,alpha,*beta*,*cumulative*)

GAMMAINV

Returns the inverse of the gamma cumulative distribution.

–GAMMAINV(*probability*,alpha,*beta*)

GAMMALN

Returns the natural logarithm of the gamma function.

=GAMMALN(*x*)

GEOMEAN

Returns the geometric mean of an array or range of positive data.

=GEOMEAN(*number1*,*number2*,...)

GROWTH

Calculates predicted exponential growth by using existing data.

=GROWTH(*known_y's*,*known_x's*,*new_x's*,*const*)

HARMEAN

Returns the harmonic mean of a data set.

=HARMEAN(*number1*,*number2*,...)

HYPGEOMDIST

Returns the hypergeometric distribution.

=HYPERGEOMDIST(*sample_s,number_sample,population_s,number_population*)

INTERCEPT

Calculates the point at which a line will intersect the y-axis by using existing x-values and y-values.

=INTERCEPT(*known_y's,known_x's*)

KURT

Returns the Kurtosis of a data set.

=KURT(*number1,number2,...*)

LARGE

Returns the k-th largest value in a data set.

=LARGE(*array,k*)

LINEST

Calculates the statistics for a line by using the "least squares" method to calculate a straight line that best fits your data, and returns an array that describes the line.

=LINEST(*known_y's,known_x's,const,stats*)

LOGEST

In regression analysis, calculates an exponential curve that fits your data and returns an array of values that describes the curve.

=LOGEST(*known_y's,known_x's,const,stats*)

LOGINV

Returns the inverse of the lognormal cumulative distribution function of x, wherein (x) is normally distributed with parameters *mean* and *standard_dev*.

=LOGINV(*probability,mean,standard_dev*)

LOGNORMDIST

Returns the cumulative lognormal distribution of x, wherein (x) is normally distributed with parameters *mean* and *standard_dev*.

=LOGNORMDIST(*x,mean,standard_dev*)

MAX

Returns the largest value in a set of values.

=MAX(*number1*,*number2*,...)

MAXA

Returns the largest value in a list of arguments.

=MAXA(*value1*,*value2*,...)

MEDIAN

Returns the median of a given set of numbers.

=MEDIAN(*number1*,*number2*,...)

MIN

Returns the smallest number in a set of values. Nonnumeric values are ignored.

=MIN(*number1*,*number2*,...)

MINA

Returns the smallest value in a list of arguments including text and logical values such as "No Grade", TRUE, and FALSE. TRUE evaluates to 1. All other nonnumeric values evaluate to 0.

=MINA(*value1*,*value2*,...)

MODE

Returns the most frequently occurring, or repetitive, value in an array or range of data.

=MODE(*number1*,*number2*,...)

NEGBINOMDIST

Returns the negative binomial distribution.

=NEGBINOMDIST(*number_f*,*number_s*,*probability_s*)

NORMDIST

Returns the normal cumulative distribution for the specified mean and standard deviation.

=NORMDIST(*x*,*mean*,*standard_dev*,*cumulative*)

NORMINV

Returns the inverse of the normal cumulative distribution for the specified mean and standard deviation.

=NORMINV(*probability*,*mean*,*standard_dev*)

NORMSDIST

Returns the standard normal cumulative distribution function.

=NORMSDIST(*z*)

NORMSINV

Returns the inverse of the standard normal cumulative distribution.

=NORMSINV(*probability*)

PEARSON

Returns the Pearson product moment correlation coefficient, r, a dimensionless index ranges from –1.0 to 1.0 inclusive and reflects the extent of a linear relationship between two data sets.

=PEARSON(*array1,array2*)

PERCENTILE

Returns the *k*-th percentile of values in a range.

=PERCENTILE(*array,k*)

PERCENTRANK

Returns the rank of a value in a data set as a percentage of the data set.

=PERCENTRANK(*array,x,significance*)

PERMUT

Returns the number of permutations for a given number of objects that can be selected from *number* objects.

=PERMUT(*number,number_chosen*)

POISSON

Returns the Poisson distribution.

=POISSON(*x,mean,cumulative*)

PROB

Returns the probability that values in a range are between two specified limits.

=PROB(*x_range,prob_range,lower_limit,upper_limit*)

QUARTILE

Returns the quartile of a data set.

=QUARTILE(*array,quart*)

RANK

Returns the rank of a number in a list of numbers.

=RANK(*number*,*ref*,*order*)

RSQ

Returns the square of the Pearson product moment correlation coefficient through data points in *known_y's* and *known_x's*.

=RSQ(*known_y's*,*known_x's*)

SKEW

Returns the skewness of a distribution.

=SKEW(*number1*,*number2*,...)

SLOPE

Returns the slope of the regression line through data points in *known_y's* and *known_x's*.

=SLOPE(*known_y's*,*known_x's*)

SMALL

Returns the *k*-th smallest value in a data set.

=SMALL(*array*,*k*)

PART

X

APP

A

STANDARDIZE

Returns a normalized value from a distribution characterized by *mean* and *standard_dev*.

=STANDARDIZE(*x*,*mean*,*standard_dev*)

STDEV

Estimates standard deviation based on a sample. Nonnumeric values are ignored.

=STDEV(*number1*,*number2*,...)

STDEVA

Estimates standard deviation based on a sample including text and logical values such as "None", TRUE, and FALSE. TRUE evaluates to 1. All other nonnumeric values evaluate to 0.

=STDEVA(*value1*,*value2*,...)

STDEVP

Calculates standard deviation based on the entire population given as arguments. Nonnumeric values are ignored.

=STDEVP(*number1*,*number2*,...)

STDEVPA

Calculates standard deviation based on the entire population given as arguments including text and logical values such as "None", TRUE, and FALSE. TRUE evaluates to 1. All other nonnumeric values evaluate to 0.

=STDEVPA(*value1*,*value2*,...)

STEYX

Returns the standard error of the predicted *y* value for each *x* in the regression.

=STEYX(*known_y's*,*known_x's*)

TDIST

Returns the student's t-distribution.

TDIST(*x*,*degrees_freedom*,*tails*)

TINV

Returns the inverse of the student's t-distribution for the specified degrees of freedom.

=TINV(*probability*,*degrees_freedom*)

TREND

Returns values along a linear trend.

=TREND(*known_y's*,*known_x's*,*new_x's*,*const*)

TRIMMEAN

Returns the mean of the interior of a data set.

=TRIMMEAN(*array*,*percent*)

TTEST

Returns the probability associated with the student's t-test.

=TTEST(*array1*,*array2*,*tails*,*type*)

VAR

Estimates variance based on a sample, with from 1 to 30 arguments.

=VAR(*number1*,*number2*,...)

VARA

Estimates variance based on a sample including text and logical values such as "None", TRUE, and FALSE. TRUE evaluates to 1. All other nonnumeric values evaluate to 0.

=VARA(*value1*,*value2*,...)

VARP

Calculates variance based on the entire population. Nonnumeric values are ignored.

=VARP(*number1,number2,...*)

VARPA

Calculates variance based on the entire population, including text and logical values such as "None", TRUE, and FALSE. TRUE evaluates to 1. All other nonnumeric values evaluate to 0.

=VARPA(*value1,value2,...*)

WEIBULL

Returns the Weibull distribution.

=WEIBULL(*x,alpha,beta,cumulative*)

ZTEST

Returns the two-tailed P-value of a z-test.

=ZTEST(*array,x,sigma*)

TEXT FUNCTIONS

CHAR

Returns the character specified by a number.

=CHAR(*number*)

CLEAN

Removes all nonprintable characters from text.

=CLEAN(*text*)

CODE

Returns a numeric code from the first character in a text string.

=CODE(*text*)

CONCATENATE

Joins several text strings into one text string.

=CONCATENATE(*text1,text2,...*)

DOLLAR

Converts a number to text using Currency format, with the decimals rounded to the specified place. The format used is $#,##0.00_);($#,##0.00).

=DOLLAR(*number*,*decimals*)

EXACT

Compares two text strings and returns TRUE if they're exactly the same, and FALSE otherwise. EXACT is case sensitive.

=EXACT(*text1*,*text2*)

FIND

Finds one text string with another text string, and returns the number of the starting position of *find_text* from the leftmost character of *within_text*. FIND is case sensitive and cannot include wildcard characters.

=FIND(*find_text*,*within_text*,*start_num*)

FINDB

Finds one text string with another text string, and returns the number of the starting position of *find_text*, from the leftmost character of *within_text*. FINDB is case sensitive and cannot include wildcard characters. This function is for use with double-byte characters.

=FINDB(*find_text*,*within_text*,*start_num*)

FIXED

Rounds a number to a specified number of decimals, formats the number in decimal format using a period and commas, and returns the result as text.

=FIXED(*number*,*decimals*,*no_commas*)

LEFT

Returns the first character or characters in a text string.

=LEFT(*text*,*num_char*)

LEN

Returns the number of characters in a text string.

=LEN(*text*)

LOWER

Converts all uppercase letters in a text string to lowercase.

=LOWER(*text*)

MID

Returns a specific number of characters from a text string, starting at the position you specify.

`=MID(text,start_num,num_char)`

PROPER

Capitalizes the first letter in a text string and any other letters in text that follow any character other than a letter.

`=PROPER(text)`

REPLACE

Replaces part of a text string with a different text string based on the number of characters you specify.

`=REPLACE(old_text,start_num,num_chars,new_text)`

REPLACEB

Replaces part of a text string with a different text string, based on the number of bytes you specify.

`=REPLACEB(old_text,start_num,num_bytes,new_text)`

REPT

Repeats text a given number of times.

`=REPT(text,number_times)`

RIGHT

Returns the last character or characters in a text string.

`=RIGHT(text,num_chars)`

SEARCH

Returns the number of the character at which a specific character or text string is first found, reading from left to right. SEARCH is not case sensitive and can include wildcard characters.

`=SEARCH(find_text,within_text,start_num)`

SEARCHB

Returns the number of the double-byte character at which a specific character or text string is first found, reading from left to right. SEARCHB is not case sensitive and can include wildcard characters.

`=SEARCHB(find_text,within_text,start_num)`

SUBSTITUTE

Substitutes *new_text* for *old_text* in a text string.

`=SUBSTITUTE(text,old_text,new_text,instance_num)`

T

Returns the text referred to by *value*.

`=T(value)`

TEXT

Converts a value to text in a specific number format.

`=TEXT(value,format_text)`

TRIM

Removes all spaces from text except for single spaces between words.

`=TRIM(text)`

UPPER

Converts text to uppercase.

`=UPPER(text)`

VALUE

Converts a text string that represents a number to a number.

`=VALUE(text)`

WHAT'S ON THE CD?

In this appendix

by Patrick D. Blattner
Patrick@BlattnerBooks.com

EXCEL WORKBOOKS

One of the keys to learning is by working with "live" examples and understanding the underlying structure behind the examples. How formulas work, how the examples in the book look on your computer—and, after all, why re-create examples that were already created once by someone else?

I've often found it frustrating that book content rarely showed up on the CD, or the CD content was just static images. Not very useful, is it? In this book, however, the workbooks, charts, Gantt charts, formulas, PivotTables, and form controls you see in the screen shots are included on the CD. In addition, I believe that this CD includes more examples and useful "live" information than any other Excel CD ever created. The CD itself is worth the value of the entire book. The following sections provide a brief description of some of the items you'll find on the CD.

> **Caution**
>
> When opening workbooks with links, click No when Excel asks whether you want to update links. Do not update the links.
>
> When opening workbooks with macros, Excel offers you the option to enable or disable the macros. Choose Enable Macros.

WORKBOOKS FROM *SPECIAL EDITION USING MICROSOFT EXCEL 2000*

Special Edition Using Microsoft Excel 2000 features workbooks from the book. Although the pictures and examples in the book are a nice feature in learning how to be more effective with Microsoft Excel, we've taken it one step further and included just about all of them on the CD. If you have questions as to setup, formula referencing, or formatting, you can refer to the CD for the sample workbooks. Just save the workbook with a new name on your hard drive and manipulate it to fit your style or situation.

GANTT CHART WORKBOOKS

For the first time ever, we show techniques on how to use Excel for project management. Although you could create Gantt charts with a chart from the Chart Wizard (and yes, that's been done), it's not really helpful. The goal here is to show you how to manipulate a worksheet to solve problems that occur over time. This issue is addressed in Chapter 23, "Innovative Ways to Use Excel," but the CD provides extended examples on how to apply these techniques with cash flow, widgets, units, and so on to help you understand the flexibility of Excel as a time-management tool.

Since 1995, I've been using Excel as a powerful time-management and resource-loading tool that far outperforms any application software on the market. For the first time ever, we show you how to combine spreadsheet information with charts and create visuals that are far beyond any previously published book on Excel.

FORMULAS WORKBOOK

Because so many people are becoming intermediate to advanced users in the marketplace, this CD provides a helpful formula workbook that shows examples of formulas in use. The front page of this extensive formula book has hyperlinks to take you to each specific formula, so you don't need to waste your time searching for the type of formula you want.

BONUS BOOKS

The CD includes electronic copies of the text of this book and the *Excel Function Reference* (both of which are electronically searchable for easy use) and also provides two additional electronic books: *Creating Charts in Excel* and *Working with the Small Business Tools*, which are described in the following sections.

FUNCTION REFERENCE

More than 400 functions are documented in the Function Reference, with syntax and description. Because Excel houses so many functions, it's helpful to have these functions with the description and syntax at your fingertips. No Excel user should be without this great reference, which is in HTML format for easy browsing with your browser software.

ELECTRONIC COPY OF *SPECIAL EDITION USING MICROSOFT EXCEL 2000*

Although a printed book is still the most useful format for a reference book on Excel 2000, there are times when you may find it handy to have an electronic copy of the book as well. With this full electronic copy of the book, you can quickly search for any text anywhere in the book and use this when you can't have the printed book with you.

Please note that this electronic copy of the book is for your use only. You may not copy it to a network, another CD-ROM, or the Internet for others to use. The print capability of this version has also been disabled (you already have a printed copy of the book so you shouldn't need to print this) and you cannot copy and paste material from this electronic book.

This electronic book is in Adobe Acrobat format and all of the Acrobat software needed to use it is included on the CD as well.

CREATING CHARTS IN EXCEL

Creating Charts in Excel is a 400+ page step-by-step PowerPoint book authored by Patrick Blattner. This book is in full color and shows you the final chart to be created, then takes you step by step through the process of creating the chart in Excel. You can also print the whole presentation and bind it as your own chart reference book. This is by far the most in-depth chart reference guide ever created, and is a powerful add-on to *Special Edition Using Microsoft Excel 2000*. By having *Creating Charts in Excel* on CD, you can save it to your hard drive and take it with you anywhere!

PART

X

APP

B

Working with the Small Business Tools

Office 2000 includes a Small Business Tools utility to help businesses get more out of the Office suite of applications. The components—The Small Business Financial Manager, The Business Planner, The Direct Mail Planner, and The Small Business Customer Manager—are described in this small electronic book.

Que's *Special Edition* Showcase

Que publishes a full line of books about the programs in Microsoft Office 2000, including many other books in the *Special Edition Using* series. Que's showcase features additional electronic coverage of other books in the *Special Edition Using* series and more.

- *Special Edition Using Microsoft Office 2000* by Ed Bott and Woody Leonhard (ISBN: 0-7897-1842-1)
- *Special Edition Using Microsoft Word 2000* by Bill Camarda (ISBN: 0-7897-1852-9)
- *Special Edition Using Microsoft PowerPoint 2000* by Patrice Rutledge (ISBN: 0-7897-1904-5)

Although this is an initial list, please see the CD for any additional books included on the CD.

Third-Party Software

In addition to having included electronic versions of the book, excerpts from other books, and an additional book, *Creating Charts in Excel*, the CD team at Macmillan has compiled links to other useful Excel sites and third-party shareware. Instead of listing all the shareware, here are a few examples of additional software and helpful add-ins on the CD:

- **The Spreadsheet Detective.** By adding graphical documentation to existing spreadsheets, the Spreadsheet Detective highlights errors that otherwise could easily be overlooked. These errors include inconsistent copies of formulas and Year 2000 problems. The Spreadsheet Detective also clarifies the meaning of cryptic cell references, such as =D34-D35, by adding AutoNames based on cell labels, and can compare different versions of a worksheet.

- **Additional Templates from KMT.** These templates are already created and can be adjusted to fit your needs or those of your business. Following is a partial list:
  - 24-month sales forecast
  - Business indebtedness
  - Business acquisition worksheet
  - Balloon payment loan
  - Arm mortgage comparison
  - Accounts payable voucher

- Accounts payable aging
- 401(k) reallocation planner
- Financial statement ratio analysis
- Extra payment analyzer
- Dollar cost averaging worksheet
- Daily employee timesheet
- Comparative business income analysis
- Cash flow sensitivity analysis
- Lower of cost or market value inventory
- Job price estimate
- Job order ledger
- Invoice record
- Out-of-stock report
- Merchandise return
- Material requisition
- Marketing calculators
- Manufacturing overhead budget
- Quarterly budget analysis
- Startup cash outlay forecast
- Startup capitalization
- Startup budget
- Small business valuation
- Weekly materials analysis
- Weekly direct labor analysis
- Wall-covering calculator
- Trade show budget

In addition to the previous templates and software, the following list highlights some additional third-party software found on the CD. See the CD for a full list of CD software, templates, and add-ins.

- **Passkeeper.** Keeps track of passwords.
- **The Spreadsheet Assistant.** Add-in that adds over 200 features.
- **Interactive Charts.** A group of charts with various interactivity options.
- **Precision Tree.** Data analysis add-in for Microsoft Excel.
- **Edwin's Power Tools.** Tools that extend Excel's capabilities.
- **Prime for Excel 2000.** A variety of Office-related tools.
- **Power Utility Pak.** Over 70 utilities, functions, and so on.

PART

X

APP

B

INDEX

B

J-K

Canon

SPECIAL OFFER

The OfficeReady™ templates you're using are just a selection from the 650 templates offered in the complete version of OfficeReady.

If you're enjoying the time-saving benefits of these professionally designed, ready-to-use templates, just imagine having templates for nearly every task you perform using Microsoft® Office.

It's easy. All the additional templates are already located on *Que's Special Edition WOPR 2000 Pack* CD-ROM. You'll immediately be able to use them for all of the work you do using Microsoft Office. Even better, you'll have all 650 templates for only $19.95. That's 50% off the normal retail price!

Ordering is easy. Just call 1-(800) 385-2155. All the additional templates are already located on your CD-ROM. You'll be issued a password to unlock the templates.

Designing documents in Microsoft Office can take up hours of your valuable time. Now, for only $19.95, you can save that time, and devote it to something that makes sense – like your business.

Offer subject to availability. Prices subject to change without notice.